AUSTRIA

BELGIUM

FRANCE

GERMANY

GREAT BRITAIN

IRELAND

ITALY

THE NETHERLANDS

PORTUGAL

SPAIN

SWITZERLAND

The **AA** **KEY**Guide

Western European Cities

Contents

KEY TO SYMBOLS

✚ Map reference
✉ Address
☎ Telephone number
🕐 Opening times
💲 Admission prices
🚌 Bus number
🚆 Train station
⛴ Ferry/boat
🚗 Driving directions
ℹ Tourist office
🎫 Tours
📖 Guidebook
🍴 Restaurant
☕ Café
🍷 Bar
🏬 Shop
🚻 Toilets
🛏 Number of rooms
🚭 No smoking
❄ Air conditioning
🏊 Swimming pool
🏋 Gym
❓ Other useful
   information
🛍 Shopping
🎭 Entertainment
🌙 Nightlife
🏃 Sports
⭐ Activities
❤ Health and Beauty
👫 For Children
▷ Cross reference

HOW TO USE THIS BOOK	RESTAURANT PRICES

Understanding Western European Cities is an introduction to the area, its geography, politics and people.

For detailed advice on getting to Western Europe—and getting around once you are there—turn to **On the Move** sections within each country. For useful information, from weather to emergency services, go to **Planning**.

Each country is divided into cities with Sights and What to Do, Eating and Staying listings. Cities and places of interest are listed alphabetically within each country.

Map references for the Sights refer to the city street plans within each country or the area map on pages 4–5. For example, Buckingham Palace has the reference 143 F4, indicating the page on which the map is found (143) and the grid square in which Buckingham Palace sits (D8).

Restaurant prices are the average for a two-course lunch (L) and a three course à la carte dinner (D) for one person and the least expensive bottle of wine. Service charges are not included.

Kristiansund
Ålesund
Florø
Bergen
Haugesund
Stavanger
Kristiansand

Trondheim
Lillehammer
Mora
Hønefoss
OSLO
Karlstad
Hirtshals

Østersund
Sundsvall

Umeå
Vaasa
Vasa

Kokkola
Karle
Iisalmi
Idensalmi
FIN
Kuopio
Joensuu
Jyväskylä

S
N

Tampere
Tammerfors
Pori
Björneborg
Turku
Åbo

Lappeenranta
Villmanstrand
Lahti
Lahtis
Sankt-Peterburg

Gävle
Borlänge
Uppsala
Örebro

Ahvenanmaa
Åland

HELSINKI
HELSINGFORS

STOCKHOLM
Kappelskär
Hiiumaa

TALLINN
EST
Tartu
Pärnu
Pskov

Norrköping
Göteborg Boras
Frederikshavn
Aalborg

Jönköping
Visby
Gotland

Saaremaa

RĪGA
LV

Kalmar
Öland
Liepāja
Daugavpils
Šiauliai
Panevežys

DK
Helsingborg
Kristianstad
Arhus
Esbjerg
KØBENHAVN

LT
Klaipėda
Kaunas
RUS
VILNIUS

Odense
Rødbyhavn
Ystad
Bornholm
DK

Kiel
Gedser
Sassnitz
Puttgarden

Kaliningrad
Gdańsk
Augustów
Hrodno
MINSK

Cuxhaven
Lübeck
Rostock
Koszalin

Wilhelmshaven
Groningen
Emden
Hamburg
Swinoujście
Szczecin

Den
Haag
NL
Bremen
Neubrandenburg
Bydgoszcz
Torun
Białystok
BY
Baranavichy

AMSTERDAM
Hannover
BERLIN
Poznań
PL
WARSZAWA
Pinsk

Rotterdam
Arnhem
Osnabrück
Magdeburg
Brest
Antwerpen
Düsseldorf
Dortmund
D
Halle
Łódź

B
Kassel
Leipzig
Radom
Lublin
BRUSSEL
BRUXELLES
Köln
Bonn
Erfurt
Wrocław
Częstochowa
Luts'k
Rivne

Koblenz
Frankfurt
Am Main
Dresden
UA

LUXEMBOURG
Würzburg
PRAHA
Katowice
Rzeszów
L'viv

Metz
Mannheim
Nürnberg
CZ
Ostrava
Kraków
Ternopil'

Saarbrücken
Plzeň
Olomouc

Nancy
Regensburg
Tábor
Brno

Strasbourg
Stuttgart
České
Budějovice
SK
Košice
Uzhorod
Chernivtsi

Dijon
Basel
Augsburg
Linz
WIEN
BRATISLAVA
Miskolc
Satu Mare

Besançon
Zürich
Bregenz
München
Salzburg
Győr
BUDAPEST
Debrecen

Lausanne
BERN
FL
Innsbruck
A
Graz
Székesfehérvár
Oradea
Cluj Napoca
Băcău

CH
Bolzano
Bozen
H
Szeged
Arad
RO
Genève
LJUBLJANA
Pécs

Grenoble
Verona
Trieste
SLO
ZAGREB
Osijek
Timişoara
Braşov

Milano
Padova
Venezia
Rijeka
HR
Novi Sad

Torino
Genova
Bihać
Banja
Luka
BUCUREŞTI

Sisteron
Bologna
Ravenna
BEOGRAD
Craiova

Nice
MONACO
Firenze
Zadar
BIH
SARAJEVO
Vidin
Calafat
Ruse

MC
Livorno
RSM
Ancona
Split
Užice
SRB
Niš
Pleven
Veliko
Tŭrnovo

Toulon
Isola
d'Elba
Siena
Perugia
Mostar
CG
BG

Bastia
Pescara
Dubrovnik
Priština
ŠOFIYA
Stara
Zagora

Corse
I
PODGORICA
Shkodër
SKOPJE
Plovdiv
Edirne

Ajaccio
ROMA
V
Manfredonia
TIRANË
MK
Ohrid
Kavála

Bonifacio
Foggia
Bari
AL
Thessaloniki

Porto
Torres
Olbia
Napoli
Potenza
Brindisi
Lecce
GR
Lárisa

Sardegna
Taranto
Igoumenitsa
Ioánnina
Vólos

Iglésias
Lamía
Ewoia

Cagliari
Catanzaro
Pátra
ATHÍNA
Kórinthos

Palermo
Messina
Reggio di
Calabria
Kalamáta
Areópoli
Monemvasía

Trapani
Sicilia
Catania

Agrigento
Gela

D
E
F

WESTERN EUROPEAN CITIES

Western Europe's countries have been the scene of some of the most momentous events in history, from invasions and migrations to revolutions and world wars, from great discoveries and inventions to the flowering of the arts and architecture, and from political and economic innovation to religious and philosophical debate. Reminders of these times can be found in every city of the region, as can the vibrant, cutting-edge, modern culture for which it is renowned. These are destinations that have it all.

Enjoying a picnic in the Hohe Tauern   *The market square in Bruges from the air*

For such a small region, western Europe certainly packs a lot of punch. Where else could you pass your morning walking in the footsteps of Roman centurions, while away the afternoon gazing up at the splendour of a Gothic cathedral, and then spend the evening dining on fusion cuisine in a boutique restaurant run by a celebrity chef?

GEOGRAPHICAL DIVERSITY

So what exactly is Europe? It's the world's second-smallest continent after Australia, but has one of the densest concentrations of people, with about 12 per cent of the world's population. It stretches from the Ural Mountains of Russia at its eastern end to Ireland in the west, perched on the edge of the Atlantic Ocean. It reaches from the arctic Scandinavian countries in the north through to the hot Mediterranean in the south, which separates the continent from North Africa.

While the geographical centre of Europe clearly lies in one of its eastern countries, the heart and power of the continent have always been in western Europe, the area covered by this book. Countries like France, Spain, Portugal, The Netherlands, Germany, Italy and Great Britain all built up strong empires around the world, thanks to the exploits of their adventurers, explorers, scientists and traders. At various times they also fought one another—usually bitterly—for control of more European territory. And if that didn't work, the royal families extended their kingdoms through marriage.

POLITICAL UNION

Today, a marriage of sorts continues to exist between the major European nations, by way of the EU (European Union), although at times it's a fairly stormy relationship. The union was originally created for economic reasons back in 1957 as the European Economic Community (EEC), consisting of just six member states. Today, 27 nations are members, including a number of former eastern European countries, and several others—classed as membership candidates and potential candidates—are waiting in the wings.

Together, the member states form a single market that aims to allow the free flow of goods, services, money and people within it. As such, border controls have been abolished between many member states, and the euro currency was introduced in 2002 and has replaced several national currencies.

However, not all member states of the EU share the euro, and not even all countries belong to the 'family'. Some, like Norway and Switzerland, have not joined the EU, while others, including Great Britain and Denmark, are members but do not use the euro. Just to complicate the issue further, some countries that are not members of the EU (like the Vatican and Monaco) have decided to use the euro anyway.

SIMILAR…

The countless migrations and conquests that have taken place across the region have resulted in a population that is more closely related than may first seem to be the case. One of the earliest influences on Europe came from Rome, whose empire extended across most of the continent and brought with it systems of government and law, as well as language, architecture and engineering.

Following the decline of the Roman empire came the Dark Ages, a period characterized by the movements and invasions of various tribes, like pieces shifting across a chessboard. These included the Goths, Huns, Celts, Franks, Angles and Saxons, followed later by the Vikings and Normans. Subsequent centuries saw wars between all the European nations as they struggled to gain land and power, and with it the redefining of borders and the redrawing of maps

The result today is that visitors are often struck by the similarities between neighbouring countries. For example, the seat of the European part of the continent. It is this diversity that makes the cities of western Europe such a delight to visit, while their shared bond makes travel between them an easy undertaking.

TOURISM IN EUROPE

Given the wealth of experiences on the average western European's doorstep, it isn't surprising that modern tourism started here. The Grand Tour was the first travel itinerary through Europe, becoming popular from the 17th century. Wealthy young men (and later women, accompanied by a chaperone) undertook the tour as part of their education, visiting classical ruins, viewing Renaissance paintings and immersing themselves in high society.

In 1828, the first guidebook was published in Germany, covering a stretch of the River Rhine.

View to Interlaken from Jungfraujoch rail station   *Amsterdam's Bloemenmarkt*

Parliament is in Strasbourg, capital of the French region of Alsace, and travellers crossing the border from there into Germany's Baden-Württemberg would expect to see immediate differences between the two. Instead, they are invariably surprised by how similar they are. Alsace has switched from being German to French and back again several times during the course of its history, and many of its residents speak German as their second language. In Baden-Württemberg, meanwhile, many people speak a local dialect that is more comprehensible to people on the French side of the border than it is to other Germans on their side. And, of course, the wines and foods are similar on both sides of the border, because grapes and cattle owe no national allegiance.

...YET DIFFERENT
Shared history aside, the western European countries are fiercely proud of their individual identities and heritage. Such differences have been summed up by an old joke, which says that in heaven the cooks are French, the policemen are English, the mechanics are German, the lovers are Italian and the bankers are Swiss. In hell, meanwhile, the cooks are English, the policemen are German, the mechanics are French, the lovers are Swiss and the bankers are Italian.

Of course, such stereotypes are rather corny, and in any case the English are now among the best cooks in Europe, but the joke does help to explain a lot about the wonderful diversity of this

It was acquired by a young German publisher named Karl Baedeker, who in 1832 produced a French edition of the book, an indication that numbers of French people were already touring the area. In 1836, the venerable London publishing house of John Murray brought out *A Handbook for Travellers on the Continent*.

With the advent of mass rail transport in the 1820s, travel became accessible to a wider population, something English Baptist minister Thomas Cook hit upon in 1841 when he organized a trip for some fellow temperance campaigners from Leicester to Loughborough. The fact that Cook was a minister didn't stop him from taking a cut of the proceeds, and by 1844 he was running his own business organizing what were effectively primitive package holidays.

A few years later Cook was bankrupt, but he bounced back and in 1855 was organizing his first overseas tour, taking people to the Paris Exhibition. Although individuals had long been enjoying the pleasures of visiting Paris and elsewhere, it was the first time that the man in the street, in numbers, was able to travel abroad and have everything arranged in advance. By 1856 Cook was offering the first grand circular tour of Europe, including several of the places we're still visiting today. The package tour and the foreign city break were born.

VISITING WESTERN EUROPE TODAY
Travel has changed dramatically since the days of the first guidebooks and Cook's tours. Back then, in the mid-19th century, there were fewer

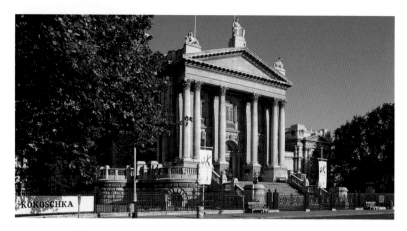

Tate Britain art gallery in London

restaurants and hotels, and far fewer attractions. Most cities had a main museum, and zoos were very popular, but otherwise it was castles and cathedrals that people went to see. Times were also much more unsettled across the region, and so travel took courage and a sense of adventure, as well as plenty of money. It also took a willingness to suffer discomfort, as most journeys had to be undertaken by coach at speeds averaging just 15kph (9mph)—the 960km (595-mile) journey from Paris to Nice alone took several days.

Today, the same journey takes just nine hours by car or a painless 90 minutes by plane. Improvements in transport, and especially the boom in budget airlines, has made short city breaks both easy and accessible. A brief flight will take a resident of Copenhagen to the very different city of Barcelona, transport someone living in Lisbon to London, or allow a Berliner to enjoy the *craic* in Dublin.

The growth in airline travel has not only made getting around western Europe easier, but has also made the region more accessible to the rest of the world. As a result, travellers from such 'new world' countries as the US, Australia and New Zealand can now afford to see at first hand the famous buildings, works of art and historical sites their predecessors could only read about in books.

It is this wealth of experiences that sets the cities of western Europe aside from all others. Here, you can immerse yourself in history by exploring such iconic buildings as Rome's Colosseum, London's St. Paul's Cathedral or Granada's Alhambra; admire such masterpieces as da Vinci's *Mona Lisa* in the Louvre, Michelangelo's ceiling fresco in the Vatican's Sistine Chapel and Botticelli's *Birth of Venus* in the Galleria degli Uffizi in Florence; or simply wander the canals of Venice, Amsterdam or Bruges, the lanes of Cork, Porto or Oxford, or the grand avenues of Paris, Vienna or Geneva.

If you were born to shop, you can browse the latest designs of the great fashion houses of Paris and Milan, stock up on Christmas gifts at the Christkindlmarkts of Salzburg and Strasbourg, or purchase fine chocolates in Brussels and Zürich. If food and drink are your passion, take tea at Claridge's in London, lunch at Maxim's in Paris or sip a Bellini at Harry's Bar in Venice. Then, if you still have energy at the end of the day, let yourself be mesmerized by an opera at Milan's La Scala, enjoy a beer and a sing-along at Munich's Oktoberfest, or laugh the night away at the Edinburgh Fringe Festival.

THE FUTURE IS GREEN

While budget flights have brought huge advantages in terms of making travel less expensive and therefore more accessible to a wider range of people across the globe, focus has recently turned to the environmental costs of this form of transport in particular and to tourism in general. The term 'carbon footprint' has quickly become familiar to everyone. Air travel is a huge contributor to carbon dioxide emissions and hence global warming, while high-impact tourism developments further damage the environment and are wasteful of resources. The effects, too, that mass tourism can have on local communties should not be underestimated.

The transition to greener forms of tourism has been embraced across western Europe, the stronghold of the modern Green movement. Here, such organizations as the UK-based Climate Care help travellers offset the harmful emissions of their transport by making equivalent reductions in atmospheric carbon dioxide through such projects as tree-planting schemes. The relatively small size of the region and its usually excellent public transport services also mean that air travel is not the only viable option when it comes to getting around. The concept of slow travel—eschewing air travel and short breaks in long-haul destinations in favour of taking your time and experiencing the journey itself—is gaining ground. And on the smaller scale, there are such environmentally friendly options as walking, cycling and sailing tours, and countless hotels and lodges are now offering accommodation that is sensitive to both ecological and social concerns. As has been the case throughout its history, western Europe is leading the way in a changing world.

AUSTRIA

UNDERSTANDING AUSTRIA

Mountains, forests and lakes cover two-thirds of landlocked Austria, providing walkers, climbers, hikers and skiers with first-rate facilities amid spectacular scenery. Vineyards coat the castle-dotted banks of the River Danube as it flows through the fertile Wachau valley. Snow-capped peaks form a backdrop to historic towns; museum- and art-filled cities proclaim some of the finest architecture in Europe. Music packs the cultural calendar, restaurants are atmospheric, public transport is good, and the people are warm and friendly. It's little wonder that Austria welcomes 20 million foreign visitors a year.

Inside a Viennese Heuriger *or wine tavern*

Hallstatt in the Salzkammergut

POLITICS

The Republic of Austria was created at the end of World War I, after six centuries of rule by the imperial Hapsburgs. Hitler incorporated the country into the German Reich in 1938 (the *Anschluss*), naming it Ostmark. Following Germany's defeat in World War II, Austria was occupied for 10 years by the Allied Powers of USSR, US, UK and France.

The State Treaty signed in May 1955 committed independent Austria to 'permanent neutrality', and during the Cold War years the country's location in central Europe was a useful buffer between the West and the Soviet bloc. Today it hosts a number of United Nations agencies, the Organization of the Petroleum Exporting Countries (OPEC), top international conferences and summit meetings.

Since Austria joined the European Union in 1995, its neutrality is less absolute—Austria participated in NATO- and EU-led missions in the former Yugoslavia—but the sense of being a neutral country has become ingrained in the Austrian psyche.

Austria is a Federal Republic, made up of nine independent federal states—Burgenland, Carinthia, Lower Austria, Upper Austria, Salzburg, Styria, Tirol, Vorarlberg and Vienna—with their own provincial governments. The federal parliament has two chambers, the Nationalrat, to which members are directly elected, and the Bundesrat, the Upper House, elected by the provincial assemblies.

In the elections of October 2006, the Social Democrat Party (SPÖ) under its leader, Alfred Gusenbauer, won with a 1 per cent lead over the ruling conservative People's Party (ÖVP) under Chancellor Schüssel. The Greens came third, just ahead of the right-wing Freedom Party (FPÖ), followed, a good way behind, by the Alliance for the Future of Austria (BZÖ), led by the controversial Jörg Haider. A Grand Coalition government between the SPÖ and ÖVP was announced in January 2007.

PEOPLE

Austria has a population of 8.3 million, 98 per cent of whom speak German, the national language. There's a wide variety of regional accents and numerous dialects. In the past, when the Alps were impassable, valley communities were isolated and maintained distinct differences in dialects and traditions. But the highly educated Austrians can switch easily between their local dialect and standard *Hochdeutsch* (High German) and, especially in the cities and tourist regions, a large number of people speak excellent English.

In a country where '*Grüss Gott*' is the customary greeting, it isn't surprising to find that religion plays an important role in many people's lives. About 74 per cent of Austrians are Roman Catholic, 5 per cent Protestant, with a mix of other faiths accounted for in the remaining population. You'll see small shrines adorned with fresh flowers out in the countryside, where church bells peal out loudly from lovingly cared-for village churches and little happens on Sunday until everyone returns from the morning service. Even in Vienna, few shops are open on Sunday.

GEOGRAPHY

The Alps dominate the Austrian landscape. Two thirds of the country's 83,858sq km (32,369sq miles) are mountainous, with three ranges running west to east. The Northern Limestone Alps form a natural barrier with Germany, the Southern Limestone Alps with Italy and Slovenia. In the Central Alps, the Grossglockner peaks at 3,797m (12,457ft) and few of its neighbours are lower than 3,000m (9,842ft). Here glaciers feed waterfalls and raw mountain scenery is at its most spectacular.

At 280km (174 miles) from north to south, and 560km (348 miles) east to west, Austria is

construction materials a priority. Recycling is a way of life, the sale of leaded fuel is banned, and a referendum held back in 1978 led to the Nuclear Prohibition Law being passed.

Austrians are very eco-conscious and a substantial amount of government money goes into projects concerned with protecting the environment. Investment in water treatment and drainage systems has resulted in most of the country's lakes being of drinking-water quality.

Environmentally friendly public transport is in use in cities, bicycles are popular, and Austrians are great walkers. In Vienna, the Eco-label denotes environmentally aware hotels, restaurants and wine taverns, while Biobauernhof is a network of 'ecological' farms.

MUSIC

To visit Austria and not become immersed in its music is to miss part of the essential soul of the

View from the summit of Austria's highest mountain pass   Rathaus *in St. Gilgen*

not a big country, but its position—bordered by Germany, the Czech Republic, Slovakia, Hungary, Slovenia, Italy and Switzerland—has always given it great importance as the crossroad between eastern and western Europe.

The Danube River flows from Germany through the regions of Upper Austria and, most scenically, Lower Austria, where the fertile Danube valley is heavily cultivated and famed for its wine-growing regions. Other important rivers are the Inn and the Salzach, the Mur and the Drau.

For a magnificent combination of lakes and mountains, the Salzkammergut area east of Salzburg is hard to beat. Carinthia in the warmer south is famed for its lakes, especially the Wörthersee, which is warmed by thermal springs. Austria has around 100 large lakes and almost 1,000 smaller ones, including tarns and mountain lakes. Lake Neusiedl in Burgenland is Central Europe's only steppe lake. Never more than 1.8m (6ft) deep, it is ideal for swimming and water sports and is so popular with people living in Vienna that it is often referred to as the 'Viennese Sea'.

ENVIRONMENT

Austria was 'green' before most of the rest of the world started waking up to the effects of environmental damage. Natural forms of energy, including wind and solar power, are actively encouraged, and subsidies are given for ecological building, with low energy consumption and the use of environmentally friendly

country. Of the great composers, Mozart was born in Salzburg, Franz Joseph Haydn in Lower Austria, Anton Bruckner near Linz, Franz Schubert and Arnold Schönberg in Vienna. At 18, Beethoven was sent to Vienna to study with Mozart, and later with Haydn, and stayed for the rest of his life. Brahms spent 35 years in Vienna, Gustav Mahler was director of the Vienna Court Opera and Richard Strauss of the Staatsoper.

The waltz originated in Vienna with the Johan Strausses, father and son. It was Johan Strauss the Younger who, inspired by his surroundings, composed *The Blue Danube* and *Tales from the Vienna Woods*. The Ball Season in Vienna epitomizes glamour, while the Vienna Philharmonic and the Vienna Boys Choir are world renowned.

Throughout the year, in cities and small towns, Austria abounds with festivals, many of them, like the Salzburg Festival in summer, highlights of the world's cultural calendar. Linz has its Bruckner Festival, alpine Schwarzenberg its Schubertiade, Innsbruck its Early Music and Summer Dance festivals; Eisenstadt celebrates Franz Joseph Haydn, and the Bregenz Festival of music and theatre is magically staged on Austria's portion of Lake Constance.

But it's not all classical. Founded in 1988, the annual Wien Modern is one of the widest-ranging contemporary music festivals in the world. Jazz thrives, and pop, rock and electronic music festivals attract top international bands.

THE BEST OF AUSTRIA

CARINTHIA

Klagenfurt Explore beautifully restored Renaissance and baroque buildings, and myriad arcaded courtyards, before heading out to the beaches, boats, walks and entertainments of Wörthersee.

Hohe Tauern-Grossglockner National Park Hike amid high peaks–the park has more than 300 mountains above 3,000m (9,840ft)–ski among glaciers, walk in lush valleys, alongside rivers, lakes and waterfalls, or drive the spectacular Glockner High Alpine Road in Europe's biggest national park.

LOWER AUSTRIA

Danube Valley Cycle the Danube Bike Path or take a boat trip past the castles, churches, villages and vineyards of the Wachau region. Don't miss the Baroque splendour of Melk Abbey.

Innsbruck (above)

SALZBURG

Salzburg (▷ 13) Soak up Mozart, a magical Old Town, the trick fountains of Schloss Hellbrunn, and venture into *Sound of Music* country.

STYRIA

Graz Walk and shop in the medieval Old Town, be amazed by the architecture and art of the Kunsthaus, see the world's largest collection of weaponry in the Landhaushof, listen to live jazz in a courtyard, drink on the innovative Island in the Mur, and get panoramic views from the tree-clothed Schlossberg hill.

Mur Island, Graz (above)

TIROL

Innsbruck See the landmark Goldenes Dachl, a shimmering golden-tiled roof dating from the 16th century, the Hofburg's grand apartments, and the alpine inhabitants of the Alpenzoo. Shop in designer boutiques, thrill to panoramic views from the Bergisel ski jump, try paragliding or a scary bungee jump from the Europabrücke bridge.

Kitzbühel Go in winter for the glitz and glamour of this fashionable ski resort, in summer for the scenic walking trails, swimming in the Schwarzsee lake and the Triathlon World Cup.

Statue of Mozart outside the Hofburg in Vienna (below)

UPPER AUSTRIA

Linz Contrast the baroque squares and patrician houses of the Old Town with the virtual world of the Ars Electronica Centre, in the European Capital of Culture 2009.

Hallstadt Gaze at the views of this picturesque and historic little town clinging to the foot of a mountain on Hallstättersee lake.

St. Wolfgang Enjoy the lakeside home of the White Horse Inn of operetta fame, but don't miss the Gothic pilgrimage church, where Michael Pacher's 15th-century high altar is mesmerizing.

VIENNA

Vienna (▷ 16–17) Marvel at the museums, music and stunning architecture of this truly capital city.

VORARLBERG

Bregenz Stroll among frescoed houses and cobbled streets, and alongside Bodensee (Lake Constance), summer scene of the international Bregenz Festival.

Hohensalzburg Fortress overlooks Salzburg's rooftops

SALZBURG

Mozart's mountain-ringed city of music, festivals and glorious architecture captivates all the senses. History abounds in the Old Town's churches and squares, and the views are unforgettable.

Salzburg lies close to Austria's border with Germany, and while its history goes back well before it was Roman Luvavum, it was the Prince-Archbishops ruling in the 17th and 18th centuries who, using their wealth from the salt trade, created the magnificent baroque architecture that thrills visitors today. The hilltop Hohensalzburg Fortress has stood guard over the city for over 900 years. Ride the funicular up there for panoramic views and the splendid State Apartments (May, Jun, Sep daily 9–6; Jul, Aug 9–7; Jan–end Apr, Oct–end Dec 9.30–5). The glacial green River Salzach winds through town and into the green pastures of *Sound of Music* country.

THE OLD TOWN (ALTSTADT)
The narrow streets and gracious squares of Salzburg's beguiling Altstadt (Old Town) are packed with fabulous old churches–the Stiftskirche St. Peter, dating from 847, and the atmospheric Franziskanerkirche are unmissable–and grand buildings, like the Residenz, seat of the Prince-Archbishops (Tue–Sun 9–5). The glorious Cathedral (summer daily 6.30am–7pm, winter 6.30–5) is where Mozart was baptized, and his birthplace in picturesque Getreidegasse is a highlight museum (Jul, Aug daily 9–7; Sep–end Jun 9–6).

Cross the river for iconic views of the Altstadt's pastel-painted buildings, its spires and domes, and the powerful fortress, all set against a mountain backdrop, and take a boat trip to Hellbrunn Palace with its trick fountains (guided tours Jul, Aug, 9am–10pm; May, Jun, Sep, 9–5.30; Apr, Oct 9–4.30).

CITY OF MUSIC
From Mozart Week in January to the November Jazz Festival and pre-Christmas carols, over 4,000 cultural events pack Salzburg's year. Music fills churches, palaces and the streets, but the most coveted tickets are for the stylish Salzburg Festival (five weeks to the end of August).

RATINGS
Historic interest	●●●●●
Cultural interest	●●●●●
Photo stops	●●●●●
Walkability	●●●●

BASICS

⊞ 5 E3

ℹ Mozartplatz 5, tel 088 987330; Jul, Aug daily 9–7, Easter–end Jun, Sep, Oct, Dec daily 9–6; Jan–Easter, Nov Mon–Sat 9–6. Staff will book hotels, theatre tickets, audio and sightseeing tours

🚆 Salzburg

www.salzburg.info
The Salzburg tourist office website, in 11 languages, has details of attractions, forthcoming events, shops, restaurants and special offers, and you can book accommodation online.

TIPS
● The Salzburg Card, which gives free single admission to all the city's museums and attractions, travel on public transport and discounts on various tours and excursions, is good value. It costs €23 for 24 hours, €32 for 48 hours and €36 for 72 hours (and a couple of euros less in winter).
● Pack an umbrella!

DON'T MISS
Be on Residenzplatz at 11am or 6pm to hear the Glockenspiel play a Mozart tune.

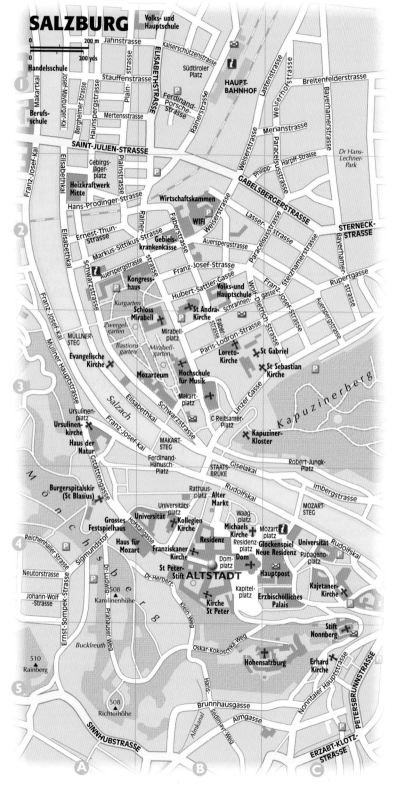

SALZBURG

Volks- und
Hauptschule

0 _____ 200 m
0 _____ 200 yds

Jahnstrasse

Handelsschule

Berufs-
schule

Makartkai

Josef-Mayer-Kai

Berghelner Strasse

Haunspergstrasse

Stauffenstrasse

Plainstrasse

Mertensstrasse

ELISABETHSTRASSE

Kaiserschützenstrasse

Südtiroler
Platz

Ferdinand-
Porsche-
Strasse

Rainerstrasse

HAUPT-
BAHNHOF

Südtiroler
Platz

Lastenstrasse

Weiserstrasse

Merianstrasse

Paracelsusstrasse

Breitenfelderstrasse

Bayerhamerstrasse

Dr Hans-
Lechner-
Park

SAINT-JULIEN-STRASSE

Franz-Josef-Kai

Elisabethkai

Gebirgs-
jäger-
platz

Heizkraftwerk
Mitte

Hans-Prodinger-Strasse

Ernest-Thun-
Strasse

Markus-Sittikus-Strasse

Elisabethkai

Schwarzstrasse

Rainerstrasse

Faberstrasse

GABELSBERGERSTRASSE

Wirtschaftskammern

WIFI

Gebiels-
krankenkasse

Auerspergstrasse

Weiserstrasse

Lasser-
strasse

Philipp-
Harpff-Strasse

Paracelsusstrasse

STERNECK-
STRASSE

Auerspergstrasse

Franz-Josef-Strasse

Franz-Josef-Strasse

Steinhamerstrasse

Bayerhamer-
strasse

Rupertgasse

Auerspergstrasse

strasse

Franz-Josef-Kai

Müllner Hauptstrasse

Kongress-
haus

Kurgarten

Schloss
Mirabell

Zwergel-
garten

Bastions-
garten

Mirabell-
garten

Hubert-Sattler-Gasse

Volks-und
Hauptschule

St Andrä-
Kirche

Mirabell-
platz

Paris-Lodron-Strasse

Fabergasse

Wolf-Dietrich-Strasse

schranner-
gasse

Franz-Josef-Strasse

MÜLLNER-
STEG

Evangelische
Kirche

Mozarteum

Salzach

Elisabethkai

Schwarzstrasse

Hochschule
für Musik

Makart-
platz

Loreto-
Kirche

St Gabriel

St Sebastian
Kirche

Linzer Gasse

Kapuzinerberg

Ursulinen-
platz

Ursulinen-
kirche

Haus der
Natur

Franz-Josef-Kai

MAKART-
STEG

Ferdinand-
Hanusch-
Platz

C Reitsamer-
Platz

Kapuziner-
Kloster

Robert-Jungk-
Platz

Giselakai

STAATS-
BRÜKE

Rudolfskai

Imbergstrasse

Mönchsberg

Reichenhaller Strasse

Burgerspitalskir
(St Blasius)

Grosses
Festspielhaus

Haus für
Mozart

Gstättengasse

Hofstallgasse

Sigmundstor

Universitäts-
platz

Universität

Kollegien
Kirche

Franziskaner
Kirche

Rathaus-
platz

Alter
Markt

Residenz

Waag-
platz

Michaels
Kirche

Residenz
platz

Dom-
platz

Dom

Mozart
platz

Glockenspiel
Neue Residenz

MOZART-
STEG

Universität

Rudolfskai

Papageno-
platz

Neutorstrasse

Johann-Wolf
-Strasse

Dr-Ludwig-

Ernst-Sompek-Strasse

508
Karolinenhöhe

510
Rainberg

Dr-Herbert-

St Peter-
Stift

Kapitel-
platz

Kirche
St Peter

ALTSTADT

Hauptpost

Erzbischölliches
Palais

Kajetaner-
Kirche

Stift
Nonnberg

Klein-Weg

Prahauser-Weg

Bucklreuth

508
Richterhöhe

SINNHUBSTRASSE

Oskar-Kokoseva-Weg

Hohensalzburg

Erhard
Kirche

Hans-

Almkanal

Sedlmayr Weg

Brunnhausgasse

Almgasse

PETERSBRUNNSTRASSE

Nonntaler Hauptstrasse

ERZABT-KLOTZ-
STRASSE

A   B   C

1   2   3   4   5

WHAT TO DO

⊕ CONFISERIE JOSEF HOLZERMAYR

Alter Markt 7
Tel 0662 842365
www.holzermayr.at
Shop for delicious handmade chocolates, fresh cream truffles and gingerbread, as well as the famous Mozartkugeln (Mozart Balls), which have been made here since 1890. There's a special counter of diabetic treats, too.
⊙ Mon–Sat 9–6, Sun 10–5 🚌 Bus 3, 5, 6, 7, 8, 10, 25, 26

⊕ SALZBURGER HEIMATWERK

Residenzplatz 9
Tel 0662 844110
www.sbg.heimatwerk.at
For something truly Austrian, this shop on the Old Town's grandest square has beautifully made traditional Austrian costumes (Trachten), high-quality crafts, fabrics and lovely things for the home.
⊙ Mon–Fri 9–6, Sat 9–5 🚌 Bus 3, 5, 6, 7, 8, 10, 25, 26

⊕ SPORER

Getreidegasse 39
Tel 0662 845431
www.sporer.at
Pedestrian Getreidegasse is the Old Town's most famous shopping street. Family-owned Sporer sells traditional liqueurs, herb bitters, schnapps and, in winter, spiced teas and punch.
⊙ Mon–Fri 9–12, 2.30–7, Sat 8.30–5 🚌 1, 4, 7, 8, 10, 15, 16, 18, 24, 27

⑦ MIRABELL PALACE CONCERTS

Mirabellplatz 4
Tel 0662 848586
www.salzburger-schlosskonzerte.at
Salzburger Schlosskonzerte are held in the stunning Marble Hall, where the Mozart family played, built in the baroque style by the Prince-Archbishops.
⊙ Box office Mon–Fri 9–6, Sat 9–12
💶 €29–€35 🚌 1, 2, 3, 4, 5, 6

⑦ ROCKHOUSE

Schallmooser Hauptstrasse 46
Tel 0662 884914
www.rockhouse.at
The music here spans jazz, punk, pop, rock, folk, blues, heavy metal, contemporary, crossover and more, with local and international bands.
⊙ Box office Mon–Fri 9.30–12.30, 5.30–7. Bar and food Mon–Thu 6pm–2am, Fri, Sat 6pm–4am 🚌 4 to Canavalstrasse 💶 €18–€40

EATING

CAFÉ BAZAR

Schwarzstrasse 3
Tel 0662 874278
www.cafe-bazar.at
The tree-shaded terrace has great views of Salzburg's Old Town across the river; inside there's an elegant coffeehouse atmosphere. Prosciutto, carpaccio and ricotta cheese ravioli with mint reveal Italian flair.
⊙ Mon–Sat 7.30am–11pm, Sun 7.30–6
🍴 L €11, D €20, Wine €15
🚌 1, 3, 4, 5, 15, 16, 25, 27 to Theatergasse

K&K RESTAURANT AM WAAGPLATZ

Waagplatz 2
Tel 0662 842156
www.kkhotels.com
Eight restaurants, each with its own character, occupy a historic building near the Cathedral. On the first floor, where the food is as elegant as the setting, seasonal highlights include superb asparagus and venison.
⊙ Daily 10am–12am
🍴 L €22, D €33, Wine €22
🚌 Bus 3, 5, 6, 7, 8, 10, 25, 26

STIFTSKELLER ST. PETER

St. Peter-Bezirk 1–4
Tel 0662 841268
www.haslauer.at
Dating back to AD803, this wood-panelled restaurant with a maze of small rooms next to the Stiftskirche oozes history. Try the saddle of wild boar with red cabbage, gnocchi and cranberry juice.
⊙ Mon–Sat 11am–12am, Sun 10am–12am
🍴 3-course set menu €26, 2-course lunch €28, D €40, Wine €23.50
🚌 Bus 3, 5, 6, 7, 8, 10, 25, 26

DIE WEISSE BRAUEREI

Rupertgasse 10
Tel 0662 8722460
www.dieweisse.at
Tucked away in the New Town, this popular modern bierkeller brews its own malty beer and serves up good, hearty Austrian food.
⊙ Mon–Sat 10.30am–12am
🍴 L €10, D €13, Beer 0.5l €4
🚌 4

STAYING

ALTSTADTHOTEL WEISSE TAUBE

Kaigasse 9, A-5020 Salzburg
Tel 0662 842404
www.weissetaube.at
Built in 1365, this family-owned hotel next to Mozartplatz has been welcoming visitors since 1809. It is traditionally furnished, with wood ceilings and an inviting breakfast room.
🛏 €100, including Austrian breakfast
🛈 30 (smoking rooms may be available)
🅿 8 minutes' walk away, €9.50 per day
🚌 3, 5, 6, 25 to Mozartsteg

BLAUE GANS

Getreidegasse 41–43, A-5020 Salzburg
Tel 0662 842491
www.blauegans.at
In the Old Town's most famous street, the building may be medieval but the interior is pure arthotel with white rooms simply furnished in contemporary style. Fresh local produce stars in the notable cellar restaurant.
🛏 €145, including buffet breakfast
🛈 10 non-smoking
🚌 Bus 1, 4, 7, 8, 10, 15, 16, 18, 24, 27
🅿 Public parking nearby, €15 per day

HOTEL ALTSTADT RADISSON SAS

Rudolfskai 25, A-5020 Salzburg
Tel 0662 848571
www.radisson.com
One of Salzburg's oldest inns, this is now a 5-star gem furnished with antiques. A combination of luxury and tradition, its river/Old Town location ensures great views.
🛏 €245 per person, excluding breakfast (€22)
🛈 62 (smoking rooms on request)
🚌 Bus 3, 5, 6, 7, 8, 10, 25, 26, 77
🅿 €26 per day

Vienna

Imperial palaces and glass skyrises, Old Masters and modern art, traditional coffeehouses and trendy restaurants, designer shopping and Christmas markets, stylish waltzes, prancing horses, Mozart and more.

The Spanish Riding School in the Hofburg

Kunsthistorisches Museum (left).
Frescoed ceiling in the Great Gallery of Schloss Schönbrunn (right)

RATINGS

Cultural interest	● ● ● ● ●
Historic interest	● ● ● ● ●
Good for food	● ● ● ●
Specialist shopping	● ● ● ●

BASICS

✚ 5 E3

ℹ Albertinaplatz, close to the Vienna State Opera, tel 01 24555; daily 9–7

🚆 Westbahnhof, Südbahnhof, Franz Josefs Bahnhof, Wien Mitte

www.wien.info
Comprehensive information on all the sights, current exhibitions and shows, hotel bookings, shopping, and loads of ideas.

TIP

● The Vienna Card, €18.50, gives a reduction or benefit at 210 museums, sights, shops, restaurants and more, plus 72 hours unlimited travel by metro, bus and tram. Valid on the day of issue and the following three days, you can buy it at hotels and tourist information desks. With each adult Vienna Card purchased, one child aged up to 15 (ID proof of age required) also travels free on public transport.

SEEING VIENNA

With its baroque architecture, fabulous palaces, brilliant museums, sinuous art nouveau buildings and the great Ringstrasse—a broad boulevard encircling an Old Town so rich it's a UNESCO World Heritage Site—Vienna has a foot in the past. But look across the River Danube at the concrete and glass UNO-city, or at the exciting MuseumsQuartier, and you soon see that Vienna embraces the 21st century too.

Alongside narrow streets, elegant squares and ornate façades are big, tranquil parks perfumed with flowers. The Vienna Woods lie just a tram ride away. The 100-year-old Ferris wheel made famous in *The Third Man* defines the Prater amusement park, a former Hapsburg hunting ground. Mozart composed *The Marriage of Figaro* here; today the city has fabulous opera, great concerts, theatre, jazz and clubs.

HIGHLIGHTS

HAUS DER MUSIK

✚ 19 D4 • Seilerstätte 30 ☎ 01 51648 🕐 Daily 10–10 💶 Adult €10, child (3–12) €5.50, child (under 3) free, family ticket (2 adults, 3 children under 12) €26
www.hdm.at
Opened in 2000, the House of Music gives you musicians and composers as you've never experienced them before: hands-on, interactive and simply brilliant.

HOFBURG

✚ 18 C4 • Michaelerkuppel ☎ 01 553 7570 🕐 Daily 9–5 💶 Imperial Apartments, Sisi Museum and Imperial Silver Collection €9.90 with audio guide, child (6–18) €4.90 🚇 Herrengasse 🚌 2A, 3A Hofburg; tram 1, 2, D, J Burgring
www.hofburg-wien.at
The imperial seat of power for centuries, the Hofburg complex is huge, comprising 18 buildings and 2,600 rooms. As well as the Imperial Apartments, here you'll find the Spanish Riding School and performing Lippizaner horses, and the Chapel where the Vienna Boys Choir sings on Sundays.

KUNSTHISTORISCHES MUSEUM

🕂 18 B4 • Maria Theresien-Platz ☎ 01 5252 44025 ⏰ Tue–Sun 10–6, Thu 10–9 💶 Adult €10, child €3.50, family ticket (2 adults and up to 3 children) €20 Ⓜ Volkstheater 🚌 2A, 57A; tram D, J, 1, 2 www.khm.at

The Viennese Museum of Fine Art is one of the world's great museums. Immerse yourself in works by Titian, Tintoretto, Rembrandt, Rubens, Raphael, and especially Breughel, in opulent surroundings.

SCHÖNBRUNN

🕂 18 off C5 • Schönbrunner Schlossstrasse ☎ 01 8111 3239 ⏰ Palace daily Jul, Aug 8.30–6; Apr–end Jun, Sep–end Oct 8.30–5; Nov–end Mar 8.30–4.30 💶 Palace tours with audio guide from €9.50, child (6–18) from €4.90 Ⓜ Schönbrunn 🚌 10A, tram 10, 58 Schönbrunn www.schoenbrunn.at

Art installation in the Secession

The Hapsburgs' grand summer palace demands as much of a day as you're prepared to give it. The State Rooms and Great Gallery are superb, while the park offers avenues of shady trees, the giant Palm House, a zoo, a maze and more. Come in December for the Christmas market.

SECESSION

🕂 18 C5 • Friedrichstrasse 12 ☎ 01 587 5307 ⏰ Tue–Sun, public hols 10–6, Thu 10–8 💶 Exhibitions and Beethoven Frieze €6; children under 10 not admitted Ⓜ Karlsplatz/Oper 🚌 Bus and tram Karlsplatz/Oper www.secession.at

Art nouveau fans will love this bright white building topped with a dome of gilded laurel leaves. Klimt's 34m (112ft) *Beethoven Frieze*, a pictorial interpretation of the Ninth Symphony painted in 1902, is stunning. Klimt's most famous painting, *The Kiss*, is in the Austrian Gallery, amid the exquisite gardens of the Belvedere Palace.

STEPHANSDOM

🕂 19 D3 • Stephansplatz 1 ☎ 01 5155 23526 ⏰ Mon–Sat 6am–10pm; Sun, public hols 7am–10pm 💶 Guided tour of the Cathedral (Mon–Sat at 10.30, 3; Sun at 3. In English Apr–Oct at 3.45): Adult €4, child (under 15) €1.50, student (15–18) €2.50. Guided tour of the Catacombs (Mon–Sat 10–11.30, 1.30–4.30): Adult €4; children (under 15) €1.50, students (15–18) €2.50 Ⓜ Stephansplatz www.stephanskirche.at

Heart and soul of the city, the Gothic cathedral of St. Stephen is full of treasures under its stripey-tiled roof, not least the icon that attracts visitors until late.

MORE TO SEE

KUNSTHAUSWIEN

🕂 19 off F2 • Untere Weissgerberstrasse 13 ☎ 01 7120491 ⏰ Daily 10–7 💶 Adult €9, child (under 10) free, family ticket €20; Mon half price 🚌 Tram N, O, Radetzkyplatz www.kunsthauswien.com

See the imaginative work of artist, architect and ecologist Friedensreich Hundertwasser at the KunstHausWien, and don't miss his jazzy social housing project nearby.

BACKGROUND

In the 1st to the 4th centuries AD, Roman Vindobona grew up and flourished in what is now Vienna's Inner City (Innenstadt), and the Roman emperor Probus encouraged the planting of vineyards in the Vienna Woods in the 3rd century. In the Middle Ages it was the seat of the Bavarian Babenbergs, from whom it received its city charter in 1221, and the Hapsburg dynasties followed. Under their reign, especially during the 18th and 19th centuries, Vienna became a city renowned for culture and music. It thrived, too, as the capital of the Austro-Hungarian Empire, hosting the World Fair in 1873. Incorporated into Germany under Hitler, liberated by Soviet troops in 1945 and occupied by Allies until 1955, during the Cold War years Vienna was a hotbed of intrigue.

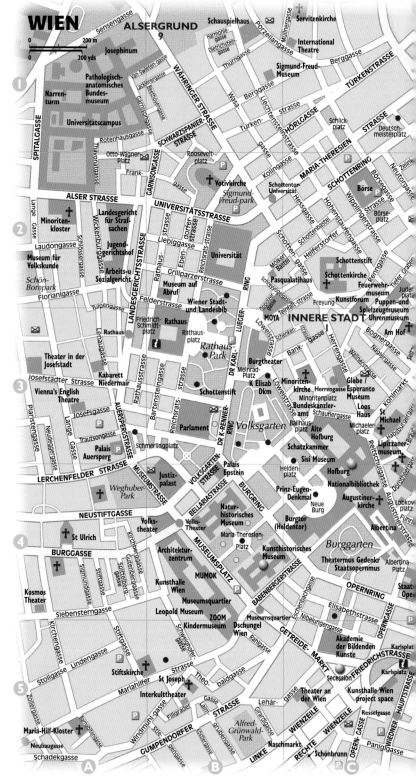

WIEN

ALSERGRUND
9

0 ____ 200 m
0 ____ 200 yds

Sensengasse

Schauspielhaus

Servitenkirche

International Theatre

Josephinum

Pathologisch-anatomisches Bundes-museum

Harmonie-gasse
Dietrichstein-gasse

Thurngasse

Porzellangasse

Müllnergasse

Berggasse

Sigmund-Freud-Museum

TÜRKENSTRASSE

Narren-turm

Universitätscampus

Rotenhausgasse

Van-Swieten-gasse
Lackierergasse

Carminigasse

Wasa-

Berggasse

Türken-

Liechtensteinstrasse

strasse

HORLGASSE

Schlick-platz

STRASSE

Deutsch-meisterplatz

SPITALGASSE

Thavonatgasse

Otto-Wagner-Platz

Frank-

Roosevelt-platz

gasse

Kolingasse

MARIA-THERESIEN

SCHOTTENRING

Börse

Neutorgasse

Zelini

ALSER STRASSE

gasse

Votivkirche

Sigmund-Freud-park

Schottentor-Universität

Hessgasse

Hohenstaufengasse

Wipplingerstrasse

Börse-platz

Börsegasse

UNIVERSITÄTSSTRASSE

Lange

Minoriten-kloster

Landesgericht für Straf-sachen

WICKENBURGGASSE

Schlösselgasse

strasse

Liebiggasse

dorfer-strasse

Reichsrats-strasse

Universität

SCHWARZSPANIER-STRASSE

Schotten-gasse

Schottenbastei

Möker-Bastei

Schottenstift

Schottenkirche

Feuerwehr-museum

Juden-platz

gasse

Laudongasse

Museum für Volkskunde

Schön-Bornpark

Florianigasse

Tulpengasse

JUGEND-GERICHTSHOF
Jugend-gerichtshof

Arbeits-u Sozialgericht

Grillparzerstrasse

Rathaus-

Eben-

LANDESGERICHTSSTRASSE

Felderstrasse

Museum auf Abruf

Wiener Stadt- und Landesbib

Freyung

Pasqualatihaus

Kunstforum

Löwel-strasse

Schottengasse

Schenken-gasse

Teinfalt-strasse

Schenken-gasse

Kunstforum Puppen-und Spielzeugmuseum Uhrenmuseum

Am Hof

Bognergasse

Naglergasse

MOYA

INNERE STADT

Friedrich-Schmidt-platz

Rathaus

Rathaus-platz

Rathaus-Park

Bank-

Herrengasse

Wallnerstrasse

Theater in der Josefstadt

LUEGER

RING

Burgtheater

Meinrad-Platz

Minoriten-kirche

Herrengasse

Kohlmarkt

DR-KARL-

K Elisab Dkm

Minoritenplatz

Esperanto Museum

Globe /

Loos Haus

St Michael

Kabarett Niedermair

Josefstädter Strasse

Vienna's English Theatre

Josefsgasse

AUERSPERGSTRASSE

Rathausstrasse

Bartensteingasse

Reichsrats-

strasse

DR KARL

Schottenstift

Bundeskanzler-amt

Schauflergasse

Alte Hofburg

Michaeler-platz

Lipizzaner-museum

Habsburgergasse

Trautsongasse

Palais Auersperg

Schmerlingplatz

Parlament

Volksgarten

Ballhaus-platz

Schatzkammer

Sisi Museum

Reitschulgasse

Bräunerstrasse

Dorotheergasse

Plankengasse
Neudeggergasse
Lange Gasse

LERCHENFELDER STRASSE

MUSEUMSGASSE

Justiz-palast

Weghuber Park

NEUSTIFTGASSE

VOLKSGARTEN

DR K-RENNER

RING

Palais Epstein

Heiden-platz

Hofburg

Prinz-Eugen-Denkmal

Neue Burg

Nationalbibliothek

Augustiner-kirche

Lobkov platz

Führi

Augustinerstrasse

St Ulrich

BURGGASSE

Kosmos Theater

Siebensterngasse

Volks-theater

BELLARIASTRASSE

Natur-historisches Museum

Volks-Theater

Maria-Theresien-Platz

BURGRING

Burgtor (Heldentor)

Kunsthistorisches Museum

Burggarten

Theatermus Gedenkr Staatsopernmus

Albertina Platz

Albertina

Sigmundsgasse

Architektur-zentrum

MUSEUMSPLATZ

BABENBERGERSTRASSE

OPERNRING

Staat Ope

Kunsthalle Wien

MUMOK

Eschenbachgasse

Elisabethstrasse

Nibelungengasse

OPERNGASSE

P

Kirchengasse

Spitelberg-gasse
Gutenberggasse

Stiftgasse

Schottenfeldgasse

Leopold Museum

Museumsquartier

ZOOM Kindermuseum

Dschungel Wien

Rahlgasse

GETREIDE. MARKT

Akademie der Bildenden Künste

Karlspl

FRIEDRICHSTRASSE

Windmühl-gasse

Stiftskirche

St Joseph

Schweighofer-gasse

Mariahilfer

Strasse

Theo-baldgasse

Karlsplatz

Secession

Kunsthalle Wien project space

Stollgasse

Lindengasse

Interkulttheater

Lehár-

Theater an der Wien

WIENZEILE

Resselgasse

Maria-Hilf-Kloster

Neubaugasse

Schadekgasse

GUMPENDORFER STRASSE

Fillgradergasse

Laim-grubengasse

Girardigasse

STRASSE

gasse

Alfred-Grünwald-Park

Naschmarkt

LINKE

RECHTE

WIENZEILE

OPERN-GASSE

Panigigasse

Schönbrunn

WIENER HAUPTSTRASSE

Capistrangasse

A   B   C

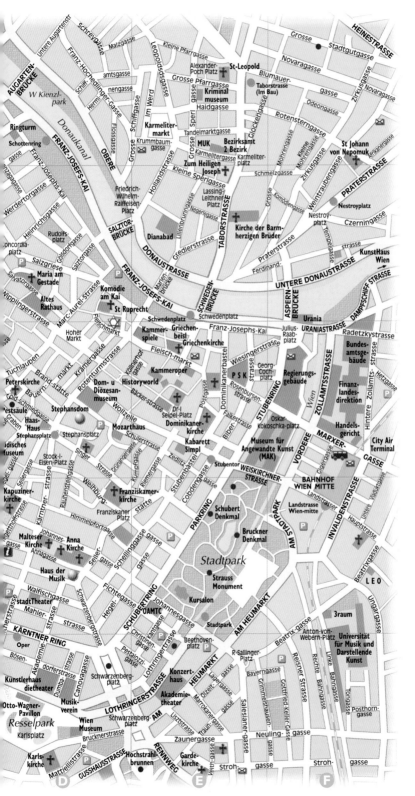

KEY TO SYMBOLS

- ⊕ Shopping
- ⊕ Entertainment
- ⊗ Nightlife
- ⊗ Sports
- ⊗ Activities
- ⊗ Health and Beauty
- ⊗ For Children

WHAT TO DO

⊕ JULIUS MEINL AM GRABEN

Graben 19
Tel 01 532 3334
www.meinlamgraben.at
This unforgettable gourmet food shop with an amazing deli is packed with temptations, from designer coffees to luxurious chocolates. It even has a top-class restaurant and an exceedingly well-stocked wine bar.
⊕ Mon–Wed 8.30–7.30,Thu, Fri 8–7.30, Sat 9–6 ⊕ Stephansplatz, Graben exit ⊟ A1 Bognergasse

⊕ PARK

Mondscheingasse 20
Tel 01 526 44144
www.park.co.at
This smart concept store near the trendy Mariahilferstrasse shopping mile displays designer fashion and accessories for men and women, with top European names and new young talent.
⊕ Mon–Fri 10–7, Sat 10–6 ⊕ Neubaugasse ⊟ 13A, Tram 49 Westbahnstrasse

⊕ JAZZLAND

Franz-Josefs-Kai 29
Tel 01 553 2575
www.jazzland.at
In a cellar under St. Ruprecht's Church, this celebrated jazz venue has been attracting international stars for 35 years alongside noted jazz, blues and swing musicians.
⊕ Mon–Sat 7pm–2am (live music from 9pm) ⊞ €11–€18 ⊕ Schwedenplatz

⊕ THEATER AN DER WIEN

Linke Wienzeile 6
Tel 01 58885
www.theater-wien.at
Unlike the Opera House, this atmospheric and historic theatre, built by the *Magic Flute* librettist, Emanuel Schikaneder, is open all year. Productions span ballet, opera, concerts, operetta and modern dance and music.

⊕ Box office daily 10–7 ⊕ Karlsplatz, exit Secession ⊟ 57A, 59A

⊕ WIENER STAATSOPER

Opernring 2
Tel 01 51444 2250
www.staatsoper.at
Just being in the spectacular Vienna Opera House building is exciting. Standing room tickets go on sale 80 minutes before the night's performance. Guided tours cost €6.50.
⊕ Season runs Sep–Jun ⊞ From €2–€254. ⊕ Karlsplatz/Oper ⊟ 59A, tram 1, 2, D, J, 62, 65

⊗ VOLKSGARTEN

Burgring/Volksgarten
Tel 01 532 4241
www.volksgarten.at
Vienna pounds with trendy bars and clubs. This is one of the most popular discos, which also has a restaurant and palm-decked gardens with a big dance floor so you could also swing, tango, salsa or jive the night away in summer.
⊞ From €5 ⊕ Disco: Tue–Sat from 11.30pm (from 9.30pm when there are live acts). Garden: May–early Sep Sat, Sun, 7pm–12am ⊕ Volkstheater

EATING

CAFÉ DRECHSLER

Linke Wienzeile 22n
Tel 01 581 2044
www.cafedrechsler.at
The legendary café on the Naschmarkt, updated by design guru Terence Conran, has a daily-changing menu of Viennese specialties.
⊕ Tue–Sat 3am–2am, Sun 3am–12am, Mon 8am–2am ⊞ L set menu €7.20, D €17, Wine €18 ⊕ Karlsplatz

FIGLMÜLLER

Wollzeile 5
Tel 01 512 6177
www.figlmueller.at
If you're looking for traditional Austrian fare, this is a good choice. Figlmüller, close to the Cathedral, is famous for Wienerschnitzels so big they overhang the plate.
⊕ Sep–end Jul daily 11–10.30 ⊞ L €15, D €22, Wine €15 ⊕ Stephansplatz

PALMENHAUS

Burggarten
Tel 01 5331033
www.palmenhaus.at

Sit among palms and tropical plants under high-domed glass in this stylish café/brasserie/bar in what was originally Kaiser Franz Josef's palace Orangery. Try the chilled soup of white chocolate with apricots for dessert.
⊕ Mar–end Oct daily 10am–2am, Nov–end Feb Mon–Thu 11.30am–12am, Fri 11.30am–2am, Sat 10am–2am, Sun 10am–12pm ⊞ L €16, D €21, Wine €28 ⊕ Stephansplatz

STAYING

ALTSTADT VIENNA

Kirchengasse 41, A-1070 Wien
Tel 01 522 6666
www.altstadt.at
The globetrotting owner believes you should feel at home in a hotel, so he has created a residence like no other, with rooms and suites from designer to homey within the historic house.
⊞ Double room from €139, including buffet breakfast ⊕ 42 (all non-smoking) ⊕ Museumsquartier

HOTEL AM STEPHANSPLATZ

Stephansplatz 9, A-1010 Wien
Tel 01 534050
www.hotelamstephansplatz.at
Opposite the Cathedral and moments from the pedestrian-only Kärntnerstrasse, this is the perfect location for sightseeing and shopping. It's a friendly hotel with modern, well-designed rooms and good service.
⊞ Double room from €210 including buffet breakfast ⊕ 56 (three floors non-smoking) ⊗ ⊕ Stephansplatz

HOTEL RATHAUS

Langegasse 13, A-1080 Wien
Tel 01 400 1122
www.hotel-rathaus-wien.at
Wine and contemporary design, including spectacular bathrooms, combine in this unusual hotel. The family owners are vinophiles and each individually furnished room is dedicated to an Austrian winemaker, whose wines are stocked in the room's minibar.
⊞ Double room from €148, buffet breakfast €13 per person ⊕ 39 (all non-smoking) ⊕ Volkstheater

ARRIVING

BY AIR

Vienna International Airport (www.viennaairport.com), served by 68 scheduled airlines from 173 destinations worldwide, is the main entry point to Austria. It has very good facilities and the transfer time between connecting flights is one of the fastest in Europe.

The airport is 16km (9 miles) from the heart of Vienna. The sleek City Airport Train (CAT) travels non-stop to the City Air Terminal at Wien-Mitte station in 16 minutes. Tickets cost €9 one way, or €16 round trip. A family ticket costs €25 and there are discounts if you book online. Under-fives travel free, as does one child aged 6–14 when accompanied by an adult. Trains depart every 30 minutes between 5.38am and 11.35pm daily. Airport Express Buses travel to Franz-Josefs-Kai in about 25 minutes. A one-way ticket costs €6, round trip €11. The Airport City Train (Schnellbahn) S7 reaches Wien-Mitte station in 32 minutes and costs €4.40. Depending on traffic, a car trip takes about 25 minutes. A taxi will cost from €30, and there's an airport surcharge of €10.

Austria's other international airports, at Graz, Innsbruck, Klagenfurt, Linz and Salzburg, handle scheduled and charter flights within Europe.

The national carrier is Austrian Airlines, which flies to 122 destinations in 64 countries and is a member of the global Star Alliance.

BY CAR

Bringing your own car to Austria is not complicated. Fast, well-maintained roads link Austria with all the surrounding countries and the main border checkpoints are open day and night.

Essential documentation includes proof of ownership of the vehicle (the original Vehicle Registration Document), your motor insurance certificate, valid full driver's licence and passport. If your driver's licence was not issued by a member state of the European Union, you'll need an International Driving Permit.

Your car must show a country sticker or licence plates that include the euro-symbol (Euro-plates) and carry a warning triangle, fire extinguisher, reflective jacket (security vest) and first aid kit at all times. Between 1 November and 15 April it is compulsory for your vehicle to be driven with snow tyres and for snow chains to be carried in the vehicle. If you are driving from the UK, headlight adjustments are required. To use Austria's motorways (expressways) you'll need a vignette (toll sticker; Driving, ▷ 22).

Car rental can be arranged at airports and in all cities and major towns. It is best to reserve a car in advance, before you leave home, if possible.

BY TRAIN

Continental Europe's excellent rail network and high-speed trains make it easy to reach Austria in comfort. A map on the website www.railteam.eu indicates the hubs where multilingual staff and information points help make connections simple.

BY BUS

Eurolines (www.eurolines.com) has air-conditioned long distance buses with reclining seats that travel across Europe to Austria. It has services to Vienna, Linz and Salzburg from London.

VISITORS WITH A DISABILITY

Vienna has worked hard to provide better access for visitors with disabilities and wheelchair users, especially on public transport, at major attractions and in hotels. Some restaurants provide menus for people with visual impairment. You'll find a useful article, *Vienna for Visitors with Disabilities*, on the website www.wien.info. The wheelchair-friendly airport has an Airport Transfer Service (tel 01 7007 35910) in special buses that accommodate up to two persons with wheelchairs and six escorts, and the City Airport Train is fully accessible.

The Austrian Railways' website, www.oebb.at, reveals a number of facilities for passengers with special needs. Around the country local tourist offices have information on accessibility.

Relevant Austrian associations with websites include: Information Center for Persons with Disabilities (www.bizeps.or.at, in German); Austrian Union of the Blind and the Visually Impaired (www.oebsv.at) and Austrian Association for the Hearing-Impaired (www.oeglb.at, in German).

In the UK, Holiday Care Service (tel 0845 124 9971; www.holidaycare.org.uk) has an information factsheet on Austria. In the US use Mobility International (tel 541/343-1284; www.miusa.org).

GETTING AROUND

DRIVING

Driving is on the right, the wearing of seatbelts is compulsory, drink/drive laws are strict and Austria's traffic regulations are similar to those of other European countries. But there are some essentials to know:

• You must keep your vehicle lights on when driving, day and night.

• To drive on Austrian motorways (expressways) you'll need a vignette (toll sticker) displayed on the upper middle or left side of the windscreen (windshield). They can be bought at filling stations, tobacconists, post offices and at border entry points. A 10-day vignette costs €7.60. Vignettes are also sold with a validity of two months, or there's an annual charge

• Roads are good, and traffic conditions are broadcast daily in English, 6am–6pm, on FM4 Radio.

• The minimum driving age is 17.

BY TRAIN

The Austrian Federal Railways (www.oebb.at) network is good, the services are efficient and the clean trains have comfortable seating. Although advance reservations can be made, they're probably only necessary if you are travelling long distances or at peak travel times like Christmas.

Austrian Railways issues VORTEILScards, valid for one year, giving up to 50 per cent discounts for families, students and seniors. UK and other European residents can buy an InterRail Austria Pass for unlimited travel on Austria's railway network plus some bonus discounts, from €109. An Austrian Railpass is available to visitors from the US and non-European countries. These passes can only be bought outside Austria—see www.interrailnet.com.

Other helpful websites include www.seat61.com, www.raileurope.co.uk and www.europeanrailguide.com.

BY BUS

Buses can reach places that trains can't and are a good adjunct to the rail system. Austria boasts more than 2,800 scheduled routes. Central bus information tel 01 71101.

OTHER TRANSPORT OPTIONS

• Taxis are generally metered, have a basic fee (€2.50 in Vienna) and the rate is calculated according to time and kilometres driven. A 5 to 10 per cent tip is customary.

• Bicycling is very popular and regional tourist boards have brochures on facilities and routes.

• Boats sail the River Danube and Austria's lakes. Between mid-April and the end of September, DDSG Blue Danube (www.ddsg-blue-danube.at) has daily departures between Vienna and Dürnstein for €19.50 one way or €26 round trip.

• Austria has around 3,200 cable cars, chairlifts and T-bars to get you up the mountains, some of them reaching altitudes of 3,000m (3,842ft).

GETTING AROUND IN VIENNA

Vienna's integrated public transport system of U-Bahn (subway), trams (streetcars), buses and S-Bahn city trains is one of the world's best. Buy tickets, valid for use on all the public transport, at tobacconists or VOR vending machines in stations—paying on board incurs a €0.50 surcharge. One ride costs €1.70, including transfers.

The best bargains are 24-hour tickets at €5.70, 72-hour tickets at €13.60, and the Vienna Card, available at hotels and tourist information points, which costs €18.50, gives great discounts and includes 72 hours' unlimited travel on public transport. At the start of the ride be sure to validate your ticket in the blue boxes found inside buses and trams or by escalators in the U-Bahn. Children under six travel free; under-15s go free on Sundays, public holidays and during Vienna's school holidays (proof of age required).

Trams 1 and 2 travel right around the Inner Ring, in both directions, and are a good way to get your bearings in the city. Big, brightly painted sightseeing buses (www.redbuscitytours.at) offer city tours for around €13, you can rent a bicycle from Pedal Power Vienna (www.pedalpower.at) for €27 a day, or take the fast Twin City Liner catamaran (www.twincityliner.com) for a day in Slovakia's capital, Bratislava, for €27 round trip.

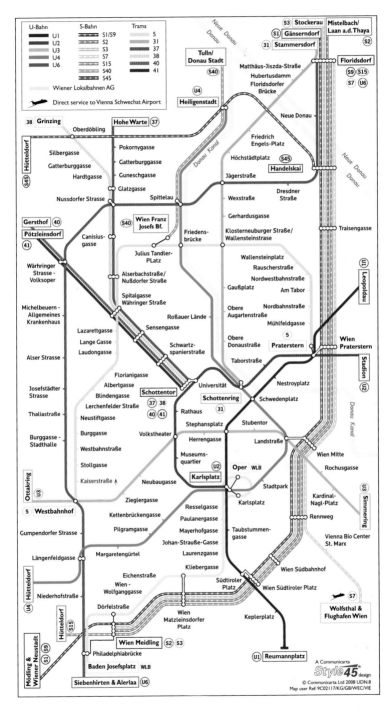

U-Bahn
U1
U2
U3
U4
U6

S-Bahn
S1/S9
S2
S3
S7
S15
S40
S45

Wiener Lokalbahnen AG

Trams
5
31
37
38
40
41

✈ Direct service to Vienna Schwechat Airport

S3 Stockerau
S1 Gänserndorf
31 Stammersdorf

Mistelbach/
Laan a.d. Thaya
S2

Neue Donau
Donau

Tulln/
Donau Stadt
S40

38 Grinzing
Oberdöbling

Hohe Warte 37

Silbergasse
Gatterburggasse
Hardtgasse

Gatterburggasse
Guneschgasse
Glatzgasse

Nussdorfer Strasse
Spittelau

Gerthof 40
Pötzleinsdorf
41

Canisius-
gasse

Wien Franz
Josefs Bf. S40

Friedens-
brücke

Matthäus-Jiszda-Straße
Hubertusdamm
Floridsdorfer
Brücke

Neue Donau

Friedrich
Engels-Platz
Höchstädtplatz S45
Jägerstraße
Handelskai

Wexstraße
Dresdner
Straße

Gerhardusgasse
Klosterneuburger Straße/
Wallensteinstrasse

Floridsdorf
S9 S15
S7 U6

Neue Donau
Donau

Traisengasse

Wärhringer
Strasse -
Volksoper

Michelbeuern -
Allgemeines
Krankenhaus

Alser Strasse

Josefstädter
Strasse

Thaliastraße

Burggasse -
Stadthalle

Julius Tandler-
PLatz

Alserbachstraße/
Nußdorfer Straße

Spitalgasse
Währinger Straße

Lazarettgasse
Lange Gasse
Laudongasse

Florianigasse
Albertgasse
Blindengasse
Lerchenfelder Straße
Neustiftgasse

Burggasse
Westbahnstraße
Stollgasse

Roßauer Lände

Sensengasse

Schwartz-
spanierstraße

Universität

Schottentor
37 38
40 41

Schottenring
31

Rathaus

Volkstheater

Stephansplatz

Herrengasse

Wallensteinplatz
Rauscherstraße
Nordwestbahnstraße
Gaußplatz

Obere
Augartenstraße

Obere
Donaustraße

Taborstraße

Nordbahnstraße
Am Tabor

Mühlfeldgasse

5
Praterstern

Nestroyplatz

Schwedenplatz

Stubentor

Leopoldau U1

Wien
Praterstern

Stadion U2

Donau Kanal

Ottakring U3

5 Westbahnhof

Gumpendorfer Strasse

Längenfeldgasse

Hütteldorf U4

Niederhofstraße

Mödling &
Wiener Neustadt
S1 S9

Kaiserstraße ↑

Neubaugasse

Zieglergasse

Kettenbrückengasse

Pilgramgasse

Margaretengürtel

Eichenstraße
Wien -
Wolfganggasse

Dörfelstraße

Hütteldorf S15

Museums-
quartier
U2
Karlsplatz

Resselgasse
Paulanergasse
Mayerhofgasse
Johan-Strauße-Gasse
Laurenzgasse
Kliebergasse

Südtiroler
Platz

Wien
Matzleinsdorfer
Platz

Oper WLB

Karlsplatz

Taubstummen-
gasse

Stadtpark

Landstraße

Wien Mitte
Rochusgasse

Kardinal-
Nagl-Platz

Rennweg

Wien Südbahnhof

Wien Südtiroler Platz

Keplerplatz

Simmering U3

Vienna Bio Center
St. Marx

✈ S7

Wolfsthal &
Flughafen Wien

Wien Meidling S2 S3
Philadelphiabrücke
Baden Josefsplatz WLB
Siebenhirten & Alerlaa U6

U1 Reumannplatz

Donau Kanal

A Communicarta
Style 45 design
© Communicarta Ltd 2008 UDN.8
Map user Ref:9C02117/KG/GB/WEC/VIE

Heiligenstadt U4

Hohe Warte 37

Pokornygasse

Hütteldorf S45

BELGIUM

UNDERSTANDING BELGIUM

Belgium, a small country at the heart of Europe, is often the country people travel through en route to one of the larger neighbouring countries, but it deserves a visit in its own right. The main cities, Brussels, Antwerp, Ghent and Bruges, have a wealth of medieval architecture, world-class art collections and a buzzing nightlife. Although not as famous or as refined as French cuisine, Belgian food is excellent, and the selection of beers and chocolates is unlike anywhere else in the world. Belgians, sometimes reserved at first, tend to warm up after a drink, and are always willing to help visitors to appreciate their country as much as they do.

Windmill on the banks of the Damme   *Life-size puppets outside Brussels' Grand' Place*

LANDSCAPE
With a surface of 30,528sq km (11,787sq miles), Belgium is about the size of Maryland in the US, with just 66.5km (41 miles) of coastline, on the North Sea. The northwest of the country has flat coastal plains at sea level, there are rolling hills in the centre and more rugged hills in the Ardennes Forest in the south, with the highest point at Botrange (694m/2,277ft). The country borders The Netherlands in the north, Germany and Luxemburg in the southeast, France in the south, and the North Sea in the west.

The environment is under severe pressure from the dense urbanization and transport network as well as the extensive animal breeding and cultivation of the land. So far the authorities have been slow in tackling environmental problems, as the matter is often caught between the national and federal governments.

LANGUAGE AND POPULATION
The population of Belgium is about 10.3 million, of whom 60 per cent are Flemish and 40 per cent French, and a tiny proportion are German-speaking. The population growth is 0.15 per cent, which makes for a fast-aging population. More than 75 per cent of Belgians are Catholic, and most of the rest are Protestant.

Brussels is often seen as a city of bureaucrats. The city is home to the national parliament as well as NATO's headquarters and the European Parliament, which alone has over 30,000

employees. There is a huge diplomatic presence as well, with diplomats to both Belgium and the European Union.

Belgium has officially three languages: Flemish, which is very similar to Dutch, is spoken in Flanders, French in Wallonia and German in a small area near the German border. This complex language structure reflects the country's long and complicated history, and has a strong influence on governance and daily life around the country. Brussels is on the language divide, so both French and Flemish are spoken and most street signs are in both languages, although the majority of people in the centre are French-speaking. In the text we have for convenience only used French in Brussels. The least complicated solution is to speak English, as it might offend a Flemish person to be asked a question in French, and equally it might offend a French speaker when spoken to in Flemish, while most people have some understanding of English.

ECONOMY
Belgium's economy is based on services, transportation, trade and industry. The land is very fertile and receives plenty of rain for agriculture, but only a small percentage of the workforce is employed in this field. Wheat, oats, rye, barley, sugar beets, potatoes and flax are the main crops.

The coal mining in the south of the country had declined by the end of the 20th century, but steel production has taken over. Belgium has a well-established metal products industry, which includes manufacture of heavy machinery, cars, rolling stock, bridges, industrial equipment and munitions. The petrochemical industry is concentrated near the oil refineries in the harbour of Antwerp, while the chemical industry produces plastics, fertilizers and pharmaceuticals.

Many cities in Flanders grew rich in the medieval cloth trade, and the textile industry is still important today, producing carpets and blankets, linen, wool and synthetic fibres. Bruges and Brussels are traditionally famous for their hand-made lace, although much of the cheaper lace for sale in the shops comes from China.

Antwerp is world-renowned for the cutting of diamonds. The city is known as the diamond capital of the world and an estimated 60 per cent of the world's uncut stones are polished in workshops in the jewellery quarter. The industry relies heavily on the import of raw materials,

married the non-royal but aristocratic Mathilde d'Udekem d'Acoz, and when their daughter was born the constitution was changed so that the firstborn becomes heir to the throne, be it a girl or a boy.

Belgium's political institutions are now pretty complex. The prime minister of the national parliament is the head of government, based on a multi-party system. The government exercises executive power and shares the legislative power with the two chambers of parliament: the senate and the chamber of representatives. Since the 1970s the important national parties have split into representations of each community. Belgian politics are heavily influenced by the trade unions and employers' organizations. There are three main political parties, all hovering close to the middle: more right-wing Liberals, the socio-conservative Christian Democrats and the left-wing Socialists. More recently, the younger party of the Green environmentalists has gained more

BELGIUM

European Parliament distirict in Brussels   Belgian chocolates (right). Atomium in Brussels (below)

particularly metals like iron, copper, zinc, lead and tin. Exports include a lot of iron and steel transport equipment, particularly trains, petroleum products and diamonds. The country's electricity comes largely (75 per cent) from nuclear power. The industrial centres are linked to each other and to the port of Antwerp by the rivers Meuse and Scheldt and canals.

POLITICS

Belgium has a federal parliamentary democratic monarchy. The Belgian Constitution was established on 7 February 1831, with a major revision in 1970, when the unitary state was declared obsolete in view of the rising conflict between Flemish- and French-speaking communities in Brussels and on the language dividing line. The decision to devolve powers to the different regions did not however settle the problem, and on 14 July 1993, the constitution was amended again to make Belgium a federal state.

The current king, Albert II, succeeded his brother King Baudouin I after his death in 1993. The king is officially the head of state, but plays more of a ceremonial and symbolic role. He mainly assigns a political leader to form a new cabinet after an election or after the resignation of the cabinet. He also plays an important unifying role, representing the common Belgian identity in a divided country. In 1999 the heir to the throne, Philippe, broke with tradition and

ground, and in Flanders, the far-right nationalist and separatist Flemish party Vlaams Belang has seen a steady rise, despite allegations of racism. For the last few years the government was led by Guy Verhofstadt, a Liberal who led a four-party coalition, but the Liberals suffered heavy losses at the last elections in June 2007. The Christian Democrats came out as winners, but reaching consensus on a workable coalition to govern was to prove elusive, resulting in political crisis. A temporary six-month solution was finally wrenched from the party political mire in December 2007 allowing Verhofstadt to continue in power and a 2008 federal budget to be agreed. The cross language group of Liberals, Christian Democrats and Socialists will also attempt to find solutions to the seemingly diverging viewpoints of the Dutch- and French-speaking communities to avoid another political meltdown. The Verhofstadt period was marked by a balanced budget, one of the few in the European Union, a nuclear phase-out legislation, more permissive legislation on euthanasia and same-sex marriages and opposition to military intervention in Iraq.

THE BEST OF BELGIUM

FLANDERS

Ypres The city itself has many 12th-century monuments, but visitors come here mainly to visit one of the 170 war cemeteries in the area and the Flanders Field Museum, which tells the story of World War I in the region.

Ghent The long history of this university city is reflected in its wealth of architecture and art, including Jan Van Eyck's most famous work, *The Adoration of the Lamb,* in St. Baaf's Cathedral. Take a boat trip on the canals to see the city's hidden corners and the majestic guildhouses. For a change of scene, try the S.M.A.K., the Contemporary Art Museum, which has a collection of modern and contemporary art of international repute.

The Flanders coastline (above). Barman pouring beer in the tradtional manner (below). An oil painting by Jordans in the Groeninge Museum, Bruges (bottom)

Antwerp Take in the beautiful churches and rich art collections in Rubens' city, then party in this city with its wild nightlife. Spot the fashionistas at the exhibitions in the superb MoMu fashion museum.

Ostend Take a walk along the seafront in 'The Queen of Belgian Beach Resorts', then stop for lunch in one of the many fish restaurants in the port. The afternoon can be spent visiting the excellent Museum of Modern Art or the Museum of Fine Arts.

BRUGES

Groeninge Museum (▷ 30) Trace the development of Flemish painting and admire the attention for detail in the Flemish Primitives.

Burg (▷ 29–30) Feel the power in this medieval square and sense the devotion at the Chapel of the Holy Blood.

Onze-Lieve-Vrouwekerk (▷ 30) Admire one of Europe's earliest and most impressive towers built entirely in brick.

THE SOUTH AND THE ARDENNES

Waterloo Picture the scene as Napoleon was finally defeated here by the Duke of Wellington in 1815.

The Ardennes The largest stretch of forest in the country, this is the perfect place for hiking and a dinner of game.

Beer Belgium has more brewers and more beer varieties than anywhere else, so check out the bars all over the country as well as the monasteries that produce the dark and strong trappist beer, such as the monastery of Maredsous.

Waterloo battlefield

BRUSSELS

Grand' Place (▷ 32–33) Marvel at the different façades of one Europe's most beautiful squares.

Musées d'Art Moderne et Ancien (▷ 33) Delve into the astonishingly rich collection of paintings by Flemish and other European masters from the 14th century to the present day.

Victor Horta Museum (▷ 33) Enjoy the marvellous sense of space and light at the renowned art nouveau architect's own house.

Art nouveau architecture Get the art nouveau map from the Brussels tourist office (www.brusselsartnouveau.be) and have a peek at the many private art nouveau houses in St-Gilles and Ixelles.

View of the market from the 13th-century belfry on Markt

Bruges

Bruges, a UNESCO World Heritage Site since 2000, not only has intimate cobbled streets, picturesque canals, medieval architecture and surprising art collections, but it also has excellent restaurants, bars and concert halls.

SEEING BRUGES

The medieval core of the city is well preserved, with its many monuments and museums easily explored on foot. The tourist office sells a combination ticket (€15), with entry to five museums, or entry to three museums, a drink, and a bicycle for the day. Start off at the Burg and walk through the Vismarkt towards the Onze-Lieve-Vrouwekerk church, near the Groeninge and Memling Museum, and then further along to the Begijnhof. Bruges is a popular destination, so if it gets too crowded during the summer, wander off towards the windmills at the end of the Carmerstraat, built on the old ramparts, from where you can walk around the entire city.

HIGHLIGHTS

BEGIJNHOF
✉ Begijnhof 1 ☎ 050 360140 🕐 Church and Begijnhof: daily 9–6.30. Museum: Mon–Sat 10–12, 1.45–5, Sun 10.45–12, 1.45–5 ✋ Church and Begijnhof: free. Museum: adult €2, child (13–26) €1 🚌 1, 2
Bruges' Begijnhof is one of the oldest and most beautiful 'closed courts' in Belgium. From 1245 onwards, pious women who lost their husbands to the Crusades lived in these cottages, taking vows of obedience to God and making lace for a living. Near the gate, a 17th-century *béguine's* house is now a museum.

BURG
✉ Burg 🕐 Gothic Room: Tue–Sun 9.30–5; Museum: Brugse Vrije Tue–Sun 9.30–12.30, 1.30–5; Museum and Chapel of Holy Blood: Apr–end Sep daily 9.30–12, 2–6; Oct–end Mar Thu–Tue 10–12, 2–4, Wed 10–12 ✋ Museum and Gothic Room: €2.50, incl audioguide. Chapel of Holy Blood €1.50, child under 13 free 🚌 All buses to Markt

MORE TO SEE

CHOCOLATE MUSEUM

✉ Wijnzakstraat 2, St-Jansplein
☎ 050 612237 🕐 Daily 10–5; closed
9–13 and 16–20 Jan 🖐 Adults €6,
student €5, child (6–12) €4 🚍 1
🛗 🏛
www.choco-story.be
The fascinating museum tells all
about chocolate from when
traces of cocoa were found in
terracotta pots used by the
Maya of Central America in
600BC. At the end there is a
demonstration of how chocolates are made and—most
importantly—a tasting.

BOAT TRIPS

✉ Departure points: Vismarkt,
Wollestraat, Rozenhoedkaai, Dijver,
Mariastraat 🕐 Mid-Mar to end Nov
daily 10-6 🖐 Adult €5.70, child
(4–11) €2.80 🚍 All buses to Markt
Bruges with its *reien* or canals is
often called 'the Venice of the
North', and taking a boat is the
best way to explore these
romantic waterways and the
heart of the city.

Until the 18th century, the walled-in Burg square was the hub of
civic and religious power in Bruges. Behind the turreted façade of
the Town Hall (1376–1420) is the Gothic Room, with its exquisite
ceiling. The Chapel of the Holy Blood actually contains two
chapels: downstairs is the atmospheric 12th-century Romanesque
chapel dedicated to St. Basilius, and upstairs the 19th-century
neo-Gothic chapel where the crystal phial containing Jesus's blood
is actually kept. The 18th-century Palace of the Brugse Vrije has
several works by local Renaissance artists. Over the foundations of
the ruined 10th-century St. Donatius's Church is the thoroughly
modern rectangular Pavillion built by Japanese architect Toyo Ito
in 2002.

GROENINGE MUSEUM

✉ Dijver 12 ☎ 050 448743 🕐 Tue–Sun 9.30–5 🖐 Adult €8, child (13–26)
€6 🚍 1
This excellent museum shows the wealth of six centuries of
mostly Flemish and Dutch paintings, from the 14th century
onwards. The Flemish Primitives include Jan Van Eyck's portrait of
his wife, Gerard David's gruesome *Judgement of Cambyses*, and
works by Hans Memling and Rogier van der Weyden. With such
a rich old collection, modern Belgian masters such as Constant
Permeke, Marcel Broodthaers, Paul Delvaux and René Magritte
are often overlooked.

MARKT

✉ Markt 🕐 Belfry: Tue–Sun 9.30–5 🖐 Free. Belfry: Adult €5, child (under-13)
free 🚍 All buses to Markt
This interesting square is lined with Gothic guildhouses. The Hallen
contained the treasury, while the bells of the 13th-century belfry
used to warn citizens against approaching danger; now they are
used for regular carillon concerts (mid-Jun to end Sep Mon, Wed,
Sat 9–10pm, Sun 2.15–3; Oct to mid-Jun Wed, Sat, Sun 2.15–3).
In the middle of the square stands the bronze statue (1887) of
two medieval Brugean heroes, Jan Breydel and Pieter de Coninck,
who led the 1302 revolt against the French.

ONZE-LIEVE-VROUWEKERK

✉ Mariastraat 🕐 Church: Mon–Sat 9.30–4.50, Sun 7.30–4.50; no sightseeing
during services. Museum: Tue–Fri 9.30–5, Sat 9.30–4.45, Sun 1.30–5 🖐 Church:
free. Museum: €2.50, child under 13 free 🚍 1
The 118m-high (400ft) brick tower, the façade and the choir of
the Church of Our Lady represent a triumph of 13th-century
workmanship. The church houses important artworks, including
Michelangelo's *Madonna and Child* and 16th-century Flemish
paintings by Pieter Pourbus and Gerard David. Charles the Bold and
Mary of Burgundy, who died in 1477 and 1482 respectively, are
buried here in two exquisite mausoleums.

ST-JANSHOSPITAAL

✉ Mariastraat 38 ☎ 050 448743 🕐 Tue–Sun 9.30–5; closed on Mon 🖐 €8
incl audioguide, child under 13 free 🚍 1
The 12th-century hospice of St. John, one of Europe's oldest,
treated pilgrims and patients until 1976, when the hospital
moved to the modern building behind. The medieval dispensary
is now a medical museum, and the wards are used to show the
works collected by the St. John friars, including the six magnificent
paintings they commissioned from the 15th-century master
Hans Memling.

BACKGROUND

In the 13th century Bruges, then a port, became an important
base of the cloth trade. High-quality English wool was
imported and made into clothing that was exported all over
Europe and the known world. When the River Zwin, the town's
connection to the North Sea, silted up during the 15th century,
the trade and most of the wealth of the city dried up too.

*Detail of one of the houses on
the Burg*

WHAT TO DO

⊕ L'HEROINE

Noordzandstraat 32
Tel 050 335657
This small boutique sells the best selection of Belgian designers, including Dries Van Noten, Kaat Tilley, Chris Janssens and younger Belgians such as Frieda Degeyter.
⊕ Mon–Sat 10–6.30 🚍 All buses to Markt

⊕ SPEGHELAERE

Ezelstraat 92
Tel 050 336052
The chocolate shop in Bruges where locals shop, with delicious handmade pralines and the house special: bunches of marzipan grapes covered in chocolate.
⊕ Tue–Sat 8.15–12.15, 1.15–7, Sun 9–1 🚍 3, 13

ⓘ BRUGGE ANNO 1468

Vlamingstraat 86
Tel 050 347572
www.celebrations-entertainment.be
Enjoy the re-enactment of the wedding of Charles the Bold to Margaret of York with jesters, minstrels, dancers, and fire-eaters, while a four-course medieval banquet is served at the neo-Gothic former Jesuit Heilige Hartkerk. Several set menus are available.
ⓘ Apr–end Oct Fri, Sat 7.30–10.45pm; Nov–end Mar Sat 7.30–10.45pm 💶 Adult from €30, child (11–14) €15, child (6–10) €12.50
🚍 3, 4, 8

EATING

CHRISTOPHE

Garenmarkt 34
Tel 050 344892
Most restaurants in Bruges close early, but not this snug bistro. On the menu is straightforward cuisine with classic Belgian dishes such as fish soup, *croquettes au crevettes* (fried shrimp patties) and excellent *steak frites* served until the early morning. Call ahead and make a reservation, as this is a popular place.
ⓘ Thu–Mon 7pm–2am
💶 D €40, Wine €14
🚍 1

HEER HALEWIJN

Walplein 10
Tel 050 339220
This much-loved wine bar, with bare brick walls and lots of candles, oozes charm and has an excellent wine list as well as a small menu of items grilled on the open fire, salads and French cheeses.
ⓘ Wed–Sun 6.30pm–10pm
💶 D €25–30, Wine €14
🚍 1

DE KARMELIET

Langestraat 19
Tel 050 338259
www.dekarmeliet.be
Bruges' top restaurant occupies a grand house with garden and is run by Geert Van Hecke, the first Belgian chef to receive three Michelin stars. The focus is on gourmet French cuisine using the best Belgian ingredients. The gourmet set menu with a nine-course selection of small dishes is the perfect introduction to Van Hecke's inventive cuisine.
ⓘ Tue–Sat lunch & dinner; closed 1–17 Jan, 24 Jun–12 Jul, 1–10 Oct
💶 L €90, D €120, Wine €25
🚍 All buses to Markt

ROCK FORT

Langestraat 15
Tel 050 334113
www.rock-fort.be
The stylish contemporary interior of this wonderful restaurant sets the tone for inventive French-Mediterranean cuisine served with humour and love. The two friends who run this brasserie serve what they like to eat, from Belgian steak to Provençal fish stew.
ⓘ Mon–Fri 12–2, 6.30–11
💶 L €45, D €50, Wine €17
🚍 All buses to Markt

STAYING

BED-AND-BREAKFAST MARIE-PAULE

Oostproosse 14, 8000 Bruges
Tel 050 339246
www.geocities.com/gastenkamermariepaule
Excellent B&B in a peaceful back street within easy walking distance of the sights. The rooms are comfortable and quiet, the reception is friendly and the delicious copious breakfast is served in a room with view of the garden.
💶 €50–€60
🚫
ⓘ 3
🚍 7, 14
🅿

DE GOEZEPUT

Goezeputstraat 29, 8000 Bruges
Tel 050 342694
www.hotelgoezeput.be
In a quiet street right in the heart of town is this charming little hotel in an 18th-century monastery. The rooms are full of period character and very comfortable, the lounge has a snug fireplace and a corner for children to play. The cellar bar is popular with locals.
💶 €85–€95
ⓘ 16

HOTEL MONTANUS

Nieuwe Gentweg 78, 8000 Bruges
Tel 050 331176
www.montanus.be
This beautiful family-run boutique hotel is in a grand 17th-century mansion near the Begijnhof. The rooms are sumptuously and stylishly decorated and the reception is very helpful and friendly.
💶 €155–€180
ⓘ 23
🅿 🚭

DE ORANGERIE

Karthuiserinnenstraat 10, 8000 Bruges
Tel 050 341649
www.hotelorangerie.com
This hotel in a 15th-century convent clad in ivy overlooks one of Bruges' most beautiful canals. It has been tastefully and luxuriously converted into one of the city's most attractive boutique hotels by the owner, who is also an antiques dealer and interior designer.
💶 €175–€255
ⓘ 20
🅿 🚭

Brussels

The Belgian capital is a surprisingly cosmopolitan city, with a rich cultural heritage and a vibrant restaurant, bar and nightlife scene.

'Carpet of Flowers' festival on Grand'Place

Inside the Museé de Victor Horta (left). A café on Grand' Place (right)

RATINGS

Cultural interest	●●●●●
Good for kids	●●●
Good for food	●●●●●
Specialist shopping	●●●●●

BASICS

✚ 5 D3

🛈 Info Brussels International, Hôtel de Ville, Grand' Place, tel: 02 513 8940; May–end Sep daily 9–6; Easter–end Apr, Oct–end Dec Mon–Sat 9–6, Sun 10–2; Jan–Easter Mon–Sat 9–6

🚆 Brussels has three main stations: Gare du Nord (Brussel Noord), Gare Centrale (Brussel Centraal) and Gare du Midi (Brussel Zuid), which is the international station, with regular trains to most cities in Belgium as well as international connections with Amsterdam, Paris, London by Eurostar and other cities

www.brusselsinternational.be
The official website of the Tourism and Convention Bureau has details of attractions, events, restaurants and nightlife and suggested walks.

SEEING BRUSSELS

The middle of the city is divided into the Upper Town, with the Royal Palace, wide boulevards and grand houses, and the Lower Town, with labyrinthine streets around the Grand' Place. Many sights are within walking distance of the Grand' Place, others require renting a bike or using the excellent public transport. The neighbourhoods of St-Gilles and Ixelles have a wealth of art nouveau buildings, as well as trendy bars and restaurants. As the city is on the language divide between the Flemish and the French-speaking Walloons, both languages are spoken, as well as English by the large international community.

HIGHLIGHTS

ATOMIUM

✚ 34 off C1 • Atomium Square, 1020 Bruxelles ☎ 02 475 4777 🕐 Daily 10–6. 24, 25, 31 Dec, 1 Jan 10–4. Last admittance 30 mins before closing 💶 Adult €9, child (12–18) €7 🚇 Heysel 🚊 Tram 23, 52
www.atomium.be; www.kmkg-mrah.be
The leafy suburb of Heysel has the city's shiniest and much-loved landmark, the Atomium (102m/335ft high), built for the World Exhibition of 1958. The nine steel balls represent the atoms of a metal crystal enlarged 165 times, and hold temporary exhibitions, a kids' zone and an excellent restaurant. Nearby, on Avenue Van Praet, are a Chinese Pavilion and Japanese Pagoda, commissioned in 1900 by King Leopold II, now museums of Oriental art (Tue–Sun 10–5).

GRAND' PLACE

✚ 34 C3 • Grand' Place 🚇 Bourse, Gare Centrale 🚊 Tram 3, 52, 55, 56, 81
A marketplace since the 13th century, this magnificent square is lined with the gilded Gothic, Renaissance and baroque façades of guildhouses. The 15th-century Town Hall (guided tours only, Apr–end Sep Tue, Wed 3.15, Sun 10.45, 12.15; Oct–end Mar Tue, Wed 3.15) is a masterpiece of Flemish Gothic architecture, and its Gothic Hall is adorned with sumptuous 19th-century tapestries

representing the city's main guilds. The Maison du Roi is the Museum of Brussels (Tue–Sun 10–5), devoted to the city's history, as well as keeper of Manneken Pis' wardrobe.

MANNEKEN PIS
34 C3 • Corner of rue de l'Étuve and rue du Chènet 🚇 Bourse, Gare Centrale 🚊 Tram 23, 52, 55, 56, 81
The tiny cherub-like sculpture of Manneken Pis, literally 'little pissing man', has been the city's mascot since its creation in 1619, when it was known as 'Petit Julien' (Little Julien). It has been kidnapped several times, and it has received hundreds of costumes, including one from French King Louis XV, now at the Museum of Brussels (▷ above).

MUSÉES D'ART ANCIEN ET D'ART MODERNE
35 D4 (Ancien). 35 D3 (Moderne) • Musée d'Art Ancien: rue de la Régence 3. Musée d'Art Moderne: Place Royale 1–2 ☎ 02 508 3211 🕐 Tue–Sun 10–5 🎫 Adult €5, child (12–18) €2; free 1st Wed afternoon of the month 🚇 Gare Centrale, Parc 🚊 54, tram 92, 94
www.fine-arts-museum.be
The Museums of Old and Modern Art were founded by Napoleon in 1801. The Old Art Museum has an immensely rich collection of Flemish and other European masters covering the 14th–17th centuries, including Flemish Primitives, Rubens, Breughel and Rembrandt. The underground Modern Art Museum shows 20th-century Belgian artists in a broader European context, with works by Rik Wouters, Paul Delvaux and René Magritte among those by Max Ernst, James Ensor and Oscar Kokoshka.

MUSÉE DE VICTOR HORTA
35 off D5 • Rue Américaine 25, St-Gilles ☎ 02 543 0490 🕐 Tue–Sun 2–5.30 🎫 Adult €7, students and seniors €3.50, child (5–18) €2.50 🚇 Horta 🚊 Tram 81, 92
www.hortamuseum.be
The two houses built by art nouveau architect Victor Horta (1861–1947) as his home and studio are a clear break from tradition, with elegant spacious rooms flooded with light and colours. It is the perfect place to start your exploration of the many other art nouveau buildings in the area.

BACKGROUND
A community settled near the River Senne during the 6th century, in today's St-Géry quarter near the Grand' Place. By the 13th century the Grand' Place had become a marketplace for food and textiles produced by the flourishing cloth industry. Invaders came and went, but when Belgium won independence in 1830, Brussels was its capital. In the 1960s it also became the capital of the European Union and home to NATO.

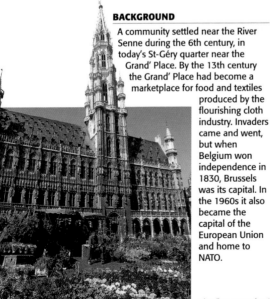

The flower market in front of the town hall on Grand'Place

MORE TO SEE
MUSÉE DES INSTRUMENTS DE MUSIQUE
35 D3 • Rue Montagne de la Cour 2 ☎ 02 545 0130 🕐 Tue–Fri 9.30–5, Sat, Sun 10–5 🎫 Adult €5, youth (13–26) €4 🚇 Gare Centrale, Parc 🚊 Tram 92, 93, 94 🍽 Fri 10.30–12
www.mim.fgov.be
The vast collection of musical instruments here, more than 7,000 of them, are beautifully displayed in the stunning art nouveau Old England department store. With the headset you can listen to each instrument play.

LE SABLON
34 C4 • Place Sablon 🚊 20, 48; tram 91, 92, 93, 94
In the 17th century the aristocracy lived round this elegant square; now it's known for its cafés, including Patisserie Wittamer and the famed chocolate maker Pierre Marcolino. There are also smart antiques shops and an antiques market on the weekends (Sat 9–6, Sun 9–2).

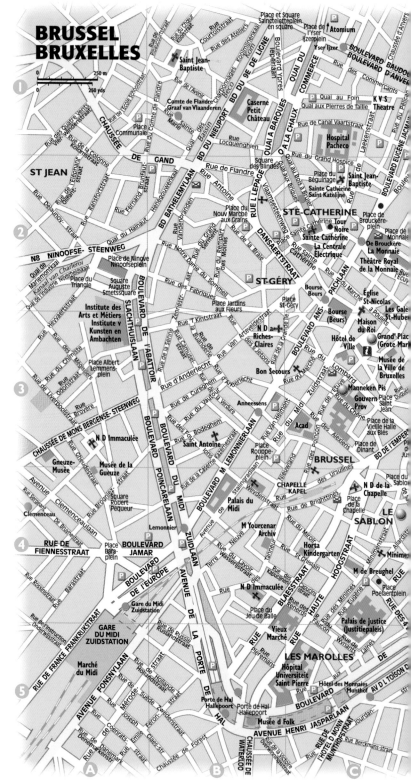

BRUSSEL BRUXELLES

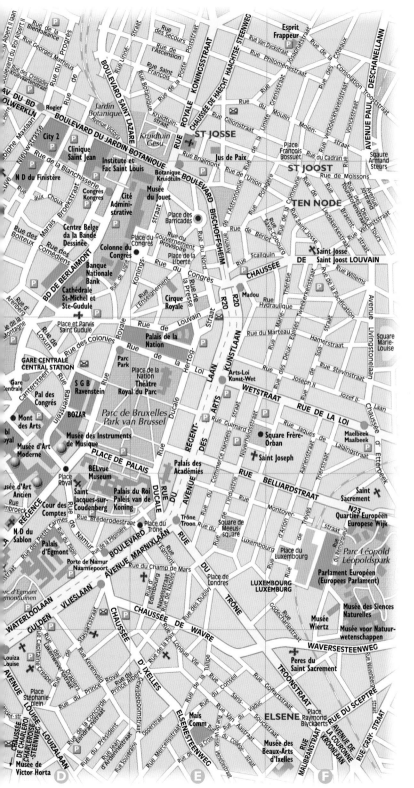

KEY TO SYMBOLS

- ⊕ Shopping
- ⊙ Entertainment
- ⊗ Nightlife
- ⊗ Sports
- ✪ Activities
- ♡ Health and Beauty
- ⊗ For Children

WHAT TO DO

⊕ IDEB LIFESTORE
Boulevard de Waterloo 49
Tel 02 289 1110
www.ideb.be
Luxury department store
set in a grand house with
sweeping stairways, with an
excellent selection of men's
and women's fashions, a spa
and cosmetics, a bookstore
and a great bar-restaurant.
🕐 Mon–Fri 10.30–7, Sat 11–7
🚇 Louise

⊕ STIJL
Rue Antoine Dansaert 74
Tel 02 512 0313
The place to buy Belgian
fashion designers, including
Dries Van Noten and Anne
Demeulemeester, also has a
hip kids' shop, Kat en Muis,
down the road at No. 33. At
No. 47 is Stijl Underwear.
🕐 Mon–Sat 10.30–6.30 🚇 Bourse,
Ste-Catherine

⊙ BEURSSCHOUWBURG
Rue Auguste Orts 20–28
Tel 02 550 0350
www.beursschouwburg.be
This is the best and most cen-
tral venue for rock concerts,
world music and avant garde
Belgian theatre and dance.
🚇 Bourse

⊙ LA MONNAIE
Place de la Monnaie
Tel 02 229 1200
www.lamonnaie.be
This royal theatre is
renowned for its outstanding
opera performances.
🚇 De Brouckère

EATING

BELGAQUEEN
Rue Fossé au Loups 32
Tel 02 217 2187
www.belgaqueen.be
Oyster bar, beer and cigar bar
and an excellent brasserie,
Belgaqueen is thoroughly
Belgian, from the grand architecture to the ingredients. The
inventive cuisine includes
roast cuckoo from Malines on

gingerbread and a tartare of
Charolais beef with caviar.
🕐 Daily 12–3.30, 7–12
🍴 L €38, D €50, Wine €18
🚇 De Brouckère
🚋 Tram 23, 52, 55, 56, 81

RESOURCE
Rue du Midi 164
Tel 02 514 3223
www.restaurantresource.be
The two gourmet chefs serve
a Slow Food Menu (€65) that
involves several courses of
sheer pleasure, including
ravioli with truffle, smoked
and fried foie gras, turbot
with crab and dill, scallops
la plancha and a selection
of desserts and cheeses.
🕐 Tue–Fri 12–2.30, 7–10, Sat 7–10
🍴 Fixed menus: L €20, D €40–€65,
Wine €23
🚇 Anneessens

TAVERNE DU PASSAGE
Galerie de la Reine 30
Tel 02 512 3731
www.tavernedupassage.com
Elegant brasserie that serves
all the classic Belgian dishes
such as shrimp croquettes
(patties), mussels in white
wine and steak au poivre
(pepper steak).
🕐 Daily 12–12
🍴 L €25, D €35, Wine €16
🚇 Gare Centrale

VINCENT
Rue des Dominicains 8/10, off rue des
Bouchers
Tel 02 511 2607
www.restaurantvincent.com
A Brussels institution, this
brasserie serves excellent
Belgian cuisine in traditional
style. The extremely profes-
sional waiters prepare steak
tartare or flambé at your table.
🕐 Daily 12–2.45, 6.30–11.30
🍴 L €30, D €40, Wine €16
🚇 De Brouckère, Gare Centrale

VIVA M'BOMA
Rue de Flandre 17
Tel 02 512 15 93
Set in an old white-tiled
butcher shop, this delightful
restaurant serves Belgian
food. The focus is on meat
dishes and offal, although
there is fish too. Try a Brussels
classic such as waterzooi
(soup of chicken and vegetables with cream). The wine
list is excellent.
🕐 Thu–Sat 12–2.30, 7–10.30,

Mon–Tue 12–2.30
🍴 L €25, D €35, Wine €18
🚇 Ste. Catherine

STAYING

LE DIXSEPTIÈME
Rue de la Madeleine 25,
1000 Bruxelles
Tel 02 517 1717
www.ledixseptieme.be
The stylish rooms in this
small, central boutique
hotel in a 17th-century
ambassador's residence are
all different and arranged
around a peaceful courtyard.
🍴 €200
🛏 20
⊗
🚇 Gare Centrale

HOTEL AMIGO
Rue del'Amigo, 1000 Bruxelles
Tel 02 547 4747
www.hotelamigo.com
Arguably Brussels' best hotel,
right in the heart of town, the
Amigo is popular with media
stars and politicians. The
room are luxurious, with a
very contemporary feel and
many references to local
culture, including Tintin and
Magritte's paintings.
🍴 €620–€750
🛏 176
🏊 P ⊙ ⊗
🚋 34, 48, 94
🚇 Gare Centrale/Bourse

HOTEL SAINT MICHEL
Grand' Place, 1000 Bruxelles
Tel 02 511 0956
www.hotelsaintmichel.be
The only hotel on the Grand'
Place was recently refur-
bished and offers comfortable
and clean rooms in the House
of the Duke of Brabant.
🍴 €85–€150
🛏 14
🚇 Gare Centrale

METROPOLE
Place de Brouckère 31, 1000 Bruxelles
Tel 02 217 2300
www.hotelmetropole.com
This central five-star hotel is
in a grand 19th-century
building. The rooms, while
comfortable, no longer have
much character. The elegant
dining room offers gourmet
Belgian-French cuisine.
🍴 €240
🛏 305
P
🚋 Tram 23, 52, 55, 56, 81

BY AIR

You can fly direct from most capitals to Brussels. Belgium's main airport is Brussels International Airport (tel 0900 70000 or 0032 2 753 7753 from outside Belgium; www.brusselsairport.be) at Zaventem, 14km (9 miles) northeast of Brussels. The airport has a tourist information desk in the arrivals hall. The Airport City Express shuttle train (tel 02 528 2828; www.b-rail.be) runs every 15–20 minutes from and to Brussels' three main stations (20–30 minutes' journey time) between 6.40am and 9.50pm. The Airport Line (tel 02 515 2000; www.stib.irisnet.be) runs bus No. 12 from the airport to the centre (35 minutes) from 5.10am to 11.35pm. Tickets cost €3. De Lijn (tel 02 526 2820; www.delijn.be) runs buses to the Gare du Nord (45 minutes). Car rental is available in the arrivals hall. There is a taxi stand outside the arrivals hall, but taxis are expensive (€35) and not all accept credit cards.

Low-cost airlines, including Ryanair, fly to Brussels Airport in Charlerloi (www.charleroi-airport.com), 50km (32 miles) south of Brussels, with regular buses going from the terminal to Brussels' Gare du Midi (1 hour, €19 one way, €35 round trip) and car rental is available.

BY CAR

Belgium is well connected to the neighbouring countries by excellent highways, which are free in Belgium. The country has open borders with its neighbours and although you should stop if requested, most border posts are now unmanned. To enter Belgium by car you will need a valid driving licence, and it is advisable to take out a breakdown policy. You should also have the vehicle registration document or a letter giving you permission to drive if the vehichle doesn't belong to you. Make sure that you carry a fire extinguisher and a high visibility vest in case of accident.

Fines for speeding or other motoring offences have to be paid on the spot, usually by cash or credit card.

BY TRAIN

The Eurostar train (www.eurostar.com) connects Brussels Gare du Midi with London (2 hours and 40 minutes). High-speed TGV trains connect the city with Paris and other cities in France, and there are excellent connections with many other European cities from the same station (tel 02 528 2828; www.b-rail.be). Thalys trains (www.thalys.com) provide high-speed services that link Brussels Midi/Zuid station with Amsterdam, Paris and Cologne. The Gare du Midi is in a potentially unsafe area of Brussels so when arriving at night it is advisable to take a taxi instead of walking out of the station. Bruges has a few international connections too.

BY BUS

Eurolines buses (www.eurolines.com) connect Brussels with all major European cities. The international bus station is CCN Gare du Nord (rue du Progrès 80, tel 02 274 1350).

BY FERRY

P&O (www.poferries.com) runs the only ferry route still operating between Britain and Belgium from Hull to Zeebrugge (14 hours); it takes 15 minutes to get to Bruges, and 1 hour and 15 minutes to Brussels from here.

You can take your car by train via the Eurotunnel from Folkestone to Calais (35 minutes; tel 08705 353535; www.eurotunnel.com). To drive from Calais to Bruges take the E40 (1 hour 20 minutes) and to Brussels the E15 (2 hours). However, the French ferry ports of Calais and Dunkeque are around 30 minutes from the Belgium border to the southwest and offer easy routes into the country from the UK.

VISITORS WITH A DISABILITY

Public transport in Belgium has few facilities for people with disabilities, but in Brussels a minibus service equipped for wheelchairs is available at low cost from the network STIB (tel 02 515 2365; www.stib.be). For more information contact Mobility International (Boulevard Baudouin 18, 1000 Bruxelles; tel 02 201 5608).

GETTING AROUND

DRIVING

Belgians drive on the right side of the road. The speed limit is 120kph (75mph) on highways and 90kph (56mph) on other roads, but locals often drive faster. Despite a strong campaign against drink-driving, there is still quite a lot of it, so be extra vigilant when driving on weekend nights.

The roads and highways are good and well-maintained, and toll free.

TRAINS

Bruges has just one train station, but Brussels confusingly has three main stations named in French and Flemish: Gare du Nord/Brussel Noord, Gare Centrale/Brussel Centraal and Gare du Midi/Brussel Zuid. Almost all the domestic trains stop at all three stations, while international trains stop only at Gare du Midi. Timetables and other train information are available from the Belgian railway company SNCB (tel 02 528 2828; www.b-rail.be). There are two trains an hour from Brussels to Bruges, a one-hour trip, and regular connections to most other places in Belgium.

Tickets, first or second class, should be bought at the station and not on the train. They are checked on the train and a fine will apply if you don't have one. Distances are small so there is no need to reserve domestic trains. Prices are relatively good value, cheaper on weekend returns (round-trips), and there are promotions for train tickets combined with entry to an exhibition or tourist attraction.

BUSES

Belgium has an extensive rail network so few locals travel by bus, except for short distances to villages outside the towns. Those buses usually leave from

the train stations; in Brussels Gare du Nord is the main bus terminal.

BICYCLING

Cycling is very popular in Belgium, both as a sport and as a way to get around, as the country is mostly flat. Cycling paths are often marked in red and separated from the cars in the road. The Fédération Belge du Cyclotourisme (tel 02 521 8640; www.cyclo.be) organizes many cycle rides and provide information on cycling routes. Bicycle rental is available from Provélo which has three pick-up points in Brussels; the central location is at rue de Londres 15 (tel 02 217 0158; www.provelo.be; €10 per day; metro: Trône); and in Bruges from the train station (tel 050 308 027; €10 per day) or Bauhaus Bike Rental, with a wide selection of bikes, scooters and wheelchair bikes (Langestraat 145, tel 050 341 093 €9 per day). QuasiMundo organizes bike tours in Bruges and the surrounding area (tel 050 330 775; www.quasimundo.com) and in Brussels Provélo also organizes interesting city tours by bicycle. The Belgian railways operate a Train-plus-Vélo scheme with bike rental included in the train ticket.

TAXIS

Taxis can be picked up from taxi stands in the cities and are metered, with a fixed tariff per kilometre inside the city, and a higher one, nearly double, outside. Belgians rarely take taxis between cities as it is

expensive and the rail network is excellent and tickets are good value for money.

CITY TRANSPORT

Many attractions are within walking distance in the middle of Brussels, but otherwise the combination of metro and trams is the easiest way to get around.

● Information on metro, tram and buses is available from STIB (tel 070 23 2000; www.stib.be).

● Brussels' metro stations are indicated by a white letter 'M'. Several lines cover most of the city.

● One-way tickets are available at metro stations, from bus or tram drivers and newsagents with the STIB sign.

● Tickets must be validated on bus, tram or metro.

● The most economical way to travel is to buy a book of five or ten tickets or a 12-hour unlimited pass. The Tourist Office sells a Brussels Card for €19–€32 which includes free public transport up to 72 hours, free entry to many museums, and reductions in private museums, restaurants and shops.

● Taxis are metered and only allowed to pick up at or near a taxi stand. You can call a taxi on 02 349 4949 or 02 349 4646.

● In Bruges calèches (horses and carts) are a popular way to see the historical part of the city, and can be picked up on the Markt or Burg squares (€30 per cart); in winter blankets are provided. For a taxi, call 050 334 444.

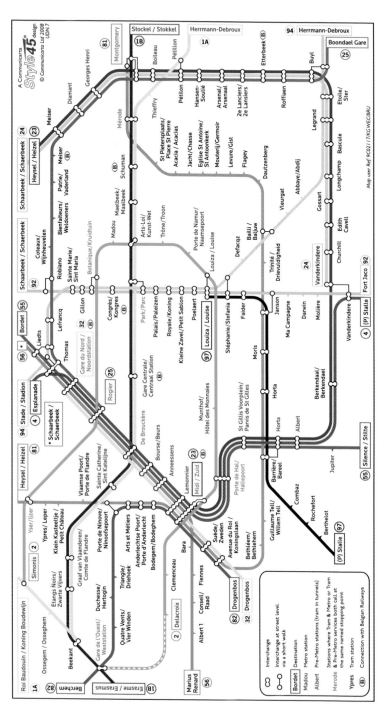

FRANCE

UNDERSTANDING FRANCE

With memorable food, world-renowned art collections and magnificent chateaux, France would be worth visiting even without the wonderful scenery. No wonder it is one of the world's most popular holiday destinations, clocking up more than 75 million visitors each year. It is the largest country in Western Europe and has a population of nearly 63 million. Each part of the country has managed to retain its own character and this regional diversity can be seen especially in French food and wine, which inspire fierce local pride. The diversity is evident in the very landscape itself, with unending rows of vines in one region, followed by flocks of sheep, goats or cattle in the next, olive groves in the southeast and apple orchards in the northwest.

A horse and cart on the beach at Barfleur

Flowers brighten up the courtyard of a farmhouse in Issenhausen

Strolling in the grounds of the Château de Chambord

ECONOMY

Until recently there was a strong division between France's wealthier cities and its poorer industrial and mining areas. But intelligent use of the high-speed rail network and budget air services has diluted the divide. Abandoned mining towns in the north are now home to many major international financial institutions, only an hour from Paris and within two hours of several European capitals. Likewise, workers in Paris can now buy homes near the Mediterranean and commute to the capital, injecting new blood and new money into formerly run-down provincial villages. There has also been investment in discount shopping malls and low-rent business complexes far from the principal cities.

Food and wine are key factors in the national economy. Famously, former president Charles de Gaulle bemoaned the impossibility of governing a nation that produces over 350 different cheeses. Bordeaux and Burgundy provide some of the world's top wines—and many of the more distinguished chateau estates are owned and managed by international financial institutions. The Champagne region is the source of the entire global supply of champagne, and the vast vineyards of Languedoc-Roussillon are Europe's principal suppliers of inexpensive and reliable supermarket table wines. Food is also a key lure to visitors, and restaurants and hotels pocket a fair share of the €36 billion spent annually by people coming from abroad.

POLITICS

French presidents manage to stamp their personalities onto the country in a way that most world leaders can only envy. This is because elections are held only once in seven years and a two-term tenure will outspan a decade, giving the incumbent the freedom to implement long-term policies without having to worry about short-term popularity. François Mitterrand was able to implement policies that brought about enormous social change and monumental architectural projects with only one interruption in the name of democracy. This situation can also lead to voter apathy, with the population feeling impotent mid-term. Thus, the extreme right candidate Jean-Marie Le Pen nudged his way into second place in the first round of the 2002 presidential elections. Socialists found themselves voting for conservative Jacques Chirac at the final poll in order to keep Le Pen out of the Elysée Palace. Extremism is usually kept at bay by parliamentary elections held midway through a presidential term, where opposition to the president is often reflected in the appointment of a prime minister from a rival party. This 'cohabitation' leads to workmanlike compromise. The other important elected official in France is the local mayor, whose powers are wide-ranging. Even a village mayor can decide to reduce the working hours of local police, or personally intervene to stop house purchases, and Paris mayors are major political figures on the national stage. However, while politicians may grab the headlines, true power lies with the workers, whose lightning strikes are greeted philosophically by a population used to days without rail and air travel.

LANGUAGE AND SOCIETY

France was originally many kingdoms and the regions retain the languages and cultures of other times. But there is fierce pride in the French language itself, reflected in occasional campaigns to remove English words from the national vocabulary (*le weekend, le sandwich* and others). This pride is maintained by the Académie Française, who insist that email is called *mél*, with an accent to disguise its American origins. Other tongues are fiercely defended in various corners of the country. Brittany celebrates its heritage with an annual gathering of Celts from Ireland, Wales, Scotland

part of the year visitors can choose to ski, sunbathe or both. There are six mountain ranges (including the Alps, Jura, Vosges and Pyrenees) and 5,500km (3,418 miles) of coastline on the Channel, Atlantic and Mediterranean. Some dramatic river gorges cleave through the country and there are 15 million hectares (37 million acres) of forest. The landscape is both typically northern and typically southern European—lush hedgerows in Normandy, huge tracts of dusty scrubland in Languedoc, rich verdant undulating hills in Auvergne and heady fields of lavender in Provence.

VISITING FRANCE

France is a large country so don't be over-ambitious when deciding what to see during your visit. It is probably best to base yourself in one

Pinot Noir grapes

The game of boules is a popular pastime in France

A field of bright sunflowers

and even farther afield at the Interceltic fortnight in August. It is said that a Breton fisherman and his counterpart from Cornwall in England, can converse freely in their native tongues. In the southwest, French Basques are less volatile than the ETA activists across the Spanish border, but their language and rituals are celebrated with pride. On the southern side of the Pyrenees, another cross-border culture, Catalan, is almost a national identity in its own right. Across the southwest, bilingual road signs include place names in Occitan—the Langue d'Oc that gives a region its name. In most of modern France, however, multiculturalism refers more to new communities than the old kingdoms. This stirs up notorious agitation from the right-wing National Front, whose support in the south stems from scaremongering about both immigration from North Africa (in the cities) and European regulation (in the agricultural and fishing communities). Conversely, Montpellier, with its large Arab population, has been a haven of tolerance for centuries and even houses its Islamic and Jewish cultural facilities in the same building. One poster in the Arab Quarter wryly announced during election year, 'Send us home and we take the Cup with us', a reference to the multi-ethnic team that won France the soccer World Cup in 1998.

LANDSCAPE

France's distinctive borders give it the nickname The Hexagon. The sheer scale of it—the country is the size of Texas—means that for

region—they are all quite different—and really get to know it, rather than travel up and down the *autoroutes* ticking off as many sights as possible. In addition to the must-see sights, each region offers its own blend of leisure activities—do you want a weekend of culture and style in Paris, or a week of walking in the Pyrenees, skiing in the Alps or relaxing on a beach on the Côte d'Azur?

If you're taking your car, it's a good idea to plan an overnight stop on longer drives. If you're moving around by train, consider buying a rail pass before you leave home, as this can save you money. Regions can vary greatly depending on the season, so bear this in mind when planning your trip. For example, Paris is quiet but stiflingly hot in August, while much of the south of France is packed with people and traffic; some of the trails in the breathtaking Pyrenees are impassable during the colder months, while this, obviously, is an ideal time for skiing in the Alps.

The shimmering white basilica of Sacré-Cœur is a Paris landmark

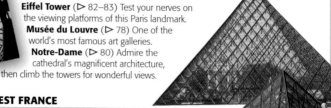

THE BEST OF FRANCE

PARIS AND THE ÎLE DE FRANCE

Eiffel Tower (▷ 82–83) Test your nerves on the viewing platforms of this Paris landmark.
Musée du Louvre (▷ 78) One of the world's most famous art galleries.
Notre-Dame (▷ 80) Admire the cathedral's magnificent architecture, then climb the towers for wonderful views.

NORTHWEST FRANCE

Bayeux See the famous 11th-century tapestry.
D–Day Beaches Visit the beaches where Allied forces landed on 6 June 1944.
Mont St-Michel Cross to this mystical abbey on its rocky mount and enjoy wonderful views of the bay.
Rouen Normandy's capital has an attractive old town, good shopping and a cathedral made famous by Monet.

The Louvre's striking Pyramid (above).
The wonderful station clock at the Musée d'Orsay (top left).
Looking across to Mont St-Michel (below)

NORTH AND NORTHEAST FRANCE

Champagne-tasting Visit a Maison du Champagne at Reims and remind yourself why bubbly has been prized for centuries.
Lille (▷ 49–53) France's fourth-largest city has a prestigious art gallery, vast shopping mall and 17th-century Citadelle.
Strasbourg This city, near the German border, is the seat of the European Parliament.
Troyes An attractive village of half-timbered houses, cobbled streets and vivid stained-glass windows.

THE LOIRE

Chartres See the awesome Notre-Dame-de-Chartres cathedral.
Chateaux of the Loire This scenic region is dotted with fairy-tale chateaux.
Saumur The town has half-timbered houses, chic boutiques and wonderful views.
Tours A thriving city, between the Loire and Cher rivers, with a rich historical, cultural and architectural heritage.

CENTRAL FRANCE AND THE ALPS

The Alps The most exhilarating way to experience these mountains is on skis or a snowboard.
Dijon This easily walkable, historic town is a hub of the Burgundy wine trade.
The Gorges de l'Ardèche Canoe along the river and underneath the natural archway, the Pont d'Arc.
Lac d'Annecy For boat trips, watersports and outdoor activities in a beautiful mountain setting, Annecy is hard to beat.
Lyon (▷ 54–57) A must-see city, great for culture and nightlife.

Historical Tours (above)

SOUTHEAST FRANCE

Avignon The main draws are the magnificent Palais des Papes and the huge drama and dance festival held in July.
Cannes Shop 'til you drop in Provence's most glamorous destination.
Marseille (▷ 58–62) Soak up the history in the Vieux Port and Le Panier districts of this ancient city.
Nice (▷ 67–68) Experience the city's hectic nightlife.

The splendid spire of St-Maurice church, in Lille

Bordeaux
●

This elegant city is world-famous for the quality of its wines. Other attractions include a superb 18th-century theatre, a 1,000-year-old cathedral and a fine arts museum.

Pont St-Pierre, spanning the Garonne river

An eye-catching art installation in a parking area

Looking across Bordeaux from the Basilique St-Michel

SEEING BORDEAUX

Bordeaux, a World Heritage Site, is an elegant city with a long history and plenty of attractions. The principal sights are relatively close together and most are easily reached from the magnificent Grand Théâtre or from the central square, Esplanade des Quinconces. A new tram system promises to make the city's main attractions even more accessible, although the works have caused major disruptions, with road diversions and the closure of some sights. The first section was opened in 2004, but work will continue until the end of 2008.

If this is your first visit to Bordeaux, be sure to walk out onto the Pont de Pierre, Bordeaux's oldest bridge, for great views of the Porte de Bourgogne and the stone buildings lining the quayside, where a regeneration project is bringing new life. If the sun is shining, it will be obvious why the city was often called Bordeaux la Blonde.

HIGHLIGHTS

GRAND THÉÂTRE
⊞ 46 C3 • place de la Comédie ☎ 05 56 00 85 95; tours 05 56 00 85 95 ⓒ Depends on rehearsal schedules
This striking venue, with its 12 lofty Corinthian columns topped by statues of the nine Muses and three goddesses, dominates place de la Comédie. It was built between 1773 and 1780 by Victor Louis, the restorer of Chartres cathedral, and is almost 90m (295ft) long and 50m (165ft) wide. Restored to its original glory in 1991, its auditorium is known for its exceptional acoustics, and the tiered boxes drip with gold leaf. The sweeping grand staircase was a model for Garnier's lobby in the Opéra Palais Garnier in Paris. You won't be able to see inside if a rehearsal is under way, so it's worth checking earlier in the day for any scheduled break in rehearsals later.

RATINGS				
Cultural interest	●	●	●	●
Good for wine	●	●	●	●
Historic interest	●	●	●	●

BASICS
⊞ 4 C4 ℹ 12 cours 30 Juillet, 33080, tel 05 56 00 66 00; Jul, Aug Mon–Sat 9–7.30, Sun 9.30–6.30; May, Jun Mon–Sat 9–7, Sun 9.30–6.30; Sep, Oct Mon–Sat 9–6, Sun 9–30–6.30; Nov–end Apr Mon–Sat 9–6.30, Sun 9.45–6.30 (except first Sun of the month 9.45–4.30)
🚉 Gare St-Jean
www.bordeaux-tourisme.com

TIPS
● The Maison du Vin, opposite the tourist office, has information on vineyard tours.
● On the last Friday of each month, in-line skaters take over the allée de Bristol, on the north side of esplanade des Quinconces, for *La Nuit du Roller*.
● Explore the city with a bicycle that comments on the main sights in English—contact the tourist office for information.

Médoc (left), produced in the Bordeaux area

CATHÉDRALE ST-ANDRÉ AND TOUR PEY-BERLAND

✚ 46 B4 • place Pey-Berland ☎ 05 56 52 68 10 🕐 Cathedral Jul, Aug daily 10–6;
Sep–end Jun Mon 10–11.30, 2–6.30, Tue–Sat 7.30–11.30, 2–6, Sun 8–12.30, 2–5.30
(closed Sun in winter). Tower Tue–Sun 10–12.30, 2–5.30 💶 Tower €5

This 1,000-year-old cathedral, whose delicate twin spires can be seen
from all over the city, is a UNESCO World Heritage Site. The huge nave
is said to be where Eleanor of Aquitaine married the future Henry II of
England in 1152. The north and south doors of the transept, the choir
and the Porte Royale on the north wall are decorated with medieval
sculptures and scenes from the Last Judgement. Next to the cathedral
is the 15th-century Tour Pey-Berland. On its pinnacle, 50m (165ft) up,
is the statue of Notre-Dame-d'Aquitaine. The view from the top is
tremendous, as is the noise if you're up there when the 11-tonne bell,
Ferdinand-André, is tolling.

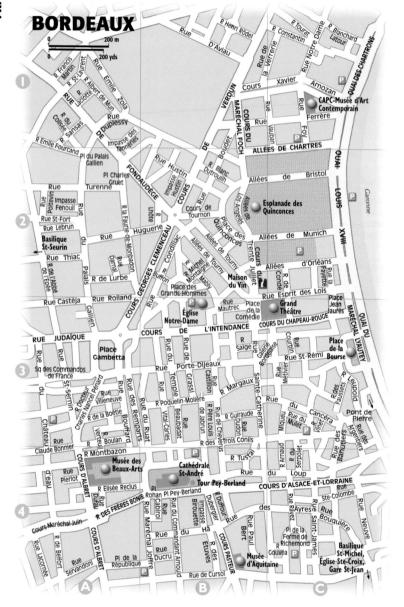

BORDEAUX

A fountain at the Esplanade des Quinconces

MUSÉE DES BEAUX-ARTS

✚ 46 A4 • 20 cours d'Albret ☎ 05 56 10 20 56 🕐 Wed–Mon 11–6 🍴 Guided tours Wed 12.30 and other times by arrangement

The fine arts museum is in the gardens of the Palais Rohan. Its permanent collection covers the main art movements from the Renaissance to World War II. Temporary exhibitions are held in the Galerie des Beaux-Arts opposite. Although relatively small, the museum's collection includes works by masters such as Titian, Van Dyck, Delacroix, Rubens and Matisse.

ÉGLISE NOTRE-DAME

✚ 46 B3 • place du Chapelet ☎ 05 56 81 01 37 🕐 Mon–Sat 8.30–5, Sun 1.30–5

Once associated with the nearby Dominican convent, this imposing church was completed in 1707 by Pierre Michel, an architect already engaged to construct the nearby fortress. The elaborate decoration of the church contrasts with the simplicity of its construction. The central nave, flanked by a series of small side chapels, extends beyond two ornate gilded wrought-iron gates to a baroque altar. On the west wall, an elaborate bas-relief depicts St. Dominic's vision of the Virgin Mary handing him a rosary.

BASILIQUE ST-SEURIN

✚ 46 off A2 • place des Martyrs de la Résistance ☎ 05 56 93 89 28 🕐 Daily 2–7 🎫 €3 🍴 Guided tours Sat 2.30–5.30, Sun 4–6

St-Seurin church was granted the title of basilica by the Pope in 1873, because of its significance to the Christian faith. It is also a UNESCO World Heritage Site, with origins dating back to Gallo-Roman times. You'll find an eclectic collection of styles and forms from the 11th to the 18th centuries, with both austere and lavish types of decoration. Excavations in 1910 revealed a huge Christian burial ground dating from the fourth century.

BACKGROUND

Bordeaux is one of France's oldest trading ports, with its wealth built on wine. The Romans were among those who took advantage of the city's coastal position and proximity to plentiful vineyards. When the marriage of Eleanor of Aquitaine and the future Henry II brought the western half of France under English rule in the 12th century, the city enjoyed a vast upsurge in revenue. Many wine merchants became wealthy and their legacy lives on in the elegant mansions and palaces they built.

The 18th century, in particular, sealed the city's reputation, and many of the great monuments date from that time. Like Paris only a century earlier, the city was rationalized with the creation of wide boulevards, public gardens and the colonnaded Grand Théâtre. During this time, wealth was also boosted from trade with the colonies in sugar, spices and coffee.

BASILIQUE ST-MICHEL

✚ 46 off C4 • place Meynard ☎ 05 56 94 30 50 🕐 Daily 2–7

This triple-naved Flamboyant Gothic basilica, now a UNESCO-listed site, became a focal point for pilgrims throughout the Bordeaux area. Its freestanding bell tower gives a wonderful panorama of the city and river.

CAPC–MUSÉE D'ART CONTEMPORAIN

✚ 46 C1 • 7 rue Ferrère ☎ 05 56 00 81 50 🕐 Tue–Sun 11–6 (also Wed 6–8pm) 🍴 Guided tours Sat, Sun 4, other times by appointment

A 19th-century converted warehouse is now a multimedia exhibition space, with cutting-edge exhibits and lively temporary exhibitions.

ÉGLISE SAINTE-CROIX

✚ 46 off C4 • place Pierre Renaudel ☎ 05 56 94 30 50 🕐 Thu 10–12

Outside, there are 12th-century sculptures above the main door. Inside, look for the baroque organ and an unusual collection of 17th-century religious paintings.

ESPLANADE DES QUINCONCES

✚ 46 B2

This huge tree-lined space, on the site of the 15th-century Château de Trompette, is said to be the largest centrally located square of any city in Europe.

MUSÉE D'AQUITAINE

✚ 46 B4 • 20 cours Pasteur ☎ 05 56 01 51 00 🕐 Tue–Sun 11–6

The history of Bordeaux from prehistoric times to today is covered in this museum, on the site of a convent. Objects from other cultures underline the city's role in exploration and trade.

PLACE DE LA BOURSE

✚ 46 C3

A sculpture of Neptune symbolically opening the road to trade stands in front of this elegant semicircular sweep of golden buildings looking out over the quayside.

FRANCE

WHAT TO DO

⊕ BAILLARDRAN

Galerie des Grands Hommes
Tel 05 56 79 05 89
www.baillardran.com
Come here to try *cannelé*, a small cake still produced according to an old, not-so-secret recipe. It has a creamy inside hidden beneath a caramelized outer crêpe-like layer infused with rum, orange-flower water and vanilla.
◉ Mon–Sat 10–7.30

⊕ BRADLEY'S BOOKSHOP

8 cours d'Albret
Tel 05 56 52 10 57
www.bradleys-bookshop.com
This is the place to come for English-language books in Bordeaux. It has the full range of guidebooks, phrasebooks and holiday reading, plus a large selection of original-language videos and DVDs.
◉ Mon 2–7, Tue–Sat 9.30–7

⊕ GALERIE DES REMPARTS

63 rue des Remparts
Tel 05 56 52 22 25
www.galeriedesremparts.com
The gallery and art shop are dedicated to the promotion of a wide selection of international painters, such as Loilier and Dubuc, with a focus on contemporary artists. The gallery holds regular exhibitions and offers a good service for resale and valuation. The staff are highly knowledgeable.
◉ Tue–Sat 10.30–1, 2.30–7

⊕ L'INTENDANT

2 allées de Tourny
Tel 05 56 48 01 29
This extraordinary wine shop is in a circular tower, climate-controlled to protect the 15,000 bottles of wine lining the walls, with the top floor reserved for the oldest vintages.
◉ Mon–Sat 10–7.30

⊕ MARCHÉ BIOLOGIQUE

quai des Chartrons
Tel 05 56 00 66 00 (tourist information)
This organic market is a recent addition to Bordeaux's market scene and one not to be missed. It is held opposite warehouse 5 on the quay.
◉ Thu 6am–4pm

⊕ ESPACE CULTUREL DU PIN GALANT

34 avenue du Maréchal de Lattre de Tassigny, Mérignac
Tel 05 56 97 82 82
www.lepingalant.com
You'll find this modern cultural venue near Bordeaux's Mérignac airport. There's an extensive and international schedule, with events ranging from opera, musicals, classical and modern concerts, to jazz, dance and theatre. Reserve your seats in advance.
◉ Performance times vary ◉ Varies

⊕ LE GRAND THÉÂTRE

place de la Comédie
Tel 05 56 00 85 95
www.opera-bordeaux.com
This magnificent neoclassical building, home to the National Opera of Bordeaux, is worth a visit for the architecture alone. There are guided tours when rehearsals and performances allow. Performances take place most days.
◉ All year ◉ Tour and performance from €11.40

♥ HERALD'S PUB

5 rue du Parlement Sainte-Catherine
Tel 05 56 81 37 37
You'll find this relaxed bar, where jazz plays in the background, in a building under stone arches off place du Parlement. Order whisky or champagne at the beautiful bar inlaid with brass.
◉ Daily 7.30pm–1am

⊕ GOLF DE BORDEAUX-LAC

avenue de Pernon, Bordeaux-Lac
Tel 05 56 50 92 72
Close to flower gardens and the Bordeaux woods are two 18-hole golf courses and a covered driving range with 25 posts. Group lessons and courses are available and there's a golf shop. Credit cards are not accepted.
◉ Daily 8–6 ◉ Entry free, but call ahead to book a time slot

⊕ IN-LINE SKATING

www.bordeaux-roller.com
Downtown Bordeaux is a pedestrian-only zone and attracts large numbers of in-line skaters. There is a regular in-line skating night when more than 500 bladers take over the heart of the city.
◉ First Sun of the month, times vary ◉ Free

EATING

LE FRANCHOUILLARD

21 rue Maucoudinat
Tel 05 56 44 95 86
www.lefranchouillard.com
This restaurant has *France à la carte*–a menu that changes every few weeks so you can sample the cuisine of different regions of the country; it's reasonably priced.
◉ Mon–Sat 12–3, 6pm–1am
◉ L €21, D €30, Wine €12

RESTAURANT DE FROMAGES BAUD ET MILET

19 rue Huguerie
Tel 05 56 79 05 77
This restaurant serves up a selection of more than 200 kinds of cheese, a choice of an all-you-can-eat cheese platter and traditional cheese-based dishes including *tartiflette* (a baked cheese and potato dish) and *raclette* (melted cheese served with potatoes, pickles and pearl onions).
◉ Mon–Sat 10am–11pm
◉ L €28, D €40, Wine €12

STAYING

HÔTEL DE FRANCE

7 rue Franklin, 33000 Bordeaux
Tel 05 56 48 24 11
This basic but clean hotel is a great choice for those on a budget. All the rooms have a private bathroom; the hotel's position makes it easy to get to the city's many attractions.
◉ €55, excluding breakfast (€7)
◉ 20 ◉

LES 4 SOEURS

6 cours du 30 Juillet, 33000 Bordeaux
Tel 05 57 81 19 20
A hotel with character and a great location. Some of the rooms are small and basic, but there are a few larger rooms overlooking the square. Some bedrooms sleep up to five people, making them a good choice for families.
◉ €80–€100, excluding breakfast (€8)
◉ 34 ◉

FRANCE

Lille

European City of Culture in 2004, Lille has one of France's most prestigious art museums—the Palais des Beaux-Arts—as well as a citadel built for Louis XIV and a cobbled old town.

Place du Général de Gaulle   *A florist on rue Lepelletier*   *Busy market stalls in the street*

SEEING LILLE

Lille is a thriving city with a compelling mixture of old and new. It is the fourth-largest city in France, capital of the Nord-Pas-de-Calais region, with a population of 1.5 million. Attractions include the Palais des Beaux-Arts, the vast Centre Euralille shopping mall and the warren of cobbled streets in the old town. Here, the 17th-century buildings are built of Lezennes white stone and Armentières brick, with intricately carved wheat sheaves and cherubs crowning the doorways. The heart of the city is the Grand' Place, officially known as place du Général de Gaulle. This square is often used for city celebrations, and the fountain is a popular meeting point. There are many bars and restaurants on the streets between here and nearby place Rihour and place du Théâtre. Lille's newer part is farther east, in the Euralille district.

Getting to Lille is simple: There are good train links with Brussels (40 minutes), Paris (one hour) and London, which is only two hours away on the Eurostar. The city has an efficient Métro, bus and tram system.

HIGHLIGHTS

PALAIS DES BEAUX-ARTS

➕ 50 B2 • place de la République ☎ 03 20 06 78 00 🕐 Mon 2–6, Wed–Sun 10–6. Closed public hols and first weekend in Sep 🚇 République 🚌 14 💶 Adult €5, child (12–18) €3.50, under 12 free

This magnificent late 19th-century palace, enlarged in the 1990s, houses France's second national museum after the Louvre in Paris, with a collection of masterpieces spanning more than 400 years. Artists represented range from Flemish and Dutch masters to the Impressionists, including Monet, Renoir and Van Gogh. There's 19th-century French sculpture in a hall on the ground floor, while the basement contains the medieval and Renaissance collection, including 40 sketches by Raphael and Donatello's bas-relief *Herod's Feast*. Other highlights are 18th-century relief maps of northern France's fortified cities, and Vauban's models for his Citadelle. Look for the stained-glass windows near the main staircases.

RATINGS

Cultural interest	●●●●●
Historic interest	●●●
Photo stops	●●●
Shopping	●●●●

BASICS

➕ 4 C3 ℹ️ Palais Rihour, place Rihour, BP 205, 59002, tel 03 59 57 94 00 from outside France or 0891 562004 within France; Mon–Fri 9–6.30, Sat 9.30–6.30, Sun 10–12, 2–5

🚇 Two Métro lines serve the city and surrounding area

🚌 Most buses leave from place des Buisses, between Lille's two train stations. There are also two tram routes

🚆 Lille-Europe station has Eurostar trains from London, Ebbsfleet and Ashford (UK), TGV trains from Paris and all over France, and Thalys trains from Brussels. Regional services arrive at Lille-Flandres station

✈️ Lille Lesquin airport, 12km (7 miles) from the city centre, has international and domestic flights

www.lilletourisme.com
French and English; a lively site with information on getting to Lille, eating out, visiting the sights, shopping and more.

TIPS

- If you are using the Métro, buses or trams, remember to punch your ticket at the start of your journey.
- A City Pass gives you unlimited use of the buses, Métro and trams within Lille, as well as entry to some museums (1 day €18, 2 days €30, 3 days €45).
- For a weekend hotel bargain, contact the tourist office (at least eight days in advance) for details of the two-for-one Bon Weekend offers.
- Town stewards, wearing yellow jackets, give advice and directions to visitors.

CITADELLE

✚ 50 A1 • avenue du 43ème Régiment d'Infantrie ☎ Tourist office: 03 20 21 94 21 🕐 Guided tours only, Sun 3–5. You must reserve in advance at the tourist office (tel 0891 562004) 🚌 14 💷 Adult €7, child (under 16) €6

The architecture in Lille's historic heart is an appealing mix of Flemish and French, but the Citadelle, just outside Vieux Lille, is entirely French, built by Louis XIV's military engineer Vauban. The vast fortress—a mini-town—is in the shape of a five-pointed star and inspired the design for the US Pentagon. It was completed in 1670, after only three years of building work. The main entrance, the Porte Royale, was intended to reflect the grandeur of Louis XIV, but security was another key concern—the gateway is at an angle to the drawbridge to avoid enemy fire and the walls are 4m (13ft) thick. The Citadelle is still home to 1,000 soldiers.

EURALILLE

✚ 50 C1 • avenue Le Corbusier ☎ 03 20 14 52 20 🕐 Euralille: Mon–Sat 10–8. Hypermarket: 9am–10pm. Restaurants: 9am–10pm 🚇 Gare Lille-Europe and Gare Lille-Flandres

This futuristic shopping, business and leisure district opened in 1994 to coincide with the launch of the Eurostar rail service. It sits on 70ha (170 acres) of land on the eastern side of the city, sandwiched between Lille's two train stations, and was laid out by Dutch architect Rem Koolhaas. You can choose from around 140 shops at the Centre Euralille mall or attend a concert in the 5,000-seat Grand Palais, and there are restaurants, a hypermar-

Christmas rides

ket, a hotel and holiday apartments. The modernistic Gare Lille-Europe is crowned by Christian de Portzampac's Tour Crédit Lyonnais, popularly known as the 'ski boot'.

MUSÉE DE L'HOSPICE COMTESSE

✚ 50 B1 • 32 rue de la Monnaie ☎ 03 28 36 84 00 🕐 Wed–Sun 10–12.30, 2–6, Mon 2–6 🚇 Rihour 💷 Adult €2.30, child €1.50

This former hospital takes you back to the 15th to 17th centuries, with French, Flemish and Dutch paintings, period furniture and rare musical instruments. Don't miss the tapestries by local weaver Guillaume Werniers and the kitchen decorated in Dutch style. The museum sits discreetly behind the shopfronts of the rue de la

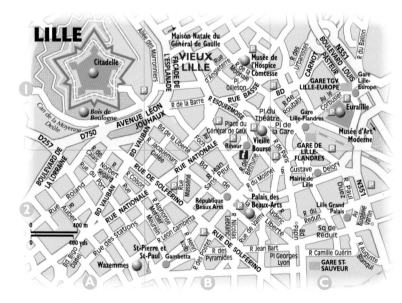

Monnaie, one of Lille's oldest streets. A hospital was founded here in 1237 by Jeanne de Constantinople, Countess of Flanders.

WAZEMMES

➕ 50 A2 • place de la Nouvelle Aventure 🕐 Sun, Tue, Thu 7am–2pm Ⓜ Gambetta

There is a carnival atmosphere at the Sunday morning Wazemmes market, which is more an event than a shopping opportunity. The sound of accordions and the aroma of Sunday lunch waft past stands selling anything from puppies and kittens to bric-a-brac. You'll find the pet market near Gambetta Métro station and antiques and bric-a-brac on the streets around the church of St-Paul-et-St-Pierre. Toys, clothes, fruit and vegetables are sold on place de la Nouvelle Aventure, and cheese, meat and fish in the market hall.

Try Euralille for retail therapy   *The 'ski boot' building*

BACKGROUND

Lille began life as a village surrounded by tributaries of the river Deûle, giving rise to its name (*l'île*—the island). Gradually, canals and a river port were created from the waterways, attracting merchants and prosperity to the burgeoning market town. From the Middle Ages onwards Lille passed from kingdom to kingdom, belonging to France, Spain, Burgundy, Flanders and the Netherlands. Louis XIV captured the city in 1667 and it was officially handed over to France as part of the Treaty of Utrecht in 1713. The Germans invaded in World War I, and again in World War II. More recently, in 1994, the launch of the Eurostar linked Lille with London, making the city an attractive day-trip destination for visitors from the UK. Lille's status was further enhanced by its designation as European City of Culture in 2004.

Lille's most famous sons are the pioneering microbiologist Louis Pasteur (1822–95), who came to the city in 1854 as Dean of the university's science faculty, and Charles de Gaulle (1890–1970), who was born on rue Princesse.

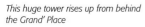

This huge tower rises up from behind the Grand' Place

BOIS DE BOULOGNE

➕ 50 A1 🕐 Daily 🚌 14

This park is wrapped around the Citadelle and bordered by the canal of the river Deûle. It is popular with bicyclists and joggers and there is also a zoo.

MAISON NATALE DU GÉNÉRAL DE GAULLE

➕ 50 off B1 • 9 rue Princesse ☎ 03 28 38 12 05 🕐 Wed–Sun 10–1 (last ticket 12), 2–5 🚌 3, 6 💶 €5

War hero and first president of the French Fifth Republic Charles de Gaulle was born here, in his grandmother's house, on 22 November 1890. It is now a museum of his life.

MUSÉE D'ART MODERNE

➕ 50 off C1 • 1 allée du Musée, Villeneuve d'Ascq ☎ 03 20 19 68 68 🕐 Wed–Mon 10–6. Reopening following refurbishment and extension, in Spring 2009 Ⓜ Pont de Bois, then bus 41 to Parc Urbain–Musée 💶 Adult €6.50, child (12–25) €1.50, child under 12 free

The modern art museum, a short Métro and bus ride out from the city, displays works by Picasso, Modigliani, Braque and others in its light, airy galleries. Sculptures embellish the gardens.

VIEILLE BOURSE

➕ 50 B1 • place du Général de Gaulle 🕐 Tue–Sun 1–7 Ⓜ Rihour 💶 Free

The opulent 17th-century trading exchange is arguably the most beautiful building in Lille, with its intricate carvings and cloistered courtyard. Merchants once traded here—today you can browse the second-hand book market or watch the chess players.

FRANCE

WHAT TO DO

⊕ LE CÈDRE ROUGE
Parvis de La Treille, 3 place Gilleson
Tel 03 20 51 96 96
www.lecedrerouge.com
An institution in Lille, this shop gathers together high-quality handicrafts and furnishings from all over the world to complement the house and garden. Among its offerings are terracotta from Tuscany, teak from Indonesia and high-quality porcelain from France.
⊙ Mon 2–7, Tue–Sat 10.30–7

⊕ CHARLES ET CHARLUS
4 rue Basse
Tel 03 20 51 01 01
Sells contemporary bags and other leather goods made using traditional methods. There is a choice of leathers and a wide range of shades.
⊙ Mon–Fri 10.30–1, 2–7, Sat 10.30–7

⊕ MARCHÉ AUX LIVRES
Cloîtres de la Vieille Bourse
This small market selling books is held inside the courtyard of the old stock exchange building, a marvel of 17th-century Flemish architecture. It's worth stopping here just to admire the surroundings, but the old books are tempting too. Credit cards are not accepted.
⊙ Tue–Sun 1–7 ⓡ Rihour

⊕ MARCHÉ DE WAZEMMES
place de la Nouvelle-Aventure
This interesting market is popular with locals who like to shop here on their Sunday stroll. Most of the stalls are set around Wazemmes church, but there is also a covered section. It's the place to buy cheap vegetables and some North African products, and there's also a small antiques section.
⊙ Sun, Tue and Thu 7–2 ⓡ Wazemmes

⊕ N DE B HAUTE MODE
6 rue Jean-Jacques Rousseau
Tel 03 20 42 19 79
This tiny shop on a picturesque street sells unique hats, bags, gloves and hair accessories to discerning but budget-conscious customers. The designs and quality are as good as haute couture, but the prices remain affordable. Special pieces can be made to order.
⊙ Tue 2–7, Wed–Sat 10.30–12, 2–7

ⓐ LE MÉTROPOLE
26 rue des Ponts de Comines
Tel 0892 680 073
www.lemetropole.com
This modern building with a glass façade has a repertory cinema showing films in their original language.
⊙ Daily 11–9 (last show) ⓓ Adult €7.30 ⓡ Gare Lille Flandres

ⓥ LE KREMLIN
51 rue Jean-Jacques Rousseau
Tel 03 20 51 85 79
There's a Russian theme to this bar, including an imposing bust of Lenin. It has 40 varieties of vodka.
⊙ Mon–Sat 6pm–2am

EATING

ALCIDE
5 rue Debris St-Étienne
Tel 03 20 12 06 95
A high-class brasserie that has been here since 1873. *Moules frites* (mussels and chips) and *potjevleesch* (cold cuts in aspic) are just two examples of the classic brasserie dishes.
⊙ Mon–Sat 12–2, 7–10; Sun 12–2
ⓛ L €30, D €40, Wine €16

LA CAVE AUX FIOLES
39 rue de Gand
Tel 03 20 55 18 43
www.lacaveauxfioles.com
The setting of this restaurant is romantic—at the heart of Lille's old town on a cobbled street in an 18th-century house. The food, served by candlelight, has inventive interpretations of local dishes, such as scallops in a light vanilla sauce and Flemish-style lobster.
⊙ Mon–Fri 12–2, 8–11, Sat 8–11
ⓛ L €28, D €43, Wine €18

LA CHICORÉE
15 place Rihour
Tel 03 20 54 81 52
This brasserie, named after the vegetable of the region, has an extensive menu of seafood platters, fish stew, onion soup and rabbit.
⊙ Daily 10am–6am
ⓛ L €30, D €45, Wine €12

À L'HUITRIÈRE
3 rue des Chats Bossus
Tel 03 20 55 43 41
www.huitriere.fr
At this restored 18th-century house, expect classic seafood dishes, such as cod in cream with caviar from Aquitaine, and a well-stocked wine cellar. The restaurant's fish shop has mosaics and stained-glass windows depicting the sea.
⊙ Mon–Sat 12–2, 7–9.30, Sun 12–2
ⓛ L €90, D €240, Wine €28

STAYING

LE GRAND HÔTEL BELLEVUE
5 rue Jean Roisin, 59000 Lille
Tel 03 20 57 45 64
www.grandhotelbellevue.com
There are great views over Grand' Place from the renovated bedrooms at this good-value hotel. Rooms have en-suite bathrooms.
ⓛ €130–€150
ⓘ 60
ⓡ Rihour

L'HERMITAGE GANTOIS
224 rue de Paris, 59000 Lille
Tel 03 20 85 30 30
www.hotelhermitagegantois.com
The only luxury four-star hotel in Lille, L'Hermitage Gantois is a cluster of restored 15th-century hospice buildings. Guests and those patronizing the hotel bar can wander through the courtyards, library and chapel for free.
ⓛ €198–€275
ⓘ 67
ⓡ Mairie de Lille

HÔTEL BRUEGHEL
5 parvis St-Maurice, 59000 Lille
Tel 03 20 06 06 69
www.hotel-brueghel.com
You'll be near the station here. Named after Flemish painter Pieter Brueghel, the interior pays homage to his style. Bedrooms are tastefully decorated.
ⓛ €66–€130, excluding breakfast (€8)
ⓘ 66

FRANCE

Lyon

Lyon was once the Roman capital of Gaul and is now France's third-largest city (by population). Its Renaissance old quarter is listed as a UNESCO World Heritage Site and the city is known for its gastronomy.

Basilique Notre-Dame de Fourvière

Detail of carving on a building in place Bellecour

Cathédrale St-Jean

RATINGS

Cultural interest	● ● ● ●
Good for food	● ● ● ●
Historic interest	● ● ● ●

TIPS

- A Lyon City Card (€19 for 1 day, €29 for 2 days and €39 for 3 days), available from the tourist office, entitles you to entry to 20 museums, guided and audioguided city tours, river cruises, lunchtime classical concerts, public transport within the city and a traditional puppet show.
- The Métro system has four lines, running from 5am until midnight. In Vieux Lyon the Métro links with a funicular to the top of the Fourvière hill.
- Parc de la Tête d'Or, by the Musée d'Art Contemporain, has plenty of places to stroll and sit in the sunshine. There's a lake, rose garden, glasshouses, playground, small zoo, *petit train* and mini-golf.
- River cruises with Naviginter include lunch or dinner and depart from 13 bis quai Rambaud. Tours without meals leave from quai des Célestins, where there is also a ticket office.

SEEING LYON

The city sits at the confluence of the Rhône and Saône rivers, with the medieval quarter on the west bank of the Saône, the modern suburbs on the east bank of the Rhône, and the heart of the city on the narrow peninsula (the Presqu'île) between the two. Like Paris, Lyon is divided into administrative *arrondissements*. Its Métro system makes it easy to get around. A trip to Lyon isn't just about what to see—its unique *bouchon* eateries serve some of the world's best food, and the city has a lively social scene, with clubs, drama and live performance. It is also known for a type of puppet theatre known as *guignol*.

HIGHLIGHTS

FOURVIÈRE AND VIEUX LYON

Head across the river Saône to find Vieux Lyon, the wonderfully atmospheric old quarter. Its pedestrian-only streets cover three districts (St-Georges, St-Jean and St-Paul), lined with four-floor mansions, the whole constituting one of the most complete Renaissance towns in Europe. The main streets, rue St-Jean and rue du Boeuf, run parallel to the river, and here you'll find the typical *traboules* of Lyon—the arched galleries, courtyards and vaulted walk-ways that cut under the Renaissance mansions to make a warren of hidden alleyways. This side of the river is great for browsing in antiques shops and galleries and has some of the best-value *bouchon* bistros in the city. *Lugdunum*, the Roman capital of Gaul, was set above here on top of the hill now known as Fourvière. You can walk or take the funicular to the Roman remains.

CATHÉDRALE ST-JEAN

⊞ 55 B3 • place St-Jean, 69005 🕓 Mon–Fri 8–12, 2–7, Sat–Sun 8–12, 2–5 🚇 Vieux Lyon

The cathedral anchors Vieux Lyon. Built on the site of an earlier church, the oldest part is the cloister wall, dating from the 11th century, although building went on throughout the 13th century. The resulting church is one of the finest examples of a transitional Romanesque/Gothic building. The vaults of the apse, for instance, are Romanesque at the base and topped with classic Gothic vaulting. There's some stunning stained glass, such as the rose windows in the transepts, and a rare astronomical clock dating from the 14th century. Pope John XXII was crowned here in 1316 and Henri IV married Marie de Medici here in 1600. The church received a visit by Napoleon in 1805 and was the site of the world's first recorded organ recital in 1928.

MUSÉE GALLO-ROMAIN

✚ 55 A3 • 17 rue Cléberg, 69005 ☎ 04 72 38 49 30 🕐 Tue–Sun 10–6 🎫 Adult €3.80, under 18 free; free to all on Thu
This museum, on Fourvière hill, is in an innovative subterranean building. Its 17 rooms display objects found in Lyon and the Ain and Isère regions. Highlights include the 'Claudius Tablet', part of a bronze

BASICS

✚ 4 C4 ℹ️ place Bellecour, 69002, tel 04 72 77 69 69; May–end Sep Mon–Sat 9.30–6.30, Sun 10–5.30; Oct–end Apr daily 9–6

🚇 Lyon's Métro system has four lines
🚉 There are two main stations in Lyon. Gare de la Part-Dieu is where most TGV services from Paris terminate, but some trains go on to the more central Perrache station

✈️ Lyon St-Exupéry airport, 24km (15 miles) east of Lyon
www.lyon-france.com

FRANCE

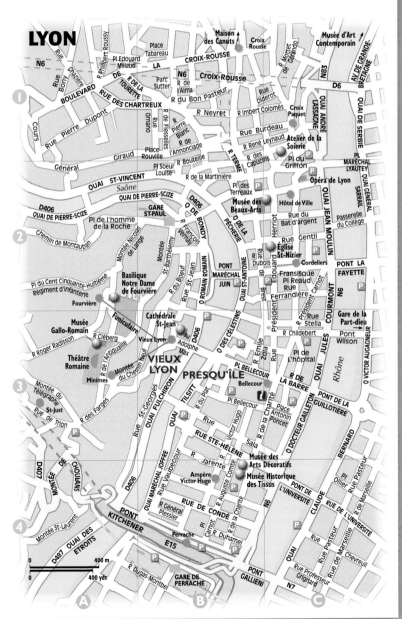

tablet inscribed with a speech given by Emperor Claudius to the Senate in AD48, in which he put forward the rights of the Gallic people to hold public office. Don't miss the rare mosaic showing a Roman circus, along with a vivid depiction of a chariot race.

BASILIQUE NOTRE-DAME DE FOURVIÈRE
✚ 55 A2 • Esplanade de Fourvière ⊙ Daily 8–7; chapel 7–7 🚇 Vieux Lyon then Funiculaire Fourvière

Despite its Roman connections, Fourvière is today famous for a much more modern edifice, the Basilique Notre-Dame de Fourvière, built on the site of the Roman forum and an 11th-century chapel. Its white marble façade, with four turrets and a rounded apse, can be seen from much of the city. In 1870 the people of Lyon, threatened by Prussian forces, prayed to the Virgin Mary (the city's patron) to spare their city. The enemy never breached the city walls and the grateful public donated enough money to build this magnificent basilica. The interior has exceptional Belle-Époque mosaics and vividly detailed stained glass depicting scenes from the life of the Virgin. The church's primary treasure is a golden statue of Mary in the 18th-century chapel adjoining the basilica.

MUSÉE DES BEAUX-ARTS
✚ 55 C2 • 20 place des Terreaux, 69001 ☎ 04 72 10 17 40 ⊙ Permanent collections: Sat–Mon, Wed–Thu 10–6, Fri 10.30–6. Closed 1–8 May, Easter Mon, Whit Mon, Ascension Day, 14 Jul and 15 Aug. First-floor rooms closed 11.55–1.05; second-floor rooms closed 1.05–2.15 🚇 Hôtel de Ville 💶 Permanent collection: adult €6, child €4. Temporary exhibitions: adult €10, under 18 free

In the Presqu'île district, the Palais St-Pierre, a former Benedictine monastery, now houses the art gallery—one of the best in France outside Paris. There are more than 1,800 paintings, shown in chronological order. Look for the fine altarpiece of *The Ascension of Christ* by Perugino from the Quattrocentro, and works by 17th-century Dutch and Flemish artists including Rembrandt and Rubens. The 18th-century Italian gallery has works by Tintoretto and Veronese. The museum is particularly strong on paintings by 19th- and early 20th-century artists including Dégas, Gauguin, Manet, Monet and Picasso. There are 16 rooms devoted to ancient civilizations, with outstanding collections of Greek, Roman and Egyptian items. A further 17 rooms

have varied collections, including Byzantine ivories, Limoges enamels, Islamic art and rare Japanese tea sets. The interior courtyard of the museum is now a formal garden.

BACKGROUND

The Gallo-Roman settlement on Fourvière hill was founded by Julius Caesar in 44BC and became the Roman capital of Gaul. But with the fall of the Roman Empire, the town moved down to the riverside, to what is now Vieux Lyon. An episcopal complex was established in the fifth century and power stayed in the hands of the bishops until the 14th century, when the monarchy introduced a secular government and law courts. In the 15th century, Lyon became an important European hub for currency dealing and printing, and began hosting huge trade fairs. The silk trade came into its own at this time and the city entered a golden age, leading to the building of the Renaissance town. Today Lyon is still at the forefront of architecture, with the ultramodern TGV station and the dramatic St-Exupéry airport, by Santiago Calatrava.

FRANCE

ATELIER DE LA SOIERIE
✚ 55 C1 • 33 rue Romarin, 69001 ☎ 04 72 07 97 83 ⊙ Mon–Sat 9–12, 2–7 🚇 Hôtel de Ville

This is one of the few working silk workshops left in the city. Watch the material being screen-printed and made into scarves, then browse the shop.

ÉGLISE ST-NIZIER
✚ 55 C2 • place St-Nizier ☎ 04 72 51 18 05 ⊙ Jun to mid-Sep daily 10–7.45; Mid-Sep to end May Mon–Sat 8.30–7.45, Sun 2.30–6

This church sits on the site of a 5th-century basilica. Begun in the early 14th century, its exterior is an excellent example of Flamboyant Gothic architecture.

MAISON DES CANUTS
✚ 55 off B1 • 12 rue d'Ivry, 69004 ☎ 04 78 28 62 04 ⊙ Tue–Sat 11–3.30 🚇 Croix Rousse 💶 Adult €5, child €2.40

The museum re-creates the old system of silk production in an original house with working handlooms. Dyeing and spinning took place on the ground floors of the tall 18th- and 19th-century houses in the Croix Rousse district, while the workers' families lived above.

MUSÉE D'ART CONTEMPORAIN
✚ 55 off C1 • 81 quai Charles des Gaulle, 69006 ☎ 04 72 69 17 17 ⊙ Tue–Sun 12–7, Fri also 7–10 🚌 4, 47 💶 Adult €5, under 18 free

In a spectacular building designed by Renzo Piano, this museum concentrates on 20th- and 21st-century art forms. It leans strongly towards installation art and computer-generated art.

MUSÉE DES TISSUS AND MUSÉE DES ARTS DÉCORATIFS
✚ 55 B4 • 34 rue de la Charité ☎ 04 78 38 42 00 ⊙ Musée des Tissus: Tue–Sun 10–5.30. Musée des Arts Décoratifs: Tue–Sun 10–12, 2–5.30 💶 €5 for both museums

These museums are in the 17th-century Hôtel de Villeroy. Learn about the use of silk and other textiles in clothing and soft furnishings.

A quiet side street in Lyon (above left)

WHAT TO DO

⊕ BERNACHON

42 cours Franklin Roosevelt
Tel 04 78 24 37 98
www.bernachon.com
Chocolate shop and tea room in the 6th *arrondissement* (take Métro line A to Foch). This chocolate heaven is filled with a variety of beautifully packaged sweets (candy). Prices are high, but the quality is worth it. The tea room serves refreshments and lunch. Try the hot chocolate.
🅖 Shop: Jun–end Aug Tue–Sat 8.30–7; May, Sep Mon–Sat 8.30–7, Sun 8.30–1; Oct–end Apr Mon–Sat 8.30–7, Sun 8.30–5. Tea room: Tue–Sat 9–6.30

⊕ DECITRE

6 place Bellecour
Tel 04 26 68 00 12
www.decitre.fr
A bookworm's paradise in the heart of the city. Subjects include travel, cookery, language and educational material as well as maps and calendars. There is a huge section of paperback fiction in English at the shop entrance and English is spoken here.
🅖 Mon–Sat 9.30–7
🚇 Lines A and D: Bellecour

⊕ MARCHÉ DE LA CROIX ROUSSE

boulevard de la Croix Rousse
Tel 08 25 08 15 15
www.lyon.fr
Covering almost the entire length of boulevard de la Croix Rousse, the Tuesday morning street market sells fruit, flowers and vegetables, household goods, clothes, shoes, pottery, fabric, baskets and beds. From Wednesday to Sunday the market sells only food and on Saturday morning there is also organic produce. Arrive early to avoid the crowds.
🅖 Wed–Thu 6–12.30; Tue, Fri, Sat–Sun 6–1.30 🚌 13, 18

⊕ L'OPÉRA NATIONALE DE LYON

place de la Comédie
Tel 0826 305 325 (toll call)
www.opera-lyon.com
Built in 1831, the opera building was altered in 1993 by Jean Nouvel, who created a profoundly different building surrounding the old theatre. Inside, the Italianate auditorium has retained its character. There is a restaurant on site.
🅖 Box office: Mon–Sat 11–7 ⊘ Opera up to €95, concerts and ballet up to €42 🚇 Lines B and C to Hôtel de Ville

✪ PARC DE LA TÊTE D'OR

69006
Tel 04 72 69 47 60
www.lyon.fr
Dating from 1856, this park includes botanic gardens, a zoo, a rose garden, a boating lake, children's play areas and a café/restaurant. You can walk, jog or rollerblade in the park, or rent a bicycle.
🅖 Mid-Apr to mid-Oct daily 5.30am–10.30pm; late Oct–early Apr daily 5.30am–8.30pm; botanical gardens 9–11.30, 1.30–3.45 ⊘ Free entry to the park 🚌 4, 47 🚇 Masséna

EATING

L'ASSIETTE DU MARCHÉ

21 Grande Rue de Vaise
Tel 04 78 83 84 90
This popular restaurant is great value, so it's a good idea to reserve. There are two dining rooms (one smoking, one not). The restaurant specializes in fish and unusually there is no formal menu, although there are always two dishes of the day (one meat, one fish). Dishes might include tuna gratin, fish soup or pikeperch.
🅖 Mon–Sat 12–2
⊘ L €14.80, Wine €6.50,

LA BRASSERIE DES BROTTEAUX

1 place Jules Ferry
Tel 04 72 74 03 98
www.brasseriedesbrotteaux.com
Established in 1913, this elegant brasserie is beautifully decorated with antiques, bright tiles, glass and mirrors. Opt for one of the wonderful prix-fixe menus or try a salad or the Aberdeen Angus beef.
🅖 Mon–Fri 7.30am–midnight, Sat 10–3, 6.30–12. Last order 10.30pm
⊘ L €35, D €45, Wine €18
✪

RELAIS GOURMAND PIERRE ORSI

3 place Kléber
Tel 04 78 89 57 68
www.pierreorsi.com
Pierre Orsi and his wife preside over this temple to gastronomy. The service is formal and impeccable and the menus are some of the most exciting in the industry.
🅖 Tue–Sat 12–1.30, 8–9.30
⊘ L €40, D €60, Wine €36

STAYING

HÔTEL ATHENA

45 boulevard Marius Vivier Merle, 69003 Lyon
Tel 04 72 68 88 44
www.athena-hotel.com
This hotel, outside the SNCF and TGV train station—as well as near bus, Métro and tram stations—is a modern, two-star hotel where rooms have satellite TV, telephone and radio. Parking costs €7 per day.
⊘ €85–€95, excluding breakfast (€8.50)
ⓘ 122 ✪

HÔTEL GLOBE ET CECIL

21 rue Gasparin, 69002 Lyon
Tel 04 78 42 58 95
www.globeetcecilhotel.com
A refurbished 19th-century hotel with early connections to the Vatican, the rooms are tastefully and individually decorated, though on the compact side. There are lots of shops and restaurants nearby.
⊘ €155, including breakfast
ⓘ 60

LA REINE ASTRID

26 boulevard de Belges, 69006 Lyon
Tel 04 72 82 18 00
www.warwickastrid.com
In a residential area convenient for Parc Tête d'Or, this four-star all-suite hotel is within easy walking distance of local shops and restaurants. The suites come with one or two bedrooms, bathroom, kitchen, satellite TV and internet access. There is a cocktail bar, a reading lounge, parking and a restaurant with a terrace.
⊘ €130–€210, excluding breakfast (€15)
ⓘ 88 suites
✪ ⊘

Marseille

This ancient yet dynamic city is a Mediterranean melting pot, with an intriguing atmosphere and exhilarating joie de vivre.

The Cathédrale de la Major soars above the traffic

Relaxing in the sunshine in the heart of Marseille

View of Marseille, looking across the port

RATINGS

Cultural interest	● ● ●
Good for food (fish)	● ● ● ●
Historic interest	● ● ● ●

BASICS

➕ 4 C4 ℹ️ 4 La Canebière, 13001, tel 04 91 13 89 00; Mon–Sat 9–7, Sun 10–5; longer hours in peak season

🚉 Gare St-Charles

www.marseille-tourisme.com
In English and French, with information on sights, guided tours and the City Pass.

SEEING MARSEILLE

On the west coast of Provence, close to the Camargue, Marseille is an energetic city with a long history. It is France's premier Mediterranean sea gateway and has a distinctive mix of ethnic and cultural influences. The city has plenty to offer, including many museums and art galleries, and boat trips to offshore islands. There are two Métro lines. The grandly beautiful Vieux Port (Old Port) and its surrounding streets form Marseille's focal point. Here are bars, art galleries, music venues and scores of little restaurants. You can walk or drive the shore road a few minutes south from Le Vieux Port to the old-fashioned little harbour at Anse des Auffes, where bright fishing boats are pulled up in front of a choice of fish restaurants. And the city makes a good base for some out-of-town sightseeing on the western Provence coast. While there are areas where you should be careful, on the whole the 'crime and drugs' image of the city is exaggerated.

HIGHLIGHTS

VIEUX PORT

➕ 60 A2

Visitors and residents alike tend to gravitate to the large, rectangular, westward-facing Vieux Port. It is fortified, enclosed by 17th-century Italianate quays and surrounded by pale stone façades and red roofs. Thousands of boats jostle one another. Steep hillsides slope down to the waterside, overlooked on the south side by the Fort St-Nicolas defences (no entry to visitors) and the powerfully fortified Basilique St-Victor, which has a fifth-century crypt. North of the Vieux Port, the extensive modern docks extend along the shore.

A massive gilded Madonna crowns the belfry of the basilica of Notre-Dame-de-la-Garde

MUSÉE D'HISTOIRE DE MARSEILLE

➕ 60 B2 • square Belsunce, Centre Bourse, 13001 ☎ 04 91 90 42 22 🕐 Mon–Sat
12–7 💶 Adult €2, under 5 free

*Fresh produce at the daily fish
market on the quai des Belges*

The fascinating Musée d'Histoire de Marseille stands alongside the
Jardin des Vestiges. It sets out the complete history of the city, with a
third-century Roman ship as its focal point. The Jardin des Vestiges
is an archaeological site now transformed into a pretty garden. A
walkway enables an overview of the ruins of the original Greek
ramparts, traces of a roadway and parts of the dock as it was in the
first century AD. Many of the items found in the excavations are now
in the museum.

LE PANIER

➕ 60 A2

Stepped alleys and rundown tenements with washing lines strung
between windows climb the Panier hill from the docks. In 1943
the occupying Nazi regime destroyed 2,000 buildings here and
expelled or murdered around 25,000 residents. Among the buildings
that survived is the 16th-century Maison Diamantée, so-called for a
façade of stones carved into diamond-like points. It houses the
Musée du Vieux Marseille, with sections dedicated to Provençal

furnishings, *santons* (Nativity scene figurines) and the esoteric playing cards called the Tarot Marseillaise. Another survival, in Grand Rue, is the 16th-century Hôtel de Cabre. After World War II, it was taken apart and rebuilt in a different street, which is why it says Rue de la Bonneterie on the wall. At the top of the Le Panier district is the former 17th-century hospice called La Vieille Charité, a rectangle of lovely, three-tiered arcaded galleries, set around a large courtyard with a small baroque chapel. Originally a place of detention and shelter for vagrants, La Vieille Charité now hosts art exhibitions and the Musée de l'Archéologie Meditéranéenne (Jun–end Sep Tue–Sun 11–6; Oct–end May 10–5). Beyond is the 19th-century neo-Byzantine Cathédrale de la Major, with its domes and striped façade. The sad, damaged little building beside it is the 12th-century Romanesque Ancienne Cathédrale de la Major (closed).

FRANCE

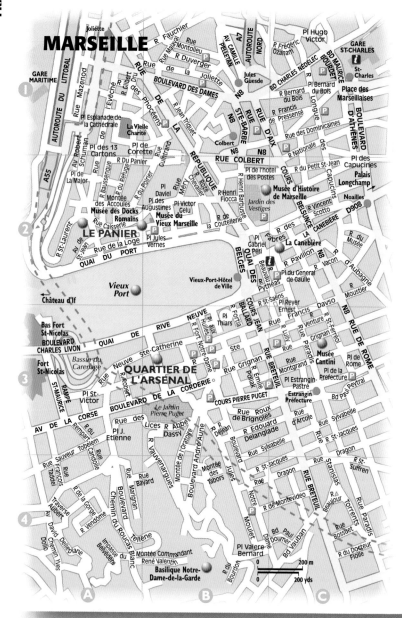

MARSEILLE

The Marché aux Capucins (left)

LA CANEBIÈRE
➕ 60 C2

Leading through the heart of the city in a majestic straight line directly from the Vieux Port's quai des Belges is the broad central avenue called La Canebière. Built in the 17th century, the street was for a long time rather seedy, but today it is an inspiring sight. Most of the main shopping streets are turnings off La Canebière.

MUSÉE CANTINI
➕ 60 C3 • 19 rue Grignan, 13006
☎ 04 91 54 77 75 🕐 Jun–end Sep Tue–Sun 11–6; Oct–end May 10–5
🎟 Adult €3, under 5 free
🚇 Estangin-Préfecture

This modern art gallery, with a good Surrealist collection and works by Matisse, Dufy, Miró, Kandinsky and Picasso, was a private home in the 17th century.

MUSÉE DES DOCKS ROMAINS
➕ 60 A2 • 28 place Vivaux, 13002
☎ 04 91 91 24 62 🕐 Jun–end Sep Tue–Sun 11–6; Oct–end May 10–5
🎟 Adult €2, child (5–17) €1, under 5 free

At the foot of the Le Panier district are several important relics and museums of the Classical period. The Musée des Docks Romains (Museum of the Roman Docks) displays a collection of first- to third-century Roman objects discovered during post-war rebuilding work. It has a good collection of Roman *dolia* (large ceramic storage jars).

NOTRE-DAME-DE-LA-GARDE
➕ 60 B4

About 1km (0.6 miles) south of the old port is the hilltop Notre-Dame-de-la-Garde, a 19th-century basilica with a huge gilded Virgin, strikingly lit at night, believed by locals to give divine protection to the city.

QUARTIER DE L'ARSENAL
➕ 60 B3

Close to the port (to the south), behind quai de Rive Neuve, is the grid of streets called the Quartier de l'Arsenal. Once a notorious shipyards area where galley slaves were housed among the workshops, it is now full of restaurants.

PALAIS LONGCHAMP
➕ 60 off C2 • 142 boulevard Longchamp, 13004 ☎ Palais: 04 91 14 59 50; Musée des Beaux-Arts: 04 91 62 21 17 🕐 Musée des Beaux-Arts: closed throughout 2008 for renovation. Musée d'Histoire Naturelle: Tue–Sun 10–5 🎟 Musée d'Histoire Naturelle: €4 🚇 Longchamp-Cinq Avenues

This palace is home to the Musée d'Histoire Naturelle which has a zoo behind it, and the Musée des Beaux-Arts. The latter has 16th- and 17th-century French and Italian paintings, a room devoted to local architect, sculptor and painter Pierre Puget, and another room dedicated to local painter Honoré Daumier.

CHÂTEAU D'IF
➕ 60 off A2 ☎ 04 91 59 02 30 🕐 May–end Sep daily 9.30–6.30; Oct–end Apr Tue– Sun 9.30–5.30 🎟 Adult €5, under 18 free 🚢 Ferries leave from quai des Belges
It's a 15-minute ferry journey to the island of If, with its nightmarish prison fortress, made famous by Alexandre Dumas in *The Count of Monte Cristo*. The journey gives great views of the city and guided tours take you to the cells once occupied by the 'Man in the Iron Mask' and other aristocratic prisoners.

BACKGROUND

Founded as the trading port of Massalia by the Greeks 2,600 years ago, Marseille has been the western Mediterranean's main port ever since. After the Roman conquest of Provence, the port was sacked and stripped of its fleet. A period of decline followed the Saracen and other raids of the seventh century, which curtailed all Mediterranean trade. By the 11th century, the city had revived and continued to develop until the plague arrived in 1720, killing 50,000 residents. By the 1760s, the city was the major port trading with the Caribbean and Latin America. The republican zeal of Marseille's oppressed workers proved a backbone of the Revolution, the city giving its name to the new national anthem, *La Marseillaise*, even though it was composed in Alsace. The city sustained extensive damage during World War II. In the second half of the 20th century, large numbers of people from Africa, particularly North Africa, moved to the city. Today, Marseille has a total population of around one million.

FRANCE

FRANCE

WHAT TO DO

⊕ LE PELLE-MÊLE
8 place aux Huiles
Tel 04 91 54 85 26
France's greatest jazz musicians have played here on the small stage. The leather and wood interior creates a warm atmosphere and an intimate setting for gigs.
⊕ Tue–Sat 6pm–3am ⊕ Varies according to performance

⊕ BAR DE LA MARINE
15 quai de Rive-Neuve
Tel 04 91 54 95 42
Facing the old harbour, this authentic local bar is evocative of scenes described by Provençal author Marcel Pagnol. It's a fashionable place with a cool atmosphere and a soundtrack of acid jazz.
⊕ Daily 7am–2am

⊕ BAR DE LA SAMARITAINE
2 quai du Port
Tel 04 91 90 31 41
Remaining true to its quintessential 1930s character, this bar is a local institution. Its terrace, facing the picturesque old harbour, becomes a piano bar from Thursday to Saturday.
⊕ Daily 6am–10pm (to 2am, Jul, Aug)

⊕ CENTRE DE LOISIRS DES GOUDES
2 boulevard Alexandre Delabre
Tel 04 91 25 13 16
www.goudes-plongee.com
This company will take you diving in the bay of Marseille, around the Rioux archipelago, where caves and old wrecks are host to extraordinary flora and fauna. Some packages include all meals, use of kayaks and mountain bikes for a weekend or longer.
⊕ Summer only daily 8am–10pm
⊕ €196 for a weekend
⊕ 19 to Les Goudes

⊕ STADE VÉLODROME
3 boulevard Michelet
Tel 04 91 76 91 76
www.olympiquedemarseille.com
This 60,000-seat stadium is home to Olympique de Marseille, the city's soccer team. The locals are passionate about the sport and every game is a big event.
⊕ 8–11pm on match nights
⊕ Adult approximately €30 per ticket

⊕ LA BALEINE QUI DIT VAGUES
59 cours Julien
Tel 04 91 48 95 60
www.labaleinequiditvagues.org
The name of this venue means 'the whale who says waves', in reference to the native American traditional tale in which a whale symbolizes the memory of the world. It hosts story-telling performances, many for children.
⊕ Fri–Sat 8pm, Wed 2.30pm, children's performances Oct–end Jun
⊕ €10

EATING

LES ARCENAULX
25 cours Estienne d'Orves
Tel 04 91 59 80 30
www.jeanne-lafitte.com
Numerous books line the walls of Marseille's majestic former arsenal, which has a beamed ceiling and long red wall seats. Sophisticated regional cuisine is on the menu, with dishes such as honey and lemon duck served with citron-scented courgette (zucchini) gratin. In the afternoons, Les Arcenaulx is a tea room.
⊕ Mon–Sat 12–2, 8–11
⊕ Fixed price seasonal menu: L €35, D €35, Wine €18

CHEZ FONFON
140 rue du Vallon des Auffes
Tel 04 91 52 14 38
www.chez-fonfon.com
The lively fishing port, now a conservation area, is the place to try bouillabaisse, the Mediterranean fish soup for which Marseille is famous. Here you are in a different world, far from the touristy restaurants of the city's old port. Chez Fonfon is an institution in town and has been run by the same family for more than 50 years. It has an elegant, Mediterranean interior with green basket-weave chairs, a white and terracotta tiled floor and Provençal fabrics.
⊕ Mon 7.30–10, Tue–Sat 12–2, 7.30–10
⊕ L €55, D €65, Wine €17

STAYING

HÔTEL LE CORBUSIER
280 boulevard Michelet, 3rd floor, 13008 Marseille
Tel 04 91 16 78 00
www.hotellecorbusier.com
The hotel is in a block of 300 apartments designed by Le Corbusier. It comes complete with play areas, shops, a cinema, a bar and a library. The bedrooms are very simple. There is private car parking and a restaurant on site.
⊕ €85–€105, excluding breakfast (€8)
⊕ 21

HÔTEL HERMÈS
2 rue Bonneterie, 13002 Marseille
Tel 04 96 11 63 63
www.hotelmarseille.com
This two-star hotel is by the Vieux Port. Although lacking the charm of the old, the soundproofed bedrooms are light and have a TV. Some have a balcony.
⊕ €68–€97, excluding breakfast (€8)
⊕ 45 ⊕

HÔTEL DE ROME ET ST-PIERRE
7 cours St-Louis, 13001 Marseille
Tel 04 91 54 19 52
www.hotelmarseille-romestpierre.com
This three-star hotel is in a 19th-century building near the Vieux Port. The refined interior (drapes and candelabra in the bedrooms) sometimes betrays art deco influences. You'll find comfortable armchairs in the reading room and wrought-iron furniture in the breakfast room. Bedrooms have a TV and minibar and there is a safe and laundry service. Business facilities include a large meeting room with a telephone and VCR, and a photocopier.
⊕ €77–€87, excluding breakfast (€9)
⊕ 47
⊕
⊕ Vieux Port, Noailles

Monaco

●

Big yachts and big money epitomize the tiny principality, which is also the site of one of Europe's best aquariums.

Luxury boats in the marina　　*Shop in the most exclusive boutiques in Monaco*　　*The Grimaldi coat of arms on the Palais du Prince*

SEEING MONACO

By a historical anomaly, this beautiful patch of rock hanging off the Provençal coast never became part of France. Instead, it has grown into a super-rich city, tax haven and millionaires' playground. It's a place that deserves to be seen, if only for the clever way it has made use of the limited space available. To accommodate the 32,000 people who live here (only 6,000 of whom are native Monégasques), the mini-state has expanded upwards in the form of skyscrapers and outwards into the sea on artificial platforms. Some streets, sitting almost on top of one another, are connected by elevators. Despite being just under 2sq km (0.75sq miles) in area, Monaco has several districts. Monaco-Ville is the original town on Le Rocher (the Rock); Monte Carlo is the larger new town, with a beach; La Condamine, the harbour district, lies between Monaco-Ville and Monte Carlo; on the steep slope between Monaco-Ville and the French border is the residential district Moneghetti; and Fontvieille is the area west of Monaco-Ville, which has been artificially extended into the sea.

HIGHLIGHTS

MONACO-VILLE

Walk through the pretty, spotlessly clean, narrow streets, with their well-kept, pastel-shaded houses, to get to Monaco's cathedral. It has a Louis Bréa altarpiece, some fine paintings and the tombs of all Monaco's past princes as well as that of Princess Grace and Prince Rainier. The main sight in Monaco-Ville, however, is the small but sturdily fortified 13th- to 17th-century Palais du Prince (Jun–end Sep daily 9.30–6; Oct 10–5), whose rooms are adorned with frescoes, tapestries and paintings. The palace also contains a museum devoted to Napoleon, with an assortment of objects, including one of his hats. In the courtyard you can watch the guardsmen, in their elegant uniforms (white in summer and black in winter), perform the Changing of the Guard (daily at 11.55). The Musée Océanographique has superb aquariums holding 350 species (Jul, Aug daily 9.30–7.30; Apr–end Jun, Sep 9.30–7; Oct–end Mar 10–6). There are fantastic views from the terrace.

RATINGS			
Cultural interest	● ● ●		
Photo stops	● ● ● ●		
Shopping (luxury)	● ● ● ●		

BASICS

✚ 5 D4

🛈 2a boulevard des Moulins, 98000, tel 92 16 61 16 (country code 377); Mon–Sat 9–7, Sun 10–12

🚉 Monaco–Monte Carlo

❓ Tourist information kiosks are set up at the train station and main sights in summer

www.visitmonaco.com
Information on the major sights, and you can order a free brochure about the principality.

A bronze statue of Princess Grace of Monaco

Flowering cacti and tropical plants in the Jardin Exotique (above). Yachts in the marina (right)

MONTE CARLO

East of the Rock is Monte Carlo, a glitzy area of restaurants, luxurious hotels, beautifully kept palm and flower gardens, and the lavishly ostentatious Belle-Époque Casino. The Salons Européens and Salons Américains (Mon–Fri from 2pm, Sat–Sun from 12 noon) in the Casino have slot machines, roulette and gaming tables. To get into the more lavish Salons Privés (Jun–end Oct Mon–Fri from 4pm, Sat, Sun from 3pm; Nov–end May from 3pm daily), which are the real Casino, not much frequented by ordinary visitors, you have to pay a fee and be appropriately dressed. A grand staircase goes down to a money-no-object nightclub. For those who have not blown all their cash at the gaming tables, there's plenty of expensive shopping around the Casino and on boulevard des Moulins.

FONTVIEILLE

Fontvieille is a residential and business quarter standing on artificial platforms of rock, with a yachting marina alongside. Its Roseraie Princesse Grace is an exquisite rose garden with more than 4,000 varieties, dedicated to Princess Grace of Monaco, the former film star Grace Kelly, who died in a car accident in 1982. There are several museums here—the Musée des Timbres et des Monnaies (stamps and currency), the Musée Naval (model ships) and the Collection des Voitures Anciennes (gleaming classic cars).

BACKGROUND

Monaco was originally a medieval fortified perched village, its castle a possession of Barbarossa. In the 13th century, the powerful aristocratic Grimaldi family of Genoa acquired the Rock and made it their headquarters, refashioning themselves as the Princes of Monaco. Under Napoleon, most of the many independent fiefdoms of Provence were incorporated by force into France, but the Grimaldi influence in Provence and Italy was so strong that Napoleon decided to make an ally of the Grimaldis instead of seizing their lands. Monaco's income had come from high taxes on its domains, but the principality found a role for itself as a refuge for the aristocracy, and in the 19th century Prince Carlo III created the glamorous zone called Monte Carlo, where the casino raised more funds for the royal family. It did so well that taxes were eventually abolished.

WHAT TO DO

⊕ CENTRE COMMERCIAL LE METROPOLE
1 avenue des Citronniers
Tel 377 93 50 15 36
www.ccmetropole.com
A stone's throw from the Casino, this shopping complex has majestic Belle-Époque decor, including marble alleys and Bohemian glass candelabras. There are three levels, with 80 boutiques specializing in fashion, beauty, household goods and leisure equipment.
⊕ Mon–Sat 10–7.30, some Sun

⊕ CLOTHING FERRAGAMO
Hôtel Hermitage, place Beaumarchais
Tel 377 93 25 12 21
The Ferragamo trademarks are elegant Italian shoes first made famous in Hollywood. Today the empire has grown into a full couture house featuring simple elegant designs for men and women.
⊕ Mon–Sat 9.30–1, 2.30–7

℗ OPÉRA DE MONTE-CARLO
place du Casino
Tel box office 377 9806 2828
www.opera.mc
Since its inauguration by actress Sarah Bernhardt in 1879, this impressive Belle-Époque opera house has welcomed the world's greatest voices. The architect, Charles Garnier, also designed the Opéra Garnier in Paris.
⊕ Varies according to performance
⊕ Varies according to performance

℗ LE SPORTING D'ÉTÉ
avenue Princesse Grace
Tel 377 92 16 36 36
www.sportingmontecarlo.com
With a sunroof and large windows facing the sea, this concert hall has a majestic setting. It welcomes the biggest international stars to the complex, which also includes a casino and a club.
⊕ End Jun–early Sep daily show 10.30pm ⊕ Varies

ⓥ CASINO DE MONTE-CARLO
place du Casino
Tel 377 92 16 20 00
www.casinomontecarlo.com
The rich and famous flock to this grand Belle-Époque gambling temple decorated with frescoes and paintings and featured in several movies, including James Bond films. You must be over 21 and well dressed to gain admittance.
⊕ Café de Paris (slot machines) opens at 10am ⊕ Entry €10 and a further €10 to enter games room

ⓢ STADE LOUIS II
7 avenue des Castelans
Tel 377 92 05 74 73 (club), 377 92 05 40 19 (stadium), 377 92 05 37 54 (ticket office)
www.asm–fc.com
Home of AS Monaco Football Club, one of the most successful in the French league. Matches are played Aug–end May.
⊕ Ticket office Tue–Sat 9–6.30
⊕ €10–€60

EATING

LE LOUIS XV
Hôtel de Paris, place du Casino
Tel 377 92 16 29 76
www.alain-ducasse.com
The height of luxury, this restaurant is within the majestic Hôtel de Paris, which was built in 1864. Here, Alain Ducasse, one of France's most celebrated chefs, practises his art. The Mediterranean-inspired menu changes with the seasons and is in themes, including the kitchen garden, hunting, the farm, the sea and rivers. The luxurious Louis XV-style interior provides the backdrop to a feast fit for a king.
⊕ Thu–Mon 12–2, 7.30–9.30; Wed dinner in Jul and Aug; closed 3 weeks in Dec and 2 weeks in mid-Feb
⊕ L €150, D €170, Wine €90

LA ROSE DES VENTS
Plage du Larvotto
Tel 377 97 70 46 96
www.larosedeventsmonaco.com
On its own private beach, La Rose des Vents combines formal dining with a day by the sea–interrupt your swimming simply to move to your table for an ample lunch under the shade of a parasol. The menu is a combination of French and Italian, with a good range of seafood. There is a buffet for Sunday lunch.
⊕ Daily 12–3.30, 7.30–10.30 (closed Mon in winter)
⊕ L €30, D €50, Wine €15

STARS N'BARS
6 quai Antoine I, La Condamine
Tel 377 97 97 95 95
www.starsnbars.com
This popular American-style bar-restaurant, with a predominantly Tex-Mex menu, is the perfect place for families tired of more formal French restaurants. The bar has lots of games to keep kids occupied. In the evenings there's a disco or live music.
⊕ Jun–end Sep daily 11am–2am; Oct–end May Tue–Sun 11am–2am. Food is served until 11pm
⊕ L €25, D €50, Wine €12

STAYING

HOTEL ALEXANDRA
35 boulevard Princesse-Charlotte, 98000 Monte-Carlo
Tel 377 93 50 63 13
www.monte-carlo.mc/alexandra
This refurbished hotel is less than 500m (550 yards) from the attractions of Monte-Carlo–the casino, restaurants, nightlife and elegant shops. The exterior has classic Belle-Époque features, while the rooms are modern. All have soundproofing, minibar and TV. The hotel is a good-value option for its location.
⊕ 56
⊕ €135–€165, excluding breakfast (€13)
⊕

HÔTEL HERMITAGE
square Beaumarchais, 98000 Monaco
Tel 377 98 06 48 12
www.montecarloresort.com
This Belle-Époque luxury hotel faces the Mediterranean Sea. It has a panoramic restaurant, Le Vistamar, and you can have breakfast under a glass ceiling designed by Gustave Eiffel. There is direct access to Les Thermes Marins de Monaco Spa and Health Resort.
⊕ €355–€850, excluding breakfast (€32)
⊕ 230 ⊕ ⊠ Outdoor ⓥ

FRANCE

The baroque Hotel Negresco, on promenade des Anglais

NICE

**The capital of the Riviera is a hectic town and an art-lover's
dream, with several major art galleries.**

Nice was developed in stages by different peoples, including the
Ligurians, Greeks and Romans. It was part of Italy until 1860,
evident by the beautiful Italianate architecture of the old quarter.
Artists began to arrive in the 1920s and there are several
important galleries.

ART AND HISTORY
At the western end of the stony beach, a handsome 19th-century
mansion contains the town's prestigious Musée des Beaux-Arts (daily
10–6). It has extensive collections of 17th- to 19th-century French
and Italian paintings and sculpture. Close by, the Kenzo Tange-
designed Musée des Arts Asiatiques (May to mid-Oct 10–6; Nov-end
Apr 10–5) has magnificent examples of Chinese and other Asian
pieces both ancient and modern that epitomize the artistic culture of
each country. On the Paillon promenade that divides the old town
from the new, there are several galleries, including the famously
avant-garde Musée d'Art Moderne et d'Art Contemporain (Tue–Sun
10–6), which has the definitive collection of works from the Nice
school of 1960s modern artists, including Andy Warhol's *Campbell's
Soup Can*. At the foot of Cimiez hill, the Musée Marc Chagall/Musée
du Message Biblique (Jul–end Sep Wed–Mon 10–6; Oct–end Jun
10–5) has a phenomenal collection of Chagall's work, including
stained glass, mosaics and vivid, dreamlike canvases. Farther up the
hill, the Musée Henri Matisse (Wed–Mon 10–6) shows the artist's
exquisite line drawings and vivid gouaches. Matisse and Dufy are both
buried in the cemetery nearby.

VIEUX NICE
The old quarter is a delightful tangle of picturesque narrow lanes, with
bars, restaurants and little shops. There are also some interesting
small baroque churches.

ROMAN REMINDERS
The Cimiez hill has the ruins of a Roman city and a Musée
Archéologique (Wed–Mon 10–6). The oval arena is a venue for
open-air performances.

*In-line skating along the
promenade des Anglais*

RATINGS	
Cultural interest	●●●○
Photo stops	●●●○
Shopping	●●●○

BASICS
✚ 5 D4 🛈 5 promenade des Anglais,
06000, tel 0892 707 407; summer
Mon–Sat 8am–8pm, Sun 9–6; rest of
year Mon–Sat 9–6
🚃 Nice
www.nice-coteazur.org
www.nicetourisme.com

TIPS
● Visit the big flower market
(Tue–Sun) on cours Saleya.
● Stroll the Nice waterfront
along the promenade des
Anglais—a long, wide walkway
edged by mimosa and palms.
● Carte Passe-Musées offers
seven days of free admittance
to 65 museums along the Côte
d'Azur in a 15-day period.

KEY TO SYMBOLS

- ⊕ Shopping
- ⊕ Entertainment
- ⊕ Nightlife
- ⊕ Sports
- ⊕ Activities
- ⊕ Health and Beauty
- ⊕ For Children

WHAT TO DO

⊕ MARCHÉ SALEYA D'ARTISANAT D'ART
Cours Saleya

Take a stroll through Nice's evening arts and crafts market after a drink at a nearby bar. You'll find Provençal handicrafts (pottery, glasswork, olive wood kitchenware), plus crafts from other regions of the world.

⊕ Jun–end Sep Tue–Sun 6pm–12.30am

⊕ MOULIN À HUILE ALZIARI
14 rue St-François-de-Paule
Tel 04 93 85 76 92
www.alziari.com.fr

The olive oil on sale in this shop comes from a mill in Nice's northwest corner, which you can visit by appointment. In addition to bottles of the oil, you can buy products containing olive oil, such as soap or olive spread.

⊕ Tue–Sat 8.30–12.30, 2.15–7

⊕ AUDITORIUM DU CONSERVATOIRE NATIONAL DE RÉGION
127 avenue de Brancolar
Tel 04 97 13 50 00
www.cnr-nice.org

Under the name *Les Lundis Kosmas*, the students at the Regional Academy of Music open their rehearsals every Monday. Established over 20 years ago in honour of the composer Kosma, the event is an institution in Nice.

⊕ Mon 6pm but closed during school holidays. Call to check schedule
⊕ Free

⊕ L'F
6 place Charles-Félix
Tel 04 93 85 74 10

On the liveliest street in town, this café has one of Nice's best terraces–and it's even heated during colder spells. Inside is a 1930s and 1940s interior with banquette seating and a black-and-white tiled floor.

⊕ Daily 7.30am–2.30am. Kitchens close 11.30pm

⊕ LE GHOST
3 rue Barillerie
Tel 04 93 92 93 37
www.leghost-pub.com

This fashionable bar has comfortable sofas, gleaming mirrors and a well-stocked library. The place packs out when the resident DJ plays techno, hip hop or soul on theme nights.

⊕ Daily 7pm–2.30am

⊕ GRAND CAFÉ DE LYON
33 avenue Jean Médecin
Tel 04 93 88 13 17
www.cafedelyon.fr

This art nouveau-style bistro is a Nice institution. It's a brasserie at lunchtime, a tea room in the afternoon and later, a good place for a drink.

⊕ Daily 7am–11pm

EATING

L'ÂNE ROUGE
7 quai des Deux-Emmanuel
Tel 04 93 89 49 63
www.anerougenice.com

Chef Michel Devilliers likes to cook fish, and his creations are tantalizing: succulent scallops roasted with chorizo, fresh and dried tomatoes and thyme flower. The warm, elegant interior has beamed ceilings, bright pictures hung on ochre walls, comfortable high-back padded chairs and a large fireplace. The flower-filled terrace has a view of the harbour.

⊕ Mon–Tue, Fri–Sun 12–2.30, 7.30–10; Wed–Thu 7.30–10
⊕ L €64, D €64, Wine €18

CHRISTIAN PLUMAIL
54 boulevard Jean Jaures
Tel 04 93 62 32 22
www.christian-plumail.com

This restaurant in the old port receives excellent reviews. It's the domain of Christian Plumail, a young and innovative chef who mixes modern recipes with traditional ingredients to put a new twist on French classical cuisine.

⊕ Tue–Fri 12–2, 7.30–10; Sat, Mon 12–2. Closed Sun
⊕ L €50, D €80, Wine €24

RESTAURANT BOCCACCIO
7 rue Masséna
Tel 04 93 87 71 76
www.boccaccio-nice.com

There are no less than six dining rooms here, all of which have a marine theme. One has a large aquarium, another with a vaulted wooden ceiling is reminiscent of the interior of a caravel (a historic small ship). The menu has Mediterranean seafood dishes such as bass in a salty crust, *bouillabaisse* and seafood platters.

⊕ Daily 12–2.30, 7–11
⊕ L €50, D €50, Wine €24

STAYING

HÔTEL DE LA BUFFA
56 rue de la Buffa, 06000 Nice
Tel 04 93 88 77 35
www.hotel-buffa.com

This two-star hotel is in an early 20th-century building. The unpretentious interior is inviting and bedrooms have Provençal fabrics, a minibar, safe and satellite TV. The street-facing rooms have double glazing and there's private car parking.

⊕ €48–€75, excluding breakfast (€8)
⊕ 14 ⊕

HÔTEL NEGRESCO
37 promenade des Anglais, 06000 Nice
Tel 04 93 16 64 00
www.hotel-negresco-nice.com

Built in 1912, this palace and its signature black dome have been given landmark status. The interior is an ode to fine art from the Renaissance to the modern: In the Salon Royal, Niki de Saint-Phalle's *Nana*, an oversized sculpture of a woman, sits happily next to classical portraits. The hotel has its own private beach.

⊕ €350–€560, excluding breakfast (€28)
⊕ 145 rooms, 24 suites
⊕

HÔTEL SUISSE
15 quai Raubà–Capéu, 06000 Nice
Tel 04 92 17 39 00
www.hotels-ocre-azur.com

Set below the peak of the chateau and a few minutes' walking distance from the beach and the delights of Nice, this beautiful ochre-coloured 19th-century building has elegant refurbished rooms with a bright Mediterranean feel. Some have balconies with fantastic views over the Baie des Anges and the old town.

⊕ €65–€165, excluding breakfast (€15)
⊕ 42

Paris

✚ 4 C3 🛈 25 rue des Pyramides, 75001, tel 0892 68 30 00; daily 9–7
www.parisinfo.com • Comprehensive information, in English or French, on the official tourist office site

SEEING PARIS

Paris has 20 districts *(arrondissements)* spiralling out from the heart of the city. Although many of the most expensive boutiques, prestigious consular offices and world-class restaurants are concentrated in the 1st *arrondissement*, each district has its own appeal and special places of interest. The 18th, for example, is where you'll find the magnificent Sacré-Cœur basilica; the graves of Oscar Wilde and Jim Morrison attract today's pilgrims to the Père-Lachaise cemetery in the 20th, and the 5th is the colourful student quarter. The River Seine divides the city in two, flowing east to west, with the area to the north known as the Right Bank and the Left Bank to the south.

The public transport system is fast, clean, efficient and inexpensive, but Paris is best discovered on foot and most *arrondissements* are less than an hour's stroll from one side to the other. With outdoor cafés offering respite for weary feet, many take a seat, order a good coffee and enjoy the people-watching; it's a fundamental pleasure for Parisians and tourists alike.

BACKGROUND

Celtic fishermen of the Parisii tribe established Lutece, the 'boatyard on the river', on the Île de la Cité around 200BC. More than 1,500 years later, in 1370, the clock was installed on the Tour de l'Horloge in the delightful place Dauphine. Today it still keeps time, having witnessed the rise and fall of monarchies and republics, the suffering of citizens during the Terror and the bloodshed of revolution and invasion, and a growing legacy of magnificent buildings, historical sites and beautiful parks.

When Georges Haussmann introduced wide tree-lined boulevards in the 19th century, he transformed the city into a jewel of urban design. Haussmann's work not only staked Paris's claim as one of the most beautiful cities on earth, but also set a standard that planners have sought to emulate ever since. Presidents, too, have left reminders of their tenure. The 20th century has seen the construction of superb, and sometimes controversial, public buildings. Who can imagine Paris today without the Centre Georges Pompidou, the glass pyramid in the Louvre or the Grande Arche? Sights such as these encapsulate the spirit of the French and their vibrant and glamorous capital city.

DON'T MISS

CHAMPS-ÉLYSÉES
Quintessential Parisian promenade topped by the Arc de Triomphe (▷ 74)
MUSÉE D'ORSAY
Visit level 3 for Impressionist and Post-Impressionist art (▷ 79)
ÎLE DE LA CITÉ
Seine river scenes, beautiful bridges and Notre-Dame cathedral. The city was founded here
MUSÉE DU LOUVRE
One of the world's premier museums, containing the *Mona Lisa* (▷ 78)
TOUR EIFFEL
View Paris's most famous landmark (▷ 82–83) from the Palais de Chaillot
NOTRE-DAME
Stunning Gothic cathedral (▷ 80) which is over 800 years old
LES INVALIDES
Napoleon's tomb and an army museum are housed in this imposing building (▷ 77)

FRANCE (side tab)

HOW TO GET THERE

✈ **Airports**
Roissy–Charles de Gaulle, Orly and Beauvais Tillé
🚆 **Train stations**
Gare du Nord is the station for Eurostar

Taking time out for a coffee in place des Vosges

TIPS

● At the Tourist Information Centre ask for the Paris Museum Pass which allows free or discounted entry into over 60 museums for 2–6 days.
● For another €5 the Mobilis day ticket provides low-cost public transport throughout zones 1 and 2.
● Children love Paris too—discover La Villette's park attractions, the magic of Métamorphosis, the Musée Grévin waxworks and the Jardin d'Acclimatation.
● *Pariscope* (€0.40) is the city's weekly pocket-size listings guide available from newsstands, detailing current cultural events and fêtes as well as the best places to eat, drink and be entertained.
● If you have a head for heights and the patience to queue, the view from the top of the Eiffel Tower is stunning—on a clear day.

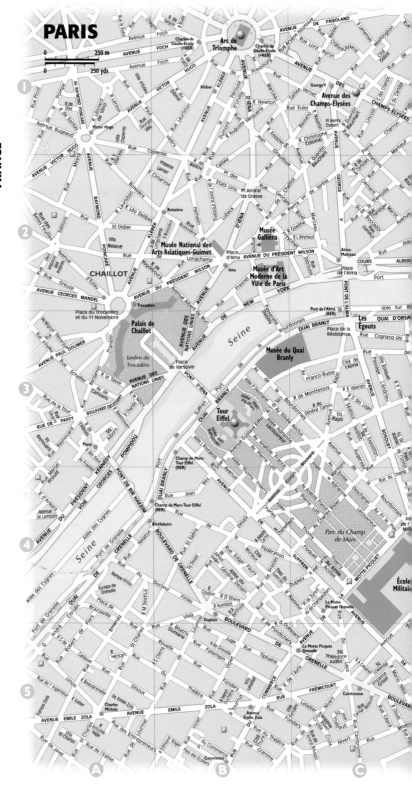

PARIS

0 — 250 m
0 — 250 yds

FRANCE

Arc de Triomphe

Charles de Gaulle-Étoile (+RER)
Charles de Gaulle-Étoile (+RER)

AVENUE FOCH
Avenue Foch
Avenue Foch

AVENUE DE FRIEDLAND

Avenue des Champs-Élysées

DES CHAMPS-ÉLYSÉES

George V
Kléber

AVENUE VICTOR HUGO
Victor Hugo

AVENUE D'IÉNA

Musée National des Arts Asiatiques-Guimet

Musée Galliéra

CHAILLOT

Musée d'Art Moderne de la Ville de Paris

AVENUE DU PRÉSIDENT WILSON

Iéna

Place de l'Alma
Alma-Marceau

COURS ALBER

Place du Trocadéro et du 11 Novembre

Trocadéro

Palais de Chaillot

Pont de l'Alma (RER)

Les Égouts

QUAI D'ORSA

Place de la Résistance

Jardins du Trocadéro

Place de Varsovie

Seine

Musée du Quai Branly

PONT D'IÉNA

QUAI BRANLY

RUE DE PASSY

BOULEVARD DELESSERT

Passy

Tour Eiffel

Champ de Mars-Tour Eiffel (RER)

VOIE GEORGES POMPIDOU

PONT DE BIR-HAKEIM

Champ de Mars-Tour Eiffel (RER)

Bir-Hakeim

Seine

Port de Grenelle

BOULEVARD DE GRENELLE

Parc du Champ de Mars

SUFFREN

MOTTE-PICQUET

École Militaire

La Motte Picquet Grenelle

BOULEVARD DE GRENELLE

La Motte Picquet Grenelle

Sq Théodore Judin

FRÉMICOURT

Cambronne

AVENUE ÉMILE ZOLA

Charles Michels

AVENUE ÉMILE ZOLA

Avenue Émile Zola

Commerce

BOULEVA

A | B | C

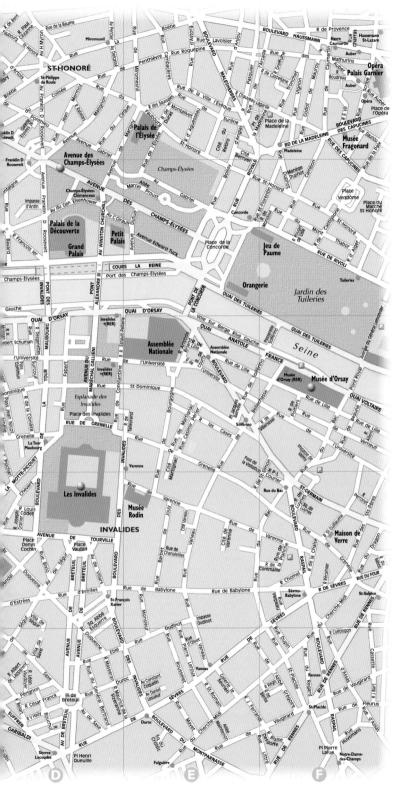

FRANCE

The Arc de Triomphe viewed from the Champs-Élysées

RATINGS

Historic interest	●●●●
Photo stops	●●●●
Shopping	●●●
Walkability	●●●

BASICS

ARC DE TRIOMPHE

⊞ 70 B1 • place Charles-de-Gaulle, 75008 ☎ 01 55 37 73 77

⊙ Apr–end Sep daily 10am–11pm; Oct–end Mar 10am–10.30pm. Closed pm on 14 Jul, 11 Nov

▨ Free to wander around the base. Rooftop: adult €8, under 18 free

⊙ Charles de Gaulle–Étoile

▣ 22, 30, 31, 52, 73, 92

▣ RER line A, Charles de Gaulle–Étoile

🏛 Gift shop 📖 €8

📞 Call Monuments Nationaux on 01 44 54 19 30

www.monuments-nationaux.fr

AVENUE DES CHAMPS-ÉLYSÉES

⊞ 70 C1 • 75008

⊙ Charles de Gaulle–Étoile, Georges V, Franklin D. Roosevelt, Champs-Élysées-Clemenceau ▣ 32, 42, 73 and others

▣ Charles de Gaulle–Étoile

TIPS

● It takes at least 30 minutes to walk from one end of the Champs-Élysées to the other and, with the heavy traffic, it is not a restful stroll. You may prefer to take the Métro—line 1 (yellow) runs underneath the entire length of the avenue.

● Most of the cafés and restaurants are at the Arc de Triomphe end.

ARC DE TRIOMPHE AND CHAMPS-ÉLYSÉES

Paris's most famous avenue is crowned by the mighty Arc de Triomphe.

The wide, leafy Champs-Élysées is a focal point for the French nation, witness to momentous events such as De Gaulle's triumphal Liberation march in 1944 and the soccer World Cup celebrations in 1998. The bustling avenue, over 2km (1.2 miles) long and 71m (232ft) wide, is packed with cinemas, shops, cafés and car show-rooms. Go there on 14 July (Bastille Day) and most of the French army will roll past you. Another good time to visit is during the Christmas illuminations.

THE EARLY DAYS

The Champs-Élysées dates back to 1616, when Marie de Medici turned the area into a fashionable driveway. Then landscape designer André Le Nôtre (of Versailles fame) added alleys of trees and gardens, prompting the name 'Elysian Fields'. Walkways and fountains were installed in 1824 and the avenue soon became crowded with cafés, restaurants and a smart clientele.

ARC DE TRIOMPHE

The Arc de Triomphe crowns the western tip of the Champs-Élysées, standing on a hectic roundabout known as L'Étoile (the star). Within its grounds are the Tomb of the Unknown Soldier, installed in 1920 after World War I, and a poignant Memorial Flame. There are wonderful views from the rooftop, 50m (164ft) above street level. From here you can admire the geometry of Baron Haussmann's web-like street design and look along the Grand Axis towards place de la Concorde in one direction and the Grande Arche in the other. At night the city shimmers with lights. Back at ground level, save some time to admire the magnificent sculpted façade, the work of three different artists. Don't miss the fearsome winged figure of Liberty on François Rude's sculpture *La Marseillaise*, calling the French to defend their nation (northeastern pillar, facing the Champs-Élysées).

Napoleon commissioned the arch in 1806, wanting an awesome memorial to the French army. In 1810 a full-size model was installed to celebrate the emperor's marriage to Marie-Louise of Austria but the real thing was not ready until 1836, 15 years after his death.

The bustling lobby of the Centre Georges Pompidou

CENTRE GEORGES POMPIDOU

Paris's wackiest building has one of the largest collections of modern art in the world.

You'll either love or hate the brazen design of the Centre Georges Pompidou, and you may well feel the same about the contemporary art it contains. The venue has sparked controversy since it opened in 1977, gracing the historic heart of Paris with an incongruously modern building that resembles a giant air-conditioning system. But while its design may not please everyone, the arts complex attracts around six million visitors each year—roughly the same as the Louvre—with its canny, ever-changing mix of visual, performance and new-media art.

THE CONCEPT

Georges Pompidou, President of France from 1969 until his death in 1974, wanted a venue where people could enjoy contemporary film, drama, dance, music and visual art. The outlandish building took five years to construct and was a controversial addition to Beaubourg, a run-down district of 18th- and 19th-century townhouses. Architects Renzo Piano and Richard Rogers turned the building 'inside out' by placing its 'guts' (all the piping) on the outside. This piping was coded: yellow for electrics, blue for air-conditioning, green for water and red for the elevators. Pompidou did not live to see the opening in 1977, but his vision proved sagacious—the venue was soon attracting 22,000 visitors a day, rivalling the Louvre in popularity. The site closed for two years for extensive renovation work in the autumn of 1997, reopening just in time for the new millennium.

MUSÉE NATIONAL D'ART MODERNE

The Museum of Modern Art takes over where the Musée d'Orsay leaves off, featuring works from 1905 to the present day. Up to 2,000 pieces from the 50,000-strong collection are on display at any one time, ranging from Cubism by Georges Braque and Pablo Picasso to Pop Art by Andy Warhol and video art by Korean artist Nam June Paik.

The Centre Pompidou's temporary exhibitions, on the first and sixth floors, are as much of a draw as the permanent collections. Other attractions include children's activities, two cinemas and a library.

Don't miss The Brancusi workshop displays a magnificent collection of works by Constantin Brancusi, the Romanian abstract sculptor.

RATINGS

Cultural interest	●●●●●
Good for kids	●●●
Photo stops (exterior and views)	●●●

BASICS

✚ 72 J3 • place Georges-Pompidou, 75004 ☎ 01 44 78 12 33
◎ Centre Georges Pompidou: Wed–Mon 11–10. Musée National d'Art Moderne and exhibitions: Wed–Mon 11–9 (last ticket 8; late night Thu until 11pm for some exhibitions).
👜 Full ticket €10; Musée National d'Art Moderne, Atelier Brancusi and Children's Gallery: adult €7, under 18 free; free to all first Sun of month. Exhibitions: prices vary
🚇 Rambuteau, Hôtel de Ville
🚌 29, 38, 47, 75
🚉 Châtelet-Les Halles
☕ Café on first floor
🍴 Georges restaurant on 6th floor
🏬 Bookshops, boutique, post office
📖 €12
www.centrepompidou.fr

TIPS

● If you're a traditionalist when it comes to art, let yourself in to the Museum of Modern Art (relatively) gently by starting with the fifth floor (1905–1960) before tackling the more bemusing fourth floor (1960 to the present day).
● If your mind is spinning from a day of modern art, enjoy a calming concert at the nearby church of St-Merri, Saturdays at 9pm and Sundays at 4pm.

Jardin du Luxembourg is especially popular on sunny days (above)

RATINGS	
Good for kids	●●●●
Photo stops	●●●
Walkability	●●●●

BASICS

✚ 72 G5 • rue de Vaugirard/rue de Médicis/boulevard St-Michel, 75006
☎ Park: 01 42 34 23 89.
Senate: 01 42 34 20 00.
Musée du Luxembourg: 01 42 34 25 95
🕐 Times vary depending on season; generally dawn to dusk
💷 Free
🚇 Odéon
🚌 38, 63, 70, 82, 83, 84, 85, 86, 87, 89, 96
🚊 RER line B, Luxembourg
☕ Open-air cafés, kiosk restaurant
🏪 Kiosk
🎧 Guided tours of the Palais du Luxembourg take place on the first Sat of each month. To book a place call 01 44 54 19 49. To sit in on a Senate debate call 01 42 34 20 00
www.senat.fr
www.museeduluxembourg.fr

JARDIN DU LUXEMBOURG

This is one of Paris's most popular parks, with a boating pond, fabulous flower displays and an Italianate palace.

The Jardin du Luxembourg forms an attractive southern boundary to St-Germain and the Latin Quarter. Students come here to relax after lectures and visitors catch some breathing space between sightseeing. It is a popular haunt of chic Montparnasse residents and their offspring, who make the most of the many children's attractions.

ATTRACTIONS

The 24ha (60-acre) park has some of the most beautiful public flower displays in Paris and is landscaped in an appealing mixture of French, English and Italian styles. The focal point is a large octagonal pond, elegantly encircled by stone urns and statues of French queens and other notable women. On the northern side, the Italianate Palais du Luxembourg is a reminder of the park's Florentine origins and is now home to the French Senate. In good weather the park is full of Parisians sunbathing, playing boules or jogging along the shady paths. Other attractions include tennis courts, a bandstand and even a bee-keeping school. The Musée du Luxembourg, in the former orangery, stages temporary art exhibitions. The Fontaine Médicis is a popular romantic spot on the eastern side of the Palais du Luxembourg.

Children are well catered for, with donkey rides (during French school holidays), puppet shows in the Théâtre du Luxembourg (Wednesday, Saturday and Sunday from 2pm) and swings and slides. They can also rent remote-control yachts to sail on the pond.

MEMORIES OF HOME

Bored with the Louvre, Marie de Medici commissioned the gardens and palace in 1615, hoping for a reminder of her native Florence. She bought the land from Duke François of Luxembourg and asked architect Salomon de Brosse to use the Pitti Palace as inspiration. Work finished in the mid-1620s but Marie, widow of Henri IV, did not have long to enjoy it. She was exiled from France by the powerful Cardinal Richelieu and died penniless in Cologne. During the Revolution, the Palais du Luxembourg became a prison, then in 1799 it became the seat of France's Upper Chamber.

A bird perches on a statue in the Jardin du Luxembourg (right)

Napoleon's grand tomb (above). The golden Église du Dôme (right)

LES INVALIDES

See Napoleon's tomb and an absorbing army museum.

Although its architecture is pompous, severe and authoritarian, Les Invalides was actually built to house wounded and elderly soldiers. Louis XIV was thinking of others for once when he commissioned Libéral Bruant to design the imposing building, with its 195m (640ft) façade. In 1674 the first soldiers moved in and were welcomed by the king himself. It took another 32 years before the gold-encrusted Église du Dôme (Church of the Dome) was completed. Today, visitors come to see a later addition, the tomb of Napoleon I, as well as the impressive Army Museum. On entering the stately grounds you'll be following in the footsteps of many a military hero, including General de Gaulle and Winston Churchill.

REMEMBERING PAST CONFLICTS

The Musée de l'Armée is one of the largest of its kind in the world, and among the extensive collections of weapons, armour, flags, uniforms and paintings are some real gems. The museum is in three wings. The west wing has reopened recently after comprehensive renovations. As you would expect, Napoleon I features prominently, and you can see his frock coat, hat, coronation saddle and even his actual horse, Vizir (not for the squeamish). Don't miss the evocative World War II exhibition, which uses film footage, photos and day-to-day objects to convey the horrors of the war and the bravery of those who fought against Hitler. On the fourth floor of the east wing, the Musée des Plans-Reliefs displays huge scale models of fortresses and French towns, which were used to plan sieges in the 17th and 18th centuries.

ÉGLISE DU DÔME

The golden dome of this stunning church rises 107m (350ft) above the ground, a glistening monument to two of France's most influential and charismatic rulers, Louis XIV and Napoleon. The church, dedicated to St. Louis, was designed by Versailles architect Jules Hardouin-Mansart and was completed in 1706. Its inauguration was a grand affair, attended by Louis XIV and members of the royal family.

Don't miss Napoleon's tomb is in a grandiose crypt directly below the dome. His remains were brought back to France in 1840, but it took another 21 years to create a mausoleum fit for an emperor.

RATINGS	
Good for kids	●●●
Historic interest	●●●●
Photo stops (exterior)	●●●

BASICS

🔖 71 D4 • Hôtel National des Invalides, 129 rue de Grenelle, 75007
☎ 01 44 42 38 77
🕐 Apr–end Sep daily 10–6, (also mid-Jun to mid-Sep 6–7pm, for the Église du Dôme); Oct–end Mar daily 10–5. Closed first Mon of each month.
💶 Adult €8 (with audioguide), under 18 free
🚇 La-Tour-Maubourg, Invalides, Varenne
🚌 28, 63, 69, 82, 83, 93
🚆 RER line C, Invalides
🎧
🎁 Gift shop/bookshop
📖 €7
🎫 Guided tours available
www.invalides.org

TIPS

● The best way to appreciate the grandeur of Les Invalides is to approach the site from Pont Alexandre III.
● The Army Museum is busiest between 11am and 1pm.
● As an antidote to the war focus of Les Invalides, unwind in the nearby gardens of the Musée Rodin.

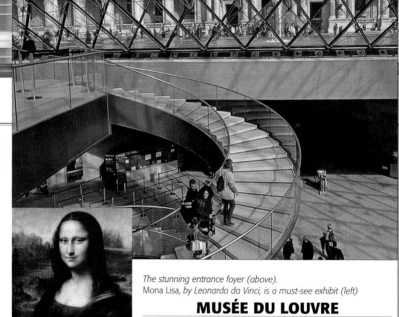

The stunning entrance foyer (above).
Mona Lisa, *by Leonardo da Vinci, is a must-see exhibit (left)*

MUSÉE DU LOUVRE

The Louvre is one of the world's largest museums. Legendary works of art include the *Mona Lisa, Venus de Milo* and a 4,000-year-old Egyptian sphinx.

The Louvre is one of the most famous art galleries in the world, with a vast collection spanning thousands of years, from ancient civilizations to mid-19th century European paintings. The main entrance is through I. M. Pei's striking glass pyramid (1989) in the Cour Napoléon. Escalators take you down to a subterranean foyer. Don't be too ambitious—there is no way you'll be able to see all 35,000 works on display in one visit.

MONA LISA

When Leonardo da Vinci set up his easel in Florence in the early 16th century to paint the *Mona Lisa*, little did he know he was creating what was to become one of the world's most famous works of art. The diminutive painting, only 77cm (30in) tall and 53cm (20in) wide, is on the first floor of the Denon wing, surrounded by bullet-proof glass and a constant crowd of admirers. The identity of the woman is not known for certain, although she is believed to be the wife of Francesco del Giocondo, hence the portrait's other name, *La Gioconda*. Da Vinci painted the work between 1503 and 1506. François I obtained the painting soon after its completion.

THE EGYPTIAN COLLECTION

The Egyptian collection is the largest of its kind outside Egypt, containing 55,000 items, around 5,000 of which are on display. The collections are presented thematically on the ground floor of the Sully wing, where topics include fishing, funerals, writing and jewellery. On the first floor and on the lower floor of the Denon wing, the displays are chronological, starting with prehistory.

BACKGROUND

Charles V transformed Philippe-Auguste's 12th-century fortress on the Louvre site into a medieval castle in the 14th century. The wily Renaissance king François I ordered considerable rebuilding and also launched an art collection. During the Revolution, an art museum opened to the public in the Grande Galerie. Napoleon's victories overseas, and the subsequent looting, added to the Louvre's stock.

RATINGS

Cultural interest	●●●●●
Historic interest	●●●●
Shopping (art books)	●●●●

BASICS

✚ 72 G3 • 99 rue de Rivoli, 75001
☎ 01 40 20 50 50. Recorded information in French and English: 01 40 20 53 17. Auditorium: 01 40 20 55 55
◙ Thu, Sat–Mon 9–6, Wed 9am–9.45pm, Fri 9am–10pm; closed Tue; some rooms closed in rotation
▣ Adult €9 (€6 after 6pm on Wed and Fri), under 18 free. Tickets are valid all day, so re-entry is allowed.
Free first Sun of month and 14 July.
Temporary exhibitions in the Hall Napoléon €9
◙ Palais Royal–Louvre
▣ 21, 24, 27, 39, 48, 67, 68, 69, 72, 74, 75, 76, 81, 85, 95
▣ Châtelet-les-Halles
▣ Range of guidebooks on sale. Free leaflet (in 9 languages) available at information desk
▮ Cafés and restaurants
▦ Large bookshop
◐ A variety of guided tours are available in English and French.
Audiotours are €5
www.louvre.fr

TIP

● The museum is most crowded on Sundays.

The Musée d'Orsay started life as a Belle-Époque train station and the ornate station clock still hangs in the main hall

MUSÉE D'ORSAY

A magnificent former train station houses this collection of world-famous Impressionist paintings, as well as other art from the mid-19th century to the early 20th century.

The collections here span 1848 to 1914, a crucial period in Western art that witnessed such giants as Monet, Renoir, Degas and Cézanne. Chronologically, the museum's collections fit neatly between those of the Louvre (▷ 78) and the Centre Georges Pompidou (▷ 75).

YOUR VISIT

Most people come to see the breathtaking Impressionist collection, which includes Monet's *Blue Waterlilies* (c1916–19), Van Gogh's *The Church at Auvers-sur-Oise* (1890) and Renoir's *Ball at the Moulin de la Galette* (1876). But Impressionism forms less than a third of the vast display, which also includes sculpture, Symbolist and historical paintings, photography and art nouveau furniture. To see the works chronologically, start with the ground floor, then take the escalators to the Impressionist works on the upper floor, before finishing on the middle floor. Even if your sole reason for visiting the museum is the Impressionist collection, don't leave without wandering through the central aisle on the ground floor, displaying 19th-century neoclassical sculpture. This is the best place to catch the feel of the building—part museum, part Belle-Époque train station—with its ornate clock and magnificent glass roof.

THE BUILDING

The imposing Orsay station and its accompanying hotel were built along the banks of the Seine in time for the Exposition Universelle in 1900. Victor Laloux designed the soaring glass and iron roof, together with the wildly ornate Belle-Époque restaurant and ballroom, all still intact. But in 1939 the advent of longer electric trains forced the station to close for long-distance travel (it was still used for suburban trains), less than 40 years after its completion. Public protest saved it from demolition, and approval was given to turn it into a museum in 1977. Italian architect Gae Aulenti masterminded the conversion of the interior, encasing both the walls and floors with stone, and President François Mitterrand opened the museum in December 1986.

Don't miss Seek out the lavishly mirrored Salles des Fêtes (Room 51).

RATINGS

Cultural interest	●●●●●
Historic interest	●●●

BASICS

🚩 71 F3 • 62 rue de Lille, 75007. Entrance on place de la Légion d'Honneur ☎ 01 40 49 48 14

🕐 Tue–Wed, Fri–Sun 9.30–6, Thu 9.30am–9.45pm. Last ticket 45 min before closing

💶 Adult €7.50, under 18 free, free to all on first Sun of month. Temporary exhibitions cost extra

Ⓜ Solférino

🚌 24, 63, 68, 73, 83, 84, 94

🚆 RER line C, Musée d'Orsay

🍴 On the middle level (11.45–2.45, 3.30–5.30; dinner 7–9.15 on Thu)

☕ Café des Hauteurs on upper level, with wonderful view of the old station clock; self-service café just above it

📖 Gift shop and bookshop

🎧 Tours in English Tue–Sat 11.30; in French Sat 11 (€6). Audioguides (€5) www.musee-orsay.fr

TIPS

● A Paris Museum Pass allows you to skip the queues, which can be long.

● Thursday evening is the quietest time to visit.

● The museum is closed on Monday, unlike the Louvre and Centre Georges Pompidou, which close on Tuesday.

● For more Impressionist paintings, visit the Musée Marmottan Monet.

Notre-Dame at night, bathed in floodlights (above).
The west front of the cathedral (left)

NOTRE-DAME

This beautiful Gothic cathedral is one of France's most visited religious sites.

Notre-Dame is as famous a symbol of Paris as the Eiffel Tower and around 10 million people enter its doors each year. The crowds are smallest in the early morning, when the cathedral is also at its brightest. Save some time for wandering around the outside to admire the architecture, including the flying buttresses. One of the best views is from the Seine, on a boat trip that circles the Île de la Cité. Finally, if your legs will agree to it, there are wonderful views from the top of the 69m (226ft) towers.

HIGHLIGHTS INSIDE THE CATHEDRAL

The south rose window, in the transept, is especially glorious when the sun shines through, adding extra vibrancy to the purple hues. Christ stands in the heart of the 13m (42ft) diameter window, encircled by angels, apostles, martyrs and scenes from the New Testament. The intricately carved and painted choir screen, created in the 14th century and restored in the 1960s, has enchanting depictions of Gospel scenes. In contrast, the bronze altar at the heart of the cathedral is strikingly modern. It depicts the four evangelists Matthew, Mark, Luke and John, as well as Old Testament prophets.

OUTSIDE AND UP THE TOWERS

The symmetrical west front is packed with statues and sculptures, originally painted and intended as a Bible for the illiterate. It's a tough climb, but it's well worth tackling the 69m (226ft) towers for views over Paris and a closer look at the grotesque gargoyles.

MORE THAN 800 YEARS OLD

Notre-Dame owes its existence to the 12th-century bishop Maurice de Sully, who decided that Paris needed its own cathedral. Pope Alexander III laid the foundation stone in 1163 and the choir was built in just under 20 years. Guilds of carpenters, stone-carvers, iron forgers and glass craftsmen worked on the grand project but it took almost 200 years to complete the building, which was finally ready in 1345. By the time Napoleon was crowned in the cathedral in 1804 the building was in a state of disrepair. Victor Hugo, author of *The Hunchback of Notre-Dame,* campaigned fervently for its restoration.

RATINGS

Historic interest	●●●○
Photo stops (views)	●●●●●

BASICS

Cathedral

✚ 72 J4 • place du Parvis Notre-Dame, 75004 ☎ 01 42 34 56 10

⊙ Daily 8–6.45 💷 Free

Ⓒ Cité, St-Michel, Châtelet

🚌 21, 24, 38, 47, 58, 70, 72, 74, 81, 82, 85, 96

🚇 RER lines B, C, St-Michel

🎫 In the cathedral and up the tower

🔁 Guided tours: in French Mon–Fri 2, 3; Sat 2, 2.30; Sun 2.30. In English Wed, Thu 2

❓ Organ recitals at 4pm on Sun

Towers

⊙ Jul–end Aug Mon–Fri 9–6.30, Sat–Sun 9am–11pm; Apr–end Jun, Sep daily 10–6.30; Oct–end Mar 10–5.30. Last admission 45 min before closing

💷 Adult €7.50, under 18 free
www.monum.fr

TIP

● Try to visit just before a service, when you feel a sense of anticipation as lights are gradually turned on and people gather to worship.

The glorious upper chapel of the Sainte-Chapelle

SAINTE-CHAPELLE

🗺 72 H4 • 4 boulevard du Palais, Île de la Cité, 75001 ☎ 01 53 40 60 97 🕙 9.30–6 👤 Adult €6.50, under 18 free. Joint ticket with Conciergerie €9.50 🚇 Cité, Châtelet 🚌 21, 24, 27, 38, 85, 96 🚉 RER line B, C, St-Michel-Notre-Dame 🔲 🔲 By appointment only (tel 01 53 40 60 93)
www.monuments-nationaux. fr

SACRÉ-CŒUR

You'll get stunning views over Paris from this gleaming white neo-Byzantine basilica.

The mighty Sacré-Cœur basilica is one of Paris's most prominent landmarks, shimmering at the top of Montmartre's hill. Its eastern-inspired dome is the second-highest point in the city and the views from the top stretch as far as 50km (30 miles). This sweeping panorama is the main attraction for many visitors. But walk into the hushed interior, especially during Mass, and it is an altogether more spiritual experience.

RATINGS	
Historic interest	●●●○
Photo stops (views)	●●●●●

BASICS	

🗺 73 b1 (inset) • Place du Parvis du Sacré-Cœur ☎ 01 53 41 89 00 🕙 Basilica: daily 6am–10.30pm. Dome and crypt: daily 9–5.45 (until 7 in summer) 👤 Basilica: free. Dome and crypt: €5 🚇 Anvers or Abbesses, then walk to base of funicular 🚌 Montmartrobus 🔲 Small bookshop/gift shop
www.sacre-coeur-montmartre.com

Sacré-Cœur was commissioned as atonement for the 58,000 people who died in the Franco-Prussian war of 1870–71 and the bloody events of the Commune. Citizens from across France donated the funds and the first stone was laid in 1875. Various problems hampered the project and the basilica was not completed until 1914. Then World War I intervened, and Parisians had to wait until 1919 for the consecration. More than 130 years after the vow to build Sacré-Cœur, priests still work in relays to maintain constant prayer for forgiveness for the horrors of war.

Bronze equestrian statues of Joan of Arc and St. Louis guard the entrance to the basilica. A stone statue of Christ stands high above them, in an arched recess. Inside, the striking golden mosaic over the choir is one of the largest of its kind, covering 475sq m (5,113sq ft). Christ stands in the middle, with outstretched arms and a golden heart. The Virgin Mary, Joan of Arc, St. Michael, the Pope and a figure representing France are among those immediately surrounding him. God the Father and the Holy Spirit are represented on the ceiling.

You'll get great views over Paris from the front terrace. If you have the time (and energy), it is worth climbing the dome for another panorama. The best view of the basilica itself is from below, in place St-Pierre.

Youngsters play in the shadow of Sacré-Cœur (above)

Stunning stained-glass windows turn this 13th-century royal chapel into a shimmering jewel. It's not quite heaven, but the celestial rays of blue, red and golden light streaming through the windows of the Sainte-Chapelle certainly seem out of this world. The chapel was commissioned by Louis IX (St. Louis) to house holy relics and to promote the king's authority as a divinely appointed leader. It was constructed within the royal palace complex (now the Palais de Justice) in less than six years. Fifteen windows, up to 15m (49ft) tall, and a glorious rose window depict more than 1,100 biblical scenes, from the Creation to the Apocalypse. The only downside is the crowds, which, as with Rome's Sistine Chapel, can detract from what should be an awe-inspiring experience.

Before reaching the upper chapel you walk through the dark lower chapel, originally used by palace staff and dedicated to the Virgin Mary. When you step into the upper chapel you are immediately hit by colour coming at you from all directions, not only from the glorious windows but also from the patterned floor, the golden columns and the painted lower walls. Two thirds of the windows are 13th-century originals, the oldest stained glass in Paris. The panels start with Genesis in the window on the left as you enter and work clockwise round the chapel to the Apocalypse in the rose window.

It's worth the wait to climb the Eiffel Tower (above).
Souvenirs of Paris's most famous sight (left)

TOUR EIFFEL

**The Eiffel Tower is the symbol of Paris and one of the
world's most famous monuments.**

The sleek iron silhouette of the Eiffel Tower, rising 324m (1,063ft)
high, finds its way into many of the city's best views. Gustave Eiffel's
extraordinary construction is a feat of late 19th-century engineering,
weighing more than 10,000 tonnes and made up of 18,000 iron
parts. It was a controversial addition to the city skyline in 1889 and
was intended to last only 20 years. More than a century on, it has had
200 million visitors.

VISITING THE TOWER

The view is the reason for climbing the Eiffel Tower, whether to take in
the magnificent sweep across the city or to test your nerves peering
down 120m (395ft) through the glass window on the floor of level 2.
From the viewing gallery on level 3 you can see up to 75km
(46 miles) on a clear day. If the vertigo-inducing top level is too much
for you, the panoramas are equally stunning on level 2, where you
can see the city in more detail. There is also a viewing gallery on level
1, with information boards. The views are often at their best in the
run-up to sunset, when the light is kinder to cameras. At night, a
totally different picture unfolds, as hundreds of thousands of lights
sketch out the city. Once you have soaked up the view, you can learn
more about the history of the tower from the short film shown at
Cineiffel (level 1). Other attractions on the first floor include the
Observatory, where you can monitor the sway at the top of the tower
(measured at 9cm/3.5in during the storms of 1999), and the
Feroscope, focusing on all things iron. You can also see the original
hydraulic lift pump and a piece of the original spiral staircase, as used
by Monsieur Eiffel himself. If you want to boast of your whereabouts
to your friends back home, you can have your postcards stamped
with 'Tour Eiffel' at the post office (daily 10–7.30).

CONSTRUCTION

Construction of the unconventional monument took only two years,
finishing just in time for the Exposition Universelle of 1889. For 40
years the tower basked in the glory of being the highest structure in
the world until New York's Chrysler building usurped the title. It gained
another 20m (66ft) in 1957 when television antennae were added.

WHAT TO DO

⊞ AGNÈS B
6 rue du Jour, 75001
Tel 01 45 08 56 56
www.agnesb.fr
Sober yet trendy, Agnès B's fashion is the epitome of young Parisian chic. Sharply cut clothes with original details are her signature, and her little waistcoat with press studs is a classic. Also worth celebrating for her artistic engagement—she sponsors many budding designers.
🕓 Mon–Sat 10–7 🚇 Les Halles

⊞ BARTHÉLÉMY (STÉ)
51 rue de Grenelle, 75007
Tel 01 42 22 82 24
Established in 1904, this is a cheese-lover's paradise: Brie, Mont d'Or (from Jura), Roquefort and much more. The old-fashioned shop supplies both the Élysée Palace and Matignon, home to France's president and prime minister respectively.
🕓 Tue–Sat 8–1, 4–7.30 🚇 Rue du Bac

⊞ CHANEL
31 rue Cambon, 75001
Tel 01 42 86 26 00
www.chanel.com
The tweed suit and the little black dress, Coco Chanel's signature outfits, keep on being reinvented by Karl Lagerfeld, head of this fashion house since 1984. Classic, sexy, feminine and chic, Chanel's designs embody Parisian elegance.
🕓 Mon–Sat 10–7 🚇 Madeleine

⊞ COMME DES GARÇONS
54 rue du Faubourg St-Honoré, 75008
Tel 01 53 30 27 27
Japanese designer Rei Kawakubo's approach to fashion is almost architectural. Her asymmetrical cuts produce sleek lines and one of her outfits can remodel a body. The collection is unique and modern, with a couture accent.
🕓 Mon–Sat 11–7
🚇 Madeleine, Concorde

⊞ FAUCHON
26 place de la Madeleine, 75008
Tel 01 70 39 38 00
www.fauchon.fr
The tastiest and probably the most expensive delicatessen in Paris. The best of French cuisine, including foie gras, fine condiments and great wines, has been sold here since 1886. And not only French: You can find Beluga caviar, the best vintages of the finest spirits from all over the world, and many more exotic delicacies. There's also a tea room here.
🕓 Mon–Sat 8am–9pm
🚇 Madeleine

⊞ GALERIES LAFAYETTE
40 boulevard Haussmann, 75009
Tel 01 42 82 34 56
www.galerieslafayette.com
Opened in 1912, the main building of this grand old department store has an impressive stained-glass dome, balconies and gilded balustrades. It's a luxurious setting for the hundreds of brands and goods that are stocked here, including fashion and beauty items, accessories, home goods and fine foods.
🕓 Mon–Wed, Fri–Sat 9.30–7.30, Thu 9.30–9 🚇 Chaussée d'Antin

⊞ MARCHÉ BEAUVAU
place d'Aligre, 75012
This is one of Paris's liveliest markets—many restaurants send staff here to shop for fresh fruit and vegetables, fish and meat. Some merchants sell by auction; it is a truly Parisian experience. The market is also known as Marché d'Aligre.
🕓 Tue–Sun 6.30am–1pm
🚇 Ledru-Rollin, Faidherbe Chaligny

⊞ MARCHÉ RASPAIL
boulevard Raspail, 75006
The fruit and vegetables sold at this strictly organic market have been grown without pesticides, so they may not always look as good as those at the local supermarket, but they certainly have more taste. You will also find organic honey, bread and wine. Another organic market is held on boulevard des Batignolles on Saturday mornings.
🕓 Tue, Fri, Sun 7–1 🚇 Rennes

⊞ PRINTEMPS
64 boulevard Haussmann, 75009
Tel 01 42 82 57 87
www.printemps.com
Since 1865 it has been this store's ambition to be the most modern of its time. Under its main building's impressive stained-glass cupola, there are six floors dedicated to women's fashion, and Europe's largest perfume department. There is also a men's store, and a department dedicated to home decoration.
🕓 Mon–Wed, Fri–Sat 9.35–7, Thu 9.35am–10pm 🚇 Havre-Caumartin

⊕ AUDITORIUM DU LOUVRE
Musée du Louvre, 75001 (entrance by the Pyramid)
Tel 01 40 20 55 00
www.louvre.fr
The impressive setting of this 420-seat auditorium, right beneath I. M. Pei's Louvre Pyramid, is matched by an excellent and varied schedule, including church music, film themes and recitals.
🕓 Concerts: Wed 8pm, Thu 12.30pm
💶 €30 (8pm concert), €10 (12.30pm concert) 🚇 Louvre-Rivoli

⊕ LA GÉODE
26 avenue Corentin-Cariou, 75019
Tel 0892 684 540
www.cite-sciences.fr
A gigantic hemispheric-screen cinema with digital stereo sound in the auditorium. You really are taken into the movie. Only films specially adapted to this technology are shown.
🕓 Tue–Sun 10.30–8.30 💶 Adult €11, child €9.50 🚇 Porte de la Villette

⊕ MAISON DE RADIO FRANCE
116 avenue du Président-Kennedy, 75016
Tel 01 56 40 15 16
www.radiofrance.fr
Top-notch symphony orchestras, jazz concerts and operas are all presented here, either as live broadcasts or recorded for subsequent broadcasting.
🕓 Varies 💶 Free (or small charge)
🚇 Kennedy Radio France

⊕ MOULIN ROUGE
82 boulevard de Clichy, 75018
Tel 01 53 09 82 82
www.moulinrouge.fr
Established in 1889, and even

FRANCE

more of an institution since the eponymous Hollywood movie. Magnificent interior within an almost authentic red windmill, where fine food is served while you enjoy the titillating 'Féerie' show.

🎦 Shows: daily 9pm, 11pm
💶 Show: €89–€99. Show and dinner: €145–€175 🚇 Blanche

🎵 LE NEW MORNING
7–9 rue des Petites-Écuries, 75010
Tel 01 45 23 51 41
www.newmorning.com
Heaven for jazz fans, this famous club has welcomed the world's most prestigious musicians over the years. Bossa nova and salsa are also played here.

🎦 Concert: 9pm (days vary)
💶 Around €25 🚇 Château d'Eau

🎵 SATELLIT CAFÉ
44 rue de la Folie-Méricourt, 75011
Tel 01 47 00 48 87
www.satellit-cafe.com
This centre for world music has room for 250 people. The varied schedule includes Latino, blues, African, Balkan and Mediterranean music.

🎦 Concert: Tue–Sat 9 💶 Around €10
🚇 Oberkampf, St-Ambroise

🎵 THÉÂTRE DES CHAMPS-ÉLYSÉES
15 avenue Montaigne, 75008
Tel 01 49 52 50 50
www.theatrechampselysees.fr
A grand auditorium, with red velvet seats and balconies, hosting performances of opera, ballet, classical and chamber music, as well as some jazz and solo variety singers.

🎦 Performances: almost daily at around 7.30–8pm 💶 Varies 🚇 Franklin D. Roosevelt, Alma-Marceau

🎵 THÉÂTRE NATIONAL DE CHAILLOT
1 place du Trocadéro, 75016
Tel 01 53 65 30 00
www.theatre-chaillot.fr
This theatre is housed in the imposing neoclassical Palais de Chaillot. The largest auditorium can accommodate productions of all kinds, including top-quality contemporary works, as well as classics.

🎦 Performances: Tue–Sat 8pm, Sun 3pm 💶 €27–€33 🚇 Trocadéro

🍸 BAR FLEUR'S
3 rue des Tournelles, 75004
Tel 01 42 71 04 51
email fleursetvodka@free.fr
Probably the most unusual bar in the city, Bar Fleur's mixes a champagne and vodka/tequila bar with a florists. The décor is ultra-cool with a vast range of fizz and distillates to try.

🕐 Daily 7pm–2am 🚇 Bastille

🎵 LA BOULE NOIRE
120 boulevard Rochechouart, 75018
Tel 01 49 25 81 75
www.laboule-noire.fr
Some of the famous names of modern times have played at this diminutive venue in the heart of Pigalle including Franz Ferdinand, Jamie Cullum, Metallica and The Dandy Warhols. It's an eclectic mix but a popular one.

🎦 Varies 💶 Varies 🚇 Pigalle

🍸 BUDDHA BAR
8 rue Boissy d'Anglas, 75008
Tel 01 53 05 90 00
www.buddha-bar.com
A trendsetting cocktail bar and restaurant that attracts both fashionistas and curious tourists. An impressive 3.6m (12ft) Buddha presides over the place, a DJ plays the latest ambient sounds, and the service is super-cool.

🕐 Bar: Mon–Fri from noon, Sat–Sun from 4. Restaurant: daily 12–3, 7–9.30 🚇 Concorde

🍸 L'ÉTOILE
12 rue de Presbourg, 75016
Tel 01 45 00 78 70
www.letoileparis.com
Dressing smartly should grant you entry into this temple of chic Parisian nightlife. Disco, dance and techno are played and the setting is beautiful with a superb view of the Arc de Triomphe from the terrace.

🎦 Wed–Sun 11pm–5am 💶 Free
🚇 Charles de Gaulle-Étoile

🎵 LE NOUVEAU CASINO
109 rue Oberkampf, 75011
Tel 01 43 57 57 40
www.nouveaucasino.net
Opened in 2001, this club didn't take long to develop a regular clientele. Excellent DJs, a beautiful interior, and a great location in a very busy district, are the keys to its success.

🕐 Thu–Sat midnight–6am; concerts

most nights at 7.30 or 8pm 💶 Around €15 🚇 Parmentier, Ménilmontant, St-Maur

⚽ PARC DES PRINCES
24 rue du Commandant-Guilbaud, 75016
Tel 0825 07 32 75 (closed Fri and public hols)
www.psg.fr
Inaugurated in 1972, the park has been home to Paris-St-Germain (PSG) soccer club since 1990. Within its boundaries you'll also find the Musée National du Sport (National Sport Museum), a shop and a restaurant.

💶 Guided tours €6 (when no sporting event is taking place). Match tickets Vary 🚇 Porte d'Auteuil, Porte de St-Cloud

☀ AQUABOULEVARD
4–6 rue Louis Armand, 75015
Tel 01 40 60 10 00
www.aquaboulevard.com
Alongside the aquapark, which has waterslides and a wave machine, there are squash courts, tennis courts, a putting range, restaurants and shops.

🕐 Mon–Thu 9am–11pm, Fri 9am–midnight, Sat 8am–midnight, Sun 8am–11pm 💶 Aquapark (6 hours): adult €20, child (3–11) €10. €2 per person per hour thereafter 🚇 Balard, Porte de Versailles

☀ FRANCE MONTGOLFIÈRES
24 rue National, 41400 Montrichard
Tel 0810 00 01 53
www.franceballoons.com
These hot-air balloon tours let you discover Paris's surroundings, soaring above villages, chateaux, rivers and forests. You can also go as far as Burgundy and the Loire. Some trips include hotels.

🕐 Tours from mid-Mar to end Nov, on booking 💶 Mon–Fri €185, Sat–Sun €225 for 3.5-hour tour
🚇 Père Lachaise

☀ PARIS HÉLICOPTÈRE
Zone Aviation Affaires, Aéroport, 93350 Le Bourget
Tel 01 48 35 90 44
www.paris-helicoptere.com
Want to see everything in less than 30 minutes? Take a tour and monument-spot across Paris. Longer tours are also available, for a bird's-eye view of the Château de Versailles and farther afield.

🕐 Sun afternoon, book ahead

🚍 €130 for a 25-minute tour
🚉 Le Bourget 🏛 152 Musée de l'Air

❽ **JARDIN D'ACCLIMATATION**
Main entry: boulevard des Sablons,
Bois de Boulogne, 75016
Tel 01 40 67 90 82
www.jardindacclimatation.fr
With its ponds and tree-lined alleys, this 'garden within a wood' is a walker's paradise. There are many activities for children including minigolf, playgrounds, bowling, wildlife discovery, theatre and sports. A trip on the little train is a good way to discover the area.
🕐 Daily 10–7 (closes 6pm winter)
🎫 Adult €2.50, children under 3 free
🚇 Les Sablons

EATING

BISTRO D'HUBERT
41 boulevard Pasteur, 75015
Tel 01 47 34 15 50
www.bistrodhubert.com
Hubert has two dining areas. The first a Provencal style informal room decorated with painted wooden dressers and pretty cotton tablecloths, the second a more formal and contemporary area. The open kitchen shows the confidence of the staff while the menu offers French cuisine touched by the latest food fashions.
🕐 Tue–Fri 12–2.30, 7–9.30; Sat, Mon 7–9.30
🍽 L €35, D €50, Wine €20
🚇 Pasteur

LA COUPOLE
102 boulevard du Montparnasse, 75014 Montparnasse
Tel 01 43 20 14 20
Follow in the footsteps of Pablo Picasso, Ernest Hemingway and Man Ray, and enjoy a meal at this elegant art deco brasserie, established in 1927. The bright and airy dining room has fresco-adorned pillars and Cubist floor tiles. All the brasserie classics are on the menu including seafood platters, sauerkraut and steak.
🕐 Sun–Fri 8.30am–1am, Sat 8.30am–1.30am
🍽 L €25, D €40, Wine €20
🚇 Vavin

GEORGES
Centre Georges Pompidou 4, place Georges-Pompidou, 75004
Les Halles
Tel 01 44 78 47 99
www.centrepompidou.fr

This restaurant on the top floor of the Centre Georges Pompidou could well be a work of modern art. There is a stunning view over the city and the nouvelle cuisine includes mushroom cappuccino (a light and foamy soup) and crab millefeuille in puff pastry. The melt-in-the-mouth chocolate cake is one of the house's signature dishes.
🕐 Wed–Mon noon–2am
🍽 L €45, D €55, Wine €20
🚇 Rambuteau

GOUMARD
9 rue Duphot, 75001
Tel 01 42 60 36 07
www.goumard.com
Exceptional cuisine in elegant surroundings, Goumard is always worth bearing in mind, especially as it opens on Sunday when many top restaurants in the heart of the city don't set a table. Housed in a mansion dating from the 1870s, the restaurant concentrates on seafood and everything is prepared with care and beautifully presented.
🕐 Daily 12.15–2.30, 7.15–10.30
🍽 L €46, D €90, Wine €21
🚇 Madeleine

STAYING

L'HÔTEL
13 rue des Beaux-Arts, 75006
St-Germain-des-Prés, Paris
Tel 01 44 41 99 00
www.l-hotel.com
At this deluxe four-star hotel the exuberantly elegant interior is by Jaques Garcia. The restaurant is closed on Sunday, Monday and all of August.
🛏 €255–€640, excluding breakfast (€17)
🛎 16 rooms, 4 suites 🔲 🔳 🔳
🚇 St-Germain-des-Prés

HOTEL ATLANTIS
4 rue du Vieux-Colombier, 75006
St-Germain-des-Prés, Paris
Tel 01 45 48 31 81
Most of the rooms in this two-star hotel face onto picturesque place St-Sulpice. All are bright and airy, and have been beautifully decorated with fine furniture and quilted bedspreads. They have telephone, satellite TV, internet connection and hairdryer.
🛏 €125–€180, excluding breakfast
🛎 27
🚇 St-Sulpice

HOTEL TILSITT
23 rue Brey, 75017 Paris
Tel 01 43 80 39 71
www.tilsitt.com
This three-star hotel is a great find in its quality/price bracket. Set close to the Arc de Triomphe, the location is good and the décor has the unique melange of sleek minimalist Scandinavian style combined with a touch of classical Greek set inside the Gallic structure. The furnishings have a luxurious feel though the rooms can be compact. Each has a wide-screen TV, safe, mini-bar and Wi-Fi access. The lounge bar opens 24 hours and there's a car park (for an extra cost).
🛏 €145–€185, excluding breakfast
🛎 38 🔲
🚇 Charles de Gaulle-Étoile
🚊 RER: Charles de Gaulle-Étoile

PAVILLON DE LA REINE
28 place des Vosges, 75003
Le Marais, Paris
Tel 01 40 29 19 19
www.pavillon-de-la-reine.com
This was the residence of Anne of Austria, Louis XIII's wife, and the exquisite interior retains many of its period features. Even the vaulted cellar where you can have breakfast has tapestries on the walls. Bedrooms have cable TV and some have canopy beds. Some bedrooms are in a second, more modern building.
🛏 €360–€440, including breakfast
🛎 34 🔲
🚇 Bastille, St-Paul

RITZ
15 place Vendôme, 75001 Opéra, Paris
Tel 01 43 16 30 30
www.ritzparis.com
This world-famous hotel has been the epitome of luxury and elegance since its opening in 1898. The lavish interior is typical of French classicism, with antiques, chandeliers and heavy drapes. The hotel has a club, several restaurants, bars, private salons and the gourmet cookery school, Ritz-Escoffier.
🛏 €710–€810, excluding breakfast (€35–€43)
🛎 135 rooms, 40 suites
🔲 🔳 Indoor 🔳
🚇 Tuileries, Madeleine, Concorde

ARRIVING

BY AIR
Paris has two airports, Roissy–Charles de Gaulle and the smaller Orly, and is also served by Beauvais Tillé airport, farther north. Other French cities with airports include Marseille, Toulouse, Lyon, Strasbourg and Bordeaux.

BY TRAIN
There are good train links between France and other European countries. If you are starting from the UK, you can take the Eurostar from London St. Pancras, through the Channel Tunnel to Paris (or Lille), where you can connect to services to destinations across France. The Eurostar also travels direct to Disneyland Resort Paris, Bourg St-Maurice and Moutiers (during the ski season only), and Avignon (weekly in summer).

BY LONG-DISTANCE BUS
● Going to France by long-distance bus can be a useful option if you're on a tight budget, although the journey from London to Paris takes almost eight hours.
● Eurolines (www.eurolines.co.uk) runs services from Victoria Coach Station to Paris up to five times a day, with pick-up points at Canterbury and Dover. They also serve more than 60 other destinations in France. The Channel crossing is made either by Eurotunnel or ferry.
● Book your ticket at least 30 days in advance for the least expensive fares.

BY FERRY
● Numerous ferries link France with the UK. The cost of crossings varies widely according to time, day and month of travel. Most companies require you to check in at least 30 minutes before departure, although extra security checks may mean you have to arrive earlier.
● P&O Ferries (tel 0870 520 2020; www.poferries.com) and Seafrance (tel 0871 663 2546; www.seafrance.co.uk) sail from Dover to Calais (journey time: 70 to 90 minutes). Once in Calais, it takes around 3 hours 15 minutes to drive to Paris.
● Speed Ferries (tel 0871 222 7456 (UK), 0044 870 22 00 570 (from outside the UK); www.speedferries.com) operates a Dover-Boulogne service (journey time: approximately 50 minutes).
● Brittany Ferries (tel 0870 907 6103; www.brittany-ferries.co.uk) sails from Portsmouth to Caen (journey time: 6 hours).
● P&O Ferries sails from Portsmouth to Le Havre (day journey time: 5 hours 30 minutes).
● Brittany Ferries sails from Poole to Cherbourg (journey time: approximately 4 hours; Fastcraft services 2 hours 15 minutes, summer only). Brittany Ferries now operates a Portsmouth to Cherbourg service (day journey time: 5 hours; Fastcraft services 3 hours, summer only).
● Brittany Ferries sails from Portsmouth to St-Malo (journey time: approximately 8 hours 30 minutes).

BY EUROTUNNEL
● Load your car onto the Shuttle train at Folkestone for the 35-minute journey under the Channel to Calais/Coquelles.
● To reach the terminal at Folkestone, leave the M20 at junction 11A and follow signs to the Channel Tunnel.
● There are up to four departures per hour, 24 hours a day, and the price is charged per car (reserve ahead).
● French border controls take place on the UK side, saving time when you arrive in Calais.
● You stay with your car during the journey, although you can go to the toilet or walk about within the air-conditioned carriage (car).
● To reach Paris from Calais you can take the A16 (E40) in the direction of Dunkerque, then join the A26 (E15). At the intersection with the A1, head south on the A1 (E15), which will take you all the way to Paris. You will have to pay *autoroute* tolls.

BY CAR
● Private vehicles registered in another country can be taken into France for up to six months without customs formalities.
● You must always carry the following documentation: a current passport or national ID card, a full (not provisional), valid national driver's licence (even if you have an International Driving Permit), a certificate of motor insurance, and the vehicle's registration document (as well as a letter of authorization from the owner if the vehicle is not registered in your name).
● You should always tell your insurer before you take your car abroad. Fully comprehensive insurance is strongly advised.

VISITORS WITH A DISABILITY
Getting around the country is becoming easier, thanks to improvements to buses and trains. Most airports have facilities for people with disabilities and Eurostar trains are accessible to wheelchair-users. But you'll still find challenges when getting around France, especially in historic towns, with their narrow, cobbled streets. Before you travel, it's worth checking what facilities are available at your arrival airport (look up www.aeroport.fr) and your hotel, as older buildings may not have an elevator.
Mobile en Ville
www.mobile-en-ville.asso.fr
A website packed with information on disability access.

GETTING AROUND

FRANCE

BY CAR

Driving in France is made easier by the country's extensive network of *autoroutes* (motorways/expressways). However, you'll have to pay a toll to use most of them. From the capital, the A1 leads to the north, the A13 to Normandy and the northwest, the A4 to the east, the A6 to the Alps and the Riviera, and the A10 to the west and southwest. Driving is the best way to tour smaller villages and towns, but is not so convenient in some of the bigger cities, especially Paris, where the traffic is heavy, the one-way systems confusing and parking difficult and expensive. Journey times can be affected by weather conditions, traffic and the season—the roads, especially in the south of France, can get very busy in the summer.

BY TRAIN

The train is one of the best ways of getting around France—it is fast, comfortable and usually runs on time. France's state railway, the Société Nationale des Chemins de Fer (SNCF), runs the services. The high-speed train service—the TGV *(Train à Grande Vitesse)*—links large cities and towns, while TER trains do regional journeys.

Overnight Trains

● Most overnight trains offer either reclining seats, couchette berths or a sleeper car.
● Reclining seats are available only in second class. They have adjustable head- and foot-rests and a reinforced foam seat for sleeping.
● In first class, couchettes are in four-berth compartments; in second class they are in six-berth compartments.
● Sleeper car compartments are for up to two people in first class and up to three people in second class.
● Overnight trains operate between Paris and Toulouse; Paris, Irun and Tarbes; Paris, Port-Bou and Latour de Carol; Strasbourg and Vintimille; Bordeaux and Nice; Lille and Vintimille; Paris and Nice; Paris and Briançon; Paris and Bourg St-Maurice; Paris and St-Gervais; Metz and Port-Bou; Strasbourg and Port-Bou; Hendaye and Geneva.
● Trains also travel to other European countries.

BY BUS

Long-distance bus travel is not an ideal option for crossing the country. Buses are really only useful for short trips in areas not served by the rail network, such as some destinations in Brittany, Normandy and the Côte d'Azur. Long-distance bus stations *(gares routières)* are usually close to train stations and major train and bus services usually coincide. Smaller towns without train stations are usually linked by bus service to the nearest station. Bus services in cities are generally excellent and inexpensive, but rural areas tend to be less well served.

Long-distance Buses

● You can buy tickets for short distances on board, but for greater distances buy tickets in advance at the bus station. You must reserve your seat on most long-distance buses.
● Buses are slightly less expensive than trains, but significantly slower.
● If you are taking a bus operated by SNCF (www.sncf.com), you may be able to use an SNCF rail pass, if you have one. Check before you travel.
● Timetables tend to be constructed to suit working, market and school hours, so there will often be one bus in the morning and one in the evening.
● For information on SNCF-run buses, telephone 3635 (24 hours; €0.34 per minute).
● Few bus stations have a left-luggage office but some have information desks that can double as luggage rooms.

BY TAXI

● Taking a taxi is not the most cost-effective way of getting about but you may consider it worthwhile for convenience.
● There is a pick-up charge and a charge per kilometre (0.6 miles), plus an extra charge for luggage and journeys during the evening or on Sundays. All taxis use a meter *(compteur)*.
● The best way to find a taxi is to head to a taxi stand, marked by a blue Taxis sign. You can phone for a taxi but this can be more expensive as the meter may start running as soon as the taxi sets off to collect you.
● All taxis are non-smoking.
● Always check the meter is reset when you enter the taxi.
● Some taxis accept bank cards, but it is best to have cash available. It is usual to leave a tip of around 10 per cent.
● If you want a receipt, ask for *un reçu*.

Taxis in Paris

● You can hail a taxi in the street, if you can find one that is free. A white light on the roof indicates the taxi is available. When the light is off, the taxi is already occupied.
● Taxi charges are based on area and time—it is more expensive in the suburbs and at night. The tariff is shown on the meter.
● Journeys in central Paris average €10–€16. The meter starts at €2.10, with a minimum charge of €5.60. There is a surcharge of €1 for each piece of luggage and an extra €0.70 if you are picked up at a mainline station.
● Most drivers will not take more than three people; transport of a fourth person is charged at €2.75.

GETTING AROUND IN PARIS

Paris has an efficient and relatively inexpensive transport network and you should have few problems finding your way around the city. The Métro (underground/subway) is the backbone of the network. Other useful options include buses, riverboats and the suburban RER trains. Finally, don't forget your own two feet—central Paris is compact and walking is a great way to get your bearings.

TICKETS
● The Métro and buses use the same tickets and travel cards, and these can also be used on the RER within central Paris.
● The city is divided into fare zones. Most of the key sights are in Zone 1, although the Grande Arche is in Zone 3, Orly airport is in Zone 4 and Roissy–Charles de Gaulle airport is in Zone 5.
● Buy tickets at Métro stations, on buses (one-way tickets only) and at some newsstands.
● Children under four travel free, and children between the ages of four and nine travel for half price.

PARIS MÉTRO
● The Métro (*Métropolitain*) is the quickest way to travel for most journeys within the city. It runs from 5.30am to around 12.30am.
● Each line is colour-coded and numbered (1–14, 3b and 7b).
● Stations are identified either by a large M or by the famous art nouveau Métro signs.
● Steps lead down into a lobby, where you can buy tickets from either a manned booth or a machine.
● To reach the platforms, validate (*composter*) your ticket by slotting it into the machine at the automatic barrier, then collect it and keep it with you—inspectors make random checks.
● You'll often have a fairly long walk to the platform, so follow direction signs carefully. Signs will show the line number and colour. You also need to know the final destination of the train in the direction you wish to travel.
● An orange *correspondance* sign on the platform gives directions to connecting lines. Blue *sortie* signs show the exits.
● You can pick up free Métro maps at every station.
● To speak to an adviser (in French only) call 32 46.
● The RATP website (www.ratp.fr) has a helpful route planner and also gives up-to-date traffic and travel information.

Click on Paris Visite for advice for visitors.
● When planning your route, don't confuse Métro lines with the suburban RER lines—both are usually shown on Métro maps. RER lines have letters rather than numbers and will usually flow off the map.
● To estimate your journey time, allow two minutes between each station. Bear in mind that it could take five minutes to walk from the station entrance to the actual platform (especially in warrens such as Châtelet).
● If you need to change lines, don't exit the interchange station or you will invalidate your ticket.
● Keep your bags close to you and watch out for pickpockets.

BUSES
Paris has a comprehensive network of buses, but don't expect to get anywhere quickly— the average speed is less than 13kph (8mph)!
● Most buses are painted easy-to-see turquoise and run from 7am to 8.30pm, although some continue into the evening, until around 12.30am. You're unlikely to have to wait more than 5 or 10 minutes from Monday to Saturday, but services are reduced or, on some routes, non-existent, on Sunday.
● The route number is displayed on the front of the bus, along with the final destination.
● Hold out your hand to stop the bus.
● If you need to buy a ticket, have the exact change ready as drivers don't carry much change.
● Enter at the front of the bus and show your travelcard or *carnet* ticket to the driver. *Carnet* tickets or single tickets must be stamped in the machine next to the driver.
● In rush hour, you are unlikely to get a seat. Be prepared for a long and uncomfortable stand.
● Just before your stop, press the red button to alert the driver that you want to get off. You'll see the *arrêt demandé* (stop

requested) sign light up.
● Leave by the central doors.
● Buses use the same tickets as the Métro. A single ticket is valid for most central routes but you are not allowed to change buses on one ticket.
● You can only buy single tickets on board.
● Always stamp single tickets (including *carnet* tickets) in the machine near the driver, but not *Paris Visite*, *Mobilis* or *Carte Orange* passes. Keep your ticket until you have left the bus.

Night Buses
Night buses, called Noctilien, link Châtelet with the suburbs from 1am to 5.30am. Buses are identified by a letter. Ticket prices are based on the RATP t+ ticket rate of €1.50, with a €1.50 ticket being valid for two zones. For 1–3 zones the cost will be €3 (the price of two tickets). Stops have a black-and-yellow owl logo. With waits of up to one hour, you may prefer to take a taxi.

RER
RER (Réseau Express Régional) trains travel through the city en route to the suburbs and can be a good time-saver if you are going from one side of town to the other. But reaching the correct platform can be a lengthy and confusing process, so for a short trip you're usually better off taking the Métro.
● A single Métro ticket is valid for RER journeys in central Paris and you can change lines (including Métro lines) on the same ticket. For journeys farther afield, you'll need to buy a separate ticket valid for the destination.
● Travelcards are valid if they cover all the zones you are going through.
● Keep hold of your ticket as you'll need to slot it through the automatic barrier to exit the station.
● Trains run from around 5.30am to 12.30am.

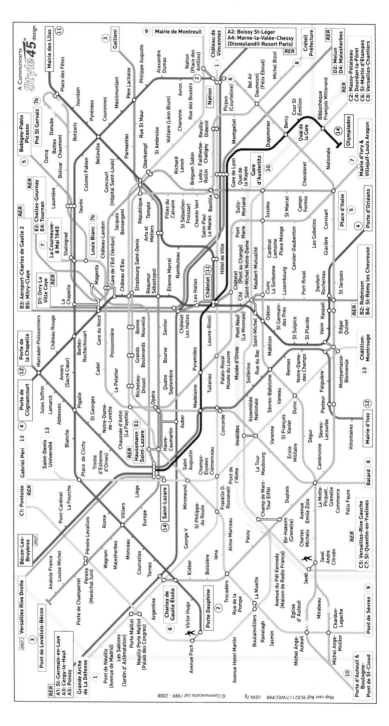

FRANCE

GERMANY

UNDERSTANDING GERMANY

Germany is not only blessed with varied and beautiful scenery, but also has a multifaceted past that has endowed it with a rich tapestry of historic buildings, art collections and fascinating towns and cities. Perhaps the most misrepresented country in western Europe, the new Germany has much to offer curious and open-minded visitors, from a bracing dip in the Baltic Sea off its northern shores to culture of every kind in Berlin and skiing and hiking in the Alps. Germany is divided into 16 administrative regions, known as *Länder*. Some of these *Länder*, like Berlin and Bremen, are city states, while others, like Bavaria, cover hundreds of square kilometres. Some 130 years after Chancellor Otto von Bismarck brought the disparate German states together, regional identities remain strong, and visitors will still discover distinctive local traditions and accents today.

LANDSCAPE

With an area of 357,022sq km (137,846sq miles), Germany is one of western Europe's biggest nations. It is about 640km (397 miles) at its widest and some 876km (544 miles) long, and it has 907km (564 miles) of coastline along the North and Baltic seas. The internal border separating the former German Democratic Republic (GDR) and Federal Republic of Germany (FDR) cut off 118,885sq km (45,901sq miles) to the east and ran for 1,393km (866 miles). Germany shares a border with nine other European countries: France, the Netherlands, Belgium, Luxembourg, Switzerland, Austria, the Czech Republic, Poland and Denmark.

North-flowing rivers delimit large stretches of both Germany's western and eastern borders, while the Bavarian Alps mark the country's southern edges and contain the Zugspitze, its highest peak at 2,962m (9,718ft). Along the western border is the Rhine valley, whose steep castle-topped banks are the quintessence of Romantic Germany. The Schwarzwald (Black Forest), and Swabian, Harz and Bohemian ranges are all lower than the Alps, but are still high enough for winter sports. Elsewhere, the landscape is characterized by fertile valleys, hills cloaked in deciduous and spruce trees, and, to the north, low-lying plains.

POLITICS

Since reunification in 1989, political life has largely followed the relatively stable model established in post-war West Germany. The head of state is the president, elected for a renewable five-year term of office by an equal number of national and regional deputies. Day-to-day decision-making power, however, lies with the chancellor, who is elected by the 614 members of the Bundestag (lower house) on a proposal from the president. Willy Brandt, former mayor of Berlin and the first leader to begin negotiations with the GDR, and Helmut Kohl, who presided over German reunification, are the best-known chancellors.

The Bundestag's members are voted for in parliamentary elections, while the upper house, the Bundesrat, is made up of representatives from the 16 *Länder*. The two main post-war parties have been the Christian Democrats (CDU) and the Social Democrats (SDU), but the Green Party, one of Europe's strongest, has now taken over the Free Democrats' former role as king-maker. At the regional level, each of the 16 *Länder* has its own *Landrat*, or parliament, and these exert considerable influence through the Bundesrat. Built on consensus, the German federal system does not easily lend itself to swift or radical change, and has been criticized in recent years for holding back much-needed reform.

ECONOMY

The first years of the 21st century have seen Germany's economy stumble as the 'miracle' of post-war reconstruction gives way to the harsh realities of globalization, an ageing workforce and increased labour unrest. Politicians are reluctant to administer an overdue but painful revamp of the generous state welfare system, while the banks and business managers press for urgent structural changes, lower taxation and greater flexibility in employment legislation.

Growth has been slower than predicted in recent years, unemployment has remained high, especially in the east, and the European Union has expressed dissatisfaction at a budget deficit that exceeds 3 per cent. Despite this, the general standard of living remains higher than in many other European countries, and Germany continues to play a leading role in the motor vehicle, electronic goods, electrical machinery and metal industries, as well as in the chemical and pharmaceutical industries. Former industrial areas such as the Ruhr have suffered badly following the decline of heavy industry and mining, and regional authorities are making efforts to develop a strong tertiary sector—although competition from eastern European countries with cheaper workforces poses challenges.

The Zugspitze (left). Mountain-climbing (middle). The Rhine (right). The German flag (opposite)

GERMANY'S REGIONS

NORTHERN GERMANY

Bremen is a city state that was formerly a member of the Hanseatic League, an alliance of trade ports that stretched across northern Europe and the Baltics.

Hamburg is another city state and is Germany's second-largest metropolitan area, with a long history that reflects its strategic maritime role.

Niedersachsen (Lower Saxony) is second only to Bavaria in size, and stretches from the North Sea to the Harz mountains. It is one of the least densely populated regions in Germany.

Mecklenburg-Vorpommern (Mecklenburg-Lower Pomerania) remains a largely agricultural state, with thousands of lakes and a diverse coastline edging the Baltic Sea.

Schleswig-Holstein lies between the North and the Baltic seas, and as the most northerly of Germany's states has complex linguistic and historical traditions.

WESTERN GERMANY

Hessen (Hesse) is a prosperous region that lies at the heart of modern German life: Frankfurt am Main is a major financial and commercial hub.

Nordrhein-Westfalen (North Rhine-Westphalia) was once dependent on heavy industry, but service industries now employ more than 60 per cent of the workforce.

Rheinland-Pfalz (Rhineland-Palatinate) is a wonderfully scenic region, where vine-covered slopes rise from the winding Rhine and tributaries such as the Mosel.

Saarland, the country's smallest region, nestles in the hilly triangle where Germany shares its borders with Luxembourg and France.

BERLIN

As the country's political hub, Berlin is at the heart of the new Germany's transformation.

EASTERN GERMANY

Brandenburg is a largely rural region, although its capital, Potsdam, contains some of Germany's most attractive palaces and formal gardens.

Sachsen (Saxony) has as its biggest draw the beautiful city of Dresden, while Leipzig is another town of considerable historical and cultural interest.

Sachsen-Anhalt (Saxony-Anhalt) has a varied landscape, with the splendid Harz Mountains to the southwest, flat land to the north and heavily industrialized areas to the east.

Thüringen (Thuringia) is sometimes called the 'green heart' of Germany and is a region that preserves many aspects of its traditional lifestyles.

SOUTHERN GERMANY

Baden-Württemberg is both a prosperous and picturesque region of southern Germany. The Schwarzwald (Black Forest) and Bodensee (Lake Constance) are just two of its many attractive natural areas.

Bayern (Bavaria) is Germany's largest state, and has some of its loveliest scenery. The modern region still has a strong regional identity.

THE BEST OF GERMANY

NORTHERN GERMANY

Bremen Wander round the Kunsthalle's impressive art collection or explore the quirky historic district of Schnoorviertel.
Hamburg A bustling city with great architecture, a cosmopolitan feel and a strong maritime tradition.
Kiel Try to visit during the *Kieler Woche*, the glamorous annual regatta held in June.
Lübeck This historically important town is famous for its unique brickwork architecture.

The quayside at Hamburg (left)

WESTERN GERMANY

Cologne (▷ 111–117) Explore the Dom, one of Europe's most splendid Gothic buildings.
Rheintal The Rhine flows north along its valley past fortresses and steep vine-covered slopes.
Ruhrgebiet The Ruhr area has a fascinating industrial legacy, as well as important design museums and art galleries.
Saarland This region's UNESCO-listed Völklingen ironworks commemorates a bygone industrial heritage.

Life in Kiel is focused around its harbour

BERLIN

Fernsehturm (▷ 101) Take in a 360-degree view of Berlin from the top of the television tower.
Brandenburger Tor A symbol of historical and contemporary upheaval, the Brandenburg Gate is one of Berlin's most recognizable landmarks.
Reichstag (▷ 107) Weighted with historical significance and now topped with a symbol of transparent government, Germany's parliament building is a must-see.

Brandenburger Tor in Berlin

EASTERN GERMANY

Colditz This grim prison fortress housed Allied prisoners during World War II.
Dresden Having overcome wartime bombing, flooding and neglect, Dresden is once again a visually stunning city.
Potsdam Brandenburg's capital is best known for its palaces and its magnificent Sanssouci park.
Weimar This town is the historic heart of German literary and intellectual life.

Köln's towering cathedral (above). Dresden (below)

MUNICH

Hofbräuhaus (▷ 124–125) Come to this huge beerhall and shaded beer garden for the archetypal Bavarian experience.
Deutsches Museum (▷ 122-123) 'How does it work?' This vast and fascinating museum provides the answers.
Englischer Garten (▷ 123) Surf, paddle, stroll or sunbathe in Munich's own central park.
Marienplatz (▷ 124) Sit over a beer in the summer, or hunt for presents in the Christmas market—this is the city's real heart.

Hofbräuhaus (below)

SOUTHERN GERMANY

Heidelberg Stroll along the Philosopher's Way, cross the Neckar on the old stone bridge or catch an open-air performance in the grounds of the imposing Schloss.
Nürnberg Medieval and modern history combine in the busy town of Nuremberg.
Schloss Neuschwanstein Soak up the atmosphere of the original fairy-tale castle and its beautiful setting.
Stuttgart Pay homage to the German motor car industry at the Mercedes Benz Museum.

Ishtar Gate, Berlin (right)

GERMANY

Berlin

✚ 5 E3 🛈 Tourist Info Center Europa-Center, Budapester Strasse 45, tel 030 250025 🚇 Zoologischer Garten
🛈 Tourist Info Center Brandenburger Tor (side wing), tel 030 250025 🚇 Unter den Linden
🛈 Tourist Info Café unter dem Fernsehturm, am Alexanderplatz, tel 030 250025 🚇 Alexanderplatz
www.berlin-tourist-information.de

The west tower of the Gedächtniskirche

Sir Norman Foster's Reichstag

A boat passes through the grounds of Schloss Charlottenburg

TIP

● For a less costly alternative to sightseeing tours, catch the No. 100 or 200 bus from Zoologischer Garten station in the west to the Prenzlauer Berg district in the east.

WELCOME CARD

The €21 Welcome Card, available from tourist offices, BVG and S-Bahn ticket offices and many hotels, allows one adult and up to three children (under 14) three days' travel on buses and trains in zones A, B and C. It comes with discount vouchers for tourist attractions.

The ultramodern Berlin Congress Hall (below)

TV Tower (right)

SEEING BERLIN

Berlin is a great mix of old and new and is constantly redefining itself. Your first port of call should be the top of the Fernsehturm (Television Tower) in Alexanderplatz (▷ 101), where you can get a 360-degree view over the city. Another great way to get your bearings is to take a guided tour or hop on a sightseeing bus.

Most cities have one heart, but Berlin has two, the western heart revolving around the Kurfürstendamm and the Kaiser Wilhelm Gedächtniskirche, and the eastern heart extending from Pariser Platz and the Brandenburger Tor to Alexanderplatz and the Fernsehturm. A regenerated commercial and entertainment hub is also emerging around Potsdamer Platz (▷ 106). There are many ways to get to know the city—on foot, by bus, on a boat, by bicycle or by tram. The S- and U-Bahn are fast and efficient, but sometimes a bus, tram or bicycle ride is a better way to appreciate Berlin's various parts. A Museums Pass costs €15 and provides entry to more than 50 museums, including all the Berlin State Museums, over a period of 3 consecutive days.

BACKGROUND

Berlin was founded in 1237, when a treaty was signed between the margraves of Brandenburg and the Bishop to settle a dispute about the right to levy taxes. The Thirty Years' War (1618–48) hit the city hard and it was left to Friedrich Wilhelm I, the Great Elector, to reconstruct it. By 1701, Berlin had been built up enough to be

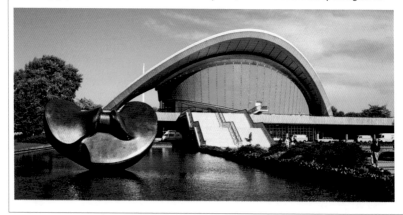

named the capital of Prussia under King Friedrich I. Things were fairly stable for a century, but during the Franco-Prussian war in 1806, Napoleon entered the city through the Brandenburg Gate, starting a French occupation that was to last for two years. When Berlin was liberated, Berliners elected their first municipal assembly, but it took another half century before the city became the capital of the newly created German Reich in 1871.

At the end of World War I, food shortages, currency devaluation and rationing prompted strikes. Adolf Hitler took power in 1933 and Berliners felt the consequences almost immediately. The Nazis destroyed the Reichstag and set up the head-quarters of their secret police (Gestapo) in the capital. On 9 November 1938, Berlin was the scene of the Reichskristallnacht, a pogrom in which synagogues and Jewish shops and businesses were destroyed. Before the Nazi regime, there were 160,000 Jewish people living in the capital—today there are only 10,000.

During World War II, Allied bombing destroyed many historic buildings. At the end of the war, Berlin was divided into four zones, administered by American, British, French and Soviet forces. In 1949, when Germany was divided in two, the border ran through the heart of the city. The GDR (East Germany) built the notorious Berlin Wall in 1961, dividing East and West Berlin. The border was heavily guarded, and in the 28 years the Wall stood, 152 people died trying to escape East Germany.

In 1989, the Berlin Wall came down, followed in 1990 by elections for the newly unified Germany. Today, Berliners have moved on from the division, but rebuilding has bankrupted the city and there is still much to do. Yet despite its troubled past, Berlin now looks forward to the future.

BERLIN'S DISTRICTS

● Commercial Mitte is in the middle of the city. Although it is Berlin's smallest district, it is the historical, political and cultural heart of the city. The area around Unter den Linden has some of the best historical buildings.

● Prenzlauer Berg in the northeast is a young, lively district, but still has the flair of old Berlin.

● Schöneberg is an easy-going district.

● Motzstrasse and Nollendorfplatz are at the heart of the gay scene.

● Charlottenburg and Wilmersdorff are leafy residential boroughs in the west of the city, bordered by the bustling Kurfürstendamm shopping street and the Tiergarten in the east.

● Kreuzberg, in the southeast, is the heart of the Turkish community. It has experienced riots, but a decade of stability has transformed it into one of the most interesting areas of the city, with international restaurants and cafés.

● Off the beaten track, Friedrichshain, in the east, is an up-and-coming area popular with students.

The vast Ishtar Gate, in the Pergamonmuseum (below)

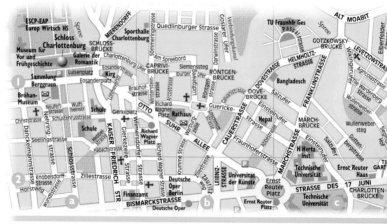

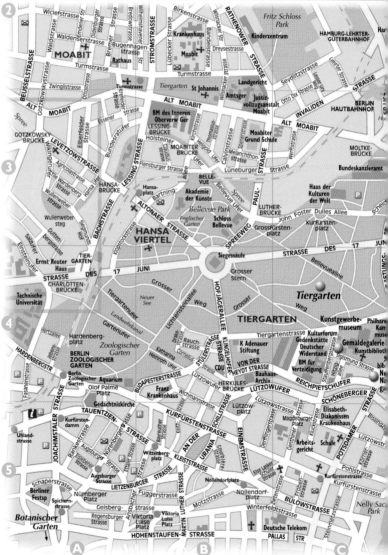

BERLIN

0   500 m
0   500 yds

Volkspark

HUMBOLDTHAIN
GESUNDBRUNNEN

TU

BIG

Kirchh
Dorothst

Schwartzkopff-
strasse

NORD-
BAHNHOF

Museum für
Naturkunde
B Amt für
Geologie
Bündn 90 Die
Grünen
Platz vor dem
Neuen Tor

Brecht
Haus

Universität

Deutsche
Bischofsknof

R Koch
Platz

Charité

Humboldt
Universität
Ananatom

BM für
Bildg u
Forschg

Max Planck
Institut für
Infektionsbiologie

Reinhardt-
Karl-
strasse

ul Löbe Haus
(Bundestag)

Reichstaguferr
Bundespres-
seeamt

Reichstag

DOROTHEEN-
STRASSE

Dorotheen-

der
blik

ndenburger
Tor

Pariser
Platz

Unter den
Linden

UNTER DEN LINDEN

Holocaust
Memorial

Leipziger
Platz

Potsdamer
Platz

Museum für
Post und
Kommunikation

Abgeordneten-
haus von Berlin

Topographie
des Terrors

Haus am
Checkpoint
Charlie

ANHALTER
STRASSE

ANHALTER
BAHNHOF

Schule

Landes-
arbeitsamt

KOCHSTRASSE

Kochstrasse

KREUZBERG

Jüdisches
Museum

Amtsger

Mehring-
platz

Patent-
amt

Deutsches
chnikmuseum

Haus Amerika
Gedenkbibliothek

Voltastrasse

Schule

Volks-
park

St Elisabeth

Lazaruskirchhaus

Pappel-
platz

Stilles
Museum

Oranienburger
Tor

ORANIENBURGER
STRASSE

Neue Synagoge

Kinderbad

Bode
Museum

Monbijou
park

Pergamonmuseum

Altes Museum/
Ägyptisches
Museum

Alte Nationalgalerie

Humboldt
Festungs
Universität

SCHLOSS-
BRÜCKE

Schinkel-
platz

Schloss-
platz

Staats-
oper

Bebel-
platz

Behrenstrasse

FRANZÖSISCHE STR

Gendarmen-
markt

Werderscher
Markt

Hausvogtei-
platz

Amtsger

Stadtmitte
Kronenstrasse

Spittelmarkt

Vineta-
platz

Mauer-
park

Zionskirch-
platz

Teutoburger
Platz

Senefelder-
platz

Rosenthaler
Platz

TORSTRASSE

Rosa Luxemburg
Platz

Marienkirche

Berliner
Dom

Rotes
Rathaus

Former
Palast der
Republik

Ehem
Staatsrat

Auswärtiges

MITTE

Märkisches
Museum

Neue
Jakobstr

Waldeck-
park

ORANIENSTRASSE

Moritz-
platz

Schule

Schule

Moritz-
torstrasse

Wassertor-
platz

GITSCHINER
STRASSE

Prinzen-
strasse

SCHÖNHAUSER
ALLEE

Eberswalder
Strasse

Wörther
Strasse

Senefelder-
platz

HACKESCHER
MARKT

ALEXANDER-
PLATZ
Fernsehturm

Alexander-
platz

Neptunbrunnen

Molken-
markt

Nikolaiviertel

STRALAUER STRASSE

MÜHLEN-
DAMM-
BRÜCKE

Märkisches
Museum

Heinrich-Heine-
strasse

Wassertor-
platz

The famous bust of Queen Nefertiti

ÄGYPTISCHES MUSEUM

**This collection of 2,000 ancient masterpieces spans three millenia.
Come here to admire the bust of Queen Nefertiti.**

BASICS

✚ 99 E3 • Am Lustgarten, 10178 Berlin (Mitte)

☎ 030 2090 5544

🕐 Daily 10–6 (Thu till 10pm)

🎟 Adult €8, child €4 (combined ticket for Mitte Museums: adult €12, child €6)

🚇 Friedrichstrasse

🚌 100, 200, 348

📷 Guided tours tel 030 2090 5566

🛍 📖 Gift shop selling souvenirs and books on Ancient Egyptian history and archaeology. Small bookshop where they also serve coffee ☕

www.smb.spk-berlin.de/amp/s.html

TIP

● Until the museum moves to its new permanent home, extend your archaeological tour by moving on from the Egyptian collection to enjoy the Classical Greek collection on the ground floor of the Altes Museum.

The Egyptian Museum has had several homes in the last few years. After some time at Schloss Charlottenburg, it has moved to a temporary home at Altes Musuem before it moves to a purpose-built facility at Mitte (Museum Island) in 2009. The current exhibition focuses predominantly on excavations in the Tell of Amarna and ranges from finds from Metjen's burial chamber, dating from around 2600BC, to Roman mummy masks from the first and second centuries AD. Illuminated by a spotlight in the dark room on the right of the foyer is the undisputed highlight of the museum: the famous bust of Nefertiti.

NEFERTITI

The wife of Pharaoh Akhenaton, Queen Nefertiti was given more rights and responsibility than any other royal Egyptian consort before or after her. Her bust portrait was discovered in 1912, along with other royal portraits, in what had been the house of Thutmose, a sculptor. Made from limestone and plaster, the bust dates from around 1340BC and is almost perfectly preserved. The symmetrical model is thought to have functioned as a teaching tool for sculptors, hence the empty socket revealing the artist's techniques. Although precise, the bags under the eyes and the soft, warm skin lend vitality to the expression. The life-like portrayal appears to embody the contemporary western ideal of femininity and timeless beauty, and she has been a hit with visitors since the day she was first put on display in the 1920s.

THE TEMPLE GATE OF KALABSHA

The Temple Gate was a gift from the Egyptian government to the German Federal Republic, thanking them for their assistance during an international archaeological rescue mission, when the monuments of the Nubian Nile Valley were threatened by the construction of the Aswan High Dam. The Roman Emperor Augustus built the Temple Gate in 20BC, ten years after he had taken control of Egypt following Queen Cleopatra's suicide. The gate is covered in reliefs, depicting the Roman Emperor as an Egyptian Pharaoh.

Don't miss The Hippopotamus figurines on display were placed inside burial tombs to guarantee eternal life (1800BC)—the ones with open mouths were thought to ward off evil spirits and banish curses.

GERMANY

ALEXANDERPLATZ

Modern architects have transformed this historic square into a bustling meeting place and transport hub.
Enjoy a panoramic view from the top of the Fernsehturm.

Alexanderplatz was named after the Russian Tsar Alexander I in 1805. In the 1920s and 30s it became a bustling crossroads for Berlin's traffic and a popular meeting place. Destroyed during World War II, it was transformed into a pedestrianized square during the 1960s, but today it is generally visited for the sights around it.

FERNSEHTURM

At 368m (1,207ft), the Television Tower, affectionately known to locals as the Tele Asparagus, is the tallest building in Berlin (Mar–end Oct daily 9am–midnight; Nov–end Feb daily 10am–midnight). Inside, elevators whisk you up to the viewing platform in the silver sphere, 203m (666ft) above the ground, at an ear-popping 5m per second (16.5ft per second) for a 360-degree view of the city. Above the viewing gallery is the Telecafé (Mar–end Oct daily 10am–midnight; Nov–end Feb daily 10am–midnight), where you can sit in the revolving restaurant and enjoy the panoramic view over *Kaffee und Kuchen* or a light meal.

MARIENKIRCHE

The Marienkirche (Apr–end Oct daily 10–9, Nov–end Mar daily 10–6) is the second-oldest parish church in Berlin, after Nikolaikirche. It was first mentioned in records as early as 1294, but burned down in 1380 and was later rebuilt. Highlights include the alabaster baroque pulpit (1703) by Andreas Schlüter, decorated with reliefs of John the Baptist and personifications of the Virtues, and the *Dance of Death* (1490) fresco in the vestibule, rediscovered by August Stüler in 1860 behind the whitewash walls.

ROTES RATHAUS

The Rotes Rathaus (Mon–Fri 9–6; closed during official events) is the official seat of the Mayor of Berlin and contains the magistrates' offices and state rooms. The frieze known as the 'stone chronicle' was added in 1879 and depicts historical figures and economic and scientific events that shaped the city. The building suffered extensive damage during World War II and was rebuilt in the 1950s when it was the seat of the East Berlin authorities. After reunification the Rotes Rathaus became the base for the city's officials. Inside, climb the red-carpeted staircase to admire the modern stained-glass windows.

The Fernsehturm and Rotes Rathaus (above). A mural on the side of a house (top)

RATINGS					
Photo stops	●	●	●	●	●
Historic interest	●	●	●		
Walkability	●	●	●	●	

BASICS

🗺 99 F3 • 10178 Berlin (Mitte)
🚇 Alexanderplatz
🚌 100, 157, 200, 348; Tram 2, 3, 4, 5, 6, N54, N92
🚻 Public toilets in the Alexanderplatz U-Bahn station, around the kiosks near the Rotes Rathaus and in the Fernsehturm

TIP

● The entrance to the Fernsehturm is on the eastern side of the tower, opposite the station at Alexanderplatz.
● If you are going to the Telecafé you will need to check your coats and bags in at the cloakroom near the toilets in the viewing gallery. You may have to wait to be shown to a table during busy times.
● There are regular classical music recitals in the Marienkirche—pick up a leaflet, call 030 242 4467 or check online (www.marienkirche-berlin.de) for the latest details.

Come to the Old National Gallery for some of the best examples of modern painting and sculpture in Berlin

RATINGS

Cultural interest	●●●●●
Historic interest	●●●●
Value for money	●●●

BASICS

✚ 99 E3 • Bodestrasse 1–3, 10178 Berlin (Mitte)
☎ 030 2090 5801
🕐 Tue–Sun 10–6, Thu 10–10
💶 Adult €8, child €4
🚇 Friedrichstrasse
🚌 100, 200, 348
🚌 Guided tours tel 030 2090 5566
📷 🍴 📖 Small bookshop where they also serve coffee
👥

www.alte-nationalgalerie.de
This is part of the official state museums website. You can find out more about the collection and the history behind it, and there is up-to-date information on temporary exhibitions. English and German.

ALTE NATIONALGALERIE

A comprehensive collection of 19th-century German painting. There are French Impressionist works by Monet, Manet and Renoir.

In 1861, the Berlin banker Joachin Heinrich Wilhelm Wagener left his collection of 262 paintings to Prince Wilhelm (later King and Emperor Wilhelm I). The gallery first opened its doors to the public on the King's birthday, 21 March 1876.

THIRD LEVEL

Begin at the top of the red-carpeted marble staircase on the third level. At the top of the stairs, lean on the balustrade and look across to Anselm Feverbach's huge painting *The Symposium* (1871–73). It illustrates an episode in Plato's *Symposium* when the poet Alcibiades makes a drunken entrance. The philosopher Socrates stands on the right, the poet is in the middle and the figure of Desire is depicted on the left. The elaborate frame is painted and incorporated into the picture, prompting the viewer to question the nature of reality and illusion. Room 3.06 is dedicated to the painter Casper David Friedrich. The artist is famous for his nighttime landscapes and depictions of moonlight reflected over water. *Moonrise over the Sea* (1822) shows two women and a man sitting on a rock, looking out to the sea and waiting for the returning ships. The group symbolizes companionship and safety, while the moonlight backdrop hints at the vast expanse of the universe. Return to room 3.04 and continue your tour clockwise round the third floor.

SECOND LEVEL

Room 2.03, the large room in the middle at the far end of the second level, is dedicated to the French Impressionists. Auguste Rodin's statue *The Thinker* (1881–83) is also in this room. A larger-than-life version stands on his grave, but this smaller version is the original. Look closely and you can detect Rodin's fingerprints and tool marks, left behind in the clay model before it was forged in bronze.

FIRST LEVEL

The first level focuses predominantly on realist painting, including works by John Constable, Gustav Courbet and Adolph Menzel. The main attraction is the neoclassical sculpture in the first long room you come to on the first floor, room 1.01. The *Double Statue of Crown Princess Luise and Friederike of Prussia* (1795–97) by Schadow is the first life-size neoclassical double statue ever made.

GEMÄLDEGALERIE

This gallery holds some 2,700 European paintings dating from the 13th to 18th centuries. Come here to see ground-breaking works by Rembrandt, Caravaggio and Bruegel.

The Gemäldegalerie collection began with various European private collections, brought together and then supplemented by others from the royal palaces. Following World War II, the paintings were divided between East and West Berlin. In 1965, a competition was held to design a complex for the museums of European art, which would stand opposite the Philharmonic Hall. The architect Rolf Gutbrod won the competition and submitted his final designs in 1966, but political and financial debate plagued the project, and it wasn't until 1985 that building work could go ahead. Gutbrod's original drawings were reworked into what is now known as the Kulturforum. After years of discussions and planning, the collection was moved to the Kulturforum and opened to the public in 1998.

THE FLEMISH PROVERBS BY PIETER BRUEGEL, IN ROOM 7

Bruegel brings together 100 proverbs in an absurd, slightly surreal village scene, reminiscent of the work of his predecessor Bosch. Painted in 1559, the painting was originally called *The Upside-Down World*, in reference to the inverted globe on the side of the house, reflecting the topsy-turvy scene. The devil occupies the chapel and takes confession, while Jesus sits outside on the right in front of a hut. A servant covers his face with a flax beard, the mask of a hypocrite. Chaos is the guiding principle, as money is thrown into the water and roses are cast before swine. The old sayings were meant used to illustrate man's foolishness and sinfulness in a world without the guidance of God.

CHILD WITH BIRD BY RUBENS, IN ROOM 9

Rubens painted this portrait of his nephew Philip in 1624. Philip was born in 1611 and was the son of Rubens' brother, who died at a young age. Rubens captures the intuitive character of children through the boy's interaction with the bird and reflects his innocence with his white clothes, pale complexion and angelic features.

ST. SEBASTIAN BY SANDRO BOTTICELLI, IN ROOM XVIII

Botticelli painted his dedication to the martyr St. Sebastian in 1474 for the church of San Francesco Maggiore in Florence. The figure is shown in the contrapposto position, with his head and upper body twisted in the opposite direction to his hips and legs.

The Dance or Iris (1719–20) by Jean Antoine Watteau

BASICS

⊞ 98 C4 • Kulturforum, Mattäikirch-platz, 10785 Berlin (Tiergarten)

☎ 030 266 2101; information 030 266 2951

🕐 Tue–Sun 10–6, Thu 10–10

💶 Adult €8, child €4 (ticket for all Tiergarten musuems)

Ⓟ Potsdamer Platz

🚌 M29, M41, M48, 200, 347

🎧 Guided tours tel 030 2090 5566; free audioguide

🛍 📖 Shop selling a wide range of art books, postcards and posters 🚻 Ⓟ

www.smb.spk-berlin.de/gg
Part of the official state museums website. There are pictures of some of the famous pieces in the gallery and you can find out more about the history of the collection. English and German.

TIP

● The air in the gallery is kept very dry to preserve the art, but you can take a break every so often by the water sculpture *5–7–9 Series* by Walter de Maria in the central hall.

The sculpture garden (above). A bronze sculpture (top) at the entrance to Neue Nationalgalerie

RATINGS

Cultural interest	●●●●●
Historic interest	●●●
Value for money	●●●

BASICS

✚ 98 C4 • Kulturforum am Potsdamer Platz, Potsdamer Strasse 50, 10785 Berlin (Tiergarten)
☎ 030 266 2651
🕐 Tue–Fri 10–6, (Thu till 10pm) Sat–Sun 11–6
💶 Adult €8, child €4
🚇 Potsdamer Platz
🚌 M29, M41, M48, 200, 347
🎧 Guided tours tel 030 2090 5566
📷
🏛 Small art bookshop
👫
🅿 Kulturforum

www.smb.spk-berlin.de/nng/e/s.html
This is part of the official state museums website. Find out about the collection and about visiting exhibitions. English and German.

NEUE NATIONALGALERIE

An outstanding collection of 20th-century painting and sculpture, with works by famous artists such as Salvador Dalí, Paul Klee and Pablo Picasso.

At the edge of the Tiergarten near the Kulturforum, the New National Gallery was designed by Bauhaus architect Ludwig Mies van der Rohe and built between 1965 and 1968. The square steel structure and glazed walls sit on a raised terrace, creating a spacious and versatile exhibition space for this collection, ranging from early modernism to art of the 1960s and 1970s. Contemporary exhibitions are also held on the upper floor.

SCULPTURE

The Dancer (1911–12) made Georg Kolbe famous and established his reputation as a sensitive sculptor of the human form. It was first shown at the Berlin Seccession in 1912 and was snapped up by the Nationalgalerie. Kolbe was inspired by the work of Rodin, particularly the way in which he conveyed energy and the impression of fluid movement in his sculpture. You can also see one of Alexander Calder's mobiles, *Dancing Star* (1940), a carefully balanced and delicate sculpture made from thin wire and painted metal shapes that dance around with the slightest movement of air. Artist Käthe Kollwitz lost her son Peter, who was a soldier, in 1914. She confronts her loss in the sculpture *Pietá* (1937–38) by reworking the famous religious image into a universal expression of maternal grief. *Woman on a Bench* (1957) is one of Henry Moore's series of seated figures, which all refer to the struggle of life, and the pregnant woman is a comment on the natural process of birth, growth and decay.

PAINTING

Max Liebermann painted many self-portraits. *Self-Portrait* (1925) shows the 78-year-old artist, who was then president of the Prussian Academy of Arts, seated facing the viewer in his studio before a canvas with a brush and palette in his hand. There are two examples of Picasso's analytic cubism on display, *Woman Seated in an Armchair* (1909) and *Woman Playing a Violin* (1911). *Potsdamer Platz* (1914), by Ernst Ludwig Kirchner, shows the famous square at night in autumn 1914. The building with the arcaded loggia in the middle is Potsdam Station. Two life-size female figures, intended to be prostitutes, stand on a traffic island in the foreground with the dark figures of potential clients in the background. These women contrast with the pink figures of the 'respectable' women in the distance.

PERGAMONMUSEUM

This houses the city's most impressive collections of archaeological discoveries.

The Pergamonmuseum is at the heart of the Museum Island complex. It is actually three museums in one: the Collection of Classical Antiquities, the Museum of Ancient Near-Eastern Art and the Museum of Islamic Art. Your ticket covers admission to all of the museum collections, and you can wander freely between them.

THE PERGAMON ALTAR
In 1876, Carl Humann began uncovering the remains of this ancient altar on the Acropolis of Pergamon in the Aegean area of Turkey. The Altar was built by King Eumenes II (197–158BC) and stood on the Acropolis in the Roman capital of the Asian province of Pergamon. The Altar was encircled by a relief frieze, over 2m (6.5ft) high and 120m (394ft) long, which illustrated the war between gods and giants that was finally settled by the heroic Hercules. Known as the Great Frieze, it captures the climax of the battle.

THE ISHTAR GATE AND THE FAÇADE OF THE THRONE ROOM
As early as 1851, French archaeologists found pieces of glazed bricks around the El-Kasr hill ruin that they believed formed part of a frieze. The Ishtar Gate is just one of at least eight double gates that led into the city of Babylon and formed the northern entrance into King Nebuchadnezzar II's capital. Because of its size, only the smaller outer gate could be reconstructed in the museum.

On the narrow walls on either side of the Ishtar gate are two sections of the reconstructed façade of the Throne Room from the southern palace of Nebuchadnezzar II. The Babylonian craftsmen who built the royal palace of Babylon in the sixth century BC coded each individual brick, which allowed Walter Andrae to reconstruct the façade of the throne room here between 1899 and 1901. The palace façade was 56m (184ft) wide, but its true height remains uncertain—its present height is determined by the dimensions of the gallery space.

BACKGROUND
It wasn't until the completion of the first phase of excavations at the Acropolis of Pergamon in 1886 that the question of where to keep these huge architectural discoveries was raised. A provisional home for the collection was opened to the public in 1901 but was only just big enough for the reconstructed altar. The new and much bigger Pergamonmuseum was built between 1910 and 1930.

It needed a vast building (top) to house the Pergamon Altar. Looking down from the Pergamon Altar (above)

RATINGS	
Cultural interest	●●●●●
Historic interest	●●●●●
Value for money	●●●●●

BASICS
99 E3 • Museuminsel, Am Kupfergraben, 10178 Berlin (Mitte)

☎ 030 2090 5577

🕐 Tue–Sun 10–6, Thu 10–10

💶 Adult €8, child €4

🚇 Hackescher Markt, Friedrichstrasse

🚌 100, 200, 348; tram 1, 2, 3, 4, 5, 6, 13, 15, 50, 53

Guided tours tel 030 2090 5566; free audioguide

Two shops sell souvenirs and books

www.smb.spk-berlin.de
Find out more about the history of the museum; there are links from here to pages dedicated to the three individual collections; English and German.

TIP
● A rolling schedule of restoration of the Pergamonmuseum starts in 2008 but some galleries will remain open throughout.

The dome of the Sony Center (above). A section of the Berlin Wall (below)

RATINGS	
Photo stops	● ● ● ● ●
Cultural interest	● ● ● ●
Historic interest	● ●

BASICS

✚ 99 D4 • 10785 Berlin (Tiergarten)
◉ Potsdamer Platz
🚌 142, 148, 248, 348
www.potsdamerplatz.de

TIPS

● The cafés and restaurants on Potsdamer Platz are a short walk from the Kulturforum, making it the ideal place to wind down after time spent in the museums.
● Throughout December there is a Christmas market here, with an ice-skating rink.

POTSDAMER PLATZ

This redeveloped area is constantly expanding, and is rapidly growing into a cultural hot spot and sleek business district.

Potsdamer Platz was once the heart of the city, a major crossroads for the traffic of Berlin. The 'Stammbahn' rail route, which passed through the newly built Potsdamer Station towards Potsdam, was opened in 1838, and brought the first signs of hustle and bustle to the square. Potsdamer Platz marked the point where five major roads intersected and provided a link between the middle of the city and the developing West. Famous hotels, department stores and restaurants lined the streets, and the area became popular with artists and the politicians and diplomats who were based nearby.

REBUILDING

Most of the buildings in Potsdamer Platz were destroyed by bombing raids during World War II, and later the Berlin Wall ran right through the middle of the square, so the few buildings that remained standing fell into disrepair. Shiny skyscrapers of big corporations such as Daimler Benz now dominate the skyline, and the square has become a key financial and business hub.

THE SONY CENTER

Designed by Helmut Jahn and built between 1996 and 2000, the Sony Center is one of Berlin's greatest architectural attractions. The steel and glass dome measures 4,013sq m (43,195sq ft) and shelters the light, spacious piazza beneath. The fountains and trees at its heart are surrounded by gleaming office buildings, alfresco dining establishments and the glass-fronted Sony Style Store, packed with the latest home entertainment gadgets.

FILM

Movie buffs will find plenty here to keep them occupied. There is a plethora of cinemas to choose from, including two 3D Imax theatres in the Sony Center and an art-house cinema on the ground floor of the Filmhaus, underneath the Berlin Film Museum (Tue–Sun 10–6, Thu 10–8). The museum, too, is an audiovisual feast; catch the film *Asphalt* by Joe May (1929) in room 4, which re-creates Potsdamer Platz at its prime in the late 1920s, before the World War II bombing. At the heart of the museum is a shrine to the German film star Marlene Dietrich.

Don't miss A line of metal plaques is imbedded in the street paving marks where the Berlin Wall once stood.

REICHSTAG

Walk up Sir Norman Foster's dome, an impressive architectural statement, to get an inside look at the seat of the German Parliament.

The original Reichstag was built in 1894 by Paul Wallot as the seat of the German Parliament. An inscription above the wide staircase, cast in bronze in 1916, reads 'Dem Deutschen Volke', meaning 'The German People'. The building was damaged by fire on 27 February 1933 and was completely devastated as a result of heavy fighting around the building during World War II. After extensive restoration, the building was handed to the Federal Administration in 1973, and the first session of the reunified German Parliament was held here on 4 October 1990.

SIR NORMAN FOSTER
In June 1993, the British architect Sir Norman Foster was awarded the commission to restore the Reichstag. Foster preserved the original features and functions of the building, while adding glass walls, a symbol of the transparency of democracy, and a glass roof and chamber that bring light to the heart of the structure. Sections marked by bullet holes and Red Army graffiti have been left exposed in the lobbies and corridors as a reminder of the building's turbulent history.

The new building is self-sustaining and nothing is wasted. The water supply, heating and electricity for the parliament complex is powered by two engines fired by rapeseed oil, a clean and renewable energy source. Any excess heat generated in the summer is stored for the winter in a brine lake 300m (985ft) below ground.

THE DOME
Foster's dome is visible for miles around and has a powerful presence on Berlin's skyline. It has also become a symbol of popular rule, and every day thousands of people climb to the top. Visitors are reflected in the central mirrored funnel as they walk up the gently sloping spiral walkway. From the top you can look down into the chamber, representing open democratic rule. There are information panels around the base of the funnel documenting the history of the Reichstag, and you can walk out of the dome onto the roof terrace to appreciate the view over the city.

Don't miss The 21m (69ft) flag-like panel in the western hall, called Black, Red and Gold (1999), by German artist Gerhard Richter is made from recycled glass.

Sir Norman Foster's glass dome is a popular attraction

BASICS

✚ 99 D3 • Deutscher Bundestag, Plenarbereich, Reichstagsgebäude, Platz der Republik, 11011 Berlin (Tiergarten)
☎ 030 2273 2152
🕐 Daily 8am–midnight, last admission 10pm 🎟 Free
🚇 Unter den Linden
🚌 100, 248, 257, 348; tram 100
📢 Lectures by prior arrangement
♿

www.reichstag.de
This German website provides links to sites related to the Reichstag and the government, including historical resources, tourist information and state-run services.

TIPS

● All visitors have to pass through security checks before entering the building, so be prepared to wait.
● An elevator takes you up to the public roof terrace and the base of the dome, but you have to walk up the sloping spiral path to reach the top.
● The Reichstag is open until midnight (last entry at 10), and there are some great night-time views of the city from the viewing gallery.

Schloss Charlottenburg

RATINGS

Photo stops	●●●○
Historic interest	●●●●●
Value for money	●●●●●
Walkability	●●○

BASICS

✚ 98 a1 (inset) • Spandauer Damm 20–24, 14059 Berlin (Charlottenburg)
☎ 030 3209 1440 ◉ Altes Schloss daily 9–5 (the State rooms on the ground floor can only be visited by guided tour); Neuer Flügel Apr–end Oct Tue–Sun 10–5, Nov–end Mar Tue–Sun 11–5; Neuer Pavilion Tue–Sun 10–5; Mausoleum Apr–end Oct Tue–Sun 12–6, Nov–end Mar Tue–Sun 12–5; Belvedere Apr–end Oct Tue–Sun 12–6, Nov–end Mar Tue–Sun 12–5; Grosse Orangerie closed to visitors
🎫 Altes Schloss: Adult €10, child €7; Neuer Flügel: Adult €6, child €5; Neuer Pavilion: Adult €2, child €1.50; Mausoleum: €1; Belvedere: Adult €2, child €1.50
Ⓢ Sophie-Charlotte-Platz, Richard-Wagner-Platz, Westend
🚌 109, 145, 210, X21
🎧 Guided tours in German (information sheets available in other languages): Adult €8, child €5; Neuer Flügel free audioguide
▯ ⊞
www.spsg.de

Statue atop the palace gates (right)

SCHLOSS CHARLOTTENBURG

Wander around the private apartments of kings and queens, where fine furniture and art from the 17th to the 20th centuries fill every room.

Charlottenburg started out in 1699 as a summer residence, then called Lietzenburg Country House. The palace became the official royal residence of King Friedrich I (1688–1705), which he shared with his wife Queen Sophie Charlotte. In 1705, the palace was renamed Charlottenburg, following the death of the Queen. Over the next 100 years, the complex was extended.

THE STATE ROOMS AND APARTMENTS

After passing through the guest suite, you come to the Glass Bedchamber of Queen Sophie Charlotte, decorated with alternating strips of mirror and green damask. From the intimate surroundings of the Queen's Apartments you pass into the more formal chambers of King Frederick I. The tour of the intersecting rooms on the ground floor, from east to west, ends with the Porcelain Cabinet.

THE WHITE HALL AND THE GOLDEN GALLERY

The White Hall on the top floor of the Neuer Flügel (New Wing) was Friedrich the Great's banqueting hall and throne room. The room suffered extensive damage during World War II and was reconstructed using the paintings of Friedrich Wilhelm Höder as a guide. The light-filled hall is lined with arched windows and Corinthian pilasters topped with gold stucco capitals. Originally bright pink, the room has faded to white. The Golden Gallery was the venue for dancing and musical recitals during Friedrich the Great's banquets and parties. The gallery is one of the best examples of a rococo banqueting hall in Germany, its long, bright hall lined with floor-to-ceiling windows and console mirrors increasing the sense of space and reflecting the baroque gardens outside.

THE GARDENS

The palace grounds were originally laid out in 1697 in the French baroque formal style, with swirling paths and neatly trimmed hedges. In 1819, Friedrich Wilhelm III replaced the topiary and circular flowerbeds with broad lawns and forest areas, akin to those seen in English romantic gardens.

TIERGARTEN

This peaceful green haven at the heart of the city, with an abundance of ornamental gardens, lakes and wooded areas to explore makes an ideal place to stroll, take a boat or bicycle tour or simply relax with a picnic.

The Strasse des 17. Juni cuts a swathe through the Tiergarten

At 202ha (500 acres), the Tiergarten is the city's biggest park, bordered by the River Spree in the north and Potsdamer Platz, the Kulturforum and the Bauhaus Archiv in the south. A network of footpaths and bicycle routes criss-crosses the park, connecting Unter den Linden in the east with the sights around the Kürfurstendamm and Zoologischer Garten in the west. The Grosser Stern and the towering Siegessäule are useful navigational landmarks at the heart of the park, which is intersected by the wide avenue of the Strasse des 17. Juni.

SIEGESSÄULE

This tower, in the middle of the Tiergarten, is at the heart of Berlin. King Wilhelm I ordered the construction of the monument, which originally stood in Platz der Republik, in 1864, following the victory of Prussia and Austria over Denmark. In 1938, it was moved to the Tiergarten to make room for the rebuilding of the city under the Third Reich. The Siegessäule, designed to convey German strength and dominance, is now a symbol of peace and acceptance.

Climb to the top and you will reach the final viewing platform, beneath the gilded angel of Victory. The main attraction is the 360-degree view. If you look down Strasse des 17. Juni towards Brandenburger Tor, you can see all the way down Unter den Linden, with the Reichstag on the left and the Fernsehturm in the distance.

ZOOLOGISCHER GARTEN

The zoo dates back to 1841, when Friedrich Wilhelm IV, the King of Prussia, donated his pheasant gardens and exotic animal collection to the citizens of Berlin. It suffered serious damage during World War II: Only 91 animals survived and many of the enclosures and buildings were beyond repair. The new director, Dr. Katharina Heinroth, began the lengthy process of rebuilding the zoo and reintroducing animals. Today it has developed into one of the most important zoos in the world, with over 14,000 animals and 1,500 species represented.

AQUARIUM

The aquarium is occupied by a huge variety of fish, frogs, lizards, snakes, crocodiles and turtles from all over the world. The Komodo dragons dominate the reptile area on the second floor.

BASICS

✚ 98 C4 • 10785 Berlin (Tiergarten)
🚇 Zoologischer Garten, Tiergarten
🚌 100, 109, 119, 129, 145, 146, 149, 187, 245, 249, 341, X9, X34
🚻 Public toilets near the Siegessäule and in the Zoo and Aquarium
🅿 Am ZooBogen, €2.30 an hour
www.zoo-berlin.de

The guilded statue of Viktoria looks over the Tiergarten

KEY TO SYMBOLS

- 🏬 Shopping
- 🎭 Entertainment
- 🍸 Nightlife
- 🏊 Sports
- ✪ Activities
- ♥ Health and Beauty
- ✹ For Children

WHAT TO DO

🏬 KADEWE—KAUFHAUS DES WESTENS

Tauenzienstrasse 21–24 (Schöneberg)
Tel 030 21210
www.kadewe.de
KaDeWe is the largest department store in mainland Europe. Its legendary delicatessen is popular with visitors and locals alike, who are attracted by the feast of luxury chocolates, vintage wines and spirits and gourmet ingredients. There is a great view from the top-floor café.
🕐 Mon–Thu 10–8, Fri 10-10, Sat 9.30–8 🚇 Wittenbergplatz 🚌 M19, M29, M46, 343 🅿

🏬 TÜRKISCHER BASAR

Maybachufer (Neukölln)
The Turkish Bazaar, popular since the 1970s, is the liveliest and cheapest market in Berlin. It is a great place to sample Turkish cuisine, soak up exotic sights and smells, and get a genuine feel for Berlin's multicultural way of life.
🕐 Tue and Fri noon–6.30
🚇 Schönleinstrasse

🎭 DEUTSCHE OPER BERLIN

Bismarkstrasse 35 (Charlottenburg)
Tel 030 348 8401
www.deutscheoperberlin.de
The Deutsche Oper company has been staging classical and modern opera and ballet, plus symphony and chamber concerts, since 1912. Performances since World War II have been held in Fritz Bornemann's contemporary glass-fronted building.
🕐 Ticket office: Mon–Sat 11am until start of performance or 7pm, Sun 10–2 and 1 hour before performance
💶 €10–€112 🚇 Deutsche Oper, Bismarkstrasse, Charlottenburg
🚌 101, 109

🎭 FRIEDRICHSTADTPALAST

Friedrichstrasse 107 (Mitte)
Tel 030 2326 2326 (box office)
www.friedrichstadtpalast.de
This is Berlin's largest cabaret theatre and the largest costume

revue venue in Europe. The show is a fantastic glitzy spectacle of dance, circus, music and chorus. They have their own high-kicking troupe of 66 dancers, plus an orchestra.
🕐 Ticket hotline: Mon 9–6, Tue–Sat 9–8 and 1 hour before performance. Main revue: daily 8pm (also Sat–Sun 4pm) 💶 €60–€100 🚇 Oranienburger Tor, Friedrichstrasse 🚌 Bus 147; tram 1, 50

🍸 BAR AM LÜTZOWPLATZ

Lützowplatz 7 (Tiergarten)
Tel 030 262 6807
www.baramluetzowplatz.com
Designed by architect Jürgen Sawade, this sophisticated cocktail bar is one of the largest in Berlin and boasts 126 different varieties of champagne. The happy hour attracts many of Berlin's business types after work.
🕐 Daily 2pm–4am. Happy hour: 2pm–9pm 🚌 100, 129, 187

🍸 B-FLAT

Rosenthaler Strasse 13 (Mitte)
Tel 030 283 3123
www.b-flat-berlin.de
This club in the heart of the city has acoustic music and jazz. Drinks are cheaper before 10pm, and happy hour is between 1am and 2am. There are open-mike sessions on Wednesdays; the club screens art-house films and shorts on Thursday; and Sunday night from 10pm is 'Tango Time'.
🕐 Sun–Thu from 8pm, Fri–Sat from 9pm 💶 €4–8, free Wed–Thu
🚇 Hackescher Markt, Weinmeisterstrasse 🚌 Tram 13, 53

EATING

CAFÉ IM LITERATURHAUS 'WINTERGARTEN'

Fasanenstrasse 23 (Charlottenburg)
Tel 030 882 5414
On the ground floor of a beautiful 19th-century villa, this traditional coffeehouse is one of Berlin's most popular Sunday brunch hot spots. It is a great place to escape the bustling shops on the Kufürstendamm. Waiters introduce you to the extensive cake buffet, and you can sit in the lovely garden in summer. Credit cards are not accepted.
🕐 Daily 9.30am–1am
💶 L €12.50, D €15, Wine €16
🚇 Kurfürstendamm

GOURMET RESTAURANT LORENZ ADLON

Hotel Adlon, Unter den Linden 77, 10117 (Mitte)
Tel 030 22610
www.hotel-adlon.de
Sample some of the best gourmet fusion food in the city at this exclusive experimental restaurant. Seafood from Brittany, Bresse poultry, fine wines, lobster, caviar and regional dishes are all on the menu. Whether you opt for an exquisite breakfast or brunch, or a gala dinner you are guaranteed a memorable meal and first-class service.
🕐 Tue–Sat 7pm–10.30pm
💶 D €100, Wine €35
🚇 Unter den Linden

STAYING

HOTEL ADLON KEMPINSKI

Unter den Linden 77, 10117 Berlin (Mitte)
Tel 030 22 61 11 11
www.hotel-adlon.de
The original Hotel Adlon was opened in 1907 at a ceremony attended by Kaiser Wilhelm II. It was one of the most luxurious hotels in the world. In May 1945 a fire demolished part of the hotel and in 1984 it was torn down. The current building, equally luxurious, opened in 1997. Its Gourmet Restaurant Lorenz Adlon is one of the best in the city (▷ above).
💶 €240–€530, excluding breakfast (€34)
🛏 104 (some non-smoking)
🍴
🏊 Indoor ♥
🚇 Unter den Linden
🚌 100

HOTEL AGON AM ALEXANDERPLATZ

Mollstrasse 4, 10178 Berlin (Mitte)
Tel 030 275 7270
www.agon-alexanderplatz.de
The guest rooms are functional and have everything you will need for a comfortable stay, including bath or shower and toilet, television, fax and internet line. The suites also have a small kitchenette.
💶 €66–€149, breakfast included
🛏 150
🅿
🚇 Alexanderplatz
🚌 100, 142, 200, 257, 340

Cologne

The mighty Dom, with its delicately filigreed twin spires and its forest of flying buttresses, is one of the most magnificent cathedrals in Europe. Cologne has stylish shops, fabulous restaurants and a thriving cultural scene.

Cologne's famous skyline

Reliquary busts from the church of St. Ursula

One of the cathedral's highlights, the Gero Cross

SEEING COLOGNE

The skyline of Cologne (Köln) is dominated by the twin towers, 157m (515ft) tall, of its massive cathedral, which is without doubt one of the architectural highlights of the entire country. Nearby is the Roman-Germanic Museum—home to one of the most important Roman collections in Europe—and the ultra-modern Ludwig Museum and Concert Hall.

To the south of the cathedral, strung out along the riverfront and surrounding the medieval Altermarkt, is the immaculately restored Altstadt, which is crammed with intimate cafés, welcoming bars and superb traditional restaurants. Culinary highlights are also thick on the ground either side of the Hohenzollernring, about a kilometre (0.6 miles) to the west of the city, while on the other side of the river are the wide-open spaces of the Rheinpark, and the warm, soporific waters of the Claudius Thermal Baths. Finally, to the south of the Altstadt, on the banks of the Rhine just a short walk beyond Deutzer Brücke, is Cologne's famous Chocolate Museum, right next door to the equally fascinating Museum of German Sport.

HIGHLIGHTS

KÖLNER DOM

🔲 113 B1 • Domforum, Domkloster 3, 50667 Köln ☎ 0221 1794 0100 🕐 Mon–Fri 10–6.30, Sat 10–5, Sun 1–5 💶 Cathedral: free; tower: Adult €2, child €1; guided tours (Mon–Sat 11, 12.30, 2, 3.30, Sun 2, 3.30): Adult €4, child €2 (in English); Multivision multi-media show, various languages (Mon–Sat 10.30, 2.30, Sun 2.30): Adult €1.50, child €1
www.koelner-dom.de
Cologne Cathedral was begun in the 13th century, but because of funding problems it wasn't actually completed until the end of the 19th century. Throughout this time, however, far-sighted architects remained faithful to the original drawings, which miraculously survived. (The original drawing of the west façade still hangs in the ambulatory, but is kept behind a curtain to protect it from the light.) The resulting harmony of structure and decoration, achieved on such

RATINGS	
Historic interest	●●●●●
Cultural interest	●●●●●
Walkability	●●●●
Good for food	●●●●

BASICS

🔲 5 D3
ℹ️ Unter Fettenhennen 19, 50667 Köln (Dom), tel 0221 2213 0400; Jul–end Sep Mon–Sat 9am–10pm, Sun 10–6; Oct–end Jun Mon–Sat 9–9, Sun 10–6
💳 Welcome Card (free public transport and cut-price tours, plus reductions in many museums, music venues and churches): €9 for 24 hrs and €14 for 48 hrs
🚉 Köln

www.koeln.de
This superb website is a one-stop shop for all things Cologne. There's comprehensive information on walking tours, exhibitions and events, museums, the cathedral and other attractions, spectator sports and facilities, and of course eateries and hotels (although the online hotel reservation service is available only in German).

KÖLSCH

As well as being the name of the dialect spoken by natives of Cologne, Kölsch is also the name of the city's traditional beer, which is served in every single bar, bistro and restaurant in town. A light, refreshing brew, it is invariably served in small, narrow glasses. Since 1986, the name Kölsch has been protected by law, and can only be given to beer brewed in or near Cologne.

a massive scale, made it one of the most awe-inspiring and audacious Gothic structures ever built, and at the time of its completion in 1880, it was the tallest structure in the world (although it was superseded just 10 years later by the Eiffel Tower).

Externally, its sheer mass is relieved by the miraculous delicacy of its flying buttresses and its lace-like masonry, while internally it seems hard to believe that the towering nave is barely a quarter of the height of the soaring spires. Indeed, the best way to appreciate just how tall these spires are is to climb the 519 steps to the platform at the base of the southern steeple. On the way, you'll pass St. Peter, the largest working bell in the world. Sadly, the platform itself is covered with graffiti, but this doesn't detract from its magnificent views.

The cathedral's other highlights include its vast expanses of priceless stained glass, which if laid flat would cover the floor of the

Riverside buildings near the heart of the city

At least part of the cathedral will be covered by scaffolding when you visit

The cathedral has an incomparable collection of stained glass, some of which dates from the 13th century

cathedral twice over: the Gerokreuz (Gero Cross), a wooden crucifix dating from AD970, which is unusual for showing Christ with his eyes closed, not as a resplendent Messiah, but as a dying man; the Shrine of the Three Magi, an unimaginably ornate, jewel-encrusted sarcophagus built between 1180 and 1225 and said to contain the bones of the Three Kings; and the largest choir stalls in Germany, carved from oak at the beginning of the 14th century. More modern, but no less striking, is the vast floor mosaic in the choir and ambulatory. Made by Villeroy & Boch at the end of the 19th century, its allegorical scenes depict important events from throughout the cathedral's history.

Look for the workshop, at the southeast corner of the cathedral. Only by seeing the individual blocks of masonry on the workshop floor can you fully appreciate the scale of the walls and buttresses above. Something you can't fail to miss, however, is the scaffolding attached to various parts of the building. For first-time visitors this can be something of a disappointment, but the locals are used to the constant repair work and have a saying: 'The day the cathedral is finished will be the day of Judgement.'

RÖMISCH-GERMANISCHES MUSEUM

🏛 113 B1 • Roncalliplatz 4, 50667, Köln ☎ 0221 2212 4438
🕐 Tue–Sun 10–5 💶 Adult €5, child €3
www.museenkoeln.de/roemisch-germanisches-museum
If you are interested in ancient history, or indeed Roman art and architecture, a visit to the Roman-Germanic Museum is a must. Built in 1974 on the south side of the Dom, over the exquisite Dionysus Mosaic, it is home to the best collection of Roman ruins and everyday items on the Rhine. The mosaic itself was discovered in 1941 during the building of an air-raid shelter; it measures a remarkable 10m (33ft) by 7.5m (25ft), and is one of the best-preserved examples of its kind anywhere in the world. It takes

its name from the images of Dionysus, the Greek god of wine, who is also known as Bacchus. It is thought to have been the dining-room floor of a merchant's villa in 220–230AD.

Under the Romans, Cologne was an important area of glass production, so the museum also has a collection of glassware. The most famous items on display are the Serpentine Thread Glasses dating from the 2nd century AD, and the 4th-century Cage Cup, with its astonishingly intricate surface decoration. Equally beguiling are everyday items like jewellery and toys, which help to give everything a more human context. Exhibit captions are in English as well as German.

Nearby are the ruins of the Roman gateway at Domplatz, and the foundations of the old city walls that have been preserved in a parking area beneath the main square.

The Wallraf-Richardz-Museum: An old collection in a modern building

Tall, pastel houses near the church of Gross St. Martin

WALLRAF-RICHARTZ-MUSEUM FONDATION CORBOUD

➕ 113 B2 • Martinstrasse 39, 50667 Köln
☎ 0221 2212 1119 🕐 Tue 10–8, Wed–Fri
10–6, Sat, Sun 11–6 💶 Adult €6.50,
child €4
www.museenkoeln.de/
wallraf-richartz-museum

Founded in 1861, the Wallraf-Richartz-Museum is the oldest museum in Cologne, but its original home was destroyed in World War II. It wasn't until 2001 that it finally found a permanent home, in a purpose-built, postmodern building designed by Cologne's architect of the moment Oswald Mathias Ungers. His simple design, with its clean lines and wide, open spaces, has been a hit with architects and gallery-goers alike. The building was deliberately positioned at the heart of the Altstadt, which during the Middle Ages would have housed the workshops of the Cologne Masters, whose works form an important part of the museum's collection. Rubens and Rembrandt are also well represented, as are early 19th-century romantics like Caspar David Friedrich.

Enjoy the views from Köln's Rhineside promenade

EAU DE COLOGNE

The world's most famous fragrance was first manufactured by an Italian immigrant early in the 18th century and was originally sold for medicinal purposes, to treat everything from gout to gangrene. In 1810, however, Napoleon decreed that the formula of all medicines must be revealed for the good of the people, something which the manufacturers of the Eau Admirable were understandably keen to avoid. Their simple but ingenious solution was to re-classify it as a product 'for the care of the body'. Overnight, miracle water became toilet water, and Eau de Cologne was born.

MUSEUM LUDWIG

➕ 113 B1 • Bischofsgartenstrasse 1, 50667 Köln ☎ 0221 2212 6165 🕐 Tue–Thu 10–6, Fri 11–6 (1st Fri of each month 11–11), Sat, Sun 10–6 💶 Adult €7.50, child €5.50, audioguide €2
www.museenkoeln.de.museum-ludwig

The Ludwig Museum, with its vast underground concert hall and industrial-looking roofline, houses one of the best collections of 20th-century art in Germany. The ubiquitous Andy Warhol is much in evidence, as are German expressionists George Baselitz and Max Beckmann. There's also plenty on offer for those who prefer the early years of modern art, with the likes of Marc Chagall, Pablo Picasso and Paul Klee all getting a showing. There's little information provided about the paintings or artists, so unless you're an expert, you'd be well advised to get an audioguide. Its intimate café is popular (▷ 117).

SCHOKOLADEN MUSEUM

➕ 113 C3 • ✉ Rheinauhafen 1a, 50678 Köln ☎ 0221 931 8880 🕐 Tue–Fri 10–6, Sat, Sun, holidays 11–7 💶 Adult €6.50, child €4
www.schokoladenmuseum.de

Officially known as the Imhoff-Stollwerck-Museum, Cologne's fabulous Chocolate Museum, on the banks of the Rhine just south of the Altstadt, is a must for children of all ages. In a well-ordered sequence of exhibits, it tells the fascinating story of chocolate production, from the harvesting of cocoa beans to the making of Easter eggs, and all of the information is presented in English as well as German. At the beginning there's a lot of information to take in, but once you get to the working production line, all you have to do is look on in wonder as ingredients are mixed, heated, rolled and churned, before being moulded, cooled, wrapped and bagged. Many of the machines have cutaways so you can see what's going on inside them, and it's also possible to sample rationed amounts of liquid chocolate from a chocolate fountain.

Everything about the cathedral is massive, including this arched doorway

DEUTSCHES SPORT UND OLYMPIA MUSEUM

➕ 113 C3 • In Zollhafen 1, 50678 Köln ☎ 0221 336090 🕐 Tue–Fri 10–6, Sat, Sun 11–7 💶 Adult €5, child €2.50
www.sportmuseum.info

Right next door to the Chocolate Museum, this enthralling sports museum is the perfect opportunity to work off any calories—both real and imagined—that might have been gained while gazing at tumbling truffles. You are guided through a series of exhibition areas that follow a time-line from ancient Greece to the present day. Many of the captions are in English as well as German, and there's not so much

TIPS

● It's often a good idea to take a quick guided tour of a city just to get your bearings, and nowhere is this more true than in Cologne. The city is so full of history, and so rich in significant sites, that only a local expert can really do it justice. The same goes for the cathedral, which is crammed from top to bottom with fascinating little details. Ask at the tourist office for details.

● The best time to see the outside of the cathedral is at night, when the whole thing gives off a green, ethereal glow. It perhaps looks most striking from the footpath that crosses the railway bridge (or Hohenzollernbrücke) at the east end of the cathedral, or from the far side of the Rhine, from where you can really appreciate the intricacies of the flying buttresses that surround the ambulatory.

GERMANY

information that you feel overwhelmed. Obviously, the focus is on German sport, but this only serves to make it all the more interesting, particularly when it comes to the role sport played in the rise of the Third Reich. The Berlin Olympics of 1936 are well covered, and there is a section on Jesse Owens, all but hidden behind another display. But the highlights are the interactive exhibits: the triple-jump runway showing how far Britain's Jonathan Edwards jumped when he set a world record of 18.29m (60ft) at the 1995 Gothenburg World Championships; the wind tunnel, where you can cycle until your legs scream; and the multi-media screen, where you can watch a selection of the best goals ever scored by German soccer players (and there are some real corkers). Just don't try the standing jump too many times, or you might not be able to walk properly the next day.

BACKGROUND

Founded by the Romans in 38BC, Cologne was granted city status less than a hundred years later by Julia Agrippina, the wife of Emperor Claudius, who was born and raised here. Its importance as a Roman outpost is reflected in exquisite workmanship of the vast Dionysus Mosaic, which today forms the focus of the Römisch-Germanisches Museum, opposite the Dom (laid out well below street level, the mosaic can be glimpsed through display windows at the northwest corner of the museum). By the Middle Ages, Cologne had become the largest city in Germany, an accolade it held well into the 19th century. In 1942, the city was the target of the first Allied 1000-bomber raid, and over the next three years 90 per cent of the buildings in the Altstadt were destroyed; remarkably, the 700-year-old cathedral seemed to withstand the worst of the blasts, but it suffered structural damage that continues to plague it to this day. Following the war, the Altstadt was sympathetically restored, although the rest of Cologne seems to have been rebuilt with varying degrees of sensitivity (and success). However, its former street pattern has been preserved, a measure which has helped it to retain some of its historic feel.

The baroque Golden Chamber (above) in the church of St. Ursula

Hohe Strasse (below) is great for shopping

WHAT TO DO

⊕ SHOPPING DISTRICTS

Bearing in mind Cologne's size (it's the fourth-largest city in Germany), it has a reassuringly compact downtown area. Its three main shopping precincts are the area around Domplatz, at the northern end of the Altstadt; Hohe Strasse and its offshoots, stretching to the south of Domplatz for almost 1km (0.5 mile); and the area around Neumarkt, about 1km (0.5 mile) to the west of Hohe Strasse. Domplatz itself is dominated by glitzy designer shops, but as you head south, you'll see the more main-stream stores of Hohe Strasse, including Benetton, Gap and Zara. Neumarkt, meanwhile, is home to the Neumarkt Passage, a small, street-like mall specializing in gifts, clothes and shoes. Beyond Neumarkt, dozens of little side-street shops sell everything from fine art to furniture.

⊕ PHILHARMONIE

KölnMusik, Bischofsgartenstrasse 1
Tel 0221 204080
www.koelner-philharmonie.de
This vast, cavernous concert hall, next door to the cathedral beneath Heinrich-Böll-Platz, is home to two world-renowned orchestras: the Gürzenich Orchestra Cologne and the WDR Symphony Orchestra Cologne. It puts on more than 350 concerts a year.
⊕ Performances almost daily year-round ⊕ €12–€50 depending on concert/seat ⊕ Tram to Domplatz or Hauptbahnhof

⊕ BRASSERIE BREUGEL

Hohenzollernring 17
Tel 0221 252579
www.bruegel.de
The effortlessly cool Brasserie Breugel, just to the north of Rudolfplatz, doubles as a jazz bar from 11pm until late every night. One end of its elegantly furnished main dining area is overlooked by a lofty gallery lined with candlelit tables for two. Breugel serves up some of the country's biggest names in jazz and soul.
⊕ Mon–Fri noon–3am, Sat, Sun 6pm–3am ⊕ Starters €6–12, main courses €15–22.50 ⊕ Tram to Rudolfplatz

⊕ HOTELUX SOVIETBAR

Rathenauplatz 22
Tel 0221 241136
www.hotelux.de
This plush, bright red bar, steeped in Soviet nostalgia, serves 28 different sorts of vodka and over 40 different cocktails.
⊕ Daily 8pm–5am ⊕ Tram to Zülpicher Platz

⊕ CLAUDIUS THERME

Sachsenbergstrasse 1
Tel 0221 981440
www.claudius-therme.de
Tucked away in a corner of Cologne's restful Rheinpark, these thermal baths are an oasis of calm. The facilities here include a spa area with massage jets, neck showers and a whirlpool, plus a sauna area offering all kinds of steam rooms.
⊕ Daily 9am–midnight ⊕ €14 (€16 weekends) for 2 hours, €19.50 (€21.50 weekends) for 4 hours, €25.50 (€27.50 weekends) for day pass ⊕ Bus to Claudius Therme ⊕

EATING

CAFÉ HOLTMANN'S

Am Museum Ludwig,
Bischofsgartenstrasse 1
Tel 0221 2509 9977
www.holtmanns.com
Housed in Köln's famous Museum Ludwig, Café Holtmann's is one of the most popular and relaxing eateries in the middle of the city, and as such is worth a visit in its own right. It serves a wide range of freshly made cakes, baguettes, quiches and salads, all at surprisingly reasonable prices considering its location. The sofas lining one of the walls provide the perfect place for burying your head in a book or newspaper, and live jazz is played every Friday, Saturday and Sunday afternoon.
⊕ Tue–Sun 10–6 ⊕ Snacks/lunches €3–€10 ⊕ Bus/tram to Domplatz

PETERS BRAUHAUS

Mühlengasse 1
Tel 0221 257 3950
www.peters-brauhaus.de
Peters Brauhaus is one of the traditional taverns in the Altstadt, and it's also one of the best, thanks to its friendly service, welcoming atmosphere and excellent food. Traditional staples such as bratwurst with sauerkraut and Wiener schnitzel with potatoes are the mainstay of the menu here, and everything is invariably washed down with a few glasses of Kölsch, the city's local brew.
⊕ Daily 11am–12.30am (food served 11.30am–midnight)
⊕ L €10, D €30, Wine served by the glass only
⊕ Hauptbahnhof

STAYING

CITYCLASS HOTEL CAPRICE AM DOM

Auf dem Rothenberg 7–9, 50667 Köln
Tel 0221 920540
www.cityclass.de
Despite its rather bland exterior, the Caprice offers understated luxury in the heart of Cologne's Altstadt. All rooms are simply but stylishly fur-nished, and have gleaming bathrooms, cable TV and a well-stocked mini-bar. There's a health area with a whirl-pool, sauna and Jacuzzi.
⊕ €60–€100
⊕ 53
⊕ Sauna, whirlpool and Jacuzzi
⊕ Bus/tram to Heumarkt

DAS KLEINE STAPELHÄUSCHEN

Fischmarkt 1–3, 50667 Köln
Tel 0221 257 7862
www.koeln-altstadt.de/stapelhaeuschen
This is one of Köln's oldest and most romantic hotels. In the heart of the old town, it's full of wood-panelled walls, antique furniture and creaking floorboards. Many of the rooms have beamed ceilings, some come with enormous old baths.The friendly owners run an intimate restaurant on the first floor, serving traditional dishes, such as pork knuckle with sauerkraut and potato.
⊕ €65–€141, including breakfast
⊕ 60 beds
⊕
⊕ Bus/tram to Heumarkt

GERMANY

Munich

✦ 5 D3 ℹ Sendlinger Strasse 1, 80331, tel 089 230 0180, Mon–Fri 9–5 🚇 Marienplatz
ℹ Marienplatz, 80331, tel 089 2339 6500; Mon–Fri 10–8, Sat 10–4 🚇 Marienplatz

GETTING AROUND

- Munich has an underground/subway (U-Bahn), an overground railway (S-Bahn), trams and buses. For more details, look up www.mvv-muenchen.de.
- The CityTourCard includes a day of public transport and an attraction discount card. Cards are vaild for 1 day (€9.80) or 3 days (€18.80). For more details see www.citytourcard.com

SEEING MUNICH

Munich (München in German) is a thousand-year-old city that is extremely proud to be Bavarian. And while the traditional beer-and-*Lederhosen* image still exists, it doesn't reflect the city's world-class art galleries, Italian-designer-clad citizens and fashionable bars and restaurants. Two days is enough to get a taste of the city, but it would take you two weeks to get through all the galleries, museums, castles and other sights.

The best way to see Munich is on foot—many of the main attractions are within an area bounded by Odeonsplatz to the north, the old city gates of Isartor to the east, Sendlingertor to the south and Karlstor to the west. A good way to get your bearings is to stroll round the Old Town (Altstadt). If you have less time, take a bus tour.

The heart of the city is Marienplatz (▷ 124). Be there at 11am to see the famous *Glockenspiel* come to life. For great views, go up the tower of the Rathaus in Marienplatz, or climb the 300 steps to the top of Alter Peter, the tower of Peterskirche. This is Munich's oldest church and is between Marienplatz and the Viktualienmarkt. For the best views of the city and the surrounding area, head out to Olympiapark and take the elevator up the Olympiaturm (▷ 125) where, on a clear day, you can see as far as the Alps.

BACKGROUND

In the 10th century, monks established a settlement on the banks of the River Isar, which became known as Munichen. The city's monastic origins are still evident in Munich's coat of arms, which depicts a monk.

In 1158, Heinrich der Löwe (Henry the Lion), the Duke of Saxony, took control of Bavaria. He ensured his own power over the growing city of München by destroying his rival's toll bridge and building his own nearby.

A century later, Munich became the main residence of the Wittelsbach dynasty, and in 1505 the city became the capital of Bavaria.

From 1618 until 1648, during the Thirty Years War,

Inside the Pinakothek der Moderne (above right). A statue at Schloss Nymphenburg (right)

GERMANY

Gustav Adolph of Sweden occupied the city. The statue of the Mariensäule was erected in Marienplatz to give thanks to God because the Swedes did not destroy the city during their occupation. In fact, Munich had to pay Sweden not to destroy the city.

In the first half of the 19th century, Ludwig I commissioned the construction of many classical buildings, such as those in Königsplatz, leading to Munich's alternative name of Athens-on-the-Isar. Many of these buildings have now been turned into museums, such as the Glyptothek.

The November Revolution of 1919 led to the last Wittelsbach ruler, Ludwig III, and his family fleeing the city in the middle of

the night. Ludwig abdicated a few days later. Political unrest continued through the early 20th century, and in 1923, a young Adolf Hitler attempted to instigate a socialist revolution by storming a beer hall with armed troops. The *putsch* failed and Hitler spent the next year in prison, where he began writing *Mein Kampf (My Struggle)*.

After suffering heavy bomb damage during World War II, Munich was rebuilt and during the second half of the 20th century, it became the economic heart of Germany, with companies such as BMW and Siemens choosing the city for their headquarters.

TIPS

● Be aware that many pavements (sidewalks) have a dividing line painted down the middle, with one half designated for pedestrians and the other half for cyclists.

● Jaywalking (crossing the street without regard for traffic) is a crime in Germany and the citizens of Munich obey pedestrian crossing signals faithfully, even when there are no cars in sight. Do the same or you face prosecution.

● The easiest way to buy transport tickets is from the ticket machines at stations. Remember to validate your ticket in the machine before you start your journey.

GERMANY

Munich's Rathaus (above left).
Munich is famous for its
beer (left).
A Biergarten (below)

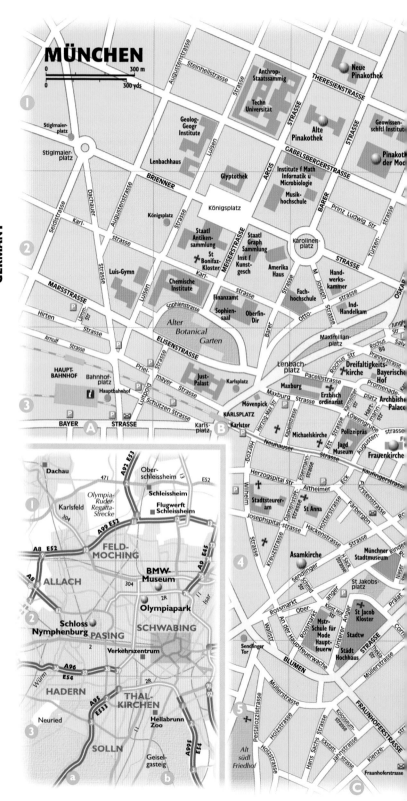

MÜNCHEN

0   300 m
0   300 yds

GERMANY

Steinheilstrasse

Augustenstrasse

THERESIENSTRASSE

Neue Pinakothek

Anthrop-Staatssammlg

Techn Universität

Geolog-Geogr Institute

Alte Pinakothek

STRASSE

Geowissen-schftl Institut

Lenbachhaus

GABELSBERGERSTRASSE

Pinakoth der Mod

Glyptothek

Institute f Math Informatik u Microbiologie

Stiglmaier-platz

Stiglmaier-platz

BRIENNER

ARCIS

Musik-hochschule

Prinz Ludwig Str

Karl-

strasse

Königsplatz

Königsplatz

BARER

Karolinen-platz

STRASSE

Seidlstrasse

Dachauer

Augustenstrasse

Luisen

MEISERSTRASSE

Staatl Antiken-sammlung

Staatl Graph Sammlung

Türken-

St Bonifaz-Kloster

Inst f Kunst-gesch

Amerika Haus

M Joseph

Hand-werks-kammer

OSKAR

Luis-Gymn

Kari-

strasse

Fach-hochschule

Ind-Handelkam

MARSSTRASSE

Chemische Institute

Finanzamt

Sophien-saal

Oberfin-Dir

Barer

Otto-

Jungfe Str

Hirten

Lämm

sophienstrasse

Alter Botanical Garten

Maximilian-platz

Rochus Str

Salv

Arnulf strasse

Strasse

ELISENSTRASSE

Lenbach-platz

Pacellistrasse

Prannerstrasse

Rochus Bg

HAUPT-BAHNHOF

Bahnhof-platz

Priel-

mayer Strasse

Just-Palast

Karlsplatz

Maxburg

Maxburg Strasse

Erzbisch ordinariat

Dreifaltigkeits-kirche

Bayerische Hof

Archbishe Palace

Promenade-platz

Hauptbahnhof

Luitpold

schützen strasse

Karls-platz

KARLSPLATZ

Mövenpick

Max Str

Löwengrube

Hart-mann-

strasse

BAYER

STRASSE

Karlstor

Karls-platz

Herzog-

Kapelien-strasse

Michaelskirche

Eisenm

Ett-

Jagd Museum

Polizeipräs

Frauenkirche

Neuhauser

Augusten-

strasse

Fr

Herzogspital Str

Eisenmann-strasse

Altheimer

ECK

Kaufingerstrasse

Wilhelm

Stadtsteurer-am

Dienerstr

St Anna

Färbergr

Fürstenfelderstrasse

Josephspital-strasse

Hackenstrasse

Kreuzstrasse

Asamkirche

Sendlinger Str

Sterk-

Str

Munchner Stadtmuseum

St Jakobs-platz

Prälat

Rossmarkt

Ober-

Kost Hof

An der Hauptfeuerwache

Rossmarkt

Mstr-Schule für Mode Haupt-feuerw

St Jacob Kloster

Stadtw

STRASSE

Sendlinger Tor

Wallstr

Unterer Anger

Städt Hochhaus

Müllerstrasse

BLUMEN

FRAUNHOFERSTRASSE

Pestalozzistrasse

Müllerstrasse

Holzstrasse

Hans Sachs Strasse

Jahnstrasse

Klenze-strasse

Fraunhoferstrasse

Alt südl Friedhof

Kolosseum-strasse

Ickstatt

Inset map

Dachau

A92 E53

Ober-schleissheim

E52

Karlsfeld

Olympia-Ruder-Regatta-Strecke

Schleissheim

Flugwerft Schleissheim

A99 E52

FELD-MOCHING

471

304

A8 E52

BMW-Museum

A9 E45

ALLACH

304

A8

2R

Olympiapark

Isar

Schloss Nymphenburg

PASING

SCHWABING

Verkehrszentrum

2

A96 E54

2R

Würm

HADERN

A95 E533

THAL-KIRCHEN

Neuried

Hellabrunn Zoo

A95 E54

SOLLN

Geisel-gasteig

a   b

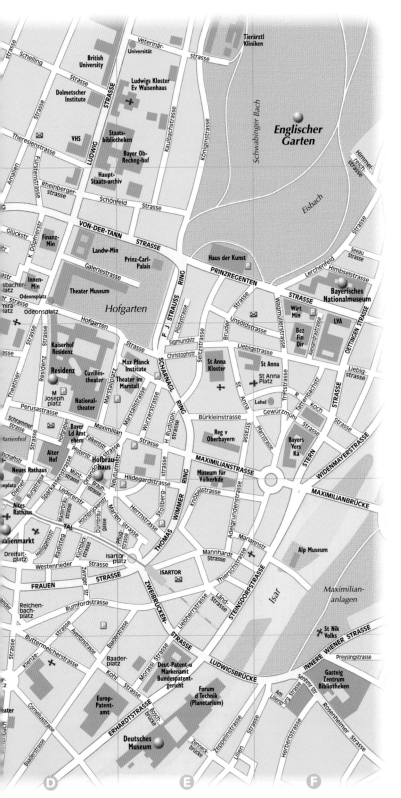

GERMANY

Strasse
Schelling
British University
Strasse
Veterinär-Universität
Tierärztl Kliniken

Dolmetscher Institute
Ludwigs Kloster Ev Waisenhaus

LUDWIG
Strasse
Kaulbachstrasse
Königinstrasse

Theresienstrasse
VHS
Staats-bibliotheken
Bayer Ob-Rechng-hof

Fürstenstrasse
Amalien
Rheinberger-strasse
Haupt-Staats-archiv
Schönfeld
Strasse

Glückstr
Finanz-Min
Odeonsplatz
Landw-Min
Prinz-Carl-Palais
Galeriestrasse
Haus der Kunst

Innen-Min
Theater Museum
Hofgarten
Hofgarten

VON-DER-TANN STRASSE
F J STRAUSS RING
PRINZREGENTEN STRASSE

Englischer Garten

Schwabinger Bach

Eisbach

Himmel-reich-strasse

Seeau strasse
Lerchenfeld
Himbselstrasse

Bayerisches Nationalmuseum

Wirt Min
LVA
OETTINGEN STRASSE

Kaiserhof Residenz
Residenz
Joseph platz
Cuvilliés-theater
National-theater
Max Planck Institute
Theater im Marstall

Theatiner
Residenz
Perusastrasse
Marstallplatz
SCHARNAGL RING
Wurzerstrasse

Schrammer Strasse
Marienhof
Bayer Ld Amt ehem
Maximilian
Alter Hof
Hofbräu haus
Neues Rathaus
Altes Rathaus

Unsöldstrasse
Bruder
Liebigstrasse
St Anna Kloster
St Anna
St Anna Platz
Liebig-strasse

Sigmundstr
Christophstr
Seitzstrasse
St Anna
Lehel
Gewürzmühl
Triftstrasse
Tattenbachstr
Koch
STERN
WIDENMAYERSTRASSE

Bürkleinstrasse
Reg v Oberbayern
Bayers Vers Ka

Falkenturm
Pfisterstr
MAXIMILIANSTRASSE

Dienerstr
Burgstrasse
Sparkassenstrasse
Ledererstr
Maderbräustrasse
Hochbrückenstrasse
Sparkassenstrasse
Minz-strasse
Orlandostr
Brau-strasse

Hildegardstrasse
Museum für Völkerkde
MAXIMILIANBRÜCKE

TAL
Heiliggeiststr
Radlsteg
Klosterbäckergässchen
Dumbtsgässle
Gries
Marien Strasse
Hermstrasse
Knöbelstrasse
Adelgrundenstrasse
MAXIMILIAN RING
THOMAS WIMMER RING
Stollbergstrasse

Dreifalt-platz
Alienmarkt
Isartor platz
Westenrieder Strasse
ISARTOR
Mannhardt Strasse
Marlannstr
Thierschstrasse
STEINSDORFSTRASSE

Alp Museum

Maximilian-anlagen

FRAUEN Str
STRASSE
Reichen-bach-platz
Zwinger Str
ZWEIBRÜCKEN-STRASSE
Rumfordstrasse
Liebherrstrasse
Länd-Strasse
Isar

Buttermelcherstrasse
Baaderstrasse
Aventinstrasse
Baader-platz
Baader-strasse
Kohl Strasse
Morassi Strasse
Kienze
Conneliusstrasse
Europ-Patent-amt
ERHARDTSTRASSE
Deut-Patent-u Markenamt Bundespatent-gericht
Forum d Technik (Planetarium)
LUDWIGSBRÜCKE
Deutsches Museum
Zenneck-brücke
Zeppelinstrasse
Lilien

St Nik Volks
INNERE WIENER STRASSE
Preysingstrasse
Gasteig Zentrum Bibliotheken
Rosenheimer Strasse
Herbertstrasse
Sanhm str
Am Lilien

D   E   F

Munich

There is more to Munich than beer, sausages and *Lederhosen*. The Bavarian
capital manages to be both traditional and cosmopolitan, with historic palaces,
parks and churches, as well as world-class museums, upmarket shops
and restaurants.

*The façade of the Alte
Pinakothek*

Aircraft on display in the Deutsches Museum

RATINGS	
Historic interest	●●●●●
Shopping	●●●●●
Photo stops	●●●●○
Value for money	●●●○○

An early Mercedes Benz

HIGHLIGHTS

ALTE PINAKOTHEK

✚ 120 C1 • Barerstrasse 27, 80333 München ☎ 089 2380 5216 🕐 Wed–Sun
10–6, Tue 10–8; closed Shrove Tue, May 1, Dec 24, 25, 31 🎫 Adult €5.50, child €4;
Sun all visitors €1
www.pinakothek.de

The Alte Pinakothek is a magnificent gallery, with paintings by
European artists from the 14th to the 18th centuries. The collection
is of the same high quality as the Louvre in Paris or the Uffizi in
Florence, but unlike those galleries, it is a manageable size and it is
possible to see everything in one visit. The gallery houses the world's
finest collection of paintings by the Flemish painter Peter Paul
Rubens (1577–1640), while Renaissance masters such as Raphael
(1483–1520), Titian (1488–1576), Leonardo da Vinci (1452–1519)
and Sandro Botticelli (1445–1510) are all well represented. Many of
the works in the Alte Pinakothek used to be in a much smaller gallery
in the Residenz, but when the collection outgrew it, Ludwig I commissioned architect Leo von Klenze to design a new building to hold the
collection. The gallery, which took 10 years to construct, was designed
in the style of a Venetian Renaissance palace and was finished in
1836. The building itself was so well received that other galleries in
Europe have used it as a model.

DEUTSCHES MUSEUM

✚ 121 E5 • Museuminsel 1, 80538 München ☎ 089 21791 🕐 Daily 9–5; closed 1
Jan, Fasching Tuesday (usually last Tue in Feb), Good Friday, 1 May, 1 Nov, 24, 25
and 31 Dec; closes at 1pm on 2nd Wed in Dec 🎫 Adult €8.50, child €3, under 6
free, family €15; Tower lift €2. Planetarium €2. Combined ticket for Deutsches
Museum, Flugwerft Schleissheim, Verkehrszentrum and shuttle bus to
Verkehrszentrum €15
www.deutsches-museum.de

The museum was founded in 1903 by the engineer Oskar
von Miller. The collection moved to its present home in
1925. Since then, the number of exhibits has topped
18,000. This is Germany's most visited attraction and one
of the largest science and technology museums in the
world, but you don't need to be a science buff or have any

specialist knowledge to appreciate the cars, planes, helicopters, model railway or re-creation of a mine, to name just a few of the thousands of exhibits. The museum is in the heart of the city, on an island on the Isar, and is accessible from either side of the river.

The Deutsches Museum also has two other museums—the Verkehrszentrum (Theresienhöhe 14a, 80339 Munich) and Flugwerft Schleissheim (Effnerstrasse 18, 85764, Oberschleissheim). The Verkehrszentrum is a transport museum designed from a 21st-century point of view, and it contains every kind of car and bicycle imaginable, as well as buses and steam locomotives. The Flugweft site is on an old airfield at Schleissheim, 13km (8 miles) from downtown Munich, and was originally built for the Bavarian Royal Flying Corps. There are helicopters (including one used by the police), gliders, planes, including a MiG fighter jet, and even a rocket.

ENGLISCHER GARTEN

✚ 121 F1 • Stretching from Prinzregentenstrasse in the south to the outskirts of the city in the north ☎ 089 3866 6390 ◷ Daily dawn to dusk ✍ Free
At 5km (3 miles) long and a kilometre (0.6 miles) wide, the Englischer Garten is more to the people of Munich than just a large park. Often referred to as 'the lungs of Munich', the English Garden is a place to relax and Münchners flock here on weekends and sunny days. Prince Elector Karl Theodor commissioned the park, which had been the hunting grounds of the Wittelsbach dynasty, in the 18th century. The design was unusual for its time; it broke away from the fashion for more formal, manicured gardens and was instead an open, natural-looking Volksgarten (People's Park), evident in the fields, woodland, lake, rivers and many kilometres of footpaths.

With such large open spaces, the park is ideal for a range of activities, such as bicycling, jogging, playing soccer, having a picnic, feeding the ducks and boating or paddling in the lake. Some paths are suitable for pushchairs (strollers) and there are playgrounds, making this a great place for children. Most of the attractions are in the section south of the main road—the Isar Ring. Here is the Kleinhesseloher See, where you can rent a boat, or enjoy a beer or a meal at the Seehaus restaurant, where brass bands play and there's a festival atmosphere. If you follow the Eisbach creek south, you'll come to the Chinesischer Turm (Chinese Pagoda), where there's a 7,000-seat beer garden. At the far south of the garden is the Japanese Tea House, a gift to the city of Munich from Japan for the 1972 Olympic Games.

Cycling in the Englischer Garten

MORE TO SEE
ASAMKIRCHE
✚ 120 C4 • Sendlinger Strasse 62, 80331 München ◷ Daily 8–5.30 ✍ Free
The narrow (9m/29.5ft) façade of this church gives little hint of the magnificence inside. Before you go in, notice the unhewn rock on either side of the columns and, above the door, the statue of St. John Nepomuk, who gave the church its official name. The church is commonly known as Asamkirche after the Asam brothers who designed, built and decorated it between 1733 and 1746. The brothers' efforts have resulted in a lavish rococo interior with sculptures of angels and gold leaf.

BAYERISCHES NATIONAL MUSEUM
✚ 121 F2 • Prinzregentenstrasse 3, 80538 München ☎ 089 211 2401 ◷ Tue, Wed, Fri–Sun 10–5, Thu 10–8 ✍ Adult €5, under 18 free, Sun free
www.bayerisches-nationalmuseum.de
The Bavarian National Museum is an art and cultural history museum with collections of arts and crafts from Bavaria and farther afield. Pick up a plan of the museum, available in English. This is invaluable, as the museum has large collections spread over three floors. These include musical instruments, porcelain, suits of armour, traditional clothes, furniture, baroque and rococo tapestries, Gothic sculpture and paintings from the 13th century through to art nouveau.

GERMANY

BMW-MUSEUM

⊞ 120 b2 (inset) • Am Spiridon-Louis-Ring, Parkdeck, 80809 München
☎ 089 3822 3307 ⊙ Reopening in 2009 after renovation work 🚻 Adult €2, child €1.50
www.bmw.com

Within walking distance of the Olympiapark, this unusual building, shaped like four cylinders and designed by Karl Schwanzer in 1970, is the headquarters of BMW. The windowless silver building shaped like a bowl next to it is the BMW Museum, the most popular company museum in the country. The 'Time Horizons' exhibition traces the company's history and technological developments. There are plenty of shining models to admire, including rare and new sports cars and motorcycles.

FRAUENKIRCHE

⊞ 120 C3 • Frauenplatz 12, 80331 Munich ☎ 089 290 0820

The enduring image of Munich is the Italian Renaissance onion domes of the twin towers (100m/330ft high) of the city's cathedral, the Frauenkirche. The church was built between 1468 and 1488, although what you see today was rebuilt after the church was reduced to rubble in World War II. The distinctive green onion domes were originally only added to the towers in 1524 as a temporary measure, but proved so popular that they became a permanent feature. You can climb the south tower of the cathedral (Apr–end Oct Mon–Sat 10–5) for wonderful views of the city.

HOFBRÄUHAUS

⊞ 121 D3 • Platzl 9, 80331 München ⊙ Daily 9am–midnight
www.hofbraeuhaus.de

If you're looking for traditional dirndl-clad waitresses serving frothy steins of beer and thigh-

MARIENPLATZ

⊞ 121 D3

If the Englischer Garten represents the lungs of Munich, then Marienplatz is surely its heart. The square has many purposes, not least as a central point where Münchners meet up with their friends, but is also the place where citizens converge to hold political demonstrations. Many years ago, public executions took place here. Today the place has a lively buzz about it, with visitors taking photos of the City Hall and the famous Glockenspiel, locals sitting outside enjoying a beer in summer and, in December, the traditional Christmas market.

Marienplatz takes its name from the Mariensäule, the golden figure of the Virgin Mary on a column, 11m (36ft) high, in the middle of the square. It was created by Hubert Gerhart and was erected in Marienplatz at the request of Elector Maximilian in 1638. It marks the saving of the city during the period of Swedish occupation in the Thirty Years War. The 19th-century Neues Rathaus (New City Hall) dominates the square. On the front of the main tower is the Glockenspiel. Get here at 11, noon or 5 to see the brightly painted figures move and chime. At the east side of the square is the Altes Rathaus (Old City Hall). It dates from the 15th century and contains the Spielzeug-Museum (Toy Museum), which has collections of teddy bears, dolls, doll's houses and model railways.

Marienplatz as seen from the Rathaus

Der Olymp by Jenssens, in the Neue Pinakothek

NEUE PINAKOTHEK

⊞ 120 C1 • Barerstrasse 29, 80799 München (Schwabing) ☎ 089 2380 5195
⊙ Thu–Mon 10–6, Wed 10–8; closed Tue, Dec 24, 25, 31, Shrove Tue, 1 May
🚻 Adult €5.50, child €3.50; Sun free; day ticket for all three Pinakothek galleries adult €12, child €7
www.neue-pinakothek.de

The Neue Pinakothek is in a glass, granite and concrete building designed by Munich architect Alexander von Branca, and is sometimes referred to as Palazzo Branca. It contains hundreds of European paintings and sculptures from the late 18th to the early 20th centuries, focusing on the development of German art. There are particularly fine collections of 19th-century German art, landscapes by French, English and Spanish painters and a sizeable French Impressionism section. Throughout the gallery are sculptures, including works by Auguste Rodin, Edgar Degas and Pablo Picasso.

OLYMPIAPARK

⊞ 120 b2 (inset) • Spiridon-Louis-Ring, München ☎ 089 3067 2414; information hotline 0180 530 6730 ⊙ Stadium: mid-Apr to mid-Oct daily 8.30–8.30; mid-Oct to mid-Apr daily 9–4.30. Tower: daily 9am–midnight
🚻 Entrance to the site free. Stadium: adult €2, child €1. Tower: adult €2, child €2.50
www.olympiapark-muenchen.de

When it was announced that the 1972 Olympic Games were to be held in Munich, the city set about building a comprehensive set of sports facilities on the site of the old airport. The site, which you can tour on the park train in the summer, is known for its unusual and expensive roof, which looks like a spider's web. It covers the Olympic Hall, where rock and pop concerts are held, the Olympic swimming pool and the stadium. Other facilities include the ice rink, gym and spa complex, which are all open to the public. If you prefer spending time outside, you can walk around the artificial lake, the Olympiasee, or climb 53m (174 ft) up the man-made hill, made of rubble from World War II.

Built between 1965 and 1968, and standing 290m (951ft) high, the Olympic tower is now as much part of the Munich skyline as the twin onion domes of the Frauenkirche. You whizz up to the top in a matter of seconds in the high speed lift (elevator), and it is certainly worth the trip as, on a clear day, you can see as far as the Alps. When you get to the top, make sure you go outside for unimpeded views over the whole city and fantastic photo opportunities.

RESIDENZ

✚ 121 D3 • Residenzstrasse/Max-Joseph-Platz 3 ☎ 29 06 71 ⏱ Apr–end Oct daily 9–6; Nov–end Mar daily 10–5 💶 Adult €6
www.residenz-muenchen.de
The Munich Residenz, the largest building in Munich's Altstadt, was the residence of the dukes and kings of Bavaria for more than 400 years, from the beginning of the 16th century to the early 20th century. The complex includes the Antiquarium (a large Renaissance Hall), a rococo theatre, Royal Apartments in the Königsbau (Royal Palace), museums and the Treasury, filled with priceless jewels, crowns, chains and ornaments.

slapping oompah-band music, this beer hall is the place to go The Hofbräuhaus is one of the world's most famous pubs.

The brewery was founded in 1589 when Wilhelm V wanted a dark beer to drink at court. The beer remained unavailable to the public until the brewery became an inn in 1828.

PINAKOTHEK DER MODERNE

✚ 120 C1 • Barerstrasse 40, 80333 München ☎ 089 2380 5360
⏱ Tue–Wed, Sat–Sun 10–6, Thu 10–8; closed Shrove Tue, 1 May, 24, 25, 31 Dec 💶 Adult €9, child €5; free to all on Sun; day ticket for all three Pinakothek galleries adult €12, child €7
www.pinakothek-der-moderne.de
The Pinakothek der Moderne, which opened in 2002, brings

The Antiquarium in the Residenz   *Schloss Nymphenburg*

The Residenz was built as a small castle and was begun in 1385. The Wittelsbach dynasty, which ruled Bavaria for nearly 800 years, added to the original building over the years until it became the palace, with more than 130 rooms, that exists today. The complex is built around seven courtyards, filled with valuable paintings and sculptures, furniture, clocks, tapestries, porcelain and sacred vestments.

Decide before you arrive what you would like to see. In the Residenz itself, about half the rooms are open to the public in the morning, then closed in the afternoon, when the rest of the rooms are open. This means that to see all the rooms you will have to visit before and after lunch or go straight through at the changeover time (12.30 in winter and 1.30 in the summer).

SCHLOSS NYMPHENBURG

✚ 120 a2 (inset) • Schloss Nymphenburg, 80638 München ☎ 089 179080
⏱ Apr–end Sep daily 9–6, Oct–end Mar daily 10–4; closed 1 Jan, Shrove Tue, 24, 25, 31 Dec; Pagodenburg, Badenburg and Magdalenenburg closed mid-Oct to end Mar 💶 Palace only: adult €5; Marstallmuseum (Carriage Museum) and Porcelain Museum: adult €4; Amalienburg only: adult €2; combined ticket for palace, carriage museum and porcelain museum: adult €10. Child (under 18) free
This baroque castle, 15 minutes from downtown Munich by tram, was used by the kings of Bavaria as a summer residence. There is plenty here to fill a day, including the palace rooms, three museums and landscaped parkland with four pavilions, each of which merit a visit. Between 1664 and 1757, five rulers from the Wittelsbach family—Ferdinand Maria, Max Emanuel, Karl Albrecht, Max III Joseph and Max IV Joseph—contributed to the construction of the baroque palace and gardens at Nymphenburg. The Palace was begun by Elector Ferdinand Maria (ruled 1651–1679) in 1664 to celebrate the birth of his son and heir Max Emanuel, who himself added to the building.

Munich's art collection right into the 21st century. The gallery's collection of 20th- and 21st-century art and sculpture, architecture, design and works on paper is displayed in a modern building designed by Stephan Braunfels. When you enter the building on the ground floor (Level 2), pick up an orientation guide.

VIKTUALIENMARKT

✚ 121 D4 • By Peterskirche near Marienplatz ⏱ Mon–Fri 7–6, Sat 7–4, closed Sun
The Viktualienmarkt (with a Latin derivation meaning 'food market') is the city's produce market. It used to be in Marienplatz but moved to its present site by Peterskirche 200 years ago. Anything and everything you could want to eat is here: Fruit, vegetables, fish, meat, cheese, honey, bread, cakes and wine are just some of the produce on sale. There are also plenty of non-German items, including Italian cheeses and French wines.

WHAT TO DO

🛍 7 HIMMEL

Hans-Sach-Strasse 17 (Isarvorstadt)
Tel 089 267053
www.siebterhimmel.com
Siebter Himmel (Seventh Heaven) is a women's clothing store with bright, funky, individual clothes at reasonable prices. Across the street is Schuhhimmel (Shoe Heaven).
🕐 Mon–Fri 11–7, Sat 10–6
🚇 Sendlinger Tor

🛍 DALLMAYR

Dienerstrasse 14–15 (Altstadt)
Tel 089 213 5130
www.dallmayr.de
This traditional high-quality Munich delicatessen is rather like Harrods' food halls in London. Separate counters sell such delicacies as beautifully decorated cakes, cold meats and sausages, chocolate, tea leaves, coffee beans and fruit. There is also a cigar shop and a small champagne bar.
🕐 Mon–Fri 9.30–7, Sat 9.30–4
🚇 Marienplatz 🚊 Marienplatz

🛍 GALERIA KAUFHOF

Kaufingerstrasse 1–5 (Marienplatz)
Tel 089 231851
www.galeria-kaufhof.de
Kaufhof is a well-known Munich department store (with branches in Marienplatz, Karlsplatz and Rotkreuzplatz), and is not as expensive as the more classy Ludwig Beck and Loden Frey. It has several floors with menswear, womenswear, a perfumery, books, stationery and food. As with Kaufhof's rival department store Karstadt, head to the basement for the best bargains.
🕐 Mon–Sat 9–8 🚇 Marienplatz
🚊 Marienplatz

🛍 MAX KRUG

Neuhauserstrasse 2 (Altstadt)
Tel 089 224501
www.max-krug.com
Lined from floor to ceiling with beer steins, musical boxes, toys, Christmas decorations and wooden cuckoo clocks, hand-made in Bavaria's Black Forest, this is the shop for you if you're looking for a cute Bavarian gift. Buying larger items is made easier as they accept credit cards, there's tax-free shopping for non-EU visitors and they can send purchases home for you.
🕐 Mon–Sat 9.30–8 🚇 Karlsplatz Stachus, Marienplatz 🚊 Karlsplatz Stachus, Marienplatz

🎭 DEUTSCHES THEATER

Schwanthalerstrasse 13 (Hauptbahnhof)
Tel 089 5523 4444
www.deutsches-theater.de
The Deutsches Theater hosts ballet performances, musicals and revues, and during Fasching there are many fancy-dress balls and events held here.
🕐 Box office Mon–Fri 12–7, Sat 10.30am–1.30pm 💶 €19–€69
🚇 Karlsplatz 🚊 Karlsplatz 🔲

🎭 GASTEIG

Rosenheimerstrasse 5 (Haidhausen)
Tel 089 5481 8181
www.gasteig.de
www.mphil.de
The huge Gasteig complex is the home of the Munich Philharmonic Orchestra and it also plays host to visiting orchestras such as the English Chamber Orchestra and the London Philharmonic Orchestra. Many other different kinds of performances are also held here, from the Chinese State Circus to Frank Sinatra tributes, The Phantom of the Opera and jazz.
🕐 Box office Mon–Fri 9–8, Sat 10–4
💶 Varies 🚊 Tram 18 to Am Gasteig; tram 15, 25 to Rosenheimerplatz
🚊 Rosenheimerplatz

🎭 NATIONALTHEATER

Max-Joseph-Platz 1 (Altstadt)
Tel 089 2185 1920
www.staatstheater.bayern.de
www.staatsoper.de
The Nationaltheater, in a building reminiscent of a Greek temple in Max-Joseph-Platz, is home to the Bavarian State Opera and stages performances of Verdi, Wagner and Strauss during the opera season. You can watch a performance or join a tour, which takes in the foyer, the plush auditorium with its large chandelier and the machinery, essential for today's high-tech productions.
🕐 Box office: Mon–Fri 10–6, Sat 10–1. Tours: 2pm 💶 €6–240
🚇 Marienplatz, Odeonsplatz
🚌 Bus 52 to Marienplatz; bus 53 to Odeonsplatz; tram 19 to Nationaltheater
🚊 Marienplatz

▽ CHINESISCHER TURM

Englischer Garten (Schwabing)
Tel 089 3838 730
www.chinaturm.de
You can't beat the setting of this beer garden at the Chinese Tower in the Englischer Garten, where there are plenty of people and there's always a good atmosphere, even in winter. It can seat up to 7,000 people at its trestle tables, and there are food stalls and children's playparks.
🕐 Daily 10am–11pm 🚌 Bus 54, 154

▽ MUFFATHALLE

Zellstrasse 4 (Haidhausen)
Tel 089 4587 5010
www.muffathalle.de
This cultural venue on the other side of the Isar hosts a constantly changing line-up of gigs. There are also club nights on Thursdays, Fridays and Saturdays, with DJs playing reggae, rare groove, funk, Latin, drum and bass, and hip-hop. See the website for what's on. Muffathalle also has a café and a beer garden selling organic beer.
🕐 Beer garden: Mon–Fri 4pm–1am, Sat–Sun noon–1am. Clubs from 7pm
💶 Varies 🚊 Tram 18 to Gasteig

▽ NEKTAR

Stubenvollstrasse 1 (Haidhausen)
Tel 089 4591 1311
www.nektar.de
An evening in Nektar is a unique experience, starting with the slippers you are given to wear to your dinner, which you eat horizontally, lying down on cushions. Expect films, cabaret and live music.
🕐 Sun–Thu 7pm–2am, Fri–Sat 7pm–3am 🚊 Tram 15, 25 to Rosenheimerplatz
🚊 Rosenheimerplatz

SANTA MARGARITA SCHÖNHEITSSALON

Reichenbachstrasse 24 (Glockenbach)
Tel 089 201 0961
www.santa-margarita.de
This salon uses Aveda and Vagheggi products for facials and different types of massage, including the Aveda mood massage.
🕐 Mon 8.30–4, Tue 11–7, Wed 10–6, Thu–Fri 11–9, Sat 9.30–6 💶 1-hour body massage €74; 1-hour Aveda mood massage €68; pedicure €60
🚇 Fraunhoferstrasse

EATING

AUGUSTINER

Neuhauserstrasse 27 (Altstadt)
Tel 089 2318 3257
www.augustiner-restaurant.com
This beer hall and restaurant belongs to the Augustiner brewery and dates from the 14th century. Here 200 members of staff cater for up to 1,500 people. Try Bavarian top-sellers such as suckling pig roasted in dark beer and served with dumplings, meatloaf, boiled beef with potato salad or sausages. Vegetarians, steer clear!
🕐 Beerhall: Daily 9am–midnight. Restaurant: Daily 10am–midnight
💶 L €17, D €21, Wine €12
🚇 Karlsplatz, Marienplatz
🚋 Karlsplatz, Marienplatz

CAFÉ AM BEETHOVENPLATZ

Goethestrasse 51 (Hauptbahnhof)
Tel 089 5440 4348
It's hard to describe this café, which dates from 1899. With its high-ceilinged rooms and chandeliers, it's like a Viennese coffeehouse during the day, while at night it becomes a restaurant serving international food. It's also a music bar, with classical, jazz or blues bands playing live almost every night.
🕐 Daily 9am–1am
💶 L €7.50, D €15, Wine €13
🚇 Goetheplatz

HOFBRÄUHAUS

Platzl 9 (Altstadt)
Tel 089 2901 3610
www.hofbraeuhaus.de
You're more likely to come here for the beer, atmosphere, singing and oompah bands than for the cuisine. However, it's always good to have something hearty to eat with your beer, so you can order a sausage with your next drink.
🕐 Daily 9am–midnight
💶 L €10, D €14, Wine €13.30
🚇 Marienplatz
🚋 Marienplatz

PFISTERMÜHLE

Pfisterstrasse 4 (Altstadt)
Tel 089 2370 3865
www.platzl.de
Pfistermühle is an elegant restaurant in a historic setting—it's in the vaults of a 16th-century former mill, right in the heart of town near Marienplatz and the Hofbräuhaus. The food is high-quality Bavarian fare, and there's an excellent selection of wines, as well as draught beer from the Aying family brewery (the Aying family owns this restaurant, the brewery and the beautiful Platzl Hotel nearby). In summer, dine outside in the little beer garden.
🕐 Mon–Sat 11.30am–midnight (kitchen 12–11)
💶 L €18, D €25, Wine €20
🚇 Marienplatz
🚋 Marienplatz

STAYING

ADMIRAL

Kohlstrasse 9, 80469 München (Isarvorstadt)
Tel 089 216350
www.hotel-admiral.de
The rooms in this four-star hotel, close to the River Isar and the Deutsches Museum, are extremely comfortable. All rooms also have internet access, a television, telephone, desk and hairdryer.
💶 €200, breakfast included
🛏 33 (8 non-smoking)
🅿 Parking spaces for €12 per day, public parking area nearby
🚇 Fraunhoferstrasse

HOTEL BAYERISCHER HOF

Promenadeplatz 2–6, 80333 München (Altstadt)
Tel 089 21200
www.bayerischerhof.de
The Volkhardt family has run this five-star hotel since 1897. You're in absolute luxury here and could enjoy a day without even leaving the building, as there are three restaurants, several bars, designer boutiques, a beauty and hair salon, a rooftop pool, a sauna and steam bath, a gym and a sun terrace. Rooms have 21st-century technology in the form of internet access and even PlayStations.
💶 €513–€740
🛏 337 rooms and 58 suites (half non-smoking)
🍴
🅿
🌡 🏊 Outdoor 🚭
🚇 Karlsplatz, Marienplatz
🚋 Tram 19

HOTEL GÄSTEHAUS ENGLISCHER GARTEN

Liebergesellstrasse 8, 80802 München (Schwabing)
Tel 089 383 9410
www.hotelenglishgarden.de
It would be difficult to find a place to stay with more charm than this 200-year-old converted watermill right by the Englischer Garten. There are only 12 rooms (six with bathroom and six without), so you'll need to book early. For families, there are 17 furnished apartments in a more modern building opposite.
💶 €71–€180, excluding breakfast (€9.50)
🛏 12 rooms, 17 apartments
🚇 Münchner Freiheit

PENSION GEIGER

Steinheilstrasse 1, 80333 München (Maxvorstadt)
Tel 089 521556
www.pensiongeiger.de
This bright but basic pension is close to the Pinakothek galleries. There are rooms with or without a shower, and rooms with three beds. Only six rooms have a television, so if you would like one in your room, request it when you make your reservation. Credit cards are not accepted.
💶 €60–€76, breakfast included
🛏 17
🚇 Theresienstrasse

ARRIVING

BY AIR

Although Berlin has regained its status as Germany's capital city, the country's largest and most important airport is not here but in Frankfurt. As West Germany's financial hub, centrally located Frankfurt was the logical place to develop a major international airport. It is here that the national airline, Lufthansa, has its base, and it is here that the majority of international flights arrive and depart, connecting with services to and from all major German cities.

Berlin is served not by a single airport, but by three, a reflection of the city's divided past. A pre-war, inner-city airport, Tempelhof, is used mostly by smaller airlines and charter flights. Schönefeld was built by the Communist regime to serve East Berlin and much of the GDR, and is some distance away from the middle of the city on its southeastern outskirts. It is used by a number of international carriers, including budget airlines and charter flights. Most international carriers land at Tegel, the modern airport built in the western suburbs to serve West Berlin.

Elsewhere in Germany, a number of cities are served by international airlines, notably Munich and Düsseldorf, but also Cologne/Bonn, Hannover, Hamburg, Leipzig/Halle and Dresden. Budget airlines have exploited the low charges of smaller airports such as Erfurt, Friedrichshafen (for Lake Constance), Hahn (for Frankfurt), Niederrrhein and Lübeck (for Hamburg).

BY FERRY

The only direct car and passenger ferry service from Britain to Germany is operated by DFDS Seaways (tel 0871 522 9955 from the UK; www.dfds.co.uk) between Harwich and the port town of Cuxhaven at the mouth of the River Elbe. The well-equipped boat sails on alternate days and the crossing takes 20 hours. Cuxhaven has a direct connection to the autobahn network and is 120km (75 miles) by main road from Hamburg. A bus to and from Hamburg connects with the ferry's arrival and departure.

Scandlines (tel 0381 54 350 from Germany; www.scandlines.de) run services linking the Baltic Coast towns.

BY TRAIN

International trains connect most European countries to the German rail network. There is no direct link from Britain, but Eurostar services (tel 08705 186 186 from the UK; www.eurostar .com) through the Channel Tunnel connect in Brussels with the high-speed Thalys service (www.thalys.com) to Cologne or Amsterdam, making this route an attractive alternative to air travel. From Cologne there are good connections to all major German cities. An early evening train from London connects at Brussels with a DB Nachtzug sleeper train to a number of German cities, including Berlin and Hamburg. Eurostar trains depart from London St. Pancras. Check-in at St. Pancras is 30 minutes before departure, and you are allowed two suitcases and one item of hand luggage, all of which must be labelled with your name, address and seat number. You should not change your seat during the journey. Passports are

required. Return (round-trip) ticket prices London–Cologne are from around £200, and the journey time is 4.5 hours.

BY CAR

To take your own car to Germany you will need a valid driving licence. Your home licence is normally sufficient if you are from other European countries or the US, but bring an international permit if you have one. Residents of countries other than these will need an international permit and the car registration document. Vehicles must be insured and display a sign at the rear indicating the country of origin.

Germany is connected to its neighbours by a dense network of motorways and main and minor roads. Frontier installations with EU countries have been progressively dismantled and controls relaxed, so border hold-ups are few. The most popular route for motorists driving from Britain begins with the Channel Tunnel or the short sea crossing from Dover to Calais. At Calais, you join the European motorway network. The E40 leads through Belgium to Aachen, Cologne and beyond, while the E42 and E25 lead through Belgium and Luxembourg to the central Rhineland and the southwest of the country.

VISITORS WITH A DISABILITY

Compared with many other countries, Germany is well equipped to receive visitors with a disability, particularly in terms of public transport and access to buildings. All modern facilities are designed to allow wheelchair access and many (but not all) older buildings have been suitably adapted. A wealth of information is available from a variety of sources to help visitors plan their trip and move easily around the country.

Useful Organizations:
Mobility International USA
www.miusa.org

Bundesarbeitsgemeinschaft der Clubs Behinderter und ihrer Freunde e.V.
www.bagcbf.de

GETTING AROUND

BY CAR

The quality of the German road network makes driving an excellent way to explore the country. Although constant driving at high speed can be tiring, the autobahn makes it possible to cover long distances in a short time, enabling you to move easily from one area of interest to another. A car is the best way of getting around if you aim to explore smaller towns and villages and the countryside. If your interest is confined to a city or group of cities, public transport will almost certainly be your better option.

With a total length approaching 12,000km (7,500 miles), the autobahn network connects all major cities and towns. Many places are linked to the system by more than one interchange, and it is sensible to check the map to see which exit suits you best. Interchanges are numbered. Signs show the distance between service areas, which are generally closely spaced. In addition, there are rest areas with basic facilities, plus picnic areas, particularly on scenic stretches. Service areas vary in their provision of facilities; some have hotels, and all have refreshments and well-maintained toilets. Vehicles joining the autobahn must give way to traffic already on it. Keep to the right-hand lane except when overtaking, and indicate your intention before you change lanes. Emergency telephones are placed at regular intervals, their location indicated by arrows.

BY TRAIN

Germany has a comprehensive rail network totalling some 42,000km (27,000 miles) of track linking all places of any size. Overall control is exercised by Deutsche Bahn (German Rail), which has several operating arms. There has been heavy public investment in the rail system over many years and services generally are of a very high standard. The efficiency and near-complete cover of the system, combined with the availability of a range of special tickets, make travel by rail a very attractive option for a holiday in Germany. Nearly all trains have separate smoking coaches or compartments, and first- and second-class accommodation, and many also have toilets for people with a disability.

Types of Train

● InterCityExpress (ICE) are state-of-the-art trains that run at speeds up to 319kph (198mph). The latest has a first-class lounge giving passengers a spectacular driver's-eye view of the track.
● Metropolitan (MET) is a prestige train linking Hamburg with Essen, Düsseldorf and Cologne. There is a choice of three seating zones: 'Office', with fax, etc.; 'Silence', which is mobile- and computer-free; and 'Club', with DVD facilities, etc.
● InterCity (IC) trains are only marginally less luxurious and swift than ICE trains, and link major cities and towns across the country. They are air-conditioned and have a restaurant or bistro.
● InterRegio Express (IRE) fast trains connect regional hubs with the national network. They have buffet or bistro facilities or a refreshment trolley.
● StädteExpress (SE) are fast, limited-stop local trains, often with double-decker coaches.
● RegionalBahn (RB) local trains are usually diesel-powered and stop at all stations.
● S-Bahn trains are the suburban trains in large cities and the Ruhr conurbation.

Overnight Services

● DB Nachtzug (NZ) are domestic and international night trains with modern sleepers, couchettes or reclining seats.
● CityNightLine (CNL) has luxury cabin, standard and couchette accommodation on services between German cities and to Austria and Switzerland.
● DB AutoZug carries cars on double-decker wagons while passengers sit in coaches or stay overnight in sleeping accommodation. These trains link major German cities with popular summer and winter destinations in Germany and abroad.

BY LONG-DISTANCE BUS

The comprehensive extent of the German rail system means that the country has an under-developed long-distance bus network, certainly compared with other countries. Local and regional bus services are operated by municipalities, an array of private companies and by Deutsche Bahn. Many bus routes make connections with rail services, and through ticketing may be available. Tickets can be obtained from bus offices and from the driver.

BY TAXI

Universally identifiable by their cream hue, German taxis are available at stands in all towns and cities or can be ordered by phone. There are stands at rail stations, public transport interchanges, airports and key downtown locations. It may not be easy to hail a taxi on the street. Licensing is carefully administered, and most taxis are vehicles of a high standard (Mercedes or similar) and are well maintained. Fares are shown on a meter and consist of a minimum fee of around €3.50 plus a charge per kilometre of around €1.40. Evening and weekend rates may be higher and there is a small extra charge for each item of luggage. It is customary to round up the fare as a tip. Public transport operators in some larger cities can arrange for a taxi to meet passengers at a particular stop or station, particularly at night.

BY BICYCLE

Bicyclists are well provided for in Germany. The network of long-distance bicycling trails is well maintained and signposted, and a bicycling holiday in Germany is an attractive proposition. Many Germans take their bicycles with them on vacation, particularly when camping, and use them for excursions from their holiday base. Bicyclists can be just as territorial as other vehicle users about their allotted space, so pedestrians are advised not to loiter on cycleways.

GETTING AROUND IN BERLIN

Comprising underground (U-Bahn) and overhead (S-Bahn) trains, plus buses, trams and ferries, Berlin's fully integrated public transport network makes it possible to explore the whole city without ever needing a car. The system is run by BVG (Berliner Verkehrs-Betriebe, or Berlin Traffic Enterprises).

INFORMATION

There is a BVG information pavilion (tel 030 19449; www.bvg.de; Mon–Fri 6.30–8.30, Sat, Sun 9–3.30) at the entrance to the Hardenbergplatz bus station in front of Bahnhof Zoologischer Garten (Zoo Station) where the staff can provide you with tickets and travel information, including a basic public transport map. There is also a public transport information desk at Tegel airport.

Public transportation maps are also available at all stations, and tourist information offices dispense travel information.

THE NETWORK

Berlin's public transport system is fully integrated, and many journeys will be made using a ticket or pass that allows you to change from one mode of travel to another.

● The S-Bahn (*Stadt-Bahn*, or City Rail), identified by a large letter 'S', runs through the middle of the city, linking it to the suburbs and beyond. It runs mostly on overhead tracks, although some sections are underground. The elevated section between Savignyplatz and Zoologischer Garten in the west to Friedrichstrasse, Alexanderplatz and Ostbahnhof in the east is particularly useful for visitors and offers a glimpse of key parts of the city. Trains run at approximately 10-minute intervals between 4am and 1am. An hourly night service is provided on lines 3 to 10.

● The U-Bahn (*Untergrundbahn*, or Underground) has nine lines and 163 stations, the latter identified by a prominent letter 'U'. U55 is currently being extended. Work will continue until 2010. The network is densest in the central parts of the city, though some lines penetrate far into the suburbs, where they may run at ground level. There is even a curious elevated section between Nollendorfplatz and Warschauerplatz, which gives

an interesting view of the Landwehr canal and the attractions of Kreuzberg. Trains run at approximately 10-minute intervals between 4am and 1am. Lines 1, 9 and 15 provide an all-night service at 15-minute intervals.

● Berlin's extensive fleet of yellow-painted double-decker buses run from 4.30am–1am, as well as a number of night services. Bus stops (as everywhere in Germany) are identified by a green 'H' on a yellow background. Always enter the bus by the front doors and leave by the middle or rear doors.

● Before 1989 trams were confined to East Berlin. There are 30 tram lines, some of which have been extended into western Berlin.

TICKETS

Tickets come in various forms, including short-distance, single-journey, day and week tickets, ranging from €1.20 to €24.50, and it is worth considering carefully what trips you are likely to make during your stay before any purchase is made. All tickets except the short-distance ticket allow you to make as many transfers as you need between

lines or from one mode of travel to another. Berlin is divided into three travel zones, A, B and C; most visitor trips will be within the two inner zones (A and B). The outer zone (C) includes Potsdam.

You can buy tickets that are valid for up to one day from the orange and yellow vending machines at the entrances to the stations. Instructions are in English as well as German. Coins and sometimes notes are accepted and change is given. Tickets must be validated before travel by being stamped in one of the red machines on the platform or aboard buses and trams. Single-journey and day tickets may also be purchased from bus drivers and on board trams.

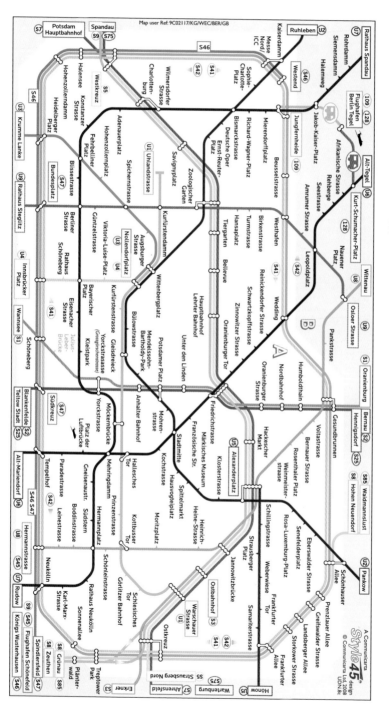

GERMANY

GREAT BRITAIN

UNDERSTANDING GREAT BRITAIN

On a map of the world Britain looks surprisingly small. But don't assume that you can see the whole country in just a week or two. Unrivalled variety, from world-class culture in dynamic cities to a beautiful, subtle patchwork of landscapes shaped by thousands of years of history, is concentrated in this densely populated island. Britain's inhabitants can be contradictory. They can prize both order and individuality, and value tradition but look forward rather than back. They've made their mark on their island with prehistoric monuments, castles, stately homes and elegant abbeys, all playing a part in Britain's dramatic history. And they've changed the world with the English language, the Industrial Revolution...and the gin and tonic.

A cottage in the English countryside (left). Rugby union is the national sport of Wales (middle). Scottish clans identify themselves by wearing different tartans (right). Big Ben (below right)

WHAT IS BRITAIN?

Even to those who live there, the word 'Britain' is a source of confusion. It covers England, Wales and Scotland. Britain plus Northern Ireland equals the United Kingdom, the political entity that is governed from the capital city, London. The Republic of Ireland is a separate country, but the islands of Ireland and Britain plus the Channel Islands make up the British Isles. A government survey in 2001 found that fewer than half of Britons thought of themselves as British; they much preferred to describe themselves as English, Welsh or Scottish.

At 50,331sq miles (130,357sq km) England is the largest nation in Britain, followed by Scotland at 30,405sq miles (77,080sq km), then Wales at 8,188sq miles (20,758sq km).

In a country where every hillside and woodland is named, it isn't surprising that Britain's regions have a proliferation of names. England, Wales and Scotland consist of areas of local government known as counties. Most counties have very long histories, have distinct characters and attract fierce loyalties.

THE ECONOMY

In the 19th century, Britain was the world's superpower and its empire stretched across one quarter of the world's surface. Two world wars diminished the country's strength and influence considerably. Today the UK is one of the top three European economies and a member of the G8 group of leading industrialized nations. Services and the financial sector are superseding manufacturing and industry as the basis of the economy. Unemployment is low when compared to some European countries, but there are pockets of deprivation in most cities, and rural economies are increasingly threadbare as the younger generation relocate to the cities to find work.

POLITICS

Despite being one of the first countries to develop a parliamentary democracy, Britain retains a monarch, currently Queen Elizabeth II. Decisions are made in two debating chambers: the House of Lords and the House of Commons. The Commons, where ultimate legislative power rests, consists of 646 Members of Parliament (MPs) who each represent a constituency in the UK. There are three main political parties: Labour, Liberal Democrat and Conservative (Tory). Britain's 'first past the post' electoral system, in which the MP who wins the most votes in their constituency then represents their party in Parliament, generally means that one party is in overall control and forms the government. Since 1997 the official Opposition has been the Conservatives (the Tories), with the Liberal Democrats also wielding considerable influence. The current Labour government is led by Prime Minister Gordon Brown. One of the first policies to be put into effect by his government was to devolve power to Scotland, Wales and Northern Ireland. The Welsh Assembly in Cardiff has 60 members and Scotland's new Parliament has 129 MSPs (Members of the Scottish Parliament). These bodies make decisions about their respective countries' domestic issues such as health and education.

Britain is a member of the European Union (EU) and the North Atlantic Treaty Organization (NATO), and is one of the five permanent members of the United Nations Security Council. Relations with other European nations are usually good, if complex, and Britain often acts as a transatlantic intermediary between the United States and the rest of Europe.

HERITAGE
Look beyond the modern veneer of Britain and you find links to the past everywhere. Many British cities and towns have Roman origins: place names ending with 'caster' or 'chester', for example, come from the Roman word *castrum*, meaning a military base. So unruly were the locals that Britain was the only province in the Roman Empire to have a permanent garrison of soldiers, and walls were erected to protect many towns. Those of York, Chester and Conwy remain intact.

By early medieval times most of today's settlements were already on the map. Their names are not far removed from the originals. The suffixes -ham, -ton and -ing suggest Saxon origins; Vikings from Scandinavia settled in eastern England in places that carry the suffix -by (such as Whitby).

For many centuries, Britain's most impressive buildings were castles, stately homes and places of worship. Castles were erected to defend coasts, towns and borders. Many were deliberately 'slighted' (rendered unusable) by invaders—notably during the Civil War in the 17th century—and now stand as jagged ruins. Kenilworth Castle is one of the finest of these. The opulent stately homes of Britain's landed gentry can also be hugely impressive, and today many are open to the public.

Religious buildings provide another key to the country's past. While Saxon church architecture is rare, the Normans introduced a huge scheme of church building. Their rounded arches gave way in turn to elaborate Gothic flourishes. Meanwhile, monasteries were among the richest landowners of medieval Britain. Their dissolution in the 1530s by Henry VIII ended a centuries-old way of life. Most

became roofless ruins; many stand today as poignant landmarks.

Britain's countryside has been shaped by its people. Over the centuries, settlers have largely removed Britain's ancient forest, leaving tracts of moorland on higher ground, consisting of heather, bogs and ferns. At lower levels, fields are bounded by hedges and drystone walls.

Pre-Roman settlers left numerous reminders of their existence. The early farming communities of the Neolithic period and Bronze Age erected ceremonial sites, such as stone circles, standing stones and burial mounds. You can find some of Britain's richest concentrations of such prehistoric sites in western Cornwall, Dartmoor (in Devon), Wiltshire and the Orkney Islands in Scotland.

LANGUAGE
English owes its roots to a mixture of Teutonic and Latin languages, reflecting waves of invasion

Sunrise at Stonehenge: The summer solstice draws many people to this ancient monument

during the early medieval period. Through Britain's vast colonial expansion it has become the first language of around 350 million people, and is understood by many more.

Traditional English dialects have been steadily eroded over the past century. Where there are differences, they tend to be minor. But somehow accents have survived to a surprising degree. The Scottish accent is unmistakable; the West Coast accent (especially around Glasgow) can be incomprehensible to outsiders. Speakers in Yorkshire and Lancashire tend to use broad vowel sounds, and there are subtle local variations. Liverpudlian has been immortalized by the Beatles, Brummy is the key signature of the West Midlands, South Wales has a singsong quality and the West Country has a distinct burr. In the South East the differences have blurred, with 'Estuary English' gaining ground over the crisp Home Counties accent.

Welsh, an old Celtic language that the Iron Age peoples spoke before the Romans arrived, is still spoken by around a quarter of the population of Wales. Banned by Henry VIII when Wales was officially united with England in 1535, it survived and is now taught in schools, and appears on bilingual signs. In Scotland, Gaelic is another ancient Celtic language, but it is less widely spoken than Welsh.

THE BEST OF GREAT BRITAIN

THE WEST COUNTRY

Avebury, Wiltshire Surrounded by prehistoric barrows, Avebury is home to Britain's largest stone circle.

Lost Gardens of Heligan, Cornwall Thankfully found and being restored, there are exotic plants, summer houses, pools and a grotto to discover.

Westonbirt Arboretum, Gloucestershire A diverse collection of 18,000 trees, including many rare species.

LONDON

British Museum, London (▷ 146–147) Nothing less than an anthology of civilization; highlights include the Egyptian Room.

Royal Botanic Gardens, Kew, Surrey Awarded World Heritage Site status in 2003, Kew's Royal Botanic Gardens have an unparalleled collection of plants.

Avebury stone circle

THE SOUTH EAST AND EAST ANGLIA

Bignor Roman Villa, West Sussex Bignor's second-century owners commissioned breathtaking mosaics for their house

Dover Castle, Kent From the Iron Age to the Cold War, this fortress has defended Britain's shores; exhibitions tell its story.

Windsor Castle Have a look around the Queen's principal residence and the largest occupied castle in the world.

WALES

Caernarfon Castle, Gwynedd Dwarfing the town, this harbourside castle was built by Edward I in 1283.

Wye Valley The River Wye builds up to a glorious finale as it meanders through the steep-sided wooded Wye Valley.

British Museum (above).
Dover Castle overlooks the town (left)

THE MIDLANDS

Stratford-upon-Avon Home of Britain's greatest playwright. A wealth of Tudor architecture awaits.

Warwick Castle, Warwick A slickly run showpiece castle, with lots of holiday events.

THE NORTH

Baltic Centre for Contemporary Art, Newcastle upon Tyne An art gallery leading the way in a city's regeneration.

Hadrian's Wall, Northumberland One Roman emperor's attempt to keep northern barbarians out is now Britain's most spectacular Roman ruin.

Rievaulx Abbey, Yorkshire Perhaps the most beautiful and moving of England's ruined monasteries.

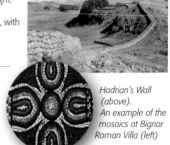

Hadrian's Wall (above).
An example of the mosaics at Bignor Roman Villa (left)

SCOTLAND

Burrell Collection, Glasgow (▷ 172) An outstanding collection of art, textiles and objects from around the world.

Eilean Donan Castle, Highlands Eilean Donan is *the* classic Scottish castle beside a misty loch.

Inverewe Gardens, Highlands Plants from the Himalayas, the Antipodes and South America flourish here.

Maes Howe, Orkney This burial chamber dates from 2800BC and may be the only World Heritage Site with Viking graffiti.

Eilean Donan Castle

Bath

Britain's most complete Georgian city, and one of the most elegant, Bath is home of the country's only hot spring, producing up to one million litres (26,000 gallons) of water a day.

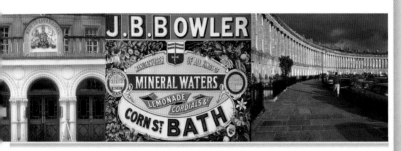

The Georgian Theatre Royal opened in 1805

Mineral waters have been available in Bath for centuries

The Royal Crescent is the grandest of Bath's streets

SEEING BATH

It is difficult to imagine a more beautiful city than Bath—great architecture, plenty to see and compact enough to explore on foot—and its World Heritage Site status has ensured its preservation. The city is built from eye-pleasing, honey limestone, and has a striking setting amid seven hills, where the Cotswolds meet the Mendip Hills, and on the banks of the River Avon and the Kennet and Avon Canal. The hills can make walking tiring, but you are compensated by the views. With more than 20 museums and historic sites, a huge choice of accommodation and plenty of specialist shops—including a daily antiques market in Bartlett Street—there is definitely something for everyone. In between sightseeing, you can take in vibrant streetlife from any number of cafés in the form of street entertainment. If you're based in London, Bath makes a great day out, as it's only about two hours by fast train from London Paddington.

RATINGS	
Good for kids	● ● ● ○
Historic interest	● ● ● ●
Specialist shopping	● ● ● ●
Walkability	● ● ● ○

TIPS

● Bath is ideal for a weekend break, with a huge choice of accommodation at all prices.
● Go early to the Pump Room and Roman Baths in order to avoid the crowds.
● Parking in the city is a real problem, so either come by public transport or use the park-and-ride service.

HIGHLIGHTS

PUMP ROOM

✚ 139 B2 • Stall Street BA1 1LZ ☎ 01225 477785
🕐 Mar–end Jun and Sep–end Oct daily 9–5; Jul–end Aug daily 9–9; Nov–end Feb daily 9.30–4.30,
www.romanbaths.co.uk

The high-ceilinged, chandelier-lit Georgian Pump Room (1796) is a great Bath institution, where a chamber trio provides accompaniment to afternoon tea (or you can sample the hot spa water, which may be an acquired taste), within sight of the King's Bath. This room was originally built for a serious purpose: A group of doctors, led by William Oliver (inventor of the Bath Oliver biscuit), felt that invalids should be able to come together to drink Bath's mineral waters. But Richard 'Beau' Nash, the city's Master of Ceremonies, had greater

Characters in period costume

GREAT BRITAIN BATH **137**

BUILDING OF BATH MUSEUM

✚ 139 B1 • Countess of Huntingdon's Chapel, The Vineyards, The Paragon BA1 5NA ☎ 01225 333895 ⊙ Mid-Feb to end Nov Tue–Sun and public holidays 10.30–5

This highly informative museum explains how Bath developed into the place it is.

JANE AUSTEN CENTRE

✚ 139 B1 • 40 Gay Street BA1 2NT ☎ 01225 443000 ⊙ Mar–end Oct daily 9.45–5.30; Nov–end Feb daily 11–4.30

An exhibition charts the life and works of the great novelist (1775–1817) who made two long visits to Bath in the 18th century, and also lived here from 1801 to 1806. The city features in *Persuasion* (published posthumously in 1817) and *Northanger Abbey* (1818).

AMERICAN MUSEUM IN BRITAIN

✚ 139 off C1 • Claverton Manor BA2 7BD ☎ 01225 460503 ⊙ Late Mar–end Oct Tue–Sun 2–5.30. Gardens: late Mar–Oct Tue–Sun 12–5 www.americanmuseum.org

This gracious manor house has re-creations of American homes from different states from the 17th to 19th centuries, as well as folk art and exhibits about Native Americans and the Shakers—a Christian sect known for their elegant furniture.

THERMAE BATH SPA

✚ 139 B2 • The Hetling Pump Room, Hot Bath Street BA1 1SJ ☎ 0844 888 0844 ⊙ New Royal Bath daily 9am–10pm; Cross Bath daily 10–8 www.thermaebathspa.com

Occupying two fantastic, former spa buildings, Bath's most contemporary spa experience includes a steam room, massage rooms, gym, rooftop open-air pool and a whirlpool.

ambitions. Realizing that a Pump Room could be useful as a meeting place, he hired musicians to play and fashionable visitors flocked in.

ROMAN BATHS

✚ 139 B2 • Stall Street BA1 1LZ ☎ 01225 477785 ⊙ Mar–end Jun and Sep–end Oct daily 9–5; Jul–end Aug daily 9–9; Nov–end Feb daily 9.30–4.30

From the genteel elegance of the Georgian Pump Room you suddenly walk into Roman times in the finest bath-house site in Britain. A self-guiding tour leads past displays of finds from the site down to the waters. The highlights of a visit are the pool and the Roman Bath (the Great Bath). The spring, still bubbling up at a constant 46ºC (116ºF), was sacred to the goddess Sulis, who was thought to possess curative powers. The Romans made a sanctuary around the spring, dedicated to Sulis Minerva, and both Celts and Romans bathed and made offerings.

The Sun God from the Temple of Sulis Minerva (below)   *Wedding dresses are on display in the Museum of Costume*

BATH ABBEY

✚ 139 C2 • 12, Kingston Buildings BA1 1LT ☎ 01225 422462 ⊙ Easter–late Oct Mon–Sat 9–6, Sun 1.15–2.45, 4.30–5.30; Nov–Easter Mon–Sat 9–4.30, Sun 1–2.30, 4.30–5.30

Not in fact an abbey but a church, this building (begun in 1499) represents one of the crowning examples of the Perpendicular style. Legend has it that the shape of the church was dictated to its founder, Bishop Oliver King, in a dream by angels. This story is immortalized on the west front, which shows the carved angels ascending and descending on ladders, and the founder's signature—a carving of olive trees surmounted by crowns. The airy interior is most notable for the size of its windows and the delicate fan vaulting, completed by George Gilbert Scott in the late 19th century. The huge east window depicts 56 scenes from Christ's life, while the floor and walls, crammed with elaborate memorials and Georgian inscriptions, make fascinating reading. The Norman Chapel (also known as the Gethsemane Chapel) has clear traces of the older, Norman chapel on this site.

MUSEUM OF COSTUME AND ASSEMBLY ROOMS

✚ 139 B1 • ✉ Bennett Street BA1 2QH ☎ 01225 477173 ⊙ Mar–end Oct daily 10–6; Nov–end Feb daily 11–5

This large and prestigious collection displays fashionable dress for men and women dating from the late 16th century to the present. The star attraction is the silver tissue dress dating from the 1660s, although many visitors are interested in the early 19th-century clothes, familiar to many from film adaptations of Jane Austen's novels.

NO. 1 ROYAL CRESCENT

✚ 139 A1 • ✉ 1 Royal Crescent BA1 2LR ☎ 01225 428126 ⊙ Mid-Feb to end Oct Tue–Sun 10.30–5; Nov Tue–Sun 10.30–4; Dec to mid-Feb Sat–Sun 10.30–4

This house was designed by John Wood the Younger (1767–74) and offers a chance to see inside one of the town houses in Bath's most celebrated architectural set piece, the Royal Crescent. It has been restored to its appearance of 200 years ago, with pictures, china and furniture of the period and a kitchen with a dog-powered spit used to roast meat in front of the fire. The first-floor windows are the only ones of the original height—all the

others were lengthened in the 19th century. Wood's father (also John) was the architect of The Circus (1754–70), a circular piazza close by.

BACKGROUND

Roman Bath was founded in AD44 as the settlement of *Aquae Sulis*. Bath prospered through the wool trade in medieval times, but its modern importance dates from the 18th century, after its Roman hot springs were rediscovered in 1755. They were made fashionable by the Welsh dandy Richard 'Beau' Nash (1674–1762), who carried out his role as official Master of Ceremonies with panache. He was paramount in attracting London's high society to the baths and springs, as well as to the grand balls and assemblies.

BASICS

✚ 4 C3

ℹ️ Abbey Chambers, Abbey Church Yard, Bath BA1 1LY, tel 0906 711 2000 (60p a minute); May–end Sep Mon–Sat 9.30–6, Sun 10–4; Oct–end Apr Mon–Sat 9.30–5, Sun 10–4

❓ Bath Visitor Card (www.visitorcards.co.uk/bath), valid for three weeks, offers discounted entry to seven musuems plus discounts at a host of eateries and shops

🚆 Bath Spa, 1.5km (1 mile) from central Bath

www.visitbath.co.uk
An informative website with details on attractions, accommodation, shopping, spa treatments, famous people, a virtual tour and what's on. Links to most of the main sights.

The Royal Crescent's green is used for all kinds of events

Bath Abbey took its present form in the 17th century

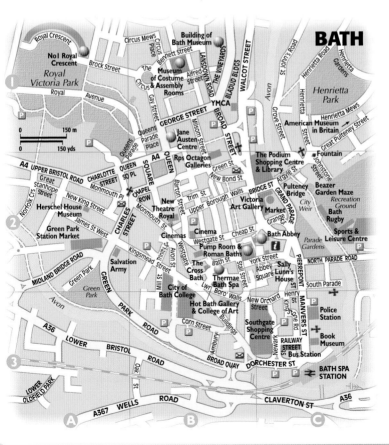

KEY TO SYMBOLS

⊕	Shopping
⊙	Entertainment
⊙	Nightlife
⊗	Sports
⊙	Activities
♡	Health and Beauty
⊙	For Children

WHAT TO DO

⊕ CAROLINE NEVILL MINIATURES

22A Broad Street
Tel 01225 443091

A leading supplier of dolls' houses and miniature furniture. The range includes Tudor, Regency and Victorian styles, as well as more contemporary designs. The tiny contents, including furniture, books, paintings and silverware, are exquisitely crafted.

⊙ Mon–Sat 10.30–5

⊕ GEORGE BAYNTUN

Manvers Street
Tel 01225 466000
www.georgebayntun.com

This bookshop is engaged in buying, selling, binding and restoring old and rare books since 1829. It specializes in English literature, particularly classics and modern first editions, plus antique prints (including views of Bath). The shop has retained much of its 19th-century character.

⊙ Mon–Fri 9–1, 2–5.30, Sat 9.30–1

⊕ GUILDHALL MARKET

High Street
Tel 01225 477945
www.bathguildhallmarket.co.uk

A traditional market experience in an 18th-century building—a market has existed on this site since its Royal Charter of 1284. The huge range of items includes antique and modern jewellery, rugs, food, electrical supplies, tools and old-fashioned sweets (candy).

⊙ Mon–Sat (also Sun in Dec) 8–5.30 (times for individual traders vary)

⊡

⊙ THEATRE ROYAL BATH

Sawclose
Tel 01225 448844
www.theatreroyal.org.uk

Opened in 1805, and steeped in history, with drama, opera, ballet; plus fringe productions and jazz in the Ustinov Studio.

⊙ Box office: Mon–Sat 10–8, Sun and public holidays 12–8 ⊞ £10–£30, 40

standby tickets costing £5 available from 12 on day of performance ⊞ ⊡

⊙ WOODS

9–13 Alfred Street
Tel 01225 314812

This is a stylish bar in a Georgian building and is popular with visiting actors and a glitzy crowd.

⊙ Closed Sun evening

♡ THERMAE BATH SPA

Hetling Pump Room, Hot Bath Street
Tel 01225 331234 (reservations)
www.thermaebathspa.com

Opened in 2006 after a long renovation and rebuilding programme, this spa draws on natural thermal springs. Bathers can enjoy an open-air roof-top pool, steam rooms, massage and treatments.

⊙ Daily 9am–10pm (last entry 8pm)

⊞ Two hours £19, 4 hours £29, all day £45 (not including treatments)

⊞ ⊡ ⊕

EATING

BATH PRIORY HOTEL AND RESTAURANT

Weston Road
Tel 01225 331922
www.thebathpriory.co.uk

The high quality of the cuisine served here has received many accolades including a coveted Michelin star. Head chef Chris Horridge counts renowned chef Raymond Blanc as his mentor. The cuisine is classic European with many ingredients coming fresh from the gardens of the hotel. The dining room has wonderful views over the gardens.

⊙ Daily 12–1.45, 7–9.30

⊞ L £20, D £55, Wine £24.50

SALLY LUNN'S

4 North Parade
Tel 01225 461634
www.sallylunns.co.uk

Sally Lunn began baking bread more than 300 years ago and her legacy has lived on at this old fashioned tearoom/café. Come to enjoy a typical English afternoon tea, or hearty home-style dishes including pies, all accompanied by Sally's bread buns.

⊙ Daily 10–10

⊞ L £12, afternoon tea £5.50, Wine £11.08

STAYING

APSLEY HOUSE HOTEL

Newbridge Hill, Bath BA1 3PT
Tel: 01225 336966
www.apsley-house.co.uk

Apsley House bed-and-breakfast is conveniently located within walking distance of the heart of the city. The house is extremely stylish and elegant, and the spacious bedrooms (one with a king-size four-poster bed) have fine views. There's also a bar, lounge and garden. Light suppers are served by prior arrangement.

⊙ Closed one week at Christmas

⊞ £70–£190

⊞ 10

⊟ On A431, 1.5km (1 mile) west of city

⊟ Bath Spa

THE QUEENSBERRY HOTEL

Russel Street, Bath BA1 2QF
Tel 01225 447928
www.thequeensberry.co.uk

This delightful hotel in four town houses is on a quiet street near the city centre. Spacious bedrooms are tastefully furnished, and deep armchairs and marble bathrooms add to their appeal. There are comfortable lounges, a small bar and a courtyard garden. The Olive Tree restaurant offers rustic but modern food. There is a valet parking service. Dogs are not allowed.

⊞ £160–£260

⊞ 29

THE WINDSOR GUEST HOUSE

69 Great Pulteney Street, Bath BA2 4DL
Tel 01225 422100
www.bathwindsorguesthouse.co.uk

This Georgian town house is a short, level walk from the heart of town. The historic terraced house has been refurbished to a high standard and furnished with antiques. Children under 12 and dogs are not welcome.

⊙ Closed one week at Christmas

⊞ £85–£150

⊞ 10

⊟ M4 junction 18 onto A4, turn left onto A36, then turn right at next mini roundabout and take second turning on left for Great Pulteney Street

⊟ £6

⊟ Bath Spa

London

✚ 4 C3 ℹ Britain and London Visitor Centre, 1 Lower Regent Street, London SW1Y 4XT, tel 0870 156 6366 (information on London only, 4p per minute); Mon 9.30–6.30, Tue–Fri 9–6.30, Sat–Sun 10–4 (Jun–end Oct Sat 9–5)
www.visitbritain.com • Information on Britain
www.visitlondon.com • Information on London

HOW TO GET THERE

✈ Airports
London Heathrow, 19km (12 miles) west of central London
London Gatwick, 48km (30 miles) south of central London
Also, **Stansted**, **Luton** and **London City** (mainly short-haul destinations)

🚆 Train stations
Mainline stations: Charing Cross, Euston, Fenchurch Street, King's Cross, Liverpool Street, London Bridge, Marylebone, Paddington, St. Pancras, Victoria and Waterloo.

The famous clock tower housing Big Ben

TIPS

● Ride the British Airways London Eye (▷ 151) for unrivalled views of London.
● Go to Harrods (▷ 152). Even if you don't want to buy anything, it's worth visiting this huge, luxurious store.
● Take a boat trip on the Thames for a different perspective of the city.
● Skip lunch and take afternoon tea at Fortnum and Mason (▷ 152).
● Wander off the beaten track; take a street map and explore areas such as Bloomsbury or the City on foot.
● Outside term time, the London School of Economics and Political Science rents student rooms to visitors, providing a basic but inexpensive base in central London.

SEEING LONDON

London is a bustling metropolis with some of the best monuments, museums and galleries in the world. Many of its attractions are some distance apart and you'll need to use its extensive public transport system to reach them. The Underground (Tube) is the quickest way to get around but buses offer views as well as a chance to get to grips with the geography of London. Taxis are everywhere in the centre and are useful for short distances but longer journeys are expensive. Another option is to take one of the open-top bus tours of the main tourist sights of central London, with a commentary in several languages, and the opportunity to get on and get off as many times as you like.

If you set out determined to see everything London has to offer you'll end up frustrated and exhausted. To get the most out of a visit, choose carefully—visit museums, for instance, in which you have a particular interest. It's also worth buying a London Pass as it includes free entry to more than 60 attractions and allows you to jump the queue at selected attractions. It costs from £36 per day (with an option to include free travel on public transport) and is available from the Britain and London Visitor Centre (▷ above), tel 01664 485 020 or www.londonpass.com.

BACKGROUND

Although it is very much a 21st-century city, London retains a strong sense of its past. Its roots go back to the first century AD, when the Romans established a garrison at a site on the north bank of the Thames after their invasion of Britain in AD43. Its importance was underlined in the 11th century, when William the Conqueror built the Tower of London. Most of the medieval city was devoured by the Great Fire of 1666, but London soon recovered, and continued to grow in Georgian times, when elegant streets and squares were laid out in Mayfair and fashionable shops opened in Bond Street and Oxford Street.

At the Great Exhibition of 1851 in Hyde Park, London was displayed to the world as the largest city on the planet. By the beginning of the 20th century, London was the capital of the largest empire the world had ever known. After the devastation of World War II came the 'swinging London' of the 1960s and the youth culture of coffee bars and boutiques, while skyscrapers and concrete high-rises changed the city skyline forever. The late 1990s heralded a boom that saw London riding high on a wave of prosperity and self-confidence, which looks set to continue, and ensure its reputation as one of the world's most vibrant cities.

DON'T MISS

BRITISH MUSEUM
A vast array of antiquities from around the world (▷ 146–147)
NATURAL HISTORY MUSEUM
Dinosaurs to lichens: millions of specimens from the natural world (▷ 151)
ST. PAUL'S CATHEDRAL
Its iconic dome dominates the London skyline (▷ 149)
SCIENCE MUSEUM
Innovative hands-on museum that brings science to life
TATE BRITAIN
Superb art (▷ 151)
TOWER OF LONDON
Symbolizes nearly 1,000 years of Britain's royal history (▷ 150)

GREAT BRITAIN

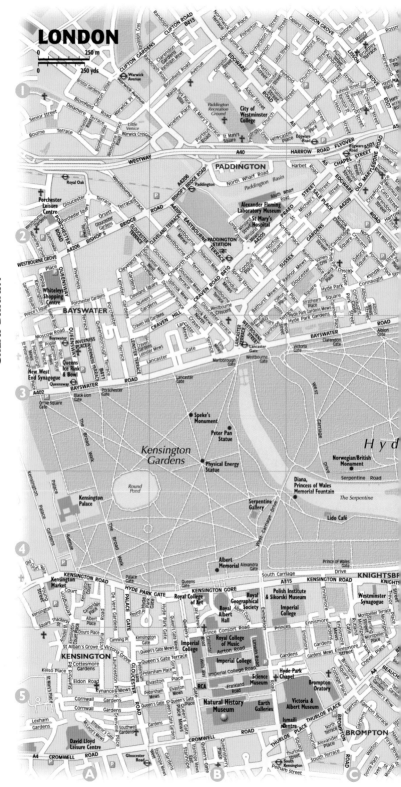

LONDON

0   250 m

0   250 yds

CLIFTON GARDENS

WARWICK AVENUE

Randolph

CLIFTON ROAD B415

LISSON GROVE

EDGWARE

Blomfield Avenue

Maida

GROVE

Senior Street

Blomfield Road

Bourne Terrace

Delamere Terrace

Little Venice

Warwick Crescent

Paddington Recreation Ground

City of Westminster College

HARROW ROAD

WESTWAY

A40

EDGWARE ROAD FLYOVER

CHAPEL STREET

PADDINGTON

Royal Oak

North Wharf Road

Paddington Basin

Harbet

Porchester Leisure Centre

BISHOP'S BRIDGE ROAD

Paddington

Paddington Basin

PRAED

OLD MARYLEBONE

A4206

A4209

EASTBOURNE

CLEVELAND TERRACE

PADDINGTON STATION

Alexander Fleming Laboratory Museum

St Mary's Hospital

EDGWARE ROAD

WESTBOURNE GROVE

QUEENSWAY

CLEVELAND

GLOUCESTER

BRIDGE ROAD

CRAVEN ROAD B410

SUSSEX GARDENS

Whiteleys Shopping Centre

BAYSWATER

CRAVEN HILL

Hyde Park

LEINSTER TERRACE

LANCASTER GATE

SUSSEX

WESTBOURNE STREET

Hyde Park Gardens

ROAD

BAYSWATER

Lancaster Gate

Clarendon Place

Albion Gate

New West End Synagogue

Queens Ice Rink & Bowl

BAYSWATER

Marlborough Gate

Westbourne Gate

Victoria Gate

A402

A402

Black Lion Gate

Ormie square Gate

Portchester Terrace

Lancaster Gate

Speke's Monument

Peter Pan Statue

H y d

The Broad Walk

Kensington Gardens

Physical Energy Statue

Norwegian/British Monument

Serpentine Road

Round Pond

Diana, Princess of Wales Memorial Fountain

The Serpentine

Kensington Palace

Serpentine Gallery

Lido Café

Palace Avenue

The Broad Walk

West Carriage Drive

Kensington Palace Gardens

Albert Memorial

Alexandra Gate

Prince of Wales Gate

Kensington Market

KENSINGTON ROAD

Palace Gate

Queens Gate

KENSINGTON GORE

South Carriage

KENSINGTON ROAD

A315

KNIGHTSBR

KNIGHT

De Vere Gardens

HYDE PARK GATE

Royal College of Art

Royal Geographical Society

Polish Institute & Sikorski Museum

Westminster Synagogue

Albert Place

Canning Pl

PALACE GATE

Royal Albert Hall

Imperial College

Ennismore Gardens

Montpelier Terrace

Montpelier Place

St Alban's Grove

Kensington Gate

Prince consort Road

Royal College of Music

Imperial College

Ennismore

Montpelier Street

KENSINGTON

Victoria Grove

Queen's Gate Terrace

Ayrton Road

Imperial College

Imperial College Road

Science Museum

Hyde Park Chapel

Cheval Place

BEAUCH

Cottesmore Gardens

Petersham Place

Frankland Road

Brompton Oratory

Kelso Place

Eldon Road

Kynance Mews

RCA

Victoria & Albert Museum

BROMPTON

Cornwall Gardens

Petersham Mews

Elvaston Mews

Natural History Museum

Earth Galleries

THURLOE PLACE

Lexham Gardens

Cornwall Gardens

Southwell Gardens

Queen's Gate

Ismaili Centre

THURLOE PLACE

North Terrace

BROMPTON

David Lloyd Leisure Centre

A4 CROMWELL ROAD

Gloucester Road

CROMWELL ROAD

Queensberry Place

Thurloe Place

South Kensington

Pelham Street

Alexander Place

South Terrace

ROAD

A   B   C

1

2

3

4

5

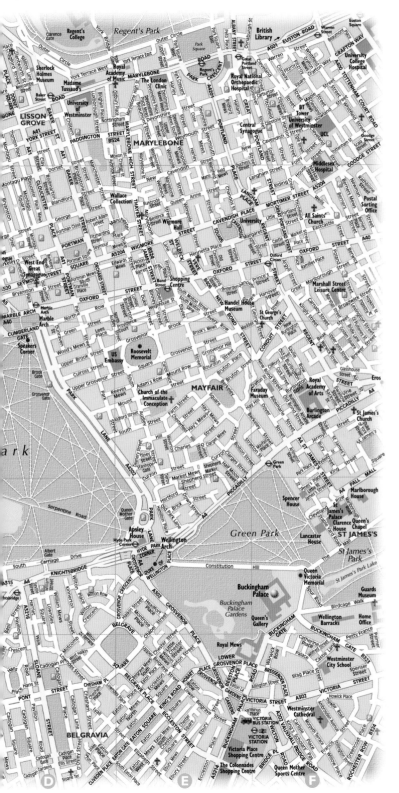

GREAT BRITAIN

Percival David Foundation of Chinese Art
Brunswick Shopping Centre
Coram's Fields
Mount Pleasant Postal Sorting Office
CLERKENWELL

University of London
RADA
National Hospital for Neurology & Neurosurgery
National Hospital for Sick Children (Great Ormond St)
Charles Dickens Museum
London Weather Centre
CLERKENWELL ROAD
FARRINGDON STATION

BLOOMSBURY
University of London
Gray's Inn
HATTON
FARRINGDON

British Museum
Conway Hall
Gray's Inn

HOLBORN HIGH HOLBORN
HOLBORN CIRCUS
City Temp

YMCA
ST GILES CIRCUS
Centre Point
Tottenham Court Road
ST GILES
New Oxford Street
HIGH HOLBORN
Sir John Soane's Museum
Royal College of Surgeons
Lincoln's Inn
London Silver Vaults
Public Record Office
Dr Johnson's House

Oasis Sports Centre
New Connaught Rooms
Old Curiosity Shop
London School of Economics and Political Science
Royal Courts of Justice
FLEET STREET
Temple Church

CHINATOWN
CAMBRIDGE CIRCUS
Photographers' Gallery
Royal Opera House
St Paul's Church
Covent Garden
ALDWYCH
Bush House
Australia House
St Clement Danes
India House
Inns of Court
Temple
Middle Temple
Inner Temple

St Paul's Church
St Peter's Hospital
Covent Garden
London Transport Museum
Courtauld Gallery
Somerset House
Old Roman Bath
King's College
Hermitage Rooms
Gilbert Collection

STRAND
Royal Society of Arts
HQS Wellington (Master Mariners)
HMS President
Blackfriars Millennium

National Portrait Gallery
St Martin-in-the-Fields
Proud Gallery
Savoy Pier
WATERLOO BRIDGE

Thames

Oxo Tower

National Gallery
Trafalgar Square
Nelson's Column
Cleopatra's Needle
Embankment Pier
Festival Pier
The London Television Centre
STAMFORD

Canada House
COCKSPUR STREET
PALL MALL
CHARING CROSS STATION
Embankment
HUNGERFORD BRIDGE
Queen Elizabeth Hall
Royal National Theatre
National Film Theatre
London City
Schiller College International
London Nautical School

Admiralty Arch
Old Admiralty
Government Offices
DEFRA
Hispaniola
Southbank Centre
Hayward Gallery
Royal Festival Hall
BFI London IMAX Cinema

Institute of Contemporary Arts (ICA)
Old War Office
Shell Centre
WATERLOO EAST STATION

Horse Guards Parade
Banqueting House
Victoria Embankment
Jubilee Gardens
WATERLOO STATION
Southwa Colle

ST JAMES'S
St James's Park
Privy Council Office
Downing St
Ministry of Defence
British Airways London Eye
Waterloo Millennium Pier
INTERNATIONAL RAIL TERMINAL

Foreign & Commonwealth Office
King Charles Street
Cenotaph
Government Offices
Dali Universe
County Hall

Churchill Museum and Cabinet War Rooms
Treasury
Portcullis House
Westminster Millennium Pier
London Aquarium
WESTMINSTER BRIDGE ROAD

Central Hall
Queen Elizabeth II Conference Centre
Middlesex Guildhall
St Margaret Westminster
Big Ben
Florence Nightingale Museum

Department of Trade and Industry
Westminster Abbey
Palace of Westminster
WESTMINSTER BRIDGE
LAMBETH
St Thomas' Hospital

Church House
Westminster School
Jewel Tower
Victoria Tower Gardens
Archbishop's Park
Imperial War Museum

Civil Service Recreation Centre
St John's Concert Hall
Lambeth Palace
NEWINGTON

HORSEFERRY ROAD
LAMBETH BRIDGE
Museum of Garden History
Geraldine Mary Harmsworth Park

WESTMINSTER
↓ Tate Britain

G   H   J

British Museum

●

Britain's largest museum, covering 33ha (81.5 acres), has more than
four million objects on display in around 90 galleries. It is unrivalled for the
variety and quality of its treasures, the result of more than 200 years of
collecting, excavation and unashamed looting.

*The Egyptian Sculpture Gallery
(above) displays ancient
discoveries, and elsewhere there
are jewel-encrusted treasures like
this helmet (right). The façade of
the British Museum (below) is all
neoclassical elegance*

TIPS
● Get your bearings in the
Great Court, where you can
pick up floor plans and
information.
● Don't expect to see
everything in a day; focus on
what interests you and make
for one or two galleries, or on
one or two collections.
● Visit in the evening, when
the Great Court's restaurants
and shops are open. On
Thursdays and Fridays the
major galleries stay open late.

SEEING THE BRITISH MUSEUM

There are two entrances: one (the main entrance) on Great
Russell Street (south) and the other on Montague Place
(north). Both lead into the covered Great Court, the hub of the
museum and the main information office. The collections are
arranged by geography, culture and theme, but the layout and
size of the place can be bewildering. Note that collections from
the same culture are not necessarily on the same floor.

HIGHLIGHTS

GREAT COURT AND READING ROOM
Sir Robert Smirke's imposing, neoclassical building is entered via the
Great Court, added in 2000 and designed by Norman Foster. The
curved glass canopy has created a huge, light space and it's worth
lingering here to enjoy the sculpture displays.

At the heart of the court is the circular Reading Room, completed in
1857 to the design of Smirke's brother, Sydney. Karl Marx and other
intellectuals once beavered away here.

MAIN FLOOR
Rosetta Stone (Room 4)
Though not impressive to look at, the Rosetta Stone was instrumental
in solving puzzles of the ancient Egyptian world. The black basalt slab,
discovered by Napoleon's army in the Nile Delta in 1799, reproduces
the same text in three languages: Greek, Demotic and Egyptian. This
offered the first opportunity for modern scholars to crack the code of
Egyptian hieroglyphics by comparing them with known scripts.

Elgin Marbles (Room 18)
The question of where they should be—in Greece or in Britain—still
causes passionate debate. These frieze reliefs, carved between 447
and 431BC, were taken by Lord Elgin, then British ambassador in
Constantinople, from the Parthenon in Athens. Elgin obtained a
licence from the Turkish Sultan to remove the stones, which had
suffered severe damage in 1687, and, arguing that they would not
survive if they remained in Greece, brought them to Britain.

UPPER FLOORS
Portland Vase (Room 70)
This ancient cameo-glass vase was probably made in Rome between
AD5 and 25. It eventually reached the hands of the third Duke of
Portland in 1786, who lent it to potter Josiah Wedgwood, who copied
its cameo design and made it famous.

Sutton Hoo Ship Burial (Room 41)
These treasures are from an Anglo-Saxon royal burial ship that survived
intact in Suffolk and was excavated in 1939. The ship was probably a
monument to Raedwald, the last pagan king of East Anglia, who died
in about 625. Besides fine gold jewels, the boat contained silver bowls
and plates, silver drinking horns, a shield, a sword with jewelled gold
hilt and an iron helmet with bronze and silver fittings.

Lewis Chessmen (Room 42)

Carved from the tusks of walruses, these squat figures were discovered on the island of Lewis in the Outer Hebrides of Scotland in 1831 by a crofter. Scandinavian in origin, they depict the figures used on a chess board and are believed to date from the 12th century.

Egyptian Mummies (Rooms 61–66)

Rows of preserved bodies wrapped in bandages and surrounded by their prized possessions and preferred foods have a gruesome fascination. The craftsmanship and elegance of the items are breathtaking.

Lindow Man (Room 37)

Nicknamed 'Pete Marsh' by the archaeologists who found him in a peat bog in Cheshire, Lindow Man is a well-preserved 2,000-year-old corpse. Among several theories is one that he was sacrificed during a Druid ceremony. There are signs of a blow to his head and a wound to his throat, and mistletoe grains were found in his gut, suggesting that he was fed a hallucinatory meal before being knocked out, strangled and drowned.

LOWER FLOORS

Assyrian Reliefs

Vivid carved figures taking part in daily activities or military campaigns, were cut into panels for the Assyrian kings' palaces and temples, and have survived from 880–612BC. Some of the most striking friezes come from the great palace of King Sennacherib, who came to the throne of Assyria in 704BC.

BACKGROUND

Wealthy physician Sir Hans Sloane (1660–1753) spent his life collecting assorted coins, books and natural history specimens, which, on his death, amounted to 80,000 items. The government bought the collection and put it on display as the British Museum in 1759. As the collection grew, more galleries were added, but space was a major problem and in 1998 the British Library was moved and the Great Court was given an overhaul.

BASICS

🏛 144 G1 • Great Russell Street WC1B 3DG

☎ 020 7323 8299

🕐 Sat–Wed 10–5.30, Thu–Fri 10–8.30. Great Court: Sun–Wed 9–6, Thu–Sat 9am–11pm. Check times for temporary exhibitions

💷 Free; charges for some temporary exhibitions

🚇 Holborn, Tottenham Court Road, Russell Square, Goodge Street

🎧 90-min tours of highlights: daily 10.30, 1, 3, adult £8, child (under 11) £5. 'eyeOpener' 50-min introductory tours: daily every half hour 11–3.30, free. Audiotours in several languages, £3.50. Foreign language tours: 020 7323 8181

📖 £5 (English only) and £6 (in several languages)

🍴 Court Restaurant on upper floor of Great Court: Sat–Wed 11–5.30 (last orders), Thu–Fri 11–10.30. Reservations, 020 7323 8990

☕ Court Café (Great Court): Sun–Wed 9–5.30, Thu–Sat 10–9. Gallery Café, next to Room 12: daily 10–5

📚 Bookshop, selling art, history and archaeology titles, children's shop and guide shop

www.britishmuseum.org
Good level of practical information and educational links; plenty of background and attractive illustrations.

Buckingham Palace is open for two months of the year

RATINGS

Value for money	● ● ●
Good for kids	● ●
Historic interest	● ● ● ● ●

BASICS

 143 F4 • Buckingham Gate SW1A 1AA

☎ General: 020 7766 7324. Credit card booking line: 020 7766 7300

🕐 Late Jul–late Sep (precise dates vary) daily 9.45–6 (last admission 4.15); timed ticket system with admission every 15 min

💷 Adult £15.50, child (5–17) £8.75, family £38.50

Ⓥ Victoria, Green Park, Hyde Park Corner

🚶 Self-guiding tours

📖 Official guidebook £4.95 in English, Chinese, French, German, Italian, Japanese, Russian and Spanish

🏛 🍴

www.royal.gov.uk
Informative, accessible site.

BUCKINGHAM PALACE

Buckingham Palace is a world-famous symbol of monarchy and focus for ceremonial and public occasions as well as one of Queen Elizabeth II's main residences.

The palace so familiar to millions from newsreels and postcards has had centuries of piecemeal architectural changes. Originally plain Buckingham House, it was built in 1702 as the Duke of Buckingham's city mansion. King George III snapped it up as a private residence in 1761 and work began on embellishments and additions. When Queen Victoria and Prince Albert moved into the palace in 1837, a whole new wing was added to accommodate their fast-growing family, closing off the three-sided quadrangle and removing the Marble Arch that provided its grand entrance. The present forecourt, where the Changing the Guard ceremony takes place, was formed in 1911, as part of the Victoria Memorial scheme.

THE STATE ROOMS

Of the palace's 660 rooms, visitors can see about 20. Enter the palace through the Ambassadors' Court and go through John Nash's dramatic Grand Hall to climb the curving marble of the Grand Staircase, with its gilt-bronze balustrade, to the first-floor State Rooms. Beyond the small Guard Room, hung with Gobelin tapestries, is the Green Drawing Room, an ante-chamber to the Throne Room, where official visitors gather before being presented to the Queen. Some of George IV's fine Sèvres porcelain can be seen here. Ahead is the Throne Room, a theatrical 20m (65ft) space leading up to the chairs of state.

This leads into the 47m (155ft) Picture Gallery, displaying works by Peter Paul Rubens, Rembrandt van Rijn and Anthony van Dyck. The Silk Tapestry Room, with its monumental French pedestal clock, links the Picture Gallery with the East Gallery, leading into the Ball Supper Room and the vast Ballroom, used for investitures and state banquets.

More Gobelin tapestries are displayed in the West Gallery, which leads to the State Dining Room, in white and gold with deep-red walls. Next is the sumptuous Blue Drawing Room, with a dazzling Nash ceiling and huge Corinthian columns. The opulence continues in the Music Room, with its domed ceiling and columns of lapis lazuli.

A blaze of white and gold greets you in the White Drawing Room, where there is more wonderful French furniture, such as a veneered roll-top desk from 1775. The intricately designed Minister's Staircase leads to the ground floor and the Marble Hall, displaying statues of nymphs. Other attractions are the Queen's Gallery, with an important collection of paintings, and the nearby Royal Mews.

Looking down the aisle towards the altar (above).
The cathedral illuminated at night (right)

ST. PAUL'S CATHEDRAL

Britain's only domed cathedral, St. Paul's is second only in size to St. Peter's in Rome.

Sir Christopher Wren's masterpiece is a dramatic combination of vast, airy spaces and elaborate decoration. A wide flight of steps leads up to the west front entrance, flanked by two clock towers.

THE DOME AND GALLERIES
Eight pillars support the huge dome, 111m (364ft) high and weighing about 65,000 tonnes. The acoustics are such that someone standing on the opposite side of the gallery will hear your whispers clearly after several seconds' delay. The frescoes on the dome depict scenes from the life of St. Paul and were painted by Sir James Thornhill between 1716 and 1719. The Golden Gallery runs around the outer dome, a breathtaking 85m (280ft) from the cathedral floor. A hole in the floor gives a dizzying view down.

THE CHANCEL
This part of the cathedral is a riot of 19th-century Byzantine-style gilding. In the north choir aisle is a marble sculpture, *Mother and Child,* by Henry Moore (1898–1986). A marble effigy of poet John Donne (1572–1631) stands in the south choir aisle. This is one of the few effigies that survived the Great Fire of London in 1666, and you can make out scorch marks on its base.

The Duke of Wellington (1769–1852), hero of the Napoleonic Wars and prime minister from 1828 to 1830, lies in a simple Cornish granite casket. Admiral Nelson (1758–1805), who died in action at the Battle of Trafalgar, lies in the middle of the crypt. Nelson's coffin went with him into battle, and after his death he was preserved in it in French brandy for the journey home. At Gibraltar the coffin was put into a lead-lined casket and steeped in distilled wine. Finally his remains were encased in two more coffins before being buried under Cardinal Wolsey's 16th-century sarcophagus.

THE CATHEDRAL'S HISTORY
The first St. Paul's was founded in 604 by King Ethelbert of Kent. It was rebuilt 300 years later after a Viking attack and replaced by a Norman cathedral, Old St. Paul's, in 1087. After its destruction in the Great Fire of 1666, Sir Christopher Wren (1632–1723), who was appointed King's Surveyor-General, was commissioned to build a new one. It was finally completed in 1710.

RATINGS				
Good for kids	● ●			
Historic interest	● ● ● ● ●			
Value for money	● ● ● ● ●			

BASICS

✚ 145 K2 • St. Paul's Churchyard EC4M 8AD

☎ 020 7246 8350

🕐 Mon–Sat 8.30–4.30. Daily for services. Triforium tours (Library, West End Gallery, Trophy Room and Wren's Great Model); advance reservation required, tel: 020 7246 8357 (Mon–Fri 9–2); £12

🎫 Cathedral, Crypt and Galleries: adult £9.50, child (6–16) £3.50, family £22.50

🚇 St. Paul's, Blackfriars

🚉 Blackfriars

🚌 £4

🎧 Guided tours (in English only) Mon–Sat 11, 11.30, 1.30 and 2. Adult £3, under 16 £1. Audio tours (9.45–3): £3.50 in English, French, German, Italian and Spanish

🍴 Refectory restaurant

☕ Crypt Café

♿ 🚻

www.stpauls.co.uk
Virtual tour of the cathedral. Good to look at, but a fairly basic level of background and information.

TIP
● There are free organ recitals at 5pm every Sunday, but bring some loose change for the collection at the end.

RATINGS

Historic interest	● ● ● ● ●
Good for kids	● ● ● ● ○
Value for money	● ● ● ● ○

BASICS

✚ 145 M3 • Tower of London EC3N
4AB ☎ 0870 756 6060 (recording),
0870 756 7070 (tickets) ◑ Mar–end
Oct Tue–Sat 9–6, Sun–Mon 10–6;
Nov–end Feb Tue–Sat 9–4.30, Sun–Mon
10–4.30. Last admission 1 hour before
closing. All internal buildings close 30
min after last admission; Tower closes 1
hr after last admission. To watch the
Ceremony of the Keys apply in writing
at least 6–8 weeks in advance for free
tickets to The Ceremony of the Keys
Office, HM Tower of London, London
EC3N 4AB 🎟 Adult £16, child (5–15)
£9.50, family £45 🚇 Tower Hill, Tower
Gateway DLR 🚢 Tower Millennium
Pier 🚌 £3.95, English, French, German,
Italian, Japanese, Russian, Spanish
🎧 Audioguide, £3.50, in English,
French, German, Italian, Japanese,
Russian, Spanish
🍴 🛍 🏧 🚻

www.hrp.org.uk
Straightforward site with links, historical
background and full visitor information.

TIPS

• Crowds can be a problem in
the summer. To save waiting,
buy tickets in advance by
telephoning 0870 756 7070 or
online at www.hrp.org.uk.
• There are free daily guided
tours by yeoman warders;
times are posted every
morning at the main entrance.

Crime and punishment: Prisoners rarely left the Tower in one piece

TOWER OF LONDON

**Prison, palace, home to the Crown Jewels and symbol of
1,000 years of Britain's royal history.**

In previous centuries, prisoners accused of treason would enter the
Tower of London by boat through Traitors' Gate–some, such as Henry
VIII's second wife, Anne Boleyn, taking their final journey. Today the
visitors' entrance is through the Middle Tower and you'll probably get
out alive.

THE WHITE TOWER

At the heart of the Tower is its oldest medieval building, the White
Tower, thought to date from 1078 and built to serve as a fortress and
a royal residence. There's an exhibition about small arms, from the
Royal Armouries collection, and spiral stairs lead to the gloriously
simple Chapel of St. John the Evangelist. John Flamsteed
(1646–1719), Charles II's astronomer, observed the stars from the
turrets before moving to new headquarters at Greenwich.

THE CROWN JEWELS

First stop for many visitors is the Jewel House, where displays tell
the history of the Coronation Regalia (Crown Jewels) before
reaching the Treasury, where the jewels are kept. An excellent visual
story of the jewels entertains those waiting to view the exhibits, and
it is possible to repeat the circuit round the jewels immediately for a
second look.

The jewels mainly date from the restoration of the monarchy in 1660.
Among the priceless stones in the collection is the world's biggest cut
diamond, the 530-carat First Star of Africa.

TOWER GREEN

The famous prisoners incarcerated and executed here over the years
provide the human interest. The Bloody Tower gets its name from the
supposed murder of the two princes, Edward and Richard, sons of
Edward IV and allegedly the victims of their ambitious uncle, Richard
III. The Queen's House, a black-and-white building next to the Bloody
Tower, was the scene of failed regicide Guy Fawkes' interrogation in
1605 and of a daring escape when the Earl of Nithsdale, imprisoned
after the 1715 Jacobite rebellion, made his getaway dressed as a
woman. The high-ranking prisoners were kept in the 13th-century
Beauchamp Tower. Tower Green was the main focus for suffering and
heroics, and was where Anne Boleyn, among others, was beheaded.

Follow the story of evolution at the Natural History Museum

Looking out over the city from a London Eye capsule

BRITISH AIRWAYS LONDON EYE

144 H4 • Westminster Bridge Road SE1 7PB ☎ 0870 5000 600 (reservations) ⏰ Jul–end Aug daily 10–9; May–end Jun, Sep daily 9.30–9; Sep–end Apr daily 10–8 💷 Adult £15, child (5–15) £7.50 🚇 Waterloo, Westminster, Embankment, Charing Cross 🚢 Riverboat to Waterloo Millennium Pier ℹ️ Arrive 30 min before the flight 📖 Souvenir book and guide £5, in English, French, German, Spanish and braille 📷 In the Flight Zone, County Hall, and outside in Jubilee Gardens 🏛️ Jubilee Gardens www.ba-londoneye.com

The world's largest observation wheel offers the best overview of London from 135m (443ft) above the Thames. The capsules have unobstructed views from large windows and the wheel is in constant, very slow motion. Reservations recommended, especially at peak times.

NATURAL HISTORY MUSEUM

142 B5 • Cromwell Road SW7 5BD ☎ 020 7942 5000 ⏰ Daily 10–5.50. Last admittance 5.30. Wildlife Garden: Apr–end Oct daily 12–5 (except during bad weather) 💷 Free. Special exhibitions around £5, child (5–16) £3 🚇 South Kensington 🚶 Tours of Darwin Centre (over 10s only), free, reservations required 📖 £3.50, English only 🍴 📷 🏛️ 🚻 www.nhm.ac.uk

England's most significant collection of dinosaur remains, and more than 70 million items (not all on display) from whales to meteorites, are kept at the outstanding Natural History Museum.

The galleries are divided into the Life Galleries and the Earth Galleries, where state-of-the-art displays explain the making of the planet. Dinosaurs (Gallery 21) is one of the most popular galleries: the lighting is low, and there is an animatronic re-creation of a *Tyrannosaurus rex* in action. For a new take on arthropods (Gallery 33) visit Creepy Crawlies to see how many millions of insects, spiders and crustacea inhabit our world.

The Earth Galleries include Visions of Earth, a dramatic, ethereal space highlighting some fantastic geological specimens. Power Within focuses on volcanoes and earthquakes, including a simulation of the earthquake that shook Kobe, in Japan, in 1995. Other galleries focus on Earth's natural treasury of gemstones.

PALACE OF WESTMINSTER

144 G4 • Parliament Square SW1A 0AA ☎ 020 7219 4272 (House of Commons Information Office), 0870 906 3773 (summer tours tickets) ⏰ Tours during summer recess, Aug, Mon, Tue, Fri, Sat 9.15–4.30, Wed, Thu 1.15–4.30; Sep–early Oct Mon, Fri, Sat 9.15–4.30, Tue–Thu 1.15–4.30; Clock Tower Mon–Fri 10.30, 11.30, 2.30 💷 Public Gallery (House of Commons) and Visitors Gallery (House of Lords) and Clock Tower free; tours see below 🚇 Westminster 🚢 Westminster Millennium Pier 🚶 Tour during summer recess: adult £7, child (4–16) £5, family £22 📖 Free 📷 🏛️ 🚻 www.parliament.uk

Despite their appearance, the Houses of Parliament, which form the main part of the Palace of Westminster, are 19th-century buildings. The original medieval palace was virtually destroyed by fire in 1834 and the competition to design a replacement in Elizabethan style was won by architect Charles Barry (1795–1860) and his assistant, Augustus Pugin (1812–52). The famous clock tower housing Big Ben (the hour bell), was completed in 1858.

The Jewel Tower (Apr–end Oct daily 10–5; Nov–end Mar daily 10–4) was used to store Edward III's treasures. An exhibition in the tower explains the history of Parliament.

TATE BRITAIN

144 off G5 • Millbank SW1P 4RG ☎ 020 7887 8008 (recording), 020 7887 8000 ⏰ Daily 10–5.50 💷 Free, donations welcome. Charge for special exhibitions 🚇 Pimlico, Vauxhall, Westminster 🚢 From Tate Modern (every 40 min) 🚶 Mon–Fri 11, 12, 1.15, 2, 3; Sat–Sun 12, 2.30, 3. Free. Audiotours free, English, French, German, Italian, Spanish 📖 £4.99 🍴 📷 🏛️ 🚻 www.tate.org.uk/britain/

The Tate Gallery, now Tate Britain, transferred its international collection to Tate Modern in 2000, allowing its British collection from 1500 to the present day (the world's largest) to spread out considerably. Despite this, the gallery still owns far more than it can display, and the paintings on show, presented chronologically, are changed every year. All the great names of British art are represented, from Nicholas Hilliard's 16th-century portrait of Queen Elizabeth I and fashionable 17th-century portraits by Sir Peter Lely and Sir Godfrey Kneller, through the work of major 18th-century figures such as William Hogarth, Joshua Reynolds and Thomas Gainsborough, and progressing into innovative 19th-century paintings by William Blake, John Constable and J. M. W. Turner, who is especially well represented. The Pre-Raphaelites are represented in force, and the collection moves into the 20th century with work by J. S. Lowry, Francis Bacon, David Hockney and Lucian Freud.

WHAT TO DO

⊕ AGENT PROVOCATEUR
16 Pont Street SW1X 9EN
Tel 020 7235 0229
www.agentprovocateur.com
Seductive underwear sold in a boudoir-style shop by the son and daughter-in-law of Vivienne Westwood, famous for her punk designs in the 1970s.
🕐 Mon–Sat 11–7 🚇 Knightsbridge, Sloane Square

⊕ CHRISTIE'S
85 Old Brompton Road SW7 3LD
Tel 020 7930 6074
www.christies.com
James Christie conducted his first sale in 1766, and went on to hold the greatest auctions of his time. Christie's sale-rooms are now world famous, auctioning major artworks. Most auctions are free and public; some require a ticket, which should be reserved in advance.
🕐 Variable 🚇 South Kensington

⊕ FORTNUM AND MASON
181 Piccadilly W1A 1ER
Tel 020 7734 8040
www.fortnumandmason.co.uk
Founded in 1707 as a grocery, this famous store is wood-panelled and lit with chandeliers. The ground-floor food hall is fantastic.
🕐 Mon–Sat 10–8, Sun (Food Hall, Lower Ground Floor and Patio Restaurant only) 12–6
🚇 Green Park, Piccadilly Circus

⊕ HAMLEYS
188–196 Regent Street W1B 5BT
Tel 0800 2802 444
www.hamleys.co.uk
The 'World's Finest Toyshop' and certainly one of the biggest. Five large floors full of toys. Staff demonstrate the latest gadgets.
🕐 Mon–Fri 10–8, Sat 9.30–8, Sun 12–6
🚇 Oxford Circus

⊕ HARRODS
87–135 Brompton Road SW1 7XL
Tel 020 7730 1234
www.harrods.com

Harrods' vast, terracotta building belies its origins as a small grocer's shop in 1849. There are 330-plus departments. The ground-floor food halls are a highlight.
🕐 Mon–Sat 10–7 🚇 Knightsbridge

⊕ LIBERTY
210–220 Regent Street W1B 5AH
Tel 020 7734 1234
www.liberty.co.uk
The mock-Tudor building was actually built in the 1920s. The interior contains a varied stock, ranging from ornaments and rugs that seem to have been gathered on some explorer's travels to up-to-date fashion designer apparel.
🕐 Mon–Thu 10–8, Sat 10–7, Sun 12–6
🚇 Oxford Circus

⊕ MOLTON BROWN
8 Jubilee Place, Canary Wharf E14 5NY
Tel 020 718 8761
www.moltonbrown.co.uk
Molton Brown luxury toiletries are stocked by the world's best hotels, and it all started in London in 1973 at South Molton Street. The company has several outlets in the city where you also buy home fragrances.
🕐 Mon–Wed 9–7, Thu–Fri 9–8, Sat 10–6, Sun 12–6 🚇 DLR Canary Wharf

⊕ PORTOBELLO ROAD
Famous market with hundreds of stalls selling antiques, vintage clothing, and *objets d'art*. Not cheap and there is a lot of junk, but fun to catch the 'Notting Hill' vibe. Runs from Pembridge Road (Notting Hill Gate Underground) north up to Westbourne Park Road (Ladbroke Grove Underground).
🕐 Mon–Wed, Sat 8–7, Thu 8–1, Fri 8–6 🚇 Notting Hill Gate, Ladbroke Grove

⊕ SELFRIDGES
400 Oxford Street W1A 2LR
Tel 08708 377377
www.selfridges.com
A Victorian façade hides this popular store, now a modern emporium filled with designer clothes, accessories and a huge beauty hall. There is also an eclectically stocked food hall and 18 places to eat and drink.
🕐 Mon–Wed 10–8, Thu–Sat 9.30–8, Sun 12–6 🚇 Marble Arch, Bond Street

⊕ IMAX CINEMA
1 Charlie Chaplin Walk, South Bank SE1 8XR
Tel 08707 872525
www.bfi.org.uk/imax
A 480-seat cinema housed in a space-age balloon, with the biggest film screen in Britain. Visually overwhelming but limited number of films.
🚇 Embankment, Waterloo

🎭 JAZZ CAFÉ
5 Parkway, Camden Town NW1 7PG
Tel 0870 630 3777
www.meanfiddler.com
Live jazz, soul, world music, hip-hop, R&B—it's all here.
🎟 £10–£20 🚇 Camden Town

🎭 NATIONAL THEATRE
South Bank SE1 9PX
Tel 020 7452 3000
www.nationaltheatre.org.uk
Base of the National Theatre Company. Three auditoriums: the Cottesloe, with no fixed seats or staging; the Lyttleton; and the Olivier, named after Sir Laurence Olivier, the NT's first director.
🎟 £10–£34 🚇 Waterloo

🎭 RONNIE SCOTT'S
47 Frith Street W1D 4HT
Tel: 020 7439 0747
www.ronniescotts.co.uk
Britain's top jazz venue and one of the world's most famous jazz clubs, where the best players perform.
🎟 £15–£25; more for special gigs
🚇 Tottenham Court Road

🎭 ROYAL ALBERT HALL
Kensington Gore SW7 2AP
Tel 020 7589 3203 (info), 020 7589 8212 (reservations)
www.royalalberthall.com
Renowned venue for major concerts and the Proms; cheap tickets are sold on a first-come, first-served basis.
🎟 £3–£50 🚇 South Kensington

🎭 ROYAL OPERA HOUSE
Bow Street WC2E 9DD
Tel 020 7304 4000
www.royaloperahouse.org
This is the principal venue for world-class classical music, opera and ballet. It is also home to the Royal Ballet.
🎟 £3–£180 🚇 Covent Garden

GREAT BRITAIN

SADLER'S WELLS THEATRE
Rosebery Avenue EC1R 4TN
Tel 020 7863 8000
www.sadlerswells.com
Europe's finest dance venue,
offering classical ballet,
modern dance and opera.
£10–£40 Angel

FABRIC
77A Charterhouse Street EC1M 3HN
Tel 020 7336 8898
www.fabriclondon.com
Fabulously cool Fabric is one
of London's superclubs and a
cutting-edge venue, playing
eclectic dance music for an
easy-going 20-something
crowd. It is next to Spitalfields
market in Farringdon.
Fri 9.30pm–5am, Sat 10pm–7am
£12–£18 Farringdon

MARKET PLACE
11 Market Place W1W 8AH
Tel 020 7079 2020
www.marketplace-london.com
Set on two floors, Market Place
is a classic London DJ bar with
panelled walls and very good
food. Downstairs is larger,
with room to dance and
alcove tables.
Mon–Wed noon–midnight, Thu–Sat
11am–1am, Sun 1pm–11pm Free–£7
Oxford Circus

MASH
19–21 Great Portland Street W1W 8QB
Tel 020 7637 5555
Popular retro bar where beers
are brewed on the premises.
Good pizzas, bar food and
serious dining too. DJs four
nights a week.
Mon–Sat noon–2am Free
Oxford Circus

MINISTRY OF SOUND
103 Gaunt Street SE1 6DP
Tel 0870 602 0010
www.ministryofsound.com
Perhaps London's most famous
club, the Ministry is a huge
place where you can experience every aspect of house
music. Never mind the
unfriendly bouncers, long
queues and high admission
prices—just party past dawn.
Fri–Sat 3pm–7am £12–£20
Elephant and Castle

THE SCALA
275 Pentonville Road N1 9NL
Tel 020 7833 2022
www.scala-london.co.uk
Former cinema turned

clubbing venue with three
floors and several bars.
Hosts hip-hop and breakbeat
nights. Friday is Popstarz, a
gay indie night attracting
many straight clubbers.
Fri 10pm–5am, Sat 10pm–6am
£8–£15 King's Cross

ZOO BAR
13–17 Bear Street WC2H 7AS
Tel 020 7839 4188
www.zoobar.co.uk
Central London bar popular
with Londoners after work and
buzzing with a party
atmosphere. Features a
comprehensive cocktail list
with a happy hour until 7pm.
Mon–Fri noon–2.30am, Sat
noon–3am Free Leicester Square

ALL ENGLAND LAWN
TENNIS AND CROQUET CLUB
PO Box 98, Church Road, Wimbledon
SW19 5AE
Tel 020 8944 1066
www.wimbledon.org
Private club founded in 1868.
Centre and No. 1 courts used
only for the Championships;
others used all year by club
members and LTA-sponsored
players.
Southfields Wimbledon

ARSENAL
Arsenal Stadium, 75 Drayton Park,
Highbury N5 1BU
Tel 020 7704 4000
www.arsenal.com
This famous north London soccer club is usually near the top
of the Premiership. It relocated
to the new Emirates Stadium
at the start of 2006–07 season.
Arsenal

CHELSEA
Stamford Bridge, Fulham Road,
Chelsea SW6 1HS
Tel 0871 984 1905
www.chelseafc.co.uk
Wealthy soccer team, owned
by a Russian billionaire, that
has played since 1905, win-
ning the League championship
50 years later and again 50
years on in 2005.
Fulham Broadway

LORD'S
St. John's Wood Road NW8 8QN
Tel MCC info: 020 7289 1611;
tickets: 020 7432 1000
www.lords.org.uk
Historic home of cricket, hosting
internationals, one-day games,

cup finals and semi-finals.
St. John's Wood

TOTTENHAM HOTSPUR
White Hart Lane, Bill Nicholson Way,
High Road, Tottenham N17 0AP
Tel 08704 205000
www.spurs.co.uk
Universally known as Spurs,
Tottenham has played at its
White Hart Lane stadium since
renting it from brewers in
1899.
White Hart Lane

TWICKENHAM STADIUM
Rugby House, 21 Rugby Road,
Twickenham TW1 1DZ
Tel 020 8892 2000;
tours: 020 8892 8877
www.rfu.com
Rugby union's major venue
also has a Museum of Rugby,
and there are tours of the
stadium.
Museum: Tue–Sat 10–5, Sun 11–5.
Closed post-match Sun. Matchdays: no
tours; museum open for match ticket
holders only Tours/museum: adult
£10, child £3 Twickenham

HYDE PARK
The Ranger's Lodge, The Old Police
House, Hyde Park W2 2UH
Tel 020 7298 2100
www.royalparks.gov.uk
The Serpentine, an 11ha
(27-acre) lake, has facilities
for rowing, canoeing and
paddle boats.
Hyde Park Corner, Marble Arch,
Knightsbridge

PORCHESTER SPA
Porchester Centre, Queensway
W2 5HS
Tel 020 7792 3980
Good-value spa in west
London. Three Turkish hot
rooms, two Russian steam
rooms, a cold plunge pool,
a whirlpool bath and an art
deco swimming pool, all for
less than £20.
Daily 10–10. Women only: Tue,
Thu–Fri, Sun (10–4). Men only: Mon,
Wed, Sat. Mixed couples: Sun 4–10
Adult £19.45. Mixed couples ticket:
£27.50 Bayswater

LONDON ZOO
Regent's Park NW1 4RY
Tel 020 7722 3333
www.londonzoo.co.uk
London Zoo opened in 1828
and is now an internationally
important conservation
centre. Check the events

schedule for feeding times, when the modernist Penguin Pool becomes crowded.

◎ Early Mar–late Oct daily 10–5.30; Nov–early Mar daily 10–4 🏠 Adult £13 (or £14.40 with a donation), child (3–15) £10 (or £11.50 with a donation), family £45 ◎ Camden Town

EATING

AL DUCA
4–5 Duke of York Street SW1Y 6LA
Tel 020 7839 3090
www.alduca-restaurant.co.uk
Reasonably priced but classy restaurant. First-rate fish (roasted cod with lentils and parsley sauce, perhaps) and pasta dishes (such as ravioli with woodpigeon and rosemary jus). The 130 or so Italian wines are evenly spread in terms of price.

◎ Mon–Sat 12–2.30, 6–11; closed Sun, Christmas, New Year, public holidays 🏠 L £17.50, D £24, Wine £16
🅂
◎ Piccadilly

LE CAPRICE RESTAURANT
Arlington House, Arlington Street SW1A 1RT
Tel 020 7629 2239
The menu at this unashamedly glamorous, retro-chic restaurant offers a tireless repertoire of uncomplicated, well-presented staples: eggs Benedict, deep-fried haddock with minted pea purée and chips, and comfort puds like banana sticky toffee pudding. Reserve in advance.

◎ Mon–Sat 12–3, 5.30–12; Sun 12–5, 6–11. Closed 1 Jan, Aug public holiday, D 24 Dec, 25–26 Dec, L 27 Dec 🏠 L £30, D £40, Wine £18.50
🅂
◎ Green Park

FIFTEEN
13 Westland Place N1 7LP
Tel 0871 330 1515
www.fifteenrestaurant.com
This venture from celebrity chef Jamie Oliver can be reserved for months in advance. But don't let that put you off this simple but creative cooking. This is food to be enjoyed. 'Please use your fingers–don't be English', says the menu after a description of a juicy partridge dish.

◎ Daily 12–3, 6–9.30; closed D Sun, public holidays 🏠 L £22, D (6 courses) £60, Wine £16 ◎ Old Street

LINDSAY HOUSE RESTAURANT
21 Romilly Street W1V 5AF
Tel 020 7439 0450
www.lindsayhouse.co.uk
Ring the bell for admission to this quirky Soho success story and succumb to the twin temptations of cutting-edge cooking and sheer indulgence. Chef Richard Corrigan and his team rarely put a foot wrong and their well-judged experiments ensure a heady journey for the diner. Adventurous starters like pink slices of veal kidney with harissa sauce and couscous might be followed by a perfectly balanced ensemble of tender pigeon breasts, pork rillette and soft foie gras, served with creamy mash. Sliced poached pear in Sauternes jelly with a quenelle of piquant blue cheese bavarois is a sensational dessert. A tasting menu offers further inventive choices for the whole table. Jacket and tie preferred but children welcome.

◎ Mon–Sat 12–2.30, 6–11; closed Sun, L Sat, one week Christmas, one week Easter
🏠 L £28, D £56, Wine £26
🅂
◎ Leicester Square

MORO
34–36 Exmouth Market, Clerkenwell EC1R 4QE
Tel 020 7833 8336
www.moro.co.uk
Packed Spanish/North African eatery with good-value meals. Many dishes are inspired by the wood-fired oven, and range from the simple grilled chicory with *jamon* and sherry vinegar to the more complex wood-roasted turbot with roast beetroot lentils and churrasco sauce. A warm goat's curd with pine nuts, raisins and orange blossom water in filo pastry provides an unusual end to the meal. The wine list is biased towards Spain and reasonably priced.

◎ Mon–Sat 12.30–2.30, 7–10.30 (tapas served all day); closed Sun, L Sat, Christmas, New Year, public holidays
🏠 L £25, D £31, Wine £12.50
◎ Farringdon Road, Angel

THE OXO TOWER RESTAURANT
8th Floor, Oxo Tower Wharf, Barge House Street SE1 9PH
Tel 020 7803 3888
www.harveynichols.co.uk
With its amazing view through floor-to-ceiling windows overlooking the river and City beyond, this cubed tower cannot fail to impress. Cooking is modern in style but not outlandish, in dishes such as lobster, tomato and basil jelly with Sevruga caviar and pan-fried veal sweetbreads with a sauce of ceps, parsley and lemon oil. Desserts might include coconut rice pudding with spiced ice cream.

◎ Mon–Sat 12–2.30, 6–11; Sun 12–3, 6.30–10. Closed 25–26 Dec
🏠 L (3-course set menu) £31, D £45, Wine £22
◎ Blackfriars

RESTAURANT GORDON RAMSAY
68 Royal Hospital Road SW3 4HP
Tel 020 7352 4441
www.gordonramsay.com
Gordon Ramsay is probably the most acclaimed chef in Britain today and Royal Hospital Road is the foundation of his empire. For somewhere with such a huge reputation, it's surprisingly intimate. Service is as good as it gets, with every dish accurately explained and plenty of help when navigating the wine list. Simplicity, integrity and lightness of touch are Ramsay hallmarks, along with determination and consistency. The quality of ingredients is irreproachable in, for example, a pan-fried fillet of wild sea bass with crushed new potatoes, braised baby pak choi, langoustines and Hermitage sauce, while timing is dead-on. Desserts are a delight. Prices, for the food, are decidedly reasonable.

◎ Mon–Fri 12–2.30, 6.45–11; closed Sat–Sun, two weeks Christmas, public holidays
🏠 L £35, D £85, Wine £12
🅂
◎ Sloane Square

THE RIVER CAFÉ
Thames Wharf, Rainville Road W6 9HA
Tel 020 7386 4200
www.rivercafe.co.uk

The River Café is still serving some of the best Italian food around. The emphasis is on the finest raw materials lovingly prepared. The twice-daily changing menu might include plump whole pigeon roasted in the wood oven, tender to the bone and accompanied by mouthwatering roasted pumpkin, fennel, celeriac and carrots. Desserts are typically Italian and fairly simple.

🕐 Daily 12.30–2.15, 7–9; closed D Sun, Easter, 22 Dec–3 Jan, public holidays
🍴 L £30, D £36, Wine £12
🚇 Hammersmith

SMITHS OF SMITHFIELD
Top Floor, 66–67 Charterhouse Street EC1M 6HJ
Tel 020 7251 7950
www.smithsofsmithfield.co.uk
The food at this large restaurant is organic and additive-free and includes pumpkin tortellini with oregano and Parmesan crisps and Welsh chicken with mushroom ravioli, tarragon and mustard sauce.

🕐 Daily 12–3.30, 6.30–12; closed L Sat, 25–26 Dec, 1 Jan
🍴 L (set menu) £27, D (set menu) £27, Wine £13.75
🚇 Farringdon, Barbican, Chancery Lane

STAYING

CLARIDGE'S
Brook Street, London W1A 2JQ
Tel 020 7629 8860
www.claridges.co.uk
Impressive standards of luxury, style and service are upheld at this iconic bastion of British hospitality. Sumptuously decorated, air-conditioned bedrooms have Victorian or art deco themes to reflect the architecture of the building. Service and dishes are excellent at the restaurant, Gordon Ramsay at Claridge's, run by Mark Sargeant, a protégé of Gordon Ramsay. Reservations are advised.

🛏 £306
🚪 203
🏊 Use of sister hotel's pool
🚇 Bond Street

THE DORCHESTER
Park Lane, London W1K 1QA
Tel 020 7629 8888
www.dorchesterhotel.com
One of London's finest hotels,

The Dorchester is sumptuously decorated. Bedrooms have individual design schemes, are beautifully furnished and have huge, luxurious baths. The Promenade is ideal for afternoon tea or drinks. In the evenings you can relax to the sound of live jazz in the bar, and enjoy a cocktail or an Italian meal. Other dining options include the traditional The Grill and The Oriental. There is a spa, gym, sauna, solarium and Jacuzzi.

🛏 £265–£495
🚪 250
🚇 Hyde Park Corner

EURO HOTEL
51–53 Cartwright Gardens, Russell Square, London WC1H 9EL
Tel 020 7387 4321
www.eurohotel.co.uk
This friendly bed-and-breakfast enjoys an ideal location in a leafy Georgian crescent. Many of the bedrooms have private bathrooms.

🛏 £76
🚪 34
🚇 Russell Square

THE GAINSBOROUGH
7–11 Queensberry Place, South Kensington, London SW7 2DL
Tel 020 7957 0000
www.hotelgainsborough.co.uk
This smart mid-Georgian town house is located in a quiet street near the Natural History Museum. Bedrooms are individually designed and decorated in fine fabrics, with quality furnishings. There is a small lounge and 24-hour room service.

🛏 £160–£200
🚪 49
🚇 South Kensington

GALLERY
8–10 Queensberry Place, South Kensington, London SW7 2EA
Tel 020 7915 0000
www.eeh.co.uk
This stylish property offers friendly hospitality, attentive service and sumptuously furnished bedrooms, some with a private terrace. Room service is available 24 hours a day.

🛏 £145–£180
🚪 36
🚇 South Kensington

HART HOUSE HOTEL
51 Gloucester Place, Portman Square, London W1U 8JF
Tel 020 7935 2288
www.harthouse.co.uk
This elegant Georgian house enjoys a prime location. Bedrooms and public areas are smartly furnished and stylishly decorated and retain much of the house's original character.

🛏 £125
🚪 16
🚇 Baker Street, Marble Arch

LINCOLN HOUSE HOTEL
33 Gloucester Place, London W1U 8HY
Tel 020 7486 7630
www.lincoln-house-hotel.co.uk
Friendly, family-run Georgian town house which has been impressively renovated.

🛏 £89
🚪 23
🚇 Marble Arch

MILLENNIUM GLOUCESTER HOTEL LONDON KENSINGTON
4–18 Harrington Gardens, London SW7 4LH
Tel 020 7373 6030
www.millenniumhotels.co.uk
Air-conditioned bedrooms are furnished in a variety of contemporary styles. Additional amenities are provided in club rooms, which have a dedicated lounge. Eating options include Italian and Singaporean cuisine.

🛏 £205–£340
🚪 610
🚇 Gloucester Road

THE SAVOY
Strand, London WC2R 0EU
Tel 020 7836 4343
www.fairmont.com
Service is impeccable at this renowned hotel and bedrooms and suites offer excellent levels of comfort. The choice of dining areas presents a predicament: whether to opt for the Grill run by chef Marcus Wareing—an alumnus of Gordon Ramsay's restaurant, the River Restaurant—or La Banquette. Jackets and ties are preferred. No visit would be complete without afternoon tea in the Thames Foyer, perhaps enjoying the regular Sunday afternoon tea dance.

🛏 £250–£500
🚪 263 🏊 Indoor
🚇 Charing Cross

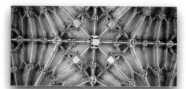

Oxford

•

Oxford rivals Cambridge as one of the world's foremost university towns, with 39 colleges and Britain's oldest library. It's also a hotbed of interesting buildings and has some pretty riverside walks.

Rowing is a big part of student life in Oxford

Is the Radcliffe Camera Britain's most attractive library?

Tradition says morris dancers must dance on May Day

RATINGS	
Good for kids	● ● ●
Historic interest	● ● ● ● ●
Specialist shopping	● ● ● ● ●
Walkability	● ● ● ● ●

TIPS
● Visit in term-time for the real student atmosphere.
● Come by public transport or use the park-and-ride services from the outer ring roads.
● They may look private, but you can visit many colleges; some have a small admission charge.
● City Sightseeing hop-on, hop-off open-top buses give a useful overview with live commentary.

Grotesques on Corpus Christi College (below).
University dignitaries (far right)

SEEING OXFORD

Enclosed by the rivers Cherwell and Thames, Oxford is a beautiful city of honey-coloured Cotswold stone. This world-famous seat of learning is a compact historic city and easily explored on foot. The university's colleges stand in cloistered seclusion displaying a wonderful array of ancient, Classical and modern architecture. Don't miss the back lanes and alleys, particularly Merton Street/Oriel Street, and Queen's Lane/New College Lane (leading beneath the Bridge of Sighs; just off here the Turf Tavern is a popular students' pub). The high street, known as The High, runs from Carfax Tower east to Magdalen Bridge over the River Cherwell, dividing the city into north and south.

HIGHLIGHTS

VIEWS OVER THE CITY
At the beginning of a visit to Oxford, it's a good idea to get your bearings from the rooftops. You can climb the tower of St. Michael's Church in Cornmarket Street, the city's oldest building, or survey the city from Carfax Tower, a remnant of the 14th-century St. Martin's Church, at the busy crossroads known as Carfax, the city's focal point. Another excellent vantage point is the University Church of St. Mary the Virgin, High Street, dating from 1280. Climb the 27m (90ft) tower to the external viewing gallery.

CHRIST CHURCH
✚ 158 B3 • St. Aldates OX1 1DP ☎ 01865 276150 ◉ College: Term time Mon–Sat 10.30–11.45 and 2.30–4.30, Sun 3–4.30; out of term Mon–Sat 9–4.30, Sun 1–4.30. Picture Gallery: Apr–end Sep Mon–Sat 10.30–5, Sun 2–5; Oct–end Mar Mon–Sat 10.30–1, 2–4.30

Founded in 1524, Oxford's largest and most visited college has the biggest quadrangle, and its chapel, Christ Church Cathedral (predating the college), is England's smallest cathedral. Within the Great Hall you will find features from the *Alice in Wonderland* stories written by former don Charles Dodgson, better known as Lewis Carroll (1832–98), while Ante Hall became Hogwarts Hall in the *Harry Potter* movies.

Christ Church Picture Gallery is the only public gallery in any college in either Oxford or Cambridge, and has a collection of 300 paintings, with Italian Old Masters—among them Tintoretto, Leonardo da Vinci, Michelangelo and Carracci—being well represented.

Balliol College and bicycles are quintessentially Oxford

THE RIVERS THAMES AND CHERWELL
➕ 158 B3, C3

These waterways slice through remarkably verdant land close to central Oxford. The tree-lined Cherwell (pronounced *charwell*) is the place for punting and provides almost rural views of Magdalen College (pronounced 'maudlin'), one of the richest and most spacious colleges, founded in 1458 and set in its own deer park—walks through here are really stunning. University rowing crews train on the Thames (also known here as the Isis). Stroll through the Oxford Botanic Garden, founded in 1621 and the oldest of its kind in Britain, to Christchurch Meadow and the confluence of the rivers, or rent a punt or rowing boat from Magdalen Bridge or the Cherwell Boathouse in Bardwell Road.

RADCLIFFE SQUARE
➕ 158 C2 • Between Broad Street and High Street ☎ Sheldonian Theatre: 01865 277299. Bodleian Library: 01865 277000 🕐 Sheldonian Theatre: daily 10–12.30, 2–4.30. Bodleian Library: guided tours Mar–end Oct Mon–Fri 10.30, 11.30, 2, 3; Sat 10.30, 11.30

This is an eye-catching architectural group belonging to the university. The Sheldonian Theatre (built between 1664 and 1668) was the first major architectural work by architect Sir Christopher Wren, who was Professor of Astronomy at the time. The interior assumes the shape of a Roman theatre and its grand ceremonial hall is used for university functions and concerts. High above, the cupola is an excellent viewpoint. Close by, the Bodleian Library is one of six copyright libraries in the UK, entitled to receive a copy of every book published in the country. The circular domed Radcliffe Camera of 1737–49, designed by James Gibbs, is a reading room for the library.

ASHMOLEAN MUSEUM
➕ 158 B2 • Beaumont Street ☎ 01865 278000 🕐 Tue–Sat 10–5 and public holidays (Jun–end Aug Thu to 7.30), Sun 12–5 (except Cast Gallery); closed during St. Giles' Fair early Sep

Britain's oldest public museum (opened in 1683), the Ashmolean houses Oxford University's priceless collections from the time of early man to the 20th century. Come here to see material about early cultures in Europe, Egypt and the Near East, and an antiquities department covering everything from the Stone Age to Victorian times. On a separate site in Beaumont Street, the Cast Gallery has a staggering 100,000 casts (not all on show at one time), which together

MORE TO SEE

PITT-RIVERS MUSEUM AND UNIVERSITY MUSEUM
➕ 158 B1 • Parks Road OX1 3PW ☎ 01865 270927 🕐 Mon–Sat 10–4.30, Sun 12–4.30

This cavernously old-fashioned museum is an anthropology collection of more than 250,000 objects—among them masks and shrunken heads. Or just admire the Victorian Gothic architecture.

MUSEUM OF OXFORD
➕ 158 B2 • Town Hall Building, St. Aldates OX1 1DZ ☎ 01865 252761 🕐 Tue–Fri 10–4, Sat 10–5, Sun 12–4

This museum gives a succinct survey of the city from prehistoric times to the present, from mammoths to Morris Motors. It has archaeological finds, including a Roman pottery kiln, paintings and furniture from houses in Oxford, and re-created interiors such as a Victorian kitchen and a student's college room.

OXFORD CASTLE–UNLOCKED
➕ 158 A2 • 44–46 Oxford Castle OX1 1AY ☎ 01865 260666 🕐 Daily 10–5 🎟 Adult £7.25, child (under 15) £5.25

Discover the secret world of Oxford Castle and the people who worked here and where imprisoned here from the Civil War era through Victorian times to the 20th century.

GREAT BRITAIN

MODERN ART OXFORD

➕ 158 B2 • 30 Pembroke Street OX1 1BP ☎ 01865 813830 🕒 Tue–Sat 10–5, Sun 12–5

This stylish gallery occupies a former brewery and is free of charge. It has changing exhibitions of contemporary art from Britain and beyond, as well as talks, live music and children's activities, plus a café selling very good cakes, and a shop.

BASICS

➕ 4 C3

🛈 15–16 Broad Street OX1 3AS, tel 01865 252200

❓ Guided walking tours of the city and colleges from the tourist information centre (first-come, first-served). Punts and rowing boats available from Magdalen Bridge or the Cherwell Boathouse, Bardwell Road

🚂 Oxford

🚌 From London services run every 10–20 min from Victoria Coach Station via Marble Arch (pay on board), then hourly throughout the night www.visitoxford.org

give a privileged overview of Classical sculpture. The University Museum nearby has fascinating collections on natural history.

OTHER HISTORIC COLLEGES

Merton College (founded 1264) has peaceful gardens and the 14th-century Mob Quad, Oxford's oldest quadrangle, while New College (founded 1379) is famous for its hall, cloister, chapel and gardens enclosed by the old city wall. Peep into St. John's College, founded 1555, with its arcaded Canterbury Quad, and Queens College (founded 1341) for buildings by Sir Christopher Wren and Nicholas Hawksmoor. Farther out in Parks Road is Keble College (1870), a relative newcomer whose elaborate red-brick buildings are a Victorian *tour de force*.

BACKGROUND

Everywhere in this city of spires and greenery you sense learning has been going on a long time: since 1167 in fact, when a number of English scholars, expelled from the Paris Sorbonne, settled here to found the university. As with its ancient rival, Cambridge, students are attached to individual colleges, mostly set around quadrangles (or quads), each with a chapel and dining hall. Most of the central colleges have medieval origins and display a mix of architectural styles, from Renaissance to modern. The colleges originated in the 13th century, when a series of town-versus-gown confrontations hastened the establishment of separate halls of residence. These were succeeded by the first colleges. Since 1974, all but one of them has admitted both men and women—St. Hilda's remains the sole women-only college.

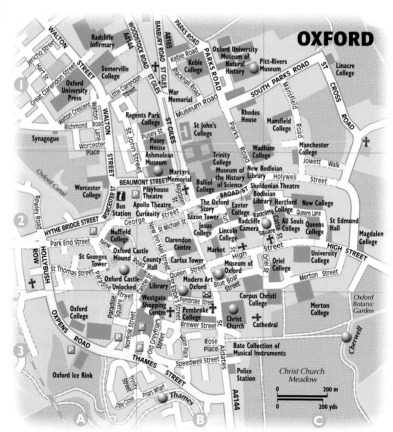

OXFORD

KEY TO SYMBOLS

- 🛍 Shopping
- 🎭 Entertainment
- 🍸 Nightlife
- 🏈 Sports
- ⚙ Activities
- ♥ Health and Beauty
- ✪ For Children

WHAT TO DO

🛍 ALICE'S SHOP
83 St. Aldate's
Tel 01865 723793
www.sheepshop.com
This is the original Old Sheep Shop (from Lewis Carroll's *Through the Looking-Glass*), from where the real-life Alice Liddell used to buy her sweets (candy). It stocks a wide range of Alice-themed gifts.
🕐 Daily 11–5 🛍

🛍 BLACKWELL'S
50 Broad Street
Tel 01865 792792
www.blackwell.co.uk
Blackwell's Oxford empire spans seven shops, including this renowned academic bookshop, the Art and Poster Shop at No. 27 and the Music Shop at Nos. 23–25.
🕐 Mon–Sat 9–6 (Tue from 9.30), Sun 11–5

🛍 THE COVERED MARKET
The High
www.oxfordcity.co.uk/shops/market
Oxford's covered market has been developing since 1773. Today it houses a wide variety of shops, from clothing and footwear to gift shops and jewellers', via butchers' and delicatessens.
🕐 Mon–Sat 8.30–5.30

🛍 THE UNIVERSITY OF OXFORD SHOP
106 High Street
Tel 01865 247414
www.oushop.com
This shop sells official University of Oxford items.
🕐 Mon–Sat 9–5.30 (also Jun Sun and public holidays 11–4; Jul–end Aug Sun 11–5)

🎭 PHOENIX PICTUREHOUSE
57 Walton Street
Tel box office: 01865 7042026; recorded information: 01865 554909 (24 hours)
www.picturehouses.co.uk
Opened in 1913, now

showing independent and classic films.
🕐 Daily 🎬 Adult £6–£7, child (3–14) £5 🛍 ✪

🍸 FREUD
119 Walton Street, Jericho
Tel 01865 311171
Housed in a converted church, this bar is popular for a late drink.
🕐 Mon–Sat 11am–2am, Sun 12–10.30

⚙ CHERWELL BOAT HOUSE
Barwell Road
Tel 01865 515978
www.cherwellboathouse.co.uk
Rent a traditional hand-crafted 'punt' (or canoe or rowing boat) and tour the waterways of Oxford.
🕐 Daily 10am–dusk 🎬 Weekdays £12 per hour, weekends £14 per hour

⚙ THE RIDGEWAY NATIONAL TRAIL
The National Trails Office, Holton
Tel 01865 810224
www.nationaltrail.co.uk/ridgeway
The Ridgeway, which follows a chalk ridge used by prehistoric man, is perhaps Britain's oldest road. It's 136km (85 miles) long and stretches from Overton Hill near Avebury to Ivinghoe Beacon in the Chilterns. There are many places to stop off at along the way.

EATING

GEE'S RESTAURANT
61 Banbury Road
Tel 01865 553540
www.gees-restaurant.co.uk
This beautiful conservatory is airy by day and romantic by night. Dishes are a mix of English and French cuisine, using mostly organic produce.
🕐 12–2.30, 6–10.30; closed 25–26 Dec
🍷 L £25, D £32, Wine £18.95
🚗 From M40, junction 8 take northern ring road and follow signs to city centre through Summertown. Gee's opposite Parktown on Banbury Road

LE PETIT BLANC BRASSERIE
71–72 Walton Street
Tel 01865 510999
www.brasserieblanc.com
At this busy yet relaxed French-style brasserie, the food clings to its Gallic roots but substitutes British ingredients wherever possible, offering satisfying brasserie favourites.

🕐 Mon–Sat 12–11, Sun 12–10; closed 25 Dec
🍷 L £30, D £40, Wine £13.25
🎭
🚗 From city centre, north along St. Giles, left into Little Clarendon Street and right at end of Walton Street
🚉 Oxford

STAYING

BURLINGTON HOUSE
374 Banbury Road, Summertown, Oxford OX2 7PP
Tel 01865 513513
www.burlington-house.co.uk
A warm welcome is assured at this immaculately maintained Victorian bed-and-breakfast. The attractive furnishing schemes complement the original features, and two of the bedrooms overlook a pretty patio garden. Memorable breakfasts are served in a homey dining room. Children 12 and dogs are not welcome.
🛏 £85
🛏 11
🚗 At Peartree roundabout follow signs to Oxford. At next roundabout take second exit A40. After about 800m (0.5 miles) at next roundabout take third exit. Hotel on corner of fourth road on left
🚉 Oxford

THE OLD BANK HOTEL
92–94 High Street, Oxford OX1 4BN
Tel 01865 799599
www.oldbank-hotel.co.uk
This former bank has been converted into a very stylish and comfortable hotel. Bedrooms are smart and have CD players and air conditioning. Public areas include the vibrant all-day Quod Bar and Restaurant, a separate residents' bar, and an outside courtyard.
🕐 Closed 25–27 Dec
🛏 £175
🛏 42 🎭

York

●

A wonderfully complete medieval city, crammed with historic treasures and outstanding museums, York is also home to Gothic York Minster, one of Britain's finest cathedrals. The city is fun to explore on foot, with plenty of entertainment out on the streets.

SEEING YORK

This strikingly beautiful city straddling the River Ouse is one of Britain's premier sights. Despite its distance from London, it is easily accessible by train, and is served by several major roads. York has a multitude of museums and buildings spanning a range of historic periods. Much of the city's compact heart is pedestrianized, so it's a great place to explore on foot, taking in its wealth of shops and vibrant street performers. York is an easy and pleasant city for walking, and a circuit of the city wall is an excellent way to get your bearings. Among the most evocative streets are The Shambles, originally a street of butchers' shops and retaining overhanging, jettied, timber-framed buildings, and Stonegate, where shop signs and frontages span several centuries. Also look for York's distinguished clutch of medieval churches (some no longer used for services). Arguably the finest is Holy Trinity (Goodramgate) with its inward-facing box pews and late 15th-century stained glass.

HIGHLIGHTS

YORK MINSTER

🚩 163 B1 • Deangate YO1 7HH ☎ 01904 557216 🕐 Mon–Sat 9–30–5 (for tourists), Sun 12–5.30 💷 Adult £5, child (under 16) free. Combined ticket (includes undercroft, treasury and crypt): adult £7, child free. Tower: adult £3, child £1
www.yorkminster.org

Dating from 1220–1472, this is Europe's largest Gothic cathedral north of the Alps, with two towers, richly traceried windows and a massive west front. Its medieval stained glass represents a quarter of all the stained glass of the period in England. Look particularly for the Five Sisters within a quintet of lancet windows, and for the depictions of Genesis and Revelation in the superb east window of 1405–08, the world's largest area of medieval stained glass within a single window. The stone choir screen is carved with images of English monarchs from William I (1028–87) to Henry VI (1421–71), while around the nave and choir are painted stone shields dating from the time when Edward II (1284–1327) held a parliament in York.

There are separate admission charges for certain other parts of the Minster—the treasury, featuring the 11th-century Horn of Ulf, and the crypt, containing part of the 11th-century church that preceded the Minster. Also below ground level, the foundations (or undercroft) reveal an absorbing cross-section of history, from the remains of a Roman fort to the drastic building works carried out in the 1960s to support the collapsing central tower (whose foundations turned out to be completely inadequate). The octagonal Chapter House has lively carvings of flowers and fruits and is unusual in that it lacks a central structural pillar. The long climb up the central tower is rewarded by a panoramic view over the city (extra admission charge).

Reconstructed streets in the Castle Museum bring York's history alive

RATINGS	
Good for kids	●●●
Historic interest	●●●●●
Specialist shopping	●●●●
Walkability	●●●●●

TIPS

● The York Pass (www.yorkpass.com) gives free entry to more than 30 attractions in and around the city, plus numerous special offers for shopping and dining (adult: one day £21, two days £27, three days £34).

● The city wall (5km/3 miles) is worth walking, but you may prefer to skip the southern part, which looks over relatively modern suburbs.

● A boat trip on the River Ouse is a great alternative way of seeing York and its surroundings, and also offers a glimpse of the Archbishop of York's palace at Bishopthorpe.

York Minster (left and inset) is the city's crowning glory

TREASURER'S HOUSE

✚ 163 B1 • Minster Yard YO1 7JL
☎ 01904 624247 ◉ Apr–end Oct
Sat–Thu 11–4.30
This house beside the Minster
was mostly rebuilt in the 17th
century—long after the post of
Treasurer to the Minster was
abolished (in 1547)—after which
it passed into private hands. The
National Trust has filled it with
French furniture and English glass
and ceramics.

*Displays in the Jorvik Viking
Centre illustrate the city's history*

THE MERCHANT ADVENTURERS' HALL

✚ 163 C2 • Fossgate YO1 9XD
☎ 01904 654818 ◉ Apr–end Sep
Mon–Thu 9–5, Fri–Sat 9–3.30, Sun
12–4; Oct–end Mar Mon–Sat 9–3.30
York's largest (27m by 12m/
89ft by 40ft) and most
impressive medieval half-
timbered building is still in use.
It has a complex roof with
vast crossbeams.

CLIFFORD'S TOWER

✚ 163 B3 • Tower Street YO1 1SA
☎ 01904 646940 ◉ Mar–end Sep
daily 10–6; Oct 10–5; Nov–end Feb
10–4
The four-lobed stone keep of
the castle dates from 1245,
and replaced a wooden tower
built by William I in 1068.

FAIRFAX HOUSE

✚ 163 B2 • Castlegate YO1 9RN
☎ 01904 655543 ◉ Mon–Thu, Sat
11–4.30, Sun 1.30–4.30; Fri guided
tours, 11 and 2
Witness wealthy living during
the 18th century at this
exceptional Georgian town
house, which was saved from
the brink of collapse in 1984.
It contains select items from
centuries past, notably a
collection of splendid 17th-
and 18th-century English clocks.

CITY WALL

You get an immense sense of historic continuity in York, which is
enclosed by its virtually complete wall, pierced by bars (gateways).
The section between Bootham Bar (on the site of the Roman
gateway) and Monk Bar gives some of the choicest views of the old
city. Monk Bar, the best-preserved gateway, houses the Richard III
Museum (Mar–end Oct daily 9–5; Nov–end Feb daily 9.30–4),
presenting the story of the monarch (1452–85) portrayed (possibly
unfairly) as a murderer by Shakespeare and others, and giving you a
chance to reach your own verdict. The heads of criminals and
enemies were placed on spikes on Micklegate Bar during the Wars of
the Roses (1455–85), and there's a small social history display inside
(Feb–end Oct daily 9–5; Nov–end Jan Sat–Sun 9–5).

THE SHAMBLES

✚ 163 C2
A short walk south from York Minster leads through some
of the city's most memorable streets, where jettied half-
timbered buildings overhang the narrow thoroughfare, the
walls lean at alarming angles and the buildings on either
side almost touch each other at roof level. This was
originally a row of butchers' stalls (hence the hooks and
rails, from which the meat was hung, still visible above
some windows). It has since been smartened up into one
of the city's most famous sights and costumed characters
such as town criers (below) entertain sightseers. Stonegate
has an array of old shop fronts and has such curios as a red
devil figurine above a former printer's shop. Farther east,
near Aldwark, is the half-timbered Merchant Taylors' Hall (all year Tue
10–4), with a 14th-century roof beyond a 17th- and 18th-
century façade, and the jettied Black Swan Inn, whose beamed
rooms and inglenook fireplace make it an interesting lunch spot.

YORK CASTLE MUSEUM

✚ 163 C3 • The Eye of York YO1 1RY ☎ 01904 087087
◉ Daily 9.30–5
Housed in the former Debtors' Prison of 1705
and Female Prison of 1780, this museum alone
justifies a visit to York. Displays include full-
size reconstructions of Victorian and
Edwardian shopping streets, collections of costumes and uniforms, and
the very cell in which notorious high-
wayman Dick Turpin (1706–39) spent
his last days before facing death on the
gallows.

JORVIK VIKING CENTRE

✚ 163 B2 • Coppergate YO1 9WT ☎ 01904 543400
◉ Apr–Oct daily 10–5; Nov–end Mar daily 10–4
Another of York's must-sees is the fruition of
an excavation that uncovered the Viking
settlement of Jorvik. The centre presents a
unique journey back to 10th-century York, with
sights, sounds and smells of life based on archaeological evidence. It ends with a display of finds
from the site and a hologram of the Viking helmet
found here—the original is in the Yorkshire
Museum in Museum Gardens.

NATIONAL RAILWAY MUSEUM

✚ 163 A2 • Leeman Road YO26 4XJ ☎ 08848 133139 ◉ Daily 10–6
Across Lendal Bridge in the west of the city, the National Railway
Museum is the definitive national collection of railwayana, and it's
free. More than 100 restored locomotives are on display here, including the record-breaking steam locomotive *Mallard*, which reached a
heady 202kph (126mph) and is the world's fastest steam engine, a
full-size working replica of the *Rocket*, originally built by railway

pioneer George Stephenson (1781–1848), the sumptuous royal saloon carriage (car) built for Queen Victoria (1819–1901), and a modern Japanese bullet train. Other displays include railway posters, paintings and photographs. Rail buffs may also like to visit York Model Railway (Mon–Sat 9–6, Sun 10–5), in York Station.

MUSEUM GARDENS
✚ 163 B2

This is a pearl of a picnic place. There are ruins of 13th-century St. Mary's Abbey, the 13th-century remains of St. Leonard's Hospital (including a chapel and vaulted undercroft, or foundation), a Roman tower known as the Multangular Tower and a large chunk of Roman wall standing at its original height. Also in the gardens is the Yorkshire Museum (daily 10–5), whose exhibits include Roman sculptures and mosaics, Anglo-Saxon finds such as the Ormside Bowl and much-embellished Gilling Sword, Viking weaponry and medieval treasures. Look for the Middleham Jewel in the Yorkshire Museum, a gold pendant adorned with a superb sapphire.

BACKGROUND

York was founded by the Roman army in AD71 as the town of Eboracum. The Roman fortress and the roads that led to it form the basis of the city's outline today, and a few remains are visible above ground, such as the walls of the fortress in the foundations of York Minster. After the Romans left, Viking settlers took over, and the town became Jorvik. They established the city's gateways and named the streets, many of them on the Roman lines. In the Middle Ages, York flourished as a trading city, and the walls that were started in Roman times were rebuilt.

BASICS
✚ 4 C2
ℹ George Hudson Street YO1 6WR, tel 01904 550099
🚉 York

www.visityork.org
Comprehensive and clearly laid out guide to visitor attractions and accommodation in the city. A to Z of themes, plus itineraries, shopping and eating.

York's defensive walls have Roman foundations

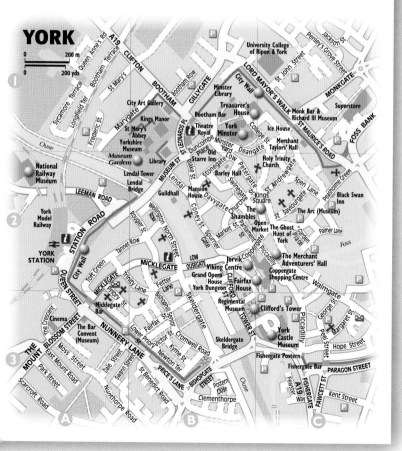

KEY TO SYMBOLS

- 🛍 Shopping
- 🎭 Entertainment
- 🍸 Nightlife
- ⚽ Sports
- ✪ Activities
- ♡ Health and Beauty
- ✹ For Children

WHAT TO DO

🛍 BARBARA CATTLE
45 Stonegate
Tel 01904 623862
www.hl-brown.co.uk
A treasure house in York's historic centre, with fine silver and jewellery, especially 18th- and 19th-century English silverware and rare York silver.
⏰ Mon–Sat 9–5.30

🛍 ROBERT THOMPSON'S CRAFTSMEN LTD
Mouseman Visitor Centre, Kilburn
Tel 01347 869100
www.robertthompsons.co.uk
Run by the grandsons of founder Robert Thompson (1876–1955), the woodcarver whose work is seen in many of Yorkshire's churches and great houses. Oak furniture and smaller items are finished with Thompson's celebrated trademark mouse.
⏰ Mon–Thu 9–5, Fri 9–3.45, Sat 10–12; closed Christmas and New Year. Visitor Centre: Easter–end Sep daily 10–5; Oct Tue–Sun 10–5; Nov, Dec Wed–Sun 11–4 🍴 🚉 Thirsk (11km/7 miles)

✪ YORK RACECOURSE
Tadcaster Road
Tel 01904 620911
www.yorkracecourse.co.uk
Race meetings here are one of the highlights of the northern social scene and it's the place to dress in style and enjoy a card filled with fine horse-flesh. Main meetings take place in May and August.
💷 Tickets £24–£77

EATING

BETTY'S TEA ROOMS
6–8 St. Helen's Square
Tel 01904 659142
www.bettys.co.uk
This café has been supplying afternoon teas to the people of York and surrounding area, and is still set in grand surroundings inspired by the liner the Queen Mary in the 1930s. Enjoy patisseries and

tea or tasty lunches. A pianist plays most evenings between 6 and 9.
⏰ Daily 9am–9pm
💷 L £12, D £16, Wine £16.95

MELTON'S RESTAURANT
7 Scarcroft Road
Tel 01904 634341
www.meltonsrestaurant.co.uk
The Modern British cooking at this inviting family-run shop-fronted restaurant has influences from Europe, Asia and North America— buckwheat blinis with beetroot gravadlax and crème fraiche— from the à la carte or set-price lunch/early evening menu. Details are impressive, from the varied canapés to the home-made cheese biscuits, and the warm service shows pride in the food.
⏰ Tue–Sat 12–2, 5.30–9.30; Mon 5.30–9.30; closed Sun, three weeks at Christmas, one week in Aug
💷 L £22, D £29, Wine £15
🚉 South from city centre across Skeldergate Bridge, opposite Bishopthorpe Road parking area

YORK PAVILION HOTEL
45 Main Street, Fulford
Tel 01904 622099
www.yorkpavilionhotel.com
Langton's brasserie, known for its seafood, occupies half a dozen rooms of this hotel. A rustic starter such as grilled peppered goats' cheese with dressed leaves and tapenade oil might be followed by a main of fillet of red mullet with chive and crayfish risotto. The wine list is admirable. Children are welcome.
⏰ Daily 12–2, 6.30–9.30
💷 L £17, D £26, Wine £14
🚉 South from city centre on A19 (Selby), hotel 3km (2 miles) on left

STAYING

ALEXANDER HOUSE
94 Bishopthorpe Road, York YO23 1JS
Tel 01904 625016
www.alexanderhouseyork.co.uk
Guests are made to feel very much at home at this Victorian terraced house, just a short walk from the city centre. The owners of this stylish bed-and-breakfast delight in sharing their home with guests, and have created four superbly equipped rooms. Delicious breakfasts featuring

quality local produce are served in the well-appointed dining room. Children under 12 are not welcome.
⏰ Closed 25 Dec–1 Jan
💷 £79
🛏 4
🚗 From A64 take A1036 York road west into city centre. Turn right at Scarcroft Road, at the end turn right and Alexander House is 100m (110 yards) on left
🚉 York

THE GRANGE HOTEL
1 Clifton, York YO30 6AA
Tel 01904 644744
www.grangehotel.co.uk
This bustling Regency town house is conveniently placed. The bedrooms have been thoughtfully equipped, and the public rooms are comfortable and stylish. There are two dining options—The Brasserie in the cellar, which has an informal atmosphere, and The Ivy, which is lavishly decorated and offers a fine dining menu.
💷 £125–£220; discount for under-12s
🛏 30
🚗 On A19 York–Thirsk road about 500m (550 yards) from city centre
🚉 York

HAZELWOOD
24–25 Portland Street, Gillygate, York YO31 7EH
Tel 01904 626548
www.thehazelwoodyork.com
The Hazelwood bed-and-breakfast is an elegant Victorian town house quietly situated in the heart of the ancient city, only 350m (400 yards) from York Minster. The bedrooms are individually styled and tastefully fitted to very high standards using designer fabrics. There's a wide choice of breakfasts. No children under eight. Dogs are not welcome.
💷 £75
🛏 14
🚗 Approaching York from north on A19 turn left before City Gate and take first turning left
🚉 York

CARDIFF

A heady mixture of greenery and Victorian civic elegance.

FROM VILLAGE TO CAPITAL

From its beginnings as the site of a Roman fort on the River Taf (Taff), Cardiff grew up as a village protected by a Norman castle and, later, a modest harbour town.

By the early 20th century it was the biggest coal-exporting dock in the world. The heart of the city has handsome Victorian and Edwardian shopfronts and arcades, a 19th-century covered market and gleaming civic buildings. Redevelopment of the docks area began in the 1980s, and the docks' connection with the city was gradually re-established. Cardiff is now the home of the National Assembly for Wales.

THE CASTLE AND CIVIC CENTRE

The focus of the city is Cardiff Castle (daily 9.30–6), a Norman fortress dating from Roman times. In the 19th century it was transformed into a flamboyant, neo-Gothic extravaganza by the third Marquess of Bute and his designer William Burges (1827–81).

Northeast of the castle, the white Portland-stone buildings of the Civic Centre, built in the 19th and 20th centuries, are laid out on broad avenues. In front is the elaborate City Hall and the National Museum and Gallery (Tue–Sun 10–5), with an Evolution of Wales exhibition and the largest collection of Impressionist and post-Impressionist paintings outside France.

Don't miss The Arab Room in Cardiff Castle has a marble and cedar-wood interior. In the Banqueting Hall is a fireplace with castle frieze.

ON THE WATERFRONT

Cardiff's docks have become vibrant Cardiff Bay, fringed with restaurants, bars and shops. Among the attractions are Techniquest (Mon–Fri 9.30–4.30, Sat–Sun 10.30–5), a science discovery complex and planetarium; arts and crafts exhibitions in a restored warehouse; Butetown History and Arts Centre (Tue–Fri 10–5, Sat–Sun 11–4.30), tracing the area's history; and the Pierhead Building (Mon–Fri 9.30–4.30), with a display about the National Assembly for Wales.

The white-wood Norwegian Church (daily 10–4) is a cultural centre with events and exhibitions, built for Scandinavian sailors who brought timber beams for the South Wales coal mines. Goleulong Lightship 2000 (Mon–Sat 10–5, Sun 2–5) has a light tower, engine room, chapel and cabins to explore. The new Millennium Centre hosts opera, ballet and musicals in a dramatic modern building opened in 2004.

Admire the Islamic ceiling in the Arab Room (above) at Cardiff Castle (above left)

RATINGS	
Good for kids	● ●
Historic interest	● ● ●
Specialist shopping	● ● ●
Walkability	● ●

BASICS
➕ 4 C3
ℹ The Old Library, The Hayes, Cardiff CF10 1AH, tel 08701 211258
🚉 Cardiff Central

www.visitcardiff.com

WHAT TO DO

⊕ CASTLE WELSH CRAFTS
1 Castle Street
Tel 029 2034 3038
Opposite the entrance to Cardiff Castle, this giftshop has good-quality traditional products such as carved love spoons, Celtic-design jewellery, slate carvings and lamps. There are also excellent handmade Welsh-language cards, artwork by Welsh artists and tapestries.
⊙ Mon–Sat 9–5.30 (also some Sun)
🚊 Cardiff Central

⊕ COAL EXCHANGE
Mount Stuart Square
Tel 029 2049 4917
www.coalexchange.co.uk
The ornate 1880s exchange building in the inner harbour of Cardiff Bay is a stylish live music venue.
⊙ Box office open daily 9–5
🚊 Cardiff Bay (trains from Cardiff Queen Street)

⊕ NEW THEATRE
Park Place
Tel 029 2087 8889
www.newtheatrecardiff.co.uk
A traditional theatre—home of Welsh National Opera—with plays, gigs and dance.
⊙ Box office: Mon–Sat 10–8 🍴 ▯
▯ 🚊 Cardiff Queen Street

⊕ SHERMAN THEATRE
Senghennydd Road, Cathays
Tel 029 2064 6900
www.shermantheatre.co.uk
A mixture of conventional and radical productions, including those by the Sherman Theatre Company.
⊙ Box office: Mon–Sat 10–8 (10–5.30 if no performance) ▯
🚊 Cardiff Queen Street

⊕ ST. DAVID'S HALL
The Hayes
Tel 029 2087 8444
www.stdavidshallcardiff.co.uk
Wales' national concert hall, home of the BBC National Orchestra of Wales and a venue for the biennial Cardiff Singer of the World. Pop, rock and classical music, comedy, children's shows and dance.
⊙ Box office: Mon–Sat 9.30–8 (or 5.30 if no performance) 🍴 Various 🍴 ▯
▯ 🚊 Cardiff Central

⊕ CLWB IFOR BACH
11 Womanby Street
Tel 029 2023 2199
www.clwb.net
Three floors with different styles—bar and dance floor on ground level; alternative music at the top.
⊙ Mon–Sat 9pm–2am 🍺 £3–£15
🚊 Cardiff Central

⊕ LIQUID
St. Mary's Street
Tel 029 2064 5464
www.liquid-online.com
This branded city-centre super-club is all lava lamps and light shows. Music is from the dance mainstream with some R&B.
⊙ Thu 9.30pm–3am, Fri 9.30pm–2.30am, Sat 9.30pm–3am
🍺 Usually free before 10, then various

⊕ GLAMORGAN CRICKET CLUB
Sophia Gardens
Tel 029 2034 3478
www.glamorgancricket.com
Welsh cricket's only first-class team hold their own with the English counties.
⊙ Apr–end Sep 🍺 £8–£15

⊕ MILLENNIUM STADIUM
Wesgate Street
Tel 0870 013 8600;
ticket hotline: 0870 5582582
www.millenniumstadium.com
State-of-the-art sports stadium with retractable roof, hosting major sports and music events.
⊙ Tours (non-match days): Mon–Sat 10–5, Sun 10–4 🍺 Tours: adult £5.50, child £3, family £17 🍴 ▯
🚊 Cardiff Central

EATING

IZAKAYA JAPANESE TAVERN
Mermaid Quay
Tel 029 2049 2939
In the style of a traditional rural Japanese tavern, Izakaya serves the kind of authentic food the Japanese enjoy every day. Five different types of seating arrangement each create a slightly different mood.
⊙ Daily 12–2.30, 6–11; closed 23–26, 31 Dec, 1 Jan
🍺 L £5.90, D £17, Wine £14

⊖ Leave M4 at junction 33 for A4232. Restaurant on first floor Mermaid Quay

THE ST. DAVID'S HOTEL AND SPA
Havannah Street
Tel 029 2045 4045
www.thestdavidshotel.com
Tides Restaurant is adjacent to this hotel's stylish cocktail bar. The menu features the best of Welsh ingredients, such as braised shank of lamb, and is supplemented by a daily market menu focusing on in-season produce.
⊙ 12.30–2.15, 6.30–10.15
🍺 L £25, D £30, Wine £15
⊖ M4 junction 33/A4232 for 15km (9 miles) for Techniquest at top exit slip road; first left at roundabout then first right
🚊 Cardiff Central

STAYING

THE BIG SLEEP HOTEL
Bute Terrace, Cardiff CF10 2FE
Tel 029 2063 6363
www.thebigsleephotel.com
This central bed-and-breakfast hotel offers well-equipped bedrooms ranging from standard to penthouse, with spectacular views over the city towards the bay. Continental breakfast is served or 'breakfast to go' is an alternative for the visitor wishing to make an early start. There is a bar on the ground floor and secure parking. Dogs are not allowed.
🍺 £50–£69; discount for under-12s
🛏 81
🚊 Cardiff Central

THE ST. DAVID'S HOTEL AND SPA
Havannah Street, Cardiff CF10 5SD
Tel 029 2045 4045
www.thestdavidshotel.com
This imposing contemporary building sits in a prime position on Cardiff Bay. The bedrooms are comfortable. A quiet lounge on the first floor suits guests seeking a place for relaxation. There is a good restaurant.
🍺 £150–£250
🛏 132 ⊕ ⊕
⊖ M4 junction 33/A4232 for 15km (9 miles) for Techniquest at top exit slip road; first left at roundabout then first right
🚊 Cardiff Central

THE ROYAL MILE
Edinburgh

A castle, a palace, an impressively long main thoroughfare and a world-famous skyline create the home city of Scotland's ruling élite. Edinburgh is drenched in history.

SEEING EDINBURGH

The Scottish capital is divided into two distinct halves by the the Water of Leith. The Old Town to the south has historic routes such as Grassmarket and Canongate and a medieval network of alleys. More breathing space can be found in the striking Georgian streets of the New Town to the north.

HIGHLIGHTS

EDINBURGH CASTLE

➕ 168 B2 • Castle Hill EH1 2NG ☎ 0131 225 9846 🕐 Apr–end Oct daily 9.30–6; Nov–end Mar daily 9.30–5 💷 Adult £11, child (under 16) £5.50 📷 Guided tours ⬛ 🏛
www.edinburghcastle.biz

Edinburgh Castle towers over the city from its volcanic rock. Bronze Age people settled on the top around 850BC, and by the Middle Ages it was a fortified site and royal residence. The views from the ramp at the entrance are great. The Half Moon Battery is the defensive wall and walkway on the east side, built after the Lang (long) Siege of 1567–73. Since 1861 a field gun has boomed out here Monday to Saturday at precisely 1pm to enable mariners to fix the time accurately. The Crown Room displays the ancient regalia of Scotland—crown, sceptre and sword—locked away after the parliamentary union with England in 1707 and unearthed by Sir Walter Scott in 1818. The Stone of Destiny is also here, on which Scottish kings were crowned. Originally at Scone Palace, it was stolen by Edward I and remained in London until recovered from Westminster Abbey in 1996. The Scotch Whisky Heritage Centre (May–end Sep daily 9.30–6.30; Oct–end Apr daily 9.30–6) is below the castle.

PALACE OF HOLYROODHOUSE

➕ 169 E1 • EH8 8DX ☎ 0131 556 5100 🕐 Apr–end Oct daily 9.30–6; Nov–end Mar daily 9.30–4.30 💷 Adult £9.50, child (under 17) £5.50, under 5 free, family £27.50 📷 Guided tours only Nov–end Mar ⬛ 🏛
www.royal.gov.uk

Filled with works of art from the Royal Collection, this towered palace sits at the foot of the Royal Mile and is the Queen's official residence in Scotland, which means it may be closed at short notice. The palace started in the 15th century as a guesthouse for Holyrood Abbey, and its name is said to come from the Holy Rood, a fragment of Christ's cross belonging to David I (c1080–1153). Bonnie Prince Charlie (1720–88) held court here in 1745, followed by George IV on his triumphant visit to the city in 1822. The state rooms, designed for Charles II and hung with Brussels tapestries, are particularly good.

MUSEUM OF SCOTLAND

➕ 168 C3 • Chambers Street EH1 1JF ☎ 0131 225 7534 🕐 Tue 10–8, Mon, Wed–Sat 10–5, Sun 12–5 💷 Free 📷 Free tours daily 🍴 ⬛ 🏛
www.nms.ac.uk

This entertaining museum showcases the Scottish collections from the Royal Museum next door. It is a superb, well-explained collection that covers the shaping of Scotland through geology and glaciation, what is known of the lives of the earliest settlers in Scotland and the founding of Scottish identity.

New Year's Eve is spectacular in Edinburgh (above)

RATINGS				
Good for kids	●	●	●	○
Historic interest	●	●	●	●
Specialist shopping	●	●	●	●
Walkability	●	●	●	●

BASICS

➕ 4 C2
ℹ 3 Princes Street (above Mall) EH2 2QP, tel 0845 225 5121; Apr, Oct Mon–Sat 9–6, Sun 10–6; May–Jun, Sep Mon–Sat 9–7, Sun 10–7; Jul–Aug Mon–Sat 9–8, Sun 10–8; Nov–Mar Mon–Sat 9–5, Sun 10–5
🚊 Edinburgh Waverley

www.edinburgh.org

TIPS

● A free bus service links the four national galleries.
● The exact fare is required for Lothian Buses and First Edinburgh, but journeys shouldn't cost much more than £1 (£2 on night buses).

MORE TO SEE
ARTHUR'S SEAT

➕ 169 off E2
Arthur's Seat is the 251m (823ft) high remains of a 325-million-year-old volcano. There is access to Holyrood's hills and lochs.

ROYAL BOTANIC GARDEN

⊕ 168 off B1 • 20A Inverlieth Row EH3
5LR ☎ 0131 552 7171 🕐 Mar and Oct
daily 10–6; Apr–end Sep daily 10–7;
Nov–end Feb daily 10–4 💷 Garden:
free; glasshouses: adult £3, child £1,
family £8
www.rbge.org.uk

The garden has 15,500 species
in 28ha (70 acres) of landscaped
grounds and 10 greenhouses.

CANONGATE KIRK

⊕ 169 E2 • Canongate EH8 8BR
☎ 0131 556 3515 🕐 Jun–end Oct Mon–
Sat 10.30–4, Sun 10–12.30 💷 Free ☐
Canongate Kirk was built in 1688
after James VI of Scotland
converted the abbey church at
Holyrood to a chapel.

NATIONAL GALLERY OF SCOTLAND

⊕ 168 C2 • The Mound EH2 2EL ☎ 0131 624 6200 🕐 Fri–Wed 10–5, Thu 10–7
💷 Free 🚌 Free bus runs between all four national galleries ☐ ♿
www.nationalgalleries.org

Designed by New Town architect William Playfair (1789–1857), the
National Gallery of Scotland has a collection of 20,000 paintings,
sculptures and drawings. The main focus are paintings by Europe's
great masters but Scottish artists are displayed in their own section
downstairs. Favourites include Sir Henry Raeburn's over-the-top tartan-
clad chieftan, *Colonel Alastair Mcdonnell of Glengarry* (1812), and the
land- and seascapes of William McTaggart (1835–1910).

NEW TOWN

⊕ 168 B1

The New Town covers 2.5sq km (1sq mile) to the north of Princes
Street, and is characterized by broad streets of grand, terraced houses
with large windows and ornamental door arches. The Georgian House
(Mar, Nov daily 11–3; Apr–end Jun, Sep, Oct 10–5; Jul, Aug 10–7),
on Charlotte Square's north side, is a meticulous re-creation of an
18th-century home, down to the Wedgwood dinner service on the
dining table.

ROYAL MILE

⊕ 168 C2

The Royal Mile is the name of the long street that links Holyrood Palace
with Edinburgh Castle. About 60 narrow closes lead off on either side.
Lady Stair's Close, near St. Giles Cathedral, is the best known and leads
through to the Writers' Museum (Mon–Sat 10–5, Sun 2–5 during
Edinburgh Festival). Drop into the Museum of Edinburgh (Aug only

*Greyfriars Bobby, a famous
city landmark (top right).
Holyroodhouse (middle right).
The Camera Obscura on the
Royal Mile (bottom right)*

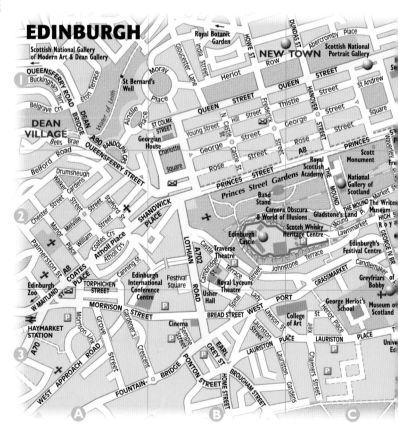

Mon–Sat 10–5, Sun 12–5) to get a feeling of the interiors of these old houses. The 1490 John Knox House (Jul–end Aug Mon–Sat 10–5.30, Sun 12–5.30), on the corner of Royal Mile, is where John Knox (c1505–72), the founder of the Church of Scotland, preached. The house shows how the medieval High Street looked.

NATIONAL GALLERY OF MODERN ART AND DEAN GALLERY
✛ 168 off A1 ✉ 74 Belford Road EH4 3DR ☎ 0131 624 6200 🕐 Daily 10–5
🎫 Free, may be a charge for temporary exhibitions ☐
A sweeping, living sculpture of grassy terraces and ponds is the first thing you see as you arrive here. Among the works in the permanent collection are those by Pablo Picasso, Georges Braque, Henri Matisse and Barbara Hepworth. The work of the early 20th-century group of painters known as the Scottish Colourists is striking. Stroll across the road to the Dean Gallery. This collection majors on Dada and the Surrealists, and the Scottish sculptor Eduardo Paolozzi (1924–2005).

BACKGROUND
The name Edinburgh derives from the city's original name Dunedin and the 12th-century term burgh, denoting a town with certain rights, such as trading or taxation. Edinburgh was a royal burgh, and by the time Robert the Bruce granted a new charter to the city in 1329, it was on the road to becoming the capital of Scotland. The 16th and 17th centuries saw religious and political turmoil, but the city survived. Unlike Glasgow (▷ 172–176), Edinburgh's people didn't get their hands dirty during the Industrial Revolution, preferring to develop services such as banking. In the 1990s, political power was devolved from London to the Scottish capital.

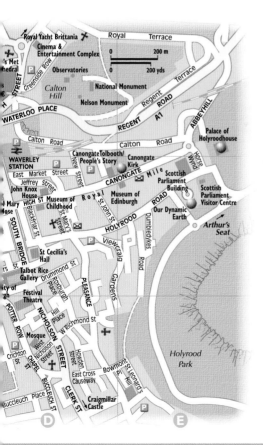

OUR DYNAMIC EARTH
✛ 169 E2 • Holyrood Road EH8 8AS
☎ 0131 550 7800 🕐 Jul–end Aug daily 10–6; Apr–end Jun, Sep–end Oct daily 10–5; Nov–end Mar Wed–Sun 10–5 (last admittance 70 mins before closing)
🎫 Adult £8.95, child £5.75
This science park tells the story of the Earth in slick, easy chunks of virtual-reality science.

GREYFRIARS BOBBY
✛ 168 C2 • George IV Bridge
This bronze statue is of a Skye terrier, Bobby, the devoted companion of a farmer who regularly dined in Greyfriars Place.

SCOTTISH NATIONAL PORTRAIT GALLERY
✛ 168 C1 • 1 Queen Street EH2 1JD
☎ 0131 624 6200 🕐 Fri–Wed 10–5, Thu 10–7 🎫 Free ☐ ♿
Scottish worthies and the national photography collection are represented in this gallery.

WHAT TO DO

⊕ JENNERS
48 Princes Street
Tel 0131 225 2442
www.jenners.com
Grander than its newest rival Harvey Nichols, Jenners is an Edinburgh institution, founded in 1838. It sells everything from high-quality clothes and shoes to toys, glassware, groceries and perfume. Slightly more expensive than Princes Street's other department stores.
⏰ Mon, Wed, Fri, Sat 9–6, Tue 9.30–6, Thu 9–8, Sun 11–5
🚉 Edinburgh Waverley

⊕ OCEAN TERMINAL CENTRE
Ocean Drive, Leith
Tel 0131 555 8888
www.oceanterminal.com
Designed by Jasper Conran and opened in 2001, Ocean Terminal is a vast shopping and cinema complex overlooking the Firth of Forth and the royal yacht *Britannia*.
⏰ Mon–Fri 10–8, Sat 10–7, Sun 11–6
🍴 Zinc Bar & Grill (tel 0131 553 8070)

⊕ ROYAL MILE WHISKIES
379 High Street, Royal Mile
Tel 0131 524 9380
www.royalmilewhiskies.com
This specialist whisky shop opposite St. Giles Cathedral stocks a vast range of malt whiskies, some of which are 100 years old. It's the best place to buy rare whiskies if you want them shipped home.
⏰ Mon–Sat 10–6, Sun 12.30–6
🚉 Edinburgh Waverley

⊕ TARTAN WEAVING MILL AND EXHIBITION
555 Castle Hill, The Royal Mile
Tel 0131 226 1555
www.tartanweavingmill.co.uk
You can hear the basement weaving looms everywhere in this massive tartan shop at the top of the Royal Mile. On the way down you can have your photo taken in full Highland rig, consult the 'Clans and Tartans Bureau' for information about your own clan history, then have a go at weaving yourself.
⏰ Daily 9–5.30 💷 Free
🚉 Edinburgh Waverley

⊕ DOMINION
18 Newbattle Terrace, Morningside
Tel 0131 447 4771 (box office)
www.dominioncinemas.net
This family-run cinema screens independent and mainstream movies, and has traditional leather Pullman seats. Bag a sofa and free wine or beer with the Gold Class service.
⏰ Daily 🚉 Edinburgh Haymarket

⊕ EDINBURGH FESTIVAL THEATRE
13–29 Nicolson Street
Tel 0131 529 6000
www.eft.co.uk
Hosting touring productions of dance, theatre, musicals and comedy, this prestigious concert venue also has ballet and Scottish Opera productions.
⏰ All year. Box office: Mon–Sat 11–8, Sun 11–4 💷 From £8
🚉 Edinburgh Waverley

⊕ EDINBURGH PLAYHOUSE
18–22 Greenside Place
Tel 0870 606 3424
www.getlive.co.uk (theatre information)
The best venue for touring productions of big-budget musicals and dance. A five-minute walk from the east end of Princes Street.
⏰ All year 💷 From £12
🚉 Edinburgh Waverley

⊕ QUEEN'S HALL
Clerk Street
Tel 0131 668 2019
www.thequeenshall.net
A more intimate venue than the Usher Hall, this is a hot spot for jazz, blues and soul, as well as classical music and comedy, attracting names such as Courtney Pine and Ruby Turner.
⏰ All year 💷 From £10
🚉 Edinburgh Waverley

⊕ USHER HALL
Lothian Road
Tel 0131 228 1155
www.usherhall.co.uk
Edinburgh's most prestigious concert hall attracts excellent orchestras. A distinctive circular building towards the West End, its high dome can be seen from many parts of the city.
⏰ All year 💷 From £10
🚉 Edinburgh Haymarket

⊕ BELUGA
30a Chambers Street
Tel 0131 624 4545
The Beluga bar-nightclub is the place to see and be seen: a laid-back lunch spot in by day, and home of the beautiful people by night. A huge waterfall dominates the opulent interior.
⏰ Daily 11am–1am 💷 Free entry
🚉 Edinburgh Waverley

⊕ BLUE MOON
1 Barony Street, New Town
Tel 0131 556 2788
Everybody is welcome at this gay bar, noted for serving the best food in the area all day. The staff are a good source of local knowledge on the best club nights (both gay and straight).
⏰ Mon–Fri 11–11, Sat–Sun 10am–11.30pm 🚉 Edinburgh Waverley

⊕ JOLLY JUDGE
7a James Court, Old Town
Tel 0131 225 2669
Seek out this 17th-century pub for its malt whiskies. At the top of the Royal Mile go down East Entry into James Court.
⏰ Mon and Thu–Sat 12–12, Tue–Wed 12–11, Sun 12.30–11

⊕ STAND COMEDY CLUB
5 York Place
Tel 0131 558 7272
www.thestand.co.uk
Enjoy live comedy from new and well-known comedians at this dark and intimate basement bar. Weekend shows often sell out, so reserving in advance is recommended.
⏰ Mon–Sat 7.30pm–1am, Sun 12.30–midnight 💷 Free–£9
🚉 Edinburgh Waverley

⊕ MURRAYFIELD STADIUM
Off Roseburn Terrace, Murrayfield
Tel 0131 346 5000
www.scottishrugby.org
Rugby is Edinburgh's most popular sport so reserving in advance for matches is essential. Behind-the-scenes tours are also available.
⏰ Call for match information. Stadium tours Mon–Fri 11 and 2.30
💷 Vary. Tour: adult £5, child (5–18) £3, family £12 🚉 Edinburgh Haymarket

GREAT BRITAIN

♥ EDINBURGH FLOATARIUM
29 North West Circus Place
Tel 0131 225 3350
Relax in a float tank, reflexology, massages and facials. The aromatherapy massage is particularly recommended.
🕐 Mon–Fri 9–8, Sat 9–6, Sun 9.30–4
💷 1-hour float £30; 1-hour aromatherapy massage £32 🈯
🚇 Edinburgh Waverley

EATING

BLUE BAR CAFÉ
10 Cambridge Street
Tel 0131 2211222
This modern brasserie goes from strength to strength with a menu that is flexible, good value and imaginative. Lunch could be as simple as a crayfish sandwich or a bowl of white bean and chorizo soup. A more substantial meal would be carpaccio of beef with Parmesan followed by corn-fed chicken with aromatic leek risotto and bacon dressing. Deftly prepared desserts include chocolate tart with caramelized oranges.
🕐 Mon–Thu 12–2.30, 5.30–10.30; Fri–Sat 12–2.30, 5.30–11. Closed Sun, 25–26 Dec
💷 L £18.50, D £24, Wine £12.95
🚇 From Princes Street turn into Lothian Road second left, first right, above the Traverse Theatre

OFF THE WALL RESTAURANT
105 High Street, Royal Mile
Tel 0131 558 1497
This Royal Mile restaurant has an uncomplicated approach to cuisine: no fussiness or unnecessary flourishes, just perfectly prepared food that speaks for itself. The interior is based on the same mantra of simplicity. Expect modern cooking made from the finest Scottish ingredients: beef fillet, perhaps, with red cabbage, port sauce and buttery truffle mash; or venison with celeriac and a chocolate sauce. And as befits its name, Off the Wall delivers a few unexpected combinations—squab pigeon with black pudding and orange sauce, for instance. Vegetarian options available on request.
🕐 Mon–Sat 12–2, 7–10; closed Sun, 25–26 Dec, 1–2 Jan
💷 L £16.50, D £38, Wine £13.95
🚇 On Royal Mile near John Knox House. Entrance via stairway next to Baillie Fyfes (first floor)

RESTAURANT MARTIN WISHART
54 The Shore, Leith
Tel 0131 553 3557
Serious French staff are intent on communicating their passion for food and wine. This is sophisticated territory. There's a juggernaut of a menu with enough eye-catching flair, luxury and creativity to compete with any national restaurant. Terrine of confit duck, foie gras with sweet and sour pear, duck bonbon and walnut toast is a flawlessly executed dish, while fillet of Buccleuch beef with confit of bone marrow, celeriac puree, beignets of salsify and *marchand de vin* sauce is similarly precise. Smart dress is preferred.
🕐 12–2, 7–10; closed L Sat, Sun–Mon, 25 Dec
💷 L £20.50, D £45, Wine £19.50
🚇 Telephone for directions

STAC POLLY
8–10 Grindlay Street
Tel 0131 229 5405
Two low-ceilinged rooms make for an intimate atmosphere in this charming restaurant in the heart of the city with its cream parchment walls, red carpet and tartan-covered chairs. Modern Scottish cuisine dominates the menu, for example baked supreme of Scottish salmon served with braised leeks, bacon dumplings and a lemon butter sauce. Desserts, and the wine list, are appealing.
🕐 Daily 12–2, 6–9.30; closed L Sat and Sun
💷 L £14.95, D £30, Wine £14.95
🚇 In town centre, beneath Castle, near Lyceum

STAYING

BONNINGTON GUEST HOUSE
202 Ferry Road, Edinburgh EH6 4NW
Tel 0131 554 7610
This Georgian house offers individually furnished bedrooms that retain many of the property's original features. The homey lounge is complemented by an attractive dining room, where a fine Scottish breakfast is served. There is a particularly warm welcome here.
💷 £60; discount for under-11s
🛏 6

🚇 On A902
🚇 Edinburgh Waverley

MALMAISON
One Tower Place Edinburgh EH6 7DB
Tel 0131 468 5000
www.malmaison.com
The stylish Malmaison overlooks the port of Leith. Bedrooms have striking décor, CD players, mini bars and a number of individual touches. Food and drink are equally important here, with brasserie-style dining and a café-bar.
💷 £145
🛏 101 🈯
🚇 A900 from city centre towards Leith. At end of Leith Walk continue over lights, through two more sets of lights, then left into Tower Street; hotel on right

THE SCOTSMAN
20 North Bridge Edinburgh EH1 1YT
Tel 0131 556 5565
www.thescotsmanhotel.co.uk
The former head office of *The Scotsman* newspaper has been transformed into this state-of-the-art boutique hotel, where traditional elegance blends seamlessly with cutting-edge technology and friendly, attentive service. Bedrooms are all smartly furnished and very well equipped. The galleried Brasserie restaurant offers an informal dining option.
💷 £270
🛏 68 🈯 🈯
🚇 A8 to city centre, left on to Charlotte Street. Right into Queen Street, right at roundabout on to Leith Street. Keep straight on, left on to North Bridge, hotel on right
🚇 Edinburgh Waverley

Glasgow

Known as a gritty but friendly city, Glasgow has some handsome architectural treasures, along with regenerated cultural pursuits. Make sure you look up—much of the finest architecture is above street level.

Rodin's The Thinker *at the Burrell Collection*

SEEING GLASGOW

Once Scotland's industrial powerhouse, Glasgow has rediscovered its artistic side in recent years. It was European City of Culture in 1990, then City of Architecture and Design in 1999—a long way from its roots in ironworks and ship-building.

HIGHLIGHTS

BURRELL COLLECTION

✚ 174 B3 • Pollok Country Park, 2060 Pollokshaws Road G43 1AT ☎ 0141 287 2550 ◷ Mon–Thu, Sat 10–5, Fri and Sun 11–5 ♿ Free; charge for some special exhibitions 🚉 Pollokshaws West ✇ Free guided tours ▯ ⊞ ⛨

This priceless collection of 9,000 pieces of art from around the world was given to Glasgow in 1944 by Sir William Burrell (1861–1958). You'll find August Rodin's *The Thinker* in the Courtyard. Intriguing old stone doorways lead into different parts of the museum. In the Ancient Greece and Rome section, look for fragments of delicate Roman mosaics. Don't overlook the Islamic Art section at the farthest end of the museum, dripping with Oriental carpets.

GALLERY OF MODERN ART (GoMA)

✚ 175 D2 • Royal Exchange Square, Queen Street G1 3AH ☎ 0141 229 1996 ◷ Mon–Wed, Sat 10–5, Thu 10–8, Fri and Sun 11–5 ♿ Free 🚉 Queen Street, Glasgow Central ✇ Tours most weekends ▯ ⊞ ⛨

GoMA, in a former tobacco baron's mansion, is set on four floors linked by a glass lift. Among the ever-changing display, look out for Peter Howson's painting *Patriots* (1991), with three loutish men and their snarling bulldogs, as well as huge striped canvases by pop artist Bridget Riley (born 1931) and works by Andy Warhol (1927–87) and David Hockney (born 1937).

GLASGOW SCIENCE CENTRE

✚ 174 C2 • 50 Pacific Quay G51 1EA ☎ 0871 540 1000 ◷ Summer daily 10–6, winter 10–5; late opening IMAX cinema Thu–Sat ♿ Science Centre: adult £7.95, child (3–16) £5.95; combination tickets available 🚉 Cessnock 🚉 Exhibition Centre ⛨ ⊞ ⛨

The main attraction at the Science Centre is the Science Mall, with four floors of 500 interactive exhibits. Highlights include distorting mirrors, seeing how an artificial arm picks up signals from your body, and a walk-on piano for those under age seven. The other main elements on the site are the 24m (80ft) screen in the IMAX theatre, and the dizzying 122m (400ft) viewing tower designed to turn 360 degrees in the wind.

GLASGOW NECROPOLIS

✚ 175 E2 ℹ 50 Cathedral Square G4 0UZ, tel 0141 552 3145 ◷ Daily 10–6 ♿ Free

This is Glasgow's 'city of the dead', stuffed with ostentatious monuments to the wealthy 19th-century industrialists who developed the city. Their competitive spirit showed even after death, with extraordinary monuments commissioned from the finest architects of the day. There's a great view of the crowded Necropolis skyline from the third floor of the St. Mungo Museum (▷ left).

RATINGS				
Good for kids	●	●	●	
Historic interest	●	●	●	●
Specialist shopping	●	●	●	
Artistic interest	●	●	●	●

BASICS

✚ 4 C2

ℹ Greater Glasgow and Clyde Valley Tourist Board, 11 George Square, Glasgow G2 1DY, tel 0141 566 0800; Mon–Sat 9–8, Sun 10–6

🚉 Glasgow Central and Queen Street

🚇 Glasgow Underground (or Clockwork Orange) links different parts of the city, tel 0141 332 6811; www.spt.co.uk/subway

www.seeglasgow.com

MORE TO SEE

ST. MUNGO MUSEUM OF RELIGIOUS LIFE AND ART

✚ 175 E2 • 2 Castle Street G4 0RH ☎ 0141 553 2557 ◷ Mon–Thu, Sat 10–5, Fri and Sun 11–5 ♿ Free 🚉 High Street ⛨ ⊞

www.glasgowmuseums.com

Enter this modern museum near the medieval cathedral through a Zen gravel garden. It is set out over three floors, with an art collection, religious items and a section about religion in Glasgow.

The Gallery of Modern Art (above).
Victorian George Square and City Chambers (right)

HUNTERIAN MUSEUM AND ART GALLERY

⊞ 174 C1 • University of Glasgow, 82 Hillhead Street G1 8QQ ☎ 0141 330 5431/
4221 🕐 Mon–Sat 9.30–5 💷 Free 🚇 Hillhead 🚆 Glasgow Queen Street 🚍 🚲
www.hunterian.gla.ac.uk

William Hunter (1718–83) was a Glasgow-trained physician who left
his scientific collections—including anatomical specimens used in
teaching—to his old university. The collection was opened for show in
1807, making this the oldest public museum in Scotland. The
magnificent art collection, in a separate building on campus, originates
from Hunter's own purchases of 17th-century Flemish, Dutch and
Italian masters. There's also a coin collection and displays of geology
and archaeology, including Roman finds from Scotland.

THE MACKINTOSH TRAIL

ℹ 11 George Square G2 1DY, tel 0141 204 4400

Charles Rennie Mackintosh (1868–1928) was born in Glasgow, and
at the age of 16 was apprenticed to a firm of architects. He was an
outstanding student, praised for the originality of his architecture, a
distinctive fusion of the flowing lines of art nouveau with the simplicity
of the Arts and Crafts Movement. He left his mark on Glasgow, with
principal points of interest forming the Rennie Mackintosh Trail, such
as the Glasgow School of Art, the Willow Tearooms and the House for
an Art Lover. At the university's Hunterian Gallery, Mackintosh House
is the exquisite re-creation of the interior of the home which
Mackintosh and his wife made together, with original furniture, as it
appeared in 1906. You can clearly see the influence of Japanese style.

BACKGROUND

**Trade and religion have shaped Glasgow. The settlement became a
royal burgh in 1611 and the Protestant Revolution later that century
allowed commerce to flourish. As a port on the west coast,
Glasgow was perfectly located for trade with the English colonies
in America. The Industrial Revolution helped Glasgow become
the workshop of the Western world.**

THE TENEMENT HOUSE

⊞ 175 D1 • 145 Buccleuch Street,
Garnethill G3 6QN ☎ 0141 333 0183
🕐 Mar–end Oct daily 2–5 💷 Adult £5,
child (5–16) £4 🚇 Cowcaddens
🚆 Charing Cross
www.nts.org.uk

In the 19th and early 20th
centuries, most Glaswegians
lived in tenement houses,
sharing communal facilities.
They could be overcrowded, with
families sharing one room. This
example was the home of Agnes
Toward from 1911. When she
died in 1975, her house became
a time capsule of social history.

TALL SHIP AT GLASGOW HARBOUR

⊞ 174 C2 • 100 Stobcross Road G3
8QQ ☎ 0141 222 2513 🕐 Mar–end
Oct daily 10–5; Nov–end Feb daily 10–4
💷 Adult £4.95, child (5–16) £2.50 (one
child free with every adult) 🚇 Partick
🚆 Finnieston/ Exhibition Centre 🚍 🚲
www.thetallship.com

The best view of this fine steel-
hulled sailing ship is from the
windows of the Science Centre
opposite. The SV *Glenlee,* built
on the Clyde in 1896, is one of
five Clyde-built ships left afloat.

PEOPLE'S PALACE

⊞ 175 E2 • Glasgow Green G40 1AT
☎ 0141 271 2962 🕐 Mon–Thu, Sat
10–5, Fri and Sun 11–5 💷 Free
🚆 High Street, Argyle Street, Bellgrove
🚍 🚲
www.glasgowmuseums.com

Set on Glasgow Green, this
museum captures the character
of the city.

SCOTTISH FOOTBALL MUSEUM

⊞ 175 D3 • Hampden Park G42 9AY
☎ 0141 616 6139 🕐 Mon–Sat 10–5,
Sun 11–5 💷 Adult £5.50, child (5–16)
£2.75, family £20 🚆 Bridge Street 🚍
www.scottishfootballmuseum.org.uk

Hampden Park is Scotland's
national football stadium.

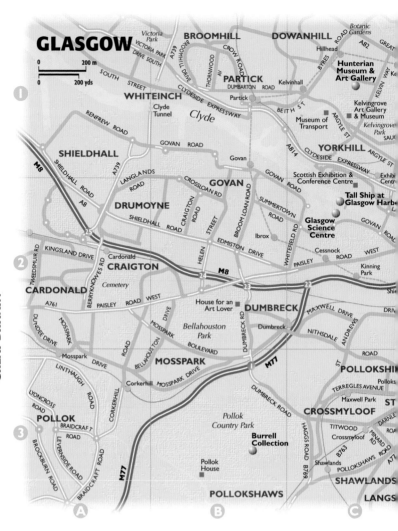

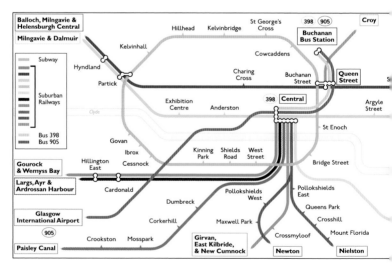

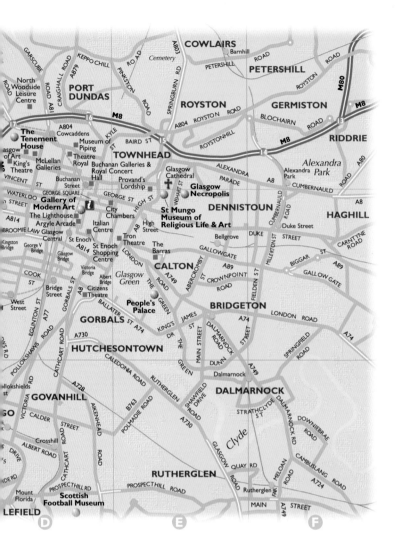

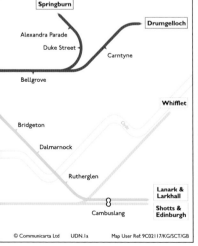

GREAT BRITAIN

GREAT BRITAIN

WHAT TO DO

🛍 GEOFFREY (TAILOR) KILTMAKERS & WEAVERS

309 Sauchiehall Street
Tel 0141 331 2388
www.geoffreykilts.co.uk
One of Scotland's top kiltmakers and Highland dress specialists, brimming with every kind of kilt, tartan and accessory. Made-to-measure outfits can be sent to you abroad.
🕒 Mon–Wed and Fri–Sat 9–5.30, Thu 9–7, Sun 11–5 🚇 Glasgow Charing Cross

🛍 PRINCES SQUARE

48 Buchanan Street
Tel 0141 221 0324
www.princessquare.co.uk
An art deco style doorway on Buchanan Street announces this chic indoor shopping complex. Good shops sell clothes, shoes and gifts, including Jo Malone perfumes.
🕒 Mon–Wed and Fri 9.30–6, Thu 9.30–8, Sat 9–6, Sun 12–5 🚇 🍴
🚇 Glasgow Argyle Street

🛍 TISO GLASGOW OUTDOOR EXPERIENCE

Couper Street, off Kyle Street
Tel 0141 559 5450
www.tiso.com
A great selection of outdoor equipment, clothing and books. The interactive features–a 15m (50ft) rock pinnacle, waterfall and 7m (23ft) ice wall–enable you to try out the gear.
🕒 Mon–Tue, Fri–Sat 9–6, Wed 9.30–6, Thu 9–7, Sun 11–5
🚇 Glasgow Queen Street

🎭 BARROWLANDS

244 Gallowgate
Tel 0141 552 4601; 0870 903 3444
www.glasgow-barrowland.com
Big-name pop and rock acts play at this engaging venue. For tickets call Ticket Scotland on 0141 204 5151.
🕒 All year 💷 From £9 ⚽
🚇 St. Enoch 🚇 Glasgow Central, Queen Street

🎭 GLASGOW ROYAL CONCERT HALL

2 Sauchiehall Street
Tel 0141 353 8000
www.grch.com
Glasgow's most prestigious venue and home of the Royal Scottish National Orchestra, this concert hall has a varied schedule of classical, pop and rock music and holds the Celtic Connections winter festival of concerts and ceilidhs.
🕒 All year 💷 Varies 🍴 🚇 🛍
🚇 Buchanan Street
🚇 Glasgow Queen Street

🎭 KING TUT'S WAH WAH HUT

272a St. Vincent Street
Tel 0141 221 5279
www.kingtuts.co.uk
The heart of the Glasgow music scene. It's an unpretentious, relaxed venue playing cutting-edge indie, pop and rock. Get your tickets from Ticketmaster.
🕒 All year 💷 From £4.50
🚇 🚇 Glasgow Central, Queen Street

🎭 THEATRE ROYAL

282 Hope Street
Tel 0141 060 6647
www.theatreroyalglasgow.com
The best in opera, ballet, dance and theatre can be found at the home of Scottish Opera and Scottish Ballet.
🕒 All year 💷 From £4 🍴 🚇
🚇 Cowcaddens, Buchanan Street
🚇 Queen Street

🍸 ARCHES

253 Argyle Street
Tel 0141 565 1000
www.thearches.co.uk
The nightclub in the Arches complex, with its industrial-style interior, is Glasgow's biggest. The music varies and can include hip-hop, house, soul or big name DJs.
🕒 Club nights Fri–Sun, until late
💷 From £5 🚇 St. Enoch
🚇 Glasgow Central

🍸 SCOTIA BAR

112–114 Stockwell Street
Tel 0141 552 8681
This traditional pub is Glasgow's oldest, established in 1792. Live folk music on most evenings and poetry readings on Sundays.
🕒 Mon–Sat 11am–midnight, Sun 12–12 🚇 St. Enoch
🚇 Glasgow Central

EATING

LUX

1051 Great Western Road
Tel 0141 576 7576
www.luxstazione.co.uk
Lux serves Scottish produce cooked by adventurous chef/proprietor Stephen Johnson, such as pan-fried fillet of Scottish beef with red Thai paste and bean sprouts with a coriander (cilantro) sour cream. Children under 12 are not welcome.
🕒 D only from 6; closed Sun, 25–26 Dec, 1–2 Jan
💷 D £35.50, Wine £16.75
🚇 At the traffic lights signed Gartnavel Hospital

STAYING

CROWNE PLAZA HOTEL

Congress Road,Glasgow G3 8QT
Tel 0870 443 1691
www.ichotelsgroup.com
Instantly recognizable from its mirrored glass exterior, most of the bedrooms at this modern hotel have panoramic views. There are two restaurants.
💷 £99–£199
🛏 283 🛁 🚭
🅿 300
🚇 From M8 exit 19 follow signs for SECC, hotel adjacent to centre

HOLIDAY INN

161 West Nile Street, Glasgow G1 2RL
Tel 0141 352 8300
www.higlasgow.com
This hotel includes the Bonne Auberge restaurant, a bar area and conservatory. Some suites are available.
💷 Double from £90–£170
🛏 113 🚭 Mini gym
🚇 M8 exit 16, follow signs for Royal Concert Hall, hotel is opposite

VICTORIAN HOUSE

212 Renfrew Street, Glasgow G3 6TX
Tel 0141 332 0129
www.thevictorian.co.uk
This raised terraced (row) house offers a range of well-equipped bedrooms, in both modern and traditional décor. The breakfast room serves buffet style meals.
💷 Double from £46–£60
🛏 58
🚇 Turn left into Garnet Street at 1st set of traffic lights on Sauchiehall Street, east of Charing Cross. Go right into Renfrew Street, hotel is 91m (100 yards) on left

ARRIVING

BY AIR

This is the most common method of entering the UK, and London, Britain's principal gateway, has air connections to all major world cities. Most long-haul flights arrive at either Heathrow or Gatwick, while the capital's three other airports—Stansted, Luton and London City—serve mainly short-haul destinations.

All airports have information desks, shops, banks, restaurants, car-rental companies, hotel reservation desks and left-luggage facilities. If departing from Heathrow or Gatwick make sure you know which terminal you need. Taxis are usually available outside the terminals.

A number of airports in other parts of the country also accept international flights. These include Birmingham International, Edinburgh, Glasgow (International and Prestwick), Manchester, Southampton and Leeds Bradford.

Useful contacts

Gatwick Express Tel 0845 850 1530; www.gatwickexpress.co.uk
Heathrow Express
Tel 0845 600 1515;
www.heathrowexpress.com
London City
Tel 020 7646 0000;
www.londoncityairport.com. For shuttle bus tel 020 7646 0000
National Express
Tel 08705 808080;
www.nationalexpress.com
Stansted Express
Tel 0845 600 7245;
www.stanstedexpress.co.uk
Thameslink Tel 0845 026 4700; www.firstcapitalconnect.co.uk

BY TRAIN

Eurostar trains from France (Paris, Avignon and Lille) and Belgium (Brussels) speed to St. Pancras International Station (www.stpancras.com) in less than three hours. Passports are required for travel and, on arrival, you must also clear customs. There are escalators and elevators to the main St. Pancras complex and signs to the Underground (Victoria, Hammersmith & City, Piccadilly, Circle, Metropolitan and Northern lines) and buses. A taxi stand is outside the station.

Trains from other parts of Britain arrive at one of London's main terminals, all of which have Underground and bus links.

BY COACH

If you travel to Britain by coach (long-distance bus) you will probably arrive at London's Victoria Coach Station (VCS), a 10-minute walk from Victoria railway station. There is a taxi stand outside the coach station. The main coach company is National Express, but Greenline coaches also connect local cities and airports to London.

● **Victoria Coach Station**
164 Buckingham Palace Road,
London SW1W 9TP
Tel 020 7730 3466
● **National Express**
Tel 08705 808080;
www.nationalexpress.com
● **Greenline**
Arriva, Admiral Way, Doxford International Business Park,
Sunderland SR3 3XP; tel 0844 801 7261; www.greenline.co.uk

BY CAR

Eurotunnel operates the train service for cars, caravans and motorcycles through the Channel Tunnel. The journey from Calais to Folkestone takes 20 minutes, and drivers and passengers remain in their vehicles. At Folkestone, the terminal joins the M20 north at junction 11a, and the drive to London takes about 1 hour 30 minutes.

Car Rental

Arranging to rent a car through your travel agent before arriving can save money and allows you to find out about deposits, drop-off charges, cancellation penalties and insurance costs in advance. However, the usual established car rental companies have offices throughout Britain. Smaller, local companies and online agents may offer better deals.
● You must have a valid driver's licence. An International Driving Permit may be useful if your licence is not in English.
● Most rental firms require the driver to be at least 23 years old and have at least 12 months' driving experience.

● Rental rates usually include free unlimited mileage.
● It is important to ensure that you have some form of personal insurance along with Collision Damage Waiver (CDW). Many companies also offer Damage Excess Reduction (DER) and Theft Protection for an additional premium. You will also have to pay more for additional drivers.
● Most cars use unleaded fuel; make sure you know what's required (unleaded or diesel) before filling the tank.
● Although reputable companies operate new fleets and service them to a high standard, make your own checks before accepting a rental car, including checking for tyre wear. Insist on a different vehicle if you are unhappy.

BY FERRY

Ferries now face stiff competition from Eurostar and Eurotunnel, so they can be a relatively inexpensive way of crossing the Channel. Various companies operate passenger and vehicle services between Britain and Europe. Trains run from ports on the south coast—Dover, Folkestone, Ramsgate and Newhaven—to London Victoria. The train operator 'one' runs a service from Harwich to Liverpool Street. Along with regular ferry services, certain ports, such as Calais, operate faster Seacat and Superseacat vessels.

VISITORS WITH A DISABILTIY

While the majority of Britain's tourist attractions are accessible to visitors with disabilities, public transport still lags behind. Avoid peak times if possible. Guide dogs are welcome on all forms of public transport. Shopping malls and main streets in major towns sometimes have motorized buggies on loan (often free). All London black taxis have wheelchair access, as have an increasing number of modern cabs in larger towns and cities.

The Royal Association for Disability and Rehabilitation (RADAR)
Tel 020 7250 3222;
www.radar.org.uk

GETTING AROUND

BY CAR
One of the best ways of seeing Britain is by car. On the whole, motorists drive safely, roads are good, if busy, and signposting is efficient. In some parts of Britain, this is the only way of getting around, as local transport can be limited. The network of narrow, crooked lanes between small towns and villages makes a delightful opportunity to see the country, while the fast motorways link major towns and cities. Note that you must drive on the left-hand side of the road.

Motorways
Britain has a vast network of motorways serving all parts of the country. The major arteries are the M1 north, M2 to the southeast, M3 south, M4 west, M5 southwest, the M6/M74 to Scotland, the M62 across the Pennines and the M8 across Scotland's central belt. The M6 has an alternative toll section that avoids a notorious congested area, between junctions 4 and 11 around Birmingham.
● When joining the motorway from a slip road, give priority to traffic already on the motorway.
● Do not overtake on the inside—this is against the law—except where traffic is stationary and the lane you are in is moving faster than the outer lanes, or where a slip road (exit ramp) is indicated off the motorway by a short dotted line.
● Do not exceed the 70mph (113kph) speed limit.
● Do not drive on the hard shoulder except in an emergency or if you are directed to do so.

BY TRAIN
The railway is a British invention and, unfortunately for passengers, much of the 19th-century network is still in operation. However, the services generally work fairly efficiently and are not oppressively crowded outside peak periods. Following denationalization and the breakup of the British Rail network, more than 20 different companies now operate the trains. This can lead to differing facilities and some curious price

anomalies as each company determines its own fare structure. In some cases it is worth checking whether another company serving the same region can offer an alternative route or lower price.
● Detailed information for the whole network—including operating companies, timetables, fares and restrictions—is available from National Rail Enquiries. Tel 08457 484950; textphone 0845 605 0600; www.nationalrail.co.uk.

BY COACH
Coaches (long-distance buses) run from London's Victoria Coach Station (VCS) to all parts of the country and are a slower but much less expensive alternative to train travel. The main operator in Britain is National Express, whose routes cover the whole country. Journey times can be long (with some changes necessary), but coaches are comfortable, with air-conditioning, toilets and sometimes refreshments.

At Victoria Coach Station you can buy or reserve airport coach tickets, tours and excursions, London travelcards, theatre and concert tickets, domestic and European rail tickets, ferry and hovercraft tickets and travel insurance. The travel office can also arrange Western Union money transfer and organize car rental and hotel accommodation.
● **National Express**
Tel 08705 808080 (bookings, daily 8am–10pm); www.nationalexpress.com. For detailed information, routes, timetables and bookings.
● Scottish **Citylink** connects 200 towns and cities in Scotland and beyond.
Tel 08705 505050; www.citylink.co.uk
● **Green Line Travel Office**
4a Fountain Square, 123–151 Buckingham Palace Road, London SW1W 0SR; tel 0844 801 7261; www.greenline.co.uk. Services between London and local cities and airports.

BY BUS
Buses often make a pleasant alternative to trains. Major towns and cities usually have frequent buses, but services can be erratic elsewhere, especially in rural areas. Some night services (buses have an 'N' prefix) are available in major towns and cities. Tourist information offices can provide information and timetables, but these can be complicated, so check carefully for services that run only on certain days or are otherwise restricted.

BY BICYCLE
Thanks to organizations such as Sustrans (Sustainable Transport), Britain's network of cycle routes now covers more than 11,340km (7,000 miles). Routes are suitable for a range of journeys and include off-road sections, such as canal towpaths, holiday routes for experienced riders, and urban routes for commuters, school runs or shopping trips.

There are also countless outlets all over the country offering bicycle and equipment rental and practical advice. Local tourist information offices should have details.

BY TAXI
Taxis are a relatively expensive way of getting around, but are useful in certain circumstances, such as airport trips for groups. There are essentially two types of taxi: licensed taxis (which should have meters), such as the traditional black London cab (not confined to the capital), which display a licence on the rear of the vehicle and the private hire operator or minicab.

GETTING AROUND IN LONDON

You'll need to tackle the public transport system to cross London. The Underground train network (known as the Tube), the world's oldest, is quicker than taking a bus, but it can be hot and stuffy. Buses can be a pleasant alternative, offering views from the top deck. Riverboats run from quays along the River Thames to certain attractions, while taxis are a convenient but expensive option. Or you could walk—many Tube stations are actually very close to each other.

THE UNDERGROUND

London Underground operates nearly 500 trains between 260 stations. Twelve colour-coded lines make up the Greater London Underground system, each with its own name.

● Most stations have electronic ticket gates. If your ticket does not work, find a member of staff. You will need your ticket to leave the station; don't discard it.
● Trains run Mon–Sat 5.30am–midnight (Sun 7am–11pm).
● Try to avoid the rush hours (7–9.30am, 4.30–7pm).
● It is cheaper to travel after 9.30am and at weekends.
● If you cannot produce a valid ticket you will be fined £20.
● Space is limited so don't take too much luggage.
● Watch out for pickpockets.

BUSES

London's iconic red double-decker buses are a good way to make short journeys.

● Main bus stops (red circle on a white background) have timetables and route information. Buses stop automatically.
● At request stops (white circle on a red background) you must hail buses.
● At night treat all stops as request stops. Night buses (number preceded by 'N') run 11pm–6am on main routes.
● Each route is identified by a number on the front of the bus.
● In central London you must buy a ticket from a roadside machine before boarding.
● The Riverside service links the South Bank to the West End, with 40 attractions along the route.
● A one-way adult fare on most routes within Greater London is £2. Children under 14 travel free. 14–15 year olds may travel free if they have photo ID.

TICKETS

You can buy tickets for all forms of public transport at most Underground stations, train stations, information offices and many other outlets. Carry small change so you can use ticket machines instead of queuing at a ticket office. You can buy individual tickets for all types of transport, but the best option is a Travelcard. These are valid for the entire network in selected zones and give unlimited travel in the paid-for zone. Central London occupies Zone 1, with Zones 2–6 following in progressively wider concentric rings, which are colour-coded on Tube maps. It is sensible to pay a little extra to allow travel in more zones.

RIVERBOATS

Most services start from Westminster Pier and run 6.20am–9.30pm. The route runs as fas as Hampton Court Palace to the west and the Thames Barrier to the east.

GREAT BRITAIN

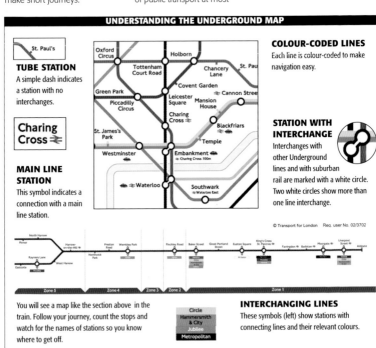

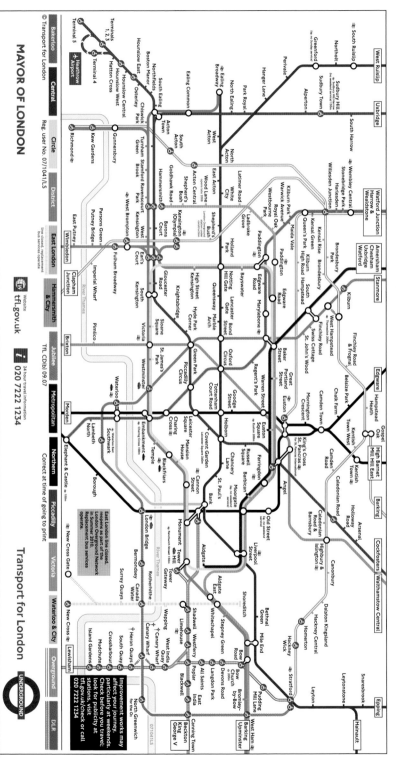

IRELAND

UNDERSTANDING IRELAND

The most striking feature of Ireland is the legendary 40 shades of green that make up this Emerald Isle. You may have to put up with the unpredictable showers of its maritime climate, but your reward is the dazzling spectrum of colour on the lush pastures and rolling hills when the sun breaks through. Some 7 million visitors come to Ireland every year to see its prehistoric monuments, castles and high crosses, crumbling monasteries and stately homes. But although the island looks small on a map, don't assume you can tour it quickly. Its winding country roads and beautiful scenery demand a leisurely pace. Besides, it's almost a sacrilege to hurry in Ireland. Take time to chat with the locals, linger in the brightly painted coastal towns or vibrant cities, share a story or a song in a local pub. Through the people, as well as the places, you will discover the magic of Ireland.

WHAT IS IRELAND?

Officially, this North Atlantic island nation goes by its ancient name of Éire. More widely known in English as Ireland, it measures 84,421sq km (32,924sq miles) and is part of the British Isles. The independent Republic of Ireland is made up of 26 counties—five-sixths of the island—while the six northeastern counties that make up Northern Ireland are part of the United Kingdom. However, 20th-century political divisions cannot erase Ireland's strong ties to its united past. Its four provinces reflect the island's ancient kingdoms: Leinster in the east, Connacht in the west, Ulster in the north and Munster in the south. Even though they hold no official significance today, they are still important historically and culturally, featuring in regional literature, and often referred to in poetry and song as 'the four green fields'.

Ireland's landscape is surprisingly varied given its size. Much of the coastline is backed by a rim of mountains and sea cliffs, while a limestone plain spreads across the interior, where the terrain ranges from flat pasture to rolling hills, with winding rivers and lakeland regions. Much of the land is agricultural. The ancient oak forests are long gone, but there are still vast stretches of peat bog in the central and northwestern regions.

POLITICS

Although the violent clashes known as 'the Troubles' came largely to an end with the Good Friday Agreement of 1998, peace in Northern Ireland remains the biggest political issue on the island. The problems of the province are often simplified by outsiders as being a religious conflict between Catholics and Protestants, but the reality involves more complex economic, social and political issues. About 60 per cent of the population of Northern Ireland are Protestant. Both the Unionists (who want the status quo of union with Britain) and the Nationalists (who wish for Irish unity) have long historical ties to their positions.

The implementation of a devolved Assembly in Northern Ireland, with the main opposing parties sharing power, has been difficult. Between 2002 and 2007, the Democratic Unionists, led by the Reverend Ian Paisley, have refused to sit in government with Sinn Féin, led by Gerry Adams, over concerns that a rogue branch of the Irish Republican Army—called the Real IRA—is still active. However, talks brokered by both the UK and Eire governments eventually brought about a resolution and the Assembly was restored in May 2007. The body has legislative powers over social and economic policy in Northern Ireland. Only time will tell if the province becomes part of a united Ireland at some point in the future or remains part of the UK.

The Republic is a parliamentary democracy. The Oireachtas (National Parliament) consists of the president and two houses: Dáil Éireann (House of Representatives), with 166 members (Teachta Dála or TDs), and Seanad Éireann (Senate), with 60 senators. Both are elected through a system of proportional representation.

The president is the head of state and is elected directly by the people for a term of seven years, with a limit of two terms. Although the president does not have an executive or policy-making role, he or she may still influence legislation. Mary Robinson, a lawyer who served as president from 1990 to 1997, championed civil liberties. Under her term of office, homosexuality was decriminalized and divorce was made legal, despite fierce opposition from the Catholic Church. She was succeeded by Mary McAleese, the current president, now in her second term.

The Head of the Government, or Taoiseach, is nominated by the Dáil and appointed by the President. Bertie Ahern has served as Taoiseach since 1997. The two main political parties are Fianna Fáil and Fine Gael, and there are several smaller parties as well. The last general election, in May 2007, resulted in a coalition government led by the Fianna Fáil party. The Republic of Ireland is a member of the European Union.

as the Bronze Age. These skills were enhanced by the Celtic people who came to Ireland from Europe in the sixth century BC. Celtic art features interlaced geometric patterns and stylized animals, often carved on stonework.

The early Christian era gave Ireland some of its most striking architecture. The slender round towers, unique to the island, and tall, elaborately carved high crosses are key features of monastic sites around the country. From the seventh to the ninth centuries, while the rest of Europe was in the Dark Ages, art and learning flourished in Ireland's monasteries. Celtic decorative arts reached their zenith in magnificent

A gift shop on the Aran Islands, selling the famous knitwear (left). Crossing Carrick-a-Rede rope bridge at sunset (middle). Misty clouds hang over the mountains of the Ring of Kerry (right)

ECONOMICS

Ireland joined the European Economic Community, forerunner of the European Union (EU), in 1973, and by the 1990s it was one of Europe's biggest success stories. The lowering of trade barriers expanded the market for Irish goods, while EU aid helped Ireland to modernize its economy. Ireland enthusiastically embraced the euro as its official currency in 2002. Between 1995 and 2002, annual growth averaged an impressive 8 per cent, making it the fastest grow-ing economy in the industrialized world. Ireland became known as the Celtic Tiger, and for the first time in decades, Ireland's young people no longer had to seek work abroad. Despite the global slowdown of the past couple of years, Ireland outranks the four big European economies in per capita GDP by 10 per cent.

Around 60 per cent of Irish workers are employed in the services sector, which now accounts for half of the country's GDP. Electronics, pharmaceuticals, financial services and telemarketing are other leading industries. Tourism is one of the fastest growing economic sectors. Agriculture remains an important factor in the economy, particularly livestock production.

HERITAGE

Ireland's rich heritage stretches back to prehistoric times. Megalithic tombs, cairns and stone circles scattered throughout the countryside are testi-mony to an ancient and mysterious race. Along with remnants of primitive dwellings, such as ring forts and *crannógs* (artificial islands built on lakes), they lend a sense of wonder and timeless-ness to an exploration of the island.

Early Irish craftsmen were making impressive weapons and exquisite gold jewellery as far back

illustrated manuscripts such as the Book of Kells.

The Anglo-Normans brought Romanesque and Gothic churches, and monastic sites such as Jerpoint Abbey. In eastern counties, you can find the ruins of a few of the early Norman castles. Most of Ireland's 2,500 castles and fortified tower houses date from the late 12th to the 16th cen-turies and are in the west and southwest. During the 1700s and early 1800s, the aristocracy built splendid neoclassical mansions such as Castle Coole and Bantry House, and Dublin acquired the elegant Georgian squares for which it is famous.

The art, literature, music, theatre and culture of Ireland are again in the spotlight, as Cork was one of the cities to be a European Capital of Culture in 2005.

THE IRISH

The Republic of Ireland is a nation of 4.2 million people. Its population is young, with about 37 per cent under the age of 25. About 1.7 million people live in Northern Ireland.

The official language of the Republic of Ireland is Irish, one of the Celtic languages. Around 35 per cent of the population have a knowledge of it, and it's widely spoken on the west coast, in Gaeltacht areas. The second official language, English, is spoken almost everywhere.

Though attitudes are becoming more relaxed in certain respects, many people in Ireland remain deeply religious. In the Republic around 92 per cent are Roman Catholic (around 40 per cent in Northern Ireland). The importance of religion is noticeable in just about every aspect of life, from conversation and statues to law and politics.

The Irish are famous for their friendly humour and wit. There's no better place to enjoy it than the pub, the hub of Irish social life.

UNDERSTANDING IRELAND 185

THE BEST OF IRELAND

DUBLIN

Book of Kells (▷ 204–205) This magnificent ninth-century illuminated manuscript in the Old Library at Trinity College represents the height of Celtic artistic achievement.

Christ Church Cathedral (▷ 198) **and St. Patrick's Cathedral** Dublin's two grand cathedrals are filled with monuments to historic figures, from Strongbow to Jonathan Swift.

Guinness Storehouse (▷ 199) Drink a pint of Ireland's most famous brew while enjoying the view from the rooftop bar.

THE EAST

Boyne Valley Drive through beautiful scenery to visit fine monastic sites and the seat of the High Kings at Tara.

Brú na Bóinne Tour the mysterious passage tombs at Newgrange and Knowth, over 5,000 years old and among the world's most important prehistoric sites.

Kilkenny After touring the magnificent cathedral, castle and Black Abbey, explore the medieval alleyways and lively streets of this delightful historic town.

THE SOUTH

Blarney Castle Kiss the Blarney Stone at one of Ireland's most famous castles.

Cork City (▷ 187–189) Explore the picturesque lanes of the old French Quarter, in the heart of Ireland's second city.

Ring of Kerry Drive the most famous scenic route in western Ireland.

THE WEST

The Burren Walk out across the limestone and look for the tiny wild flowers.

Connemara Mountains, lakes, boglands and a jagged coastline of rocky bays and islets make this one of the most scenic areas of the country.

Galway City Bright shop-fronts and medieval buildings line the cobbled streets in this lively university town.

THE MIDLANDS

Blackwater Bog Take a trip on a narrow-gauge train for a close-up look at the boglands.

Clonmacnoise Admire the elaborate stone-carved high crosses, round towers and ruined churches at this important early Christian monastery.

Strokestown Park and Famine Museum Visit the Famine Museum, where the tragedy of the famine years is movingly portrayed.

NORTHERN IRELAND

Belfast (▷ 208–214) Attend a performance to see the lavish interior of the city's Grand Opera House.

Derry Walk around the ramparts of the 17th-century town walls and admire the historic buildings within.

Giant's Causeway Walk (carefully) along the volcanic stepping stones of Northern Ireland's most popular sight.

THERE IS NO CHARGE FOR KISSING THE BLARNEY STONE. REMOVE HATS, GLASSES AND SECURE JACKET POCKETS.

Sign at Blarney Castle (above)

Dublin's Georgian architecture (above)

Molly Malone statue (above), one of many fine examples of sculpture in Dublin. St. Fiachra's Garden, Kildare (below)

Belfast Opera house (above)

Lofty view over Derrynane on the Ring of Kerry (below)

IRELAND

Cork

The second city of the Republic, and a European Capital of Culture in 2005,
Cork is a community with top-class shopping
and a buzzing cultural life.

SEEING CORK

Cork is a vibrant, modern industrial and university city. Its status
as a European Capital of Culture for 2005 has resulted in major
refurbishment, visible in the improvements along Patrick Street
(a main artery of the shopping district) and increased pedestrian-
ization. The level heart of the city lies between the North and
South Channels of the River Lee, and waterways and bridges
have given it the soubriquet of Ireland's Venice. Three-spired
St. Fin Barre's Cathedral (1870) lies to the south.

HIGHLIGHTS

ST. PATRICK'S STREET
☐ 191 B3

Cork is second only to Dublin for the quality and variety of its
shopping, and exploring is easy in such a compact district. St. Patrick's
Street (known locally as Patrick Street) is the hub, curving south from
the North Channel, and you'll find all the big name shops and department stores here including Roches (which started out in Cork),
Dunnes, Penneys and Brown Thomas, and all the chain stores. Step
off the main drag and pedestrianized lanes branching north to Paul
Street and south to Oliver Plunkett Street (named after a 17th-century
martyr) are lined with classy retailers and appealing eateries.

ENGLISH MARKET
☐ 191 B3

For the very essence of the city, visit this covered food emporium, in
a building designed by Sir John Benson in 1881, and restored after a
fire in 1980 (access is from Grand Parade, St. Patrick's
Street, Princes Street and Oliver Plunkett Street; Mon–Sat
8.30–5.30). In the early morning you'll see top local
restaurateurs in here, picking out the best of the meat,
vegetables and fabulous fresh fish: flatfish, langoustines
and conger eels, as well as salt cod, mackerel and
smoked salmon.

Be brave and buy the traditional
Cork dish of tripe (cow's stomach
lining) and drisheen (black pudding)
from the array of butchers' stalls. Iago
sells the best Irish cheeses, including
delicately smoked Gubbeen (West
Cork), Benoskee (Dingle), Cashel Blue
and Brie-like Maighen (both from
Tipperary)—taste before you buy. Odd
corners hold unexpected delights,
such as the tiny Good Yarns
bookshop, packed from floor
to ceiling; and the barber
shop (hot towel, shave and
massage €19). Sit in the
upstairs café and watch Cork
life passing below.

Footbridge over the River Lee

IRELAND

TIPS

● The Visitor Centre is at the
eastern end of Grand Parade
beside the Grafton multi-level
parking; you can buy disks for
on-street parking here, and
also get tickets for the open-
top bus tours which take
around 1 hour.
● You can learn more about
Cork's history at the Cork
Vision Centre on North Main
Street (Tue–Sat 10–5) and
the Public Museum in
Fitzgerald Park (Mon–Fri 11–1,
2.15–5, Sun 3–5).

*A market trader selling organic
fruit and vegetables*

Parliament Bridge, over the Lee (above). A tribute to rock legend Rory Gallagher, on Rory Gallagher Square (right)

CRAWFORD ART GALLERY

✚ 191 B3 • Emmet Place ☎ 021 490 7855 🕐 Mon–Sat 10–5

This outstanding municipal collection is housed in a red-brick building, erected in 1724 as the custom house, when Emmet Street was the King's Dock. As well as rotating exhibitions from the permanent collection of paintings, and the Sculpture Room, there is a modern space for temporary shows which may include video and photography. Up the big staircase (with brilliant stained glass by James Scanlon, 1995) the displays on the upper floor include depictions of Aran islanders by Charles Lamb RHA (1893–1964), and a portrait of actress Fiona Shaw by Victoria Russell (1964–). Séan Keating's icon of Irish nationalism, *Men of the South* (1921) is here, as are impressionistic landscapes by Jack B. Yeats (1871–1957).

CORK CITY GAOL HERITAGE CENTRE

✚ 191 off A3 • Sunday's Well ☎ 021 430 5022 🕐 Mar–end Oct daily 9.30–6; Nov–end Feb daily 9.30–5 (last admittance 1 hour before closing)

Whatever time of year you visit, it's always bone-cold inside the walls of this grim, castle-like structure on a steep hillside to the northwest of the city. Inside, the cells and corridors resonate with the unhappiness of the men and women incarcerated here between 1824 and 1928. Cells are furnished in 19th- to early 20th-century style, and the audio tour and audio-visual presentation bring it all to life with the stories of individual prisoners. In the early days felons were isolated in single cells to avoid further corruption, and left in silence to contemplate their crimes. In reality, such treatment often led to madness. In the 1950s the buildings became the headquarters of Radio Éireann, which could get a good signal this high above the city. A radio museum is upstairs.

BACKGROUND

Cork's history dates back to the founding of a monastery on marshland here by St. Finbarr in the mid-seventh century. The Vikings built a town, and walls were constructed around the core; these were demolished in the 17th century, after a siege by William of Orange's men. Cork's 19th-century prosperity was founded on sea trade, notably shipping butter to Australia and South America. Part of the city was burned in 1921 by the English during the nationalist uprisings.

BASICS

✚ 4 B2

ℹ Áras Fáilte, Grand Parade, Cork, Co. Cork, tel 021 4255100; Jul, Aug Mon–Fri 9–6, Sat, Sun 9.30–4.30; Sep–end Jun Mon–Fri 9–5, Sat 9.30–4.30

🚉 Cork

⛴ Ferries from Roscoff and Swansea; ferry port at Ringaskiddy, tel 021 486 6000, 16km (10 miles) southeast

www.cork-guide.ie
www.corkkerry.ie
Useful site covering the whole Cork region, with listings of accommodation, nightclubs, attractions and more.

IRELAND

KEY TO SYMBOLS
Shopping
Entertainment
Nightlife
Sports
Activities
Health and Beauty
For Children

WHAT TO DO

BUTLERS CHOCOLATE CAFÉ
0 Oliver Plunkett Street
Tel 021 427 8866
www.butlerschocolates.com
Butlers chocolate is famed throughout Ireland and this ultra-modern chocolatier and sip-café is the fashionable place to recharge the batteries during a day's sightseeing. You can by chocolates loose or beautifully boxed.
Mon–Fri 7.30–7, Sat 9–6.30, Sun 1–6.30

LA GALERIE
2 Grand Parade
Tel 021 427 7376
Original modern landscapes and seascape paintings of Ireland are on sale at this classy art gallery on Grand Parade.
Mon–Fri 9.30–1.30, 2.15–5.30, Sat 10–1.30, 2.30–5

THE HEMP COMPANY
Lancaster House, Western Road
Tel 021 427 8958
www.thehempcompany.ie
With an eye on the green sustainability market, The Hemp Company produce an eclectic range of products made from various parts of the hemp plant, from clothing and material to cosmetic and foodstuffs.
Mon–Sat 10–5.30

IMB DESIGN
10a Paul Street
Tel 021 425 1800
www.imbdesign.com
Exquisite jewellery handcrafted in silver and gold is the pride of this tiny shop by the entrance to Paul Street Mall, off the west side of Patrick Street. One of the young owners is usually to be seen in the corner workshop. The results are beautiful, and understandably expensive.
Mon–Sat 10–5.30

VERO MODA
31–32 Patrick Street
Tel 021 427 6072
www.veramoda.dk
The very best in cool Danish women's street fashion can be found in this modern boutique. Clothes are understated and co-ordinated but very much of the moment.
Mon–Sat 9–5.30

AN BODHRÁN
42 Oliver Plunkett Street
Tel 021 427 4544
Live traditional music and occasional rock bands are featured seven nights a week through most of the year at this lively pub. The outside is bright yellow and red; the inside is wooden, snug and welcoming.
Mon–Wed 10.30am–11.30pm, Thu–Sat 10.30am–12.30am, Sun 10.30am–11pm

CORK OPERA HOUSE
Emmet Place
Tel 021 427 0022
www.corkoperahouse.ie
Musical drama and family entertainment, from jazz concerts and pantomime (vaudeville-style fairy tales) to international touring ballet, set the scene at this modern, glass-fronted venue. The back stage door gives access to the Half Moon Theatre, with more experimental drama, live music and a nightclub.
Box Office Mon–Sat 9–5.30 (8.30 on performance nights) From €11

EVERYMAN PALACE THEATRE
15 MacCurtain Street
Tel 021 450 1673
www.everymanpalace.com
A lively mixture of comedy, touring theatre and opera productions, with pantomime (vaudeville-style fairy tales) over the Christmas period, are staged in this Victorian building. Irish plays dominate the summer season.
Box office Mon–Sat 10–6 (7.30 on performance nights), Sun 2–7.30 on performance nights only From €10

THE GATE MULTIPLEX
North Main Street
Tel 021 427 9890
www.corkcinemas.com
If the rain is falling in southern Ireland you may want to head to the multiplex cinema to enjoy the latest box-office hits.
Daily from around 11am; last showings Mon–Thu at 9.30pm, Fri–Sun at 11.30pm Before 5pm €5.50, after 5pm €8, child (5–15) €5.50; family ticket daytime €20, evening €23

GRANARY
Mardyke
Tel box office 021 490 4275
www.granary.ie
Works in a full range of artistic genres are produced and performed at Granary. It's a space for theatre, music, live art and dance. More than 100 performing arts students are based here so it's a lively forum throughout the day and the ASYLUM theatre company is based here.
Mon–Sat 9–5.30 Vary

LE CHATEAU
93 Patrick Street
Tel 021 427 0370
Established in 1793, this bright yellow pub is the perfect place to relax for a while when you're dropping from your shopping. Food is served all day, and you can also get hot drinks, including Irish coffee, hot whiskey and the traditional hot port.
Mon–Thu 10.30am–11.30pm, Fri–Sat 10.30am–12.30am, Sun noon–11pm

SCOTTS OF CAROLINE STREET
Caroline Street
Tel 021 422 2779
www.scotts.ie
This is an elegant and streamlined bar, where glasses and bottles gleam in the soft lighting and tall bucket seats are gathered round the tables. There's a nightclub upstairs, open Friday and Saturday; patrons under 21 must produce some form of photo-ID.
Lunch 12–3.30, Dinner 4–9; Bar Sun–Wed to 12.30am, Thu–Sat to 2am

CURRAHEEN PARK GREYHOUND STADIUM
Curraheen
Tel 021 454 3095/1850 525575
Cork's state-of-the-art stadium is a modern temple to greyhound racing. It includes not only the excitement of 10 races a night, but also live music afterwards, not to mention the comforts of tote

IRELAND

betting from your restaurant table. Curraheen Park offers a memorable and very Irish complete night out.

🏇 Racing Thu–Sat from 7.50, doors open 6.45 🎟 Adult from €10, child (4–16) from €1 🚌 Bus 8 from city; shuttle bus (€2) to city every 20 min between 10.30pm–12.30am

🍴 Laurels Restaurant, advance booking essential, tel 021 493 3154 🍽 🏧

CAFÉ PARADISO
16 Lancaster Quay, Western Road
Tel 021 427 7939
www.cafeparadiso.ie

A lively vegetarian restaurant in a great spot just a 5-minute walk from University College Cork. The imaginative lunch menu offers choices such as feta, pine nut and couscous cake with lemon and cumin wilted spinach, while the dinner menu may list sage-grilled portobello mushrooms with tomato and glazed walnut dressing with red onion jam, smoked gubeen (cheese) mashed potatoes and braised cannellini beans. The wine list emphasizes Italian and New Zealand wines.

🕐 Tue–Sat 12–3, 6.30–10.30 🍷 L from €25, D from €50, Wine from €22

🚗 Follow Washington Street in the direction of Universtiy College Cork, opposite the entrance to Jurys Hotel

GALLERY RESTAURANT
Rochestown Park Hotel, Rochestown Road, Douglas
Tel 021 489 0800
www.rochestownpark.com

The Gallery Restaurant offers a wide choice from simple fish dishes (pan-fried sole with lemon and parsley butter) to more complex carnivorous fare (sautéed pheasant, braised cabbage, lardons and red wine jus). Or you could plump for steak with onions, mushrooms and french fries if you're in the mood for something more down to earth.

🕐 Mon–Sat 12.30–2.30, 6.30–9.45, Sun 12.30–2.30, 5.30–8 🍷 L €25.20, D €65, Wine from €25 🚗 From central Cork take south link road. Take the third exit at the roundabout (traffic circle) for Rochestown. At the small roundabout take the third exit into Rochestown Road

JACOBS
30a South Mall
Tel 021 425 1530
www.jacobsonthemall.com

The high ceilings and contemporary furnishings give Jacobs a light, airy feel, a modern oasis in the bustling financial district of the city. Add to that the skilful, creative menus using top-notch ingredients, and it is no wonder that this restaurant is ever popular. Lunch might be duck confit potato cakes with spinach, caramelized onion and green peppercorn jus followed by a milk chocolate and caramel brulée with strawberries. The dinner menu has such choices as crispy salmon with couscous served with marinated grilled vegetables and harissa, expertly presented. There is a good selection of dessert wines and port to finish your meal.

🕐 Mon–Sat 12.30–2.30, 6.30–10 🍷 L €40, D €65, Wine €21 🚗 In the heart of the city

CRAWFORD HOUSE
Western Road, Cork
Tel 021 427 9000

This Victorian bed-and-breakfast mixes traditional architecture with modern Irish décor. Rooms are contemporary yet intimate with warm oak furnishings and comfy linens. The bright conservatory makes an ideal breakfast room. There is on site parking and some rooms have Jacuzzis.

🕐 Closed Christmas 🛏 €50–€60 ⓘ 12 🅿 On-site, no charge 🛏 8

GARNISH HOUSE
1 Aldergrove, Western Road, Cork
Tel 021 427 5111
www.garnish.ie

Rooms here are tasteful, and some have a private Jacuzzi. The breakfast menu provides a huge choice. It's convenient for the ferry and airport, and has 24-hour reception. Five minutes walk to the heart of the city.

🛏 €90–€140 ⓘ 13 🚗 Opposite Cork University College

GRESHAM METROPOLE
MacCurtain Street, Cork
Tel 021 464 3700
www.gresham-hotles.com

This city hotel has good conference facilities with natural daylight and air conditioning. Bedrooms very in size but are well equipped and comfortable. There is a leisure suite, waterside restaurant and a café. Ask reception for car parking information.

🛏 €149–£189 ⓘ 113 🏊 Indoor 🛏 🚗 In the middle of the city

HAYFIELD MANOR
Perrott Avenue, College Road, Cork
Tel 021 484 5900
www.hayfieldmanor.ie

Part of a grand estate with lovely gardens in its 1ha (2.5 acres) of grounds, this fine secluded hotel has every modern amenity and a tranquil atmosphere. Bedrooms offer high levels of comfort, with many thoughtful extras. Elegant public rooms have fine furnishings and real fires.

🛏 €220–€280 ⓘ 88 🏊 Indoor 🛏 🚗 Take N22 towards Killarney, in 2km (1 mile) turn left at University Gates off Western Road. Turn right into College Road, then left into Perrott Avenue

THE WATER'S EDGE HOTEL
Yacht Club Quay, Cobh
Tel 021 481 5566
www.watersedgehotel.ie

This hotel sits on the coast outside the city in the picturesque town of Cobh. Many rooms have views across the bay and there's a long veranda on which to enjoy a drink and the panorama. Though the building is modern the elegant interior harks back to Cobh's Victorian heyday. Rooms are well appointed and many are wheelchair accessible. There's a fine-dining restaurant on site.

🛏 €70–€100 ⓘ 44 🚗 🚆 20 minutes from Cork with bus and rail service from the city

IRELAND

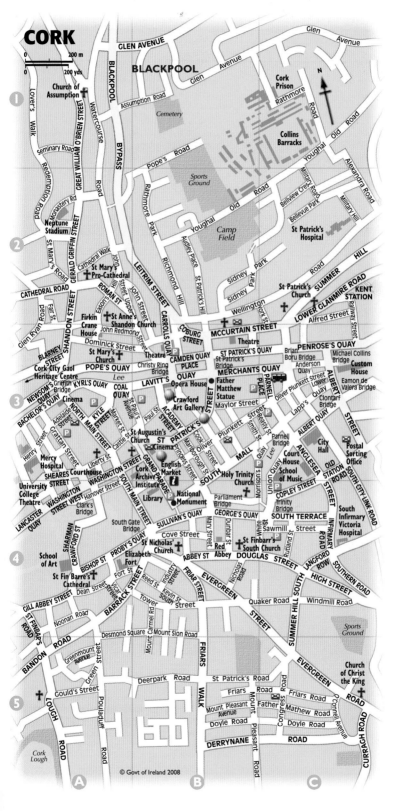

CORK

0 — 200 m
0 — 200 yds

BLACKPOOL

GLEN AVENUE

Glen Avenue

Church of Assumption

Cork Prison

Collins Barracks

Cemetery

Sports Ground

St Mary's Pro-Cathedral

Neptune Stadium

Camp Field

St Patrick's Hospital

St Anne's Shandon Church

Firkin Crane House

St Patrick's Church

KENT STATION

Theatre

MCCURTAIN STREET

St Mary's Church

Cork City Gaol Heritage Centre

Opera House

Christy Ring Bridge

St Patrick's Bridge

MERCHANTS QUAY

Michael Collins Bridge

Custom House

Cinema

Crawford Art Gallery

Father Matthew Statue

Maylor Street

Eamon de Valera Bridge

Mercy Hospital

St Augustin's Church

Cinema

City Hall

Postal Sorting Office

Courthouse

English Market

Court House School of Music

University College Theatre

Grand Archive Institute

National Monument

Holy Trinity Church

South Infirmary Victoria Hospital

School of Art

St Nicholas' Church

Elizabeth Fort

Red Abbey

St Finbarr's South Church

St Fin Barre's Cathedral

Church of Christ the King

Cork Lough

© Govt of Ireland 2008

IRELAND

Dublin

✚ 4 B2 🏛 St. Andrew's Church, Suffolk Street, Dublin 2 ☎ 01 605 7700 🕐 Jul, Aug Mon–Sat 9–7, Sun 10.30–7; Jun, Sep Mon–Sat 9–7, Sun 10.30–3, Oct–end May Mon–Sat 9–5.30, Sun 10–3.30. Public holidays 10.30–3. Closed 25–26 Dec, 1 Jan
www.visitdublin.com • Excellent, informative English-language site

HOW TO GET THERE

✈ Airport
Dublin International Airport, 11km (7 miles) north of city

🚆 Railway stations
Connolly Station, the main station, is in the middle of the city and is also on the DART line; **Heuston Station** is 3km (2 miles) west of the city, and linked to it by bus

Inside the Oliver St. John Gogarty pub in Temple Bar (above). The Dublin City Arms (right). Ha'Penny Bridge (below)

TIPS

● Allow plenty of time at the Chester Beatty Library. Its unpromising name conceals one of the city's real hidden gems.
● The city's hop-on/hop-off tour buses are convenient for getting to the sights that are outside the main hub of the city.
● Summer weekends are a nightmare at Trinity College. If at all possible, visit on a week-day to avoid the crowds.
● Outside term time, Trinity College rents student rooms to visitors, providing a basic but inexpensive central base in a very special place.

SEEING DUBLIN

Dublin is a compact city and easy to walk around. Several of the main attractions, though, such as Kilmainham Gaol and the Irish Museum of Modern Art, will need taxis or public transport to reach them, the latter being generally good and inexpensive. Another option is to take one of the open-top bus tours, which link the attractions and allow you to get on and off as many times as you like. You should decide in advance which sights you want to see, and how many you can manage in a day. It's worth buying a Dublin Pass as it includes free entry to 30 attractions with the chance to jump the lines, and transport from the airport into the city. It costs from €31 per day and is available from Dublin Tourism offices in the airport arrivals hall or in the city (main offices at Suffolk Street and O'Connell Street).

While you could cover the main sights on a weekend visit, there are so many attractions that a week would not be too long. Part of the city's charm is its people, and it would be a shame not to have a chance to relax in the bars and cafés and talk to people. Rushing around is not the best way to experience Dublin.

BACKGROUND

In recent years Dublin has become one of the hottest city destinations in Europe. But its roots go back to Viking times, and it celebrated a thousand years of history in 1988. Its location on the River Liffey was ideal for defence and for trade, and it is less than 112km (70 miles) from the British mainland. In the 12th century English invaders arrived, leading to several centuries of Anglo-Irish strife that is still unresolved in Northern Ireland.

The English presence did help the city to flourish, and left its mark in many of today's splendid houses, especially the Georgian areas around Merrion Square and other fine city squares. By the 18th century the independence movement was gaining ground, but it was not until the early 20th century that the final break from England was made. By 1972 Ireland was a member of the European Union, initiating the boom that really flourished in the 1990s, when not just the economy but fashion, the arts, food and Irish culture all blossomed and turned Dublin into the vibrant city that it is today.

DON'T MISS

TRINITY COLLEGE LIBRARY
The Library and the Book of Kells are essential (▷ 204–205)
CHESTER BEATTY LIBRARY
One of the best museums in Ireland (▷ 197)
KILMAINHAM GAOL
Powerful, moving and historically fascinating (▷ 200–201)
GUINNESS STOREHOUSE
Educational, entertaining, inventive, and one of the best views in Dublin (▷ 199)
NATIONAL MUSEUM
Unrivalled national collection of antiquities (▷ 202–203)
NATIONAL MUSEUM OF DECORATIVE ARTS AND HISTORY
Impressive branch of the National Museum, within Collins Barracks (▷ 203)

IRELAND DUBLIN **193**

DUBLIN

Dublin's Georgian Custom House was built on a bed of pine planks to prevent it from sinking into the marshy bank of the Liffey

A Celtic cross in Glasnevin Cemetery

Picturesque Malahide Castle spans many centuries

The magnificent reading room of the National Library

Dublin Castle and the Chester Beatty Library

The interior was largely rebuilt in the 18th and 19th centuries

RATINGS	
Cultural interest	● ● ● ● ●
Good for kids	● ● ●
Historic interest	● ● ● ●

BASICS

✚ 195 D3 • Dame Street, Dublin 2
☎ 01 677 7129
◉ Mon–Fri 10–4.45, Sat–Sun 2–4.45. Closed during state business
💷 State Apartments, Undercroft, Chapel Royal: adult €4.50, child (over 12) €2
🚌 50, 50A, 54, 56A, 77, 77A, 77B, 123
🎫 Access by 45-min guided tour only
🍴 Castle Vaults Bistro in Lower Yard
♿ Castle foyer and Chester Beatty Library

www.dublincastle.ie
A very clever site that's easy to navigate.

TIPS

● The State Apartments are often closed for security reasons ahead of important events and state occasions so call in advance to make sure you can join a tour.
● The best view of the Dubh Linn Garden is from the rooftop garden of the Chester Beatty Library; if this is closed, try the top floor of the Record Tower (Garda Museum).

SEEING DUBLIN CASTLE AND THE CHESTER BEATTY LIBRARY

Long the symbol of Anglo-Norman power, the Dublin Castle complex is a mix of vice-regal classicism, medieval buildings, modern offices and a world-renowned museum. The Chester Beatty Library and Gallery of Oriental Art contains a collection of early religious manuscripts including fragments of second-century biblical tracts and ninth-century Koranic texts. On view at the castle itself are its fine State Apartments, its Undercroft, showing traces of the Viking fortress that was the earliest incarnation of the city of Dublin, and its Chapel Royal, a neo-Gothic gem of a church built in 1814.

HIGHLIGHTS

STATE APARTMENTS

The State Apartments were designed to reflect the extravagant and fashionable lifestyle of the vice-regal court. Following a disastrous fire in 1684, they were remodelled by Sir William Robinson, who also designed the Royal Hospital at Kilmainham. He planned the Upper and Lower courtyards to complement the remaining buildings. From the entrance in the Upper Yard, a guided tour visits the Throne Room dating from 1740, where the throne is said to have been presented to William of Orange to commemorate his victory at the Battle of the Boyne. St. Patrick's Hall is hung with banners of the old order of the Knights of St. Patrick. Its ceiling, painted by Vincenzo Valdré in 1778, depicts links between Ireland and Britain. The apartments, with Killybegs carpets and Waterford crystal chandeliers, are used for presidential inaugurations and other ceremonial occasions.

The Undercroft was revealed when work was done on the Lower Yard in 1990. The city walls join the castle here and a small archway allowed boats to land provisions at the Postern Gate, also visible. In the base of the Norman Powder Tower, the original Viking defensive bank can be made out.

CHAPEL ROYAL

The Chapel Royal (officially the Church of the Most Holy Trinity) was designed by Francis Johnston and is best known for its ornate plaster decorations by George Stapleton and Richard Stewart's woodcarvings.

GARDA MUSEUM

✉ The Garda (Police) Museum, Dublin Castle, Dublin 2 ☎ 01 671 9597
◉ Mon–Fri 9.30–4.30, Sat, Sun by appointment
The Garda Museum moved to the Record Tower in 1997. The museum displays uniforms and equipment charting policing in Ireland from the days of the Royal Irish Constabulary to the Civic Guard of 1922 (later renamed Garda Síochána na hÉireann). The top floor has the best view of the Dubh Linn Garden, and exhibits on the worldwide role of the Garda, working for the United Nations.

CHESTER BEATTY LIBRARY

✉ Chester Beatty Library and Gallery of Oriental Art, Dublin Castle, Dublin 2
☎ 01 407 0750 🕐 May–end Sep Mon–Fri 10–5, Sat 11–5, Sun 1–5; Oct–end
Apr Tue–Fri 10–5, Sat 11–5, Sun 1–5 💷 Free 🚪

The Chester Beatty Library and Gallery of Oriental Art houses the
collection of Sir Alfred Chester Beatty, a wealthy North American
mining magnate of Irish descent, who died in 1968. Chief
among the exhibits are the fragments of early religious texts.
There are over 300 Korans, Babylonian tablets over 6,000 years
old, Coptic Bibles, Jewish texts, Confucian scrolls and Buddhist
literature, with explanations on these religions. The displays and
exhibits are supported by touch-screen computers giving more
information about the world's religions and the artwork inspired
by them. Popular exhibits are the exquisite Burmese and
Siamese *parabaiks* describing folk tales and drawn on paper
made from mulberry leaves. There are also exhibition spaces
here, housing collections of contemporary work. Don't miss the
Pauline letters from AD180–200, and the gospels from AD250—
the oldest full collections in the world; the delicate papyrus fragment of St. John's Gospel, taken from the Bodmer codex, the
oldest New Testament scripture in existence; and the Chinese
jade books, engraved then filled with gold.

BACKGROUND

Dublin takes its name from the 'Dubh Linn', the Black Pool at
the confluence of the Liffey and Poddle rivers. The castle
gardens now occupy that site and their Celtic-design parterre
cleverly doubles as a helicopter pad for visiting dignitaries.
The castle was built for King John in the 13th century and was
renovated for use as a vice-regal palace in the 16th century. The
oldest remaining part is the Record Tower, once used as a top-
security prison. Red Hugh O'Donnell, son of a Donegal chieftain,
was held here in 1592 for rebelling against the Crown. He
escaped and, together with Hugh O'Neill, led the Nine Years War.
Today the Record Tower houses a simple museum documenting
the history of Ireland's police force.

*Chinese ceiling of the Chester
Beatty Library (top).
Two examples of the Oriental
art in the Chester Beatty
Library (above)*

The early Gothic nave dates from around 1226

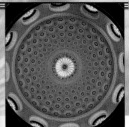

The dome of City Hall bathes the rotunda with natural light

CHRIST CHURCH CATHEDRAL

Dublin's second cathedral has a historical role as the seat of Irish bishops from the time of Viking Dublin. Next door, Dvblinia tells the history of the city.

⊕ 195 D3 • Christchurch Place, Dublin 8 ☎ 01 677 8099
🕐 Jun–end Aug daily 9–6; Sep–end May 9.45–5. Check website for times of services 💷 Donation €5 waged, children (5–12; accompanied) free 🚌 49, 50, 51B, 54A, 56A, 65, 77A, 78A, 123, 90 from Tara Street DART station 🚃 DART Tara Street, 25-min walk 🔛
www.cccdub.ie

DVBLINIA
⊕ 195 D3 • St. Michael's Hill, Christchurch, Dublin 8 ☎ 01 679 4611
🕐 Apr–end Sep daily 10–5; Oct–end Mar Mon–Sat 11–4, Sun, public holidays 10–4 💷 Adult €6.25, child (5–18) €3.75, family €17 🍴 Jun–end Aug
www.dublinia.ie

TIP

● You can access Christ Church Cathedral from Dvblinia across the bridge over St. Michael's Hill, but you are not allowed to go the other way, so visit Dvblinia first.

St. Laurence's heart is in this casket

This Gothic jumble of buttresses and spires has been a Protestant stronghold in Catholic southern Ireland since the Reformation and seat of Irish bishops for 1,000 years. Within its overtly Victorian walls lies a medieval core, and until 1871 it was the main church of the state. Strongbow was responsible for turning the wooden Viking church to stone in 1172, and his tomb of 1176 is one of Christ Church's oldest remains. The Chapel of St. Laud holds the heart of St. Laurence O'Toole (died 1180), archbishop and patron saint of Dublin.

Much of the building collapsed in 1562 and had to be rebuilt, but the north wall, now disturbingly out of line with the rest of the building, is original. The transepts and part of the choir retain their Norman features, and there is an impressive eagle lectern dating from the 13th century. Don't miss the cathedral's crypt and its peculiar cornucopia of remnants.

DVBLINIA
Multimedia presentations of medieval Dublin here include the arrival of Strongbow, a merchant's house and the dockside at Wood Quay and a scale model of the city in 1500. There's a wonderful view over the city from St. Michael's Tower.

CITY HALL
⊕ 195 D3 • Cork Hill, Dame Street, Dublin 2 ☎ 01 672 2204 🕐 Mon–Sat 10–5.15, Sun, public holidays 2–5. Closed Good Fri, 24–26 Dec 💷 Adult €4, child €1.50 🚌 54 (from Burgh Quay), 50, 56A, 77A (from Eden Quay), 123, 150 🎧 On request 🍴 Queen of Tarts restaurant
www.dublincity.ie/cityhall

The magnificent Corinthian portico of Thomas Cooley's Royal Exchange of 1779, in front of Dublin Castle on Lord Edward Street, has been the public face of the Dublin Corporation since 1852 and is still the City Hall, their principal meeting place. 'The Story of the Capital' exhibition on the ground floor relates the city's history, while the restored rotunda has statues and an Arts and Crafts mural depicting Dublin's past. Ireland's first President, Arthur Griffiths, lay in state here, as did Michael Collins after his assassination in 1922.

CUSTOM HOUSE
⊕ 195 F2 • Custom House Quay, Dublin 1 ☎ 01 888 2538 🕐 Mid-Mar to end Oct Mon–Fri 10–12.30, Sat, Sun, public holidays 2–5; Nov to mid-Mar Wed–Fri 10–12.30, Sun 2–5 💷 Adult €1, family €3 🚌 Busáras, 5-min walk 🚃 DART Tara Street 🍴 Access to staff restaurant

One of the most prominent buildings on Dublin's waterfront, the Custom House was designed by James Gandon and completed in 1791. The classical façade, best seen from the opposite bank of the river downstream from O'Connell Bridge, is 114m (125 yards) long, and the huge green copper cupola is 38m (125ft) high. Today, it houses government offices and a small Visitor Centre explaining the building's history and restoration.

IRELAND

A Celtic cross in Glasnevin Cemetery

DRIMNAGH CASTLE

⊞ 194 off B4 • Long Mile Road, Drimnagh, Dublin 12 ☎ 01 450 2530
🕐 Wed 12–3, Sun 2–5 (last tour at 4)
🎫 Adult €4.50, child (4–18) €3 🚌 77, 77A, 56, 18 🚇 🏛

Drimnagh Castle is a medieval, moated castle with a wonderfully restored 17th-century garden. The tower gateway leads into a walled courtyard, a world away from the surroundings. Inhabited for over 500 years, the castle was abandoned in the 1950s and slid into ruin.

Restoration began in the late 1980s, using traditional craft skills to bring the masonry and woodwork back to their former condition, and 5,500 tiles were specially made for the great hall in 1991. Outside, the moat once more flows with clear water.

GLASNEVIN CEMETERY

⊞ 194 off C1 • Finglas Road, Glasnevin, Dublin 11 ☎ 01 830 1133
🕐 Mon–Sat 8.30–4.30, Sun 9–4.30
🚌 19, 40, 40A 🖵 Wed, Fri 2.30, tel 01 830 1133
www.glasnevin-cemetery.ie

Established in 1832, when Catholics were finally allowed to conduct funerals, the list of occupants of Glasnevin Cemetery reads like a roll call of the key players in Ireland's story from the last 180 years. Daniel O'Connell is commemorated by a round tower standing 49m (160ft) high, Charles Stewart Parnell by a big lump of granite. Michael Collins, Countess Markiewicz, Brendan Behan and Alfred Chester Beatty are among the other names familiar to any visitor to Dublin. There are sad reminders of famine and poverty in the many paupers' graves, and sections devoted to the Irish army and other services.

A mountain of barrels in this temple to the art of brewing

GUINNESS STOREHOUSE

See how the brewing giant turns water, barley, hops and yeast into Ireland's national drink.

⊞ 194 B3 • St. James's Gate, Dublin 8
☎ 01 408 4800, information line 01 453 8364 🕐 Jul, Aug daily 9.30–7; Sep–end Jun 9.30–5 🎫 Adult €14, child (6–12) €5, under 6 free
🚌 51B, 78A (from Aston Quay), 123 (from O'Connell Street)
🎧 Self-guided 🍴 Three bars and a restaurant 🚇 🏛
www.guinness-storehouse.com
Slick, nicely designed site, packed with information about Guinness.

RATINGS	
Cultural interest	● ● ●
Good for Guinness	● ● ● ● ●
Good for kids	● ● ● ●

TIPS

• Use public transport so you can enjoy the free Guinness.
• Make time to visit the excellent Guinness merchandise shop on the ground floor.

The Gravity Bar atop the Storehouse has great views

For many people a trip to Dublin involves, in some way, a search for the mythical 'best pint of Guinness'. The Dublin brewer's status as a world brand ensures that a ready stream of visiting drinkers arrive to take up the challenge. The Guinness Storehouse off St. James's Gate is a good place to start. Here, an old warehouse next to the vast brewery has been transformed into a cathedral to the creation of this ale.

Seven floors of dramatic exhibits take you through the process from the water (it doesn't really come from the Liffey as the legends say), Irish barley, hops and yeast to the finished product. On the way you learn how the beer developed from a dark porter-style ale popular among Irish migrant workers in London to the distinctive global superbrand it is today. Escalators connect the floors in a pleasingly futuristic style redolent of Fritz Lang's classic 1920s film *Metropolis*. The labyrinthine displays include sections dedicated to the transport that has carried Guinness around world. You get a free pint in the seventh floor Gravity Bar, now reputed to be the best pint in Dublin. The views over the city to the docks and the mountains are impressive. Back on the ground floor, is a large, comprehensive Guinness merchandise shop.

Kilmainham Gaol

No other sight captures the iconography of the Irish struggle for independence quite like this well-preserved prison on a low hill in west Dublin.

Prison life was more comfortable for some

The main compound of the prison forms the heart of the museum (above). The gates are now open wide—for visitors (above right)

IRELAND

RATINGS	
Cultural interest	●●●○
Historic interest	●●●●
Photo stops	●●●

BASICS

✚ 194 off A3 • Inchicore Road, Kilmainham, Dublin 8

☎ 01 453 5984

🕐 Apr–end Sep daily 9.30–5; Oct–end Mar Mon–Sat 9.30–4, Sun 10–5. Last tour 1 hour before closing

💶 Adult €5.30, child (4–16) €2.10, family €11.50

🚌 51B, 78A, 79

🚉 Heuston Station, 20-min walk

🎫 Access by guided tour only. Allow at least 1 hour plus 30 min to see exhibition

♿ Tours by prior arrangement. Some older parts of the prison are difficult for wheelchair users

☕ Tea room by exhibition

🛍 Beyond front desk

www.heritageireland.ie

SEEING KILMAINHAM GAOL

This sinister place is where the leaders of the 1916 rising were executed. Its last prisoner, released in 1924, was Eamonn de Valera, who went on to become Taoiseach, and two-time president. Viewing is by guided tour only. After a video presentation in the basement you are led through the east wing, the chapel, the west wing, then the prison yards. A museum has some grim exhibits illustrating the lives and deaths of former inmates. The tours, accompanied by an enthusiastic and knowledgeable curator, last around 70 minutes and run every half hour. The gaol's history is put in context, not just as a place for political prisoners, but also for its role as a prison for common criminals.

HIGHLIGHTS

THE EAST WING

This is a painstakingly restored example of a 19th-century cell block. A three-floor shell, open to skylights in the roof, is ringed by tiny cells opening onto iron lattice landings. From the central ground floor, where the prisoners would eat, every cell door is visible and from the landings observation hatches allow warders to see inside every cell. Unlike older prisons, inmates here could not hide in the shadows; their behaviour was monitored 24 hours a day.

THE WEST WING

There's a stark contrast in the West Wing, with its labyrinth of dank, dilapidated corridors and tight, dimly lit cells. Recent graffiti in some corridors enhances the sense of squalor. Connecting the two is the prison chapel, where Joseph Plunkett married Grace Gifford the night before his execution in 1916. They spent 10 minutes together as a married couple before he was led away. Each cell is labelled with the names of the most significant occupants. With risings against British rule in 1798, 1803, 1848, 1867, 1883 and 1916, it is easy to understand the gaol's reputation as the place to hold political prisoners, and graffiti over one doorway threatens the gaolers with the 'vengeance of the risen people'. Charles Stewart Parnell was held here in 1883, in a pleasant suite of rooms that befitted his political standing. Other

prisoners were not so lucky and overcrowding was a significant problem. During the famine years, when thousands flocked to Dublin to find food, there were over 7,000 men and women crammed into the cells.

THE YARDS

The exercise yards are where the 14 leaders of the Easter Rising were executed by firing squad and a cross marks the spot where the injured James Connolly was strapped to a chair so he could be upright when he was shot. However, the 1916 rising was not well-supported at the time, and its leaders were not portrayed as heroes until much later. In the civil war that followed independence, the Free State government dispatched a further 77 anti-treaty fighters against these grey walls.

THE MUSEUM

Among the grim items in the museum is a darkened room devoted to *memento mori* of each of the 1916 executed. You can also see the block of wood on which Robert Emmet's head was removed following his hanging in 1803. Emmet had hoped to bring Napoleonic firepower to the fight against the British, but it didn't materialize in the way he had planned. On a lighter note, there are many fine banners from the various Irish struggles; a charming home-made selection from the Irish Land League in 1879 declare 'the land for the people'.

BACKGROUND

The main body of the prison was built in 1789, and was restored by enthusiasts in the 1960s. It is the largest unused prison in Europe and has been in great demand as a film set since the 1960s. Bizarrely, the gaol scenes from that most English film *The Italian Job* (1966) were filmed here. More recently it reprised its real-life role in *Michael Collins* (1996), with Liam Neeson in the title role as the Irish military leader.

A prisoner's-eye view of the main compound through the bars of a sturdy cell door (top). Names that are now writ large in the history of Ireland feature on this plaque commemorating those executed after the Easter Rising (above)

TIPS

● Wait for the rest of the tour group to leave before you take photos of the panoptican east win; the effect is much greater.

● Avoid the busiest times; come early in summer, or later in winter after the school groups.

IRELAND

National Museum

The Kildare Street site houses such national treasures as the Ardagh Chalice and Tara Brooch. The Collins Barracks site is worth visiting for the building alone.

RATINGS

Cultural interest	● ● ● ● ●
Historic interest	● ● ● ● ●
Specialist shopping	● ● ● ● ●

BASICS

NATIONAL MUSEUM OF ARCHAEOLOGY AND HISTORY

⊞ 195 F3 • Kildare Street, Dublin 2
☎ 01 677 7444
◉ Tue–Sat 10–5, Sun 2–5
🎟 Free
🚌 7, 7A, 10, 11, 13
🚉 DART Pearse
🎧 Tours last 40 min and depart from main entrance at regular intervals; adult €2, child (under 16) free
🍴 Museum café on ground floor 🏛
♿ By back entrance

NATIONAL MUSEUM OF DECORATIVE ARTS AND HISTORY

⊞ 194 B2 • Collins Barracks, Benburb Street, Dublin 7
◉ Opening times as Kildare Street site
🎟 Free
🚌 25, 25A, 66, 67, 90
🎧 Tours available by advance reservation (tel 01 677 7444) 🏛 🏛

www.museum.ie
Excellent, easy to use website, covering all branches of the National Museum.

SEEING THE NATIONAL MUSEUM

The National Museum safeguards some of Ireland's most precious and important treasures—gold and silverware found in bogs, caves and burial mounds all across the country and memorabilia from the 20th-century struggle for independence. The Kildare Street site is based around a glorious marble-halled rotunda, the Benburb Street site is the old Collins Barracks, a fascinating building in its own right.

HIGHLIGHTS

PREHISTORIC IRELAND

The Prehistoric Ireland displays include tools and weaponry from the Stone Age and Bronze Age, with explanations of burial customs and reconstructed graves. One of the most impressive exhibits is the Lurgan Bog Boat, over 13m (43ft) long, pulled from a Galway bog in 1902 and dated to around 2500BC. There is a huge collection of Sheela na Gigs here too. These weird, often comically sexy, stone carvings of women date from a pre-Christian era.

ÓR—IRELAND'S GOLD

Bronze Age Ireland produced a wealth of gold jewellery and other items which may come as a surprise to anyone with preconceptions about this 'uncivilized' era. The collection includes gold lunulae dating back as far as 2000BC, and more sophisticated works such as the Gleninsheen Collar, which was made around 700BC.

THE TREASURY

The best-known pieces of ancient Irish craftsmanship are preserved in the Treasury. The Tara Brooch, only 5cm (2in) across yet intricately patterned with Celtic motifs is believed to have been made in the eighth century AD, of white bronze, silver gilt, amber and glass, and symbolizes the inspirational early Christian design that flourished here while much of the British Isles languished in the Dark Ages. The superb Ardagh Chalice is also from that period—gilded and studded in multi-hued glass and decorated in gold filigree. The exquisite crozier from Clonmacnoise shows the wealth and power of the early church.

THE ROAD TO INDEPENDENCE–AR THOIRE NA SAOOIRSE
This part of the museum charts the rise of nationalism in the 19th century then concentrates on the first two decades of the 20th century. The 1916 Easter Rising is heavily represented with a collection of weapons that belonged to notable individuals.

OTHER EXHIBITS
Viking Ireland is explored upstairs, particularly the peaceful trading aspects of the Scandinavians who established their port at Dublin. A new exhibition reveals the wealth of artefacts discovered at the site of the Iron Age bog bodies discovered in County Meath in 2003.

The impressive exterior of Collins Barracks (below left), housing the National Museum of Decorative Arts and History

The great hall of the National Museum of Archaeology and History (below middle), and its colonnaded exterior (below right)

IRELAND

NATIONAL MUSEUM OF DECORATIVE ARTS AND HISTORY
The layout at the Collins Barracks is a little more confusing, with 13 galleries on four floors around two sides of the central courtyard, but there's a leaflet to help you navigate, available from the reception desk. The section devoted to Irish Silver takes the silversmith's craft from the early 17th to the 20th century, and another section deals with coinage. It was the Vikings who first brought the concept of currency to Ireland's shores and this exhibition follows its history, from 10th-century hoards to the ATM. 'The Way We Wore' displays 250 years of Irish clothing, and the influence of European trends on local materials. Curator's Choice is an eclectic selection chosen for interesting stories or significance, and include a wedding gift from Oliver Cromwell to his daughter, King William's gauntlets from the day of the Battle of the Boyne in 1690, and a hurling ball love token.

The Ardagh Chalice (left), a wonder of early Celtic art, is in the museum's Treasury

BACKGROUND
The Kildare Street site, opened in 1896, was designed by Thomas Newenham and Thomas Manley Deane, in a style known as Victorian Palladian, with a dome that rises to 19m (62ft). The Collins Barracks, on the other hand, began life as the main barracks for the British garrison in Dublin and were built in 1700. The Irish Free State took them over in 1922 and they remained in military hands until the 1990s, renamed after Michael Collins. In the superb courtyard-cum-parade ground, you can still see 100 marching paces marked off against the wall.

TIPS
● Combine a trip out to the Collins Barracks with a visit to Kilmainham or the Museum of Modern Art.
● The Kildare Street museum isn't a large space, and can seem very congested, so try to avoid times when it is most likely to be crowded, for example weekend afternoons in summer.

Trinity College Library

The iconic intricacy of the Book of Kells draws visitors to Trinity College, Ireland's premier seat of learning. A fascinating exhibition puts the art of the ninth-century scribe in perspective.

Trinity's busy main entrance (above). Sphere Within a Sphere (right) by Arnaldo Pomodoro, outside the Berkeley Library

The spacious campus (above)

RATINGS	
Cultural interest	●●●●
Historic interest	●●●●
Specialist shopping	●●●
Walkability	●●●

BASICS

➕ 195 E3 • College Street, Dublin 2
☎ 01 608 2320
🕐 Jun–end Sep Mon–Sat 9.30–5, Sun 9.30–4.30; Oct–end May Mon–Sat 9.30–5, Sun 12–4.30. Closed 10 days over Christmas and New Year
💶 Adult €8, family €16
🚌 All cross city buses
🚉 DART Tara Street

www.tcd.ie/library/
Comprehensive information about the college.

TIPS

● Visit on a Sunday morning in June for the best view of the campus with the fewest students and other visitors.
● You can wander around the main courtyards and admire the historic buildings for free, but remember it's a working university and private property.
● Take your time at the Book of Kells; its intricacy is scarcely credible at first glance.

SEEING TRINITY COLLEGE LIBRARY

No visit to Dublin is complete without seeing one of the most famous illuminated manuscripts in the world. The intricate beauty of the Book of Kells has been imitated countless times, but to see the pages themselves, and those of the similarly ornate books of Durrow and Armagh, is really memorable. There is more here than just these revered texts though. The exhibition 'Turning Darkness into Light' brings a context to the works, and upstairs, the barrel-ceilinged Long Room is filled with the intoxicating musk of over 200,000 ancient leather-bound books.

The entrance to the Old Library is through the gap in the square on the right-hand side. It faces a group of modern buildings including the Berkeley Library, which was designed by Paul Koralek in 1967. The exhibition is reached through the shop at street level.

HIGHLIGHTS

EXHIBITION

'Turning Darkness into Light' is the name of the exhibition in the Old Library that leads you up to the displayed pages of the Book of Kells. It explains the context of the book, follows the development of writing and illuminating manuscripts and has examples of Ogham and Ethiopian scripts. Pages, and individual illustrations, have been enlarged to the size of a person, so you can stand back and identify the truly stunning detail of the monastic scribe's art.

THE BOOK OF KELLS

The Book of Kells itself is displayed in a darkened room known as the Treasury. The book is bound in four volumes, two of which are always on display, so you are able to see two double-page spreads at a time, and these are turned every three months. It was written, if that is the right word for its spectacularly ornate pages, in the ninth century AD by monks at St. Columba's monastery at Iona on the west coast of Scotland. The book was transferred to the monastery at Kells in

County Meath for safekeeping during the Viking raids and then its history is less certain. It arrived in Dublin in 1653, during the Cromwellian upheavals, and was acquired by Trinity College in 1661. Its brilliantly elaborate pages reveal both the craft and the wit of its scribes. The text is the four Christian gospels, written in Latin. Each evangelist is portrayed in minute detail and each gospel begins with just a few words on a magnificently decorated page. Some of the pages, known as 'carpet pages', have no words at all, just the swirling abstract ornamentation which has become the hallmark of

this incredible era of Celtic art. Also on display in the Treasury are the equally fabulous, but less well-known books of Durrow and Armagh, which may originate from the seventh century AD. They, too, demonstrate the tremendous scope and vision of the monastic scribes, again displaying an intricacy of penmanship that could scarcely have been visible in that distant age before electric lighting and artificial magnification.

Intricate Celtic art frames a portrait of St. John in the Book of Kells (above)

THE LONG ROOM

The Long Room is up the stairs from the Treasury. As in Marsh's Library at St. Patrick's Cathedral, the smell of old books hits you as you walk in. They are piled high to the ceiling, which was extended in 1860 to fit more in. The gallery bookcases were added at this point. The central aisle is lined with busts of scholars and there is also a harp on display, believed to be the oldest in existence, though its 15th-century provenance means it can't be the legendary harp of Brian Boru, the 11th-century High King of Ireland, as one story claims. Another display has a rare copy of the Proclamation of the Irish Republic, as read out by Padraig Pearse from the steps of the GPO in 1916, Robert Emmet's arrest warrant and other papers from the struggle for independence.

BACKGROUND

Trinity College is a modern working university and so, unless you visit on Sunday morning or in high summer, its courtyards are usually teeming with students and their bicycles. Founded by Queen Elizabeth I in 1592, it is Ireland's oldest university. Although this Georgian building (1759) is grand in its own right, its impact is lessened by the proximity of the traffic and the more overt classicism of James Gandon's east front of the Bank of Ireland across the road. This dates from 1785 and was added to an older building, which once housed the Irish parliament.

Past the Porter's Lodge you come out into Parliament Square, with the chapel, built in 1798, to the left and the Examination Room, of 1791, to the right. Ahead of you is the Campanile, a bell tower 30m (98ft) high added to the square in 1853. Beyond it, the red-brick building is known as the Rubrics. With its origins around 1700, this is the oldest surviving building on the campus. The playwright Oliver Goldsmith had chambers on the top right-hand side next to the Old Library. Before the rebuilding work of the 1980s, the Book of Kells was kept upstairs in the Long Room, and the area known as the Colonnades below, where the shop, exhibition and Treasury are now, was a crowded storage area for the library's overflowing book collection.

Oliver Goldsmith (below) was one of many illustrious students

WHAT TO DO

⊕ ARNOTTS
12 Henry Street
Tel 01 805 0400
www.arnotts.ie
A huge, long-established department store just off O'Connell Street, Arnotts is popular with Dubliners and visitors alike for fashion, sportswear and childrenswear as well as perfume, gifts and home furnishings. It also has a good selection of Irish crystal and other indigenous products.
◎ Mon, Wed, Fri, Sat 9–7; Tue 9.30–7; Thu 9–9; Sun 12–6 🚌 Any O'Connell Street bus 🚉 DART Connolly

⊕ CELTIC WHISKEY SHOP
27–28 Dawson Street
Tel 01 675 9744
www.celticwhiskeyshop.com
Boasting one of the best selections of Irish whiskeys in town, the Celtic Whiskey Shop also features a range of handmade chocolates and a rich assortment of wines and liqueurs.
◎ Mon–Sat 10.30–8, Sun 12.30–6 🚌 Most cross-city buses 🚉 DART Pearse

⊕ PATAGONIA
24–26 Exchequer Street
Tel 01 670 5748
www.patagonia.com
The Patagonia shop is one of only four outlet stores in Europe (and the only one in the British Isles) for this iconic brand of eco-friendly outdoor wear.
◎ Mon–Fri 10–6 (Thu 10–8), Sat 9.30–6, Sun 1–5 🚌 Most cross-city buses 🚉 DART Tara Street

🎭 NATIONAL CONCERT HALL
Earlsfort Terrace
Tel 01 417 0000
www.nch.ie
Dublin's biggest classical music venue was built for the International Exhibition of Arts and Manufactures in 1865. In addition to hosting the greatest visiting musicians of the

day, it is home to the RTÉ National Symphony Orchestra.
◎ All year 🎭 Varies ⬛ 📞 🚌 10, 11, 13, 14/A, 15/A/B/C, 27C, 44, 46A/B, 48A, 86 🚉 DART Pearse

🎭 WHELAN'S
25 Wexford Street
Tel 01 478 0766
www.whelanslive.com
You'll see an eclectic line-up at this smaller rock and pop venue with late club bar from Wednesday to Saturday. Licensed to serve alcohol since 1772, renovation work in the early 1990s revealed the original wood and stonework, which is now a feature.
◎ All year 📞 🚌 16/A, 19/A., 65/B, 83 🚉 DART Pearse/Tara Street

🍸 MULLIGANS
8 Poolbeg Street
Tel 01 677 5582
www.mulligans.ie
A pub since 1820, Mulligans is a Guinness drinkers' institution. Retaining its Victorian mahogany furnishings, it has resisted change and would probably have looked the same when John F. Kennedy drank here, as a journalist, in 1947.
◎ Sun–Fri 10.30am–11.30pm, Sat and evenings before a public holiday 10.30am–12.30am

🍸 THE VAULTS
IFSC (under Connolly Station)
Tel 01 605 4700
www.thevaults.ie
A busy mainstream nightclub in the International Financial Services Centre, where Friday is Smooth Grooves mixed up with some hip-hop and R'n'B, and Saturday nights are given over to R'n'B and '80s soul.
◎ Mon–Thu 12pm–11.30pm, Fri–Sat 12pm–2.30am, (Sun open bank holiday weekends only)

✹ THE ARK
11a Eustace Street, Temple Bar
Tel 01 670 7788
www.ark.ie
This is a cultural venue especially for 4–14 year olds. It stages varied performances by children and for children in both the indoor theatre and outdoor amphitheatre.
◎ Call for opening times and performances 🚉 DART Tara Street

EATING

BRAZEN HEAD
20 Lower Bridge Street
Tel Restaurant: 01 677 9549
Bar: 01 679 5186
www.brazenhead.com
Ireland's oldest pub dates back 800 years and remains the archetypal Irish pub, with a lively atmosphere, good music, food and beer. The Courtyard Restaurant attached to the pub serves a mix of traditional Irish and international cuisine, accompanied by a good range of wines. The Brazen Head was frequented by James Joyce, who mentioned it in *Ulysses*.
◎ Pub: Mon–Wed 11–11, Thu–Sat 11am–midnight; carvery: Mon–Fri 12–2.30; a la carte food: Mon–Sat 2.30–9, Sun 12–7
🍽 L (carvery) €40, D €50, Wine €18
🚉 DART Tara Street
🚌 Short walk from the heart of the city on the left-hand side of Bridge Street, just before the bridge

BROWNES RESTAURANT
22 St. Stephen's Green North
Tel 01 638 3939
www.brownesrestaurant.com
In a Georgian town house facing St. Stephen's Green in the heart of Dublin, Brownes provides romantic dining at its best. The spectacular dining room boasts chandeliers and Italian-style friezes and is considered one of the most stylish in the city. Executive chef David Willcocks chooses Irish ingredients but serves them in a contemporary style, including exceptional seafood dishes.
◎ Mon–Fri 12–2, 6–7 (pre-theatre set menu), 7–10; Sat 6–7 (pre-theatre set menu), 7–10; Sun 12.30–2.30
🍽 L €19 (limited menu), D €60, Wine €18
🚌 Cross-city buses
🚉 DART Pearse

CHAPTER ONE
18–19 Parnell Square
Tel 01 8732266
www.chapteronerestaurant.com
Chapter One, in the basement of the Dublin Writers Museum, puts a modern twist to consistently excellent classic French cooking, which includes grilled skate with creamed leeks, roast salsify, red wine butter and boulangère potato. For wine lovers, a look at the impressive

stocks of the wine cellar is a must.

🕒 Tue–Fri 12.30–2, 6–11; Sat 6–11
🍽 L €35, D €90, Wine €25
🚌 1, 2, 46
🚆 DART Connolly
📍 To the north of the city hub

HALÓ RESTAURANT
The Morrison Hotel, Lower Ormond Quay
Tel 01 887 2400
www.morrisonhotel.ie
This hotel was designed by the renowned John Rocha and Douglas Wallace. Wood, stone and natural fabrics are combined with vibrant hues to create a relaxing environment that follows through to the dining room. The contemporary menu offers sophisticated, beautifully presented dishes along the lines of ballotine of foie gras with spiced pineapple compote and toasted brioche, and duck breast, sweet potato and celeriac gnocchi with spiced plum and garlic greens. Desserts are equally delicious and there is a good wine list.

🕒 Daily 7pm–9.30pm
🍽 D €50, Wine €22
🚌 7
🚆 DART Tara Street
📍 On the north bank of the River Liffey, opposite Temple Bar

NUDE
21 Suffolk Street
Tel 01 677 4804
An eco-friendly café with a commitment to Fairtrade and recycling based on social concerns about protecting the environment. Their own range of organic products, such as wraps, salads, soup, low-fat desserts, smoothies and juices are free from additives and contain ingredients like ginseng and bee pollen. These healthy options can be taken away or eaten at the pinewood refectory tables set against lime green paintwork and milk crates, lined up waiting for the empties.

🕒 Mon–Fri 8am–9pm, Sat 10–9, Sun until 7pm
🍽 L €9, D €14
🚌 Cross-city buses
🚆 DART Pearse

ROLY'S BISTRO
7 Ballsbridge Terrace
Tel 01 668 2611
www.rolysbistro.ie

This popular and lively bistro provides robust retro cooking, for example the parsnip and apple soup with curry cream or the roast pumpkin risotto with parmesan cheese shavings. Popular dishes such as warm chocolate brownie and vanilla ice cream with nutty chocolate sauce grace the dessert menu. The bistro is renowned for its homemade breads.

🕒 Daily 12–2.45, 6–9.45
🍽 L €25, D €50, Wine €25
🚌 5, 7, 45
🚆 DART Lansdowne Road
📍 A 5- to 10-min drive south of the city on Northumberland Road; close to Herbert Park

STAYING

ARIEL HOUSE
50–54 Lansdowne Road, Ballsbridge, Dublin 4
Tel 01 668 5512
www.ariel-house.net
This gracious Victorian house is in a southeastern suburb, near the rugby ground. Luxurious premier rooms and more contemporary standard rooms are available, and healthy and vegetarian options are on offer at breakfast. Staff are friendly and there are professional aromatherapy and reflexology treatments, plus free secure parking.

🕒 Closed 23–27 Dec
🛏 €99–€190
🛌 37
🚌 7, 45
🚆 DART Lansdowne Road
📍 From Merrion Square, take Northumberland Road to Ballsbridge. Turn left at Jurys Hotel and Ariel House is on left past the traffic lights

CHARLEVILLE LODGE
268–272 North Circular Road, Phibsborough, Dublin 7
Tel 01 838 6633
www.charlevillelodge.ie
In a northern suburb, near Phoenix Park, this elegant Victorian terrace has been beautifully restored. Lounges are welcoming, and a choice of breakfasts is available in the smart dining room. Bedrooms are very comfortable, and there's secure parking.

🕒 Closed 21–26 Dec
🛏 €75–€105
🛌 30 (4 ground floor)
🚌 10
📍 Near to St. Peter's Church

THE CLARENCE
6–8 Wellington Quay, Dublin
Tel 01 407 0800
www.theclarence.ie
The Clarence is at the heart of Dublin City, on the banks of the River Liffey, within walking distance of the shopping areas, museums and galleries. This is a very individual hotel, where contemporary design is tastefully incorporated into the original features of the 1850 building. The unobtrusive professional staff are extremely careful.

🛏 €350–€380 (suites €720–€2,600)
🛌 50
🚌 7, 10, 45
🚆 DART Tara Street
📍 From O'Connell Bridge, go west along quays, and the hotel is 500m (550 yards) beyond the first set of lights (at the Ha'Penny Bridge)

HARDING HOTEL
Cooper Alley, Fishamble Street, Christchurch, Dublin 2
Tel 01 679 6500
www.hardinghotel.ie
Fully renovated during 2007, the Harding offers discreet yet contemporary interiors in the bustling Temple Bar area. The hotel features a bistro and an Irish restaurant with live music, making it a popular meeting place.

🕒 Closed 23–26 Dec
🛏 €89–€120, exluding breakfast (€6.50)
🛌 52
🚌 7, 45
🚆 DART Connolly
📍 Top of Dame Street beside Christ Church Cathedral

MOUNT HERBERT HOTEL
Herbert Road, Sandymount, Dublin 4
Tel 01 668 4321
www.mountherberthotel.ie
Near local places of interest, this hotel has comfortable public rooms, well-equipped bedrooms and a friendly atmosphere. There is a spacious lounge, a TV room, a cocktail bar and a lovely, good-value restaurant overlooking the floodlit gardens. There is also a children's playground.

🛏 Double €133–€200
🛌 168
🚌 10, 45
🚆 DART Lansdowne Road (200m/ 220 yards)
📍 Close to rugby stadium

IRELAND

Belfast

Northern Ireland's biggest, most important and lively city has a fascinating, sometimes grim, history. The capital offers vibrant nightlife and Belfast people have a great taste for black humour.

City Hall (above left). A Shankill Road mural (middle). The Botanic Garden (above right)

IRELAND

RATINGS	
Cultural interest	●●●●●
Good for kids	●●●●
Historic interest	●●●
Photo stops	●●●

BASICS

✚ 4 C2

ℹ Belfast Welcome Centre, 47 Donegall Place, Belfast, BT1 5AD, tel 028 9024 6609; Jun–end Sep Mon–Sat 9–7, Sun 11–4; Oct–end May Mon–Sat 9–5.30, Sun 11–4

🚉 Belfast

www.gotobelfast.com
Full information; good events section.

A festival character in front of the Albert Clock (below)

SEEING BELFAST

The River Lagan flows north through Belfast into Belfast Lough, cutting the city in two; just about everything that a visitor would want to see or do is west of the river. Most of the grand public buildings, such as St. Anne's Cathedral and the Town Hall, are in the middle of the city, while along the river are the Lagan Lookout, Sinclair Seamen's Church, Waterfront Hall and the other riverside attractions. Just to the west are the Falls and Shankill roads with their vivid murals—black taxi-tour territory. About 1.5km (1 mile) to the south of the city lies Belfast's university quarter with Queen's University, the Botanic Gardens, the Ulster Museum and some fine parks.

HIGHLIGHTS

DONEGALL SQUARE

✚ 212 B3

The heart of Belfast is Donegall Square, whose broad pavements and flowerbeds surround the giant City Hall (▷ below). Buildings to admire around Donegall Square include the Italianate sandstone Marks & Spencer, the Scottish Provident Building with its cavorting dolphins and guardian lions, and the Linenhall Library (tel 028 9032 1707, Mon–Fri 9.30–5.30 Sat 9.30–1), a wonderful, hushed, old-fashioned library (with a tea room that's a Belfast institution) whose Political Collection offers an overview of the recent Troubles.

CITY HALL

✚ 212 B3 • Donegall Square, BT1 5GS ☎ 028 9027 0456 ◉ Closed for renovation until mid-2009 💷 Free

The great green dome of the City Hall (opened in 1906) rises 53m (173ft) into the sky and is a prime Belfast landmark. Patterned Italian marble and elaborate stucco greet you in the hall, from where tours of the building ascend beneath the dome to the oak-panelled Council Chamber. This splendid civic apartment contains two tellingly contrasted items. One is the Lord Mayor's handsomely carved throne. The other is an icon for all Orangemen: the plain and simple round wooden table at which the Unionist leader, Sir Edward Carson, signed the Solemn League and Covenant of Resistance against

STORMONT CASTLE

✚ 213 off D3

Seat of the on-off Northern Ireland Assembly, Stormont Castle lies 8km (5 miles) east of the city, and is easily accessible by City bus 16, 17 or 20. The very imposing castle at the end of its mile-long drive is only open to the public by appointment, but there are great walks in the woods and across the open parkland that surround Stormont.

Waterfront Hall (above)

The Crown Liquor Saloon (left)

AN CULTÚRLANN MACADAM O'FIAICH

✚ 212 off A3 • 216 Falls Road, BT12 6AH ☎ 028 9096 4180 ◷ Sun–Wed 9–9, Thu–Sat 9–10

Here exhibitions, music concerts and a bookshop promote the Irish language and culture.

ST. MALACHY'S CHURCH

✚ 212 C4 • Alfred Street, BT2 8EN ☎ 028 9032 1713 ◷ Daily 8–5.45

The church may look unprepossessing from the outside with its dingy red-brick and lurid pink paintwork, but it shouldn't be judged by its cover. Inside you'll find an early Victorian extravaganza of elaborate stucco, fanvaulting that's said to be a tribute to King Henry VII's chapel in Westminster Abbey and a fine altarpiece carved by the Piccioni family (from the Tirol).

ST. GEORGE'S MARKET

✚ 212 C4

This handsome 1896 red-brick and stone building is Belfast's only surviving Victorian market hall. Organic produce, flowers, knick-knacks and a lively fish market, under a restored roof of glass and cast iron, are the focus for shoppers on Tuesdays and Fridays.

Home Rule on 28 September 1912. Over 400,000 Ulster Protestants were to follow him as signatories, some in their own blood.

GRAND OPERA HOUSE

✚ 212 A4 • 2–4 Great Victoria Street, BT2 7BA ☎ 028 9024 1919/3411 ◷ Box office: Mon–Fri 8.30am–9pm, Sat 8.30–6; tours: Wed–Sat 11am 👜 Adult £5, child £3 (including post tour tea and pastry at Lucianos)
www.goh.co.uk

The Grand Opera House is a splendid example of a late Victorian music hall. Ornate outside and all overblown opulence within, it has suffered various vicissitudes down the years, from relegation to a second-class cinema in the 1950s to a brace of IRA bombs in 1991 and 1993, which damaged but failed to destroy it. Yet one look at the giant gilt elephants, the cherubs and swags of golden fruit and flowers tells you of its aspirations when it was opened in 1895. Nowadays restored and refurbished, the Grand Opera House puts on a wide variety of entertainment that includes live music, comedies, dramas, musicals, pantomime, Shakespeare, ballet…and, of course, opera productions.

CROWN LIQUOR SALOON

✚ 212 A4 • 48 Great Victoria Street, BT2 7BA ☎ 028 9027 9901 ◷ Mon–Sat 11.30am–midnight, Sun 12.30–11pm

IRELAND

THE HARBOUR COMMISSIONER'S OFFICE

✚ 212 C1 • Corporation Square, BT1 3AL, off Donegall Quay near Lagan Lookout ☎ 028 9055 4422 ☞ Tours for booked parties only

The city has few grander buildings than this one, built in 1854 to reflect Belfast's Victorian prosperity. The interior has wonderful floors of mosaic and inlaid marble, heavy plaster mouldings and stained-glass

This Victorian 'temple of intemperance' is, as its owners the National Trust proudly claim, 'the most famous pub in Belfast'. The Trust bought the pub in 1978 and spent £400,000 restoring it because they recognized it for what it was: a supreme example of the Golden Age of public house design. From the colonnaded gilt and marble frontage to the interior with its curved bar and embossed ceiling, the Crown Liquor Saloon is gloriously over the top. The inlaid crown on the floor at the entrance was installed in 1895 by the nationalist owner Patrick Flanagan, so that all his customers could tread it underfoot.

PUBS

A good way to sample the best of Belfast pubs is to join the Historical Pub Tour of Belfast (tel 028 9268 3665; www.belfastpubtours.com;

The Crown Liquor Saloon's interior is pure Victoriana

The Harland & Wolff shipyard cranes are a city landmark

A maritime theme pervades the Sinclair Seamen's Church

IRELAND

windows. Upstairs there are maritime paintings, and in the barrel-roofed Barnet Room the stained-glass windows depict the arms of old colonial partners in trade such as Canada, Australia, India and the United States.

ORMEAU BATHS GALLERY

✚ 212 B4 • 18a Ormeau Road, BT2 8HS ☎ 028 9032 1402 ◎ Tue–Sat 10–6

Frequently changing exhibitions of contemporary art from Ireland and elsewhere are displayed on two floors of an imaginatively converted old public bathhouse.

The Barrel Man sculpture on Portside

May–end Oct Thu 7, Sat 4) that starts at Flannigan's (upstairs at the Crown Liquor Saloon, ▷ above). Belfast's most atmospheric pubs include White's (tel 028 9024 3080)—Belfast's oldest pub (so it claims)—in Winecellar Entry, and the Morning Star (tel 028 9023 5986) in Pottinger's Entry, a pub with a superb semi-elliptical bar and a menu that can include emu, kangaroo and crocodile. Guess the nationality of the licensee! Bittles Bar (tel 028 9031 1088) in Victoria Street is a wedge-shaped corner pub with some splendid paintings of Irish literary figures; the Kitchen Bar (tel 028 9032 4901) on Victoria Square offers local real ales and traditional music; Kelly's Cellars (tel 028 9024 6058) in Bank Street is a dark, delightful old place.

SINCLAIR SEAMEN'S CHURCH

✚ 212 C1 • Corporation Square, BT1 3AJ ☎ 028 9071 5997 ◎ Wed 2–5, Sun for services at 11.30 and 7 🎫 Free

This is an L-shaped Presbyterian church of 1857, furnished in a nautical style to attract visiting sailors. The font is a ship's binnacle; the pulpit resembles the prow of a ship; nautical themes feature in the stained-glass windows; the mast of a Guinness barge and ships' riding lights decorate the walls. Services commence with the ringing of HMS *Hood*'s ship's bell. Even the welcome sign by the door conveys its message by semaphore flags. Seafaring worshippers will never be turned away—50 seats are reserved for them.

BOTANIC GARDENS

✚ 212 off B5 • Stranmillis Road, BT7 1LP ☎ 028 9032 4902 ◎ Gardens: daily until dusk; Greenhouse and Tropical Ravine: Mon–Fri 10–12, 1–5, Sat, Sun 2–5 (Oct–end Mar until 4) 🎫 Free

These classic 19th-century gardens beside the river contain two pieces of High Victorian glass-and-cast-iron architecture: the great Glasshouse of 1839–40 with its Cool Wing full of bright plants and its steamy Stove Wing and mighty central dome. There's more steam in the nearby Tropical Ravine, where you stroll around a gallery looking down through the canopy of a minia-ture tropical rain forest. The wide lawns of the

Botanic Gardens provide a place to relax for students from nearby Queen's University.

ULSTER MUSEUM

✚ 212 off B5 • Botanic Gardens, Stranmillis Road, BT9 5AB ☎ 028 9038 3000
🕐 Currently closed for renovation until 2009 🎫 Free
www.ulstermuseum.org.uk

Displays in the Ulster Museum include Stone and Bronze Age implements, jewellery and religious icons of the Dark Ages and medieval Ireland, and machines and mementoes of Ulster's great industrial heritage of shipbuilding, textiles and heavy industry. The history of the Troubles is not neglected. There's also a display of the treasures dredged up from the 1588 wreck of the Spanish warship *Girona*.

Statue of Lord Edward Carson   Botanic Gardens

Stormont Castle

ST. ANNE'S CATHEDRAL

✚ 212 B2 • Donegall Street, BT1 2HB ☎ 028 9032 8332 🕐 Mon–Sat 10–4,
Sun just before services 🎫 Free
www.belfastcathedral.org

Consecrated in 1904, St. Anne's Cathedral is an impressive church built of stone from all 32 counties of Ireland. Highlights include the 'Occupations of Mankind' carvings on the capitals of the nave pillars, the glorious modern stained glass of the east window, and the maple and marble of the nave floor. Don't miss the 1920s mosaics by the Martin sisters, or the prayer book written out by hand on cigarette paper by a World War II captive in a Japanese prisoner-of-war camp.

RIVER LAGAN EXPLORATIONS

✚ 212 C2

Belfast's river frontage has seen a major regeneration programme since the turn of the millennium with new housing, entertainment projects and business parks (see www.laganside.com). More than 30 pieces of community art have been commissioned and installed at locations across the area and the river banks and water quality has been much improved. The Lagan Boat Company (tel 028 9033 0844; www.laganboatcompany.com) runs trips from Donegall Quay: upriver past the fine new developments and out into green countryside; downriver to view the shipyards of Harland & Wolff where *Titanic* was built and where the twin giant yellow cranes called Samson and Goliath are familiar Belfast landmarks. You can walk or bicycle along the Lagan's towpath, which runs south for several miles to Lisburn. Leaflet guides are available from the Belfast Welcome Centre.

BACKGROUND

Belfast is a solid Victorian city built largely on the sea trading, shipbuilding and textile trades, with large public buildings that sit grandly amid fading red-brick terraces and commercial premises. Parts of Belfast are a bit shabby, but down along the River Lagan and around the heart of the city the old place is refurbishing and modernizing itself at a great rate.

IRELAND

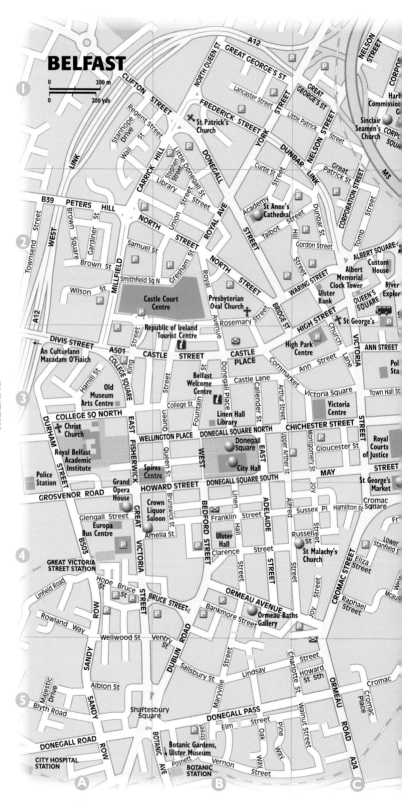

BELFAST

0 ___ 200 m
0 ___ 200 yds

St Patrick's Church
Sinclair Seamen's Church
St Anne's Cathedral
Albert Memorial Clock Tower
Custom House
Ulster Bank
Queen's Square
An Cultúrlann Macadam O'Fiaich
Republic of Ireland Tourist Centre
Castle Court Centre
Presbyterian Oval Church
High Park Centre
St George's
Old Museum Arts Centre
Belfast Welcome Centre
Linen Hall Library
Victoria Centre
Christ Church
Royal Belfast Academic Institute
Police Station
Donegall Square
City Hall
Royal Courts of Justice
Grand Opera House
Crown Liquor Saloon
Europa Bus Centre
Spires Centre
St George's Market
Ulster Hall
St Malachy's Church
Great Victoria Street Station
Ormeau Baths Gallery
Botanic Gardens, Ulster Museum
City Hospital Station
Botanic Station

IRELAND

Clarendon Dock

Abercorn Basin

Lagan

Queen's Quay

Of Man
oon
at Terminal

onegall
uay

Odyssey Arena

SYDENHAM ROAD

QUAY

BRIDGE

BRIDGE

QUEEN'S

MIDDLEPATH STREET

BRIDGE END

Stormont Castle

Laganside Walkway

Belfast Waterfront Hall, Conference & Concert Centre

Laganbank Road

Mays Meadows

Place

Lan-Yon

BRIDGE STREET

Mays Meadows

Street

BELFAST CENTRAL STATION

Stewart Street

Laganside Walkway

Lagan

ORMEAU EMBANKMENT

Ravenhill Reach

Ormeau Park

© Crown Copyright 2008

D

Stormont Castle

Crown Liquor Saloon

Albert Memorial Clock Tower

IRELAND

KEY TO SYMBOLS

- ⊕ Shopping
- ⊕ Entertainment
- ⊗ Nightlife
- ⊗ Sports
- ⊗ Activities
- ♡ Health and Beauty
- ⊗ For Children

WHAT TO DO

⊕ ARCADIA
378 Lisburn Road
Tel 028 9038 1779
Crammed into this tiny
delicatessen is a wonderful
range of good things to eat,
including a great variety of
delicious Irish cheeses.
⊙ Mon–Sat 9–5.30 🚌 Citybus 58

⊕ SMYTH & GIBSON, SHIRTMAKERS
Bedford House, Bedford Street
Tel 028 9023 0388
Smyth & Gibson make the
most beautiful shirts, following
in a tradition of expertise from
when Belfast craftsmen led the
world of shirtmakers. Irish
linen garments are a specialty.
⊙ Mon–Sat 8–5.30

⊕ THE LYRIC THEATRE
55 Ridgeway Street
Tel 028 9038 1081
www.lyrictheatre.co.uk
The Lyric began as a small
company specializing in the
plays of W. B. Yeats but it now
puts on a varied calendar, still
with an emphasis on Irish
plays. The bars overlook the
River Lagan.
⊙ Box office: Mon–Fri 10–7, Sat 4–7.
Performances: 8pm 💷 £10–£20

⊕ ODYSSEY
Queen's Quay
Tel 028 9073 9074
www.odysseyarena.com
Dozens of international eateries, bars, clubs, multiplex
cinemas, ten-pin bowling and
games rooms fill this riverside
complex, Belfast's most
popular nightspot for all ages.
There's a sports arena, which
doubles as the preferred venue
for big music events.
⊙ Box office: Mon–Sat, 10–7
💷 £12–£60

⊗ APARTMENT
2 Donegall Square
Tel 028 9050 9777
www.apartmentbelfast.com
A funky, stylish bar/restaurant
with hip décor, resident and
guest DJs, attracting a sophisticated and stylish crowd. It's
right in the middle of Belfast,
and window tables give great
views over the City Hall.
⊙ Mon–Sat 8am–1am, Sun 12–12
💷 Usually free

EATING

BEATRICE KENNEDY
44 University Road
Tel 028 9020 2290
www.beatricekennedy.co.uk
Chef/owner Jim McCarthy has
created dishes with influences
from around the world. Good-
value express menu served
from 5–7pm.
⊙ Tue–Sat 5pm–10.30pm, Sun
12.30–2.30, 5–8.15; closed Easter
💷 L £24, D £50, Wine £14
🚌 71, 69
🚗 Adjacent to Queen's University on
the main University road, A55

BOURBON
60 Great Victoria Street
Tel 028 9033 2121
www.bourbonrestaurant.com
The quirky interior combines
Victorian Gothic with a feel of
the American Deep South, and
touches of Spanish colonial
architecture. Food influences
come from America, the Far
East and Britain.
⊙ Mon–Fri 12–3, 5–11, Sat 5–11
💷 L from £15, D £25, Wine £14.50
🚗 Opposite Great Victoria Street

RESTAURANT MICHAEL DEANE
34–40 Howard Street
Tel 028 9033 1134
www.michaeldeane.co.uk
Chefs work in full view of the
guests, and meals are brought
out on huge trays. Prepare to
be smitten by the perfection of
dishes that sound quite simple
on the menu: perhaps local
scallops, foie gras and potato
bread or a main course of
pan-fried turbot and velouté
of artichoke.
⊙ Mon–Sat 12–3, 6–10
💷 L £16.50 (limited menu) D £40,
Wine £21.50
🚗 In the middle of the city, just west of
City Hall

SHU
253 Lisburn Road
Tel 028 9038 1655
www.shu-restaurant.com
Shu's minimalist ambience—
warm chocolate brown, reds
and creams, with suede seats
and leather banquettes—provides the perfect background
for the discreet, lazy jazz
soundtrack. The eclectic menu
(foie gras terrine sits alongside
sausages and mashed pota-
toes) takes a loose fusion line,
and fashionable ideas make
their mark, but all is executed
with a light touch.
⊙ Mon–Sat 12.30–2.30, 6–10; closed
12–14 Jul
💷 L £18, D £27.50, Wine £15
🚌 58, 5
🚗 From the middle of the city take
Lisburn road, A1, for 1.5km (1 mile)
southwest

STAYING

EXPRESS BY HOLIDAY INN
106a University Street, Belfast
BT7 1Hp
Tel 028 9031 1909
www.exhi-belfast.com
A modern hotel ideal for
families and business people.
Fresh and uncomplicated, the
spacious bedrooms include
satellite TV, power shower
and tea- and coffee-making
facilities.
💷 £65–£75
🛏 114
🚗 Behind Queen's University in the
south of the city. Turn left at the lights
on Botanic Avenue onto University
Street where the hotel is 500m
(550 yards) farther on left

RAMADA BELFAST
117 Milltown Road, Shaws Bridge,
Belfast BT8 7XP
Tel 028 9092 3500
www.ramadabelfast.com
The bedrooms are stylish and
furnished in bright, eye-
catching designs. The LA
Fitness club is well equipped,
and the Grand Ballroom hosts
top events. The Belfast Bar and
Grill serves innovative Irish cuisine, while the trendy Suburbia
Bar offers a lighter alternative.
💷 £95–£160, excluding breakfast
(£8.50)
🛏 120
🚌 13
🏊 Indoor 🏋
🚗 South from the city, follow Malone
Road to the roundabout (traffic circle)
and signs for Barnett Demesne. Turn
left on Milltown Road; hotel is on left

ARRIVING

BY AIR TO THE REPUBLIC OF IRELAND
The Republic is well served by international airlines, and there are three international airports at Dublin, Shannon (near Limerick) and Cork. There are regional airports on the Aran Islands and in Donegal, Galway, Kerry, Knock, Sligo and Waterford. More than 30 airlines fly into the Republic from more than 55 cities.

The national airline in Ireland is Aer Lingus; Ryanair is a privately owned Irish airline, which is the largest low-cost airline in Europe.

You can fly into Dublin and Shannon airports from North America, but if you are coming from Australasia, you will have to connect in another country (for example, London), as there are no direct flights.

BY AIR TO NORTHERN IRELAND
Northern Ireland is served by Belfast International airport, Belfast City airport and City of Derry airport. Most scheduled flights to these airports are from Britain or the Republic of Ireland and there are no flights to or from the US—you'll need to take a transatlantic flight to the Republic or to London, and then make your way to Northern Ireland.

BY FERRY
Ireland has six main ferry ports with services from Scotland, England, Wales, the Isle of Man and France run by different ferry operators. Sometimes more than one ferry operator runs services on a particular route, so it pays to shop around. You should always check crossing times as there are fast and slow services, so if time is short you may want to sail on a faster, if more expensive, service. You should remember that the Irish Sea can sometimes be quite rough, which occasionally leads to crossings being cancelled. Many ferry operators run a reduced service in January, when ships have their annual refit.

BY LONG-DISTANCE BUS AND FERRY
You can travel by long-distance bus and ferry to Ireland with Eurolines (www.eurolines.com). Inter-city bus services in Britain are operated by National Express (nationalexpress.com) and in Ireland by Bus Éireann (www.buseireann.ie), and you can travel from major UK cities, such as London, Birmingham, Oxford, Glasgow, Edinburgh, Bristol and Cardiff. The ferry routes that are used by these services are Holyhead to Dublin Port, Holyhead to Dun Laoghaire, Fishguard to Rosslare and Stranraer to Belfast.

BY TRAIN AND FERRY
It's possible to purchase one ticket (known as 'Rail and Sail') which includes a train journey to a ferryport in England and a sailing with Stena Line to a port in Ireland. For example, you can take a train from London (which stops en route at Birmingham, Leeds, Manchester, Liverpool and Chester) to Holyhead then sail to Dún Laoghaire on the Stena HSS. Alternatively, there's a service from London to the Welsh port of Fishguard (via Bristol, Cardiff and Swansea), from where you sail on the Stena *Europe* to Rosslare. For train information call National Rail Enquiries in England on 08457 484950 or see their website, www.nationalrail.co.uk

To make a reservation call 08457 484950 and state that you are travelling by train.

BY CAR
Bringing your own car to Ireland from Europe is straightforward thanks to the car ferry services to Ireland from Britain and France. Contact your insurer at least a month before you travel to check that your car is covered in the Republic and/or Northern Ireland, or to arrange insurance if it is not. In addition to your passport, you'll need to bring a valid driving licence, International Driving Permit (where necessary) and your motor insurance and vehicle registration documents.

Car Rental
You'll find the larger well-known car rental companies as well as smaller rental firms at airports, ferry ports and in towns. It is always best to reserve a car in advance. The Car Rental Council of Ireland's website www.carrentalcouncil.ie has information, although you can't actually reserve a car on this site. You must have a valid driver's licence, held for more than a year. An international licence is not acceptable.

VISITORS WITH A DISABILITY
Ireland's facilities for visitors with disabilities are improving, and any new buildings and public transport must have disabled access. With some advance planning most forms of transport are accessible, although older city buses are not accessible to wheelchair users.

Useful Organizations:
Northern Ireland
Disability Action, Portside Business Park, 189 Airport Road West, Belfast, BT3 9ED. Tel 028 9029 7880; textphone 028 9029 7882; www.disabilityaction.org

Republic of Ireland
National Disability Authority, 25 Clyde Road, Ballsbridge, Dublin 4. Tel 01 608 0400; www.nda.ie

IRELAND

GETTING AROUND

BY ROAD

If you want to travel around the countryside, stopping in little villages, realistically you're going to need a car, as smaller places are not served by public transport. In both Northern Ireland and the Republic you drive on the left and speed limits are observed and enforced. The main factor to consider, particularly when driving in the Republic, is time. On the map, distances may seem short, but a combination of country roads, less than comprehensive signage and some poorly maintained road surfaces can lead to journeys taking longer than you might anticipate. You can prepare for this by buying a detailed road map, allowing plenty of time to get to your destination and accepting the often slow speeds on Irish roads. Avoid taking a car into Dublin, particularly during the rush hour.

When several people are travelling together they may well find that taking a taxi is a sensible option for some shorter journeys. Taxis in Dublin, Belfast, Cork, Limerick and Galway have a meter. In other parts of the country you need to agree the fare with the driver in advance.

BY TRAIN

Getting around Ireland by train may not be as economical as using the bus, but it is fast— the maximum time for a long-distance journey will be less than 4 hours. There has been massive investment in improvements to major stations and in the railway network as a whole, although the network still does not cover the whole country. For example, there is no railway line that covers the west coast from north to south and no service at all in Donegal or the far southwest of the country. Getting from Dublin to Belfast is quick (2 hours) and easy, though, thanks to the excellent Enterprise service.

BY BUS

Most of Ireland is covered by some sort of bus service, although the services can be somewhat haphazard, and on long journeys you will probably have to change buses at least once. However, buses are still the least expensive way of getting around and if time is not pressing, they are a good way to see the countryside. If it's your intention to travel around the island by public transport, consider investing in a special pass, such as the Irish Rover, which gives you unlimited travel on buses in the Republic and Northern Ireland, or the Emerald Card, which covers unlimited travel both on long-distance buses and on trains.

GETTING AROUND IN DUBLIN

BY BUS

Buses in Dublin and its suburbs are operated by Bús Átha Cliath (Dublin Bus; www.dublinbus.ie). Fares for adults within the city are between €1 and €1.90 (€0.70–€0.90 for children). If you plan to use the bus at least twice a day, a Rambler ticket covers unlimited city travel for varying periods: 1 day €6, 3 days €11, 5 days €17.30, 7 days €21. A family day ticket costs €8.50. Buy them from any newsagent displaying the sign *Dublin Bus Tickets*, from the Upper O'Connell Street office or online from www.dublinbus.ie or www.ticketmaster.ie

If you don't buy a prepaid ticket, you must pay the exact fare in coins (no notes) on the bus.

CITY BUS TOURS

The Dublin City Tour is an open-top bus tour that takes in all the main attractions, with a lively commentary from the driver. The buses, operated by Dublin Bus, are beige and dark green. Tickets are valid for 24 hours from when they are stamped in the machine on board, and you can get on and off as many times as you wish during that period. Tickets are €14 for adults and €6 for children under 14.

DART

The DART (Dublin Area Rapid Transit) is a light railway system which runs along the coast, from Howth, northeast of Dublin, to Arklow to the south. You are most likely to use the DART if your hotel is outside the city, if you arrive on foot at Dún Laoghaire port, or for day trips to one of the attractions en route. You can catch the bright green DART trains from Connolly, Tara Street or Pearse stations in the city; get tickets from the ticket desk or a vending machine which accepts cash, credit cards (Eurocard/MasterCard or Visa) and debit cards (Solo). You need to validate your ticket by stamping it in the machine before you get to the platform on outward and return journeys. The DART can get crowded during rush hour.

LUAS

Opened in 2004, the Luas (www.luas.ie) operates sleek modern trams on two city-to-suburbia routes. The Red Line runs from Dublin Connolly station (where it links to the DART) west to Heuston, then to Tallaght. The Green Line links St. Stephen's Green with Sandyford. There are ticket machines, taking coins, notes and credit cards, at Luas stops, or you can buy from ticket agents, Luas or Dublin Bus (for combined Luas–bus tickets only).

BY BICYCLE

Dublin is a relatively flat and compact city and many Dubliners cycle to work. The only place you can rent bicycles is outside the middle of the city—take bus number 46a to Belfield Bike Shop, University College, Dublin 4 (tel 01 260 0749; www.cyclingsafaris.com).

BY TAXI

City taxis are metered and there are stands outside train and bus stations and at various points in the city. To call a taxi, try one of the companies listed below.

TAXIS	
COMPANY	**TELEPHONE**
Radio Cabs	01 708 9292
City Cabs	01 872 7272
Budget Cabs	01 459 9333
Pony Cabs	01 661 0101

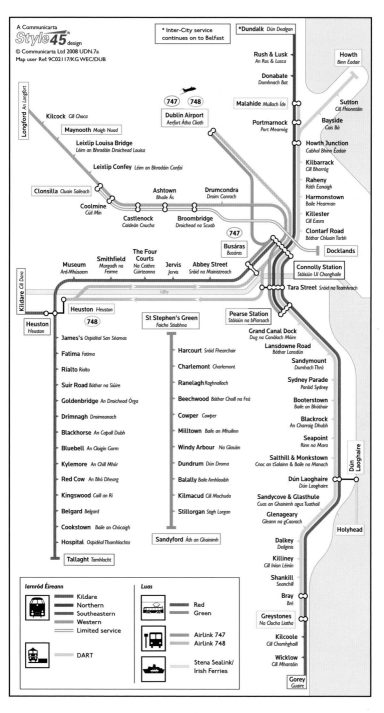

ITALY

UNDERSTANDING ITALY

From well-kept beaches and dramatic mountain scenery to historic cities with a wealth of art and architecture, and small, picturesque villages, Italy offers something for all visitors. Since Turin hosted the Winter Olympics in 2006, this northern city has been the focal point of winter sports in Italy, and the growth of European budget airline routes has opened up other regions of the country not previously thought of as main holiday destinations. Just as Rome wasn't built in a day, so Italy cannot be explored in a single visit. The country is truly a year-round holiday destination, with a vibrant arts and music scene, world-class sporting events, colourful festivals, unforgettable food and some of the best shopping in Europe.

The 14th-century Castello degli Challand, on a lofty outcrop in the Alpine foothills near the Valle d'Aosta town of Verres (left). A view over the resort of Limone Sul Garda on Lake Garda (right)

LANDSCAPE

Italy is a mountainous Mediterranean country extending south from the Alps, with two major offshore islands, Sicily and Sardinia, and several groups of smaller islands. It covers an area of about 300,000sq km (116,000sq miles) and has a coastline running for 7,600km (4,723 miles). It is over 1,500km (930 miles) long, a contrast to the width, which you can drive across in 3–4 hours.

The chain of the Apennine Mountains runs down the country from Genoa in the north to Reggio di Calabria in the south, covered in huge tracts of forest. North of Genoa lie the flat plains of the Po Valley, immensely fertile and intensively farmed. These mist-laden plains are backed by the Alps, stretching eastward from the border at Ventimiglia through to Slovenia, with the most scenic ranges, the Ortles and Dolomites, in the east. The stereotypical classic rolling hill landscape dotted with vines and lined with cypress trees is confined to central Italy, seen at its best in Tuscany and Umbria.

ECONOMY

Italy is a modern industrialized nation. Business and commerce revolve around Milan in the north, but the deep south remains one of Europe's most economically depressed areas.

Apart from natural gas, the country has few natural resources, with no substantial deposits of oil, iron or coal. Much of the land is unsuited to agriculture and Italy is a net food importer. Its economic strength lies in the processing and manufacturing of goods, primarily in family-owned firms. The major industries are car and precision machinery manufacture, textiles, clothing and footwear, ceramic and chemical production and food processing. Sixty-two per cent of the population is employed in tourism and the service industries. Major trading partners include the US and countries within the European Union, with car and fashion industries exporting worldwide.

POLITICS

The Republic of Italy was created in 1948; since then there have been well over 50 governments. The head of state is the president, chosen by an electoral college drawn from the houses of parliament and regional representatives. Decision-making lies with the lower house, the Chamber of Deputies, which is directly elected. The upper house, the Senate, is made up of six representatives from each region, plus a number of senators-for-life. The complicated proportional representation electoral system has been responsible for a series of coalition governments, many of which have been suspected of corruption at the highest level. The *Mani Pulite* (Clean Hands) investigation in the 1990s extinguished the *tangentopoli* (bribetown) climate, leading to the downfall of some of the old-established parties. Scandals continue, but there is a genuine feeling that Italy is moving forward.

ITALY

ITALY'S REGIONS

THE NORTHWEST

Lombardy is heavily industrialized, but it also has beautiful valleys and Alpine foothills and some splendid historic towns. To the north lie the lakes—Orta, Iseo, Garda and Como.

Piedmont, at the foot of the Alps, borders France and is renowned for its winter skiing and summer walking. This region is known for its stuffed pastas, red wine and the world-famous white truffles.

Liguria is Italy's Riviera, a tiny region between the Alps and the sea.

VENICE, THE NORTHEAST AND EMILIA-ROMAGNA

The Veneto is a rich and developed region spreading from the flatlands and lagoon northward into the Dolomites. Its cities include Vicenza and Verona, but **Venice** is the main draw.

Friuli-Venezia-Giulia has mountain ranges in the north, spiritual retreats in the east and Adriatic lagoon land to the south. Trieste is the regional capital.

Trentino-Alto-Adige is a German-Italian region in the far northeast, created in 1919. The Alto-Adige is German, while Trentino is distinctly Italian, a contrast of cultures evident in the region's main towns.

Emilia-Romagna is famous for its artistic towns and for its cuisine. Prosperous Bologna is the capital.

The village of Baschi in Umbria (left). The vineyards of the Chianti district (right)

FLORENCE, TUSCANY AND UMBRIA

Tuscany has an abundance of picturesque towns, attracting huge numbers of visitors each year, but leave time for the rural pleasures. **Florence** is renowned as the cradle of the Renaissance.

Umbria, whose capital is Perugia, is Italy's only landlocked region. Orvieto, with its famous cathedral, far in the west, is the other main town, while to the east lies Spoleto, a quiet, historic town that comes alive during its summer arts festival.

ROME, LAZIO AND THE MARCHE

Lazio is a quiet and low-key region with a gentle landscape. **Rome**, Italy's compelling capital, has a staggering wealth of monuments, museums, galleries and architecture spanning almost 3,000 years.

The Marche is an unspoiled region with historic towns, long stretches of coastline and a green, hilly interior. The main attraction is Urbino, a classic Renaissance ducal town.

THE SOUTH

Campania has a vibrant capital—Naples—a coastline dotted with picturesque villages, the jewel-like islands of Ischia and Capri, and a wealth of archaeological sites: Pompei, Herculaneum and Paestum.

Molise is remote and undiscovered; nearby, the **Abruzzo** is better known, chiefly for its superb Parco Nazionale d'Abruzzo, Italy's third-largest park.

Basilicata has superb mountain scenery, seen at its best in the Parco Nazionale del Pollino. Enjoy the coastline on both the Mar Tirenno and Golfo di Taranto.

Calabria, Italy's toe, is an undeveloped region with a long coastline and mountains inland. The Sila range, with its rolling plateaux and dense woodlands, shouldn't be overlooked.

Puglia, the heel of Italy, is more prosperous than other regions in the south. Highlights include the port of Bari and exuberant Lecce, one of Italy's finest baroque towns.

SICILY AND SARDINIA

Sicily, to the southwest of the toe of Italy, has enough to keep you busy for weeks. Palermo is the capital, its vitality rivalled only by grimy Catania and the ancient Greek settlement of Siracusa.

Sardinia, 200km (124 miles) to the west of the mainland, is renowned for its idyllic coastline, clear waters, classy resorts and wild interior. Walled Cagliari is the capital.

ITALY

THE BEST OF ITALY

THE NORTHWEST

The Parco Nazionale del Gran Paradiso Some excellent walking in majestic mountain scenery.

Milan (▷ 242–247) Explore the art and architecture and indulge in some of the world's best retail therapy.

When it comes to shopping for the latest styles, there's plenty of choice in Milan (left)

VENICE

The Canal Grande (▷ 280–281) Take the *vaporetto* No. 1 down this famous waterway.

The Basilica di San Marco (▷ 278–279) Appreciate this mind-blowing overview of Venetian art and history.

Burano (▷ 275), **Murano and Torcello** Spend a day exploring the lagoon islands.

THE NORTHEAST AND EMILIA-ROMAGNA

Assisi in Umbria (above)

Bologna (▷ 223–224) Spend time strolling through the arcaded streets—don't miss the Strada Maggiore.

Parma Shop for *prosciutto di Parma* (Parma ham) and Parmigiano Reggiano (Parmesan cheese).

Verona (▷ 290–294) Admire the Roman Arena before exploring the area around the Piazza delle Erbe.

A vaporetto on the Canal Grande in Venice (below)

FLORENCE

The Duomo, Campanile and Battistero (▷ 228–231) View this harmonious trio of Renaissance church buildings.

The Galleria degli Uffizi (▷ 232–233) Trace the development of Italian painting and admire the treasures.

The Galleria Palatina, Palazzo Pitti (▷ 235–236) Admire the superb Renaissance pictures and then relax in the Giardino di Boboli.

TUSCANY AND UMBRIA

Murano glassware by Stefano Toso (left)

Assisi Follow the pilgrim trail to this lovely Umbrian town that is famously the birthplace of St. Francis.

Siena Wander around this perfect medieval city.

ROME

The Basilica di San Pietro (▷ 258–259) Marvel at the overwhelming opulence of this Roman Catholic landmark.

The Musei Vaticani (▷ 265–267) Don't miss one of the world's greatest museums, home to Michelangelo's Sistine Chapel.

The Colosseo (▷ 260–261) See this ancient arena lit up at night.

The Galleria Borghese (▷ 264) Spend a morning or afternoon viewing this wonderful art collection, in verdant surroundings.

The Roman Amphitheatre in Verona (below)

LAZIO AND THE MARCHE

Tivoli Take time out surrounded by the shade and rushing water of the Villa d'Este gardens.

Ascoli Piceno Drive down the Tronto Valley to this relatively undiscovered jewel with its beguiling piazza.

Parmigiano Reggiano (right)

THE SOUTH

Naples (▷ 248–251) Explore the treasures and streets of this vibrant city, where life is theatrical and emotions run high.

Pompei Step back in time into a Roman town preserved by the eruption of Vesuvius in AD79.

ITALY

The illuminated Fontana del Nettuno in Piazza Maggiore

BOLOGNA

Capital of Emilia-Romagna, known for its beauty, wealth and fine cuisine, as well as for its left-wing politics. An ancient settlement full of history.

Bologna is endowed with beautiful streetscapes—arcades of mellow brick and stone, juxtaposed with the stark shapes characteristic of the high-tech industry that generates the money that sustains the expensive restaurants and elegant shops. Bologna is a classic Roman city that, after the Dark Ages, became a free *comune* and subsequently, in the 15th century, gave way to rule by an individual family, the Bentivoglio, until annexed by the Papal States. Its university is one of Europe's oldest and is of great importance.

THE MEDIEVAL CORE
The compact historic core is medieval in plan, scattered with churches, monuments, civic buildings and museums. Elegant porticoed streets radiate from two main squares, Piazza Maggiore and Piazza del Nettuno, with most of interest to visitors on the eastern side of the city. Around Piazza del Nettuno, named after Giambologna's Fontana del Nettuno, rise medieval civic palaces. Behind it, Piazza Maggiore is dominated by the late Gothic church of San Petronio, the Palazzo dei Notai, home to 14th-century lawyers, and the Museo Civico Archeologico (Tue–Fri 9–3, Sat–Sun 10–6.30). Farther east are some of the loveliest streets and buildings—a series of porticoes punctuated by attractive squares. Head for Via Clavatura, with its tempting food stands, before exploring the Archiginnasio complex, the oldest part of the university. More arcades lead south to the church of San Domenico, built in 1251 to house the relics of the saint, enclosed in the superb Arca di San Domenico, sculpted by Pisano and the young Michelangelo. Only two of the dozens of towers from the Middle Ages survive; climb Torre degli Asinelli (Apr–end Oct daily 9–6; Nov–end Mar daily 9–5) for great views. From here the university quarter is within striking distance.

THE UNIVERSITY
Via Zamboni leads to the heart of the university, in the medieval palaces. Palazzo Poggi has two quirky museums (Mon–Thu 9–12, 2–4.30, Fri 9–12.30; tel 051 209 1533): an idiosyncratic assemblage of anatomical waxworks, and the Specola, an observatory.

ITALY

WHAT TO DO

⊞ TAMBURINI
Via Caprarie 1
Tel 051 234726
www.tamburini.com
This is the finest delicatessen in what is considered the gastronomic capital of Italy. The large display of local produce includes fresh pasta (such as black pasta coloured with squid ink and tortelloni stuffed with pumpkin), cheeses, hams and salamis. Make sure you sample the gourmet ingredients at the self-service café (open 12–2.30).
🕐 Mon–Wed, Fri–Sat 8–7, Thu 8–2

🎭 NOSADELLA
Via Nosadella 19/21
Tel 328 329 2 666
www.nosadella.it
About 10 minutes' walk southwest of the city's hub, this two-screen cinema shows films in English on Mondays and in other languages on other days.
🕐 Four screenings daily, 4pm–midnight 🎫 Adult €5, child €4

🎭 TEATRO COMUNALE
Largo Respighi 1
Tel 051 617 4299
www.tcbo.it
Wagner preferred to premiere his operas here in Bologna's leading venue, an auditorium in the heart of the university district that first opened its doors in 1763.
🕐 Sep–end Jun 🎫 €28–€135

☻ CANTINA BENTIVOGLIO
Via Mascarella 4b
Tel 051 265416
www.cantinabentivoglio.it
This is a large, elegant bar in the university district. One of the top jazz venues in town, it has music every night from 10 and good food. There is music outdoors in July and August.
🕐 Daily 8pm–2am 🎫 €4–€10

EATING

BROCCAINDOSSO
Via Broccaindosso 7/a
Tel 051 234153
At this rustic establishment, with rough tables and long wooden benches, they only serve one course and desserts, and there is no menu; although you can order pasta, it's better to wait and see what the staff bring you. Reservations are essential. Credit cards are not accepted.
🕐 Mon–Sat 8.30pm–2am; sometimes closed Aug
🍽 D €33, Wine €10
🚌 14, 27

C'ENTRO
Via dell'Indipendenza 45
Tel 051 234216
This modern, clean restaurant has an excellent range of local dishes and salads—all at very reasonable prices. C'entro is a safe haven for vegetarians, who can pile up as many of the raw ingredients as they like on their plates.
🕐 Mon–Sat 11.45–3, 6.30–9.30pm
🍽 L €11, D €17, Wine €7
🚌 20, 27

CESARI
Via de' Carbonesi 8
Tel 051 237710
This stately establishment, five minutes' walk south of the main square, has long been a star in Bologna's gastronomic sky. Specialties include homemade ravioli stuffed with rabbit and white truffle with celery and Parmesan. The wine list is extensive and good and includes wines produced by the owner. Reservations are essential.
🕐 Mon–Sat 12.30–3, 7.30–11pm; closed Sat in Jul and Aug
🍽 L €33, D €40, Wine €12
🚌
🚌 20, 29, 38, 39, 52

FANTONI
Via del Pratello 11
Tel 051 236358
This small, lively trattoria serves simple local dishes with home-made pasta and wines and fresh fish from Thursday to Saturday. The small menu changes daily. You can sit out on the terrace in summer. Be prepared to wait at the door if you haven't made a reservaton.

Credit cards are not accepted.
🕐 Tue–Sat 12–2.30, 8–10
🍽 L €15, D €25, Wine €11

VICTORIA STATION
Via Zanardi 76
Tel 051 6346062
www.victoriastation.it
Easily recognized by the red London bus standing outside, this is a lively party place where British style meets old-fashioned Bolognese hospitality. There is a large garden area and seating for 500 guests. It is a popular hangout for trendy young Bolognesi and celebrity visitors to the city. The daily menu is viewable on the website.
🕐 Daily 7.30pm–2.30am
🍽 D €30 Wine €12

STAYING

ALBERGO CENTRALE
Via della Zecca 2, 40121 Bologna
Tel 051 225114
www.albergocentralebologna.it
Centrale is a small central third-floor hotel with elevator. It is the best-value and most pleasant of the city's cheaper hotels. The hotel is simply furnished, but there is a television in all the rooms.
🍽 €90–€120, excluding breakfast
🛏 25 ✱

GRAND HOTEL BAGLIONI
Via Indipendenza 8, 40121 Bologna
Tel 051 225445
www.baglionihotels.com
Housed in the Palazzo Ghisilardi Fava, rooms here are luxuriously furnished and superbly equipped, with 24-hour room service, adjustable heating and air conditioning, satellite television, minibar and safe. The hotel has a restaurant, parking and computer access.
🍽 €325–€420
🛏 124 ✱

OROLOGIO
Via IV Novembre 10, 40123 Bologna
Tel 051 231253
www.ghrhotels.com
The elegant rooms are well equipped, and service is excellent. Pets are welcome. Bicycles are available and there is also garage parking. Reservations are essential.
🍽 €220–€320
🛏 34 ✱

ITALY

Florence

✚ 5 D4 🏛 Piazza Stazione 4 (opposite the railway station), 50123 Firenze, tel 055 212 245; Mon—Sat 8.30—7, Sun, public holidays 8.30—2. Borgo Santa Croce 29, 50122 Firenze, tel 055 234 4044; Mon—Sat 9—5, Sun, public holidays 9—2 www.firenzeturismo.it • Helpful English-language site

HOW TO GET THERE

✈ Airports
Amerigo Vespucci (Peretola)
10km (6 miles) northwest of the city
Galileo Galilei, Pisa
80km (50 miles) west of the city (most international flights)

🚆 Railway stations
Stazione Centrale di Santa Maria Novella
The main station, centrally located, is adjacent to the city's public transit terminal.
www.trenitalia.com

The Duomo is an icon of the city

TIPS

● Be at the door when the most popular attractions open, before lines begin to form. For example, you can walk right into the Galleria dell'Accademia at 8.15am.
● To avoid coach tours at major sights, arrive just after 12, when they schedule lunch.
● Have your hotel or restaurant phone a taxi for you; it is almost impossible to find one at a stand and they will not respond to telephone calls from individuals.

SEEING FLORENCE

The historic heart, *centro storico*, of Florence is compact and walkable. In fact, walking is often the only way to navigate the narrow pedestrian streets between its major landmarks. While a few are a bit farther—hop on a bus for the views from Piazale Michelangelo, and to visit San Miniato beyond it—most major sights are within a 0.5km (500-yard) radius of Piazza della Signoria. San Marco, the Accademia and Santa Maria Novella lie just outside this circle. Although these sights are close, do not underestimate the time it will take to see them. Most are multi-faceted, with many attractions within. And the lines for the most popular ones can add up to long hours of waiting unless you reserve ahead (locking you into a schedule) or arrive very early. Florence has become Italy's—perhaps Europe's—most popular destination for students and the very young, despite the fact that it offers few after-dark youth venues, lacking the lively club and music scene of Milan or Turin. These milling throngs of the under-20 set can fill and block an entire street or piazza; in the summer, simply picking a pathway up the few steps of the Duomo can be daunting.

BACKGROUND

Florence was a magnet for the brightest and best of Italy's artists, and it is the birthplace of the Italian Renaissance. Brunelleschi's brilliantly conceived dome changed the way domes were built ever after; Michelangelo coaxed hitherto unimagined power from marble; Ghiberti's baptistery doors opened a whole world of perspective in relief metalwork; and da Vinci painted the *Mona Lisa* here. Donatello, Giotto, Fra Angelica, Pisano, della Robbia and fellow artists created masterpiece after masterpiece in Florence.

The family that encouraged—and financed much of—this artistic flowering was the Medici clan, who began their rise in the 12th century. By the 13th, their acuity in banking and commerce had made them both rich and powerful, so by the 14th they were able to lead a revolt that made them virtual dictators, setting the stage for Cosimo il Vecchio to rule. Popular and known for his largesse on the city's behalf, he set the standard that later generations would uphold, and Florence became Europe's cultural capital. Under grandson Lorenzo, the city reached even greater artistic heights, and by 1569, Cosimo I was the ruler of all Tuscany, with Florence as his capital. The Medici ruled Florence until the 1700s, although the city's prominence, both political and economical, had dwindled by then. Today, the city seems like one grand museum of that artistic legacy.

DON'T MISS

BRUNELLESCHI'S DOME
Even if you don't climb to the top, stand beneath its lantern and look up (▷ 228)
MUSEO DELL'OPERA DEL DUOMO
Michelangelo's most moving *pietà* and the original baptistery doors (▷ 230)
PIAZZALE MICHELANGELO
The classic view of the city
GALLERIA DEGLI UFFIZI
Just the Florentine Renaissance artists can take all day (▷ 232–233)
GIARDINO DI BOBOLI
A peaceful respite, where the Medici played

ITALY

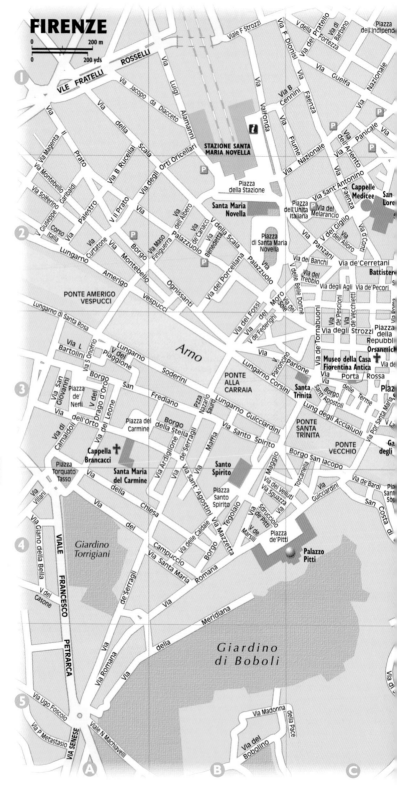

FIRENZE

0   200 m

0   200 yds

Grid references (top to bottom, left edge): 1, 2, 3, 4, 5

Grid references (bottom): A, B, C

VLE FRATELLI ROSSELLI

Via Jacopo da Diacceto

Via Luigi Alamanni

Viale F Strozzi

Via F Dionisi

Via della Fortezza

Via di Barbano

Piazza dell'Indipend

Via della Pratello

Via Magenta

Via II Prato

Via della Scala

Valfonda

Via B Cennini

Via Faenza

Via Guelfa

Via Nazionale

i

STAZIONE SANTA MARIA NOVELLA

Via Montebello

Via degli Orti Oricellari

Via B Rucellai

Via Fiume

Via Nazionale

Via Panicale

Via dell'Ariento

Via Solferino

Via Giuseppe Garibaldi

Piazza della Stazione

Santa Maria Novella

Piazza dell'Unità Italiana

Via Sant'Antonino

Via del Melarancio

Cappelle Medicee

San Lore

Corso Italia

Palestro

Curtatone

Via Montebello

Borgo

Via Maso Finiguerra

Palazzuolo

Via dell'Albero

Via de Canacci

Via della Scala

Via Benedetta

Via del Moro

Piazza di Santa Maria Novella

Via dei Panzani

Via de' Giglio

Via de' Conti

Via d'Alloro

Lungarno Amerigo Vespucci

PONTE AMERIGO VESPUCCI

Lungarno di Santa Rosa

Ognissanti

Vespucci

Via del Porcellana

Palazzuolo

Via del Sole

Via delle Belle Donne

Via dei Banchi

Via del Trebbio

Via de'Cerretani

Battister

Via degli Agli

Via de'Pecori

Arno

Via L Bartolini

Via S Onofrio

Lungarno del Piaggione

Via del Piaggione

soderini

Via dei Fossi

V de' Federighi

Via de Tornabuoni

Via de'Pescioni

Via degli Strozzi

Via de'Vecchietti

Piazza della Repubbli

Orsanmich

PONTE ALLA CARRAIA

Lungarno Corsini

Via Parione

Via Porta Rossa

Museo della Casa Fiorentina Antica

Piaz

San Giovanni

Piazza de' Nerli

Borgo San Frediano

V del Drago d'Oro

V del Leone

Pizza Nazario Sauro

Lungarno Guicciardini

Santa Trinita

Borgo Santi Apostoli

PONTE SANTA TRINITA

Via delle Terme

V La

Via di Camaldoli

Via dell'Orto

Piazza del Carmine

Borgo della Stella

Via de'Serragli

Via santo Spirito

Maggio

Borgo San Jacopo

PONTE VECCHIO

Via de Bardi

Ga degli

Cappella Brancacci

Santa Maria del Carmine

Via della Chiesa

Via Sant'Agostini

Via Ardiglione

Via Mattia

Santo Spirito

Via dei Velluti

Via Squazza

Via Maggio

Via Toscanella

Via Guicciardini

San Costa di

Pia Sant So

Piazza Torquato Tasso

Via Villani

Via delle Caldaie

Piazza Santo Spirito

Via Tegolaio

Via de' Masili

Piazza de'Pitti

Via de' Pitti

Via dello Sprone

VIALE FRANCESCO PETRARCA

Via Ciano della Bella

V del Casone

Giardino Torrigiani

Via Santa Maria

Campuccio

Via de Serragli

Borgo

Via Mazzetta

Via Romana

Palazzo Pitti

Meridiana

Via Ugo Foscolo

Via P Metastasio

VIA SENESE

Viale N Machiavelli

Giardino di Boboli

Via Madonna della Pace

Via del Bobolino

Via di

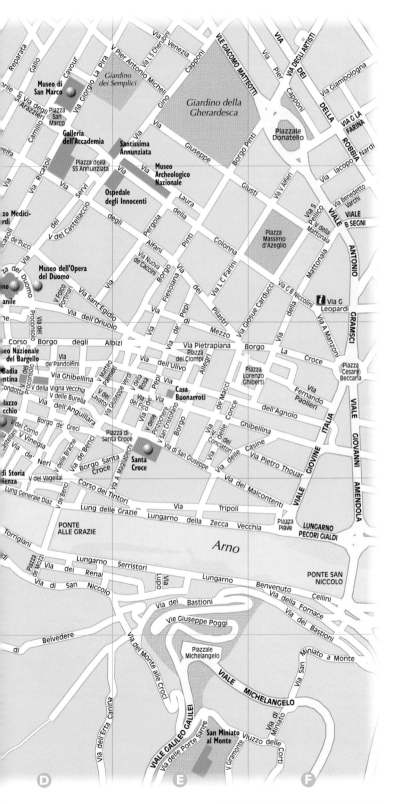

Reparata
Gallo
Cavour
V Giorgio La Pira
V Pier Antonio Micheli
Via L S Cherubini
Via Capponi
VLE GIACOMO MATTEOTTI
VIA
VIA DEGLI ARTISTI
Via Giambologna

Museo di San Marco
Via degli Arazzieri
Piazza San Marco
Giardino dei Semplici
Gino
Via Capponi
Via Pier
Via DEI
VIA DELLA
VIA G LA FARINA
Nardi
ROBBIA

Galleria dell'Accademia
Camillo
Santissima Annunziata
Giuseppe
Borgo Pinti
Piazzale Donatello
Via Iacopo

Via Ricasoli
Piazza della SS Annunziata
Museo Archeologico Nazionale
Via
Giusti
Via A Alfieri
Via S P V della Mattonaia
Via Benedetto Varchi
VIALE B SEGNI

Via Servi
Ospedale degli Innocenti
degli
Laura
Colonna
Via S Pellico
Via C B Niccolini
VIALE

zo Medici-rdi
Casoli de Pucci
del Castellaccio
Alfani
Pinti
Piazza Massimo d'Azeglio
ANTONIO

za de' Duomo
Museo dell'Opera del Duomo
V del Castellaccio
Pergola
della
Via Nuova de' Caccini
Borgo
Via C Fariri
Mattonaia
Via G B Niccolini
Via G Leopardi
GRAMSCI

anile
V Folco Portinari
Via Sant'Egidio
Via dell'Oriuolo
Via de'
Fiesolana
Pilastri
della
Via A Manzoni

seo Nazionale del Bargello
Via del Proconsolo
Corso Borgo degli Albizi
Via Pietrapiana
Mezzo
Borgo La Croce
Piazza Cesare Beccaria

Badia entina
Via de'Pandolfini
Piazza dei Ciompi
Via dell'Ulivo
Piazza Lorenzo Ghiberti
Fernando Paolieri
VIALE

lazzo cchio
Via Ghibellina
Via Matteo Palmieri
Via Giuseppe Verdi
Allegri
Via
Via dell'Agnolo
ITALIA

V della Vigna Vecchia
V delle Burella
V del Lavatoi
Via della Rosa
Via de' Pepi
Casa Buonarroti
Via de' Macci
Ghibellina
GIOVINE

Via dell'Anguillara
V del Corno
V Vinegia
V del Fico
V delle Pinzochere
Borgo
Via di San Cristofano
Via delle Conce
Via delle Casine
Via Pietro Thouar
AMENDOLA

di Storia ienza
Borgo de' Greci
V dei Neri
V delle Brache
Piazza di Santa Croce
Santa Croce
Via di San Giuseppe
Via dei Conciatori
VIALE

Lung Generale Diaz
V dei Vagellai
Borgo Santa Croce
Via A Magliabechi
Via dei Malcontenti
GIOVANNI

Torrigiani
Corso dei Tintori
Lung delle Grazie
Lungarno della Zecca Vecchia
Piazza Piave
LUNGARNO PECORI GIALDI

PONTE ALLE GRAZIE
Lung delle Grazie
Tripoli

Piazza de' Mozzi
Via dei Renai
Serristori
Arno
Lungarno
Benvenuto Cellini
PONTE SAN NICCOLO

Via di San Niccolo
Via Lupo
Lungarno
Via della Fornace

Via del Bastioni
Vle Giuseppe Poggi
Via dei Bastioni

Belvedere
di
Via del Monte alle Croci
Piazzale Michelangelo
San Miniato a Monte
Via San
Via di Miniato

Via dell'Erta Canina
VIALE MICHELANGELO

VIALE GALILEO GALILEI
Via delle Porte sante
San Miniato al Monte
V Giramonte
Viuzzo delle Corti

D   E   F

ITALY

Duomo and Museo dell' Opera del Duomo

One of the most important early-Renaissance architectural complexes in Italy. The first free-standing dome to be constructed in the post-Roman period.

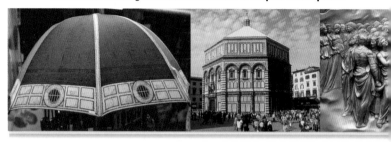

RATINGS

Historic interest	●●●●●
Cultural interest	●●●●●
Value for money	●●●●●

TIP

● Skimpy shorts and sleeveless tops are frowned upon.

Detail of Michelangelo's Pietà *in the Museo dell'Opera del Duomo (top)*

A souvenir umbrella in the style of the Duomo (above left)

The octagonal Battistero di San Giovanni decorated with marble geometric motifs (above middle)

Detail of one of the bronze panels of the Door of Paradise of the Battistero di San Giovanni (above right)

View over the Duomo (right)

SEEING THE DUOMO, BATTISTERO AND CAMPANILE

The sublime, if somewhat grimy, complex of the Duomo, Campanile and Battistero lies a few blocks north of the Piazza della Signoria and the River Arno and less than 20 minutes' walk east from the railway station. The three buildings stand in their own piazza, a clear space that is constantly busy with visitors. The best way to tackle the Duomo is to start early in the day to beat the tour groups. Many of the best artworks are displayed in the Museo dell'Opera del Duomo, behind the east end of the Duomo.

HIGHLIGHTS

THE DUOMO

The Duomo of Santa Maria del Fiore is huge—there is room inside for 20,000 people. It is worth walking right around its green-and-white striped marble exterior to appreciate the vast proportions. Several doors punctuate the walls, the most elaborate being the Porta della Mandoria with its relief of the Assumption sculpted by Nanni di Banco between 1414 and 1421. By contrast, the ornate Gothic façade dates from the 19th century; the original was destroyed in the late 1500s.

Compared with the outside, the interior is remarkably austere. Over the years many of the finest artworks have been moved to the Museo dell'Opera del Duomo, leaving the Duomo relatively bare. This enables you to appreciate the soaring space beneath the Gothic arches, the patterned marble pavements, the scale of the dome itself, and the superb mid-15th-century stained-glass windows, some of Italy's best.

There are two equestrian memorials dedicated to two of Florence's most famous *condottieri*: A monument to Niccolò da Tolentino (1456) by Andrea del Castagno, and a far sharper-edged portrait (1436) of Sir John Hawkwood, an English mercenary, by Paolo Uccello. Terracotta reliefs by Luca della Robbia decorate both north and south sacristy doors, and a superb bronze reliquary urn by Ghiberti stands in the central apse.

Steps to the ancient church of Santa Reparata lead down from the south aisle; excavated in the 1960s, this ancient and confusing space has archaeological finds and, more inspiring, the tomb of Filippo Brunelleschi, architect of the dome.

Climbing the rather claustrophobic 463 steps of the dome is a must; it is the high point of this great building, rewarded with sweeping views.

ITALY

DUOMO

✚ 227 D2 • Piazza del Duomo, 50122
Firenze ☎ 055 230 2885 🕐 Mon–Wed,
Fri 10–5, Thu 10–3.30, Sat 10–4.45, Sun
and holidays 1.30–4.45; Easter 3.30–
4.45; closed 1 Jan, Easter Day, 15 Aug
and 25 Dec 🎫 Free 🎟 Free guided
tours. Fixed audioguide points in the
Duomo, €1 📖 Guidebooks in Italian,
English, French, German and Spanish,
€10 🚻 👥 🅿 Underground parking
at Santa Maria Novella; parking for visitors with disabilities in Piazza del Duomo

Museo dell'Opera del Duomo

KEY

A Portale Maggiore with relief
   Maria in Gloria by A. Passaglia
B Porta dell Mandoria
C Crypt, with remains of old
   cathedral
D Chancel and High Altar
1. *L'Assunta* window by Ghiberti
   Incoronazione di Maria
2. Equestrian portrait of Niccoló da
   Tolentino, by A. del Castagno
3. Equestrian statue of Giovanni
   Acuto (John Hawkwood)
   painted by P. Uccello
4. 14th-century window, and
   below, *Dante and the Divine
   Comedy* by D. di Michelino
5. Marble altar (Buggiano)
6. In the door, lunette,
   Risurrezione, by Luca della
   Robbia
7. Sagrestia Nuova o della Messe
8. Above the altar, two angels
   (Luca della Robbia), below the
   altar reliquary of St. Zenobius
   by Ghiberti
9. Lunette, *Risurrezione*,
   terracotta by della Robbia
10. Sagrestia Vecchia o dei Canonici
11. Altar by Michelozzo
12. Entrance to the dome
13. Bust of Brunelleschi, by
    A. Cavalcanti
14. Stairs to the Crypt

MUSEO DELL'OPERA DEL DUOMO

The Museo dell'Opera del Duomo contains the sculptures and
paintings of the Duomo complex, too precious to be left to the mercy
of modern pollution. Ghiberti's *Gates of Paradise* (see below) probably
steals the show, but there is a *Pietà* by Michelangelo that many see as
equally exquisite. The sculptor was 80 when he created it, his last work,
and intended it to be for his own tomb, but never finished it; the figure
of Nicodemus is said to be a self-portrait. Donatello, the greatest of
Michelangelo's precursors, is represented by two works: A gaunt and
bedraggled *Mary Magdalene* and the powerful figure of the prophet
Habbakuk. Donatello carved this for the campanile and it is so realistic
he is said to have seized it, crying 'Speak, speak'. His lighter side
emerges in the choir loft from the Duomo, carved with capering *putti*
(children), the perfect contrast to Luca della Robbia's version,
ornamented with earnest angels.

GHIBERTI'S BAPTISTERY DOORS IN THE MUSEO DELL'OPERA

Having finished the north doors in the baptistery in
1425, Ghiberti set to work on the doors for the east
side, a work of such beauty that Michelangelo
named them the 'Gates of Paradise'. Completed in
1452, they are made up of 10 relief panels of
biblical subjects, exquisitely carved in low relief. Their
artistic importance is in their use of perspective,
extending the scenes far into the background—a
totally new concept at the time that became typical
of the Renaissance. The composition is far more
naturalistic than the earlier baptistery doors, with figures grouped off-
centre to intensify the drama of each scene. The baptistery doors are
Ghiberti's finest achievement. On the frame of the left-hand door is his
self-portrait—the smug-looking gentleman with a bald head.

THE BATTISTERO

The octagonal baptistery, entirely encased in green and white marble, is
one of Florence's oldest buildings, probably dating from around the
sixth to seventh centuries, and remodelled in the 11th century. It is
most famous for its three sets of bronze doors, the south set dating
from the 1330s by Andrea Pisano, and the north and east by Lorenzo
Ghiberti. Ghiberti, aged 20, who won the commission for the north
doors in a competition and worked on them from 1403 to 1424,
embarking on his finest achievement, the east set (▷ above),
immediately afterwards. The panels in the doors you see are

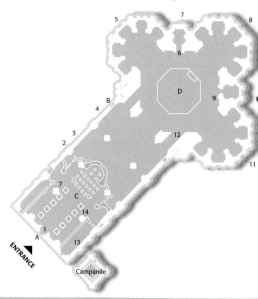

reproductions; the originals are kept away from 21st-century pollution in the Museo dell'Opera del Duomo.

The mosaic ceiling inside the Battistero

INSIDE THE DOME

The interior of the dome glitters with Florence's only mosaic cycle, the earliest dating from 1225. Begin by looking above the entrance door and follow the history of the world from the Creation to John the Baptist, before taking in the main image of Christ and the Last Judgement, together with the Apostles and the Virgin.

THE CAMPANILE

Giotto designed the campanile (bell tower) in 1334, but he died in 1337, before it was completed. Both Andrea Pisano, who took over after Giotto's death, and Talenti altered the original design considerably, strengthening the walls and adding large windows. The building is covered with bands of green, white and pink marble and is decorated with copies of sculptures and reliefs showing prophets, patriarchs and scenes from the Old Testament; the originals are in the Museo dell'Opera del Duomo. There are 414 steps to the top of the campanile, well worth it for the views of Florence and the hills.

BACKGROUND

The sixth- to seventh-century baptistery was originally Florence's cathedral, later replaced by the church of Santa Reparata, whose remains lie beneath the present building. In the 13th century, the city fathers decided to replace it, largely to flaunt the city's political clout and growing wealth and size. In 1294 the project was entrusted to Arnolfo di Cambio, and work continued throughout the 14th century, with various architects realizing his plan. The campanile was finished by 1334 and by 1418 the nave and tribunes were complete. The building awaited the massive dome planned for the crossing—the only drawback being that nobody had yet worked out how it would be built. The architect Filippo Brunelleschi offered his services, refusing to explain his solution, but exuding confidence. The building committee finally gave him the job, insisting that he work with his rival Lorenzo Ghiberti, who had been responsible for the baptistery doors. In 1436 the dome was completed, and the cathedral consecrated. The lantern was finally completed in the 1460s.

BATTISTERO

➕ 226 C2 • Piazza del Duomo, 50122 Firenze ☎ 055 230 2885 🕐 Mon–Sat 12–7, Sun and holidays 8.20–2; closed 1 Jan, Easter Day, 8 Sep, 24 and 25 Dec 💶 €3 🎧 Audioguide

MUSEO DELL'OPERA DEL DUOMO

➕ 227 D2 • Piazza del Duomo 9, 50122 Firenze ☎ 055 230 2885 🕐 Mon–Sat 9–7.30, Sun and holidays 8.30–1.30; closed 1 Jan, Easter Day, 8 Sep, 25 Dec 💶 Adult €6, under 6s free 🚻 ♿

CAMPANILE

➕ 227 D2 • Piazza del Duomo 9, 50122 Firenze ☎ 055 230 2885 🕐 Daily 8.30–7.30; closed 1 Jan, Easter Day, 8 Sep, 25 Dec 💶 Adult €6, under 6s free

SANTA REPARATA (CRYPT)

🕐 Mon–Fri 10–5, Sat 10–4.45 (first Sat of month 10–4); last admittance 45 mins before closing. Closed 1 Jan, Easter Day, 15 Aug and 25 Dec 💶 €3

DOME

🕐 Sun–Fri 8.30–7, Sat 8.30–5.40 (last admission 40 min before closing) 💶 €6

Galleria degli Uffizi

Priceless paintings and sculptures from the world's most important collection of Renaissance art.
Giotto's *Maestà*, Botticelli's *The Birth of Venus* and Titian's *Venus of Urbino*.
Superb collection of Roman and Hellenistic sculpture.

Visitors waiting in line outside the Galleria degli Uffizi

Sculpture gallery

RATINGS

Good for kids	●●●○
Cultural interest	●●●●
Specialist shopping	●●●○
Value for money	●●●○

GALLERY GUIDE

Rooms 2–6: Giotto, 14th-century Florentine, International Gothic
Rooms 7–9: Early Renaissance
Rooms 10–14: Botticelli
Room 15: Leonardo da Vinci
Rooms 16–24: Perugino, Signorelli, Giorgione, Corregio
Rooms 25–26: Michelangelo, Raphael and Andrea del Sarto
Rooms 27–29: Mannerism
Room 30: Emilian painting
Room 31: Veronese
Room 32: Tintoretto
Rooms 33–45: 16th- to 18th-century—Rubens, Caravaggio and Rembrandt

The Holy Family by Michelangelo

SEEING THE GALLERIA DEGLI UFFIZI

Set aside plenty of time to see the Uffizi—there is so much art of such importance that a flying visit is out of the question. Do not attempt to see the entire collection in one day. In a first visit concentrate on Rooms 1 through 15, which present major Florentine works, Tuscan Gothic and Early Renaissance in the East Corridor, and 16th-century artists in the West Corridor. You can avoid a wait by reserving tickets in advance.

HIGHLIGHTS

MAESTÀ: GIOTTO—ROOM 2
A painting of the Madonna enthroned, combining Byzantine tradition with the first crucial steps towards the realism of Renaissance painting.

ADORATION OF THE MAGI: GENTILE DA FABRIANO—ROOM 6
This intricate picture (1423), with its sumptuously portrayed fabrics, epitomizes the zenith of the International Gothic movement.

PORTRAIT OF THE DUKE AND DUCHESS OF URBINO: PIERO DELLA FRANCESCA—ROOM 7
A double portrait showing the sitters in profile; the Duke lost his right eye in battle and was always portrayed from the left.

MADONNA AND CHILD WITH ANGELS: FILIPPO LIPPI—ROOM 8
Painted in 1465; the beautiful model for the Virgin was Lucrezia Buti, a nun, with whom the painter eloped.

THE BOTTICELLI WORKS—ROOMS 10–14
The Uffizi's most famous paintings are *Primavera* and *The Birth of Venus*. *Primavera* symbolizes spring, with a Zephyr chasing Flora, transforming her into spring and covering her with flowers. *The Birth of Venus* is inspired by Politia's poem and shows Zephyrus and Chloris blowing Venus ashore on the edge of a scallop shell.

LEONARDO DA VINCI—ROOM 15
Early works painted by Leonardo when he was living in Florence.

See his large *Annunciation* (1475), along with the *Adoration of the Magi* (1481), noted for its busy composition, remarkable character studies and curious symbolism. Left unfinished when Leonardo moved to Milan, it is in its preparatory state, sketched out in red-earth pigment.

THE HOLY FAMILY: MICHELANGELO–ROOM 25
Also known as the *Doni Tondo*, this painting was created between 1504 and 1505 for the marriage of Agnolo Doni and Maddalena Strozzi. It's Michelangelo's only completed work in tempera, a precursor to the Sistine Chapel frescoes.

THE RAPHAEL PAINTINGS–ROOM 26
Several important works hang here, including the luminous *Madonna of the Goldfinch*, a self-portrait, and the portrait group *Leo X with Giulio de' Medici*, painted shortly before the artist's death.

SALA DI PONTORMO E DEL ROSSO FIORENTINO–ROOM 27
This is Mannerism at its most startling, with attenuated forms and vivid shades.

VENUS OF URBINO: TITIAN–ROOM 28
This sensuous nude with a wistful and chaste gaze was painted in 1538 and described by Lord Byron as 'the definitive Venus'.

BACKGROUND
The gallery in the vast Palazzo degli Uffizi extends from Piazza della Signoria to the River Arno. Originally intended to be government offices *(uffizi)*, the U-shaped building was constructed between 1560 and 1574 by Giorgio Vasari, under the orders of Cosimo I de' Medici. Succeeding Medici dukes added to the collections, which were bequeathed to the people of Florence by the last member of the family, Anna Maria Lodovica, in 1737, on the condition that the works never leave the city. The museum continues to acquire paintings and drawings. In 1993 a terrorist bomb caused great damage, and the gallery has undergone major reorganization.

Prints for sale outside the gallery (top). Raphael's Madonna of the Goldfinch *(above)*

ITALY

BASICS
➕ 226 C3 • Piazzale degli Uffizi, 50122 Firenze ☎ 055 238 8651, 294 883 (reservations)

🕐 Tue–Sun 8.15–6.50 (hours usually extended in summer); reservations in advance Mon–Fri 8.30–6.30, Sat 8.30–12.30, tel 055 294883; www.firenzemusei.it

💶 Adult €6.50, reservations €3, under 18 free

🎧 Audio tours in English, French, Spanish, German, Japanese, Italian, from €6.50

📖 Official guidebook from €4.50

☕ Café 🚻

🅿 Limited parking on Lungarno Serristori (10-minute walk); underground parking at Santa Maria Novella station (15-minute walk); parking for visitors with disabilities in Piazza della Signoria

❓ Unscheduled room closures may occur at any time

The Annunciation *by Fra Angelico*

RATINGS

Historic interest	●●●○
Cultural interest	●●●○
Value for money	●●●○

BASICS

✚ 227 D1 • Piazza San Marco 3, 50121
Firenze ☎ 055 238 8608, 055 294883
(reservations)
🕐 Mon–Fri 8.15–1.50, Sat 8.15–6.50,
Sun 8.15–7; closed 1st, 3rd and 5th Sun
and 2nd and 4th Mon of each month
and 25 Dec, 1 Jan, 1 May 💶 Adults €4,
18–26 years (EU nationals) €2, under
18s, over 65s (EU nationals) free
🎫 Official guidebook €7.50
♿ 🚻 Includes toilets for visitors
with disabilities
🅿 Parking at the Parterre (10-minute
walk); parking for visitors with
disabilities in Piazza San Marco

www.polomuseale.firenze.it
An Italian site bringing together the
major museums and galleries in
Florence. Site plans of the major
collections and pictures of the highlights.

TIPS

● The museum can be busy;
a visit out of peak season
allows you to experience
the spirituality of the place,
which may be compromised
by the crowds.
● Only 120 people are allowed
up to the dormitories at one
time, so reserve your visit in
advance (tel 055 294 883),
arrive early in the morning or
be prepared to wait.

MUSEO DI SAN MARCO

**A shrine to Fra Angelico, little changed since the 1400s.
See his paintings in their original context, the
Dominican Convent of San Marco.
Ethereal images full of endlessly fascinating detail.**

The Convent of San Marco, within which the museum resides, is
next to the church of the same name. The original convent on the
site was of the Silvestrine Order, but it was given to the Dominicans
by Cosimo il Vecchio, who commissioned the architect
Michelozzo to enlarge the existing buildings. Fra Angelico
(c1400–55), also known as Beato Angelico, lived here from
1436 to 1447. The museum was founded in 1869 and in 1921
most of Fra Angelico's panel paintings were transferred here from
other museums in Florence.

THE CLOISTERS AND THE PILGRIMS' HOSPICE

A visit starts in Michelozzo's peaceful Cloister of Sant'Antonio. In the
middle is an ancient cedar of Lebanon and at each corner is a small
lunette fresco by Fra Angelico. Off this cloister is the Pilgrims' Hospice,
a long room full of beautiful paintings by Fra Angelico, glowing in
bright jewel shades and gold leaf. At one end of the room is the
superb *Deposition from the Cross* (c1435–40), while at the other is
the famous *Linaiuoli Tabernacle* (1433) with its *Madonna Enthroned
and Saints*. The border consists of musical angels, often reproduced
on Christmas cards. In this room is also the great *Last Judgement*
altarpiece (1431) and a series of charming reliquary tabernacles in
gold frames featuring 35 tiny scenes from the life of Christ.

Other paintings here are by Fra Bartolomeo, Giovanni Sogliani,
Lorenzo Lippi and others. Before climbing the stairs to the monks'
quarters, visit two more frescoes: Fra Angelico's large *Crucifixion and
Saints* (1441–42) in the Chapter House and Domenico Ghirlandaio's
Last Supper in the small refectory.

THE MONKS' CELLS

At the top of the stairs to the dormitory is one of Fra Angelico's most
famous frescoes, the *Annunciation* (1442). The 44 tiny cells where
the monks lived each has a shuttered window and a small fresco by
Fra Angelico or his assistants. Those by the master himself are in Cells
1 to 9. Note the beautiful angel in Cell 3 and the Nativity scene in
Cell 5. Girolamo Savonarola, the rebel priest who was prior in 1491,
occupied the Prior's Cell. Other famous inhabitants include the
Florentine painter Fra Bartolommeo, who was a friar.

ITALY

Palazzo Pitti

A building of immense proportions with extensive grounds.
Florence's largest and most opulent palazzo, once the main seat of the Medicis.
Home to the Galleria Palatina, Florence's most important picture collection
after the Uffizi, and seven other collections.

SEEING THE PALAZZO PITTI

The Pitti collections are huge, so it makes sense to concentrate on
the Galleria Palatina, a suite of 26 rooms covered with paintings.
The works are displayed much as they were in the 17th century,
adorning the walls from floor to ceiling in no discernible order.
Allow 2–3 hours to fully appreciate the paintings before moving
on to another gallery that takes your fancy. Be prepared for
crowds, and also for sections or collections that are closed; you
can reserve ahead to avoid disappointment (tel 055 294883).
There is much to see, but make sure you leave time to relax
afterwards in the Giardino di Boboli.

HIGHLIGHTS

THE COURTYARD

The main entrance to the palace leads you through to Ammanati's
splendid courtyard (1560–70), an excellent example of Florentine
Mannerist architecture. It was used as a stage for lavish spectacles
between the 16th and 18th centuries, and is still the venue for
concerts and ballet in the summer.

GALLERIA PALATINA
MADONNA AND CHILD: FILIPPO LIPPI–SALA DI PROMOTEO

Painted in 1452 and known as the *Pitti Tondo*, Lippi's famous work
perfectly combines exquisite painting and intense spirituality. The eye
is drawn to the pure face of the Virgin, the central point, surrounded
by scenes from the life of her mother, St. Anne, and the Christ child
lying on her knee.

MADONNA DELLA SEGGIOLA: RAPHAEL–SALA DI SATURNO

Raphael painted this tondo in Rome in 1514, and it has been at the
Pitti since the 18th century. Although heavily influenced by Venetian
painting, evident in its use of light and shade, the painting follows a
strictly Florentine form, its shape emphasizing the tender curves of
the Virgin and Child.

PIETRO ARETINO: TITIAN–SALA DI APOLLO

Portraiture gained importance during the High Renaissance, as the
Church lost its total control on subject matter, and new money
brought self-made men to prominence. Titian painted this portrait of
the satirical poet Pietro Aretino in 1545, after Aretino had moved
from Mantova to Venice, Titian's native city.

SLEEPING CUPID: CARAVAGGIO–SALA DELL'EDUCAZIONE
DI GIOVE

This plump little sleeping Cupid is full of allegorical references to
passion and lost love. Caravaggio painted it when he was in Malta in
1608. By this time he had already lived in Rome, where he had
studied and grasped the fine details of human anatomy and was
beginning to concentrate on the development of *chiaroscuro*, the
contrast of light and dark, a technique expertly employed in his work
later on in his life.

*The vast 205m (673ft) façade
of the Palazzo Pitti*

BASICS

✚ 226 C4 • Piazza Pitti, 50125 Firenze

☎ 055 294883

🕐 Palatina, Appartamenti, Galleria
d'Arte Moderna: Tue–Sun 8.15–6.50
(last admittance 6.05); Appartimenti
closed in Jan. Costume, Argenti,
Porcellane: Daily Jun–end Aug
8.15–7.30; Apr–end May, Sep to
mid-Oct 8.15–6.30; Mar and late Oct
8.15–5.30; Nov–Feb 8.15–4.30 (last
admittance 30 mins before closing)

💶 Palatina, Appartamenti, Galleria
d'Arte Moderna: Adult €8.50 (for all
museums), under 18s (EU nationals)
free. Boboli, Porcellane, Argenti,
Costume: Adult €6 (for all museums),
under 18s (EU nationals) free

🎧 Palatina audiotours €4.65

☕ Café with a terrace on the main
courtyard

🏪 In Palatina and main courtyard

🚻 🅿 Underground parking at Santa
Maria Novella station; limited parking
on Lungarno Serristori; parking for
visitors with disabilities Piazza Pitti

www.palazzopitti.it

ITALY

GALLERY GUIDE

Galleria Palatina: The main collection, strong on 16th-century works, particularly Raphael, Titian and Andrea del Sarto. In a wing of the main palace.

Galleria d'Arte Moderna: Works spanning the mid-18th to mid-20th centuries. In the main building on the floor above the Galleria Palatina.

Museo degli Argenti: *Objets d'art*, gold and jewellery from the Medici collections. Accessed from the main courtyard.

Museo del Costume: Rotating exhibitions of historic clothes from the early 18th to mid-20th centuries. In Palazzina Meridiana in the south wing.

Museo delle Porcellane: French, Italian, German and Viennese porcelain and ceramics. In a pavilion at the top of the Boboli Gardens.

Appartamenti Reali: Lavishly decorated state apartments following on from the Palatina.

Collezione Contini Bonacossi: A picture collection on long-term loan, strong on Spanish painting. Next to the Museo del Costume in the Palazzina Meridiana.

Museo delle Carozze: Carriage collection—currently closed.

Statue in the Sala di Venere (Room 4) in the Galleria Palatina

Inside the Grotto del Buontalenti (1583–88) in the Giardino di Boboli, the formal gardens of the Palazzo Pitti

APPARTAMENTI REALI

These royal apartments have been expertly and sensitively restored to their 19th-century condition. From the 17th century onwards they were the residence of the Medici, the dukes of Lorraine, and members of the house of Savoy, including Italy's first monarch, King Umberto I. They are hard to beat in terms of extravagance; their gilding and stucco, rich damask hangings, vast chandeliers, gilt mirrors, period furnishings, paintings and sculptures are impressive.

MUSEO DEGLI ARGENTI

In a series of sumptuous state rooms, this museum concentrates on luxury *objets d'art* amassed by the Medici dukes. There is a huge range of items, from antique vases collected by Lorenzo Il Magnifico to stunningly worked, but aesthetically banal, figurines, and a vast array of inlaid pieces.

BACKGROUND

Construction began on the Palazzo Pitti in 1457, supposedly to a design by Brunelleschi. It was originally the private residence of the banker Luca Pitti, a rival of the Medici family, and his descendants, but in 1549 the family funds dried up and it was purchased by Cosimo I's wife, the Grand Duchess Eleonora. It became the official residence of the Grand Dukes and was occupied by ruling families until 1919, when it was presented to the state by Vittorio Emanuele III. Under Medici ownership it was repeatedly enlarged, notably in the 16th century, when Bartolomeo Ammanati (1511–92) lengthened the façade and built the courtyard, while the side wings were added in the 18th and 19th centuries. The Medici family began decorating and amassing the collections in the 17th century. The main galleries opened to the public in 1833 and the Galleria d'Arte Moderna, Florence's modern art museum, joined the gallery complex in 1924.

ITALY

PALAZZO VECCHIO

Florence's town hall, an outstanding example of Florentine civic purpose, with superb rooftop views from the loggia. Vast, elaborately decorated public rooms and intimate private apartments. Fine sculptures, including *Victory* by Michelangelo.

The palace stands on the site of the medieval Palazzo dei Priori, rebuilt to Arnolfo di Cambio's design. Designers of *palazzi comunali* throughout Tuscany based their designs on its battlemented structure. Cosimo il Vecchio was imprisoned in the asymmetrically placed tower before his exile in 1433. Savonarola was also imprisoned here in 1498, but went on to be burned at the stake in Piazza della Signoria.

THE COURTYARD
Past the main entrance is the courtyard, reconstructed by Michelozzo in 1453. It was elaborately decorated by Giorgio Vasari in 1565 to celebrate the marriage of the son of Cosimo I to Joanna of Austria.

FIRST FLOOR
The largest room is the Salone del Cinquecento, a meeting room for the 500-member Consiglio Maggiore. Vasari painted the frescoes to celebrate Cosimo I's triumphs over Pisa and Siena. The most notable sculpture is Michelangelo's *Victory*.

Next door, the tiny, windowless Studiolo di Francesco I has allegorical paintings by Vasari and small bronze statues by Giambologna and Ammanati. It was here that the melancholic son of Cosimo I pursued his interest in alchemy. On the same floor, Vasari and Cosimo I's assistants decorated the Quartiere di Leone X with ornate illustrations of the history of the Medici family.

SECOND FLOOR
Access to the Quartiere di Eleonora di Toledo, the private apartments of Cosimo I's wife, is via a balcony across the end of the Salone del Cinquecento, providing a close-up view of the ceiling. The chapel, decorated with frescoes of various saints, is one of Bronzino's most important works. The Sala dei Gigli owes its name to the lily *(gigli)* motif, a symbol of the city. Here also is Donatello's bronze statue, *Judith and Holofernes* (1455). Niccolò Machiavelli used the Cancelleria next door as an office from 1498 to 1512, when he was a government secretary. The *guardaroba*, or wardrobe, contains a fascinating collection of 57 detailed maps of the world as it was then known.

RATINGS	
Historic interest	● ● ● ●
Cultural interest	● ● ● ●
Value for money	● ● ●

BASICS
✚ 227 D3 • Piazza della Signoria, 50122 Firenze
☎ 055 276 8325
🕐 Mon–Fri 9–7, Sun, holidays 9–2
💶 Adult €6, child (3–17) €2, family €14
🎧 Audiotours in Italian, English, French, German, Japanese, €4.10
📖 From €4.65
♿ 🚻
🅿 Nearest parking under Santa Maria Novella Station (15-minute walk). Parking for visitors with disabilities in Piazza della Signoria

www.comune.fi.it
www.museoragazzi.it

A copy of Verrochio's Pluttino Fountain (top). A marble bust on the façade (above)

PIAZZA DELLA SIGNORIA

Florence's most noble and famous piazza—the place to get a real feel for the city. A vast open-air, traffic-free sculpture gallery with elegant cafés and restaurants.

Ammanati's statue of Neptune (above). The Calcio Storico, a football match held here each year in medieval costume (top)

This wide, open square marks the heart of the *centro storico* and is next to the Galleria degli Uffizi (▷ 232–233). The Piazza della Signoria has been the political focus of Florence since the Middle Ages. Surrounded by tall buildings, notably the vast, sombre Palazzo Vecchio (▷ 237), this is where the ruling city fathers called open-air public assemblies in times of crisis. The crowd was often provoked by speeches on the *arringhiera* (oration terrace), a raised platform, and the gatherings frequently degenerated into violence. The area in front of the Palazzo Vecchio was named Piazza del Popolo (People's Square) in 1307.

THE SCULPTURES

The enormous Loggia dei Lanzi (also known as the Loggia della Signoria) was designed to be used by dignitaries for formal meetings and ceremonies. It was completed in 1382 and has been used as an open-air sculpture museum since the late 18th century. Dominating the front is Cellini's mannerist bronze *Perseus* (1545). Considered his greatest work, it shows Perseus triumphantly holding aloft the severed head of Medusa. Near it is Giambologna's last work, the *Rape of the Sabine Women*, completed in 1583. Donatello's *Judith and Holofernes* was the first of the statues to be placed in the piazza (this is a copy—the original is in the Palazzo Vecchio). In front of the main entrance to the Palazzo Vecchio stands a copy of Michelangelo's David (the original is in the Galleria dell'Accademia. The other large statue nearby is Bandinelli's Hercules and Cacus (1534), described by his rival Cellini as an 'old sack full of melons'. At the corner of the Palazzo Vecchio is Ammanati's massive fountain (1575), with the undignified figure of Neptune. The large equestrian bronze, Giambologna's monument to Cosimo (1595), shows detailed scenes of Cosimo's coronation and victory over the Sienese. The plaque in the pavement in front of the fountain marks the spot where Girolamo Savonarola was burned at the stake as a traitor on 23 May 1498.

RATINGS

Good for kids	● ● ●
Historic interest	● ● ● ● ●
Cultural interest	● ● ● ●
Walkability	● ● ● ●

BASICS

✚ 226 C3 • Piazza della Signoria, 50122 Firenze
🅿 Parking at Lungarno Torrigiani (10-minute walk)
🚻 In Palazzo Vecchio

TIP

● An elegant, expensive, table at the Café Rivoire is a good place to people-watch. Or perch on a stone bench under the Loggia dei Lanzi.

Rape of the Sabine Women

ITALY

SANTA CROCE

The largest Franciscan church in Italy, reputedly founded by St. Francis.
Cappella dei Pazzi—one of Brunelleschi's most important works and a masterpiece of the early Renaissance.
Several important Florentines are buried here.

In the heart of one of Florence's most attractive areas, the present Santa Croce was begun in 1294 and completed in the 1450s. The original plain front was replaced in the 19th century with an elaborate neo-Gothic one. The interior is vast, with a wide nave and superb stained-glass windows by Agnolo Gaddi. Although some frescoes were damaged in the 1966 flood, there are some exceptional works.

THE NORTH AISLE

Lorenzo Ghiberti (1378–1455) is buried under the tomb-slab with the eagle on it. There is also a monument to Galileo Galilei (1564–1642), the great scientist who spent his latter years in Florence.

THE EAST END

The polygonal sanctuary in the east end is covered with vivid frescoes by Gaddi. On either side are small chapels, each dedicated to an eminent Florentine family of the day, with frescoes by Giotto. The Bardi di Libertà Chapel has frescoes by Bernardo Daddi and an altarpiece by Giovanni della Robbia. The Bardi di Vernio Chapel has frescoes by Masi di Banco, while Donatello's wooden crucifix hangs in the Bardi Chapel in the north transept. The frescoes in the Castellani Chapel are by Gaddi, whose father Taddeo was responsible for the beautiful paintings in the Baroncelli Chapel. Next to the Baroncelli Chapel a corridor leads to the Medici Chapel by Brunelleschi.

THE SOUTH AISLE

In the south aisle are the tombs of Michelangelo (designed by Vasari), the poet Dante, and Niccolò Machiavelli.

CAPPELLA DEI PAZZI

From the south aisle there is access to Brunelleschi's Cappella dei Pazzi. He was still working on this masterpiece of tranquillity when he died in 1446. Inside, in contrast to the elaborate Gothic tendencies of the age, grey *pietra serena* stone, simply carved in classical lines, is set against a white background. At the base of the elegant dome, 12 terracotta roundels by Della Robbia depict the Apostles.

RATINGS	
Historic interest	●●●○
Cultural interest	●●●○
Value for money	●●●○

BASICS

✚ 227 E3 • Piazza Santa Croce, 50122 Firenze
☎ 055 2466105
🕑 Mon–Sat 9.30–5.30, Sun 1–5.30 (last admittance 5pm)
🎫 Adult €5 (also covers museum); child (11–18) €3; child (under 11) free
🚌 Free tours in English, French, German, Spanish, Italian Mon–Sat 10–12.30, 3–5, Sun 3–5 (tours given by volunteers, so times and availability of languages may vary). Audioguides at fixed points: English, French, Spanish, Italian, €4
📖 €8
🚇 P Lungarno della Zecca Vecchia (10-minute walk); parking for visitors with disabilities in Piazza Santa Croce
www.santacroce.firenze.it

TIP

● The Calcio Storico, an established football (soccer) match, is played in medieval costume in Piazza Santa Croce or Piazza della Signoria on St. John's Day, 24 June (St. John is the patron saint of Florence). Other dates are picked from a hat on Easter Sunday.

The decorative floor tombs of illustrious Italians in the Basilica di Santa Croce (above)

ITALY

KEY TO SYMBOLS
⊕ Shopping
🎭 Entertainment
🍷 Nightlife
🏊 Sports
★ Activities
♡ Health and Beauty
👶 For Children

WHAT TO DO

⊕ FLORENTINE MARKETS
Piazza San Lorenzo, Piazza Santo Spirito, Piazza dei Ciompi and Via dell'Ariento, Piazza Lorenzo Ghiberti, Piazza della Repubblica, Via Porta Rossa, Piazza del Mercato Centrale
Tel 055 234 0444 (tourist office)
The most famous flea market is in and around Piazza San Lorenzo, where you'll find leather and other assorted goods. There are stands daily at Santo Spirito, selling bedding, shoes, clothing and haberdashery. On the second Sunday of the month there is an arts and crafts market (except during July and August). Piazza dei Ciompi holds a daily flea market (Mar–Oct daily 9–8, Nov–Feb Tue–Sun 9–7.30) where you can browse for collectibles such as ornaments, antique and period clothes and old post cards. Head towards Via dell'Ariento and the Mercatone delle Cascine (Tue 7–2) for a morning of browsing and bartering. Mercato Nuovo (Porcellino) on Via Porta Rossa (daily 9–7) is full of inexpensive reproductions of Florentine classics, which makes it a great place for souvenir-hunters. The leather bags and shoes are often a good buy, too. The Mercato Centrale (summer Mon–Sat 7–2, winter Mon–Fri 7–2, Sat 7–5) is full of mouth-watering Florentine delights—feast your eyes on the wonderful fruit and vegetable stands, and the *salumeria* counters brimming with meats and cheeses.

⊕ FRATELLI PICCINI
Ponte Vecchio 23
Tel 055 294768
www.fratellipiccini.com
If you want to go jewellery-shopping on the Ponte Vecchio, make sure you take in Piccini's. Their lovely gold charms make a nice gift. The family has been in the jewellery-making business since 1903.

⊕ Apr–end Oct daily 9.30–7.30; Nov–end Mar daily 9.30–1, 3.30–7.30
🚍 B, D

⊕ PINEIDER
Piazza della Signoria 13r
Tel 055 284655
www.pineider.it
Pineider remains Italy's original and most prestigious stationer—the letters of Napoleon, Byron and Dietrich were scribed using Pineider's beautifully crafted tinted papers and inks. It also stocks exquisite leather-bound notebooks and accessories including seals.
⊕ Tue–Sat 10–7, Mon 3–7 🚍 23

★ SCUOLA DEL CUOIO (LEATHER SCHOOL)
Piazza Santa Croce 16
Tel 055 244533
www.leatherschool.it
This workshop, at the back of the famous church, was once run by Franciscan monks. If you intend to shop for leather goods, come here first to learn how to spot quality and craftsmanship. If you make a purchase at the on-site shop, they'll personalize the goods for you with a stamp.
⊕ Mar–end Nov Mon–Sat 9.30–6, Sun 10–6 🚍 B, C, 23

🎭 PINOCCHIO LIVE JAZZ
Viale Giannotti 13
Tel 055 683388
www.pinocchiojazz.it
Jazz buffs will love this place as it attracts some of Italy's top artists, who can be heard during the club's annual two-season schedule. Members nod approvingly in this smoky venue while the musicians blow, brush and noodle their instruments into the night.
🎭 Membership fee plus various for tickets 🚍 31, 32

🎭 TEATRO COMMUNALE
Corso Italia 16
Tel 055 277 9350
www.maggiofiorentino.com
Florence's major venue for all things orchestral, balletic and operatic. The winter concert season runs from January to late March, while opera and ballet is staged between September and late March. Expect old favourites like *Macbeth* and *Coppelia* as

well as seminal composers' work from Bach to Wagner.
🎭 €30–€90

🍷 MARACANA
Via Faenza 4
Tel 055 210298
www.maracana.it
Six levels, a carnival stage and a party crowd make this club a winner with lovers of all things Brazilian. It's the place to watch carnival dancers, samba, sip *caipirinhas* (a cocktail made with lime juice and *cachaça*, Brazilian sugar cane liquor) and try some of the enormous *churrasco* (Brazilian barbequed meats).
🍷 Thu–Sat 9pm–4am 🍷 €15; free entry for women Tue, Thu and Sun 🚍 31, 32

🍷 TENAX
Via Pratese 46
Tel 055 308160
www.tenax.org
Florence's premier house-music club, attracting big international names like Dimitri from Paris, Thievery Corporation, Grace Jones and Groove Armada. It has mind-blowing lighting and sound technology, as well as some very curious art installations. Also hosts live music acts.
🍷 Thu–Sat 10pm–4am 🍷 €15
🚍 5, 29, 30, 56 🚍 A, B

★ FLORENCE BY BIKE
Via San Zanobi 120
Tel 055 488992
www.florencebybike.it
Florence by Bike has a good selection of bicycles and scooters to choose from should you wish to whizz around town or explore the countryside. Prices start at €7.50 for half a day, or €20 for a day's use of a standard mountain bicycle. Reserve a place on the daily 32km (20-mile) bicycle tour in advance.
⊕ Apr–end Oct daily 9–7; Nov–end Mar Mon–Sat 9–1, 3.30–7.30 🚲 €7.50 half day, €14 full day; mountain bike €20 per day. Prices include all accessories 🚍 20, 25, 31, 32, 33

♡ OFFICINA PROFUMO FARMACEUTICA DI SANTA MARIA NOVELLA
Via della Scala 16
Tel 055 21 62 76
www.smnovella.com
One of the world's oldest

pharmacies, this atmospheric apothecary is operated by Dominican friars, in a 14th-century chapel. Herbal compounds, from soothing eucalyptus cough drops to calendula hand creams, are sold in a fragrant environment.

🕐 Mon–Fri 9.30–7.30, Sun 10.30–6.30

🚇 A, 11, 36, 37

EATING

L'ANTICO RISTORO DI CAMBI

Via Sant'Onofrio 1r

Tel 055 217134

www.anticoristorodicambi.it

This eatery is a rare find, serving lighter dishes at lunch. The menu concentrates on fresh ingredients. Try one of the excellent salads or platters, which are piled high with fresh produce including basil, rocket (arugula), pecorino cheese, buffalo mozzarella and cured meats.

🕐 Mon–Sat 12.30–2.30, 7.30–10.30pm

🍴 L €20, D €30, Wine €12

♿

🚇 D, 6

BALDOVINO

Via San Giuseppe 22r

Tel 055 241773

www.baldovino.com

A bustling yet relaxed *trattoria* not far from Piazza Santa Croce that is especially good for those with children, as it serves great pizzas. The changing menu includes lots of soups, beef, grilled meats and some inventive plates of *pastasciutta*. The wine list includes many Tuscan classics.

🕐 Mar–Oct daily 12–2.30, 7pm–midnight; Nov–Feb Tue–Sun noon–2.30, 7pm–midnight

🍴 L €14, D €25, Wine €14

🚇 C, 14

CAFFÈ RIVOIRE

Piazza della Signoria 3r

Tel 055 214412

www.rivoire.it

The Rivoire opened in the 1870s and is a must for the chocolate connoisseur. It produces arguably the best chocolate in town. Eat an exquisite ice cream or sample the famous hot chocolate.

🕐 Tue–Sun 8am–midnight; closed for 2 weeks in Jan

🍴 Cappuccino €6, ice cream from €6 to eat in

🚇 A, B

ENOTECA PINCHIORRI

Via Ghibellina 87

Tel 055 242777

www.enotecapinchiorri.com

This French-influenced establishment is one of Italy's best. The magical rose-scented *cortile* (courtyard) and elegant dining areas are a fitting complement to the exquisite nouvelle cuisine and unrivalled wine list. A jacket is recommended for male diners.

🕐 Wed 7.30pm–10pm, Thu–Sat 12.30–2, 7.30–10; closed Sun–Tue, L Wed

🍴 L €160, D €210, Wine €28

♿

🚇 A, 14

OLIVIERO

Via delle Terme 51r

Tel 055 287643

www.ristorante-oliviero.it

Excellent service and superb Tuscan food are the main characteristics here. Specialties include wild boar, guinea fowl and rabbit. Sublime soups, exquisite vegetables and innovative pasta creations make up the rest.

🕐 Mon–Sat 7.30pm–1am; closed Aug

🍴 D €70, Wine €21

🚇 A, B, 6, 11, 36, 37

SABATINI

Via dei Panzani 9a

Tel 055 282802

www.ristorantesabatini.it

This elegant restaurant serves solid Tuscan dishes with international touches, and the restaurant is known for *bistecca alla fiorentina*. Seafood enthusiasts can opt for the *risotto con scampi*. An excellent wine list and multilingual service.

🕐 Tue–Sun 12.30–3, 7–11

🍴 L €35, D €80, Wine €14

🚇 A, 1, 4, 7, 10, 11, 22, 23, 36, 37

STAYING

CASCI

Via Cavour 13, 50129 Firenze

Tel 055 211686

www.hotelcasci.com

This family-run hotel, near the Duomo, was once the home of the opera composer Rossini. There are some original 14th-century touches, but overall it has been thoroughly modernized, with immaculate, functional rooms. The triple-glazed windows deaden street sounds. The hotel is especially

good for families. Many of the simple but comfortable rooms have balconies. Facilities include private bathroom, safe telephone, cable television and minibar.

🏨 €90–€150, breakfast included

🛏 25 ♿

🚇 1, 6, 7, 10, 11, 17, 31, 32

CRISTINA

Via della Condotta 4, 50122 Firenze

Tel 055 214484

www.hotelcristina-florence.com

This friendly, small hotel with largish rooms is a great place for families, as the owners go out of their way to make children and their parents feel at home. The rooms are clean and spacious, and four have private bathrooms. Great value for money, so you'll need to reserve well in advance.

🏨 €55–€70

🛏 9

🚇 A, 14, 23

HELVETIA & BRISTOL

Via dei Pescioni 2, 50123 Firenze

Tel 055 287814

www.thecharminghotels.com

Once popular with English ladies on the Grand Tour, this hotel preserves the refined air of the 19th century. Each room has been individually designed. Modern amenities include private bathroom, hair-dryer, television, telephone, minibar and safe. The Bristol restaurant serves contemporary Tuscan food.

🏨 €440–€650, excluding breakfast

🛏 67 ♿

🚇 A, B, 6, 11, 22, 36, 37

MONNA LISA

Borgo Pinti 27, 50121 Firenze

Tel 055 2479751

www.monnalisa.it

This 15th-century *palazzo* is a wonderful mix of old and contemporary design. The reception has stuccoed walls and a striking staircase. Many rooms have elaborate ceilings, wall hangings and antiques. Facilities include private bathroom, hair-dryer, television, telephone, minibar and safe. The flower-filled garden is perfect for relaxing with a drink.

🏨 €244–€370

🛏 55 ♿

🚇 14, 23

Milan

●

**Italy's most dynamic city, the powerhouse of the country's economy.
One of Europe's richest cities, with chic shopping and cutting-edge style in its
galleries, shops and restaurants.
An abundance of historical and artistic heritage.**

*The magnificent marble façade
of Milan's Duomo*

*A close-up view of the Duomo's exterior (above) and the glass-
roofed shopping complex of the Galleria Vittorio Emanuele II (right)*

RATINGS

Historic interest	●●●●
Shopping	●●●●●
Specialist shopping	●●●●
Value for money	●●●

BASICS

✚ 5 D4

🛈 Via Marconi 1, 20123 Milano, tel 02
72524301/2/3; Mon–Sat 8.45–1, 2–6,
Sun 9–1, 2–5

🚆 Milano Centrale, Milano Garibaldi,
Milano Lambrate, Milano Porta Genova,
Milano Nord

✈ Milano Malpensa and Milano Linate

www.milanoinfo.eu
Crammed with information: extensive
accommodation, restaurant, entertainment and shopping listings; full
information on museums and
public monuments; transport
details; up-to-date
information on what's
going on and how to
get the most out of
your visit; in English
and Italian.

*One of the Duomo's
many statues*

SEEING MILAN

Booming Milan lies in the flat country 48km (30 miles) south of
the Alps and 3 hours 30 minutes by fast train northwest of Rome.
It is a northern, grey city, with a fast pace of life and efficient
infrastructure. Milan is not immediately beguiling, but its
architecture reflects its diversity. There are a few medieval and
Renaissance buildings, but the style is predominantly neoclassical,
art nouveau and modern, and the streets are wide and busy. The
historic core lies within three concentric ring roads, and most of
the major sights are within the Cerchia dei Navigli, which follows
the path of the medieval walls. The Piazza del Duomo is the heart
of Milan: It's a good place to get your initial bearings, and most
sights are within walking distance. For farther-flung sights, simply
hop on a bus or tram or take the metro.

HIGHLIGHTS

DUOMO

✚ 244 C2 • Piazza del Duomo, 20123 Milano ☎ 02 86463456 🕒 Daily 9–6
www.duomomilano.it

Milan's Duomo is the hub of the city, the world's largest Gothic
cathedral and the third-largest church in Europe. Building began in
1386 under Duke Gian Galeazzo Visconti and finally finished nearly
500 years later. The façade, built of marble from the Lake
Maggiore area, is a strange mix of Gothic and baroque.
The brass strip on the pavement near the entrance is
part of Europe's largest sundial, laid out in 1786.
Above the chancel, the crucifix has a nail from Christ's
cross, while the nearby crypt contains the remains of
St. Charles Borromeo, who worked with Milan's poor in the
16th century. The highlight is the roof itself, a forest of
pinnacles and statues with views as far as the Alps.

PINACOTECA DI BRERA

✚ 244 C1 • Via Brera 28, 20121 Milano ☎ 02 722631 🕒 Tue–Sat
8.30–7.15 (last admittance 7) 💰 €5
www.brera.beniculturali.it

Right in the heart of the smart Brera district, the Pinacoteca di

ITALY

LA SCALA

✚ 244 C2 • Piazza della Scala, 20121 Milano ☎ Box office 02 861 827 www.teatroallascala.org
La Scala is one of the world's most famous opera houses, designed in 1778, with an opulent gilt and velvet interior that can seat over 2,000 people. It remains the social and cultural focus for the city's rich. Backstage tours Tue and Thu (tel 02 433 53521 for reservations).

SANT'AMBROGIO

✚ 244 A3 • Piazza Sant'Ambrogio 15, 20123 Milano ☎ 02 8645 0895
🕐 Daily 9–6.30
www.santambrogio-basilica.it
An outstanding Lombard-Romanesque church, founded in the fourth century by St. Ambrose, patron saint of Milan, whose remains lie in the crypt. The simple church, with relics, carving and mosaics, is reached through a colonnaded courtyard; outside is Bramante's Cortile della Canonica.

Brera is Milan's most prestigious art gallery, originally founded by Napoleon to display loot from churches, convents and displaced aristocrats. The collection is huge, with over 600 works exhibited in 40 rooms. The emphasis is on Italian Renaissance painting, and in particular the Venetian school. Early Renaissance Venetian works include pictures by Carpaccio and Giovanni and Gentile Bellini, and there is a striking *Dead Christ* by Andrea Mantegna, viewed from the soles of Jesus' feet. There is a lively Veronese *Supper in the House of Simon*, and a more spiritual *Deposition* by Tintoretto, painted in the 1560s. For a serene contrast to Venetian drama, don't miss Piero della Francesca's *Madonna with Saints and Federigo di Montefeltro*, all harmony and pellucid greys, and Raphael's sumptuously languid *Marriage of the Virgin*. For yet another experience, there is the 17th-century realism of Caravaggio and Il Pitochetto, a Lombard artist who specialized in depicting the poor.

SANTA MARIA DELLE GRAZIE

✚ 244 A2 • Piazza Santa Maria delle Grazie, Corso Magenta, 20123 Milano
☎ 02 89421146 🕐 Tue–Sun 8–7.30; reserve at least 2 days in advance; visits restricted to 25 people and for 15 mins, visitors must arrive at least 15 mins before their tour time 💶 €6.50 plus €1.50 reservation fee
The church of Santa Maria delle Grazie was begun in Gothic style in the mid-15th century, and altered considerably by Bramante in 1492 when he added the beautiful tribune, serene cloister and massive dome. What draws the crowds, however, is Leonardo da Vinci's fragile fresco of the *Last Supper* on one wall of the Old Refectory in the adjoining monastery. This huge work portrays the moment when Christ announces that one of his disciples will betray him. Da Vinci applied the tempera and oil to dry plaster, rather than using the more stable, wet-plaster technique, so his work began to deteriorate five

years after it was completed. Napoleonic troops used the fresco for target practice and the building was bombed in 1943, but amazingly the fresco survived. The work is fading fast despite continuous restoration, but against the odds, the brilliance of the artist's hand continues to shine through.

CASTELLO SFORZESCO

➕ 244 B1 • Piazza Castello, Milano ☎ 02 8846 3700 🕐 Castle: summer daily 7–7, winter 7–6. Museums: Tue–Sun 9–5.30 (last admittance 5) 💰 Castle: free. Museums: adult €3, child (under 18) free

The Castello Sforzesco is one of Milan's major landmarks. Destroyed in the 1440s, it was rebuilt by the Sforzas and, under their patronage, became the heart of one of Europe's most powerful and cultured courts. It was used as a barracks from the 15th century, when the

GALLERIA VITTORIO EMANUELE II

➕ 244 C2 • Piazza del Duomo, 20123 Milano

A monumental glass-roofed shopping arcade, built in 1867, which links the Piazza del Duomo with the Piazza della Scala. The central mosaic shows the symbols of the cities of the newly united Italy. It's considered good luck to stand on the testicles of Turin's bull. It is a great place for people-watching.

The Museo Nazionale della Scienza e della Tecnica (left) and outside La Scala opera house (right)

Sforzas fell, until it was converted into a museum complex in the 19th century. Artistic highlights include Michelangelo's unfinished *Rondanini Pietà*, works by Bellini and Mantegna, and Arcimboldo's 16th-century surrealistic portrait of *Primavera* (Spring), an image composed entirely of flowers.

BACKGROUND

Mediolanum, the Roman precursor of modern-day Milan, became the seat of the rulers of the Western Empire in AD286, and it was here that Constantine gave his approval to Christianity in AD313. From the 13th to the 16th century, Milan was ruled by dynastic families. Under the rule of the Viscontis, the city became powerful through marriage with other European royal houses, and under the Sforzas, art and culture flourished, enriching the city with some of its finest monuments. The late 16th century saw the start of 300 years of foreign rule by the French, Spanish and Austrians, an era when Milan developed into Italy's economic capital. The city was bombed extensively during World War II, and much of the city has been rebuilt since 1945.

PINACOTECA AMBROSIANA

➕ 244 B3 • Piazza Pio 2, 20123 Milano ☎ 02 80 6921 🕐 Tue–Sun 10–5.30 (last admittance 4.30) 💰 Adult €7.50, child (under 18) €4.50 www.ambrosiana.it

Cardinal Federico Borromeo founded this art gallery in the early 17th century. Highlights include Leonardo da Vinci's *Portrait of a Musician,* Raphael's cartoon for the *School of Athens* in the Vatican and Caravaggio's *Basket of Fruit*—purportedly Italy's first still life. The adjoining library also has exhibitions, and is Italy's oldest public library, founded in 1609.

MUSEO POLDI PEZZOLI

➕ 244 C2 • Via Alessandro Manzoni 12, 20123 Milano ☎ 02 794 889 🕐 Tue–Sun 10–6 💰 Adult €8, child (11–17) €5.50 🚇 Monte Napoleone

The museum has a fine collection of paintings, jewellery, clocks and *objets d'art*, bequeathed to the city by the 19th-century collector Gian Giacomo Poldi Pezzoli. There are some Renaissance pictures here, including Pollaiuolo's *Portrait of a Young Woman* and *San Nicola da Tolentino* by Piero della Francesca. The building itself contains many original features and is a good example of a late 19th-century aristocratic residence in Milan.

ITALY

WHAT TO DO

⊕ ARMANI
Via Manzoni 31
Tel 02 7231 8600
www.emporioarmani.it
This flagship Armani shop is a veritable fashion megastore. Children's clothes, lingerie, accessories, and the latest fashions are spread across eight floors.
⊕ Mon–Sat 10.30–7.30 ⊕ Monte Napoleone

⊕ LE SAC FACTORY OUTLET
Via Carnevale 13
Tel 02 376 0399
www.le-sac.it
You can find bargain bags, belts and purses (leather and snakeskin predominate) here. Many items come with chic labels, and prices range from €50 to €500—reasonable compared to some of the other big stores nearby.
⊕ Mon–Fri 9.30–2, 3.30–7.30; Sat–Sun 9.30–1, 2.30–7.30 ⊕ San Babila

⊕ LOUIS VUITTON
Via Monte Napoleone 2
Tel 02 777 1711
www.louisvuitton.com
Get your hands on the world's most distinctive luggage. Branded bags, purses and cases for the international jet set. The nearby branches of Bruno Magli and Samsonite are also useful if you need extra luggage space to take your shopping home.
⊕ Mon–Sat 10–7.30, Sun 11–7.30 ⊕ San Babila

⊕ MANDARINA DUCK
Galleria Passerella 2
Tel 02 782 2210
www.mandarinaduck.com
Mandarina Duck has two floors of funky, functional handbags and purses. The shop is close to Milan's central Piazza del Duomo, next door to the British Abbey National bank. Full sets of non-leather luggage start at around €350.
⊕ Tue–Sat 10–7.30, Mon 3–7 ⊕ Duomo

⊕ PRADA
Corso San Andrea 21
Tel 02 7600 1426
www.prada.it
The windows of this flagship store, near Via Monte Napoleone, are jam-packed—purses, bags and shoes beckon those with style and money. Immaculately turned-out staff are there to help you choose from Prada's reassuringly expensive range.
⊕ Daily 10–7.30 ⊕ San Babila

⊕ SISLEY
Via Dogana 4
Tel 02 86996191
www.sisley.com
This is very much a flagship fashion store for this smart-casual Italian label. In sight of the Duomo, Sisley's huge window displays and moderately priced clothes draw the shoppers in droves. Quality Italian shirts for men are around €40. T-shirts for women start from around €12. This branch also stocks Sisley's latest lingerie collection.
⊕ Mon–Sat 10–7.30, Sun 11–7 ⊕ Duomo

⊕ TEATRO ALLA SCALA
Piazza della Scala
Tel 02 861 827 (box office)
www.teatroallascala.org
Milan's most famous playhouse is the venue for a huge variety of classical music and operatic performances. As well as entertainment this stunningly beautiful theatre has an on-site bookshop, bar and history museum to explore. You can reserve tickets and find details of up-and-coming events on their website.
⊕ Most evenings from 8pm
⊕ €12–€170 ⊕ Monte Napoleone

⊕ ALCATRAZ
Via Valtellina 25
Tel 02 6901 6352
www.alcatrazmilano.com
This live music and disco venue is rock-oriented. One of the city's largest venues, it attracts more than 1,000 happy dancers on the weekend. It is frequented by the occasional famous face and the well dressed, so it's best to dress to impress, as with most Milanese clubs. It only really gets going after midnight.
⊕ Fri–Sat 11pm–4am ⊕ Women €6, men €10 (includes a drink) ⊕ Garibaldi

⊕ POGUE MAHONE'S
1 Via Salmini
Tel 02 5830 9726
www.poguemahones.it
Lots of Brits, Irish and Australians hang out at this friendly Irish pub. Watch football matches on the big-screen TV while enjoying a €5 pint of Guinness and a bacon sandwich. They occasionally have Irish music and dancing.
⊕ Mon 6pm–2am, Tue–Fri 10am–4pm, 6pm–2am, Sat 1pm–2am, Sun 10am–2am ⊕ Porta Romana

⊕ ROLLING STONE
Corso XXII Marzo 32
Tel 02 733172
www.rollingstone.it
Listen to live rock, punk, indie and jazz at this hangout near the Porta Vittorio rail station. It is very relaxed and there is no dress code. Listings are in Milan's free newspapers.
⊕ Fri–Sat 7.30pm–2am ⊕ Free entry unless a live band is playing ⊕ Porta Vittorio

⊕ TOCQUEVILLE 13
Via de Tocqueville 13
Tel 02 2900 2973
www.tocqueville13.it
This posh club is popular with footballers and you might spot a few famous faces. Thursday and Sunday are the big nights. Entry is easier on other nights. Pricey nibbles are available.
⊕ Wed–Sun 9pm–3am ⊕ €10–€15 ⊕ Garibaldi

⊕ AC MILAN AND INTER MILAN LIVE FOOTBALL
Via Piccolomini 5
Tel 02 404 2432
www.acmilan.com, www.inter.it
Catch one of Italy's most illustrious clubs, AC Milan or Inter Milan, at the San Siro stadium. Tickets for a match with either sell out fast, so buy your tickets in advance from their shop in Via Turati, from FNAC in Via Torino, online on their website or through TicketOne.
⊕ Sep–end Jun every other weekend ⊕ Tickets €20–€350 ⊕ Metro Lotto (free before matches)

⊕ ITALIAN GRAND PRIX
Parco di Monza, Monza
Tel 039 248 2212
www.monzanet.it

ITALY

The Italian Grand Prix at Monza is one of the highlights of the Formula 1 calendar. Phone for full details, or print a reservations form from the Monza website.

🗓 Mid-Sep 🎟 €35–€500 🚗 Monza is clearly signed 20km (12 miles) northeast of Milan

EATING

LE BICICLETTE
Via Torti angolo Corso Genova
Tel 02 8394177
www.lebiciclette.com

Housed in a former bicycle shop, this restaurant is decorated with modern paintings by emerging artists. Ultra-busy at aperitif time, when there is a giant buffet of pasta, sandwiches and tasty delights to accompany the €5 cocktails. The short menu includes artichoke salad, fish ravioli with black butter, and Argentinian steak.

🕐 Sun–Thur 8pm–2am, Fri–Sat 8pm–1am
🍴 L €21, D €30, Wine €11.50
🚇 Sant' Agosina
🚌 84

LA COZZERIA
Via Muratori 7
Tel 02 54107164

Gigantic portions at competitive prices are served at this seafood restaurant. The menu is almost entirely mussel-based—you'll find mussel soup, mussels with pepper, mussels with saffron, onions and cognac, and even curried mussels. This restaurant is quite small and the furniture is very simple, but it's certainly worth visiting.

🕐 Daily 6pm–11pm; closed Aug
🍴 D €30, Wine €10
🚇 Porta Romana

INNOCENTI EVASION 1
Via Privata della Bindellina 1
Tel 02 33001882
www.innocentievasioni.com

The beautifully presented nouvelle cuisine at this small restaurant is very affordable. Four seasonal fixed-price menus are available, including one based on truffles. The restaurant is tricky to find, as it is on a street that looks like a private road. It is advisable to make a reservation.

🕐 Tue–Sat 8pm–10pm; closed Aug
🍴 D €47, Wine €11

🌐
🚇 Certosa

JUST CAVALLI CAFÉ
Viale Camoens
Tel 02 311817
www.justcavallicafe.com

Fashion designer Roberto Cavalli owns this glitzy restaurant and his flamboyant modernist style is reflected in the interior and the menu. The menu concentrates on Italian ingredients served with a contemporary twist.

🕐 Daily 6.30pm–2am, Sun lunch from 12.30; closed Aug
🍴 L €50, D €70, Wine €14
🚇 Cadorna

OSTERIA DEL BINARI
Via Tortona 1
Tel 02 89406753

This restaurant serves fixed-price meals, which diners select from the à la carte menu. The cooking style is traditional but extremely elegant. The atmosphere is great, thanks to both the restaurant's rustic style and the beautiful garden. There is no parking for cars and no metro station nearby, so the best way to get here is by taxi.

🕐 Mon–Sat 7–11pm
🍴 D €48, Wine €13
🚇 Porta Genova

ZEN SUSHI
Via Maddalena 1
Tel 02 89013557
www.zenworld.it

Here at one of Milan's few sushi bars, you grab your rice, seaweed and raw fish as they revolve on a giant conveyor belt. The evening menu is à la carte only. This Italian-run Zen establishment is fun and friendly. Sake (rice wine) and Kirin beer are served, as well as some Italian wines.

🕐 Mon–Sat 12.30–3, 8–12; closed Aug
🍴 L €30, D €40, Wine €14
🚇 Missori

STAYING

BAVIERA
Via Castaldi 7, 20124 Milano
Tel 02 6590551
www.hotelbaviera.com

This comfortable and gracious hotel is within walking distance of Centrale rail station. The rooms have old-fashioned bedding; some rooms are larger than others, so ask for

the biggest possible.
🏨 €80–€315
🛏 50 🌐
🚇 Repubblica

BRISTOL
Via Scarlatti 32, 20124 Milano
Tel 02 6694141
www.hotelbristolmil.it

Exit Centrale rail station via the stairs and you'll find yourself at the front door of this classic, stylish hotel. There are modern amenities such as soundproofed rooms, direct-dial phones, in-room Jacuzzis and internet facilities. There is no restaurant, but the bar serves snacks and drinks until late at night.

🕐 Closed August
🏨 €200–€300
🛏 68 🌐
🚇 Centrale FS

CARLYLE BRERA HOTEL
Corso Garibaldi 84, 20121 Milano
Tel 02 29003888
www.carlylebrerahotel.com

The stylish Carlyle Brera is a cut above most business hotels. The Moscova metro station is a stone's throw from the front door. Bicycles are also available to guests, free of charge.

🏨 €300
🛏 94 rooms (2 suites) 🌐
🚇 Moscova

MICHAELANGELO
Via Scarlatti 33, 20124 Milano
Tel 02 67551
www.milanhotel.it

This elegant 4-star hotel offers hydrotherapy suites, opulent lounges and fine dining. The guest rooms are vast and most bathrooms have Jacuzzis.

🏨 €250–€350
🛏 300 rooms, 4 suites 🌐
🚇 Centrale FS

MINI HOTEL AOSTA
Piazza Duca d'Aosta 16, 20124 Milano
Tel 02 669 1951, numero verde (free in Italy) 800 719888
www.minihotel.it

Functional modern hotel right outside Milan's central train station. The rooms are soundproofed and simply furnished.

🏨 €180–€250
🛏 63 🌐
🚇 Centrale FS

Naples

A beautiful coastal setting for one of Italy's most vibrant cities.
The best place to experience southern Italian urban life.
A seemingly dilapidated city, packed with historical and artistic treasures.

A view over Naples from Castel San Elmo

A cart full of vegetables in the Porta Nolona market

Artichokes for sal

RATINGS

Good for kids	● ● ●
Historic interest	● ● ● ●
Shopping	● ● ●
Walkability	● ● ●

BASICS

➕ 5 E5

ℹ️ Piazza del Gesù Nuovo, 80134 Napoli, tel 081 551 2701; Mon–Sat 9–2

🚉 Napoli Centrale

www.inaples.it
A multilingual, comprehensive tourist authority site listing what's on in Naples.

TIPS

● Most areas are safe if you remain alert to petty crime—do not wear expensive jewels or carry much cash, and avoid back streets during the siesta or late at night.
● Traffic is chaotic and moves at a snail's pace, so use public transport and then walk.
● Opening times in general can be erratic, so be prepared to make more than one visit.

SEEING NAPLES

Naples is southern Italy's great city, pulsing with life, full of wonderful buildings and museums and flanked by an idyllic bay. Capital of the region of Campania, on Italy's west coast, it is two hours by fast train from Rome. The city is as famed for its citizens as its monuments, and there is nowhere else in Italy where you can find such a level of life lived on the streets. With more than a million inhabitants, Naples is a big, sprawling city, so be prepared to walk; the upshot will be some fascinating discoveries and fabulous views.

HIGHLIGHTS

SPACCANAPOLI

➕ 249 B1 • Via Capitelli, Piazza del Gesù Nuovo, Via Benedetto Croce, Via San Biagio dei Librai

The grid plan of streets that makes up the *centro storico* was the core of ancient Neapolis, and its three main streets—the ancient *decumani*—still slice relentlessly through the oldest part of the city. Spaccanapoli is one of these *decumani*; its name means 'split Naples' and it crosses the heart of the old city, a thoroughfare teeming with people and lined with churches, palazzi and idiosyncratic shops selling everything from books and musical instruments to religious objects and woodcarvings.

Spaccanapoli is made up of a string of streets, now mainly pedestrianized, from Piazza del Gesù Nuovo to Via Viccaria Vecchia. The heart of the university district, it has plenty of bars and restaurants, including Scaturchio, one of Naples' oldest and best *pasticcerie*. Along its length, highlights include the rococo obelisk, the Guglia dell'Immacolata in Piazza del Gesù, the Church and Convent of Santa Chiara (▷ 249), Piazza San Domenico with its obelisk and 13th-century castellated church, and some fine Renaissance palaces.

MUSEO ARCHEOLOGICO NAZIONALE

➕ 249 B1 • Piazza Museo 19, 80135 Napoli ☎ 081 211 0258 🕐 Wed–Mon 9–7.30 💶 €6.50, under 18s free

The Museo Archeologico Nazionale houses one of the world's most important collections of classical Roman sculpture, mosaics, gems,

ITALY

wall paintings, glass and silver, much of it plundered from the excavations around and to the south of Naples. The museum is badly labelled and confusingly laid out, with whole sections often closed, but it is nevertheless outstanding, and the exhibits do much to enhance visits to Pompei and Ercolano.

The ground floor is devoted to sculpture, much of it from the 17th-century Farnese collections, which were largely discovered in Rome. Highlights are the muscular *Farnese Hercules* and the *Farnese Bull* (200BC), the largest surviving classical sculptural group. There is a wonderfully vivid mosaic collection and the Gabinetto Segreto (Secret Chamber), a collection of Roman erotica from Pompei, which ranges from sensual wall paintings to phallic charms. Upstairs, rooms are filled with more finds from Pompei and Ercolano, including a naturalistic wall painting of a graceful Flora scattering spring flowers, and a *cave canem* (Beware of the Dog) mosaic from the entrance to a house in Pompei.

CERTOSA DI SAN MARTINO

✚ 249 A2 • Largo San Martino 5, 80129 Napoli ☎ 081 558 6408 ◷ Thu–Tue 8.30–7.30 ▣ €6, under 18s free

The huge hilltop Carthusian complex of the Certosa di San Martino was founded in 1325, but what you see today dates mainly from the 16th to 18th centuries. The baroque church is crammed with the best of Neapolitan painting and sculpture, and there are more riches in the choir, sacristy and treasury. Explore the expertly restored, arcaded 16th-century Chiostro Grande, the lavishly decorated Quarto del Priore and the Pinacoteca in rooms set around the cloister with views over the city and the bay. Don't miss the exhibition of *presepe*—people and animals fashioned for 18th-century Christmas cribs. The Certosa is surrounded by terraced gardens, with sweeping views.

MORE TO SEE

DUOMO DI NAPOLI

✚ 249 B1 • Via Duomo 147, 80138 Naples ☎ 081 449097 ◷ Duomo: Mon–Sat 9–12, 4.30–7, Sun 9–12. Cappella di San Gennaro: Sat 10–7 ▣ €3

A 13th-century Gothic cathedral dedicated to San Gennaro, patron saint of Naples; the first chapel on the right contains two phials of his blood, said to liquefy three times a year. Also part of the complex are the fourth-century Basilica Santa Restituta (the oldest church in Naples), a baptistery and Renaissance crypt.

PALAZZO REALE

✚ 249 B3 • Piazza del Plebiscito 1 ☎ 081 400547 ◷ Thu–Tue 9.30–7 ▣ €7.50

The 17th-century palace of the Spanish viceroys of Naples was extended in the 18th century by the Bourbons and altered in the 19th century by the French. It houses the historic Biblioteca Nazionale (National Library) and a series of grandiose state rooms.

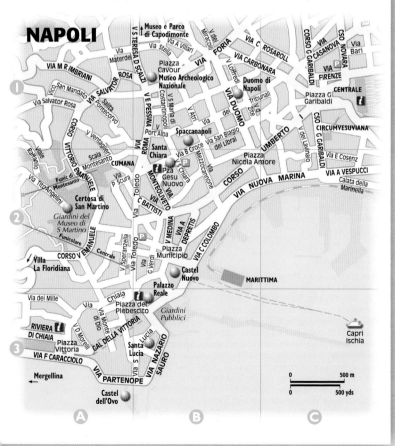

ITALY

SANTA CHIARA

✚ 249 B2 • Via Benedetto Croce/Via Santa Chiara 49, 80134 Napoli ☎ 081 552 6209 ⏰ Daily 7.30–1, 4–8

Santa Chiara is Naples' great Franciscan church, a simple and austere 14th-century Gothic conventual complex. Founded by King Robert of Anjou for his wife, Sancia, in 1310, it became a focal point for Naples' Angevin rulers, several of whom are buried here. The original church, greatly altered over the centuries, was catastrophically bombed in 1943. Rebuilding started almost at once, using whatever could be salvaged, and the church, restored to its original Gothic appearance, re-opened in 1953. Three Angevin royal tombs survive: that of Robert himself and those of his son, Carlo and daughter-in-law, Mary of Valois.

Behind the church is the 14th-century cloister, remodelled by Domenico Vaccaro in 1742. He decorated the central garden with

CASTEL NUOVO

✚ 249 B2 • Piazza Municipio, 80133 Napoli ☎ 081 749 9111 ⏰ Mon–Sat 9–7 🎫 Adult €5

A huge castle erected in 1282 by the Angevins, converted into a royal residence by the Aragonese; now accommodates the council offices and the Museo Civico.

MERGELLINA

✚ 249 off A3

The waterfront area and ferry port, with its attractive harbour

72 octagonal pillars, interspersed with benches, each of which is covered with hand-painted majolica tiles. The church's Museo dell'Opera (Thu–Tue 9–1, 4–6) lies off the cloister, also providing access to a fascinating Christmas crib scene, complete with street life, flying angels and a variety of people and animals.

MUSEO E PARCO DI CAPODIMONTE

✚ 249 off B1 • Via Miano 1, 80132 Napoli ☎ 081 749 9111 ⏰ Thu–Tue 8.30–7.30 🎫 €7.50, under 18s free

Built in 1738 as King Charles III's hunting lodge, and surrounded by a wooded park, the Palace of Capodimonte houses one of Italy's richest museums. The bulk of the collection is made up of works acquired by Charles from his mother, Elizabeth Farnese. You can wander freely through the opulent royal apartments on your way to the majolica and porcelain collection, much of it made by the Neapolitan Capodimonte factory and painted with local scenes. Upstairs is a picture gallery, a collection amassed by the Farnese and Bourbon rulers and spanning the 15th to 17th centuries, with the emphasis on Renaissance painting. Botticelli, Perugino and Pinturicchio are all represented, but it is the High Renaissance works that shine, particularly the portraits by Titian, Raphael and Sebastiano del Piombo. Leave time to wander through the shady avenues of the surrounding park.

BACKGROUND

Greek settlers founded Neapolis in 750BC, and the city prospered under both Greek and Roman rule before declaring itself independent in 763. The Normans took the city in 1139, and were soon followed by the Hohenstaufens, German rulers who held on until the Angevins took over in 1269. The Spanish moved in next in 1422 and remained in control for over 300 years. Bourbon and French rule followed before Naples became part of united Italy.

The city has a long history of foreign rule and neglect by government. Despite money pouring into the south under the Mezzogiorno scheme in the mid-20th century, unemployment and social deprivation remain common, but the late 1990s, when Antonio Bassolino was mayor, saw a burgeoning civic pride and a burst of creative activity.

and spread of chalets, ramshackle bars and ice-cream parlours; a popular place for a seafood meal.

CASTEL DELL'OVO AND SANTA LUCIA

✚ 249 A3 and B3 • Borgo Marinari, 80132 Napoli ☎ 081 240 0055 ⏰ Mon–Sat 8–6, Sun 8–2 🎫 Free

The oldest castle in Naples (ninth century) attained its present form in 1503. Restored in the 1970s after centuries of decline, it is now used for exhibitions and concerts. There are some excellent fish restaurants around the Santa Lucia district, close to the city's harbour.

VILLA LA FLORIDIANA

✚ 249 off A2 • Via Cimarosa 77, Napoli ☎ 081 578 8418 ⏰ Mon–Sat 9 until 1 hour before sunset

A beautiful villa and park in the Vomero district, once the home of the Duchess of Floridia, morganatic wife of Ferdinand I. It now houses the Museo Nazionale della Ceramica, the porcelain museum (Tue–Sun 9.30–11), with a superb Limoges and Meissen collection.

Vespas are a common sight, zipping around the streets of Naples (above left)

The Capodimonte Gardens (above right)

WHAT TO DO

⊕ IL CANTUCCIO DELLA CERAMICA
Via Benedetto Croce 38
Tel 081 5525857
You'll find this ceramics studio down a small street between Piazza del Gesù Nuovo and Piazza San Domenico Maggiore. Ceramics in a multitude of hues are for sale, but you can also take classes here and make your own.
🕐 Mon–Fri 10–6 🚇 Piazza Cavour

⊕ ENOTECA PARTENOPEA
Viale Augusto 2
Tel 081 593 7982
Don't leave Naples without tasting some of the region's fine wines. The rich volcanic soil gives the wine a remarkable richness; ask the staff for an introduction to the region's offerings and grab a few bargain bottles to take home.
🕐 Fri–Wed 9–1.30, 4.30–7.30, Thu 9–1.30 🚇 Campi Flegrei

⊕ MARINELLA
Riviera di Chiaia 287
Tel 081 764 4214
www.marinellanapoli.it
If formal style is what you're after, then Marinella should be right up your street. This well-respected Neapolitan haunt has been patronized by the likes of Kennedy, Gorbachev and Caruso. The shop is famed for made-to-measure ties in silk, wool and other fabrics.
🕐 Mon–Sat 9.30–1.30, 3.30–8 🚇 Piazza Amedeo 🚌 102, 108, 122

🎭 GRAN CAFFÈ GAMBRINUS
Via Chiaia 1 & 2
Tel 081 417582
www.caffegambrinus.com/ing/home.htm
Sit out in Piazza Trieste e Trento or inside in the beautiful old-fashioned tea room of this Naples institution for a cocktail or to enjoy a pot of tea and exquisite Neapolitan cakes.
🕐 Daily 8.30am–9pm

🎭 MURAT LIVE CLUB
Via Bellini 8
Tel 081 544 5919
This club on Piazza Dante has an adventurous music policy—the eclectic schedule includes lots of jazz and funk, all imbued with a touch of Neapolitan style.
🕐 Daily 10pm–late 🚇 Montesanto 🚌 137, 160, 161

🎭 TEATRO SAN CARLO
Via San Carlo 98F
Tel 081 797330
www.teatrosancarlo.it
The oldest opera house in Italy stages ballet as well as opera, classical concerts and short comic operas. Reserve tickets in advance.
🕐 Box office: Tue–Sun 10–1, 4.30–6.30 💶 €25–€120 🚌 C4, 140, 149

😊 EDENLANDIA
Viale Kennedy, Campi Flegrei
Tel 081 239 4090
www.edenlandia.it
This theme park is just a short train ride away from the city. There are lots of attractions for all ages, including a fantasy castle, a 3-D cinema, variety shows, water rides and the exciting Star Wars ride.
🕐 Jun–end Aug Mon–Fri 5pm–midnight, Sat 10am–midnight; rest of year most weekends 10am–midnight, hours vary 💶 Entrance €2.50 plus fee for individual rides or €10 with reduced rates for rides 🚌 152 🚋 Cumana train to Campi Flegrei

EATING

DORA
Via Ferdinando Palasciano 30
Tel 081 680519
Traditional fish dishes make up the bulk of the impressive menu here. Well worth trying is the famous *pasta alla Dora* (pasta with a tomato sauce and shellfish), and the menu also offers a choice of grilled and baked fish dishes.
🕐 Mon–Sat 12–3, 8pm–midnight 💶 L €55, D €100, Wine €15 🚇 Piazza Amedio 🚌 C18, 1, 150

EXCELSIOR
Via Partenope 48
Tel 081 7640111
www.excelsior.it
The Hotel Excelsior's restaurant, La Terrazza, is hard to beat, with its stunning views, exquisite food and luxurious touches. The wine list has been compiled by a professional sommelier. There are some inventive pasta creations and a superb mixed grill garnished with mussels.
🕐 Mon–Sat 12.30–3, 8–11pm 💶 L €70, D €100, Wine €18 💲 🚌 C52, E5, 140, 152

STAYING

GRAND HOTEL EUROPA
Corso Meridionale 14, 80143 Napoli
Tel 081 267511;
booking line 081 551 8691
www.sea-hotels.com
A convenient location and decent service make this a good bet for accommodation near the *centro storico*. Most of the soundproofed rooms have cheerful paintings hung on whitewashed walls. Facilities include television, phone, safe, hair-dryer and minibar. There is an adjoining restaurant, La Grande Abbuffata.
💶 €78–€180 🛏 80 💲 🚇 Piazza Garibaldi, Napoli Centrale 🚌 ALIBUS to Piazza Garibaldi

GRAND HOTEL VESUVIO
Via Partenope 45, 80121 Napoli
Tel 081 7640044
www.vesuvio.it
Many notable figures such as Grace Kelly and tenor Enrico Caruso have passed through the doors of the Grand Hôtel Vesuvio since it opened in 1882. Public rooms and guest rooms are filled with antiques and exquisite fabrics. Dine in style at Caruso, the rooftop restaurant, or take advantage of the fitness, health and beauty facilities.
💶 €420–€430, suites €700–€1900 🛏 163 rooms, 16 suites 💲 🏊 🚌 C52, E5, 140, 152

MIRAMARE
Via Nazario Sauro 24, 80132 Napoli
Tel 081 7647589
www.hotelmiramare.com
The American consulate in the 1950s, this beautiful building has been transformed into an attractive hotel. The bedrooms come with all modern comforts.
💶 €228–€340 🛏 31 💲 🚌 152

Rome

✚ 5 D4 ℹ Visitor Centre, Via Parigi 5, tel 06 488991; Mon–Sat 9–7
www.romaturismo.com • Excellent, informative English-language website

HOW TO GET THERE

✈ Airports

Roma Fiumicino, the main international airport 32km (20 miles) from the city with fast train links to Termini station

Ciampino, a smaller airport, located 15km (10 miles) southeast of the city, used by budget airlines, charters and internal flights. Connected to the Rome metro system and regular bus services into the city centre

🚆 Railway stations

Termini station is the main rail terminal, centrally located, served by international trains from all over Europe and routes to all Italy's main cities. Rome also has numerous suburban stations and an efficient metro (subway) train network

TIPS

• For a change from admiring ancient architecture, take a look at Renzo Piano's ultra-modern concert hall complex, the Auditorium, also known as Parco della Musica.

• Queuing for train tickets at Termini station can be time-consuming. It's quicker and easier to use self-service machines in the station concourse. You can select English-language touch screens to buy tickets and reserve seats.

• Go early in the morning to visit St. Peter's Basilica and the Vatican Museums, and avoid carrying big bags. The queues and security checks can take up a lot of your sightseeing time if you go later in the day.

• Take time to escape the city centre and visit Rome's seaside. There are regular trains from Termini to Ostia, which has modern beaches, and you can visit the remains of the ancient Roman port at Ostia Antica.

SEEING ROME

Rome is a city of 3,000 years of living history. Monuments, museums, galleries and ancient churches make it a treasure house of art, architecture and culture. At the same time it is a thriving modern capital city with a social life that positively buzzes. Rome is a patchwork of ancient, medieval and modern sights, and just as it was not built in a day, you need more than a day to explore it fully. The Forum and Colosseo (Colosseum) occupy sites of prime real estate in the historic centre *(centro storico)*, and the Vatican, dominated by St. Peter's Square, the Basilica and the Vatican Museums, is one of Rome's main attractions both as a piece of history and as the administrative centre of the modern Catholic Church. Former aristocratic villas are much in use today as offices, museums and galleries. For example, the Quirinale, once a papal residence, is now the Palace of the President of the Republic and also a concert venue. Monumental squares such as Piazza di Spagna, Piazza Navona and Piazza Venezia are places to take a break amid fabulous architecture and stylish coffee bars and restaurants. Rome is also renowned for its public fountains. Many of Rome's attractions can be seen on foot, but to get around quickly there is an efficient and inexpensive metro system and an extensive network of bus routes.

BACKGROUND

Tribes had colonized the seven hills of Rome as early as 1000BC, and Julius Caesar took control around 49BC, creating a hub of learning and civilization from which the Roman Empire grew throughout Europe and north Africa. In the Middle Ages the city was dominated by the popes, who were not only spiritual leaders but temporal lords of vast tracts of territory. It was the wealth of the Church and the artistic aspirations of successive popes that were the driving force behind Rome's artistic and architectural heritage. The city became the capital of Italy only relatively recently, with the Unification of the country in 1870. Italy was but a collection of autonomous city-states, kingdoms and the remnants of the Holy Roman Empire, until Napoleon intervened and took over the Papal States and Garibaldi occupied Rome. The Pope was confined to the Vatican, which today is recognized internationally as an independent sovereign state marooned like an island surrounded by the swirl and bustle of modern Rome. In spite of political upheavals, Rome has bloomed as a wealthy capital city amid relics of its rich and glorious past.

DON'T MISS

ST. PETER'S BASILICA AND VATICAN MUSEUMS
Admire the Colonnade in St. Peter's Square and the magnificent works of art in the Basilica and the Sistine Chapel (▷ 258–259, 265–267)

COLOSSEUM
The most famous Roman amphitheatre and site of gladiatorial contests and other imperial entertainment (▷ 260–261)

FONTANA DI TREVI
Decorated with gloriously over-the-top sculpture and set in a central square that has become a popular meeting place (▷ 253)

QUIRINALE HILL
One of the best viewpoints from which to look over the city

PIAZZA DI SPAGNA
Location of the famous Spanish Steps

VIA CONDOTTI
A shopper's paradise if you have the money for buying Prada, Gucci, Bulgari, Louis Vuitton, Cartier and the rest

ITALY

The Fontana di Trevi is even more charismatic at night

A giant foot in the Palazzo dei Conservatori at the Musei Capitolini

ARCO DI COSTANTINO

255 F5 • Piazza del Colosseo, Roma
Colosseo Tram 3, 117

Rome's best-preserved and largest Roman arch, the Arco di Costantino stands proudly alongside the old Roman triumphal way. Highly decorated and nearly 25m (82ft) high, it was built by the Senate and people of Rome in AD315 to commemorate Emperor Constantine's victory over the tyrant Maxentius, after which he granted freedom of worship to the Christians. An inscription on each side celebrates his coming to power, and scenes show combat against the Dacians and the triumphs of Constantine and his son. When first carved, the bas-reliefs between the statues of the four Dacian prisoners showed episodes in the life of Marcus Aurelius, but his features were later altered to resemble those of Constantine.

CASTEL SANT'ANGELO

254 C3 • Lungotevere del Castello 50, 00120 Roma 06 681 9111
Tue–Sun 9–7.30. Prison: Sun by guided tour Adult €7, under 18s free Ottaviano–San Pietro

Mausoleum, fortress and papal stronghold, this imposing ancient monument is now home to the Museo Nazionale's collection of ceramics, weapons, furnishings and Renaissance paintings. The frescoes in the papal apartments are not to be missed. As you approach over the Ponte Sant'Angelo, pause to enjoy the view of the Tiber and San Pietro. Commissioned in AD135 by Hadrian to be the resting place for himself and his family, the castle remained a mausoleum until Caracalla's death in AD217. Aurelian later converted it into a fortress.

Legend has it that when Rome was struck by the plague in 590 Pope Gregory the Great organized a procession to pray for the city. As the people approached the mausoleum, the statue of the Archangel Michael rose into the air holding aloft a flaming sword, signalling the end of the plague. From then on it was called Castel Sant'Angelo. In the ninth century, Leo IV linked it to the Vatican with a high defensive wall topped by the Passetto, a covered walkway. Castel Sant'Angelo has also served as a prison.

FONTANA DI TREVI

255 E3 • Piazza Trevi, 00187 Roma
Barberini

Immortalized in Federico Fellini's 1960 film *La Dolce Vita*, this is the most photographed fountain in Rome, and has stood here, at the junction of three roads (*tre vie*), since 1762.

In the middle, Neptune rides a shell-shaped chariot drawn by seahorses steered by giant tritons. Behind is a baroque façade with statues of Plenty, Health and the Four Seasons. In 19BC, General Agrippa built a 19km (12-mile) aqueduct to bring water to the baths near the Pantheon (▷ 268). The story is told in bas-reliefs: On the right a young girl leads Agrippa's soldiers to a spring; on the left he approves plans for the aqueduct. Today the water, called Acqua Virgo, runs underground in one of the few Roman canals still in use.

Toss two coins over your shoulder into the fountain, make a wish and, it is said, you will return to Rome and your wish will come true.

IL GESÙ

255 E4 • Piazza del Gesù/Via degli Astalli 16, 00186 Roma 06 697001
Daily 7–12.30, 4–7.45 Tram 8

For fans of the baroque, the highlight of this church, dedicated to the Holy Name of Jesus and completed in 1584, is the chapel of St. Ignatius of Loyola. He lived, died and founded his Jesuit order here, and this chapel is the work of the architect Andrea Pozzo.

MUSEI CAPITOLINI

255 E4 • Piazza del Campidoglio, 00186 Roma 06 8205 9127
Tue–Sun 9–8 (last admittance 7)
Adult €6.50, under 18s free
Colosseo
www.museicapitolini.org

The Palazzo dei Conservatori and the Palazzo Nuovo make up the Musei Capitolini, home to one of Rome's richest collection of sculptures, mosaics, frescoes and paintings. In 1450 the Palazzo dei Conservatori became the world's first public museum when it began to show bronze statues given to the Romans by Pope Sixtus IV. The collection was greatly expanded during the latter part of the 16th century when Pope Pius V cleared the Vatican of what the Catholic Church viewed as pagan works. Much of the monumental statuary carved in ancient times was deemed unsuitable to remain and was donated to the secular authorities of Rome, who moved it to the Capitolini.

In the courtyard are fragments of a colossal statue of Constantine. Inside, highlights include the delightful *Spinario*, a first-century Greek bronze of a boy extracting a thorn from his foot, and the famous sixth-century Etruscan bronze of the Capitoline Wolf. The art gallery has a collection of 16th- and 18th-century paintings. The Palazzo Nuovo has more excellent pieces, including carved sarcophagi and the headless *Capitoline Venus*.

ITALY

ROMA

0   250 m
0   250 yds

TRIONFALE

S Giusep

Musei

Musei

S Maria
d Grazie

CITTÀ DEL
VATICANO

Musei
Gregoriano
Etrusco

Musei
Vaticani

Casino di
Poi IV

Giardini
Vaticani

Governatorato

Cappella
Sistina

Basilica di
San Pietro

Piazza
San Pietro

Palazzo
Torlonia

S Maria
in Traspon

Palazzo dei
Penitenzieri

Sagrestia

VATICANO

Ospizio di
Santa Marta

Aula della
Udienze

S Spirito
in Sassia

Caste
Sant'Angelo

VIA AURELIA

VIA AURELIA

VIA DI PORTA CAVALLEGGERI

CALL PRINCIPE
AMEDEO SAVOIA AOSTA

San Gio
dei Fior

Campi
Cottolengo
Sportivi

Palazzo
Salviati

Sforz

VIA GREGORIO VII

Monte
del Gallo

ROMA
SAN PIETRO

Palaz
Corsi

AURELIO

Gianicolo

Orto
Botanico

Monti della Creta

Villa
Floridi

Villa
Abamelek

San Pietr
in Montori
CARIBA

VIA   AURELIA   ANTICA

VIA   AURELIA   ANTICA

Villa
Doria Pamphilj

ITALY

A   B   C

ITALY

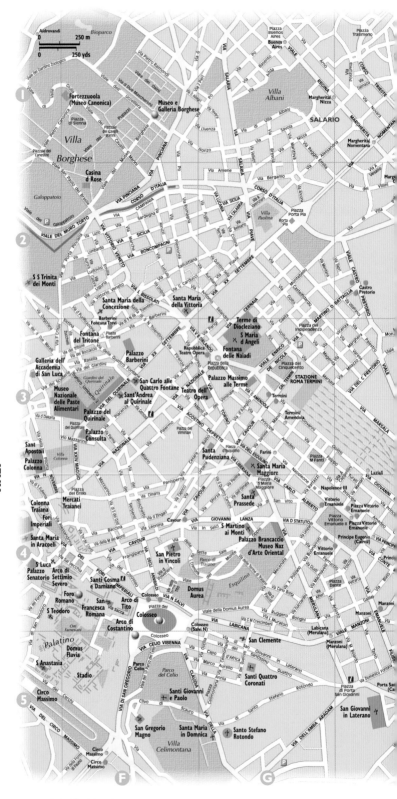

Campo dei Fiori market stalls

Basilica di San Pietro

Protestant Cemetery

Basilica di San Pietro

The most famous church in Christendom.
The spiritual capital of the Roman Catholic faith and the focus of Vatican City.
Testament to the genius of Michelangelo, architect and sculptor.

A bird's-eye view of Piazza San Pietro and Bernini's colonnade

RATINGS	
Historic interest	● ● ● ○
Cultural interest	● ● ● ● ●
Photo stops	● ● ● ● ●

Looking towards the basilica from Piazza San Pietro (below)

SEEING SAN PIETRO

It is the monumental scale of the Basilica di San Pietro (St. Peter's), the largest Roman Catholic building in the world, that is mesmerizing. The proportions are huge—it is 218m (715ft) long, 137m (450ft) high, and covers a total of 22,067sq m (237,535sq ft). It can accommodate 60,000 people. With 778 columns, 44 altars, 135 mosaics and 395 statues, the interior is overwhelming. Concentrate on the highlights: the view of and from Michelangelo's soaring dome, one of his earliest and most moving sculptures, and Bernini's contributions to the interior.

HIGHLIGHTS

THE PORTICO

The approach to the basilica is impressively grand, through the embrace of Bernini's colonnade (284 columns and 140 statues). The obelisk in the middle of the square was brought here by Caligula from Alexandria in Egypt. As you reach Bernini's broad staircase, note the central balcony above the portico, the Loggia delle Benedizioni, where the Pope stands to bless the people gathered in the square below. Inside the portico, the last bronze door on the right is the Holy Door, opened only every 25 years, in a Holy Year (the last was 2000). Over the central door is what remains of Giotto's *Navicella* mosaic (1298).

MICHELANGELO'S LA PIETÀ

The most famous of all the statues in San Pietro, now protected by bulletproof glass, is in the first chapel in the south aisle. Michelangelo's *Pietà* was begun in 1498, when he was 24 years old. It is his only signed work; he engraved his name on a band across the Virgin's breast, and an M inside her right hand. Look up to see his other contribution to the building, the vast dome, covered in mosaics.

BERNINI'S SCULPTURES

Directly under Michelangelo's dome is Bernini's *baldacchino*, an amazing bronze canopy 29m (50ft) high. Its twisted columns are decorated with golden olive and laurel branches and bees, the emblem of the Barberini, the family from which Pope Urban VIII came. It stands over the Altar of the Confession, where only the Pope may celebrate Mass.

Beneath this is St. Peter's tomb, lit by 99 lamps, and to the right sits a statue of St. Peter (attributed to Arnolfo di Cambio from the late 1220s), his right foot worn by the touch of pilgrims. Behind the *baldacchino*, in the end apse, are Bernini's baroque monument to Pope Urban VIII and his extraordinary *cattedra*, which encases a chair that was supposedly used by St. Peter.

ITALY

The rooftop statues and the dome (far left)

The bronze canopy over the altar inside (left)

Michelangelo's Pietà *(1498–99) in the Cappella della Pietà (bottom)*

Nuns ascend the wide flight of steps up to the basilica (above)

At the top of the north aisle, past the Cappella della Colonna—dedicated to St. Leo, who persuaded Attila the Hun to spare Rome—is a chapel containing the monument to Alexander VII, by Bernini, portraying Death as a skeleton. Past many more papal monuments, and almost back at the portico, is the baptistery. The basin is made from an ancient porphyry sarcophagus taken from the tomb of Hadrian.

THE GROTTOES AND THE DOME

Under one of the dome's great supporting pillars is the entrance to the Vatican grottoes, which are lined with tombs of emperors and popes. To climb the dome, take the elevator to the cupola and terrace, then climb the 330 steps for a closer look at the mosaics. The final ascent, via a spiral staircase, takes you to the top of the lantern, from where you can marvel at the panoramic views of Rome.

BACKGROUND

It was here, in about AD67, that Nero had the Apostle Peter crucified, and it was over his tomb that Constantine built the first basilica, in 324. By 1452 it had started to crumble and Nicholas V began restoring it. In 1547, Pope Paul III appointed Michelangelo to control the project. Michelangelo refused all payment, insisting that he work for the glory of God. He began rebuilding the church in the form of a Greek cross. Then, in 1606, Pope Paul V decided to make some alterations. He chose a Latin cruciform, and employed Carlo Maderno to extend the complex, making a nave and a new portico, while Bernini transformed the interior with baroque touches. San Pietro was finally consecrated in 1626.

BASICS

✚ 254 B3 • Piazza San Pietro, 00120 Roma

☎ Vatican switchboard 06 6982

🕐 Basilica: Apr–end Sep daily 7–7; Oct–end Mar daily 7–6. Cupola: Apr–end Sep daily 8–6; Oct–end Mar daily 8–5 (1 hour before closing, access by elevator only). Museo del Tesoro: Apr–end Sep daily 9–6.30; Oct–end Mar daily 9–5.30. Grottoes: Apr–end Sep daily 9–5; Oct–end Mar daily 8–5. Necropoli: Mon–Sat 9–3.30. Visits must be requested 2 weeks in advance in writing to Officio Scavi di San Pietro, tel 06 6988 5318, fax 06 6987 3017. Basilica closed during papal celebrations

🎫 Basilica: free. Dome: from €7. Museo del Tesoro: €6. Grottoes: free. Necropolis: €10. Free tickets for papal ceremony at main entrance

Ⓜ Ottaviano–San Pietro

🚌 Tours: Groups with reservation. No private tours before 10.30am (tel 06 6988 4466)

📖 €5

🚊 Via della Conciliazione, Borgo Pio

♿ 🚻 With disabled access

www.vatican.va

ITALY

Colosseo

The largest monument of imperial Rome in existence, an amphitheatre where gladiators fought to the death with wild beasts.
Rome's number one landmark and symbol of classical times.
Superbly designed sports arena that is the model for modern stadia.

Archways inside the Colosseo | The Colosseo, illuminated, viewed from Via dei Fori Imperiali | The four levels of the Colosseo

RATINGS	
Good for kids	● ● ● ○
Historic interest	● ● ● ●
Cultural interest	● ● ● ○
Photo stops	● ● ● ●

TIPS

● Buy your entrance ticket at the Palatine, as there is often a very long wait at the Colosseo.
● If you want a clearer idea of what the interior of the stadium was like, take a guided tour. The service provided by the Italian Sovrintendenza dei Beni Culturali is very good.

SEEING THE COLOSSEO

The Colosseo (Colosseum) stands just to the east of the Foro Romano, encircled by the Caelian, Palatine and Esquiline hills. The best approach is from Via dei Fori Imperiali, where you'll get a good sense of its scale and size. Walk around the outside before tackling the damaged and confusing interior. Take a guided tour or rent an audioguide to help you visualize the arena's past glory.

HIGHLIGHTS

THE EXTERIOR

The elliptical structure covers about 2.4ha (6 acres), and enough survives of the exterior to give a good idea of its original appearance, though the marble facings, painted stucco and statues have all gone. Externally, the Colosseo measures 188m by 156m (617ft by 512ft) and rises to 48m (159ft), with a façade of three tiers of arches and an attic. The tiers are faced with three-quarter Doric, Ionic and Corinthian columns, and the attic has square window openings. At the top were 240 brackets and sockets that anchored the *velarium*, a shade and bad-weather canopy that could be pulled across the interior. The holes you see on the walls once held the metal clamps that pinned the massive blocks together; they were pillaged, together with tons of stone, for later building.

THE ARCADES AND SEATING

Inside, arcades run right around the outer edge of the building on each level, linking the stairways that connect the different floors. Passages from the arcades accessed, via 80 doorways, the tiers of marble benches, some still complete. The spectators were arranged by rank, with humble citizens and women at the top, a special box, closest to

The Colosseo is the largest surviving structure of the Roman Empire

the action, naturally, for the emperor, and ringside seats for the senators and Vestal Virgins. The tickets, which were wooden plaques, carved with the entrance numbers, are still visible above the exterior arches. The system was very efficient, and the organizers could move up to 70,000 people in or out in a matter of minutes.

THE ARENA

The middle of the Colosseo is a jumble of ruins, all that's left of the labyrinthine passages beneath the arena itself. In Roman times, this area had wooden flooring covered with canvas and sand—the word 'arena' comes from the Latin word for sand. The four principal entrances were used by the gladiators, stagehands and corpse removers. Far more dramatic entrances were made through trapdoors in the floor—you can still see their outlines. These opened into the passages and lifts from where men and wild animals emerged—tens of thousands of animals, sent to Rome from all over the Empire, were slaughtered at the Colosseo. Other passages were water conduits, and the arena was regularly flooded for water battles.

Gladiatorial games began in the morning with an elaborate procession, the prelude to staged hunts when wild animals were pitted against each other or pursued by *bestiarii*, gladiators specializing in animal slaughter. The lunch break was accompanied by executions, a taster for the day's climax—the individual gladiatorial combats.

BACKGROUND

Known since the eighth century as the Colosseo, the arena was built by the three Flavian emperors, Vespasian, Titus and Domitian. Construction started in AD72, and the inaugural games were held in AD80. It was the first permanent amphitheatre built in Rome, brilliantly combining grandiose design with practicality. Games and fights were held here right up to the end of the Empire in the sixth century. During the Middle Ages the Colosseo was used as a fortress, and from the 15th century as a source of building materials for some of Rome's finest palazzi. By the late 1700s the crumbling structure was a romantic and overgrown ruin, and since 1750 it has been dedicated to the Christians killed in its arena. Conservation began in the 19th century and is ongoing.

BASICS

⊞ 256 F4 • Piazza del Colosseo, 00184 Roma

☎ 06 396 7700

🕐 Daily 9am–1 hour before sunset

💶 Adult €12.50, under 18s free. Timed tickets: Palatine and Colosseum valid 24 hours. Roma Archaeologia Card valid 7 days for Colosseum, Palatine, Baths of Caracalla, Palazzo Altemps, Palazzo Massimo, Baths of Diocletian, Crypta Balbi, Tomb of Cecilia Metella and Villa dei Quintili, €20

🚇 Colosseo (line B)

🚊 Tram 3, 8

🎧 Tours €16: Apr–end Oct daily on the hour 9–5; Nov–end Mar daily on the hour 9–3. Audiotours €4

📘 Official guide published by the Sovrintendenza dei Beni Culturali

🏛

🚻 Outside on south side (open until 6pm) and inside the Colosseum.

www.archeorm.arti.beniculturali.it
An Italian website bringing together the key archaeological sites in Rome, with photos, site maps and information on the Colosseo, the Domus Aurea, the Museo Nazionale Romano, the Terme di Caracalla, the Mausoleo di Cecilia Metella and the Villa dei Quintili.

www.ticketclic.it

ITALY

Foro Romano

The political, commercial, economic and religious focal point of Republican Rome.
One of the city's most important archaeological sites, with many famous monuments spanning more than 900 years.

The broad Via Sacra links two triumphal arches

A section of the right aisle of the ruins of the formerly lavish Basilica di Massenzio (AD308)

RATINGS	
Historic interest	●●●●
Cultural interest	●●●●●
Photo stops	●●●
Walkability	●●●●

TIPS

● The Forum can be confusing, so before you enter, get an overview of the general layout from Via del Campidoglio, the northern side of Piazza del Campidoglio or the Orti Farnesiani gardens.
● Take something to drink, as there are no bars or cafés in the immediate area.

Detail of the Arco di Settimio Severo

SEEING THE FORO ROMANO

The Roman Forum was the hub of daily life in the days of ancient Rome, and its ruins lie in what is still the heart of the city, between the Colosseum and Piazza Campidoglio and the great Victor Emmanuel monument. There are several points of entry, but the main entrance, and the best one, is from Via dei Fori Imperiali. This leads immediately onto Via Sacra, the most ancient road, which runs through the heart of the Roman Forum, linking two triumphal arches, the Arco di Settimio Severo and the Arco di Tito. The most important sights lie between these arches. At first the Forum seems nothing more than a jumbled collection of ruins with one or two intact buildings—you'll need a plan to get your bearings.

HIGHLIGHTS

VIA SACRA, TEMPIO DI ANTONINO E FAUSTINA, BASILICA AEMILIA

Via Sacra, which bisects the Forum, linked the Palatine to the Capitoline hills. Holy sanctuaries lined the way, and victorious generals led processions along the route to give thanks to Jupiter in the Temple of Jupiter Capitolinus. Near the main entrance are the remains of the Temple of Antoninus and Faustina, the best-preserved temple in the Forum, chiefly because it was converted into a Christian church in the seventh century. To the right is a large area of broken columns, the Basilica Aemilia, built in the second century AD to house the law courts.

TEMPIO DI VESTA AND TEMPIO DEI CASTORI

Back near the main entrance, by the Via Sacra, is the circular white Temple of Vesta, where the six Vestal Virgins, priestesses to the goddess of fire, kept the sacred fire alight. The women lived in the House of the Vestal Virgins next door (the central courtyard with its three pools survives), dedicating most of their lives to the service of the goddess and receiving social privileges in return.

Nearby are the three Corinthian columns that remain of the Tempio dei Castori (Temple of Castor and Pollux), built to commemorate the Battle of Lacus Regillus, during which the two divine figures helped the Romans defeat the Latins.

ITALY

BASILICA JULIA, CURIA, ARCO DI SETTIMIO SEVERO

Via Sacra runs westwards beside the steps of the ruined Basilica Julia, built by Julius Caesar after he returned from the Gallic Wars. Across the Forum from here is the remarkably intact, red-coloured Curia (senate house), politically the Roman Republic's most important building. It was here that famous orators and statesmen made their speeches.

At the western end of the complex, the triumphal Arch of Septimius Severus was built in AD203 by his sons, Caracalla and Galba, to

commemorate the 10th anniversary of the emperor's reign and his victory over the Parthians between AD197 and 202. Statues of Septimius Severus and Caracalla stand on top of the arch.

BASILICA DI MASSENZIO AND ARCO DI TITO

East of the main entrance to the Foro Romano, Via Sacra passes the Basilica di Massenzio (Basilica of Maxentius), the largest and most impressive of all the ruins, built by Constantine and Maxentius in the fourth century. Note its arches, constructed of poured cement.

At the far end of the Foro, Via Sacra is spanned by the Arco di Tito, built on the Palatine after Titus's death in AD70 to commemorate his victory over the Jews and the capture of Jerusalem.

BACKGROUND

In the eighth century BC the site of the Foro Romano was a marshy area between the Capitoline and Palatine hills, used as a burial ground and a meeting place for the leaders of the nearby agricultural settlements. The area then came under the rule of the Etruscans, who drained the land. In 497BC one of the first temples to be built here was dedicated to the Etruscan god of crops. The area developed as the hub of social, civic and political life. As Rome grew in wealth and power, triumphal arches and monuments were erected to celebrate the victories of the Roman Republic, and the area became the city's financial focus. With its *comitium*, a square in front of the Curia, and the *rostra*, where the tribunes met, the Forum became the focal point for the men who planned the future of the empire.

By 44BC, however, the Forum had become overcrowded, and Julius Caesar moved the Curia and *rostra* to the Fori Imperiali. The Mercati Traianei (Trajan's Market) became the city's commercial hub, and in AD391, with Christianity spreading, Theodosius closed the pagan temples. From then the Foro gradually fell into ruin, its buildings became a quarry for building stone, and what had been the power behind a mighty empire reverted to pasture for cattle.

The Forum began life as a market

BASICS

✠ 255 F4 • Via dei Fori Imperiali, Via Sacra, Via di San Teodoro, Via di San Gregorio (entrance to the Palatine), 00186 Roma

☎ 06 3996 7700

🕐 Foro: daily 9am–1 hour before sunset (ticket office closes 1 hour before). Groups with reservations may enter at any time. Palatine: Mar–end Oct daily 9–6.30; Nov–end Feb daily 9–3.30.

💶 Foro: free. Palatine: €8; 18–24 years (EU nationals) €4; under 18s (EU nationals) free. Timed tickets: Palatine and Colosseum valid 24 hours

🚇 Colosseo

🚋 Tram 3 🎧 Foro: €3.50; daily at 10.30 in English

www.capitolium.org
www.comune.roma.it

Detail of the remains of an architrave surmounting a solitary Corinthian column in the Foro Romano

Canova's reclining statue of Paolina Borghese, sister of Napoleon

BASICS

✚ 256 F1 • Piazzale Scipione Borghese 5, 00197 Roma (entrance in Via Pinciana)

☎ 06 841 3979

🕐 Tue–Sun 9–7 (last entry 6.30)

💶 Adult €12.50, under 18s €6. Advance reservations required, tel 06 32810

🚇 Spagna or Flaminio

🚌 2-hour tour with an art historian in English (9.10am, 11.10am) and Italian (11.10am, 1.10pm, 5.10pm), €5. Advance reservations required (through website or tel 06 855 5952). Audiotours in Italian, English, Spanish, French and German, €5

📖 💻 🏧 🚻 🅿 On Via Pinciana

www.ticketeria.it
You can make advance reservations for the Galleria Borghese via this website, along with many other famous museums and galleries in Italy that require reservation.

www.galleriaborghese.it
This site has pictures of some of the highlights in the collection.

TIPS

● If possible, reserve in advance as only 360 people are admitted every 2 hours.
● All bags must be deposited at the entrance so carry the minimum of valuables.

GALLERIA BORGHESE

**A remarkable and much-loved collection of art in the peaceful setting of the Villa Borghese.
Masterpieces include famous sculptures by Bernini and Canova, and paintings by Caravaggio, Titian and Raphael.**

Cardinal Scipione, Ortensia Borghese's son, was passionate about art and founded this outstanding collection of sculpture and painting. He was also a man without scruples, however. For example, he arranged for Raphael's *Deposition* to be stolen from a church in Perugia and put the painter Domenichino in jail for refusing to give him his *Diana*. In 1620 his collection was moved to the Villa Pinciana. At the end of the 19th century the villa was sold to the Italian State to settle debts, and in 1903 the once-secret gardens were given to the municipality of Rome.

ROOM I
The main draw is Canova's sensuous sculpture of Paolina Borghese, Napoleon Bonaparte's sister, controversial in its day for its naked depiction of a wealthy subject.

ROOMS II, III AND IV
These rooms display sculptures by Bernini. First is *David,* preparing to fight the giant Goliath. The piece is thought to be a self-portrait. In homage to Bernini's patron, Scipione Borghese, his harp features an eagle's head, a Borghese family emblem. Note how the facial expression changes as you move around the statue. Next is *Apollo and Daphne*, showing Daphne changing into a laurel tree as she escapes Apollo's advances. Bernini's energetic statue *The Rape of Proserpina* shows Pluto, god of the underworld, attempting to rape Demeter's daughter.

ROOM VIII
The six Caravaggio paintings here are noted for their use of *chiaroscuro*. This technique of highlighting figures with a shaft of light from the surrounding darkness is used beautifully in the *Madonna dei Palafreni*.

OTHER HIGHLIGHTS
Paintings by Raphael, Pinturicchio and Perugino are exhibited in Room IX. Correggio's *Danaë* illustrates Jupiter's love for the eponymous heroine. In Room XVIII is the stolen *Deposition* by Raphael (1507).

ITALY

Musei Vaticani

The largest and richest museum complex in the world—at least 1,400 rooms. Sculpture, paintings and *objets d'art* spanning more than 3,000 years, from every corner of the Classical and modern world. The Sistine Chapel and Michelangelo's famous frescoes.

SEEING THE MUSEI VATICANI

The vast complex includes the museum, galleries and parts of the papal palace, richly decorated by the world's greatest artists. The galleries, themselves of great architectural interest, have a diverse collection of art, with a particular emphasis on Western art and sculpture.

The Vatican Gardens

HIGHLIGHTS

CAPPELLA SISTINA

The Cappella Sistina (Sistine Chapel) was built by Pope Sixtus IV between 1473 and 1481, both as the pontiff's private chapel and as a venue for the conclave of cardinals that gathers to elect each new pope. It is a huge, cavernous structure, with an intricate cosmatesque mosaic floor and a marble screen by Mino da Fiesole. But, above all, it is the frescoes, entirely covering the walls and ceiling, that attract up to 20,000 visitors a day.

Even during the construction of the chapel, Sixtus was planning the interior decoration, settling on scenes from the Old and New Testaments as the subject matter, with an emphasis on the parallels between the lives of Moses and Christ. From Florence, he summoned Sandro Botticelli, together with Domenico Ghirlandaio, Cosimo Rosselli and Perugino. These artists, joined by Pinturicchio, Luca Signorelli and Piero di Cosimo, worked for 11 months, producing a series of glowing works. The two most important scenes are Perugino's *Christ Giving the Keys to Peter* and Botticelli's *The Punishment of Korah,* each showing the Arco di Costantino in the background (▷ 253).

Though undoubtedly masterpieces, they tend to be overshadowed by Michelangelo's frescoes on the ceiling and altar wall, arguably Western art's finest achievement and certainly the largest work ever planned and carried out by one man. Julius II commissioned the ceiling in 1508, and Michelangelo completed it in 1512, an artistic *tour-de-force* combining narrative scenes, architectural *trompe l'oeil* effects and statuesque figures of immense beauty. The central panels illustrate the Creation and tell the story of Noah, surrounded by the figures of the Prophets and Sibyls and containing wonderful details, including the famous *ignudi* (nude youths).

Years later, in 1535, Michelangelo was again summoned to the chapel, this time by Paul III, to decorate the altar wall with scenes of the Last Judgement, a task that occupied him until 1541. Even before it was finished, the amount of nudity offended many, not least the pope's master of ceremonies. Furious, Michelangelo depicted him in the bottom right-hand corner of Hell as Minos, the doorkeeper, complete with ass's ears. Later, Pius IV commissioned Daniele da Volterra to paint over the genitals—an exercise that earned him the name Braghettone, the trouser-maker. This alteration was reversed during the restoration of

RATINGS				
Good for kids	● ●			
Historic interest	● ● ● ● ●			
Value for money	● ● ● ●			
Walkability	● ● ●			

TIPS

● Dress respectfully—shorts and bare upper arms are unacceptable and you will be turned away from churches if you are wearing shorts, short skirts or showing shoulders.
● To avoid crowds, arrive as the museum opens, or late in the morning. Wednesday morning can be peaceful as people go to the Piazza di San Pietro for the papal blessing.

Ancient sculpture

One of several massive sculpted heads on the terrace

BASICS

✚ 254 B2 • Viale Vaticano, 00165 Roma

☎ 06 6988 4676

🕐 Mar–end Oct Mon–Fri 10–4.45 (last ticket 3.30), Sat 10–2.45 (last ticket 1.30), Nov–end Feb Mon–Sat 10–1.45 (last ticket 12.30), though some days longer hours. Closed most Sun throughout the year but open last Sun of the month with free entrance. Closed on public hols

💶 Adult €13, child (under 15) €8

🎫 2-hour guided tour, €23.50; reserve at information point or tel 06 6988 5100. Audiotours in Italian, English, French, German, Spanish, Japanese, €6

🍴 €7.50 🛍 🏛 🚻

🅿 Gianicolo underground parking

Ⓜ Cipro Musei Vaticani, Ottaviano-Vaticano

www.vatican.va
This website dedicated to Vatican City is very informative. Under the section on the Vatican Museums you can view the collection online, read about the artworks and zoom in on individual paintings for a closer look. There are also online tours and up-to-date practical information, such as opening times and prices.

the chapel frescoes of the 1980s and 1990s, a project said to have cost more than $3 million.

STANZE DI RAFFAELLO

In 1508 Julius II embarked on a major project to decorate his private apartments, today known as the Stanze di Raffaello (Raphael Rooms). The Stanza della Segnatura, the pope's study, is deservedly the most famous room and was Raphael's first major Roman commission, painted between 1508 and 1511.

The four frescoes, compositions imbued with balance and harmony, are allegories representing the humanist ideals of theology, philosophy, poetry and justice. The _School of Athens_ emphasizes truth acquired through reason, with all the great Classical thinkers represented and the central figures of Plato—probably a portrait of Leonardo da Vinci—and Aristotle dominating the scene. The figure on the left is said to be Michelangelo, added after Raphael had a sneak preview of his work in the Cappella Sistina. Opposite is the _Disputation of the Holy Sacrament_, while the side walls show _Parnassus_, home to the Muses, and the _Cardinal Virtues_.

Chronologically, the next room to be painted was the Stanza di Eliodoro, with its energy-charged _Expulsion of Heliodorus_ and serene _Miracle of Bolsena_. The latter tells the story of the medieval miracle that occurred in that town, when a priest who doubted the doctrine of transubstantiation saw the wafer bleed during Mass. The window wall has a superb night scene, showing the _Deliverance of St. Peter from Prison_.

The Stanza di Costantino depicts the life of Constantine, the first Christian emperor, while the main focus in the Stanza dell'Incendio, commissioned by Leo X, is the miraculous quenching of a _Fire in the Borgo_, which occurred when Leo IV made the sign of the cross.

One of the Pope's Swiss Guards (left)

ITALY

PINACOTECA VATICANA

The Pinacoteca, founded in 1816 by Pius VI, occupies a separate building (1932) within the museum complex. It is widely considered to be Rome's best picture gallery, with works from the early and High Renaissance to the 19th century. Among these are some of the most remarkable early paintings in Rome, with Giotto's *Stefaneschi Triptych* stealing the show (Room II). Painted in the early 1300s it shows the *Martyrdom of St. Peter and St. Paul*. St. Peter is shown being crucified, at his own request, upside down, as he felt unworthy to die the same way as Christ. The next rooms are devoted to 15th-century Italian art; look for Fra Angelico's lovely *Madonna and Child with Saints* in Room III and the serene Umbrian pictures in Room VII, particularly Perugino's luminous *Madonna and Child*. Room VIII is the Pinacoteca's finest, with a collection of Raphael's work, including

Maps of the papal lands in the Galleria delle Carte Geographiche

tapestries, woven in Brussels from his cartoons, that once hung in the Cappella Sistina. Dominating the room, however, is the *Transfiguration*, a sublime work that was hung above the artist's coffin and completed by his pupils later. The triumphant figure of the ascending Christ pulses with energy amid piercing light and lowering cloud formations, a superb contrast to the artist's first major composition, the *Coronation of the Virgin*, painted when he was only 20. The gentle *Madonna of Foligno* was commissioned in 1512 as a votive offering.

In Room IX is Leonardo da Vinci's unfinished and curiously monochrome *St. Jerome*, one of only a few of Leonardo's works whose authorship has never been disputed. Here, too, is the exquisite *Pietà* by Bellini. Venetian painting is featured heavily in Room X in two canvases by Titian, a glowing *Madonna with Saints* and the subtle *Portrait of Doge Nicolò Marcello*. There are further psychological insights in Caravaggio's despairing *Deposition* in Room XII, all muted tones and intense *chiaroscuro*.

BACKGROUND

Pope Innocent III (1179–81) began building a palace near the Basilica San Pietro, and his successors enlarged and embellished

it. Major work was carried out under Nicolò V in the mid-15th century, and in the 1470s Sixtus IV added the Cappella Sistina. Both Julius II (1503–13) and Leo X (1513–22) built and decorated further buildings—Julius commissioned Michelangelo to paint the Cappella Sistina and Raphael to decorate his private rooms. In the 18th century the collections were arranged into a museum, with galleries built to display sculpture, paintings, and *objets d'art*—a huge project that continued into the 20th century.

GALLERY GUIDE

LOWER FLOOR

Museo Pio Clementino: The cream of the classical sculpture collection is in this museum's octagonal courtyard. Two statues here influenced Renaissance sculptors more than any others, the *Laocöon* and the *Apollo Belvedere*. Highlights within include a beautiful Hellenistic *Sleeping Ariadne*, candelabra from the Villa Adriana at Tivoli, and Roman portrait busts, including a splendid Julius Caesar.

Museo Gregoriano Egizio: Founded in the 19th century by Gregory XVI, this museum displays a reconstruction of the Temple of Serapis from the Villa Adriana at Tivoli, mummy cases, mummies and tomb treasures.

Museo Gregoriano Profano: Built in 1963 and opened in 1970, a museum with a collection of antique and Christian art moved here from the Lateran Palace.

Museo Pio Cristiano: A collection of documents and objects illustrating religions of the world.

Museo Storico Vaticano: An unusual collection of papal transportation, including carriages.

Museo Chiaramonti: Another collection of Roman sculpture, in particular portrait busts.

Braccio Nuovo: A beautiful collection in a superb architectural setting.

Biblioteca Vaticana: A huge, brilliantly frescoed hall with letters from Petrarch, Michelangelo and Martin Luther, and King Henry VIII's love letters to Anne Boleyn.

UPPER FLOOR

Museo Gregoriano Etrusco: Founded in 1837, this is a major collection of Etruscan sculpture and funerary art.

Galleria delle Carte Geographiche: This upper-floor gallery links the museums with the papal palace. It was painted in 1580 by Ignazio Danti with maps of Italy, Mediterranean islands, papal possessions in France, the Siege of Malta and Venice.

Cappella di Nicolò V: Serene and delicate frescoes (1446–49) by Fra Angelico in the pope's private chapel.

A map of Sardinia in the Galleria delle Carte Geographiche (left), painted by Ignazio Danti

RATINGS

Historic interest	●●●○
Cultural interest	●●●○
Walkability	●●●○

BASICS

✚ 255 E3 • Piazza della Rotonda, 00186 Roma ☎ 06 6830 0230
🕐 Mon–Sat 8.30–7.30, Sun 9–6, public holidays 9–1. No visits during celebration of the Sun 10.30am Mass
🎫 Free
🚊 Tram 8 to Argentina
🔲 In the Square
🏛 On Piazza della Rotonda

TIPS

● There is not much information to help visitors on site, so have your guidebook handy.
● Have a drink in one of the cafés or sit around the central fountain of the piazza to enjoy the view of the Pantheon.
● The Pantheon is often very crowded, especially at the weekend. To make the most of a visit, go on a weekday or early in the morning.

Shafts of sunlight shine through the oculus, illuminating the porphyry, granite and yellow marble walls and floors

PANTHEON

**Simple, solid and austere, an architectural *tour de force* by the engineers of ancient Rome.
Pagan temple turned Christian church—now Italy's best-preserved building from antiquity.**

The original Pantheon was built by Agrippa, according to the inscription on the façade. It was erected in 27BC in honour of the heavenly gods and was also dedicated to the Julia family, thought to be direct descendants of gods. Agrippa's building was destroyed in the great fire of AD80 and the Pantheon was rebuilt in the early second century by Emperor Hadrian. In the sixth century, Emperor Phocas gave the Pantheon to Pope Boniface IV, who turned it into a Christian church. The building was then covered in bronze and lead, and despite being pillaged over the years, the covering helped to preserve the dome and other surfaces. The portico of Egyptian granite columns was once a fishmarket. Pope Urban VIII had the bronze on the ceiling removed in the 17th century for use on Bernini's *baldacchino* in San Pietro (▷ 258–259), but the bronze doors survive from ancient Rome.

THE DOME

The design is superbly simple: a dome on a circular base attached to a rectangular portico. With a diameter wider than the dome of San Pietro, this is the largest dome ever built before the introduction of reinforced concrete, testimony to the amazing ingenuity of the Roman engineers. The height of the dome from the floor is identical to its diameter, 43.3m (142ft). The walls supporting the dome are 7m (23ft) across, and the thickness of the dome itself diminishes from base to apex. The unglazed oculus, the circular hole in the middle of the dome (9m/29.5ft across), is the only source of natural light. A statue of Jove Ultor, the Avenger, who punished the murderers of Caesar, once stood directly under the oculus, and shrines and niches once held statues of the 12 Olympian gods, along with emperors Hadrian and Augustus. The tombs of Italy's first two kings and the artist Raphael are the only tombs you can see today.

PIAZZA DELLA ROTONDA

The Pantheon faces Piazza della Rotonda, a pretty square with cafés, a fountain, and a 13th-century BC Egyptian obelisk built by Ramses II, brought to Rome and used in the Temple of Isis and Serapis in Campo Marzio, then moved here by Pope Clement XI. In the evening this is a lively place with people dining or enjoying coffee and ice cream.

WHAT TO DO

⊕ BULGARI

Via Condotti 10
Tel 06 696261
www.bulgari.com

This is the most splendid jewellery shop in Rome, but it's also fantastically expensive. Andy Warhol called it the most important museum of art in the Western world. It specializes in glittering Renaissance-inspired pieces and a complete lack of refined taste.

ⓘ Daily 10–7 ⓢ Spagna

⊕ FURLA

Piazza di Spagna 22
Tel 06 6920 0363
www.furla.it

Purveyors of chic bags and practical totes in bright shades, along with scarves, shoes and jewellery. Some wild style combinations and original touches. Prices are moderate compared with other big-name accessory designers. The company has a fleet of branches all over the world, and several more in Rome.

ⓘ Daily 10–8 ⓢ Spagna 🚌 116, 117, 119, 590

⊕ PORTA PORTESE

Porta Portese

Rome's most famous flea market stretches all the way from Porta Portese to Trastevere station. It also branches off down the side streets. From trendy clothes and antiques to junk, you can find all sorts here. Arrive early for the best buys, and beware of pickpockets.

ⓘ Sun 6.30–1 🚌 Tram 3

⊕ VALENTINO

Via Condotti 13
Tel 06 679 5862
www.valentino.com

One of the few Italian fashion designers to be based in Rome rather than Milan. Valentino has been dressing the rich and famous since the late 1950s. Further branches are in Piazza

Mignanelli (haute couture), Via del Babuino and Via Bocca di Leone.

ⓘ Mon 3–7, Tue–Sat 10–7 ⓢ Spagna

⊕ VOLPETTI

Via Marmorata 47
Tel 06 574 2352
www.volpetti.com

One of the best (though not the cheapest) delis in Rome. An astounding variety of breads, cheeses, hams, salamis, fresh pasta and ready-made dishes. Service is professional and cheerful and you can sample the cheese to help you decide. Whatever happens, you won't come away empty-handed. Good for gifts. There's another, more expensive branch in Via della Scrofa in the city centre.

ⓘ Mon, Wed–Sat 8–2, 5–8.15, Tue 8–2 ⓢ Piramide 🚌 23, 30, 60, 75, 280, 716 (or any to Piramide or Via Marmorata); tram 3

ⓓ ALEXANDERPLATZ

Via Ostia 9
Tel 06 3974 2171
www.alexanderplatz.it

Rome's most famous jazz venue holds jazz festivals all year round, and organizes outdoor concerts at Villa Celimontana in summer. American bands are often on the bill. Creole cuisine is served in the restaurant.

ⓘ Daily 8pm, live music from 10pm; closed first 2 weeks of Aug 🎫 €10 per month for membership 🚌 Bus to Piazza Risorgimento or Clodio

ⓓ TEATRO DELL'OPERA DI ROMA

Piazza Benaimino Gigli
Tel 06 4816 0255 (box office)
www.operaroma.it

A hidden gem, the interior is adorned with all the trimmings of a true opera house complete with velvet boxes. Not to be missed by those who love classical dance. The theatre is beautiful and attracts first-rate dance troupes from all over the world. You are certain to see the cream of Roman society.

ⓘ Performances: Nov–end May 9pm; Box office: Tue–Sat 9–5, Sun 9–1.30 🎫 €9–€130 🚌 Bus to Via Nazionale

ⓥ CUL DE SAC

Piazza Pasquino 73
Tel 06 6880 1094

In a little piazza off Piazza Navona, this is one of the oldest wine bars in town and still one of the best. They have an excellent wine list, mouth-watering cheeses, meats and unusual dishes. Friendly service and frequent tastings.

ⓘ Daily 12–4, 7–12.30 🚌 46, 62, 64, 492 to Corso Vittorio Emanuele II (get off near Sant'Andrea della Valle); 70, 81, 87 to Corso Rinascimento; 116 to Campo de' Fiori

ⓥ THE GALLERY

Via della Maddalena 12
Tel 06 687 2316
www.thegallery.it

An enegetic, modern and elegant bar behind the Pantheon. Music from hip-hop to R&B to 1970s and 1980s revival draws a crowd that's young and ready to party.

ⓘ Tue–Fri 8pm–3am, Sat–Sun 8pm–4am 🎫 €10 🚌 116

ⓢ BIOPARCO DI ROMA

Viale del Giardino Zoologico 20
Tel 06 360 8211
www.bioparco.it

Bioparco is one of the oldest zoos in Europe but is modern and aims to promote the conservation of endangered species. It also hopes to educate visitors about the animals, some of which have been rescued from illegal trading in rare species. The zoo is set in botanical gardens and contains over 1,000 animals.

ⓘ Apr–end Oct daily 9.30–6 (7 on Sat, Sun, holidays); Nov–end Mar daily 9.30–5. Last admittance 1 hour before closing 🎫 Adult €8.50, child 3–12 €6.50 ⓢ Flaminio 🚌 52, 53, 926; tram 13, 19

ⓢ LUNEUR PARK

Via delle Tre Fontane
Tel 06 592 5933
www.luneur.it

Built in 1953, the oldest fun park in Italy has kept up with the times. Activities and rides are both traditional and adrenalin-pumping, with a puppet theatre, several haunted houses, bumper cars, a lake with motor boats, and rides called Flipper, Thriller and Space Kickers. The park is a lot bigger than it seems. Suitable for kids and teenagers.

ⓘ Apr to mid-Oct Mon–Fri 4–midnight, Sat 3–2am, Sun 10–1,

ITALY

3-midnight; late Oct–Mar Fri 3–8, Sat 3-midnight, Sun 11–8 🕃 Adult €16, child (4–12) €14 🚇 Magliana, Palasport or EUR Fermi 🚌 706, 707, 714, 717, 765, 771

🕃 TIME ELEVATOR
Via S.S. Apostoli 20
Tel 06 9774 6243
www.time-elevator.it
A multimedia experience illustrating the history of Rome from its founding to the present day. With headphones, a screen, a moving platform and other surprise special effects, this is a genuinely fun (if slightly cheesy and occasionally factually weak) introduction to the city.
🕔 Daily 10.30–7.30 🕃 Adult €11, (under 12) €8 🚌 40, 64, 170, 175 or any bus to Via del Corso or Piazza Venezia

---

EATING

AL BRIC
Via del Pellegrino 51
Tel 06 6879533
www.albric.it
This is a very stylish *osteria* and wine bar. There are many small tables in the large room overlooking Via del Pellegrino, near Campo dei Fiori. The wine list is huge, with more than a thousand labels to choose from, while the menu has a wide selection of creative dishes matched perfectly with the wine suggestions. Try spaghetti with anchovies and pecorino or pears with Gorgonzola cheese. Among the home-made desserts, don't miss the strudel with cinnamon ice cream. The bread is home-made, too.
🕔 Mon–Sat 7.20pm–11pm, Sun 11–3, 7.30–11
🍽 L €30, D €55, Wine €13
🚌 64, 87, 492 to Largo Argentina
🚋 Tram 8

PIERLUIGI
Piazza de' Ricci 144
Tel 06 6861302
www.pierluigi.it
This excellent fish restaurant is reasonably priced considering its quality and setting—on the edge of a piazza, with plenty of tables outside. The scampi risotto is fantastically smooth and tasty, as is the *carpaccio* of tuna or swordfish. The fresh fish of the day are displayed behind a glass cabinet.

🕔 Tue–Sun 12–3, 7.30pm–midnight
🍽 L €35, D €60, Wine €14
🚌 46, 62, 64, 87, 116, 492

SORA LELLA
Via di Ponte Quattro Capi 16
Tel 06 6861601
www.soralella.com
Set on Isola Tiberina, near Trastevere, this is possibly one of the most unusual places to eat in Rome. Here you will find Roman cuisine at its best. All the typical dishes, from oxtail with cinnamon, cloves, raisins and pine nuts to memorable fried artichokes. Reservations are recommended.
🕔 Mon–Sat 12.30–2.30, 8–11pm; closed Aug
🍽 L €35, D €45, Wine €13
🚌 23
🚋 Tram 8

STAYING

ANNE AND MARY
Via Cavour 325, 00184 Roma
Tel 06 69941187
www.anne-mary.com
This welcoming bed-and-breakfast occupies part of an elegant 19th-century building near the Colosseum. Rooms are simple but they are dramatically appointed, with clean lines and swooping curtains. Each has a private bathroom with an enclosed shower. Via Cavour is a large, somewhat frantic road, but the proximity of this hotel to the major sights means it is worth putting up with the noise.
🛏 €100–€150
🚪 6 🕃
🚇 Cavour, Colosseo
🚌 75, 81, 85, 87, 116, 117

HOTEL INTERNAZIONALE
Via Sistina 79, 00187 Roma
Tel 06 69941823
www.hotelinternazionale.com
Wisteria winds up the front of this palazzo, which was used as a convent in the 16th and 17th centuries. The breakfast lounge is swathed in soothing pastel shades of blue and mauve. The scheme continues throughout the hotel, from the cupids in the cupola to the moiré wall coverings in the bedrooms.
🛏 €150–€300
🚪 42 🕃
🚇 Piazza di Spagna
🚌 62

ITALIA
Via Venezia 18, 00184 Roma
Tel 06 482 8355
www.hotelitaliaroma.com
This inexpensive, family-run hotel is very central and just off the second-largest shopping street in town. The reception is on the first floor. The 19th-century building was refurbished simply in 2002. The rooms are functional with television, minibar, bathroom and hair-dryer. There is a Continental buffet breakfast.
🛏 €70–€130
🚪 23 🕃 15 rooms (€8 extra)
🚇 Repubblicà
🚌 64

LANCELOT
Via Capo D'Africa 47, 00184 Roma
Tel 06 7045 0615
www.lancelothotel.com
Don't let the high-rise appearance put you off this welcoming, family-run hotel just above the Colosseum. The lounge and dining room have period furniture and Murano glass chandeliers. There is a bar, library and a delightful courtyard. The rooms are spacious and most have wooden floors and pastel walls. All the rooms have bathrooms with a shower, a safe and satellite television. Some of the guest rooms have terraces. The breakfast is Continental.
🛏 €180–€216
🚪 60 🕃
🚇 Colosseo, San Giovanni
🚌 81, 85, 87, 117; tram 3

LORD BYRON
Via Giuseppe de Notaris 5, 00197 Roma
Tel 06 3220404
www.lordbyronhotel.com
The Lord Byron is a romantic hideaway in pastoral Parioli, overlooking the Villa Borghese. The art deco villa has been elegantly restored, with scarlet sofas, lacquered furniture, gilded mirrors and marble bathrooms. Rooms 503, 602 and 603 have spectacular views. Its restaurant, Relais Le Jardin, is considered to be one of Italy's finest.
🛏 €330–€500
🚪 32 🕃
🚇 Flaminio
🚌 117
🚗 West side of Via Giuseppe de Notaris 5, just north of Via Mangili

Turin

Splendid baroque architecture, elegant shops and excellent museums.
An important cultural hub with many contemporary art museums and
commercial galleries hosting major exhibitions.

The racetrack on top of the Lingotto Fiat factory   *The rooftops of Torino*   *The Caffè Torino*

SEEING TURIN

Turin (Torino) has had a rebirth. The 2006 Winter Olympics have
put Turin firmly on the world map for winter sports and as an all-
year place to visit. The city and its locality in the foothills of the
Alps have benefited from huge investment, including Europe's
most modern metro (subway) system. A new ice-skating
complex has changed the city's landscape and become a
modern ice palace. More than any other city in Italy, Torino has
made great strides in improving its hospitality to visitors,
whether they are drawn by the upgraded winter sports facilities
or the historic assets and cultural life that it offers all year round.
The Duomo or Cathedral is renowned as the location of the
Turin Shroud, the Mole is a grand domed tower in the city centre
and there is a rich nightlife in the Murazzi and Docks Dora areas
and on the streets of the Roman Quarter. Nestling in the
shopping arcades of Via Po, off Piazza Castello, are numerous
historic cafés and restaurants serving traditional Piedmont
dishes and wines.

HIGHLIGHTS

MUSEO EGIZIO AND GALLERIA SABAUDA

Palazzo dell'Accademia, Via Accademia delle Scienze 6, 10100 Torino
☎ 011 5617776 🕐 Museo Egizio: mid-Jun to early Sep Tue–Sun 9.30–8.30;
mid-Sep to early Jun Tue–Sun 8.30–7.30. Galleria Sabauda: Tue, Fri–Sun 8.30–2,
Wed–Thu 2–7.30 💶 Museo Egizio: €6.50; Galleria Sabauda: €4
www.museoegizio.org, www.museitorino.it/galleriasabauda
Housed in a vast baroque palace, this is the world's third most
important collection of Egyptian antiquities after those in Cairo and
London. Among the great treasures are a black granite statue of
Ramses II, the tomb of the architect Kha, and the reconstructed
temple of Ellesija. The Galleria Sabauda, in the same building, has an
exceptional collection of paintings, begun by the Dukes of Savoy, with
works of art by Piedmontese, Tuscan, Lombard and Venetian masters,
and a major Flemish and Dutch collection (Van Eyck, Memling,
Rembrandt). The museum adjoins Piazza San Carlo, a baroque
square known as the 'the drawing room of Turin'.

BASICS

➕ 5 D4
ℹ Atrium, Piazza Solferino, tel 011
535181; daily 9.30–7
Also at Torino Caselle airport and Porta
Nuova train station
🚇 Torino's new metro (underground)
line uses state-of-the-art technology
and is adapted for people with limited
mobility.
🚌 The city is served by buses, trams
and a funicular. Tickets are sold at
stations, *tabacchi*, etc. A tourist bus
takes visitors around the city with a
guide (departs from Piazza Castello)
🚆 The city is a major rail terminus.
Regular trains run to and from Milan
(1 hour 15 minutes)
✈ Turin's Sandro Pertini International
Airport in Caselle is 16km (10 miles)
north of the city, accessible
by regular bus and train services.
🎧 Guided tours for individuals or
groups tel 011 535181/535901
www.turismotorino.org

www.comune.torino.it
This website has a great deal of
information in English.

A statue of the Cavaliere d'Italia in Piazza Castello

● Torino+Piemonte Card (€18 for 2 days, €20 for 3 days €30 for 5 days and €35 for 7 days and valid for one adult and one child) covers 150 museums, monuments, castles and palaces in Turin and Piedmont, plus urban and suburban transport and river trips. It also gives reductions on services such as guided tours, car rental and theatre tickets.

● TurismoBus Torino is a hop-on hop-off tour bus with live commentary on the sights, culture and history of Torino. A ticket lasting all day costs €6 for adults and €4 for children under 12. You can buy the tickets at tourist information offices in Piazza Solferino and the Porta Nuova train station, at Torino Caselle airport, in hotels or on board the bus. TurismoBus Torino is free if you hold a Torino Card.

● The ChocoPass entitles you to sample the range of tastes and products around the city. It costs €10 for ten tastings in 24 hours or €15 for 15 tastings in 48 hours, from Turismo Torino information points.

● Just outside the city at Pessione di Chieri you can visit the premises of Martini & Rossi, makers of the famous aperitif since the mid-1800s. Visits: summer daily 9.30–7; prebook the rest of the year. Via Piazza Luigi Rossi 1, Pessione di Chieri, tel 011 941 9217.

PALAZZO CARIGNANO

Via Accademia delle Scienze 5, 10123 Torino ☎ 011 5621147 🕐 Museum: Tue–Sun 9–7 💶 €5

www.regione.piemonte.it/cultura/risorgimento/iindex.htm

The nearby Palazzo Carignano, designed by Guarino Guarini (1679), was the birthplace of Vittorio Emanuele II in 1820 and the seat of the Subalpine parliament. The Unification of Italy was proclaimed here in 1861. It is now home to the Museo del Risorgimento. You can visit the royal apartments and the Royal Armoury (separate entrance) of the Palazzo Reale (apartments Tue–Sun 8.30–7.30; garden daily 9–7).

GALLERIA CIVICA D'ARTE MODERNA E CONTEMPORANEA

Via Magenta 31, 20100 Torino ☎ 011 442 9610 🕐 Tue–Sun 10–6 (last admittance 1 hour before) 💶 Adult €7.50, young person (10–25) €4, free first Tue of month
www.gamtorino.it

If you like modern art, seek out the Galleria Civica d'Arte Moderna e Contemporanea (GAM), northwest of the station. It has 15,000 works of art including pieces by Modigliani, De Chirico, Klee and Warhol.

MOLE ANTONELLIANA

Via Montebello 20, 10124 Torino ☎ 011 813 8560 🕐 Tue–Sun 9–8, Sat 9–11 💶 Museum: Adult €6.50, child (11–15) €5, child (under 10) free. Museum and panoramic lift: Adult €8, child (11–15) €6.50, child (under 10) free
www.muzeonazionaledelcinema.org

Turin's answer to Paris's Eiffel Tower is 167m (548ft) high. Built between 1798 and 1888, it now houses an outstanding museum tracing the history of cinema.

BACKGROUND

In 1574, the house of Savoy made Turin its capital and remained here for the next eight centuries. After Unification, Turin-born Vittorio Emanuele II was proclaimed the first king of Italy in 1861 and ruled until 1865. Giovanni Agnelli founded Fiat here in 1899, and the Lingotto, the ex-Fiat car factory designed in 1914–16, has been transformed by Renzo Piano into a vast conference, exhibition and shopping space. The Dukes of Savoy were the owners of the Shroud of Turin from the mid-15th century until it passed into the hands of the Catholic Church on the death of exiled ex-King Umberto II. Turin Cathedral was erected adjoining the Ducal palace as a suitably majestic building to house the shroud, one of the most studied of the many medieval religious relics found across Europe.

KEY TO SYMBOLS

- 🛍 **Shopping**
- 🎭 **Entertainment**
- 🍸 **Nightlife**
- ⚽ **Sports**
- 🎿 **Activities**
- ❤ **Health and Beauty**
- 🧸 **For Children**

WHAT TO DO

GERLA
Corso Vittorio Emanuele II 88
Tel 011 545422
www.giandujotto.it
Thousands of tiny chocolates vie for customers' attention. The ornate chocolate cakes cost around €15. Other Piedmontese snacks and desserts—including fruit tarts, sweet breads and pastries—complete the spread.
🕐 Mon–Fri 9–7.30, Sat 8.30–1, 3.30–7.30, Sun 8.30–1 🚃 15

STICKY FINGERS
Via delle Orfane 24
Tel 011 521 7320
www.sticky-fingers.it
In the heart of the Roman Quarter, Sticky Fingers brings the 1960s and 1970s back into fashion. Beautiful faux-vintage trousers, shirts and dresses from €50 fill this tasteful shop. Check out the classy Simon Kneen boutique next door, too.
🕐 Tue–Sat 11–2, 5–10
🚃 Buses to Piazza della Repubblica

TEATRO REGIO TORINO
Piazza Castello 215
Tel 011 881 5241
www.teatroregio.torino.it
You will find this unmissable theatre on the corner of Piazza Castello next to Via Guiseppe Verdi. It hosts musicals, plays and the occasional opera all year round.
🕐 Box office: Tue–Fri 10.20–6, Sat 10.30–4 🎫 €20–€300 🚃 11, 12

JUVENTUS LIVE FOOTBALL
C so Galileo Ferraris 32
Tel 011 65631
www.juventus.com
Italy's most decorated football (soccer) club, Juve play alternate weeks at the Stadio delle Alpi. You can pay up to several hundred euros for the best seats.
🕐 Sep–end Jun every other weekend 🎫 From €18 🚃 The Stadio delle Alpi is clearly signed 4km (2.5 miles) south-west of the city centre

CIRCOLO GOLF
Via Agnelli 40, Fiano
Tel 011 923 5440
www.circologolftorino.it
This is a classy 19-hole, 72-par golf course. The club has a practice field, swimming pool, bar, fine restaurant, and jewellery and fashion shops. The summer heat tends to be quite bearable up here too.
🕐 Mar–Dec 15 Tue–Sun 8–8
🎫 A round of golf is €96 on a weekday, €156 at the weekend. Equipment rental extra 🚗 Take the Venaria Reale exit from the Tangenziale Nord from Milan

EATING

LA BADESSA
Piazza Carlo Emanuele II 17
Tel 011 835940
www.labadessa.net
Wonderfully atmospheric city centre restaurant whose tables tumble out into the Piazza Carlo Emanuele II during the summer. The vaulted interior, part of the Palazzo Coardi di Carpeneto, is divided into a number of intimate spaces, giving it a cosy feel, while the stucco walls and terracotta tiled floors feel typically Italian. The signature dishes are *baccala* and *stoccafisso* (stockfish) but the restaurant uses many ingredients made at the convent nearby.
🕐 Mon 7.30–11.30, Tue–Sun 12–2.30, 7.30–11.30. Closed Jan
🍴 L €18, D €30, Wine €12
🚃 68
🚇 Porta Nouva

FRATELLI LA COZZA
Corso Regio Parco 39
Tel 011 859900
www.lacozza.com
A traditional family trattoria which specializes in piles of tasty fresh pasta and sizzling pizzas served in the bustling atmosphere of a large dining room complete with chandelier but without any over-fancy contemporary frills. The clientele ranges from businesspeople to families.
🕐 Daily 12.30–2.30, 7.30–midnight
🍴 L €15, D €25, Wine €10
🚃 68

OSTERIA DEL CORSO
Corso Regina Margherita 252
Tel 011 408665
www.osteriadelcorso.it
A country-style restaurant with light rustic interior and a covered terrace for alfresco dining. The *osteria* serves tasty local Piemonte cuisine. Roasted piglet is a specialty.
🕐 Tue–Sun 11–2.30, 7–11.30. Closed mid-Aug to mid-Sep
🍴 L €25, D €40, W €14
🚃 29

STAYING

HOTEL BOLOGNA
Corso Vittorio Emanuele II 60, 10121 Torino
Tel 011 562 0193
www.hotelbolognasrl.it
A convenient hotel opposite Porta Nuova rail station. Most of the rooms have televisions, private bathrooms and telephones. The hotel has no restaurant, but there are plenty of eating options nearby.
🛏 €95
🔑 45
🚇 Porta Nuova

STARHOTEL MAJESTIC
Corse Vittorio Emanuel II 54, 10123 Torino
Tel 011 539153
www.starhotels.it
A modern hotel near the Porta Nuova rail station and a short walk from the city's historic sights. As well as an excellent restaurant, facilities include a babysitting service, international newspapers, movies on demand and laundry.
🛏 €210–€310
🔑 161
🚇 Porta Nuova

TURIN PALACE
Via Sacchi 8, 10128 Torino
Tel 011 5625511
www.thi.it
An elegant 4-star hotel where the rooms have giant beds. The buffet breakfast is a rich spread of Piedmontese hams, cheeses and local Lavazza coffee. Turn left out of Turin's Porta Nuova rail station and you are right outside the hotel's doors.
🛏 €200–€280
🔑 122 rooms, 2 suites
🚇 Porta Nuova

ITALY

Venice

✚ 5 D4 🏠 Palazzo Ziani, Fondamenta San Lorenzo, 30122 Venezia, tel 041 529 8711; daily 9.30–3.30
www.turismovenezia.it • Official tourist board site with English option, packed with information
www.comune.venezia.it • City council site with excellent practical information and English-language option

HOW TO GET THERE

✈ Airports

Venezia Marco Polo
At Tessera, 7km (4 miles) north of the
city centre by water
Tel 041 260 6111

Treviso Sant'Angelo
Treviso, 26km (16 miles) north of
Venice
Tel 042 231 5111

🚆 Railway stations

Venezia Santa Lucia
Trains cross the causeway linking
Venice with the mainland to terminate
at Venezia Santa Lucia, situated on
the Grand Canal; automated train
information on 041 258 0136
(Italian only)

Gondola jam!

TIPS

● If possible, avoid visiting
Venice between late June and
the end of September, when
the city is swamped by crowds.
● Reserve accommodation
well ahead and, as all luggage
has to be carried, consider the
hotel's distance from a
vaporetto stop.
● If visiting the lagoon islands,
use the *vaporetti* rather than
taking a tour—you get more
time, more flexibility and it
costs less.
● For an inexpensive gondola
experience, take one of the
traghetto gondolas that cross
the Grand Canal at fixed points.
● Bring comfortable shoes and
be prepared to walk, bearing in
mind that you will be crossing
numerous steep bridges.

SEEING VENICE

Venice is a surprisingly small city, but also a confusing maze, and
first-time visitors should follow the yellow signs, painted above
head height on buildings throughout the city. These mark the
routes to the main attractions and other key points, such as the
railway station. Longer distances will entail travelling by water,
and all parts of the city and the lagoon islands are served by
vaporetti (water buses). A journey down the Grand Canal is an
excellent way to start your sightseeing, taking you under the
iconic Rialto Bridge and past some of Venice's loveliest palaces,
before depositing you amid the glories of the Piazza San Marco.
It's worth investing in a tourist *vaporetto* pass for transport, which
is available for 12, 24, 36, 48 and 72 hours, and gives unlimited
travel on all services. It costs €13, €15, €20, €25 and €30
respectively, and is available from the ticket offices at main
vaporetto stops. Regular *vaporetto* tickets cost €6 and are vaild
for 1 hour. If you plan to do a lot of sightseeing you can buy
various museum passes, ranging in price from €17 to €23; these
are available at the museums. The APT also issues the Venice
Card, which is valid for all transport and entrance to the civic
museums. Prices range from €29.90 for 12 hours to €81.90 for
seven days. It must be reserved at least two days in advance,
either online at www.venicecard.it or by calling 0039 041 2424.
Try to walk as much as possible during your visit; it's the best way
to see the city, make serendipitous discoveries and soak up its
unique atmosphere, though even with a good map you can
expect to get lost—an essential part of the Venetian experience.

BACKGROUND

For centuries, Venice has been welcoming visitors and remains
one of the world's ultimate travel destinations. This unique city,
built on water, was founded in the fifth century by mainland
dwellers fleeing the barbarian invaders and, by the 12th century,
had established itself as a world trading and commercial hub.
A republic was established, headed by a doge (chief magistrate)
and ruled by councils, which acquired a vast overseas empire
that made Venice both feared and envied by every major power.
Wealth poured into the city to fund the building of its great
churches and palaces, adorned with paintings and sculpture, and
Venice was renowned for its marvels and sybaritic way of life. Its
power declined as other trade routes to the East were opened,
and in 1797 the Republic fell, the city becoming part of newly
unified Italy in 1866. Today, Venice faces huge problems
associated with a falling population and the effects of pollution
and climate change, but steps are being taken to counteract
these, and this superb city, a dream-like harmony of water, light
and stone, continues to enchant millions of visitors.

DON'T MISS

CANAL GRANDE
Take a trip down one of the world's most breathtaking waterways (▷ 280–281)
PALAZZO DUCALE
An airy Gothic palace with a sumptuous interior (▷ 284–285)
BASILICA DI SAN MARCO
Domed 11th-century basilica glittering with interior mosaics (▷ 278–279)
GALLERIA DELL'ACCADEMIA
Paintings from every period of Venetian art (▷ 282–283)
RIALTO
This district has vibrant markets and a famous bridge (▷ 287)

ITALY

Bright houses reflected in the waters of Burano's canal

Gothic arches under the staircase leading up from the courtyard at the Ca' d'Oro, a flamboyant Gothic palazzo

BURANO

➕ 277 off F1 🏛 Palazzo Ziani, Fondamenta San Lorenzo, 30122 Venezia, tel 041 529 8711; daily 9.30–3.30 🚤 Vaporetto: Burano www.comune.venezia.it

For a change of pace, Burano is an island tucked away in the northern part of the lagoon, whose brilliantly painted houses and miniature canals provide some of Venice's best photographic opportunities. Burano, and Mazzorbo next door, were among the first settlements in the lagoon. As Venice boomed, Mazzorbo declined, but Burano thrived as a fishing community, where the men went to sea and the women stayed home to make gossamer-fine lace, once famous all over Europe. The *rii* (canals) are still busy with boats and all the paraphernalia of fishing, and the *fondamente* (streets along the canals) are lined with houses of varying shades. Lace is still on offer everywhere, although few women make the real thing now; you can see it at the Scuola di Merletti (Lace-making School). **Don't miss** Sample the fish in the restaurants along Via Galuppi, the main street.

CA' D'ORO

➕ 276 C2 • Calle Ca' d'Oro, Cannaregio, 30121 Venezia 🕿 041 522 2349 🕐 Mon 8.15–2, Tue–Sun 8.15–7.15 💶 Adult €5, students (18–25) €2.50, under 18 and over 65 free (EU citizens) 🚤 Vaporetto: Line 1 Ca' d'Oro 🖼 Overlooking the sculpture garden 🚻 www.cadoro.org

One of the city's finest and most flamboyant examples of a Gothic palazzo, the Ca' d'Oro (Golden House) stands on the Canal Grande just above the Rialto. It was built for the Contarini family in the early 15th century, but changed hands repeatedly until it was heavily (and badly) restored in the 1850s by the Russian Prince Troubetskoy. Forty years later, Baron Franchetti bought and restored it, filling it with his painting, sculpture and coin collections. As a result, the ground floor regained its medieval layout, with a courtyard, tiny pleasure garden and main door opening onto the water. An exterior staircase leads to the upper floors, where the family lived. These floors, imaginatively converted into light and airy galleries, now house the collections, and have beautiful Gothic loggias overlooking the canal. Artistic highlights include Andrea Mantegna's powerful *St. Sebastian* and the ghostly fragments of frescoes by Giorgione that once decorated the nearby Fondaco dei Tedeschi. **Don't miss** View the water traffic on the Canal Grande from the upper loggias.

COLLEZIONE PEGGY GUGGENHEIM

➕ 276 B4 • Palazzo Venier dei Leoni (entrance on Fondamenta Venier), Dorsoduro 701, 30123 Venezia 🕿 041 240 5411 🕐 Wed–Mon 10–6 💶 Adult €10, over 65 €8, students with card €5, under 12s free 🚤 Vaporetto: 1 Salute 🍴 Snacks and lunches overlooking the sculpture garden www.guggenheim-venice.it

The Palazzo Venier is one of the Canal Grande's most eccentric buildings, an oddity whose construction began in 1759 but had progressed only as far as the first floor before the Venier money ran out. Its bizarre appearance appealed to the rich American millionairess Peggy Guggenheim (1898–1979), who realized its potential as a showcase for her collection. She began collecting contemporary art in the 1920s, buying from and dealing in the works of a whole generation of innovative abstract and Surrealist artists. She married Max Ernst, one of the greatest exponents of Surrealism, in 1941, but divorced him in 1946 and moved to Venice. Now administered by the Guggenheim Foundation, the collection is one of Venice's top attractions, its works the perfect antidote to an excess of Byzantine, Gothic and Renaissance art.

GESUITI

➕ 276 C2 • Campo dei Gesuiti, Cannaregio, 30121 Venezia 🕿 041 528 6579 🕐 Daily 10–12, 3–6 🚤 Vaporetto: Fondamenta Nove

Fans of baroque architecture must not miss the Jesuit Church of Santa Maria Assunta, known as the Gesuiti. The Jesuits, with their close ties to the papacy, were never popular in Venice and it was not until 1715 that they commissioned Domenico Rossi to build a church. He made up for the delay by going for maximum impact—a church with a vast façade and a mind-bogglingly ornate interior.

Inside you are struck by the baldachin over the altar, modelled on Bernini's version in St. Peter's in Rome (▷ 258–259), and festoons of drapery that billow from every corner and decorate every inch of wall space. What appear to be swags and drapes of figured damask and brocaded velvet are actually intricately carved and polished pieces of green and white marble. With scarcely a corner unadorned, it all adds up to a visual feast that is far more memorable than the comparatively pedestrian paintings by Palma il Giovane in the sacristy. The best painting, though badly lit and hard to see, is a night scene by Titian, the *Martyrdom of St. Laurence*.

ITALY

VENEZIA

0   200 m

0   200 yds

ITALY

CANNAREGIO

Fond Contarini

Rio di S Alvise

Tre Archi

Rio di San Girolamo

Rio del Battello

Rio della Sensa

Rio Mad

dell'Orto

Madonna dell'Orto

Calle della Cereria

Canale

Rio de S Giobbe

Canale

Rio Terra Farsetti

della Misericordia

Canale d'Misericordia

Fondar

Rio della Crea

Rio della Crae

Cannaregio

Guglio

Rio Terra san Leonardo

Campo S Geremia

San Marcuola

San Noale

Rio d S Caterina

Rio di S

Gesuiti

Calle Rielo

SS11

SANTA LUCIA

Ferrovia

Fond S Lucia

Fond San Simeon Piccolo

Riva de Biasio

San Stae

Canal

Rio d Felice

Ca' d'Oro

Ca' d'Oro

Grande

Apostoli

Rio di S S

RIO Martin

Rio d S Zan Degola

Rio Ca Tron

Rio d S Stae

Rio d Pergola

Rio delle due Torri

Ca' d'Oro

Rio di S S Apostoli

Santa Maria degli Miracoli

Ponte della Libertà

Piazzale Roma

P

Piazzale Roma

P

Rio Novo

SANTA CROCE

Rio d S Zuane

S A N

Muneghette

P O L O

Rio d S Cassiano

Beccari

Rio delle Madonetta

Rio di S

Rialto

Rialto

Grande

Rio d S Salvador

Santa Maria Gloriosa dei Frari

Campo S Polo

Rio d S Polo

San Silvestro

Calle d Fabbri

Rio d Burchielle

Rio Terra del Pensieri

Scuola Grande di San Rocco

Pescada

Rio di Ca' Foscari

Canal

Sant' Angelo

Rio d Luca

Fuseri

Bas Sar

Rio d S M Maggiore

Rio Novo

San Toma

SAN MARCO

Piazza San Marco

Scuola Grande dei Carmini

Campo S Margherita

San Samuele

Campo Santo Stefano

Campanile

Rio d Tintor

Ca' Rezzonico

Ca' Rezzonica

Rio di S Barnaba

Rio d S Vidal

Rio d Duca

Rio d Sandismo

Rio d S Maurizio

Rio d S Mois

Museo Correr

Rio Malpaga

Accademia

DORSODURO

Rio di San Nicolo

Rio d A Raffaele

Rio d S Trovaso

Rio Ognissanti

Galleria dell'Accademia

Giglio

Salute

Vallaresso (san Marco

MARITTIMA

Fond Zattere al Ponte Lungo

San Basilio

Rio d S Vio

Collezione Peggy Guggenheim

Rio della Fornace

Santa Maria della Salute

Zattere

Fond Zattere allo Spirito Santo

Canale della Giudecca

Zite

Canale dei Lavraneri

Fond San Biagio

Rio del Sa

Biagio

Fond d Convertite

S Eufemia

Fond S Eufemia

Giudecca

Redentore

Fond San Giacomo

Fond della Croce

For

Calle del Soliera

LA GIUDECCA

C delle Scuole

Calle S Giacomo

Rio del P lungo

Rio d Croce

Rio d Croce

A   B   C

1

2

3

4

5

Fonta dei Vetrai

Murano

Burano,
Torcello

Murano

San Michele
in Isola

Cimitero

Isola
di San Michele

Nuove

Ospedale

nti Giovanni
Paolo

Rio d Giustina

o d S.G Laterano

ria

Rio di S Francisco

Scuola di
San Giorgio
degli Schiavoni

Canale d Galeazze

Canale di Porta Nuova

Rio d'Vergini e S Pietro

Darsena
Grande

o d S. Lorenzo

San Giorgio
dei Greci

S Ternita

S Martino

Rio d Corne

Rio San Daniele

Isola di
S Pietro

an
ria

Rio d Greci

Rio del la Pieta

Rio Ca Dio

CASTELLO

Canale di S Pietro

degli

Schiavoni

Rio del Arsenale

Museo Storico
Navale

Rio di Quintavale

n Zaccaria

Arsenale

Rio della Tana

Via Giuseppe Garibaldi

Fond a Sant'Ana

Riva dei Sette Martiri

Viale Garibaldi

Secco Marina

Rio di S Giuseppe

Canale di San Marco

San Giorgio
Maggiore

Viale dei Giardini Pubblici

Viale trento

Via XXIV Maggio

Rio dei Giardini

Isola
di
S Elena

Via IV

Canale di S Elena

Viale Piave

Via S Elena

Isola di
San Giorgio
Maggiore

Novembre

della Grazia

D   E   F

ITALY

Basilica di San Marco

The great Byzantine-Venetian basilica—a reflection of Venice's historic role as a bridge between East and West.
The spiritual heart of Venice and the focal point of Piazza San Marco.
One of the world's finest medieval buildings.

Visitors sit on passarelle *(walkways for* aqua alta, *Venice's high water)*

The main cupola with a detailed mosaic depicting the Ascension

A view of the five domes from the Campanile

RATINGS

Historic interest	●●●●●
Cultural interest	●●●●○
Photo stops	●●●●○
Value for money	●●●●○

BASICS

✚ 276 C3 • Piazza San Marco, San Marco, 30124 Venezia

☎ 041 522 5205

🕐 Basilica, Tesoro and Pala d'Oro May–end Sep Mon–Sat 9.45–5.30, Sun 2–4.30; Oct–end Apr Mon–Sat 9.45–4.30, Sun 2–4.30

💶 Basilica, Pala d'Oro €1.50. Loggia and musuem €3. Tesoro €2 (no concessions). Tickets can be reserved at **www.**alata.it

🚤 *Vaporetto*: San Marco (Vallaresso)/San Zaccaria

🚌 Wide range at various prices. *Electra* is the best of those published in Italy; it covers various specific sights in Venice (available at the Palazzo Ducale)

🏬 Stands in atrium and Loggia selling postcards, religious souvenirs and tourist guides to Venice

SEEING THE BASILICA DI SAN MARCO

The best approach is on foot from the west end of the piazza (*vaporetto* stop San Marco (Vallaresso)). Aim to arrive early before the queues build up, and be prepared to wait. There's a fixed route around the interior. Allow your eyes to accustom to the low light levels, and take your time; this is an overwhelming building.

HIGHLIGHTS

THE LOGGIA

For a superb overview of the basilica, climb the steep stairs from the atrium to the gallery, where you'll find yourself at eye level with the mosaics (▷ below). From here you can gain access out onto the Loggia, a splendid vantage point from which to view the piazza.

THE BRONZE HORSES

Also here are replicas of the famous bronze horses (the originals are inside). These powerfully evocative creatures were looted from Constantinople in 1204 and are the only surviving four-horse chariot group from antiquity. They were thought to have been made for the Hippodrome in the third century, but they could be as much as 500 years older. Apart from a brief spell in Paris in the Napoleonic years, they have stood at San Marco for 800 years.

THE MOSAICS

The Sant'Alipio doorway, one of five leading to the atrium, is the only door with an original 13th-century mosaic. In the glittering darkness, shafts of light and slanting sunbeams illuminate more than 4,000sq m (43,000sq ft) of mosaics illustrating stories from the Bible. The early Byzantine-Venetian examples are the finest and include the Pentecost dome, nearest the entrance, the Ascension in the central dome, and Christ Emmanuel in the eastern dome. Old as it looks, the great Christ Pantocrator above the apse is actually a faithful 16th-century copy of the 11th-century original.

ITALY

The throngs in Piazza San Marco admiring the fabulous façade (left)

A glittering mosaic on the arch surmounting one of the portals (above)

THE PALA D'ORO

The focal point at ground level is the iconostasis, a Byzantine marble screen that hides the chancel and high altar. The remains of St. Mark lie beneath the altar, which is backed by the Pala d'Oro, an opulent gold and silver altarpiece. Made by a Sienese master in 1342, it is covered with more than 3,000 precious stones and 80 enamel plaques, many of which date from the 10th to 12th centuries.

CHAPEL OF THE MADONNA NICOPEIA AND THE TREASURY

To the left of the Pala d'Oro is the Chapel of the Madonna Nicopeia, a tiny, much-revered 12th-century Byzantine icon, and there is more Byzantine work in the Treasury (Tesoro). Look out for the 12th-century censer in the shape of a domed church.

BACKGROUND

The present basilica, built between 1063 and 1094, is the third to occupy this site. The original was built in 832 to house the remains of St. Mark the Evangelist, brought by merchants from Alexandria to become the city's patron saint. During the 11th century, Venice was culturally influenced by Byzantium, hence the centralized Greek cross plan and multiple domes of the newer church. The interior also owes much to the East, while the façade was altered between the 11th and 15th centuries with the addition of Gothic-style marble columns and carved stonework.

The upper portion of the red-brick Campanile (bell tower), 99m (325ft) high, viewed from Piazza San Marco (far left). Begun in 912, it also doubled as a lighthouse. It had to be totally rebuilt after collapsing in 1902, and was reopened to the public in 1912

Canal Grande

**Take a boat ride along one of the world's most mesmerizing waterways.
A host of magnificent palazzi and churches line its famous banks.
Sit back and watch the water traffic that keeps Venice alive and on the move.**

The Canal Grande—a waterway for traditional and modern boats

The Ponte di Rialto is illuminated at night

Gondolas on the Canal Grande near San Marco

RATINGS	
Historic interest	●●●●○
Cultural interest	●●●●○
Photo stops	●●●●●

TIPS

● The *vaporetto* is the cheapest and probably most entertaining way of seeing the Canal Grande. A gondola or water taxi is a more expensive option.
● It is best to begin at the station end and keep San Marco for the end of the trip.
● For the best chance of getting a good vantage point (and a seat) get on at Piazzale Roma.
● *Vaporetti* can be very crowded, particularly during the morning and evening rush hours. The best time is between 12.30 and 3 (siesta time), along with very early or late in the day.
● Few palazzi along the Canal Grande are floodlit, but a night ride is still a great experience.

SEEING THE CANAL GRANDE

Bisecting the city, the Canal Grande is Venice's main thoroughfare, a sinuous waterway lined with a succession of glorious buildings. It is 4km (2.5 miles) long and varies in width from 30m to 70m (100ft to 230ft), with an average depth of around 5m (16ft). Three *sestiere* (city districts)—Cannaregio, San Marco and Castello—lie to the east of the canal, with three more—San Polo, Santa Croce and Dorsoduro—to the west. Along its length are *traghetti* stations, from where gondolas ply back and forth. There are few places where you can walk or sit beside the canal; the best are at the railway station, at San Marcuola and Santa Sofia, by the Ponte di Rialto, on Campo San Vio, in front of Santa Maria della Salute and at San Marco. The best way to appreciate it is to board the No. 1 *vaporetto* at Piazzale Roma or Ferrovia and relax as far as San Marco (Vallaresso) or San Zaccaria. The whole trip takes 45 minutes.

HIGHLIGHTS

FERROVIA TO RIALTO

The present 1950s railway station *(ferrovia)* replaced the original 1846 construction, built when the causeway to the mainland was created; the stone-built Ponte dei Scalzi went up in 1934. On the right is the domed church of San Simeone Piccolo (1738); on the left is the ornate façade of the Scalzi (1656) and the entrance to the wide Canale di Cannaregio, the gateway to Venice in its pre-causeway days. The brick church soon after this is San Marcuola, unfinished since funds ran out in the 18th century; the two impressive buildings opposite are the Fondaco dei Turchi, trading headquarters for the Turks in Republican days, and the Deposito dei Megio, once a granary. In winter, the Casino moves to the Renaissance Palazzo Vendramin Calergi, where Richard Wagner died in 1883. Opposite, to the left, is the white baroque façade of San Stae. Two highlights are Longhena's Ca' Pesaro on the right (1652), now housing the Museo d'Arte Moderna (Apr–end Oct Tue–Sun 10–6; Nov–end Mar Tue–Sun 10–5; tel 041 524 0662), and the Gothic Ca' d'Oro (▷ 275). Across the water lie the *pescheria* (fish market) and Rialto market stands; the long building beside them is the Tribunale Nuove

ITALY

Two gondolas moored on
the Canal Grande (above)

A water taxi (left)

(1555), now the Assize Court. Opposite is the Fondaco dei Tedeschi, once home to German merchants, and overhead is the graceful Ponte di Rialto.

RIALTO TO ACCADEMIA

Highlights on the next stretch are the Gothic 13th-century Palazzo Barzizza (on the right), and the Palazzo Mocenigo (on the left), where Lord Byron lived in 1818. Beyond a sweeping bend known as La Volta, are the huge Palazzo Giustinian and Ca' Rezzonico on the right, along with the 18th-century Palazzo Grassi, one of Venice's prime exhibition venues. More Gothic façades follow before the Galleria dell'Accademia and its bridge come into view (▷ 282–283).

ACCADEMIA TO SAN MARCO

Below the bridge, Campo San Vio fronts the water on the right, followed by Palazzo Barbarigo, decorated with 19th-century mosaics, and the Palazzo Venier dei Leoni, home to the Peggy Guggenheim Collection (▷ 275). Opposite is Ca' Grande, designed by Sansovino in 1545, followed by some of Venice's grandest hotels. Look for the tiny Gothic Palazzo Dario on the right as the great plague church of Santa Maria della Salute approaches. The canal ends at the Dogana di Mare (customs), opposite which are the Giardini Reali and San Marco.

BACKGROUND

Running northwest to southeast, the Canal Grande was originally the main thoroughfare for merchants approaching the Rialto. An uninterrupted sequence of palazzi and churches, built across four centuries, lines the canal, their façades lapped by water.

BASICS

🕂 276 C2

🚏 *Vaporetti*: Piazzale Roma, Ferrovia, Riva de Biasio, San Marcuola, San Stae, Ca' d'Oro, Rialto, San Silvestro, Sant' Angelo, San Tomà, San Samuele, Ca' Rezzonico, Accademia, Giglio, Salute

ITALY

A statue in the Peggy Guggenheim Collection, housed in the 18th-century Palazzo Venier dei Leoni on the Canal Grande

Galleria dell'Accademia

●

**One of the world's great specialist collections.
Comprehensive overview of the very best of Venetian painting.
Well displayed in three historic buildings.**

A painter at the bottom of the Ponte dell'Accademia   Part of the St. Ursula Cycle *by Vittore Carpaccio*

TIPS
● Staffing shortages mean that sometimes certain rooms are closed, so if there is something specific that you want to see, ask before you buy your ticket.
● The €11 combined ticket for the Galleria dell'Accademia, Ca' d'Oro (▷ 275) and Museo Orientale is a good bargain.
● You can reserve timed tickets if you don't want to stand in line (Mon–Fri 9–6, Sat 9–2, tel 041 520 0345).

ITALY

SEEING THE GALLERIA DELL'ACCADEMIA

The Accademia's 24 rooms take a couple of hours to see properly. Pick up a plan from the entrance desk and, if you wish, an audioguide. Visit early or late to avoid the crowds—it is particularly busy on Sundays.

HIGHLIGHTS

THE SAN GIOBBE ALTARPIECE BY GIOVANNI BELLINI–ROOM 3
By the mid-15th century, the Bellini family had developed the concept of the *sacra conversazione*, a unified composition of the Madonna and saints. This superb altarpiece, all architectural detail, balance and warmth, is a prime example, painted at the time of the 1478 plague.

LA TEMPESTA BY GIORGIONE–ROOM 5
Giorgione's contribution to the development of Venetian painting was huge. In this, his most enigmatic work, its iconography still unsolved, we see the growing importance of realistic landscape and light—a far cry from the rigid gold used just over a century before.

CHRIST IN THE HOUSE OF LEVI BY VERONESE–ROOM 10
Figures stand out against a background of classical architecture in this stupendous set piece. The painting was originally titled *The Last Supper*, but was judged so secular by its patrons that Veronese faced heresy charges if he failed to change it; cleverly, he simply changed the name.

MIRACLE OF ST. MARK FREEING THE SLAVE BY TINTORETTO
Tintoretto's technical wizardry still shocks in this picture of the hurtling figure of St. Mark swooping down to help a persecuted slave, painted for the Scuola Grande di San Marco in 1547.

A further part of the St. Ursula Cycle *by Vittore Carpaccio*

GALLERY GUIDE

The rooms are arranged chronologically except for 19–24, which are specific collections.

Room 1: The Primitives—Byzantine and international Gothic gold-ground paintings, typified by Paolo Veneziano.
Rooms 2–3: 15th-century altarpieces and works by the Bellini family, Sebastiano del Piombo, Cima de Conegliano and Carpaccio.
Rooms 4–5: Giovanni Bellini, Mantegna, Piero della Francesca, Cosmè Tura and Giorgione.
Rooms 6 and 10: Titian, Jacopo Tintoretto and Paolo Veronese—the Venetian superstars.
Rooms 7–8: Lorenzo Lotto, Romanino and Jacopo Palma il Vecchio.
Room 11: Veronese and Tiepolo.
Rooms 14–18: The 17th and 18th centuries: pictures and genre paintings by Tiepolo, Canaletto, Bellotto, Guardi, Pietro Longhi and Rosalba Carriera.
Rooms 19–20: Stories of the Relic of the Cross by Vittore Carpaccio, Gentile Bellini and others.
Room 21: *St. Ursula Cycle* by Vittore Carpaccio.
Room 23: Former church of Santa Maria della Carità with 15th-century paintings by the Bellini and Vivarini families.
Room 24: Former Albergo Room of Santa Maria della Carità.

DISCOVERY OF THE TRUE CROSS BY GIAMBATTISTA TIEPOLO—ROOM 11

Painted for a church in Castello, now destroyed, this ceiling panel perfectly embodies Tiepolo's style—dizzying perspective, startling light and sugary, light-hearted hues.

PROCESSION IN THE PIAZZA DI SAN MARCO BY GENTILE BELLINI—ROOM 20

Created in 1496, this work shows the Piazza di San Marco as it was more than 500 years ago, with St. Mark's and the Doge's Palace much as they appear today. Carpaccio's painting of the Rialto nearby makes a good contrast, as there is little that's recognizable in the 21st century.

ST. URSULA CYCLE BY VITTORE CARPACCIO—ROOM 22

Crammed with charming anecdotes and details, the *St. Ursula Cycle* was painted in around 1498. It's the complicated tale, mixing reality and imagination, of a princess who, accompanied by her fiancé and 11,000 virgins, attempted to cross Europe to Rome, only to be massacred in Cologne.

PRESENTATION OF THE VIRGIN BY TITIAN—ROOM 24

This beautiful picture, painted between 1534 and 1539 for the Scuola della Carità, still hangs in its original position. The composition balances landscape, architecture and figures, with the small figure of the Virgin ascending the stairway.

BASICS

🕇 276 B4 • Campo Carità, Dorsoduro 1050, 30123 Venezia ☎ 041 520 0345
🕐 Mon 8.15–2, Tue–Sun 8.15–7.15
💶 Adult €6.50, EU citizens (18–25) €3.25, under 18 and over 65 free
🚤 *Vaporetto*: Line 1 and 82 to Accademia
🎧 Tours in English and Italian, Mon–Sat 11–1, 3.30–5, Sun 10–2, tel 041 520 0345. Audiotours in English, Italian, French and German, €4. Video guide €6
📖 Full and short illustrated guides in Italian, English, French, Spanish, German and Japanese, €15.50 and €8.20
🛍 One shop and a stand selling good postcards, prints, good-quality gifts and art books (mainly on Renaissance art and artists)
🚻 ♿
www.gallerieaccademia.org

BACKGROUND

The Accademia di Belle Arti, which houses the Galleria dell'Accademia, was founded in 1807 under Napoleon, who had suppressed dozens of churches and monasteries and needed somewhere to house their artworks. The art school still exists, but today the Accademia is primarily known as one of Europe's finest specialized art collections. It fills three connected former religious buildings, the Scuola Grande della Carità, its adjacent church of Santa Maria, and the monastery of the Lateran Canons.

Palazzo Ducale

The political and judicial hub of the Venetian government.
The biggest, grandest and most opulent civic building in Venice.
A dream-like Gothic palace—one of the architectural highlights of the city.

A close-up of the Palazzo Ducale's balcony

The delicate tracery and elegantly regular columns of the façade viewed from the water

BASICS

✚ 276 C4 • Piazza San Marco 1, San Marco, 30124 Venezia ☎ 041 271 5911
🕐 Apr–end Oct daily 9–7; Nov–end Mar daily 9–5. Itinerari Segreti (Secret Itineraries) tour must be reserved in advance
💵 Adult €12, child (6–14) free
🚤 Vaporetto: San Zaccaria, San Marco (Vallaresso)
🎧 Guided tours in English Tue–Thu, Sat 11.30, €16; audioguides in Italian, English, French, German and Spanish, €6
📖 Good Electra guidebooks available from bookshops in several languages
🍴 Bar on ground floor serving drinks, coffee and snacks
📚 Excellent bookshop, with good range of guidebooks, art books, posters, postcards and souvenirs
🚻

www.museiciviciveneziani.it

SEEING THE PALAZZO DUCALE

The Palazzo Ducale (Doge's Palace), seat of Venice's temporal power, is connected to the Basilica di San Marco at the east end of the Piazza di San Marco, a 45-minute walk or half-hour ride by *vaporetto* from the railway station. The meeting place of the councils that ruled Venice, the home to the Doge, the law courts, the civil service and the prisons, the palazzo overlooks both the piazzetta and the waters of the Bacino di San Marco. Founded as a castle in the ninth century, its present appearance as a masterpiece of Venetian Gothic architecture dates from the 14th century, a magnificent reminder of the city's past glories. Whether you approach it via the water or by strolling through the piazza, the first impressions of this fairy-tale palace are unforgettable.

HIGHLIGHTS

THE EXTERIOR, THE PORTA DELLA CARTA AND THE COURTYARD

One of the world's finest examples of Gothic architecture, the exterior of the Palazzo Ducale runs along the water's edge and the piazzetta. The waterfront façade was finished in 1419 and the side on the piazzetta was built in the 15th century. The beautiful pink-and-white frontage has an airy arcade topped by a gallery supporting the mass of the upper floors; the play of light and shade over the masonry enhances the impression of harmony. The columns and pillars at ground level are mainly copies of the 14th- to 15th-century originals, now housed in the Museo dell'Opera, off the interior courtyard.

The main entrance into the palazzo is the Porta della Carta, a grand piece of florid Gothic architecture, built by Bartolomeo and Giovanni Bon between 1438 and 1442. This provides access through a portico to the courtyard, an enclosed space with a first-floor loggia. The most imposing approach to the loggia is undoubtedly via Sansovino's 1485 Scala dei Giganti (Giant's Staircase), used by the Doge at his inauguration. There is another flamboyant Sansovino stairway, the stucco-and-gilt Scala d'Oro (Golden Stairway), leading from the loggia to the upper floors.

ITALY

THE DOGE'S APARTMENTS

The Doge, elected from Venice's patrician families, was the one politician to sit on all the major councils and the only one elected for life—a position of such potential power that it was hedged with endless restrictions to prevent abuse of power. After his election, the Doge gave his entire life over to the service of the State, and his apartments reflect this lack of privacy. They comprise a series of surprisingly intimate rooms, magnificently if austerely decorated, with splendid ceilings and superb fireplaces. Here, the Doge received deputations and ambassadors and oversaw council deliberations. The finest and biggest chamber is the Sala delle Mappe (Map Room), painted with maps of the whole of the 16th-century known world, with Venice firmly as the central focus.

THE ANTICOLLEGIO, THE COLLEGIO AND THE SALA DEL SENATO

The extraordinarily rich decoration of the state rooms in the Palazzo Ducale is intended to illustrate the history of Venice and was painted by some of the greatest 16th-century Venetian artists. The aim was to impress visiting emissaries, many of whom passed through the palace on official business. The Anticollegio served as a waiting room for ambassadors hoping to see the Doge; four mythological paintings, created in 1577–78 by Tintoretto (1518–94), hang on the walls, while facing the window is Veronese's *Rape of Europa*. From here, the ambassadors moved to the adjoining Collegio to be received. This was also the room where the inner cabinet met. The ceiling panels are by Veronese (1528–88), pure propaganda showing Justice and Peace as mere sidekicks to Venice herself. Venice triumphs yet again in Tintoretto's painting in the middle of the ceiling in the next-door Sala del Senato, where the 300-strong senate met to receive reports from returning ambassadors and debate questions of commerce, war and foreign policy.

BACKGROUND

The Palazzo Ducale was designed not only to provide a home for the Doge, but also to house the machinery of the State—the councils, committees and officials who administered the government of the city. From the 14th century only those noble families listed in the so-called *Libro d'Oro (Golden Book)* sat on the councils, and the building reflects their power, wealth and prestige as well as that of Venice itself. The Palazzo Ducale began to assume its present shape in 1340 when a new hall for the Maggior Consiglio (Great Council) was built. Much of the rest of what we see today dates from the mid-15th century. There were devastating fires in 1574 and again in 1577, but it was decided to restore the building rather than replace it with something new. Since the fall of the Republic in 1797, the Palazzo Ducale has had many different functions; today, as well as being open to the public, it houses various city offices.

TIPS

● Expect parts of the Palazzo Ducale to be closed; a building of this age requires constant restoration.
● The Museum Card for the Musei della Piazza San Marco (€17) provides entrance to all the museums in Piazza San Marco (Palazzo Ducale, Museo Correr, Museo Archeologico Nazionale, Biblioteca Nazionale Marciana).
● A Museum Pass (€23) is available for all Venice's civic museums in the Musei della Piazza San Marco (Palazzo Ducale, Museo Correr, Museo Archeologico Nazionale, Biblioteca Nazionale Marciana), the Musei del Settecento (Ca' Rezzonico, Palazzo Mocenigo, Casa di Carlo Goldini, Ca' Pesara) and the Musei delle Isole (Museo del Vetro and Museo del Merletto).

ITALY

The Sala della Bussola (above left)

Displays of weaponry, armour and a cannon in the Palazzo Ducale (below)

PIAZZA SAN MARCO AND THE CAMPANILE

The historic heart of Venice.
Some of the city's finest Byzantine, Gothic and
Renaissance architecture.
Bordered by compelling museums, chic shops and cafés.

As you emerge from the narrow surrounding streets into the piazza, its sheer scale is breathtaking—not for nothing did Napoleon describe it as 'the biggest drawing room in Europe'. Within the arcades that line three sides of the piazza are Florian's and Quadri's, two historic cafés with plush interiors, impeccable service and tables outside on the piazza. They are very expensive, but a drink here is quite an experience, often accompanied by an orchestra.

THE PIAZZETTA AND THE TORRE DELL'OROLOGIO

At the east end of the piazza's wide expanse stands the Basilica di San Marco (▷ 278–279). The open space runs down to the water's edge, St. Mark's Basin, and is flanked on the right by the Biblioteca Marciana and the Zecca, designed by Sansovino between 1527 and 1537, and the Palazzo Ducale (▷ 284–285) on the left. A winged lion, symbol of Venice, and St. Theodore, the city's first patron saint, top its two columns. On the other side of the basilica, the tiny space fronted by ancient marble lions, known as the Piazzetta dei Leoncini, is overlooked by the Torre dell'Orologio. This clocktower has a zodiacal clock with mechanical figures and is crowned with a golden lion. It was designed by Mauro Coducci and built between 1406 and 1506.

THE ARCADES AND THE CAMPANILE

The arcaded buildings that run down the long sides of the piazza are the offices of the Procurators of San Marco; the 16th-century Procuratie Vecchie, to the north, and the Procuratie Nuove, built a century later, to the south. After the fall of Venice in 1797, the two were linked by another arcaded building, the Ala Napoleonica, now home to the Museo Correr. In front of San Marco, the campanile (bell tower), a great place for city and lagoon views, was designed in 1514. What you see is a copy, as in 1902 the entire tower collapsed. No other buildings were damaged but the custodian's cat was killed. It was rebuilt *'Com'era, dov'era'* ('Like it was, where it was') and Sansovino's Loggetta at the foot of the tower was pieced together from the fragments.
Don't miss Visit the Piazzetta and the Torre dell'Orologio.

ITALY

RIALTO

The traditional setting of one of Italy's most vibrant markets. A place to jostle with the locals and experience a slice of Venetian life.

The Rialto was one of the earliest parts of the lagoon to be settled: the word *Rialto* is a corruption of *Rivoaltus*, the upper bank, the highest area and thus less likely to be flooded. By the 10th and 11th centuries, the Rialto was Venice's commercial heart and one of Europe's most important trading areas. In 1097 the market became a permanent fixture. A pontoon of boats linked the two banks, but in the 12th and 13th centuries the first of five wooden bridges was built across the canal. Venetian merchants controlled trade between Europe and the Far East, while Europe's major banks and international trading companies set up offices here. The name Rialto was as familiar to medieval moneymen as that of Wall Street or the City of London is today.

PONTE DI RIALTO
The idea of a stone bridge at the Rialto was first mooted in 1557 and a competition was held to choose the best design, with big names such as Michelangelo, Palladio and Sansovino all submitting their plans. The prize went to the aptly named Venetian Antonio da Ponte, for his revolutionary single-span suggestion. Two *fondamente* (canalside streets) stretch along either side of the water, one of the few places in Venice where you can actually stroll along the edge of the Canal Grande (▷ 280–281). The San Marco side is the Riva del Ferro, named after the iron that was once unloaded here, while opposite, the Riva del Vin is a reminder that this was originally the discharge point for wine barrels.

THE MARKET
Behind the Riva del Vin is a labyrinthine maze of narrow streets, many named after the goods sold during the great days of the Republic: Ruga de'Orefici (Goldsmiths' Row), Ruga Speziali (Spicemakers' Street), Riva dell'Olio (Oil Quay) and Campo della Pescheria (Fish Market Square). Nearby is the Rialto market and its surrounding specialist shops, the city's main place for food shopping, where people bargain for meat, fruit, vegetables and, above all, fresh fish and seafood.

The little church of San Giacomo, on the San Polo side of the bridge, is said to be Venice's oldest, founded, according to legend, on the same day as the city itself, 26 March 421. The clock above the church is famous for its inaccuracy; it has been incorrect since its installation in the 15th century.

RATINGS	
Good for kids	● ● ●
Specialist shopping	● ● ● ● ●
Photo stops	● ● ● ●
Good for food	● ● ● ●

BASICS
✚ 276 C3
🚢 *Vaporetto*: Rialto

TIP
● The fish market is closed on Mondays.

Traffic criss-crossing the Canal Grande in front of the Ponte di Rialto (top) and the Campo della Pescheria, where you can buy fresh fish and seafood, the staples of Venetian cuisine (above)

KEY TO SYMBOLS

- ⊕ Shopping
- 🎭 Entertainment
- ▼ Nightlife
- ◎ Sports
- ✪ Activities
- ♡ Health and Beauty
- ⊗ For Children

WHAT TO DO

⊕ BOTTEGA VENETA
San Marco 1337, Calle Vallaresso
Tel 041 522 8489
www.bottegaveneta.com
An elegant shop, famed for its superior leather belts, bags and wallets. This is an opportunity to get your hands on the new lines while staying in the Veneto region. A great place to buy classic gifts that are practical and enduring.
🕐 Mon–Sat 10–7.30, Sun 11–7
🚌 San Marco

⊕ GILBERTO PENZO
San Polo 2681, Calle Seconda dei Saoneri
Tel 041 719 372
www.veniceboats.com
Gilberto's practical approach to recreating Venetian boats in miniature, including gondolas, is respected the world over. His crowded workshop is fascinating and you can buy boats of all sizes, including inexpensive kits to build.
🕐 Mon–Sat 9.30–12.30, 3–7
🚌 San Toma

⊕ MONDONOVO
Rio Terà Canal, 3063 Dorsoduro
Tel 041 528 7344
www.mondonovomaschere.it
Venice's most famous mascheraio has been setting an example to other mask-makers for decades with its enormous variety of masks, handmade on the premises from papier-mâché and beautifully gilded and painted.
🕐 Mon–Sat 9–6
🚌 Ca' Rezzonico

⊕ PANTAGRUELICA
Campo San Barnaba, Dorsoduro 2844
Tel 041 523 6766
Arguably the finest food shop in Venice, Pantagruelica offers the best produce from all over Italy, lovingly tracked down by the enthusiastic owner. The emphasis is on quality, so expect to find organic produce

heavily featured. Highly recommended for cheese, salumeria (cured meats), specialty oils, dried goods and fresh truffles.
🕐 Mon–Sat 9–6.30 🚌 Ca' Rezzonico

⊕ RIALTO MARKET
Near the Rialto Bridge, on the San Polo side
Wander around the Rialto for fruit and vegetables or head down to the pescheria, or fish market, to see the strangest creatures in the lagoon. A great experience that hasn't changed for centuries.
🕐 Mon–Sat 8am–12 🚌 Rialto

⊕ VENINI
Murano 47–50, Fondamenta Vetrai
Tel 041 273 7211
www.venini.com
If you're serious about buying some Murano glass, spend an afternoon seeing how it's made. The great thing about Venini is that it's not too crowded, so you can appreciate the craftsmanship. A good balance of traditional designs and artier pieces.
🕐 Mon–Sat 9.30–7.30
🚌 Colonna, Murano

🎭 GRAN TEATRO LA FENICE
San Marco 1965, Calle del Fenice
Tel 041 756 511; box office: 041 2434
www.teatrolafenice.it
The spiritual headquarters of 19th-century opera and classical music was ravaged by fire in 1996. After lengthy delays, the building reopened for the 2004–05 winter season. Tickets are available from the Cassa di Risparmio in Campo San Luca.
🎟 €25–€180 🚌 Santa Maria del Giglio

🎭 TEATRO MALIBRAN
Calle dei Milion, 5873 Cannaregio
Tel 041 786 603; box office: 041 2434
This wonderful building stages well-known operas such as La Traviata and more modern works, as well as classical concerts and ballet. There is a full theatrical and musical programme.
🎟 €10–€60
🚌 Rialto

▼ HARRY'S BAR
San Marco 1323, Calle Vallaresso
Tel 041 528 5777
A Venice must-visit, Harry's Bar

was opened in 1931 and made famous by celebrity clients including Woody Allen, Ernest Hemingway and Truman Capote. Harry's Bar is both a bar and a restaurant and it's given the world two culinary signature items, carpaccio of beef and the Bellini cocktail.
🕐 Daily 10.30am–11pm 🚇 🚌 San Marco

◎ GONDOLA RIDE
A gondola ride, the ultimate in Venetian romance, allows visitors to see the city at its most magical and is an unforgettable experience. If you're planning a trip, you can discuss the itinerary beforehand with the gondolier; the route will depend on where you're boarding, but most gondola trips will cover either the Bacino di San Marco and some side canals, or a section of the Grand Canal and some smaller rii. Fares are set by the gondola board (tel 041 528 5075, www.gondolavenezia.it), and are based on six passengers, with no reductions for smaller numbers. Expect to pay between €65 and €80, depending on the time of day, for 50 minutes.
Gondola Stations:
- Bacino Orseolo (behind Piazza San Marco)
- Campo San Moïse (in front of Grunwald hotel)
- Ferrovia (railway station)
- Piazzetta San Marco
- Piazzale Roma
- Riva degli Schiavoni (in front of Hotel Danieli)
- Riva del Carbon (south end of Rialto Bridge)
- San Marco (Vallaresso) (next to vaporetto stop)
- San Tomà (near vaporetto stop)
- Santa Maria del Giglio (next to vaporetto stop)

EATING

AL MASCARON
Castello 5225, Calle Lunga Santa Maria Formosa
Tel 041 522 5995
Al Mascaron offers great ciccheti (Venetian tapas). It also has a menu for pasta, risotto and salads if you fancy grazing a little longer.
🕐 Mon–Sat 11–3, 6.30pm–midnight; closed over Christmas and New Year

ITALY

L €30, D €55, Wine €6.50 per carafe 🚇 San Zaccaria

FORTUNY RESTAURANT

10 Giudecca, Hotel Cipriani and Palazzo Vendramin
Tel 041 520 7744
www.hotelcipriani.it
This outstanding restaurant specializes in matchless regional Italian cuisine. The menu and wine list are very carefully thought out to ensure a memorable meal. Men over 15 should wear a jacket and tie. Children under eight are not welcome.
🕐 Daily 8–10.30, 12–2.30, 7.30–10.30
🍴 L €75, D €150, Wine €35
🚇 Giudecca

OSTERIA OLIVA NERA

Castello 3417/18, Calle della Madonna
Tel 041 522 2170
www.osteria-olivanera.com
The menu here shows that Venetian cooking can be given a contemporary edge. Delicious examples include scallops with wild mushrooms, and lamb cooked in thyme. The dessert menu includes a rich mascarpone cheesecake.
🕐 Fri–Tue 12–2.30, 7–10pm
🍴 L €28, D €47, Wine €9
🚇 San Zaccaria

DAL PAMPO (OSTERIA SANT'ELENA)

Calle Generale Chinotto, 24 Castello
Tel 041 520 8419
Dal Pampo provides hearty cooking and robust wines.
🕐 Fri–Wed 12–2.30, 7.30–9; closed Christmas, May and Aug (check to see which week)
🍴 L €17, D €22, Wine €4
🚇 Sant'Elena

VINI DA GIGIO

Cannaregio, 3628A Castello
Tel 041 528 5140
www.vinidagigio.com
This increasingly famous place is one of the best-value restaurants in Venice, known for its superlative *antipasti*, fresh fish and meat and game; in season, try the wild duck from Burano. The wines come from all over the world. Reservations are essential.
🕐 Tue–Sun 12–2.30, 7.30–10.30; closed 3 weeks Jan into Feb, 3 weeks Aug into Sep
🍴 L €35, D €45, Wine €7
🚫
🚇 Ca' d'Oro

STAYING

CA' PISANI

Dorsoduro 979/a, Rio Terra dei Foscarini, 30123 Venezia
Tel 041 240 1411
www.capisanihotel.it
Smooth lines, exposed beams and art deco furnishings mix with modern minimalist touches here. Each room is individually designed and has a relaxing, sophisticated charm. The facilities, including sauna, are excellent and the bathrooms ultra-modern. La Rivista restaurant has simple Italian cuisine.
🏨 €270–€500
ℹ 29 🚫 💻 Access
🚇 Accademia

LA FENICE ET DES ARTISTES

San Marco 1936, Campiello della Fenice 193, 30124 Venezia
Tel 041 523 2333
www.fenicehotels.com
This is popular with musicians and opera aficionados as it's close to the famous La Fenice. Exposed beams, antique furnishings and marble give it a refined yet comfortable character. The best rooms have balconies. Facilities include telephone, television, private bathroom, hair-dryer and safe. La Taverna restaurant serves Venetian dishes.
🏨 €160–€330
ℹ 67 rooms, 1 suite 🚫
🚇 San Angelo or San Marco

LOCANDA ARMIZO

Campo San Silvestro, 1104 San Polo, 30125 Venezia
Tel 041 520 6473
www.armizo.com
This small hotel in a converted merchant's premises offers excellent value and comfortable rooms. Four big, airy and spacious rooms overlook the *campo* and will sleep up to five; rates are per room, not per person. Good bathrooms, friendly welcome and well-presented breakfasts served in the bedrooms. All rooms have satellite TV.
🏨 €79–€259
ℹ 7 🚫
🚇 San Silvestro

PENSIONE ACCADEMIA

Dorsoduro 1058, Fondamenta Bollani, 30123 Venezia
Tel 041 521 0188
www.pensioneaccademi.it

Verdant courtyard gardens, Grand Canal views and helpful staff complement this hotel that is in a great location for art-lovers. Once called Villa Maravege, it is a former Russian embassy. The stately rooms have wooden floors, 19th-century furniture and chandeliers. Private bathroom, television and phone in all the rooms. Early reservations are recommended.
🏨 €140–€330
ℹ 27 🚫
🚇 Accademia

LA RESIDENZA

Castello 3608, Campo Bandiera e Moro, 30122 Venezia
Tel 041 528 5315
www.veneciaresidenza.com
The Gothic façade, with its 10th-century sculptural details, overlooks the peaceful Campo Bandiera e Moro to the south. The wonderful lobby has elegant furnishings amid ornate ceilings and walls. Request one of the refurbished rooms, which have a fresh, bright feel and period pieces. Facilities include private bathroom with shower, television, safe and minibar.
🏨 €80–€180
ℹ 15 🚫
🚇 Arsenale

SAN SAMUELE

San Marco 3358, Salizada San Samuele, 30124 Venezia
Tel 041 522 8045
www.albergosansamuele.it
This above-average 1-star hotel is in a wonderful location near the San Samuele *vaporetto* stop. Staff are friendly and the hotel is tidy and well run. For the price, the rooms are nothing special, but in contrast to the competition they are clean and comfortable. Most have shared bathrooms and basic facilities. Credit cards are not accepted.
🏨 €50–€120
ℹ 10
🚇 San Samuele

Verona

●

Impressive Roman remains, medieval castles and Romanesque and
Renaissance churches and palaces.
A beautiful city, the setting of Shakespeare's *Romeo and Juliet.*
Streets lined with expensive shops and fashionable restaurants.

*Verona's Roman amphitheatre
has capacity for 22,000 people*

SEEING VERONA

Beautiful Verona—Roman ruins, rose-red
medieval buildings and romantic dreams
of young love—is the largest city in
mainland Veneto, a quietly prosperous,
cultured place where tourism plays
second fiddle to the rest of the economy.
Most of its historic heart is enclosed by
a loop of the River Adige, with a few
other important sights on the north
bank. Wonderful churches and buildings
are scattered throughout the pleasant
streets, which are themselves punctuated by lovely squares.

HGHLIGHTS

RATINGS

Historic interest	● ● ● ●
Specialist shopping	● ● ● ● ●
Walkability	● ● ● ●
Good for food	● ● ● ● ●

BASICS

➕ 5 D4

ℹ️ Via degli Alpini 9 (Piazza Brà),
37121 Verona, tel 045 806 8680;
Mon–Sat 8.30–7.30, Sun 9–3

🚆 Verona

www.tourism.verona.it
You can send e-cards, get the latest
weather forecast or get the latest view
over Piazza Brà via the webcam at this
website dedicated to Verona and Lake
Garda. It also has a guide for visitors
and information on accommodation,
regional food and wine, events and
sport. Italian, English and German
versions.

THE ARENA

➕ 293 C2 • Piazza Brà, 37121 Verona ☎ 045 800 3204 🕐 Sep–end Jun Mon
1.45–7.30, Tue–Sun 8.30–7.30 (last admittance 6.30); Jul, Aug (opera season) daily
9–3.30; closed to visitors during performances 💷 Adult €4, child €1
Piazza Brà should be your first stop, an irregular open space
dominated by one of the city's best-known monuments, the great
Roman amphitheatre. Built in the first century AD, it is the third-largest
of the surviving Roman amphitheatres in Italy. A 13th-century
earthquake destroyed most of the exterior arcade, but the interior is
intact, with steeply pitched tiers of pink marble seats and dizzying
views from the top. Since 1913 people have flocked to Verona to
catch a performance during its summer opera season.

BASILICA DI SAN ZENO MAGGIORE

➕ 292 A2 • Piazza San Zeno, 37121 Verona 🕐 Mar–end Oct Mon–Sat 10–1,
Sun 1–5 💷 €2.50
Farther west from Castelvecchio stands San Zeno Maggiore, a
Romanesque church founded in the fourth century; a set of superb
11th-century bronze doors open into a lofty interior with Roman
columns and an altarpiece by Andrea Mantegna (c1431–1506). The
church is the burial place of Pepin the Short, king of the Franks. Father
of Charlemagne and founder of the Frankish dynasty of the Caroling-
ians, he led his army into Italy to defeat the Lombards in AD754.

PIAZZA DELLE ERBE

➕ 293 C2
Piazza delle Erbe is the setting for a lively daily market, and Piazza
dei Signori, the heart of medieval Verona. Piazza delle Erbe is
surrounded by exquisite buildings: The Torre dei Lamberti soars
above the brightly frescoed Casa Mazzanti, and there is a loggia, a
14th-century fountain and a Lion of St. Mark.

PIAZZA DEI SIGNORI

➕ 293 C2
From Piazza delle Erbe an arch leads to the old civic area, the Piazza
dei Signori, the focus of which is a statue of the Renaissance poet

Dante Alighieri (1265–1321). The candy-striped Palazzo della Ragione has a fine Romanesque-Gothic courtyard. The building behind Dante is the Renaissance Loggia del Consiglio dating from 1493, with the Tribunale next to it. Don't overlook the Scaligeri tombs, next to the Tribunale.

Cangrande II's Ponte Scaligero on the River Adige near Castelvecchio (below left)

CASA DI GIULIETTA
➕ 293 C2 • Via Capello 23, 37121 Verona ☎ 045 803 4303 ⏰ Mon 1.30–7.30, Tue–Sun 8.30–7.30 (last admittance 6.30) 🎟 Adult €4, child (8–13) €1

The ivy-clad walls and balcony of the Casa di Giulietta (below)

From Piazza delle Erbe, Via Cappello leads southeast to the so-called Casa di Giulietta (House of Juliet), a graffiti-adorned mecca for love-sick teenagers and bus tours; the balcony was added in 1935.

LA CATTEDRALE (DUOMO)
➕ 293 C1 ☎ 045 808 3711 ⏰ Mar–end Oct Mon–Sat 10–5.30, Sun 1.30–5.30; Nov–end Feb Mon–Sat 10–4, Sun 1.30–4 🎟 €2.50
On the northern point of the promontory is the Romanesque cathedral, which has a beautiful apse and a fine *Assumption* by Titian in the first chapel of the north aisle.

BACKGROUND
Verona is on the River Adige, 50km (30 miles) west of Vicenza, at the bottom of an Alpine pass, and was first colonized by the Romans in 89BC. It became a regional capital and survived the Ostrogoth and Frankish invasions of AD489 and AD754, becoming a free *comune* in 1107. Feuds and vendettas between the city's noble families dominated the next century or so and provided the basis for William Shakespeare's tale of doomed love, *Romeo and Juliet*, set in Verona. By the late 1200s one family had emerged as top dogs, the Scaligeris, a terrifyingly successful mercenary clan. They were ousted in their turn by the Milanese Viscontis in 1387. In 1402, having had their fill of lords, Verona turned to republican Venice, and remained part of *La Serenissima* (the Venetian Republic) until 1797, after which the city passed to the Austrians, who retained control until 1866, when Verona and Venice became part of the new Kingdom of Italy. The city was badly bombed during World War II, but quickly recovered to become an outstanding economic success story.

TIPS
● The historic heart is closed to traffic for most of the day, so come by train or use the parking area near the station.
● You can rent a bicycle in Piazza Brà at Zanchi (tel 045 800 5681).
● The Verona Card, valid for a day or a week, includes unlimited travel and museum admissions and is available from the tourist office. Pick up a free copy of *Passport Verona* for up-to-date listings.
● Verona is the venue for plays and musical events all year round, including great jazz and rock concerts, often in historic monuments and in open spaces outdoors. In July and August there is opera in the amphitheatre.
● Verona has a great café scene and is much livelier in the evenings than Venice. It is also a better bet for buying clothes.

ITALY

Teatro Romano in Verona was built in the 1st century AD

ITALY

Sunset over Verona

VERONA

0 ____ 300 m
0 ____ 300 yds

C COLOMBO
VIALE
PONTE CATENA

Via Tomaso da Vico
Via dei Carroccio
Via Spagna

PONTE RISORGIMENT

Via Pontida
Piazza S Zeno
VIA P SAN ZENO
Basilica di San Zeno Maggiore
Piazza Pozza
Piazza Corrubbio
Via Lenotti
Via A Rosmini
Circonvallazione P Maroncelli
Via Silvio Pellico
S Bernardino
Via Picacane
VIALE COL GALLIANO
Via Seffi
STRADONE
Via V Merighi
P
Circonvallazio
Porta Palio
Via C Camuzzoni
Via Albere
Alfredo Orieni

A

292 **ITALY** VERONA STREET PLAN

Via di San Salvatore

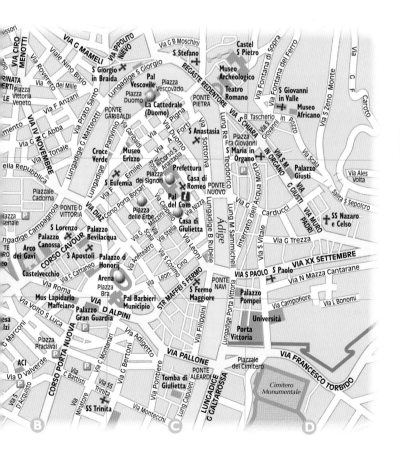

WHAT TO DO

🌐 ANTICA SALUMERIA ALBERTINI
Corso Sant'Anastasia 41
Tel 045 803 1074
www.salumeriaalbertini.it
This central shop is ideal for buying picnic food to take to the opera in the Arena. Sample the local prosciutto, wines and cheeses, or dive into the big barrel of olives.
✪ Daily 8–8

🌐 L'ENOTECA DELL'ISTITUTO ENOLOGICO ITALIANO
Via Sottoriva 7
Tel 045 590366
www.enotecaverona.com
In the old town, these old wine cellars lie beneath a 17th-century palace. Visitors have been tasting and buying top wines here for more than 40 years. There is an excellent selection, and afternoon wine-tasting sessions take place daily, with a different wine to sample every week. Pasta and jams are on sale too.
✪ Tue–Sat 9–12.30, 3.30–7.30, Mon 9–12.30

🎵 ARENA
Piazza Brà
Tel 045 800 5151
www.arena.it
This is one of the best-preserved Roman amphitheatres in Italy. Opera, concerts and other performances take place throughout the year but particularly in summer.
🎵 Evenings from 7.30 🍷 €22–€180

✹ GIARDINO GIUSTI
Via Giardino Giusti 2
Tel 045 803 4029
A magnificent garden, across the river from the heart of town. Get lost in the hedge maze or climb up to the grotto below a fearsome stone face and enjoy the view across to the city.
✪ Apr–end Sep daily 9–8; Oct–end Mar daily 9–dusk 🍷 €5

EATING

AL CARRO ARMATO
Vicolo Gatto 2/a
Tel 045 8030175
www.carroarmato.it
Delightful bar/restaurant near the Gothic church of Santa Anastasia, with its mysterious name meaning 'armoured car'. Delicious *antipasti* are served from the narrow bar or on large trestle tables in the adjoining high-ceilinged hall. The good-humoured staff occasionally burst into song. Wines are served either from the barrel or by the bottle. Card games are often played here, and there's occasional live music. Young clientele. No credit cards.
🍴 Thu–Tue 11–3, 6pm–2am, Sun 1–5, 6pm–midnight
🍷 L €13, D €33, Wine €5

OSTERIA LA PIGNA
Via Pigna 4
Tel 045 8004080
www.osteriapigna.it
At this large and elegant restaurant diners are given a glass of sparkling *prosecco* while they peruse the menu. Try the duck *pappardelle*, risotto with Amarone or *stracotto* (beef stew) and Amarone wine. A good range of wines is available.
🍴 Tue–Sat 12–3, 7–11, Sun–Mon 7–11
🍷 L €20, D €35, Wine €10
✹

TRATTORIA ALLA COLONNA
Largo Pescheria Vecchia 4
Tel 045 596718
This popular establishment takes its name from the large column in the middle of the room. It's packed with locals, so if you haven't reserved make sure you arrive before 9pm for dinner. Expect excellent regional cooking that is good value for money. Top dishes include horse meat, rabbit and *bigoli* pasta. The wines served are from the Veneto region. There is a fixed-price menu available for €13.
🍴 Mon–Sat 12–2.30, 7.30pm–2am
🍷 L €16, D €35, Wine €9

LA VECETE
Via Pellicciai 32A
Tel 045 591059
www.grupporialto.it
The best bar in town for tasting a very wide selection of wines. Five minutes' walk north from Piazza Brà, it's simply decorated with an enormous array of bottles to choose from. They also have excellent food, both snacks and full meals, served at the bar or at tables. It is advisable to make a reservation during July and August.
🍷 Mon–Sat 10.30am–1.30am
🍷 L €19, D €40, Wine €13

STAYING

COLOMBA D'ORO
Via Carlo Cattaneo 10, 37121 Verona
Tel 045 595300
www.colombahotel.com
There is beautiful antique furniture in many of the rooms at this luxury hotel. Parking is free or you can pay €20 to park in the hotel garage.
🛏 €140–€219
🛏 41 rooms, 10 suites ✹

HOTEL DUE TORRI
Piazza Sant'Anastasia 4, 37121 Verona
Tel 045 595044
www.baglionihotels.com
This luxurious hotel occupies a 13th-century palazzo in central Verona, right next to Sant'Anastasia church. It's spread over five floors, and the public areas and the guest rooms are magnificently furnished. There is a restaurant and a bar.
🛏 €220–€650
🛏 90 ✹

VICTORIA
Via Adua 8, 37121 Verona
Tel 045 590566
www.hotelvictoria.it
This friendly hotel is just southwest of the heart of the city. The rooms are equipped with satellite television, phone, safe and minibar (whirlpool baths on request). The superior class rooms are magnificent. The hotel has a bar and lounge area, and a sauna and solarium. Garage parking costs €20 per night, but advanced reservations are recommended.
🛏 €210–€325
🛏 66 ✹ 🍸

ITALY

ARRIVING

BY AIR

If you're flying direct from another continent you will arrive at Rome Fiumicino, the capital's main airport, or Milan Malpensa, serving Italy's economic capital and the Lakes. Rome and Milan each have a second airport: Rome Ciampino and Milan Linate.

Turin Caselle has doubled in size as a result of the world's attention on Turin as the venue for the 2006 Winter Olympic Games and now rivals Milan as the gateway to the north of Italy.

Venice Marco Polo is the main arrival point for north-eastern Italy, and most visitors heading for Florence arrive at Pisa, an hour's journey by road or train from the city. Naples is the South's busiest international airport.

BY FERRY

If you are planning a trip to Sicily or Sardinia, or onwards to Greece, you may want to travel by ferry. With the exception of the short hop across the Straits of Messina to Sicily, it's best to reserve a crossing in advance. You need to arrive at the departure port between 2 and 6 hours before sailing; individual companies will provide details when you reserve. The major ferry ports are clearly marked by road signs with a ship symbol, the name of the destination port and the word *traghetti* (ferries). Overnight ferries have cabins available.

For faster links to the main islands there's also the hydrofoil, though these services tend to be greatly reduced outside the peak summer season. Prices vary considerably, but reserving in advance may get you a good deal. The best way to research Italian ferries is through www.traghettionline.net/eng, a portal site linking virtually all the major operators, with an online reservations facility.

BY RAIL

From Britain you can travel by train to Italy, routing, via the Channel Tunnel, through either Brussels or Paris. The journey time via Brussels is longer, but if you choose the Paris option, you have to change from the Gare du Nord to the Gare de Lyon. Direct trains run to Rome, Florence, Milan, Turin and Venice.

The choice of routes and fares is highly complex, but it's best to use the Eurostar as far as Paris or Brussels, from where trains south are fast and frequent.

Eurostar trains link London with Paris and Brussels in under 3 hours. You must check in 30 minutes before departure and you are allowed two suitcases and one item of hand baggage. You need your passport to clear immigration and customs.

The total journey time from London to Italian destinations varies from 11 to 15 hours.

Sleepers are available from Paris on direct routes to Rome, Milan, Florence and Venice. Accommodation varies from 3-, 4- and 6-berth couchettes to single and double sleepers with integral shower and toilet.

BY BUS

Italy has few domestic long-distance bus routes, but there are international routes from major cities across Europe. **International buses** to Italy from the UK are coordinated by Eurolines (tel 08705 808080; www.nationalexpress.com), a consortium of 30 independent long-distance bus companies. Regular services run from London Victoria Coach Station to 27 cities in Italy, though most journeys involve a change in Paris. The typical adult return (round-trip) fare from London to Turin is £102, and London to Rome £112.

Destinations: Ancona, Bologna, Florence, Genoa, Milan, Naples, Padua, Parma, Pisa, Rimini, Rome, San Remo, Siena, Turin, Venice, Verona, with connections to other Italian destinations.

Journey time: London to Milan 22 hours, Florence 28 hours, Rome 30–32 hours, Naples 33–35 hours, all with a stop in Paris of 1 hour 30 minutes.

Tickets can be reserved online or at National Express travel offices. A Eurolines Pass allows you unlimited coach travel between a choice of 35 cities across Europe, including internal Italian routes between Milan and Siena and Siena and Rome (15 days £115–£198, 30 days £159–£245).

BY CAR

Driving to Italy, you will need a valid driver's licence, a vehicle registration document, a motor (auto) insurance certificate and a passport.

From the UK, you can take the ferry or use the Channel Tunnel. The main routes to Italy run through France, Switzerland and Germany. All cross the Alps; the St. Gotthard tunnel is free, but other passes range from €21–€32. To reach these take the E15 and E17 to Reims, then pick up the motorways (expressways). There are toll roads (turnpikes) all along the route. You should allow 11 to 14 hours' driving time to reach the north Italian border.

VISITORS WITH A DISABILTY

The overall picture of facilities for people with disabilities in Italy is mixed. The major problems are often not with transport, accommodation or public buildings, but in the layout and nature of the cities and towns themselves. The historic interest and architectural beauty of many of the main tourist attractions in Italy inevitably make disabled access a challenge. Italians are generally helpful, but, with some key exceptions, facilities for disabled people have not yet caught up with those in northern European countries and North America.

Accessible Italy (Regency San Marino srl): www.accessibleitaly.com

GETTING AROUND

BY CAR

Italy's road system is comprehensive, with *autostrade* (motorways/expressways) covering the entire peninsula from north to south and with trans-Apennine links at regular intervals. In addition, all regions have dual-carriageway (divided highway) and main-road alternatives and rural villages are connected by minor roads. Civil engineering is excellent, with bridges soaring over ravines and well-lit tunnels going through mountains. Given the country's north/south economic divide, the road network is at its best in the north, but even in the south driving is easy and a pleasure. However, driving in the cities, particularly in Rome, should be avoided.

As you approach the *autostrada* take the ticket from the automatic box on the left-hand side of the car or press the red button to get one. The barrier will lift. Keep your ticket safe, as you will need it to pay when you leave the *autostrada*. Cash payment is normally made to the official in the booth; the amount is displayed on a screen outside the pay window. If you are using a pass or paying by credit card, follow the signs into the Viacard booth.

Slip roads (ramps) onto and off Italian *autostrade* are short. You may have to stop and wait for traffic to pass before you can join the motorway.

Italians are fast, disciplined drivers outside the cities. Only use the outer lanes for overtaking and be prepared to move continuously between lanes to allow faster drivers behind you to overtake; they often drive up close behind you. Use the indicator before you pull out and while you are overtaking.

The Italian *autostrada* network is run by several different companies, which means that both price and frequency of tolls vary greatly. On the whole, northern toll roads tend to be more expensive, and you may find a *pedaggio* (toll station) coming up every few kilometres. South of Naples, the A1 *(Autostrada del Sole)* is

State-subsidized and free. Motorcycles under 150cc are not allowed on the motorway.

BY BUS

Italy has no national long-distance bus company. Buses are operated by myriad different companies, mainly running services within their own region, though there are a few that operate outside their own immediate area. With the low cost of rail travel, longer journeys are more efficient and less expensive by train.

If you are planning to use buses to get around a particular region, you can get timetables and information from the company office or the tourist information office.

● Bus stations are often next to the railway station. In small towns and villages, buses stop in the main piazza. Bus stations in larger towns tend to have toilets, a newsstand, bar and lost-property office.

● Tickets must normally be purchased before boarding the bus, from newsstands, shops or *tabacchi* (tobacconists).

BY TAXI

Taxis are available in all towns and cities. Government-regulated vehicles are either white or yellow. Always check that the taxi is registered and that the meter is running—avoid taxis without a meter, as they may not be insured. All charges should be listed on a rate card displayed inside the vehicle. It can be difficult to hail a cab, so it is often better to go to a taxi stand or reserve over the phone. Supplements are added for telephone reservations, luggage and additional passengers. Rates are higher at night and on Sundays and public holidays. Many city taxis have set rates from the airport to the city. Confirm the price before you begin your journey.

BY TRAIN

Italy has an extensive rail system and a variety of train types. Fares are the cheapest in Europe and train travel can be a great way to tour the country and enjoy an ever-changing view of the

landscape. Trenitalia (www.trenitalia.it), the State railway company, covers the whole country, though there are also some privately operated lines and services. Italian trains have a poor record of punctuality, which doesn't seem to bother Italians but which can be of critical importance if your journey involves several changes of trains. So be patient and allow plenty of time between arrivals and departures to make your connections.

Tickets

Ask for either *andata* (one way) or *andata e tornata* (return or round-trip) and tell the ticket clerk which train you want to take, as there may be a supplement to pay. It is cheaper to pay supplements at the time you buy the tickets, as upgrading on board the train involves an additional charge. On long journeys with changes of train at different stations, you may be issued with several tickets, representing the different legs of your journey. Keep them together as onboard inspectors may want to see them all. On the other hand, if two of you are travelling together, you may be issued with only one ticket printed with an indication of two travellers.

● Just buying a ticket is not enough for travelling on Italian trains. Whichever train you take you must validate your ticket by punching it in a yellow or red slot machine in the station booking hall before you board the train. This applies even if your ticket is for a reserved seat on a specified train. The ticket inspector may ask you to pay a surcharge of €20 if your ticket does not have the pre-boarding validation mark on it.

Night trains

Night trains are particularly good value for covering long distances. You have the choice of cabins fitted with beds *(classe)* or couchettes.

GETTING AROUND IN ROME

ATAC runs Rome's public transport system, which includes the bus, tram and metro network, all frequent, cheap and reliable. You can navigate the city easily by using just a few lines

INFORMATION
• The ATAC office is at Piazza dei Cinquecento (tel 800 431784, daily 7.30–7). Transport details, ticket information and free transport maps are available.
• Online at www.atac.roma.it

TICKETS
Buy tickets before boarding at *tabacchi* (tobacconists), shops and bars displaying the ATAC logo. Main stops and some metro stations have automatic ticket machines. You can save money by buying an 'integrated' ticket for use on buses, trams and trains.
• *Biglietto integrato a tempo* (BIT) €1—valid for 75 minutes for unlimited bus and tram travel plus one metro trip.
• *Biglietto integrato giornaliero* (BIG) €4—valid up to midnight on the day of use for unlimited travel on buses, trams, metro, Cotral and FS trains.
• *Carta integrata settimanale* (CIS) €16—valid for a week.
• **Validate** your ticket the first time it's used. The machines are inside buses and trams and just before escalators on the metro. BIT tickets must be validated again if you are using the BIT on the metro. The fine for not validating your ticket is €51 and is strictly enforced—no excuses.

BUSES
Single-decker buses cover most routes, with the historic centre served by small electric minibuses (routes 116, 117, 119). There are few seats and buses can be very crowded. Be wary of pickpockets.
• **Bus stops** *(fermata)* show the route number, the *capitolinea* (headstop where the service originates) and list the intermediate stops for buses using the stop. The

stop where you are is circled.
• Bus drivers do not sell tickets, so buy a ticket before you board.

Night Buses
Services start at midnight and drop off at stops marked with a blue owl logo. Tickets are available on board.

Taxis
There are taxi stands throughout the city centre, so it is not customary to hail a taxi as it is cruising along the street. Official metered taxis are white or yellow. The meter starts running at €2.33 7am–10pm Mon–Sat and €3.36 Sun and public holidays; €4.91 10pm–7am daily. The meter clicks in increments of 11c approximately every 20 seconds of the journey. You can phone for a taxi on 06 3570, 06 4944, 06 5551, 06 6645 or 06 8822.

METRO (LA METROPOLITANA)
There are **two lines** which intersect at Termini, the main railway station.
• **Trains** run between 5.30am and 11.30pm.
• **Entrances** are marked with a large white M on a red background.
• **Ticket machines** are below street level; be sure to validate your ticket.
• **Information boards** indicate platforms.
• The metro is always very crowded. Use the route maps displayed in the carriages to find out which side the doors will open at your stop, and start working your way towards the door well before the train stops.

TRAMS
Trams are good for getting to the outskirts. The following

routes are great for sightseeing:
3—Villa Borghese, Villa Giulia, modern art museum, zoo and Trastevere.
8—Trastevere.
19—Piazza del Risorgimento for San Pietro. Also serves Villa Borghese, Villa Giulia, the zoo and modern art museum.

DISCOUNTS
• Children under 10 travel free.
• Reductions for students holding ISIC cards.

SIGHTSEEING TOURS OF ROME
ATAC 110 City Tour Every 30 min. Hop on and off tour (stop 'n' go) ticket €16.
ATAC Archeobus From Piazza Venezia hourly. Circuit of archaeological sights including the Via Appia Antica and the catacombs, 2 hours, €10.
Appian Line Offers city tours and bus tours of Italy's finest destinations including specialist art trail tours. Piazza Esquilino 6/7, tel 06 4878 6605, fax 06 481 9712, www.appianline.it
Green Line Tours Has a two hour hop on hop off tour with 13 stops: €18 for 24 hours, €22 for 48 hours. Via del Viminale, tel 06 462 0651/06 482 8647/ 06 4877 2253, fax 06 4782 3335, www.greenlinetours.com
Stop 'n' Go CSR, Via Barberini 86, 00187 Roma, tel 06 4782 6379, fax 06 488 3167, www.romecitytours.com, €16.
ATAC Christian Rome A tour linking 15 churches from Termini Station. Prices: €13 for 24 hours, €20 for 48 hours and €28 for 72 hours.
Vastours Operates several tours of the city with varied themes. Some include lunch. Via Piedmonte 34, 00187 Roma, tel 06 48144309, www.vastours.it
A boat cruise tours the Tiber Wed–Sun from the Ponte Duca d'Aosta complete with informative audio guide. Price: €12. Further details can be found at Battelli di Roma, tel 06 678 9361, www.battellidiroma.it. The company also operate dinner cruises.

ITALY

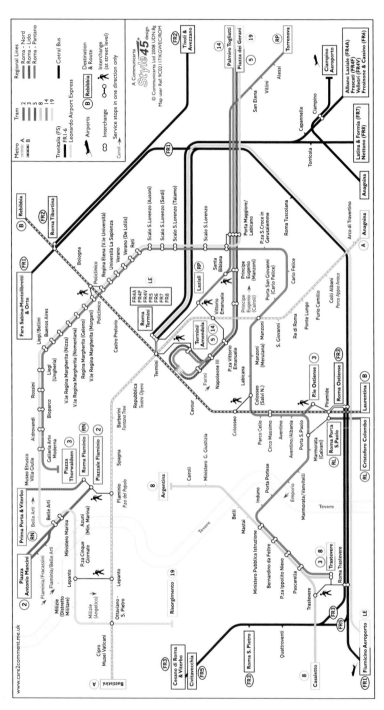

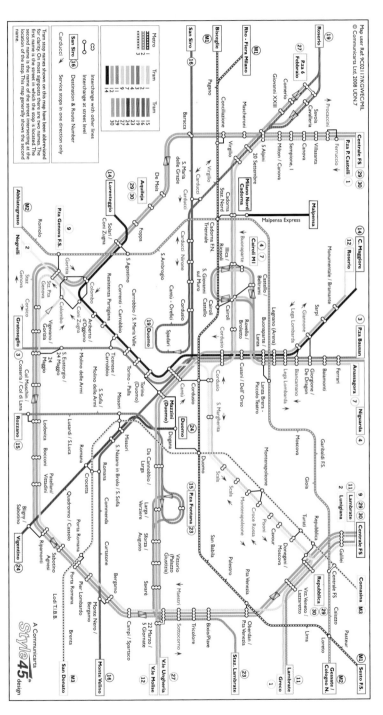

THE NETHERLANDS

UNDERSTANDING THE NETHERLANDS

The Dutch are, for the most part, a laid-back people. They don't mind that many visitors don't even get the name of their country right—it's The Netherlands, not Holland. And they don't object to visitors going to Amsterdam to see the Red Light District and the cannabis cafés: they are a tolerant lot in The Netherlands. In this country you will see all the clichés—bicycles, cheese, clogs, windmills, tulips—but much more too. People forget that this small, mostly flat country once had a big empire, controlling much of the world's trade, and has produced several of the world's greatest artists.

Sunbathing on the Singel canal   *Black and white 'cow' clogs*   *A field of red tulips*

THE NETHERLANDS

Holland doesn't exist. The Netherlands is made up of twelve provinces, which include North Holland and South Holland, both in the west of the country on the North Sea coast. The capital of South Holland is Den Haag, although the largest city is Rotterdam. The largest city in North Holland is Amsterdam, but the capital is Haarlem. Amsterdam, however, is the capital of the whole country, despite the seat of government being in Den Haag. It isn't surprising visitors are sometimes confused.

LANDSCAPE

The Dutch landscape will be familiar to many who have never been there, thanks to the work of the great Dutch landscape painters. Artists like Jan van Goyen, Jacob Isaakszoon van Ruysdael and Albert Cuyp all captured the haunting bleak beauty of the scenery—bucolic panoramas over much of the countryside that have changed little over the ensuing centuries. About half the land is less than 1m (3ft) above sea level, and much of that is actually below sea level, creating large flat—but fertile—expanses. A complicated system of sea walls, known as dikes, and pumping stations all help keep the North Sea from flooding in. The very fact that the country exists is a testimony to the determination and ingenuity of the Dutch people. There are hills in the Netherlands, notably in the south where part of the country lies in the foothills of the mountains of the Ardennes; the country's highest point is Vaalserberg (323m/1,059ft).

POLITICS

The contradictory nature of the Dutch mentality, which manages to be both liberal and conservative at the same time, is shown by its political make-up. The country is still a monarchy, like the United Kingdom, and most people have a great affection for the monarch, Queen Beatrix, who ascended to the throne in 1980. Hers is more of a ceremonial than a powerful role, as since 1848 the Netherlands has been a parliamentary democracy. It has long been renowned as a liberal country when it comes to matters such as drugs, prostitution, abortion, euthanasia, religion and race relations. However, the last two of these have been tested lately, as they have in many countries, with increases in both immigration and religious extremism. The Netherlands is a small country, yet is one of the most densely populated in the world. A huge increase in immigration has started to make the tolerant Dutch people question these freedoms, a debate which has been reflected in recent elections. The Christian Democratic Party currently rules the country in a coalition with the PvdA (Labour Party) and the Christian Union Party.

PEOPLE

At the time of the 2001 census, the population of the Netherlands was just over 16 million, and is currently estimated at about 16.5 million. Of these, about 80 per cent are of Dutch origin, and about 5 per cent are from Dutch or former Dutch territories such as Aruba, Surinam and Indonesia. There is today no predominant religion in the

Netherlands, which in the past was divided like several other European nations between rival groups of Catholics and Protestants. These days about 31 per cent of the population claims to be Catholic, and 20 per cent Protestant, but given that less than 20 per cent of the entire population say they go to church regularly, the Netherlands remains one of the most secular countries in the world.

LANGUAGE
The official language of the Netherlands is Dutch, but because it isn't one of the most widely spoken languages in the world, the Dutch have always been great learners of other languages. Almost everyone you meet speaks English, and many also speak German. A small number of people still speak some of the local languages and dialects, such as Frisian in the northwest

empire and become one of the handful of countries that dominated trade around the world from the 17th century onwards. Today it has the 16th largest economy in the world, according to the International Monetary Fund, yet is 61st in the world in the size of its population, just ahead of Kazakhstan and Burkina Faso.

That fertile Dutch landscape means that the country has a food surplus to add to those exports of flowers, which are sold all over the world. There is plenty of heavy industry too, which the average visitor never sees, and the country's ports, including Rotterdam and Amsterdam—two of the continent's largest and most efficient—see many of Europe's goods passing through them. The result is a regular trading surplus, a low inflation rate of about 1.3 per cent and the lowest unemployment rate (3.8 per cent) of all the EU countries.

Koninginnedag celebrations in Amsterdam (right). Getting around by bicycle in Amsterdam (below)

region of Friesland, and Dutch Low Saxon, in the north and east near the borders with Germany. The word Dutch, to describe the people of the Netherlands, is a corruption of the word Deutsch, or German, which English sailors used in the 17th century as they thought the Dutch were speaking German. The two languages are related, and have a few similarities, but they are very different. Don't make the mistake of confusing them.

ART
If there is one art at which the Dutch have excelled it is painting. No nation of such a comparatively small size has produced so many world-famous artists over the years; many galleries around the world have their collections of Dutch Masters. Rembrandt and Vermeer are household names, and their works and lives still fascinate us today, as is evident from such films and books as *The Girl with the Pearl Earring* and *Rembrandt's Whore*. In more recent years the names of Mondriaan, van Gogh, Escher and the Dutch-born Willem de Kooning have all achieved worldwide acclaim. Many visitors go to the Netherlands, and in particular to Amsterdam, just to see the art collections in the galleries and museums, like the Rijksmuseum and Van Gogh Museum, which stand almost side by side in the Dutch capital's Museum Quarter.

ECONOMICS
The Netherlands is an astonishingly successful nation economically. It has lost none of the ingenuity and flair that helped it create a world

THE REGIONS
Twelve administrative regions make up The Netherlands. In the extreme north there are Drenthe, Friesland and Groningen, whose capitals (and largest cities) are respectively Assen, Leeuwarden and Groningen. Along the southern borders are the three provinces of Zeeland, Limburg and North Brabant (there isn't a South Brabant). Zeeland's capital and largest city is Middelburg, while Limburg's is the name well known to EU citizens for its famous treaty: Maastricht. North Brabant's capital is 's-Hertogenbosch, better known as the more pronounceable Den Bosch, but the largest city is a more familiar one to soccer fans: Eindhoven.

Six more provinces make up the central chunk of the Netherlands: Flevoland (capital Lelystad, largest city Almere); Gelderland (capital Arnhem, largest city Nijmegen); North Holland (capital Haarlem, largest city Amsterdam); Overijssel (capital Zwolle, largest city Enschede); South Holland (capital Den Haag, largest city Rotterdam); and Utrecht (capital and largest city Utrecht).

THE NETHERLANDS

AMSTERDAM

The Van Gogh Museum (▷ 306) is both an attractive museum and an unrivalled collection of that tormented genius's work.

The Anne Frank House (▷ 305–306) is an unforgettable visit— both heartbreaking and uplifting.

A meal at La Rive in Amsterdam's InterContinental Hotel (▷ 310) will show why this has been one of the best and most consistent of Amsterdam's fine-dining restaurants, with one Michelin star.

The Albert Cuypmarkt on Albert Cuypstraat is one of the biggest and liveliest street markets in the city, and also gives a glimpse into some of Amsterdam's ethnic communities.

Rembrandt's *Night Watch* in the Rijksmuseum (▷ 306) is one of the artist's most imposing and impressive works.

Painting in the Van Gogh Museum (above)

DRENTHE, FRIESLAND AND GRONINGEN

Mud-flat walking, or *wadlopen*, is so popular with some Dutch that you will need to reserve ahead; the best places to experience it are along the coast of Friesland and Groningen.

The Groninger Museum in Groningen not only has an impressive collection, but its six pavilions are all individually designed, including one by Philippe Starck.

ZEELAND, LIMBURG AND NORTH BRABANT

Maastricht, where the European Union was effectively born, is one of the oldest and yet most modern cities in The Netherlands.

The beautiful Walcheren coast of Zeeland has some of the best designated cycle routes in the country, tucked between Rotterdam and the Belgian border.

The town of Delft (above)

NORTH HOLLAND AND SOUTH HOLLAND

Rotterdam's 'cube houses' (*kubuswoningen*), one of which can be visited, remain a startling design for city living spaces, in a city where eye-catching modern architecture is almost the norm.

The Mauritshuis in Den Haag (▷ 311) has one of the best art collections outside Amsterdam.

De Zwethheul in Rotterdam is currently the only Netherlands restaurant with two Michelin stars, making it arguably the best in the country.

Tradtional Delftware pottery (above)

FLEVOLAND, GELDERLAND, OVERIJSSEL AND UTRECHT

Delft is known for its pottery and as the home town of Vermeer, and with its old houses and canals it is picture-postcard perfect.

From the top of Utrecht's Domtoren, the tallest church bell tower in the Netherlands, you can see as far as Rotterdam and Amsterdam on clear days.

Cube houses in Rotterdam (right)

THE NETHERLANDS

Elegant buildings line the canals of Amsterdam

Amsterdam

A city of canals and culture—from high art to street culture. Attractions range from must-sees like the Van Gogh Museum, Rijksmuseum and Anne Frank House to the simple pleasures of strolling alongside its canals, and enjoying its laid-back lifestyle.

SEEING AMSTERDAM

Amsterdam's airport is one of the major gateways to Europe, making it both an easy stopover for international flyers and a great city-break vacation destination for Europeans. It is the only city that can truly rival Venice for the beauty of its canals, although it's a different kind of beauty. In Amsterdam trees as well as elegant houses line some of the canals, and the ubiquitous bicycles stamp the city's unique character on the scene.

Amsterdam is an easy city to walk around, as the centre is compact, yet it has several different faces that appeal to different visitors. For some it is the more notorious side of the city, with its Red Light District and cannabis cafés, but for others it is the city of artists, where you can visit Rembrandt's house as well as see some of his greatest works. For some it might be the city of diamonds, where shops and diamond factories are a girl's best friend, and some might yield to the seductive pleasures of its restaurants, bars and its bohemian 'brown cafés' (pubs). Or take a look at all of Amsterdam's faces, and find some new ones for yourself.

HIGHLIGHTS

ANNE FRANKHUIS

✚ 308 B2 • Prinsengracht 263 (entrance at No 267) ☎ 020 556 7105 🕐 Mid-Mar to mid-Sep daily 9–9 (Sat till 10 in Jul, Aug); mid-Sep to mid-Mar daily 9–7 🚊 Tram: 6, 13, 14 or 17 to Westermarkt 💶 Adult €7.50, child (10–17) €3.50 www.annefrank.org

Anne Frank's family fled from Germany to Amsterdam in 1933, hoping to escape the persecution the Jews were suffering there. Anne's father established the family in Amsterdam, but ultimately

RATINGS	
Historic interest	●●●●
Cultural interest	●●●●●
Good for food	●●●
Walkability	●●●●●

BASICS

✚ 5 D3
🛈 Stationsplein 10, opposite Centraal Station, tel 020 551 2525 (premium rate line); Jul, Aug daily 8–8; Sep–end Jun daily 9-5
🚉 Centraal Station

www.amsterdamtourist.nl
The official tourist office website provides all you need to know in five languages, including attractions, accommodation, dining options, events, excursions out of the city, and–especially useful–practical information on everything from parking tips to opening hours.

TIPS

● Combine getting around with seeing the canals by taking the Canal Bus (www.canal.nl), which has three different city routes linking many major attractions, and one-day and two-day ticket options.
● If you want to see Amsterdam by bicycle, but are nervous about cycling in a city, join one of the guided bicycle tours such as those organized by Yellow Bike (www.yellowbike.nl).
● The Anne Frank House is one place you really do need to get to early, if you can, as a

lot of people have to get into a small space and queues build up before opening time.

HEINEKEN EXPERIENCE

🕂 308 C5 • Stadhouserskade 78 ☎ 020 523 9666 🕙 Jun–end Aug daily 11–7 (last admission 5.45); Sep–end May Tue–Sun 10–6 (last admission 5) 🚊 Tram: 16, 24, 25 to Stadhouderskade 💶 €11, under 18 admitted with parental guidance www.heinekenexperience.com

This is no longer a working brewery but does show visitors the brewing process and tells the Heineken story (so closely tied to Amsterdam) in an enjoyable way, with a few free samples on the way. It is a very popular attraction, but is closed for renovation until summer 2008.

MUSEUM AMSTELKRING

🕂 309 D2 • Oudezijds Voorburgwal 40 ☎ 020 624 6604 🕙 Mon–Sat 10–5, Sun 1–5 🚊 Tram: 4, 9, 16, 20, 24, 25 to Damrak 💶 Adult €7, child (5–18) €1 www.museumamstelkring.nl
In the heart of the Red Light District is this mansion showing what life was like in a 17th-century merchant's house, with a complete Catholic church hidden from Protestant eyes on the upper floors.

NEMO

🕂 309 F2 • Oosterdok 2 ☎ 020 531 3233 🕙 Jul, Aug and school hols daily 10–5; Sep–end Jun term time Tue–Sun 10–5 🚉 Centraal Station 💶 €11.50, under-4s free www.e-nemo.nl
This state-of-the-art science and technology centre has interactive exhibits spread over three floors and an impressive view of Amsterdam from the rooftop.

Rijksmuseum (above)

they had to go into hiding, crammed into a few rooms above his business premises. A tour of those rooms, and an understanding of the conditions in which the family lived for two years until they were betrayed, is a moving experience whether you have read *The Diary of Anne Frank* or not. The story tells itself, but there is also an extensive archive of material here in this Amsterdam house which everyone should visit.

MUSEUM HET REMBRANDTHUIS

🕂 309 D3 • Jodenbreestraat 4 ☎ 020 520 0400 🕙 Daily 10–5 🚊 Tram: 9 or 14 to Waterlooplein 💶 Adult €8, child (6–15) €1.50 www.rembrandthuis.nl
If you see Rembrandt the artist at the Rijksmuseum, here at his Amsterdam home and studio you see Rembrandt the man. It is a much more intimate portrait, presented on three floors of the fine 17th-century town house where he lived for more than 20 years. The kitchen and the studio are highlights, and also fascinating is the collection of all kinds of objects that Rembrandt accumulated, curious about their shapes and textures. Most visitors race through the large collection of Rembrandt's drawings and sketches in the annexe quite quickly, but the house itself is one of Amsterdam's gems.

RIJKSMUSEUM

🕂 308 B5 • Jan Luijkenstraat 1 ☎ 020 674 7000 🕙 Sat–Thu 9–6, Fri 9–10 🚊 Tram: 2 or 5 to Museumplein 💶 Adult €10, under 19 free www.rijksmuseum.nl
The Netherlands' premier art collection is still undergoing renovation at the time of writing, and the reopening is now scheduled for sometime in 2009. Until then there is a display called The Masterpieces, the highlights from the museum's vast collection, on display in the Philips Wing, which has been newly refurbished. The Masterpieces naturally include Rembrandt's imposing work *The Night Watch* and other works, as well as works by Johannes Vermeer, Frans Hals and items from the fine art collections, including some exquisite items of Delftware porcelain.

VAN GOGH MUSEUM

🕂 308 A5 • Paulus Potterstraat 7 ☎ 020 570 5200 🕙 Sat–Thu 10–6, Fri 10–10 🚊 Tram: 2 or 5 to Museumplein 💶 Adult €10, child (13–17) €2.50 🏧 www.vangoghmuseum.nl
The Van Gogh Museum is the most popular attraction in Amsterdam, which isn't surprising as it has the world's best collection of work by one of the world's best-known artists. There is a fascination with the life and work of Vincent van Gogh which transcends national boundaries. Queues form early here, but the museum is spacious and can cope fairly well with the crowds. Allow plenty of time, as there are about 200 paintings and 600 drawings, not to mention 700 of the artist's original letters, many to his brother Theo. In addition there are works by contemporaries of van Gogh, including Monet and Gauguin, who either knew the artist or influenced him. The exhibits are spread across four floors, and there's an annexe that usually houses special exhibitions.

Amsterdam's history as a settlement goes back to the end of the 12th century, when a fishing community was established here, where the Amstel River flowed into the North Sea. It was the building of a dam on the Amstel which gave Amsterdam it name. The fishing community turned into a flourishing trading community from about the 14th century onwards, as those early settlers had chosen a prime spot for European trade. By the 17th century Amsterdam had become one of the richest cities in the world, at the heart of the Dutch Empire.

THE NETHERLANDS

WHAT TO DO

🛍 AMSTERDAM DIAMOND CENTER
Rokin 1–5
Tel 020 624 5787
www.amsterdamdiamondcenter.nl
This is the biggest diamond shop in the centre of Amsterdam and although it isn't one of the really old diamond factories, they have a bigger stock than many, with a wide selection of watches and jewellery, and other items such as Mont Blanc pens and cufflinks.
🕐 Daily Fri–Wed 9.30–6, Thu 9.30–8.30 🚊 Tram: 1, 2, 4, 9, 14, 16, 24 or 25 to the Dam

🛍 DE BIJENKORF
Dam 1
Tel 020 621 8080
Department stores are the same and yet different the world over, fascinating old shops that mix history with a vast array of goods. Amsterdam's much-loved 'Beehive', right on Dam Square, is no exception and also worth investigating for its excellent cafés.
🕐 Thu, Fri 9.30–9, Tue, Wed 9.30–7, Mon 11–7 🚊 Tram: 1, 2, 4, 9, 14, 16, 24 or 25 to the Dam

🎵 CONCERTGEBOUW
Concertgebouwplein 2–6
Tel 020 671 8345
www.concertgebouwworkest.nl
Amsterdam's main concert hall has housed the Royal Concertgebouw Orchestra since 1888; there are two halls inside, with some inexpensive concert options as well as grand occasions. Musicians including Ravel and Mahler have played here, so check the current programme when in Amsterdam.
🚊 Tram: 3, 5 or 12 to Museumplein or 16 to Concertgebouwplein

🎵 MUZIEKTHEATER
Waterlooplein 22
Tel 020 625 5455
http://web.het-muziektheater.nl

Amsterdam's second major concert hall alongside the Concertgebouw is the Muziektheater, where the National Ballet and Netherlands Opera are both based, and where the Netherlands Dance Theater usually performs when visiting from their base in Den Haag.
🚊 Tram: 9 or 14 to Waterlooplein

🍷 DE ADMIRAAL
Herengracht 319
Tel 020 625 4334
De Admiraal is one of the old tasting houses for the Dutch gin known as *jenever*, and even though it's the biggest such place in the city, it still gets absolutely packed. There are usually at least 16 *jenevers* and 60 or so liqueurs to choose from, with snacks and meals too.
🕐 Mon–Sat 4.30pm–12am 🚊 Tram: 1, 2 or 5 to Spui

🍷 CAFÉ GOLLEM
Raamsteeg 4
Tel 020 626 6645
www.cafegollem.nl
Not the oldest but certainly one of Amsterdam's most popular brown cafés, right in the centre, with over 200 beers for sale from all over the world, and live music too.
🕐 Sun–Thu 4–1, Fri, Sat 2–2 🚊 Tram: 1, 2, 5 to Spui

🍷 DE DRIE FLESCHJES
Gravenstraat 18
Tel 020 624 8443
This is the oldest tasting house in Amsterdam, first opened in 1650 and specializing in liqueurs rather than gins, although it does have some *jenevers* too. Visitors get a free sample, and then usually linger to try some more of the intriguing tastes on sale.
🕐 Mon–Sat 12–8.30, Sun 3–8 🚊 Tram: 1, 2, 4, 9, 14, 16, 24 or 25 to the Dam

🍷 ESCAPE
Rembrandtplein 11
Tel 020 622 1111
www.escape.nl
Amsterdam's biggest disco has become almost an institution, and you have to dress quite well to get in. It's got several dance floors and

recently added the Escape Lounge and Escape Studio Café to chill out in.
🕐 Wed, Thu, Sun 10–4, Fri, Sat 11–5, Tue 8–1 🚊 Tram: 4, 9 or 14 to Rembrandtplein

🍷 HOPPE
Spuistraat 18–20
Tel 020 420 4420
The Hoppe is the kind of place that feels like it's been packed since it first opened its doors in 1670. A drink here is one of the essential Amsterdam experiences.
🕐 Sun–Thu 8–1, Fri, Sat 8–2 🚊 Tram: 1, 2 or 5 to Spui

🍷 PARADISO
Weteringschans 6–8
Tel 020 626 4521
www.paradiso.nl
This is one of Amsterdam's most famous music clubs, in an old converted church, with everything from psychedelia and soul to rock and electronic music. It's well worth checking the schedule, as some famous names play here when in the city.
🕐 Most nights, times vary 🚊 Tram: 1, 2, 5, 7 or 10 to Leidseplein

EATING

BORDEWIJK
Noordermarkt 7
Tel 020 624 3899
www.bordewijk.nl
In the lovely Jordaan district, the Bordewijk is popular with many Amsterdammers, despite its rather unexciting interior. The cooking here might be called European fusion, ranging from Holland to the shores of the Mediterranean, including a great bouillabaisse Marseillaise.
🕐 Tue–Sun 6.30–10.30
🍴 D €35, Wine €25
🚊 Tram: 1, 2, 5, 13 or 17 to Martelaarsgracht

GIRASSOL
Weesperzijde 135
Tel 020 692 3471
The Girassol is a Portuguese restaurant with a terrace overlooking the Amstel, and service known for being more at a Mediterranean speed than the Dutch are used to. The wait is worth it, though, with authentic dishes such as sardine paté,

THE NETHERLANDS

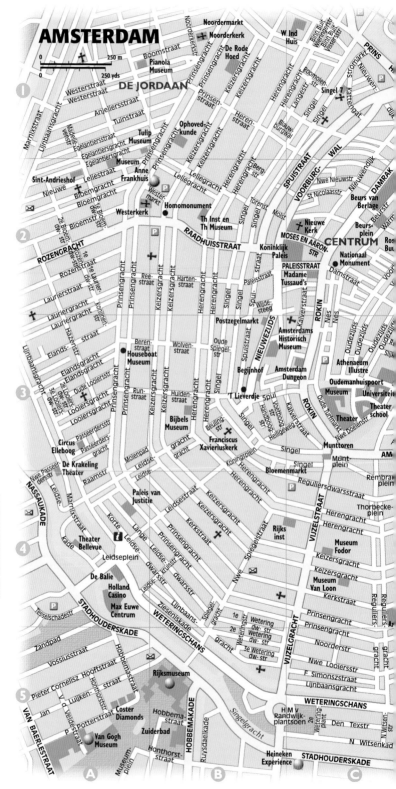

AMSTERDAM

0 ____ 250 m
0 ____ 250 yds

Noordermarkt
Noorderkerk
Noorderkerk
W Ind Huis
Blm Buit
Wiengracht
Blm Buit
Visser Buit
PRINS

Boomstraat
De Rode Hoed
Pianola Museum

Herengracht
Herengracht
Roomolen-str
Langestr
Singel 7
Kattengat
Nieuwen

Singel
Singel

DE JORDAAN
Westerstraat
Westerstraat
Anjeliersstraat
Tuinstraat

Marnixstraat
Lijnbaansgracht
Madelie- vehstr
Egelantiersstraat
Egelantiersgracht
Egelantiersgracht

Tulip Museum
Ophoved- kunde
Heren- straat
Blauw. burgwal

Prinsen- straat

Keizersgracht
Keizersgracht

WAL

VOORBURG-
SPUISTRAAT

Nwe Nieuwstr
Nieuwendijk
St Nicolaasstr

DAMRAK

Museum
Anne Frankhuis
Sint-Andrieshof
Nieuwe
Leliestraat
Bloemgracht
Bloemgracht
2e Bloem-dw str
1e Bloem-dw str

Leliegracht
Leliegracht

Herengracht
Herengracht

Berg-str

Singel
Singel

Beurs van Berlage
Beurs- plein
Beursstr
Warm

Westerkerk
Westermarkt
Homomonument

Th Inst en Th Museum

Torenst
Moist

Nieuwe Kerk

MOSES EN AARON-STR

CENTRUM
Ros
But

ROZENGRACHT
Rozengracht
2e Rozen-dw str
1e Rozen-dw str
1e Laurier dw str

RAADHUISSTRAAT

Koninklijk Paleis

PALEISSTRAAT
Madame Tussaud's

Nationaal Monument

Damstraat

Laurierstraat
Laurierstraat
Laurier- straat
Lauriergracht
Lauriergracht
Jonker-
Hazen- straat

Ree- straat
Prinsengracht
Prinsengracht

Keizersgracht
Keizersgracht

Harten- straat
Herengracht
Herengracht

Singel
Spui-str

Wijde-steeg
Paleisstraat

ROKIN
Nes
Nes

Elands- straat
Elandsgracht
Elandsgracht
2e Looiers
1e Looiers-dw str
Oude Looiersstr
Looiersgracht
Looiersgracht
Passeerdersstr
Passeerders-gracht
Lijnbaansgracht
Lijnbaansgracht

Beren- straat
Houseboat Museum
Wolven- straat
Oude Spiegel-str
Spuistraat

Postzegelmarkt

NIEUWEZIJDS
Amsterdams Historisch Museum

Oudezijds
Oudezijds
Oudezijds
Sint

Athenaeum Illustre

Bijbels Museum
Franciscus Xavieruskerk
Huiden- straat
Herengracht
Beulina-str
Handboog-str
Singel
Voetboog-str
Spui

Begijnhof
'T Lieverdje

Amsterdam Dungeon
Amsterdam Museum

Oudemanhuispoort
Universiteit

Theater
Theater school

Circus Elleboog
De Krakeling Theater

Molenpad
Run- straat
Raamstr

Koningsplein
Heiligeweg

Oude Turfmarkt
Oude Doelenstr

Munttoren
Munt- plein

AM

NASSAUKADE

Nwe Passeer dersstr

Marnixstraat

Paleis van Justitie

Leidsestraat
Keizersgracht
Kerkstraat
Prinsengracht

Herengracht

Bloemenmarkt
Reguliersdwarsstraat

Singel
Herengracht
Herengracht

VIZELSTRAAT

Thorbecke-plein
Rembrandt- plein

Reguliersdwarsstr

Theater Bellevue
Korte Leidse
Lange Leidse dwstr
Leidseplein

Spiegelstraat
Nwe Spiegelstraat

Rijks inst

Museum Fodor

Keizersgracht

Reguliers-
Reguliers-
gracht
Ar

De Balie
Holland Casino
Max Euwe Centrum

Leidse-kruisstr
Leidse-dwarsstr
Lijnbaans-
Ziesenlskade

WETERINGSCHANS

Singel
Spiegel
1e Wetering dw str
2e Wetering dw str
Weteringstr
3e Wetering dw str

Museum Van Loon
Kerkstraat

Prinsengracht
Prinsengracht
Noorderstr

VIZELGRACHT

Nwe Looiersstr
F Simonszstraat
Lijnbaansgracht

Tesselschadestr
STADHOUDERSKADE
zandpad
Vossiusstraat
Pieter Cornelisz Hoofstraat
Jan
Hobbemastraat
Hobbemakade

Rijksmuseum

Hobbema- straat

Singelgracht

WETERINGSCHANS

HM V Randwijk-plantsoen
2e Wetering plant
Den Texstr
Nwe Witsenstr
Wittenkade

VAN BAERLESTRAAT

Pieter Cornelisz Hoofstraat
v d Veldestraat
Coster Diamonds
Van Gogh Museum
Zuidbad
Museum-plein
Honthorst- straat
Ruysdaelkade

Heineken Experience
STADHOUDERSKADE
N Witsenkad

THE NETHERLANDS

A   B   C

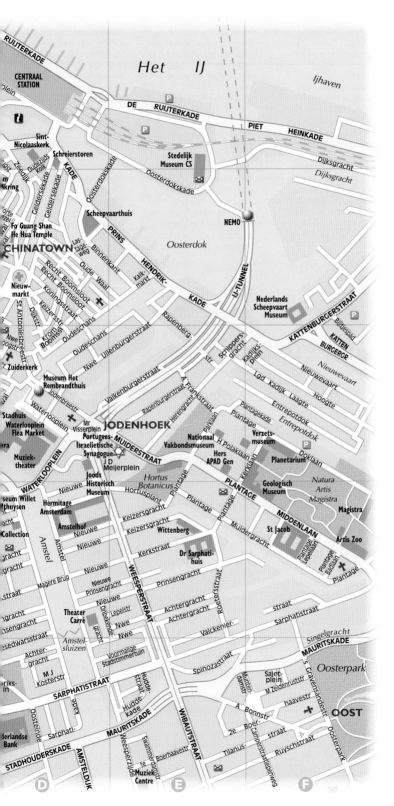

Het IJ

RUIJTERKADE

CENTRAAL
STATION

plein

ℹ️

Sint-
Nicolaaskerk

Schreierstoren

Zeedijk
Gelderskade
Gelderskade
Oudezijds Volk
kring

KADE

Oosterdoksekade

DE RUIJTERKADE

Stedelijk
Museum CS

Oosterdokskade

PIET HEINKADE

Dijksgracht

Dijksgracht

Ijhaven

Fo Guang Shan
He Hua Temple

CHINATOWN

Scheepvaarthuis

PRINS

Lastage-
weg

Binnenkant

HENDRIK

Oude Waal

Kalk-
markt

NEMO

Oosterdok

IJ-TUNNEL

KADE

Nederlands
Scheepvaart
Museum

KATTENBURGERSTRAAT

Billespad

KATTEN
BURGERGR

Nieuw-
markt

St Antoniesbreestr
acht
Nwe
Hoogstr

Zuiderkerk

Recht Boomssloot
Recht Boomssloot
Koningsstraat

Dijkstr

Keizerstr

Krom
Boomssl

Oudeschans

Oudeschans

Nwe Uilenburgerstraat

Nwe Uilenburgerstraat

Rapenburg-

Rapenburg

Schippers-
str

gracht

Kadijks-
plein

Nieuwevaart

Lgd Kadijk Laagte
Hoogte

Nieuwevaart

Museum Het
Rembrandthuis

Jodenbreestr

Valkenburgerstraat

A Frankstraat

Rapenburgerstraat

Herengracht

Parklaan

Plantagekade

Entrepotdok

Entrepotdok

Plantage

Stadhuis
Waterlooplein
Flea Market

era

Muziek-
theater

Waterlooplein

Mr
Visserplein

JODENHOEK

Portuges-
Israelietische
Synagogue

J D
Meijerplein

MUIDERSTRAAT

Nationaal
Vakbondsmuseum

Hers
APAD Gen

H Polaklaan

Kerklaan

Verzets-
museum

Planetarium

Doklaan

WATERLOOPLEIN

seum Willet
thuysen

Collection

gracht

gracht

straat

ngracht

nsengracht

esedwarsstraat

Achter-
gracht

M J
Kosterstr

riks-
in

Hermitage
Amsterdam

Amstelhof

Amstel

Amstel

Magere Brug

Joods
Historisch
Museum

Nieuwe

Nieuwe

Nieuwe

Nieuwe
Prinsengracht

Nieuwe
Lepelstr

Nwe
Omelende-
gracht

Amstel-
sluizen

Hortus
Botanicus

Hortusplant

Keizersgracht

Keizersgracht

Kerkstraat

Prinsengracht

Achtergracht

Achtergracht

Valckenier-

WEESPERSTRAAT

Plantage

Plantage

Plantage

Plantage

Wittenberg

Dr Sarphati-
huis

Roetersstraat

Muidergracht

PLANTAGE

Geologisch
Museum

St Jacob

MIDDENLAAN

Plantage Lepellaan

Plantage
Badlaan

Plantage

straat

Sarphatistraat

Singelgracht

Natura
Artis
Magistra

Magistra

Artis Zoo

Theater
Carré

Voormalige
Stadstimmertuin

Spinozastraat

MAURITSKADE

Oosterpark

Sajet-
plein

Munten-
damstr

M Zeldenruststr

s Gravensandestr

A Bonnstr

haavestr

OOST

SARPHATISTRAAT

Oosteinde

derlandse
Bank

Sarphati-

STADHOUDERSKADE

AMSTELDIJK

apel

Hudde-
straat

Hudde-
kade

MAURITSKADE

WIBAUTSTRAAT

Weesperzijde

1e Boerhaavestr

Swammerdam
straat

Muziek
Centre

2e Boer
straat

Tilanus-

Camperstraatlepenweg

straat

Ruyschstraat

Oosterpark

D

E

F

THE NETHERLANDS

and occasional fado evenings.

🅖 Mon–Fri 12–3, 6–10, Sat, Sun 6–10
🖐 L €15, D €25, Wine €15
🅠 Weesperplein

LA RIVE

Amsterdam InterContinental Hotel,
Professor Tulpplein 1
Tel 020 520 3264
www.restaurantlarive.com

Long regarded as serving the
finest food in Amsterdam,
La Rive's spacious and formal
setting is a backdrop to
Michelin-starred gastronomic
dishes such as carrot and
sweet pepper cannelloni with
Breton lobster or black
sesame and rocket lettuce
bouillon with wild thyme.

🅖 Mon–Fri 7–10.30, 12–2,
6.30–10.30, Sat 7–12, 6.30–10.30
🖐 L €75, D €85, Wine €28.25
🚋 Tram: 7 or 10 to Sarphatistraat

SUPPERCLUB

Jonge Roelensteeg 21
Tel 020 344 6400
www.supperclub.com

For more adventurous diners,
the Supperclub is as much
theatrical experience as
dinner. You lounge around
on mattresses while the fixed
meal is served to you and
any kind of event might be
happening around you–and
in Amsterdam be prepared
for anything.

🅖 Daily 8pm–1am
🖐 D €65, Wine €23
🚋 Tram: 4, 9, 14, 16, 24 or 25 to the
Dam

VAN PUFFELEN

Prinsengracht 375–377
Tel 020 624 6270
www.restaurantvanpuffelen.com

This canalside place in the
Jordaan is perfect
Amsterdam. On one hand it's
one of the city's best brown
cafés, on the other a kind of
Dutch brasserie-style restaurant, serving superb food in
the friendliest of atmospheres.

🅖 Mon–Sat 6–11, Sat 12–4,
Sun 12–4, 5.30–10
🖐 L €19.50 D €19.50 W €15
🚋 Tram: 13, 14 or 17 to Westermarkt

VERMEER

Barbizon Palace Hotel, Prins
Hendrikkade 59
Tel 020 556 4885
www.restaurantvermeer.nl

The classically elegant atmosphere here is the perfect foil

for the Michelin-quality food,
including dishes such as
Iberico pork with almond
aioli, turnips, mustard fruit
and langoustine sauce. This is
one of the best restaurants in
the city.

🅖 Mon–Fri 12–2.30, 6–10, Sat 6–10
🖐 L €65, D €75, Wine €29.50
🅠 Centraal Station

YAMAZATO

Okura Hotel, Ferdinand Bolstraat 333
Tel 020 678 8351
www.okura.nl

The Okura's traditional
Japanese restaurant has a
crisp and clean Asian décor,
and its food has been
awarded a Michelin star. It
serves some of the best sushi
in Europe.

🅖 Daily 7.30–9.30, 12–2, 6–9.30
🖐 L €65 D €65 W €24
🚋 Tram: 25 to Cornelis Troostplein

STAYING

AMSTEL BOTEL

Oosterdokskade 2–4, 1011 AE
Amsterdam
Tel 020 521 0350
www.amstelbotel.nl

A truly Amsterdam experi-
ence, staying on a floating
hotel right by Centraal
Station. The location is great,
the price is good and the
rooms are simple, but noise
can be an occasional problem.

🖐 €78
🛈 175
🅠 Centraal Station

CANAL HOUSE

Keizersgracht 148, 1015 CX Amsterdam
Tel 020 622 5182
www.canalhouse.nl

The historic Canal House is
close to the Anne Frank
House and made up of three
17th-century canal houses
that have been tastefully
renovated but retaining the
historic look and feel, with a
breakfast room which overlooks a concealed garden.

🖐 €140
🛈 26
🚋 Tram: 13, 14 or 17 to Westermarkt

THE DYLAN

Keizersgracht 384,
1016 GB Amsterdam
Tel 020 530 2010
www.dylanamsterdam.com

The Dylan is probably
Amsterdam's most stylish
boutique hotel, the haunt of

movie and rock stars, with
understated luxury and privacy guaranteed. Every room
is spacious and eye-catching,
with the Loft Room especially
having very relaxed décor and
lovely views.

🖐 €435
🛈 41
🚋 Tram: 1, 2, 5 to Spui

HOTEL ADOLESCE

Nieuwe Keizersgracht 26,
1018 DS Amsterdam
Tel 020 626 3959
www.adolesce.nl

This very small and simple
hotel close to Waterlooplein
is a tall and slender canal
house, and the best of the
modern rooms are under the
eaves–although tall people
might disagree!

🖐 €85
🛈 10
🚋 Tram: 4 to Keizersgracht

HOTEL PULITZER

Prinsengracht 315–331,
1016 GZ Amsterdam
Tel 020 523 5235
www.pulitzer.nl

Tucked between two canals,
the luxurious Pulitzer has
been converted from 25
17th-century houses,
preserving the historic feel
but providing 230 deluxe
rooms. Despite the size, it still
somehow maintains a feeling
of intimacy as you wander
along the corridors in this
maze of a building.

🖐 €465
🛈 230
🚋 Tram: 13, 14 or 17 to Westermarkt

RHO HOTEL

Nes 5–23, 1012 KC Amsterdam
Tel 020 620 7371
www.rhohotel.com

Right by the very central Dam
Square, the Rho is far from
luxurious but it's comfortable
and got great character. The
reception and lobby were
once an art deco-style
theatre, built in 1908, but
the hotel's amenities are
modern, including free wire-
less internet access.

🖐 €115
🛈 165
🚋 Tram: 4, 9, 14, 16, 24 or 25 to the
Dam

Knights' Hall in the Binnenhof

THE HAGUE

**The Netherlands' seat of government.
Home to the United Nations International Court of Justice.
A mix of lively modern life and
attractive old architecture.**

The Hague (Den Haag) is the capital of the South Holland province of The Netherlands and has been an important administrative Dutch city since the 16th century–the Old Parliament Buildings at the Binnenhof show off its historical splendour. It's still an important city today, and the presence of the Dutch Parliament and the UN's Peace Palace ensure good hotels and restaurants and a comfortably prosperous air.

BINNENHOF
The Old Dutch Parliament buildings of the Binnenhof (the name literally means Inner Court; Mon–Sat hourly tours 10–4) are one of Den Haag's most attractive features. The outside, with its waterside setting, is very photogenic, and the inside is worth seeing too on one of the regular guided tours. A highlight is the 13th-century Ridderzaal, or Knights' Hall, and other buildings date mainly from the 17th and 19th centuries.

ART COLLECTIONS
Den Haag has a lot to offer art lovers, with several major and minor museums. The most important is the Mauritshuis (Apr–end Sep Mon–Sat 10–5, Sun 11–5; Oct–end Mar Tue–Sat 10–5, Sun 11–5), home to Vermeer's famous *Girl with a Pearl Earring*. The huge collection has a breathtaking number of artists including several more Vermeers, Rembrandts and Rubens, through to Andy Warhol's portrait of Queen Beatrix.

Abraham Bredius was a Director of the Mauritshuis who amassed his own private collection, which he generously gave to the city in 1946. The surprisingly large Museum Breduis (Tue–Sun 11–5), in a lovely old house, includes works by Jan Steen, van Dyck and Rembrandt. The Hague's main art and crafts museum is the Gemeentemuseum Den Haag (Tue–Sun 11–5) with everything from Delft pottery and Den Haag silverware to modern artists including Picasso and Kandinsky. There is also a large collection of work by the renowned Dutch artist Piet Mondriaan.

BASICS

✚ 5 D3

ℹ Hofweg 1, near the Parliament Buidings, tel 0900 340 3505 (premium rate number; Mon–Fri 10–6, Sat 10–5, Sun 12–5

🚉 Den Haag Centraal Station, close to the town centre. There is another main station, Den Haag HS (Hollands Spoor), which is farther out, so make sure you alight at the right one.

www.denhaag.com
The city's official website, in eight languages, covers all the usual topics such as attractions, events, dining and accommodation; unsurprisingly, it is slanted towards business visitors.

TIP

● If you're staying in Amsterdam and visiting Den Haag, don't forget to take your *strippenkaart* tickets with you, in case you want to use Den Haag's public transport.

WHAT TO DO

⊕ NETHERLANDS DANCE THEATRE
Schedeldoekshaven 60
Tel 070 880 0100
www.ndt.nl
The Netherlands Dance Theatre is based in Den Haag and was established in 1959 by former members of the Dutch National Ballet. They have gone on to tour the world and receive great acclaim for their more modern approach to dance, injecting ballet with drama.
🚊 Den Haag Centraal

⊗ FIDDLER
Riviervismarkt 1
Tel 070 365 1955
www.fiddler.nl
This large and bustling British-style pub is a great late-night hang-out, with wood-panelling and pool tables giving it a British pub atmosphere. It serves its own ale from its own microbrewery. There's typical pub food on the menu, live jazz on winter Sundays, sport on large-screen TVs and regular quiz nights too.
⊗ Sun–Wed 12pm–1am, Thu–Sat 12pm–2am 🚊 Tram: 17 to Gravenstraat

⊗ KURZAAL BAR
Steigenberger Kurhaus Hotel, Gevers Deynootplein 30
Tel 070 416 2636
www.kurhaus.nl
The Kurzaal Bar is a Den Haag institution and a must-see place. Everyone from Maria Callas to the Rolling Stones have played in the adjoining dance hall, where there is still live music amid the grandiose décor with chandeliers and painted ceilings.
⊗ Sun–Thu 5pm–1am, Fri, Sat 5pm–2am 🚊 Tram: 11 to Strandweg

⊗ DE PAAS
Dunne Bierkade 16a
Tel 070 360 0019
www.depaas.nl
With an unassuming exterior and bare wood floors inside, you wouldn't know that De Paas is one of the best brown cafés in Den Haag. The bar runs down one side, and behind it are hundreds of bottles, showing the vast range of beers it sells. There's also another drinking area on a barge moored opposite, on one of the city's canals.
⊗ Daily 3pm–1am 🚊 Tram: 18 to Bierkade

EATING

CALLA'S
Laan van Roos en Doorn 51a
Tel 070 345 5866
For that special meal it would be hard to beat this Michelin-star winner, which serves superb creative dishes, such as shaved langoustines with caviar and celeriac cappuccino with winter truffles, in a relaxing, fairly minimalist pale-walled atmosphere.
⊗ Tue–Sat 12–2, 6.30–10
🍴 L €50, D €65, Wine €26
🚊 Den Haag Centraal

PUCK
Prinsestraat 33
Tel 070 427 7649
www.puckfoodandwines.nl
PUCK stands for Pure Unique California Kitchen, so it's no surprise to find a healthy list of American wines and dishes, such as ribs on coleslaw with pineapple, all served amid bright Californian décor.
⊗ Tue–Sat 6–10.30
🍴 L €25, D €35, Wine €25
🚊 Tram: 17 to Noordwal

SAUR
Lange Voorhout 47
Tel 070 346 2565
www.saur.nl
The Saur has been a popular choice with locals since it opened in 1928. Its crisp white tablecloths, red chairs and large wall mirrors give it a suitably French look to match the menu, where classic dishes like steak are done impeccably.
⊗ Mon–Fri 12–2.30, 6–10.30, Sat 6–10.30
🍴 L €32.50, D €42.50, Wine €19.50
🚊 Tram: 10, 16 or 17 to Korte Voorhout

STADSHERBERG 'T GOUDE HOOFT
Dagelijkse Groenmarkt 13
Tel 070 346 9713
www.tgoudehooft.nl
This venerable café-restaurant on the market square dates back to 1423, and the interior is heavy on the wood and brass. It's always lively, and the food is simple but hearty, ranging from soups and cheese plates to rib-eye steaks.
⊗ Daily 8am–12am
🍴 L €16.50, D €24, Wine €15.75
🚊 Tram: 17 to Gravenstraat

STAYING

CORONA HOTEL
Buitenhof 39, 2513 AH Den Haag
Tel 070 363 7930
www.corona.nl
The Corona is a wonderful small hotel, right by the Bonnenhof, part of which was a coffee shop back in the 18th century. Although it's a chain hotel, it still has great charm and individuality.
🍴 €170
🛏 35
🚊 Tram: 10, 16 or 17 to Buitenhof

LE MÉRIDIEN HOTEL DES INDES
Lange Voorhout 54–56, 2514 EG Den Haag
Tel 070 361 2845
www.hague.lemeridien.com
This five-star hotel is often used by visiting VIPs, the rooms having a contemporary chic feel, and there is also a brilliant Health Club with heated pool, sauna, steam bath and other facilities.
🍴 €175
🛏 92
🚊 Tram: 1 or 10 to Kneuterdijk

PARKHOTEL DEN HAAG
Molenstraat 53, 2513 BJ Den Haag
Tel 070 362 4371
www.parkhoteldenhaag.nl
The four-star Parkhotel opened in 1912 as a vegetarian hotel/restaurant, and some of the interior decoration goes back to that time. Rates include a generous breakfast, served in the Garden Room, which looks onto the gardens.
🍴 €150
🛏 120
🚊 Tram: 1 or 10 to Kneuterdijk

THE NETHERLANDS

ARRIVING

BY AIR
Amsterdam's Schiphol airport (pronounced Skipol; tel 020 794 0800; www.schiphol.nl) is served by many major carriers, including the national carrier, KLM, which has an extensive network throughout the world. Schiphol is a major gateway airport for Western Europe, so there are numerous direct flights with most of the major airlines. There are also budget flights from several UK airports.

Schiphol Airport is located about 18km (11 miles) southwest of Amsterdam city centre, and there are frequent, easy connections by train to Amsterdam's Centraal Station. The journey takes about 20 minutes, is inexpensive, and there are trains about every 10–15 minutes during the day. Taxis cost about €40–50, and there are also shared taxis which are much cheaper and which will pick up and drop off people at their different addresses. There are also hotel shuttle buses, so if you have booked your accommodation in advance, ask about this service. To travel by bus or taxi is no quicker than taking the train, as Amsterdam's canals make the streets slow to negotiate for vehicles.

There are also regular connecting trains to Den Haag from the railway station at Schiphol, which is directly under the terminal building.

BY CAR
Driving in The Netherlands is straightforward, as outside the main cities the traffic is generally (but not always) light, there is a good road network with no toll roads, and directions are well signposted and easy to understand. However, if you only plan to visit Amsterdam, then leave your car at home. The city centre is very difficult for drivers not familiar with the layout, parking is extremely hard to find, the canals and pedestrian areas make navigation tricky and, in any case, most of the major sights are easier–and much more pleasant–to get to on foot.

If you do decide to take your car then an EU or US/Canadian driver's licence is usually all that you need. Simply make sure you have adequate insurance coverage for driving overseas and consult a driving organization like the AA or AAA for current regulations and requirements in The Netherlands.

BY TRAIN
From the UK there is a Eurostar service between London and Brussels, from where it is possible to get connections to several cities in The Netherlands, including Amsterdam and Den Haag. The total journey time will be at least 6 hours, allowing for changes, so it is not as fast or as convenient as flying. There is a good rail network in The Netherlands, so getting there from other European countries is also fairly easy.

BY BUS
There are bus connections from London to Amsterdam, and it is certainly the least expensive way of travelling, but because the journey also involves taking the ferry, it can take anything from 9 to 12 hours. From Amsterdam there are onward bus and train connections to Den Haag.

BY FERRY
Taking the ferry from the UK to The Netherlands is possible but not the best option for getting there, unless you are keen to take your car. There are no direct ferries to either Den Haag or Amsterdam, the closest being the DFDS Seaways (www.dfds.co.uk) service from Newcastle to the port at IJmuiden, which takes about 14 hours. IJmuiden is about 30 minutes from Amsterdam by the connecting bus service. P&O North Sea Ferries (www.poferries.com) operate a service from Hull to Rotterdam (11 hours), from where there are train and bus connections to Amsterdam and Den Haag, while Stena Line (www.stenaline.co.uk) sails from Harwich to the Hook of Holland (6 hours 15 mins), with onward connections to Den Haag (30–40 minutes) and Amsterdam 60–75 minutes).

VISITORS WITH A DISABILITY
The Netherlands is not the easiest country if you have mobility restrictions. In theory the Dutch are very sympathetic and up to date in this area, but in practice it's impossible to improve access in some of the tall, narrow canalside buildings with steep staircases. This applies particularly to some of the more charming hotels, so you must check the question of access before booking.

Getting around the city streets is also not easy, with narrow bridges, cobble stones, numerous canals and other hazards. Using trams and buses is not ideal either, though it is improving with newer vehicles having wheelchair access. Train stations are generally fine and there are private wheelchair taxi services too, such as Garskamp (tel 020 633 3943) and Connexion Jonkcars (tel 020 606 2200).

The Dutch railway service, Netherlands Railways, has information about disabled access online (www.ns.nl), and you can call the Disabled Assistance Office (tel 030 235 7822) for help on your journeys, but do give them some notice. In the UK, contact RADAR (tel 020 7250 3222; www.radar.org.uk) or in the US Mobility International (tel 541/343-1284; www.miusa.org) for information.

THE NETHERLANDS

GETTING AROUND

BY ROAD
In The Netherlands you drive on the right, and all passengers must wear seat belts if equipped. Speed limits are: 50kph (31mph) in built-up areas; 80kph (49mph) or 100kph (62mph) outside built-up areas; 120kph (74mph) on motorways (expressways). There is no minimum speed limit on motorways.

There are on-the-spot fines for offences including parking infractions, and vehicles can be confiscated in the case of serious offences. A warning triangle or hazard warning lights must be used in case of accident or breakdown.

The blood alcohol limit is 0.05 per cent and penalties for exceeding this can be severe, including imprisonment. Note that use of a radar detector to warn against speed traps is illegal and can result in a fine and confiscation of the equipment.

BY TRAIN
The Netherlands has an excellent train network, provided by the NS, Nederlandse Spoorwegen (Dutch Railways, tel 0900 9292; www.ns.nl). Trains are comfortable, frequent and inexpensive, compared to some countries. In particular there are regular services that link Amsterdam, Rotterdam and Den Haag, also usually stopping at Schiphol Airport.

Round-trip tickets usually cost the same as two single tickets, unless returning on the same day, in which case they are less expensive. Note that in The Netherlands you can interrupt your journey and resume it later in the day, but you must continue in the same direction. For example, if going from Amsterdam to Rotterdam you can get off in Den Haag and then get back on a later Rotterdam train, but not backtrack towards Amsterdam.

BY BUS
Journeying by bus in The Netherlands is slightly more complicated than the train, as there are a number of independent companies who have franchises for different services. However, the network is good and most companies accept the *strippenkaart*. This is a nationally used public transport ticket, for which you must stamp the required number of tickets for your journey. Some of the long-distance bus journeys do not accept them, in which case you simply pay cash to the driver, but otherwise the *strippenkaart* offers the best value for getting around both within cities and within the country. Buy them in advance from local public transport offices, train stations and some tobacconists.

BY BICYCLE
Cycling is a national addiction in The Netherlands, whether in the cities or in the countryside. It's very easy and cheap to rent bikes in all kinds of places. Going by bike is easy because the country is very flat, and also people are used to cyclists, even in the heart of Amsterdam.

GETTING AROUND IN AMSTERDAM
BY FOOT
Walking is by far the best way to get round the city centre. To cross from one side to the other hardly takes more than 30 minutes, and most major sights are within easy reach. You do need a good map, however, as the curving nature of the canals and the sheer number of them makes it easy to lose your sense of direction.

BY BICYCLE
Cycling is very popular–the city is full of bikes whizzing around, and many visitors choose to get about this way. There are designated cycle lanes in many places, and renting bikes is both easy and inexpensive.

BY TAXI
Taxis are plentiful but not used as much as in other Western European cities because of the small size of Amsterdam, the difficulty in driving (making fares higher) and the excellent public transport system. That said, you will still find taxi stands everywhere, and you can also hail taxis on the street. Fares are metered but are quite expensive.

BY CANAL
The Museumboat (tel 020 530 1090; www.lovers.nl) is a popular way to float between the city's main museums, connecting with the Centraal station. A day pass costs €17, and you can get on and off as many times as you like. Alternatively, there is an €18 day pass available for the Canal Bus (tel 020 623 9886; www.canal.nl), which is more versatile, having three different routes around the city with stops at many of the major attractions.

BY METRO
Amsterdam's small metro network is less useful for visitors, being mainly aimed at commuters. There is a stop at Centraal Station, and others at Nieuwmarkt and Waterlooplein, the only three stops likely to interest the average visitor. Another more central line is being added but is not likely to open until 2011. Use the ubiquitous *strippenkaart* (▷ above) for all your journeys.

BY BUS AND TRAM
The main public transport options in Amsterdam are the bus and the tram, which both also take the *strippenkaart*. The main hub is outside Centraal Station, where the GVB public transport service (tel 0900 8011; www.gvb.nl) has its main office. You can get maps and information leaflets here, but the system is easy to negotiate as there are comprehensive maps at every stop.

THE NETHERLANDS

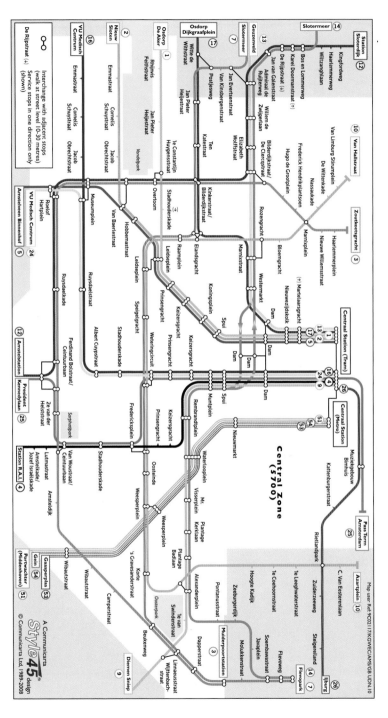

THE NETHERLANDS

Map user Ref 9C021 I 7/KGWEC/AMSIGB UDN.10

© Communicarta Ltd. 1989-2008

Style45 design

A Communicarta

THE NETHERLANDS AMSTERDAM TRANSPORT MAP **315**

PORTUGAL

UNDERSTANDING PORTUGAL

Portugal has many faces—underdeveloped and unspoiled regions coexist with sophisticated coastal resorts that have been firmly on the tourist map for more than 40 years. Lisbon, the capital, happily combines modern development with old-fashioned, idiosyncratic charm, while regional capitals, such as Porto, Coimbra and Évora, each have their own distinctive personalities. But it's the coast and sea that define Portugal both physically and historically. In short, wherever you go, you will find variety and interest; there are truly many Portugals to discover.

Fishing boats moored in Setúbal, Portugal's third-largest port

An old cottage in the Algarve, with traditional painting scheme

Porto seen from the Douro, with its bridge in the background

LANDSCAPE

Portugal is a small country (89,106sq km/ 34,404sq miles), but it enjoys immense geographical diversity. North of the Rio Tejo, the hills and upland areas are a continuation of the *meseta*, the block of high plateau and mountains that occupies much of the Iberian peninsula. The climate here makes for a green, cultivated and heavily populated landscape, particularly in the Minho and Douro regions, though much of remote, mountainous Trás-os-Montes is good for little but sheep-grazing. Farther south in the Beiras, Estremadura and Ribatejo, the countryside is predominantly fertile and undulating, rich in woodlands, vines and olives.

South of the Tejo, the vast, sun-drenched and empty Alentejan plains are Portugal's granary, where huge wheat fields are interspersed with cork oak stands, olive groves and plantations. To the south, passes lead through the low hills to the fertile Algarve and the coast. This is a sinuous 1,793km-long (1,114-mile) ribbon that includes vast sandy beaches, dramatic cliffs, headlands and hidden coves, dunes, pinewoods and marshland.

ECONOMY

At the time of the 1974 Carnation Revolution, Portugal was economically at least 50 years behind the rest of Europe thanks to the policies of António de Oliveira Salazar. Since then enormous strides have been made, particularly following the country's entry to the European Union (EU) in 1986. For much of the 1990s,

Portugal's economic growth was well above the EU average; now, its GDP stands at 70 per cent of those of the leading EU economies.

Portugal is the world's largest cork producer and among the largest producers of wine. Its leading industries include textile and footwear manufacture, papermaking and engineering. Tourism is increasingly important, while agriculture is notoriously inefficient. Many farms are little more than minute smallholdings.

POLITICS

Portugal is a republic. Administratively, the mainland is divided into 18 districts, responsible for their own health, education and financial affairs. Municipal power is in the hands of 308 *concelhos*, similar to district councils (boroughs), which are elected every four years. Madeira and the Azores are autonomous regions.

DEMOGRAPHY AND RELIGION

Portugal's population stands at around 10.5 million; the birth-rate, unlike that in many other southern European countries, is rising, albeit by a very low percentage (0.4 per cent). Most Portuguese still live on the land or in small towns, mainly close to the coast, with population levels highest in the Minho and lowest in the Alentejo.

The Portuguese are fervently Catholic; although it is falling, church attendance is much higher than in many other European Catholic countries. This is reflected in the large numbers of festivals, processions and religious pilgrimages that are still an integral part of daily life.

PORTUGAL

THE MINHO AND TRÁS-OS-MONTES

The Minho is considered by many Portuguese to be the most beautiful and varied part of the country. Here you'll find the fertile river valleys of the Minho and Lima, huge stretches of sandy beaches along the Costa Verde, and the spectacular gorges and mountains of Peneda-Gerês, Portugal's only national park.

The Trás-os-Montes, 'beyond the mountains', is a remote and sparsely populated region, unofficially divided into the southern and fertile Terra Quente (Hot Land), and the north, the Terra Fria (Cold Land), where the climate is extreme and life is still hard.

PORTO AND THE DOURO

Porto is Portugal's second-largest city, an unabashedly commercial hub near the mouth of the Rio Douro. Huge urban redevelopment has spruced up this once shabby city, and Porto today has plenty to offer in the shape of its historic riverside Ribeira area, Romanesque *Sé* (cathedral), clutch of fine buildings, good museums, and excellent shopping and entertainment.

Historic Elvas, the most beautiful of the Alentejo's frontier towns

This decorative tile is a tribute to fado, Portugal's unique music

You can buy a host of gourmet delights in Porto's old food stores

The Douro region lies on the north bank of the Rio Douro, a magnificent river that gives the area its name and cuts through some of Portugal's most impressive scenery.

THE BEIRAS

The Beiras region is divided into three parts—the Beira Alta to the northeast, the Beira Baixa in the southeast, and the Beira Litoral along the coast.

ESTREMADURA AND THE RIBATEJO

Estremadura and **the Ribatejo** are both packed with delights. Architecturally, Alcobaça and Batalha should be high on any visiting list, as should Tomar and the historic former head-quarters of the Knights Templar (later the Order of Christ).

LISBON

Lisbon is packed with history. Its main sights are its castle and Alfama area, the elegant Baixa, Chiado and Bairro Alto districts, Belém and the superb Mosteiro dos Jerónimos.

AROUND LISBON

Around Lisbon on either side of the Tejo estuary, there's the option of relaxing on the coast or visiting some of Portugal's finest royal palaces.

THE ALENTEJO

The Alentejo region falls into two parts, Alto (Upper) and Baixo (Lower). It's a vast agricultural area, its rolling plains dotted with cork plantations and scattered towns and villages.

THE ALGARVE

The Algarve is Portugal's holiday playground. To the east of Faro the coast is fringed by long, sandy offshore islands, while to the west, bays, coves and cliffs predominate.

PORTUGAL

THE BEST OF PORTUGAL

THE MINHO AND TRÁS-OS-MONTES

Barcelos Buy a ceramic cockerel at the Thursday market—the essential Portuguese souvenir.
Citânia de Briteiros One of Portugal's most impressive archaeological sites, with extensive Celtic remains.
Solar de Mateus Stroll through the glorious formal gardens.

PORTO AND THE DOURO

Cais da Ribeira (▷ 341) Explore the maze of narrow alleyways.
Fundação de Serralves (▷ 342) Exciting, cutting-edge modern art in Porto.

Torre dos Clérigos (▷ 341–342) Climb this tower in Porto for bird's-eye city views.

THE BEIRAS

Coimbra Visit the famous complex of the Velha Universidade.
Parque Arqueológico do Vale do Côa 20,000-year-old art etched into the rock.
Serra da Estrel Mainland Portugal's highest mountain range—dramatic scenery and crisp air.

ESTREMADURA AND THE RIBATEJO

Fátima Join the pilgrims at the country's greatest shrine.
Óbidos Spend a night in this walled medieval town.
Tomar Explore the Convento de Cristo, once the headquarters of the successors to the Knights Templar.

LISBON

Alfama (▷ 326–327) Wander through the picturesque streets of Lisbon's medieval quarter.
Bairro Alto (▷ 329) Spend an evening eating, drinking and listening to *fado*, Portugal's unique soul music.
Belém (▷ 330–331) Visit some of the capital's most significant monuments and important museums

AROUND LISBON

Costa da Caparica Catch the little train and hop off at one of the relaxing beaches.
Sintra Visit two of Portugal's royal palaces—the Palácio Nacional de Sintra and the Palácio Nacional de Pena.

THE ALENTEJO

Arraiolos Shop for local rugs and carpets.
Beja See some of Portugal's finest *azulejos* (tiles) at the Convento de Nossa Senhora da Conceição.
Évoramonte Climb up to the castle for superb views across the Alentejo.

THE ALGARVE

Carvoeiro Take a boat trip to see the fabulous hidden coves and rock formations.
Silves Spend time exploring this historic town, once the Algarve's Moorish capital.

Cintânia de Briteiros (above).
Barcelos's famous ceramic cockerels on display (left).
Monument to Discoveries (right)

Houses in the Ribeira, Porto's atmospheric old riverside quarter

Covento de Nossa Senhora da Conceição, Beja

PORTUGAL

Lisbon

⊞ 4 A4 🚩 Praça do Comércio, tel 210 312 810/15 🚇 Cais do Sodré
ℹ Palácio Foz, Praça dos Restauradores, tel 213 463 314 🚇 Restauradores
ℹ Estação de Santa Apolónia, Terminal Internacional, tel 218 812 606
www.atl-lisbon.pt, www.visitlisboa.com

The Baixa district (above).
Lisbon's cathedral and one of
the city's celebrated trams
(below).
The futuristic architecture of the
Parque das Nações (bottom)

SEEING LISBON

The city is a superb mix of the old and the new, spreading across hills running down to the shining waters of the Tejo estuary. Its districts are linked by steep cobbled streets, traversed by clanking trams and funicular railways, and lined with traditional shops and cafés.

Head first for the Baixa, a grid of elegant 18th-century streets built after the great earthquake of 1755, whose architectural flourish is the huge expanse of the waterfront Praça do Comércio. This is where you can find the main tourist information office—pick up maps and information, and invest in a Lisboa Card, which lets you travel free on public transport and gives excellent reductions on entry charges to many museums and other attractions. In Comércio, too, you can hop on a tram for a guided multi-language tour that covers much of downtown Lisbon—an excellent way of getting your bearings. For an alternative overview, try the parapets of the Castelo de São Jorge, the Moorish castle to the east, high above the central Baixa area. From here you can pick out the Baixa's main square, the Rossio, and look across to the slopes of the Bairro Alto, the hub of the city's nightlife, packed with restaurants and *fado* houses.

Below the castle, the slopes of the Alfama, a warren of narrow alleys around the *Sé* (cathedral) that make up Lisbon's oldest district, plunge towards the riverfront. North of this central core is the Avenida da Liberdade, linking the old city with the more modern areas that contain some of Lisbon's most prestigious museums. West along the river is Belém, with its stunning Mosteiro dos Jerónimos (▷ 331), while up-river to the east you will come to the Parque das Nações (▷ 336–337), built for Expo '98 and now a vibrant riverside entertainment and shopping area.

If it's your first visit you shouldn't miss the main attractions, but make time for simply wandering, making sure not to bypass Lisbon's many *miradouros* (lookouts), with their superb views across the city. Like many historic cities, Lisbon is best explored by walking its streets, but you can save your feet by hopping on a tram or using the funiculars. The Glória runs from Praça dos

INFORMATION AND LISTINGS
Follow Me Lisboa is a monthly free listings guide available from tourist offices. *Agenda Cultural Lisboa* is also a monthly dedicated to cultural listings.

Restauradores, the third largest of the city's central squares, to Rua São Pedro de Alcântara in the Bairro Alto, while the Bica links Rua de Boavista to Rua do Loreto. Before you leave, take the ferry or a river trip to see Lisbon from the water, the best way to appreciate its setting.

BACKGROUND

Legend has it that Lisbon (Lisboa in Portuguese) was founded by Ulysses, one of the Greek heroes of the Trojan Wars, but it was the Phoenicians who probably were the first to settle there around 1200BC. Greeks and Carthaginians followed, before the arrival of the Romans in 205BC. Their prosperous city of Olisipo was founded around 60BC by Julius Caesar.

The Romans were forced out by the Visigoths, and barbarian rule lasted until the area was captured by the Moors early in the eighth century AD. They rechristened the city Lishbuna. It and its rich hinterland prospered thanks to the trade links that were established with the Arab world. The Moors held the city for some four centuries until their expulsion and the establishment of the Portuguese monarchy in 1147. It became the capital in 1255, when Afonso III moved here from Coimbra.

Two centuries later, the city boomed as the departure point for the voyages of the great age of discoveries, when mariners such as Vasco da Gama opened up new trade routes to the east and the Americas. The city's population grew as well, from an estimated 65,000 in 1527 to around 165,000 in 1620. Wealth from overseas paid for the construction of some of the city's grandest and most historic monuments, notably at Belém, where Portugal's finest examples of the home-grown Manueline architectural style are found.

Building continued in the early 18th century, funded by the gold and diamonds pouring in from Brazil, but, in 1755, disaster struck. On 1 November Lisbon was hit by a massive earthquake, which destroyed an estimated two-thirds of the city and killed nearly 40,000 *Lisboetas*. Most of the city's population was attending Mass at the time—1 November is All Souls' Day—and the damage caused by the earthquake was exacerbated by the fires sparked off by thousands of candles. Within only a decade the city had been triumphantly rebuilt with the construction of a new and architecturally fabulous downtown area—the Baixa district (▷ 328).

This 18th-century core still defines the city, though Lisbon continues to expand. Since the 1980s, Lisbon has undergone a massive regeneration, the most obvious beneficiaries being Parque das Nações, created to house Expo '98, and the *Estádio da Luz* (Stadium of Light), which was revamped for the 2004 European Football Championship. This raised Lisbon's profile still more and helped to attract increasing numbers of international visitors.

Arco da Rua Augusta, the Baixa, (above). The Barrio Alto at night (left). The Alfama (below)

LISBOA CARD

This discount card is available from the tourist information offices and gives free travel on buses, trams, funiculars, the metro and trains to Sintra and Cascais, and free entry, or reductions on the admission charge, to 25-plus museums and other attractions. Available for 1, 2 or 3 days (€14.50, €25.50 or €31.50).

SIGHTSEEING TOURS

● CarrisTUR operates multi-lingual bus and tram tours 10–4 year-round from the Praça do Comércio; tickets available from the driver (tel 96 629 8558, www.carris.pt; adult €14, child €7).
● Cityline runs hop-on-hop-off tours from the Praça Marquês de Pombal year-round, with Portuguese and English commentary (tel 213 191 090, www.cityline-sightline.pt; €15).
● Cityrama runs half-day tours with hotel pickups as well as day trips to Fátima, Mafra, Sintra, Nazaré and Óbidos, and Lisbon by Night (tel 213 91090, www.cityrama.pt €30–€80).
● The Art Shuttle May–Sep hop-on-hop-off minibus service covers the main museums and attractions (tel 800 250 251, www.artshuttle.net, €2–€4).
● Transtejo has daily river cruises May–Oct (tel 210 244 400 or 808 203 050).

PORTUGAL

LISBOA

0 ___ 250 m
0 ___ 250 yds

Penitenciaria

Museu Calouste Gulbenkian

Estufas

Pavilhão Carlos Lopes

Parque Eduardo VII

Hospital Militar Principal

Alameda Cardeal Cerejeira

Forum Picoas
Praça José Fon

Picoas

RUA VIRIATO

AV ANTONIO AUGUSTO DE AGUIAR

AVENIDA FONTES PEREIRA DE MELO

RUA ANDR

R SOUSA MARTINS

R Ferrão

R de Andaluz
L do Andaluz

RUA MARQUES DA FONTEIRA

RUA D F MANUEL DE M

RUA VIEIRA

RUA CASTILHO

RUA RODRIGO

R P Am Vieira

R. samp Pina

M. Subserra

Rua de Sá da Pedreira

Praça Marquês de Pombal

Marquês de Pombal

AVENIDA SIDONIO PAIS

Avenida

DUQUE DE

RUA CONDE DE REDON

RUA LUCIANO

R Rctor Tasso

R C Castelo Branco

R FE
R Cre

Bernardo R F

AV C F DE SOUSA

PACHECO   R JOAQUIM A D AGUIAR

RUA DA FONSECA

RUA DE S FILIPE NERI

RUA CASTILHO

RUA BRAÇAMP

RUA ALEXANDRE

HERCULANO

AVENIDA

Hospital de Santa Marta

Tr Sta Marta

R P Cout
Tr d Parr
Tr d Lour
R Larga

Amoreiras Centro Com

AMOREIRAS

RUA DOS AMOREIRAS

RUA DE DOM JOÃO V

SILVA CARVALHO

R Gorgel do Amaral

R C Vieira

Tr Légua de Póva

Tr F D Pentes

R J Penha

C d J A Cabral

R D Palmeira

R D Mouz

da Silveira Araujo

R Rosa Barata

Salgueiro

Sampaio

RUA CASTILHO

Rato

Largo do Rato

RUA   DO   SALITRE

Avendia

RUA

DA

RUA   DO

Rua do Sol

Rua da Pascoa

Rua do J Nep

Rua do Cabo

J S J Joao

R S

Arrabida

R DE D DINIS

ALVARES CABRAL

RATO

RUA DA ESCOLA

São Mamede

T Sta Quitéria

RUA DE SÃO BENTO

RUA DE SÃO JORGE

RUA DA ESTRÊLA

Cemitério Inglês

R DE SÃO JORGE

AVENIDA

R JA ROSA

Jardim da Estrela (Guerra Jungeiro)

Praça da Estrela

Basilica da Estrela

ESTRÊLA

Hospital

CALCADA

RUA DE S BERNARDO

S Placido

Rua de Sto Amaro

RUA DA IMPRENSA

RUA BORGES CARNEIRO

R do Braga

R dos Pretores

Rua da Imprensa

R das Flores

Rua das Palmeiras

PR das Flores

Eduardo Coelho

POLITECNICA

Inst Geofisico
Museu Zoológico e antropológico

Jardim Botânico

Teatros

Universidade Internacional

Praça do Principe Real

RUA DOM PEDRO V

Praça da Alegria

Mãe de Agua

Parque Mayer

T Salitre

LIBE

Alegria

R A da C da Glória

R Antonio da Gl

Rua das Taipas

SÃO DE ALCÂN

R DE

T C Soure

R da Vinha

Tribunal Constitucional

Rua Academia Ciências

Academia das Ciências

Travs do Peixe

Jesus

T Convento Jesus

P R Nova do Loureiro

R Nova da Piedade

R do G Lusitano

T do G Mor

R da Queimar

MADRAGOA

Universidade Técnica

RUA DAS FRANCESINHAS

R d Miguel Lup

Almeida Brandão

AVENIDA DE SÃO BENTO

Palácio da Assembleia Nacional

Pr de S Bento

R da Quintinha

Polais

Cruz

R do Vale

SÉCULO

Santa Catarina

CALÇADA DO COMBRO

T das Mercês

dos Fiéis de Del

T da Espe

BAIRRO ALTO

R D LORETO

R d H Seca

R das Chagas

LAPA

RUA DO MELO

Rua das

Praças

das P

João

Quelhas

Horta

Cura Thias

Mus S Rua de Marion

CALÇADA D MARQUÊS

R de Santa

Rua de Santana

R do Combro

Tr do Combro

RUA DAS JANELAS VERDES

R S O VELHO

Calç Ribeiro Santos

Largo d Santos

SANTOS

24

AVENIDA DE JULHO

Avenida de Brasilia

Avenida de Brasilia

Museu Nacional de Arte Antiga

DOM CARLOS

CARLOS

RUA DA BOA VISTA

R D POÇO D NEGROS

T Tomás Fernandes

R inst Industrial

Dom Luis I

Praça Dom Luis I

RIBEIRA

RUA DE SÃO PAUL

Central Telefonica

R d Ribeira Nova

Cais do Sodré
CAIS DO SODRÉ

A   B   C

1   2   3   4   5

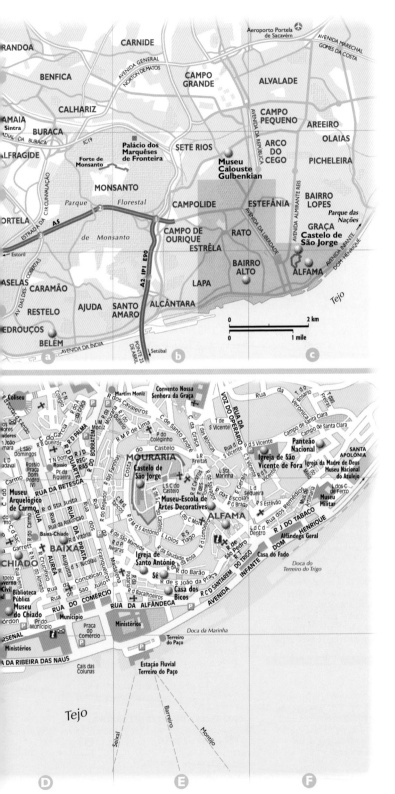

Alfama

Lisbon's evocative and atmospheric medieval quarter is a magical blend of historic buildings and picturesque streets, with great photo opportunities at every turn.

The Miradouro de Santa Luzia (left), traditional housing in the Alfama (middle), and the Casa dos Bicos (right), a 16th-century architectural curiosity

RATINGS	
Cultural interest	● ● ● ●
Historic interest	● ● ● ●
Photo stops	● ● ● ● ●
Walkability	● ● ● ●

TIPS

● If you get lost in the Alfama don't worry. Simply head downhill to get your bearings; you'll eventually emerge near the waterfront.
● Pickpockets can be a problem, so keep a close eye on your bag, wallet and camera. Narrow, ill-lit and deserted streets and alleys are best avoided after dark.
● Catch the tram up to the Graça and then walk downhill to avoid having to walk uphill.

BASICS

✚ 325 E4

www.visitlisboa.com
Lisbon's official tourist site, crammed with useful information on every aspect of the city. Portuguese-, English-, French-, Spanish- and German-language options.

SEEING THE ALFAMA

Although buses and trams serve the area, walking is by far the best option—the labyrinth of narrow alleys cannot be accessed by vehicle in many parts. Begin at the *Sé* (cathedral), then walk up the hill towards the Graça, before cutting down past Igreja de São Vicente de Fora to explore Lisbon's oldest district. There is plenty to see along the way, including some great photo stops at the *miradouros* (viewpoints). These are also good for a refreshment pause, though you might want to wait and find somewhere for lunch in the Alfama itself. Give yourself the time to explore the district to the full and to take in its buzzing street life.

HIGHLIGHTS

THE SÉ

✚ 325 E4 • Largo da Sé, 1100 Lisboa ☎ 218 866 752 ☺ Museum and cloisters: daily 10–1, 2–5. Cathedral: daily 8–8 🎟 Museum and cloisters: €1 🚌 37; Tram: 28, 12

Lisbon's cathedral—the Sé—stands on the site of the city's main mosque. It was founded by Afonso Henriques in 1150. Like the other great Portuguese Romanesque cathedrals in Évora and Coimbra, it's a fortress-like building, redolent of the troubled times when it was constructed. It has been damaged over the centuries by earthquakes, the worst occurring in 1755 when the south tower collapsed and the chancel, chapels and high altar suffered structural and fire damage. Restoration continued on and off into the 19th century, resulting in a building whose Romanesque appearance was virtually lost under baroque and neoclassical additions. This was remedied in the 1930s, when the baroque trappings were removed and the rose window and squat towers were restored.

Off to the right, you'll find the treasury and cloisters. The latter were built in the 13th century. Traces of Roman Olisipo, Visigothic remains and sections of the mosque's walls have been found here.

MUSEU-ESCOLA DE ARTES DECORATIVAS

✚ 325 E4 • Largo das Portas do Sol, 1100-411 Lisboa ☎ 218 881 991 ☺ Thu–Sun 10–5 🎟 €4; 20 per cent reduction with a Lisboa Card 🚌 37; Tram: 28, www.fress.pt

Founded in 1947 by the banker Ricardo do Espírito Santo Silva, the Museum of Applied Arts is home to both a great furniture collection

PORTUGAL

Founded in 1150, Lisbon's fortress-like cathedral (left) now looks more like it did in medieval times as much intrusive restoration has been removed

A detail from the cathedral's celebrated rose window (below)

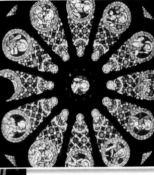

and working craft studios—you can buy their products in the museum shop. The collection is beautifully displayed in a series of reconstructed rooms, lavishly decorated with contemporary tiles and objets d'art. Other highlights include early Chinese export ware, and some exquisite silverware—don't miss the travelling toilet case, inspired by those in the French court at Versailles, but made in Lisbon.

IGREJA DE SÃO VICENTE DE FORA

✚ 325 F3 • Largo de São Vicente, 1100 Lisboa ☎ 218 810 500 🕒 Tue–Sun 10–6
💶 Church: free. Monastery and cloisters: €1 🚌 12; Tram: 28
A church dedicated to St. Vincent, patron saint of Lisbon, was first built on this site in 1147; in 1580, Philip II brought in his architect Juan Herrera to build something more in the Italian Mannerist style. Severely damaged in the 1755 earthquake, the church was restored and is now one of Lisbon's finest examples of baroque architecture. The soaring nave, with a fine coffered vault, leads the eye up to the gilded high altar with its *baldachino* (canopy), while the walls are decorated with superb tiled panels. In the cloisters, you will find still more tiles decorated with court and hunting scenes from La Fontaine's fables. The refectory is the pantheon of the Bragança dynasty.

BACKGROUND

Under the Moors, this was the grandest area of the city, and so it remained during the early years of Christian rule, but a succession of earth tremors caused the nobility to move away, leaving the Moorish character of the district untouched. This can be seen today in its labyrinthine streets—their twists and turns designed to confuse enemies—and the distinctly Arabic latticed window shutters on many houses. Because it is built on rock right against the castle hill, the area suffered relatively little damage in the 1755 earthquake and remained a vibrant, heavily populated blue-collar district. This still applies, though an element of commercialization is creeping in as Lisbon's young professionals snap up top-floor apartments and the number of visitors continues to rise.

MORE TO SEE

CASA DOS BICOS

✚ 325 E4 • Rua dos Bacalhoieros, Campo das Cebolas, 1100 Lisboa
☎ 218 810 900 🕒 Closed to public
🚌 37; Tram: 28
A 1523 merchant's house built by Brás de Albuquerque. The name comes from the *bicos* (pyramidal spikes) that decorate the façade. When it was restored in 1983, Roman and Moorish remains were found underneath.

IGREJA DE SANTO ANTÓNIO

✚ 325 E4 • Largo de Santo António da Sé, 1100 Lisboa ☎ 218 869 145
🕒 Daily 9–1, 2–6 💶 Free 🚌 37; Tram: 28
This small baroque church replaced one destroyed in 1755 and reputedly stands on the site of the birthplace of St. Anthony of Padua in 1195. There is an adjoining museum packed with mementoes of the saint.

PANTEÃO NACIONAL DE SANTA ENGRÁCIA

✚ 325 F3 • Campo de Santa Clara, 1170 Lisboa ☎ 218 881 529
🕒 Tue–Sun 10–5 💶 €1 🚌 12; Tram: 28
This church was designated the national pantheon in 1916. There are great views over the Alfama and the Tejo from the dome. The *Feira da Ladra*, Lisbon's flea market, is held outside on Tuesdays and Saturdays.

PORTUGAL

Dom José's statue (above) stands in front of a triumphal arch in the Praça do Comércio (top)

RATINGS

Historic interest	●●●●●
Specialist shopping	●●●
Walkability	●●●●●

TIPS

● Street vendors sell roast chestnuts here in winter.
● Late afternoon is a good time to explore the area and see the streets at their liveliest.

BASICS

✛ 325 D4
🚇 Rossio, Baixa-Chiado

Dom Pedro IV still regally surveys the Rossio

THE BAIXA

Rebuilt after the great earthquake, the streets, squares and houses of this district at the heart of Lisbon are a superb example of 18th-century town planning.

In 1755 Lisbon suffered one of Europe's most catastrophic recorded earthquakes, which killed thousands and destroyed much of the historic heart of the city, including the entire area behind the waterfront. The Marquês de Pombal, Portugal's first minister, decided to rebuild in the style of the time. The result is the Baixa, a carefully planned network of 18th-century streets lined with elegant, classical buildings. The main axis is the Rua Augusta, an arrow-straight thoroughfare of tiled façades, mosaic pavements and idiosyncratic shopfronts.

PRAÇA DO COMÉRCIO

Rua Augusta leads south through an over-the-top monumental arch, the Arco Triunfal, finally completed in 1873, to the Praça do Comércio, a vast waterfront square that stands on the site of the Terreiro do Paço. Pombal wanted a square that would rival any in Europe, and this huge space was the result. Lined on three sides with arcades, its fourth side is open to the Tejo, Lisbon's sea gateway.

PRAÇA DOM PEDRO IV

The district's other great open space, the Praça Dom Pedro IV, known simply as the Rossio, owes much to Pombal's 18th-century remodelling. The grand building on the north side is the Teatro Nacional de Dona Maria, built in the 1840s on the site of the old Inquisitor's palace. The statue in the middle is of Dom Pedro IV.

The Rossio opens out to the northwest into the Praça dos Restauradores and the neo-Manueline façade of Rossio station. At the top you will find the Elevador do Glória, a ramshackle funicular that links Restauradores with the Bairro Alto.

ELEVADOR DE SANTA JUSTA

Just off the Rua do Our, you will find the Elevador de Santa Justa, one of Lisbon's best-loved landmarks. Opened in 1901, the 45m-tall (147ft) elevator was constructed to link downtown Baixa with the Largo do Carmo above. It was designed by Raul Mesnier de Ponsard, a disciple of Gustave Eiffel, who designed the Eiffel Tower in Paris. The viaduct linking the tower with the Carmo is closed, but a ride up the elevator still gives you great views of the Baixa.

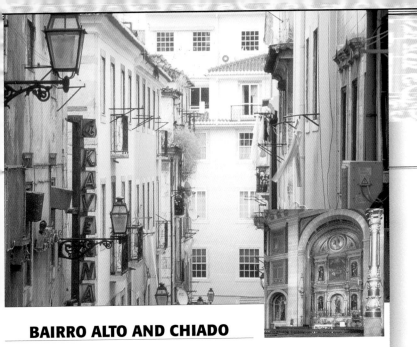

BAIRRO ALTO AND CHIADO

The narrow streets of the Bairro Alto are where you'll find some of Lisbon's best nightlife, while Chiado has traditional shops, stylish cafés and elegantly restored buildings.

BAIRRO ALTO
First laid out in the 1500s, Bairro Alto by day is a quiet residential area that's home to a broad cross-section of *Lisboetas*. It has three pleasant squares: the Largo de Trindade Coelho, bordering the upper Chiado; the Praça Luís de Camões, a square at the southern end of the *bairro* (district); and the Jardim de São Pedro de Alcântara, a garden *miradouro* (viewpoint) with great vistas over the Avenida da Liberdade district. These squares are linked by a maze of alleys and streets, where it's as easy to get lost as in the Alfama (▷ 326–327). Here you will find some of the city's quirkier shops—alternative fashion outlets, specialist record shops and second-hand booksellers near the Trindade. By night it's very different, as thousands of people throng the streets, bars and restaurants. The Bairro Alto is also one of the traditional strongholds of *fado*, Portugal's unique contribution to popular song, and the area still has more than 20 *fado* clubs, some aimed at tourists, others packed with intently listening Portuguese.

CHIADO
This district's focal point is the Largo do Carmo and the main streets of Rua Garrett and Rua do Carmo, which are both lined with some sumptuous stores. Big international names stand alongside traditional Portuguese shops selling luxury goods of all kinds, as well as the pick of the pan-European chain stores and an elegant mall at the bottom of Rua Garrett.

MUSEU ARQUEOLÓGICO DO CARMO
✚ 325 D4 • Largo do Carmo ☎ 213 460 473 ⊙ Oct–end Mar 10–5; Apr–end Sep 10–6 💶 €2.50
The museum is in the ruins of the Gothic Convento do Carmo, which was destroyed in the 1755 earthquake. The entire nave is open to the sky, with tombs on either side of the main altar. One is the resting place of Ferdinand I; nearby lies Gonçalo de Sousa, chancellor to Henry the Navigator, who is commemorated by a statue on top of his tomb. Among the rest of the somewhat eclectic collection here, look out for the pre-Columbian mummies, an Egyptian sarcophagus, Iron Age flints and arrowheads, Roman coins and ancient ceramics.

A typically narrow Bairro Alto street (top).
The Igreja de São Roque (above)

RATINGS	
Chain store shopping	●●●●○
Cultural interest	●●●●○
Specialist interest	●●●○○
Walkability	●●●●○

TIPS
● Use the *elevadores* to get up the hills.

BASICS
✚ 324 C4, 325 D4
Ⓜ Baixa-Chiado

The Elevador de Santa Justa

Belém

The departure point for the voyages of discovery, Belém's buildings span more than 600 years, including the best of Manueline architecture and a clutch of superb monuments and museums on the waterfront.

View across to Jeronimos Monastery   *Map of the world on the waterfront*   *Belém's suspensio...*

SEEING BELÉM

The suburb of Belém, 6km (4 miles) west of central Lisbon, has enough to keep you busy for a whole day. Its monuments and museums are scattered around a fairly wide area beside the Tejo, with views across the river and a plethora of spacious promenades, gardens and water features. The best way to get there is on tram 15 from the middle of the city; alternatively, you could take the train from Cais do Sodré on the Cascais line. Bear in mind that practically everything is shut on Mondays and that Sundays, when entrance to some sites is free, can be very busy. Leave enough time to stroll along the waterfront and enjoy the parks of Jardim do Ultramarino and Jardim Botânico da Ajuda.

HIGHLIGHTS

PADRÃO DOS DESCOBRIMENTOS

✉ Avenida de Brasilia, 1400-038 Lisboa ☎ 213 031 950 🕐 May–end Sep Tue–Sun 10–7, Oct–end Apr Tue–Sun 10–6 💶 €2.50 🚌 27, 28, 43, 49, 51; Tram: 15 🚆 Linha de Cascais Belém ⬛ ♿ 🅿 Surrounding streets

The idea for a monument commemorating the great age of Portuguese discoveries was first mooted in 1940 during the Exhibition of the Portuguese World, for which the Belém area was radically reconstructed. The first Padrão was temporary and the swooping white edifice you see today was erected in 1960. The jutting pediment resembles the prow of a Portuguese caravel, with a trio of curving forms behind the wind-filled sails. Its hard lines are softened by the figures crowded on the sloping prow. Dominating them is Henry the Navigator (1399–1460), holding a ship in his hand. Behind him, the 32 other figures include Manuel I, whose reign (1495–1521) coincided with some of the greatest voyages, and Luís de Camões, Portugal's most famous poet. You can take a lift to the top for great estuary views; the exhibition space inside stages temporary shows on aspects of Lisbon's history. The pavement in front combines a design of a compass and a world map showing the great Portuguese voyages and their dates, making it possible to trace their steady progress south, east and west. It was a gift from South Africa to commemorate the 500th anniversary of the death of Henry the Navigator.

The Torre de Belém

TORRE DE BELÉM

✉ Avenida de Brasilia, 1400-038 Lisboa ☎ 213 620 034 🕐 May–end Sep
Tue–Sun 10–6.30; Oct–end Apr Tue–Sun 10–5. Last admittance 30 mins before
closing 🎫 €3; 🚌 27, 28, 29, 43, 49, 51; Tram: 15 🚆 Linha de Cascais to Belém
🎁 Poor selection of expensive souvenirs 🚻 🅿 Surrounding streets
www.mosteirojeronimos.pt

Built between 1515 and 1519, the Torre de Belém, one of Portugal's
most potent national symbols, originally stood well out into the river, a
fortress designed to safeguard the western approaches to Lisbon's
harbour. The great earthquake of 1755 substantially altered the
course of the River Tejo, and the Torre today stands on the water's
edge, though still surrounded on three sides by the sea. It was
designed for Dom Manuel I by Francisco de Arruda, who had previously worked on Portuguese buildings in Morocco, and the Moorish
influence is evident in much of the architectural detail, seen at its best
in the turrets with their rounded domes. The combination of these
elements with Gothic, Venetian and Byzantine touches makes it
unique. It is also the only complete example of the Manueline style
to survive in Portugal.

Look for the armillary spheres in the decoration, which represent
navigational instruments and were Dom Manuel's personal badge,
and the cross of the military Order of Christ of which he was the
Grand Master. Don't miss the intricate stone ropework, so typical of
Manueline decoration, or the first European sculpture of a rhinoceros
under the northwest corner watchtower. From the second-floor
terrace, steps lead up to the top of the tower with wide views across
the Tejo. You can reach the terraces via the surprisingly plain and
unadorned interior, whose chief point of interest is the 'whispering
gallery', the acoustics of which amplify the tiniest whisper.

*Detail of the Monument to
Discoveries*

MOSTEIRO DOS JERÓNIMOS

✉ Praça do Império, 1400-206 Lisboa ☎ 213 620 034 🕐 Nov–end Apr Tue–Sun
10–5; May–end Sep Tue–Sun 10–6 🎫 Church: free.Cloisters: €4.50; free on Sun
until 2pm 🚌 27, 28, 29, 43, 49, 51; Tram: 15 🚆 Linha de Cascais to Belém
🎁 Sells expensive museum reproductions, china and T-shirts from all over
Portugal, plus some books (but no guides) 🚻 🅿 Surrounding streets
www.mosteirojeronimos.pt

The Mosteiro dos Jerónimos is both the triumphant symbol of
Portugal's great seafaring age and Lisbon's finest monument. It was
built on the site of an earlier church founded by Henry the Navigator,
where Vasco da Gama spent his last night on shore before setting
out on his voyage east. Dom Manuel I vowed to erect a larger church
if the voyage was successful, though it took until 1551 before the
entire complex was more or less complete. The main architects were
Diogo da Boitaca, pioneer of the Manueline style, and João de
Castilho, a Spaniard.

Inside, heavily decorated columns soar towards the superb rib-
vaulted ceiling. Under the gallery to the left, you will find the tomb of
Vasco da Gama, while that of the poet Luís de Camões lies across
the aisle.

The double-floored cloister is reached by exiting the church. The
combination of different architectural influences, the Gothic and
Renaissance contrasting with innovative touches such as the recurring
anchors, ropes and maritime motifs, makes it a perfect example of
Manueline style.

MORE TO SEE

MUSEU DA MARINHA

✉ Praça do Império, 1400–206 Lisboa
☎ 213 620 019 🕐 Oct–end Apr
Tue–Sun 10–5; May–end Sep Tue–Sun
10–6 🎫 €3 🚌 27, 28, 29, 43, 49, 51;
Tram: 15 🚆 Linha de Cascais to Belém
🚻 Moderate–expensive 🎁 🚻
🅿 Surrounding streets

Lisbon's Naval Museum is in the
west wing of the Mosteiro dos
Jerónimos, where it was moved
in 1962 following a fire in its
original home in the Arsenal. It's
among Europe's finest maritime
museums, with a huge collection. In the sections relating to
the age of discoveries, you will
find fascinating models, globes
and maps, as well as the
museum's oldest treasure, a
polychrome wooden carving of
the Archangel Gabriel said to
have accompanied Vasco da
Gama on his great voyages.

BACKGROUND

The area of Belém was once a maritime settlement right on the
water known as Restelo and was quite separate from the city of
Lisbon. Manuel I changed its name to Belém in the early 1500s,
by which time the district was synonymous with maritime exploration. The Mosteiro dos Jerónimos was built to give thanks for
da Gama's successful voyage.

The Salazar regime revamped the waterfront and laid out the
pools and gardens fronting Jerónimos. The Padrão went up in
1960, and in 1992 the Centro Cultural de Belém was built to
mark Portugal's presidency of the European Union.

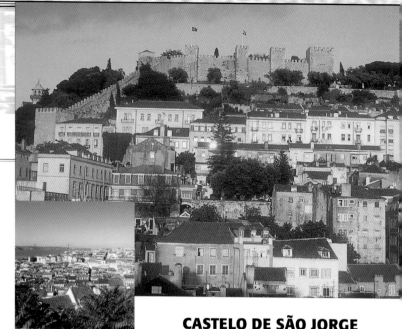

São Jorge (top) and looking down from the castle (above)

RATINGS	
Cultural interest	● ● ●
Good for kids	● ● ● ●
Historic interest	● ● ● ●
Photo stops	● ● ● ● ●

TIPS

● The castle and its gardens are a great place to spend a couple of hours during the hottest part of the day.
● The paving is uneven, so watch your step and wear comfortable, flat shoes.

BASICS

✚ 325 E4 • Castelo de São Jorge, 1100–129 Lisboa
☎ 218 800 620
◉ Olisipónia: Mar–end Oct daily 9–8.30; Nov–end Feb daily 9–5.30. Câmara Escura: Mar–end Oct daily 10–5; Nov–end Feb daily 11–2.30. Last admittance 30 mins before closing
💷 €5 for all attractions
🚌 37; Tram: 28, 12
🍴 Casa do Leão: an elegant and expensive restaurant in one of the surviving rooms of the Alcáçova
☕ Small self-service café with hot and cold drinks, snacks and ice-cream
🎁 Small shop with a limited selection of souvenirs
👫
www.castelsaojorge.egeac.pt

CASTELO DE SÃO JORGE

The birthplace of the city is an oasis of peace and cool greenery with superb views over the busy streets and the River Tejo below.

The Castelo de São Jorge has long been a defensive stronghold—a fort stood here even before the coming of the Romans in 138BC. They built a citadel on the site of the present castle, from which the Roman city spread down the hill. The Moors built a castle over the earlier Roman fortification with the Alcáçova in the middle—the palace that still stands today. Portugal's kings lived here from 1279 to 1511, moving out only after the construction of the Palácio de Ribeira.

THE RAMPARTS, WALLS AND GARDENS

Topped with battlements and crowned with 10 towers, the inner walls surround two courtyards, from where stairs provide access to the wall-top walkways. From these you can climb the towers, one of which contains an old-fashioned camera obscura. This gives bird's-eye views of the streets and people far below. More stairs lead down the hill to the outlying Torre de São Lourenço. The entire complex had a thorough facelift before Expo '98, as did the surrounding gardens, and it is now one of the best-kept parts of central Lisbon.

THE ALCÁÇOVA AND OLISIPÓNIA

The Alcáçova was the original Moorish palace, which served as the royal residence from the 14th to the 16th centuries. Little of it remains today and what there is has been heavily restored, but you will get a good idea of its original size and state in the series of chambers now housing the Olisipónia, a multimedia exhibition focusing on the history of the capital.

A series of screens and sound effects leads you through a 25-minute run-down of the city's past, with some good information on Portugal's golden age in the 15th and 16th centuries and some fascinating insights into the great earthquake of 1755. Unusually for Portugal, there is an English audio commentary.

Don't miss Take in the show at the Olisipónia for an informative overview of Lisbon's history.
Walk along the castle's ramparts for some of the best views over Lisbon and its river.
Explore the medieval quarter of Santa Cruz within the outer walls.

PORTUGAL

A tile from the National Tile Museum

MUSEU DO CHIADO

⊞ 325 D4 • Rua Serpa Pinta 6, 1200-444 ☎ 213 432 148/9 🕐 Tue–Sun 10–6 🎫 €3 🚇 Baixa-Chiado 🚋 Tram: 28, 38, 100
www.ipmuseus.pt

Founded in 1914 as Portugal's national museum of contemporary painting and sculpture, the Museu do Chiado was totally revamped after the Chiado fire of 1988. Reopened in 1994, with a contemporary facelift by the French architect Jean Michel Wilmotte, it now concentrates on Portuguese art between 1850 and 1950. The collection covers every movement, from romanticism, naturalism, modernism and surrealism to abstractionism. Artistically, works such as *A Sesta* by Almada Negreiros and *O Desterrado* by Soares dos Reis are the best, but many visitors find scenes of Lisbon, such as Carlos Botelho's *Lisboa e o Tejo*, more interesting.

MUSEU NACIONAL DO AZULEJO AND IGREJA DA MADRE DE DEUS

⊞ 325 F3 • Rua da Madre de Deus, 1900-312 Lisboa ☎ 218 100 340 🕐 Tue 2–6, Wed–Sun 10–6 🎫 Adult €3, child (under 15) free 🚇 Arroios then 🚌 18, 42, 104, 105
www.ipmuseus.pt

The museum traces the history of the *azulejo* from the 15th century to the present day. Highlights include the blue-and-white Lisbon cityscape, showing the city prior to the 1755 earthquake. There are additional stunning *azulejos* in the adjoining church. The complex received several spectacular facelifts during the 1600 and 1700s funded from Royal coffers which had been swelled by discoveries in the New World.

Intricate designs in silver, the work of Renaissance craftsmen

MUSEU NACIONAL DE ARTE ANTIGA

Portugal's national art museum is located in a beautifully converted 17th-century palace with a tranquil garden.

⊞ 324 A5 • Rua das Janelas Verdes, 1249-017 Lisboa ☎ 213 912 800 🕐 Tue 2–6, Wed–Sun 10–1, 2–6 🎫 €3 🚌 27, 40, 43, 49, 60; Tram: 28
www.ipmuseus.pt

The Museu Nacional de Arte Antiga is the place to come to see the best of Portuguese painting, enjoy an overview of other European painting schools, and take in a comprehensive collection of furniture, textiles and objects from all branches of the decorative arts. The museum's strengths are its Portuguese paintings and the Far Eastern collections, particularly the examples of late 16th-century Japanese Namban art, dating from the time the Portuguese were in Japan. They arrived there in the early 1500s and stayed until the Japanese closed the country to Europeans.

PORTUGUESE PAINTING—FLOOR 3
This covers the 15th- and 16th-century schools, when Portuguese painting was heavily influenced by Flemish artists such as Jan van Eyck and Rogier van der Weyden. The big names are Nuno Gonçalves, Grégorio Lopes and Frei Carlos. Gonçalves' star piece is the *São Vicente Polyptych*, a six-panel altarpiece showing a crowd paying homage to St. Vincent, Lisbon's patron saint.

EUROPEAN PAINTING—FLOOR 1 (GROUND)
The Flemish and German schools are strong here, the *Temptation of St. Anthony* by Hieronymous Bosch being an outstanding example of that artist's surrealistic style. There are also works by Cranach, Dürer, Raphael and Zurbarán.

FAR EASTERN ART—FLOOR 2
This is an outstanding collection of decorative art, including porcelain and metalwork, dating from the colonial period in Africa and the Far East. The ceramics and silverware rival the exhibits in the Gulbenkian (▷ 334–335), particularly the Chinese porcelain and the huge steely and lustrous 1756 silver dinner and decorative table service by F. T. Germain of Paris.

Don't miss The 16th-century Japanese screens on floor 2 depict the arrival of the Portuguese in Nagasaki; they are full of quirky European figures with long pointed noses and stork-like legs.

PORTUGAL

Museu Calouste Gulbenkian

Lisbon's only world-class museum, housed in a sleek building in lovely gardens, is home to a comprehensive but compact collection of great art, with examples from every century and from all over the world.

BASICS

✚ 325 b2 (inset) • Avenida de Berna 45, 1067-001 Lisboa
☎ 217 823 000
🕐 Tue–Sun 10–5.45
💶 Adult €4, under 12 free
🚇 Praça de Espanha, Saõ Sebastião
🚌 16, 26, 31, 46, 56
🍴 Self-service restaurant serving mediocre food and snacks throughout the day
☕ Café serving coffee, drinks and snacks; part of the restaurant
🎧 Audio guide €4
🏬 Shop selling a wide selection of art books, almost exclusively in Portuguese, and some good-quality and expensive museum reproduction souvenirs. Some smaller, less expensive objects aimed at children. No museum guidebooks or postcards
👪
www.gulbenkian.pt

TIPS

● There is no floorplan or guidebook available, so it pays to study the wall plan in the entrance hall before you start your visit.
● Allow around 2–3 hours for a leisurely visit.
● Leave time to enjoy the fine gardens that surround the Fundação Calouste Gulbenkian's buildings.
● Combine visiting the Gulbenkian with the Museu do Centro de Arte Moderna, which is also part of the foundation and situated close by to it.

The entrance to the museum (above)

SEEING THE MUSEU CALOUSTE GULBENKIAN

The Museu Calouste Gulbenkian is part of the Fundação Calouste Gulbenkian, a few minutes' walk north of Parque Eduardo VII. The collection is relatively small, but every exhibit is a superlative example of its type. The exhibits are clearly laid out in geographical and chronological groups: There are two main sections, one of which is devoted to European art and the other to the art of the ancient and oriental worlds. All the exhibits are labelled in Portuguese and English or take advantage of the new audio guide.

HIGHLIGHTS

EASTERN ISLAMIC AND ARMENIAN ART—ROOMS IV AND V
Two interconnecting galleries hold the Eastern Islamic and Armenian collections, providing an overview of all that's best from these regions, with particular emphasis on works from the 15th to 17th centuries. The silk and wool carpets, some laid flat, others used as wallhangings, are a high point, as are the numerous examples of wall tiles from the Ottoman Empire—one particularly beautiful 15th-century panel of faience tiles with a turquoise, blue and white underglaze stands out.

FAR EASTERN ART—ROOM VI
The exhibits include deep Ming bowls with a translucent celadon green glaze, though more eye-catching by far are the Chinese porcelain vases and covered pots, mainly dating from the 17th and 18th centuries. Two outstanding sets are made of enamelled porcelain, one decorated with chrysanthemums in clear pink, turquoise and green on a white ground, the other with pink and green flowers and natural motifs on a black glaze.

EUROPEAN ART—ROOMS VII–XVII PAINTING
Highlights from the painting collection include Ghirlandaio's *Portrait of a Young Woman*; she is wearing a pink dress with green sleeves, while her coral necklace draws attention to the delicate wisps of hair around her face. More young women feature in a trio of portraits by

the English artists Gainsborough, Romney and Lawrence, while Rembrandt's *Pallas Athene*, a dark depiction of the goddess with a superb shield and plumed helmet, is more sombre. Rubens is represented by a sympathetic portrait of his second wife Helena Fourment, and there is an atmospheric Turner, *The Mouth of the Seine*, all swirling water and pearly tints. Corot, Monet, Renoir and Dégas represent the French Impressionists.

Renoir's Madame Monet *(above).*
A modern sculpture (below)

SCULPTURE, FURNITURE AND PORCELAIN

Sculptures include a 15th-century Luca della Robbia medallion from Florence, a Rossellino bas-relief of the Madonna and Child, and Houdon's marble *Diana* (1780). The French Louis XV and Louis XVI furniture is superb, set off by wall hangings and tapestries. There's more French pre-Revolutionary opulence in the shape of silver and gold tableware, together with a display of Sèvres porcelain.

BACKGROUND

The Fundação Calouste Gulbenkian, a cultural foundation active throughout Portugal, funds museums and libraries and gives charitable grants. This is all possible thanks to Calouste Gulbenkian (1869–1955), an Armenian-born oil magnate, who made millions in the Middle East. Art collecting was his passion, and the Museu Calouste Gulbenkian is the result of years of astute buying. During World War II the British seized control of his assets, and it was neutral Portugal that provided the cultural patron with a home.

Parque das Nações

A stunning waterside site, whose attractions include Europe's finest oceanarium, lots of fun for the kids, and no-hassle shopping. This is a perfect family day out.

RATINGS

Chain store shopping	●●●●●
Good for kids	●●●●●
Specialist shopping	●●●●●
Value for money	●●●
Walkability	●●●●

BASICS

✚ 325 c2 (inset) • Alameda dos Oceanos, 1990-223 Lisboa
☎ 218 919 333
Ⓜ Oriente line to Oriente
www.parquedasnacoes.pt

SEEING THE PARQUE DAS NAÇÕES

It's an easy journey by Metro to the state-of-the-art Oriente station in the Parque das Nações, from where you have only to walk through the huge and tempting Vasco da Gama shopping mall to reach the park itself. The site is rambling, and distances can be deceptive, but judicious use of the miniature train and the cable car will help you to get around. Aim to visit the Oceanário before the queues build up, then spend the rest of the day exploring everything else. Although the crowds are thinner during the week, the atmosphere is best on weekends, when thousands flock here to enjoy the attractions and wander along the waterside promenades. You can also visit the park without going into Lisbon, as it's easily accessible by car.

HIGHLIGHTS

OCEANÁRIO

✉ Parque das Nações, 1800 Lisboa ☎ 218 917 002/6 🕙 Oct–end Apr daily 10–7 (ticket office closes at 6pm); May–end Sep daily 10–8 (ticket office closes at 7pm) 💶 Adult €10.50, child (4–12) €5.25, under-3s free, family (2 adults and 1 child) €25; tickets can be reserved online Ⓜ Oriente 🚌 28 📖 Illustrated floor plan in English €1.50 🏬 Excellent shop selling a wide range of ocean-related books, souvenirs, stationery and stuffed toys 🚻 🅿
www.oceanario.pt

Designed by the American architect Peter Chermayeff, the Oceanário opened in 1998 as part of Expo '98. Its role was to provide Lisbon with a permanent reminder of the Expo by neatly linking the country's maritime past with the future role of the oceans. The building crouches on the water's edge like some futuristic underwater machine, but it's the marine life inside that attracts the crowds.

The huge central tank, visible from two levels, contains more than 7 million litres (1.8 million US gallons) of salt water and is inhabited by a range of fish and sea creatures from the world's oceans—sharks, rays and great schools of smaller fish living at different depths. This is surrounded by four areas representing various oceanic ecosystems: the Atlantic, the Antarctic, the Pacific and the Indian. These exhibits have both above- and below-water habitats, allowing visitors to see birds, animals and vegetation typical of these zones above ground as well as the marine life under the water. The puffins and guillemots in the Atlantic zone are very popular, as are the Magellan penguins hopping around in the snow in the Antarctic zone and the fish-eating sea otters of the Pacific. All these creatures can be viewed underwater once you descend to the lower level, where sunlight filters through the water onto the weeds and coral, and shoals of fish glide by.

The oceanarium (above and below)

PORTUGAL

Oriente station

Additional tanks cover sea habitats as diverse as living coral reefs and mangrove forests. Highlights here are the Australian dragon fish, their camouflage so perfect that they're almost impossible to detect against the seaweeds they live in; the luminous tropical jellyfish; vivid anemones and an astounding range of crabs. There are more than 15,000 animals and plants here, with 450 different species represented. Educational interactive exhibits include information on fishing, ocean products, currents, winds, tides and conservation. Everything is clearly labelled in Portuguese and English.

CENTRO DA CIÊNCIA VIVA

✉ Alameda dos Oceanos, Parque das Nações, 1990-223 Lisboa ☎ 218 917 100 🕐 Mon–Fri 10–6, Sat–Sun 11–7
💶 Adult €6, child (7–17) €3, under-6s free, family ticket (2 adults and 2 children) €13 🚇 Oriente 🚌 28 📖 Explanatory English leaflet €1.50
🎁 Good book and gift shop with plenty of reasonably priced souvenirs 🚻 🅿
www.pavconhecimento.pt

This is another great attraction for families. It's a science park that aims—and succeeds—in getting the message across to ordinary people that science and technology are fun. There are plenty of permanent interactive exhibits, ranging from how holograms work to technology in everyday life, while kids can spend hours in the cyber-café with its free Internet access. Run by the Portuguese Ministry of Science and Technology, the site also has thematic exhibitions, drawing on the resources of the world's major scientific institutes. Highlights among these are the Unfinished House, designed by the Cité des Sciences in Paris, San Francisco's Exploratorium, and the See, Do, Learn display jointly conceived by the universities of Cardiff and Helsinki. All of these are interactive exhibits and learning zones where visitors can enjoy a real hands-on experience of science at its liveliest. Everything's clearly labelled in both English and Portuguese.

THE WATERFRONT AND GARDENS

The Tejo is up to 10km (6 miles) wide here and walkways, planted with shrubs and trees from Portugal's former colonies, run all along the water's edge from west of the Oceanário to beyond Ponte Vasco da Gama. On weekends, thousands of locals come here to relax and enjoy the fine views; during the week, though, it's one of the city's most peaceful areas. Don't miss the Jardim da Agua, where ponds are linked by stepping stones and and jet fountains spray cooling water.

BACKGROUND

Until the early 1990s the area now containing the Parque das Nações was an industrial wasteland, scarred by derelict ware-houses, an oil refinery and the municipal slaughterhouse. The site was chosen as the hub of Expo '98, Lisbon's international World's Fair, which launched the country firmly into the European mainstream. The fair ran from May to September 1998 and was a huge success, attracting many thousands of visitors.

Once Expo closed, the site was reopened as an urban district and given its present name. Construction around the park is ongoing, with the ultimate aim of creating a large-scale and well-planned residential and business zone, focused around the existing park and its huge riverside gardens. The area contains two of Lisbon's largest concert venues and a multitude of shops, cafés and restaurants. It is served by excellent public transport links via Santiago Calatrava's stunning Estação do Oriente rail, Metro and bus station.

TIPS

● The *posto de informacão* (information desk) is outside the Vasco da Gama shopping mall, and has plans of the park and details of events.

● If you want to see every-thing, consider purchasing the Cartão do Parque (adult €15.50, child €8.50). It gives access to the main sites and discounts elsewhere.

● If you don't feel like walking, a hop-on-hop-off miniature train makes the round trip through the park between 10am and 5pm. It leaves hourly on the hour from out-side the Atlantic Pavilion (adult €2.50, under-14s €1.50). You can also rent bicycles (€2 plus €5 per hour); ask at the information desk.

● It may take more than an hour to get into the Oceanário at peak times, so it can pay to get to the park early and head there first.

PORTUGAL

WHAT TO DO

⊕ ANA SALAZAR

Rua do Carmo 87
Tel 213 472 289
www.anasalazar.pt
Probably Portugal's best-known fashion designer, Ana Salazar is considered to be the pioneer of Portuguese fashion by both the national and international press. She set up her own label in the 1980s and opened a Paris showroom in 1985. Her designs often make intriguing use of stretch fabrics in neutral tones of grey, earthy browns and maroons.
🕐 Mon–Fri 10–7, Sat 10–7
🚇 Baixa-Chiado

⊕ CONFEITARIA NACIONAL

Praça da Figueira 18-B
Tel 213 424 470
Founded in 1829 and selling all kinds of delicious confectionery, this store is worth a visit just for its interior. The wood-and-glass cabinets and antique mirrors make the perfect setting for the rows upon rows of tempting sweets made from traditional recipes. The almond cookies are particularly good.
🕐 Mon–Sat 8–8 🚇 Rossio

⊕ EL CORTE INGLÉS

Avenida António Augusto de Aguiar
Tel 213 711 700
www.elcorteingles.pt
This gigantic department store, part of the Spanish chain, offers a full range of quality and designer items: clothing, accessories, perfumes and cosmetics, electrical appliances and household goods. In the basement there is a wonderful gourmet delicatessen section, restaurants and a multiscreen cinema showing films in their original language (usually English).
🕐 Mon–Thu 10–10, Fri–Sat 10am–11.30pm, Sun 10–1 🚇 São Sebastião 🚌 Bus 46, 205

⊕ MERCADO ABASTECEDOR DA RIBEIRA

Avenida 24 de Julho
Tel 213 462 966
Lisbon's largest covered market is just down from the Cais do Sodré station and is one of the city's most important fresh fish outlets. It is also good for other fresh produce, including fruit, vegetables and regional cured meats and cheeses.
🕐 Mon–Sat 6am–2pm 🚇 Cais do Sodré

⊕ SANTOS OFÍCIOS

Rua da Madalena 87, Baixa
Tel 218 872 031
www.santosoficios-artesanato.pt
This shop, opened in 1995 to promote quality, hand-selected crafts, is housed in an 18th-century stable, opposite the church of Madalena in the Baixa. Representing all regions of Portugal, it stocks an eclectic mix of pottery, rugs, embroidered linens, figurines, tiles and sculptures. A full shipping service is available.
🕐 Mon–Sat 10–8 🚇 Baixa-Chiado

⊕ FUNDAÇÃO CALOUSTE GULBENKIAN

Avenida da Berna 45
Tel 217 823 000
www.gulbenkian.pt
The most important cultural venue in the country, the Gulbenkian Foundation has its own orchestra, choir and dance company, which stages regular performances throughout the year. It also hosts national and international art exhibitions.
🕐 Box office: Mon–Fri and weekends of performances 1–7 and one hour prior to start of performance
💶 €15–€40 🚇 In auditorium 🅿
🚇 São Sebastião 🚌 Bus 56

⊕ TEATRO NACIONAL DE SÃO CARLOS

Rua Serpa Pinto 9, Baixa
Tel 213 253 027
www.saocarlos.pt
Opened in 1793, the splendid gold-leaf and red-velvet auditorium of the Teatro Nacional de São Carlos has been the stage for the country's most prestigious opera productions and major symphony concerts ever since.
🕐 Box office: Mon–Fri 1–7 or until half an hour before start of performance. Opera season: Oct–end Jun

💶 €20–€60 🚇 In auditorium 🅿
🚇 Baixa-Chiado 🚌 Bus 58; Tram 28

▼ PLATEAU

Avenida 24 de Julho, Escadinhas da Praia 7, Santos
Tel 213 965 116
Plateau was Lisbon's first true nightclub and as such enjoys legendary status. Decorated with oriental objects, it plays mainly 1980s revivalist, pop and rock to the mixed beautiful crowd lucky enough to make it past the doormen.
🕐 Wed–Sat midnight–6am 💶 Charge at discretion of doorman 🚇 Santos
🚌 Bus 28; tram E15

✪ PRAÇA DE TOUROS

Campo Pequeno, Avenida João XXI–Avenida da República
Tel 217 932 143 or 217 932 093
For a chance to appreciate the renowned horsemanship of Portuguese bullfighters, the restored 19th-century neo-Moorish bullring at Campo Pequeno is worth a visit in season. Note that in Portugal, unlike in Spain, the bulls are not killed in the ring, but skilfully wrestled to the ground.
🕐 Season: Apr–end Sep. Bullfights: Thu 8pm 💶 €20–€50 according to the line-up 🚇 Campo Pequeno 🚌 Bus 27, 36, 45

EATING

BICA DO SAPATO

Avenida Infante Dom Henrique, Armazém B, Cais Pedra, Santa Apolónia
Tel 218 810 320
Bica do Sapato is one of the trendiest of Lisbon's trendy restaurants. At a prime dockside location just across from the Santa Apolónia train station, and with a riverfront terrace and super-modern interior, it encompasses three different eating areas: the restaurant, offering the popular *sugestão da semana* (dish of the week); the café, serving traditional Portuguese dishes; and the sushi bar, where on Wednesday the fixed-price *dia dos sabores* (day of flavours) menu is good value.
🕐 Restaurant: Mon 8pm–11.30pm, Tue–Sat 12–2.30, 8–11.30. Café: Mon 7.30pm–1am, Tue–Sat 12.30–3.30, 7.30–1. Sushi bar: Mon–Sat 7.30pm–1am
💶 L €38, D €55, Wine €10
🚇 Terreiro do Paço
🚌 Bus 9, 12, 28, 46, 81, 90

PORTUGAL

CONVENTUAL

Praca das Flores 44–45, Rato
Tel 213 909 246

On one of the prettiest squares in town, this pious-sounding restaurant offers some of the best dining in the city. Appropriately decorated with antique and modern sacred art, it continues the religious theme in the names of some of its dishes, such as Pope of Avignon snails, and its excellent *doces conventuais*, highly prized egg-and-sugar-based puddings traditionally made by convent nuns. The *arroz de pato* (duck with rice) is superb.

Tue–Fri 12.30–3.30, 7.30–11, Sat, Mon and national holidays 7.30–11. Closed Aug
L €20, D €30, Wine €13
Rato
Bus 100

ENOTECA—CHAFARIZ DO VINHO

Rua Mãe d'Água/Praça da Alegria
Tel 213 422 079
www.chafarizdovinho.com

Off the Praça da Alegria, Chafariz do Vinho is an excellent place for a tapas-style meal of cured ham, spicy sausages, cheeses and a good bottle of wine. Alternatively, there's the *menu de prova*, which offers a choice of three excellent Portuguese dishes plus dessert.

Tue–Sun 6pm–2am (kitchen closes at 1am). Closed 23 Dec–10 Jan
D €15, Wine €15
Avenida

GAMBRINUS

Rua Portas de Santo Antão 23, Baixa
Tel 213 421 466

In a street packed with restaurants and eateries, Gambrinus is the most expensive and the best. With its comfortably sedate interior, sporting wood-beamed ceilings and huge fireplaces, it's a popular retreat for politicians, journalists and other Portuguese celebrities. Sit at the bar counter or in one of the two dining rooms and choose from a huge selection of seafood (prawns, lobster and crab are always available), fresh fish (seasonal choices include sea bream, sea bass and sole), and meat and game. For dessert, try the crêpes Suzette. There is a non-smoking section.

Daily noon–1.30am L €35, D €50, Wine €20 Restauradores

PAP' AÇORDA

Rua da Atalaia 57–59, Bairro Alto
Tel 213 464 811

In a converted bakery in the Bairro Alto, this fashionable restaurant has managed to maintain its iconic status. Choose from oysters, mussels or a variety of *açordas* (thick bread-and-egg stews to which such ingredients as prawns and lobster are added). The chocolate mousse is reputed to be the best in town.

Tue–Sat 12–2, 8–1. Closed first 2 weeks of Jul and Nov
L €25, D €35, Wine €20
Baixa-Chiado
Bus 58, 100

STAYING

ALBERGARIA SENHORA DO MONTE

Calçada do Monte 39, Graça, Lisboa
Tel 218 866 002
www.maisturismo.pt/sramonte.html

In a prime location up in the quiet Graça district, this hotel has uninterrupted views of the city. The rooftop breakfast bar looks across the River Tagus to the Christ statue and Ponte 25 de Abril. It's worth paying extra for a south-facing room with a terrace from where you can watch the sunset, or, even better, the sunrise. It's a short tram ride to the heart of the city.

€105–€175 including breakfast
28 (4 with terrace)
Martim Moniz
Tram 28, 12

HOTEL BORGES

Rua Garrett 108–110, Chiado, Lisboa
Tel 213 461 951
www.maisturismo.pt/hborges

This hotel in the exclusive Chiado district, next to the art nouveau A Brasileira café, with its statue of Fernando Pessoa sitting outside, is good value for money. Don't be put off by the mirrored lobby with its dated furnishings, as most rooms have been refurbished and are now freshly carpeted and well coordinated. Light sleepers should avoid the front rooms, especially on weekends, when the café stays open late.

€79–€160, including breakfast
96

Baixa-Chiado
Tram 28

LAPA PALACE

Rua do Pau da Bandeira 4, Lapa, Lisboa
Tel 213 949 494
www.lapapalace.com

Converted from what was once the 19th-century residence of the Count of Valença, and set amid tranquil gardens overlooking the River Tagus, this is one of Lisbon's plushest and most expensive hotels. At the time of writing, it is also the only one with a heated outdoor pool. Inside, the original opulence has been lovingly restored, especially in the splendidly frescoed Columbano room and the Count of Valença suite, the most luxurious room of them all. Others are decorated in art deco, *Belle Époque* and oriental styles; their facilities, somewhat incongruously, include an internet connection.

€355–€755, including breakfast
109
Indoor and outdoor
Bus 13, 27; tram 25
Santos

SOLAR DO CASTELO

Rua das Cozinhas 2, Lisboa
Tel 218 806 050
www.heritage.pt

This 18th-century palace shares its ancient walls with the Castelo de São Jorge, and its many medieval elements have been made into interesting architectural features. With only 14 intimate rooms and professionally discreet service, it feels like a private home. Bedrooms are decorated in warm tones with fine fabrics in a mix of modern and classical styles, and the Pombaline-style windows look out onto an attractive tiled patio where a good breakfast is served in warm weather.

€210–€305, excluding breakfast (€12.50)
14 rooms (non-smoking available)
Limited street parking
Bus 37

Porto

A dynamic and earthy metropolis with a superb historic heart and a vibrant cultural and entertainment scene, Portugal's second-largest city stands at the mouth of the River Douro.

RATINGS

Cultural interest	●●●
Historic interest	●●●●
Photo stops	●●●●●
Specialist shopping	●●●●

BASICS

➕ 4 A4

🛈 Rua Clube dos Fenianos 25, 4000-172 Porto; tel 223 393 472; or Rua Infante d Henrique 63 4050-297 Porto; tel 222 060 412; Oct–end Jun Mon–Fri 9–5.30, Sat– Sun 9–4.30; Jul–end Sep daily 9–7

🚉 Estação de Campanhã, Estação de São Bento

www.portoturismo.pt
This is a fast, easy-to-use site available in three languages—Portuguese, English and Spanish. Updated daily, it covers every aspect of visiting the city, with good practical and cultural information and links to other sites.

SEEING PORTO

Porto is a big, sprawling city, but it is easy for visitors to get around as most of the main sights are clustered together. If you are touring, it makes sense to tackle the place before you pick up your car: There is a shortage of parking in the city, while the entire central area is a confusing grid of one-way streets.

Porto revolves round the Avenida dos Aliados, which ends at the Praça da Liberdade, a square that is the hub of the city's public transport system and only a couple of minutes from the Estação de São Bento, one of Porto's two mainline stations. South from here, the city's historic core tumbles down the hillside towards the Cais de Ribeira, the old waterfront, with the Sé (cathedral) complex looming above to the east.

This is the most interesting quarter, so take time to explore it thoroughly before heading uphill via the Bolsa to the streets east of the Liberdade. Here you can climb the Clérigos tower for a bird's-eye view of the city. To get to other sights, use the bus or the Metro system, which is currently being expanded.

HIGHLIGHTS

SÉ

➕ 343 B3 • Terreiro da Sé, 4050-572 Porto ☎ 222 059 028 ⏰ Cathedral: Nov–end Mar Mon–Sat 8.45–12.30, 2.30–6, Sun 8.30–12.30, 2.30–6; Apr–end Oct Mon–Sat 8.45–12.30, 2.30–6, Sun 8.30–12.30, 2.30–7. Cloisters: Nov–end Mar Mon–Sat 9–12.15, 2.30–5.15, Sat 2.30–5.15; Apr–end Oct Mon–Sat 9–12.30, 2.30–6, Sun 2.30–6 💶 €2

There are expansive river views from the flagstoned Terreiro da Sé, the sweeping open space, complete with pillory, in front of Porto's cathedral. The Sé, like so many of Portugal's ancient cathedrals, is half-church, half-fortress, an austere but pleasing granite Romanesque

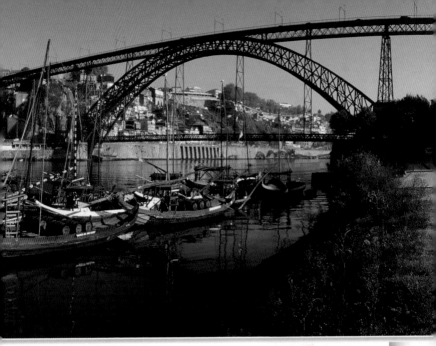

building, founded in the 12th century by Dona Teresa, mother of Afonso Henriques. The interior was remodelled in the 18th century. Gleaming in the north transept to the left of the high altar is a superb silver altarpiece, dating from the mid-17th century.

More instantly appealing than the church are the cloisters, begun in 1385 and adorned with glowing panels of 18th-century *azulejos* (tiles). From here, a fine staircase designed by the Italian architect Nicolau Nasoni, who was responsible for introducing baroque architecture into the country between 1735 and 1748, leads to the chapterhouse and terrace—there are more great river and city views from here. Outside, pause to admire the classical façade of what was once the archbishop's palace, designed by Nasoni in 1772. At the back, surrounded by a tranquil garden, is the Museu Guerra Junqueiro, Rua Dom Hugo 32 (Tue–Sat 10–12.30, 2–5, Sun 2–5, €2). It houses a fine collection of Islamic Iberian art.

RIBEIRA

343 B4 • Cais de Ribeira 4050-029 Porto ⊞ A good variety of shops, including craft shops

From the Terreiro da Sé you plunge down into the heart of Porto's oldest district, a confusing maze of narrow streets, winding steps and alleyways. Despite a recent clean-up, it is still a resolutely raucous and vibrant area, revolving around the waterfront Cais da Ribeira, where you will find a lively weekday market. West of here, the Praça da Ribeira, lined with tall, rickety old houses, is the main square, from which precipitous streets run uphill towards the more modern parts of the city. There's a great view of the two-tiered Ponte Dom Luís I bridge—walk across the bottom level to reach the port warehouses of Vila Nova de Gaia. Head west from the Praça da Ribeira and up Rua da Alfândega to take in the Casa do Infante, said to be the birthplace of Prince Henry the Navigator in 1394.

TORRE DOS CLÉRIGOS AND IGREJA DOS CLÉRIGOS

343 B2 • Rua São Felipe de Nery, 4050 Porto ☎ 222 001 729 ⓒ Church: daily 8.45–12.30, 3.30–7. Tower: Nov–end Mar daily 10–1, 2–5; Apr–end Oct daily 9.30–1, 2.30–7 🎫 Tower: €2 🚌 3, 6, 20, 52, 78

A few minutes' walk west of the Praça da Liberdade, the baroque Torre dos Clérigos soars 75.6m (248ft) into the air. It was once the tallest structure in Portugal, and the view of the city and beyond from the top is excellent for getting your bearings. It, too, was designed by

Fishing boats moored on the Douro, with the graceful Ponte Dom Luís I in the background (top) and houses in the Ribeira, Porto's oldest district (above)

Nasoni. The Igreja dos Clérigos, right beside the tower, was the first oval-plan church to be built in Portugal, and is lavishly adorned with a riot of festoons and garlands.

THE BOLSA

✚ 343 A4 • Rua Ferreira Borges, 4050-253 Porto ☎ 226 399 000 🕓 Nov–end Mar daily 9–1, 2–6; Apr–end Oct daily 9–7 💶 €5 🚌 1, 57, 91

Up the hill and west of Ribeira is Porto's temple of commerce, the Stock Exchange, a building that typifies Porto's 19th-century commercial acumen and industry. Built to impress, its neoclassical façade is the perfect expression of financial solidity and probity. Designed and erected in 1834, it is elaborately decorated inside with a profusion of precious stone, marble and wood, seen at its most lavish in the wonderfully kitsch Arabian Hall, a wonderful pastiche of Granada's

The baroque Torre dos Clérigos (above left), for a long time the tallest building in Portugal, and the Praça da Liberdade (above centre), old Porto's main square. The cloisters (above right), liberally decorated with 18th-century blue tiles, are a major feature of the cathedral, whose exterior (opposite) is pleasingly austere and Romanesque

---

TIPS

• It is worth investing in the Porto Card, a 1- or 2-day discount card. This lets you travel free on public transport and gives you free or discounted admission to monuments and museums and discounts in shops, restaurants and on river cruises. It is available at tourist information offices (1-day €7.50, 2-day €11.50, 3-day €15.50).

• River cruises are the best way to see Porto's bridges and the Douro valley. Timetables and services vary throughout the year, with few running during the winter months. Contact Barcadouro (tel 222 008 882) for further details or ask at the tourist office.

• Wear comfortable, flat shoes—Porto is very hilly, with steep cobbled streets in the historic areas.

Alhambra in Spain, complete with Moorish-style stuccowork, lavish stained glass and elaborately carved woodwork.

There is more jaw-dropping ostentation next door in the Igreja de São Francisco (Nov–end Jan daily 9–7.30; Feb–end May daily 9–6; Jun, Sep–end Oct daily 9–7; Jul–end Aug 9–8; €3), which was built for the Franciscans and began life as a plain Gothic structure with a fine rose window. The interior underwent a formidable reconstruction in the 18th century, and is now filled with golden rococo carving, the altars, walls and vaulting dripping with *putti* (children), vines, garlands and depictions of wildlife. It is said that the clergy were so shocked by its extravagance when it was unveiled that the church was promptly deconsecrated—it remains so. Don't miss the museum, beneath whose floor lies a vast *ossário*, an ossuary or bone deposit, where thousands of bones were buried before public cemeteries were instituted in Portugal in 1845.

FUNDAÇÃO DE SERRALVES

✚ 343 off A4 • Rua Dom João de Castro 210, 4150-417 Porto ☎ 226 156 571 🕓 Oct–end Mar Tue–Sun 10–7; Apr–end Sep Tue–Fri 10–7, Sat–Sun 10–8 💶 €5 🚌 3, 19, 21, 30, 35 🛍 Good art books and museum souvenirs 🚻 🅿 www.serralves.pt

Porto's modern art museum, the Fundação de Serralves, stands in a sculpture-dotted park a short distance west of the heart of the city. The permanent collection is focused on the relationship between Portuguese artists and their international counterparts from the late 1960s to the present day, and is displayed in a clean-cut ultra-modern building designed by renowned Portuguese architect Alvaro Siza. The museum also hosts temporary exhibitions in the 1930s art deco Casa de Serralves, which forms part of the museum complex.

BACKGROUND

Porto grew in importance during the Roman occupation, when two settlements grew on opposite banks of the River Douro. In 1095 the area passed to Henry of Burgundy by marriage. Under Afonso Henriques, it became the base for the Christian reconquest, and Porto eventually gave its name to the entire country.

In 1387 Porto was the setting for the marriage of João I and Philippa of Lancaster, and their son, Henry the Navigator, was born in the city. Its harbour and shipbuilding industry rapidly developed and trading links were forged with many European nations—in particular England, through treaties signed in 1654 and 1703. During the Peninsular War, British troops under Wellington recaptured the city from its French occupiers in 1809; in 1820, Porto's citizens played a major part in forcing the adoption of a more liberal constitution for the whole country.

Today, Porto is Portugal's second city, a bustling, earthy mix of merging urban areas that for many years was so busy making money that its historic treasures were neglected and began to decay. Its naming as European City of Culture in 2001 was the spark for a massive urban renewal. The Ribeira quarter, a World Heritage Site, got a major facelift, many buildings were restored, and streets and squares pedestrianized, creating a maritime promenade linking the heart of the city with the sea.

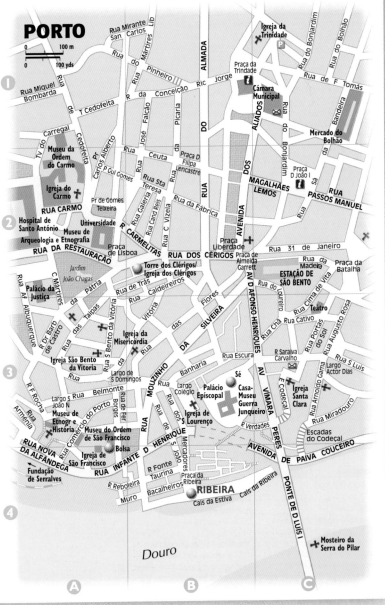

PORTUGAL

WHAT TO DO

⊕ ARTE FACTO

Rua da Reboleira 37, Ribeira
Tel 223 320 201

In an elegant 18th-century building a block back from the river, this shop stocks a great selection of good-quality local crafts. It hosts frequent craft exhibitions and workshops.

⊙ Tue–Fri 10–12, 1–6, Sat–Sun 1–7

⊗ SWING

Rua de Julio Dinis 766, Boavista
Tel 226 090 019

Off the Rotunda da Boavista is Porto's oldest club, which has remained fashionable since day one. Music styles vary during the week from 1980s student nights to dance and commercial club, and attract a mixed crowd, old and young, gay and straight.

⊙ Daily midnight–7am ⊗ €10–€20 (includes drinks)

⊗ ESTÁDIO DO DRAGÃO

FC Porto (club), Avenida Fernão de Magalhães, Antas
Tel 225 570 400 or 241 153 800 (club hotline)
www.fcporto.pt

Home to frequent national football (soccer) champions FC Porto, this impressive stadium was completed in 2003 to host the opening match of the 2004 European Football Championship. Seating 52,000, it is part of the 'sport city' complex of multi-purpose pavilions, shops and housing. For match details see *Público* or *Jornal de Notícias*.

⊙ Ticket office for matches: daily 10–1, 3–7 ⊗ Tickets €15–€50 ⊗ Antas
⊗ Bus 21

EATING

ADEGA VILA MEÃ

Rua Caldeireiros 62
Tel 222 082 967

This not-to-be-missed *adega* (wine cellar) near the famous Torre dos Clérigos serves unadorned regional food in massive portions *a moda antiga* (as in the old days). Ask

for a quarter-portion if you are on your own—that's how big they are! Each day of the week has its special dish: salt-cod fritters on Monday, roast octopus on Tuesday, braised pork on Wednesday, *cozido à Portuguesa* (boiled meats and vegetables) on Thursday, roast veal on Friday and roast kid on Saturday. Credit cards are not accepted.

⊙ Mon–Sat 12–3, 7–11 ⊗ L €10, D €15, Wine €6

CAFÉ MAJESTIC

Rua de Santa Catarina 112
Tel 222 003 887
www.cafemajestic.com

At its opening in 1921, this luxurious art nouveau coffee house attracted intellectuals and politicians. Complete with stucco cherubs, magnificent chandeliers, leather upholstery, Indian marble floors and huge Antwerp mirrors, the Majestic was meticulously restored to its former glory in the 1990s. Now probably the most beautiful café in the country, it is an ideal place to stop for a coffee and a pastry, although the liveried waiters also serve light meals at lunchtime, including salads and a dish of the day.

⊙ Mon–Sat 9.30am–midnight
⊗ Light snack and drink €10

CASA AGRÍCOLA

Rua do Bom Sucesso 241–243
Tel 226 053 350
www.casa-agricola.com

Inside an original 18th-century building (onto which the Bom Sucesso shopping mall has been added), the first-floor Casa Agrícola, with its ox-blood walls and wooden floors, is an elegant establishment. It has a choice of grilled fish, meats (including duck and succulent peppered steaks) and, most unusually for Portugal, a vegetarian menu. For dessert, try the port pudding with mango ice cream.

⊙ Mon–Sat 12–3, 8–12 ⊗ L €18, D €24, Wine €12

STAYING

ALBERGARIA MIRADOURO

Rua da Alegria 598, Porto
Tel 225 370 717

This slim 13-floor hotel with its 1950s–1960s feel seems uninspiring, until you see the views. Spread out beneath it are the

city and river Douro with the Gaia port warehouses on the opposite bank. Many of the rooms are large and well appointed; the corner rooms with dual views are the best. Day or night, enjoy a sunny breakfast or leisurely dinner in the highly acclaimed Restaurante Portucale.

⊗ €65, including breakfast
ⓘ 30
⊗ ⊕

HOTEL INFANTE SAGRES

Praça Dona Felipa de Lencastre 62, Porto
Tel 223 398 500
www.hotelinfantesagres.pt

This city landmark is just off the Avenida dos Aliados. Its sumptuous furnishings, draped fabrics and 17th-century Chinese porcelain recall a lost age of elegance. The delicate and sinuous wrought-iron staircase is worthy of special attention, as is the interior courtyard, which is used for alfresco meals as well as being a sun trap in the summer. Rooms are dressed in the same vein, with period-style furniture. The opulent dining room serves international and Portuguese cuisine.

⊗ €175–€350, including breakfast
ⓘ 72 rooms, 9 suites
⊗
⊕ Limited

RESIDENCIAL DOS ALIADOS

Rua Eliseo de Melo 27, Porto
Tel 222 004 853
www.residencialaliados.com

This *residencial* is great value for money. It is conveniently located in the heart of town, and the service is friendly. Rooms are simply but adequately furnished and all have their own bathroom. Some have small balconies and overlook the Ávenida; the ones at the back are slightly smaller, but much quieter.

⊗ €50–€95, including breakfast
ⓘ 43 ⊗

PORTUGAL

ARRIVING

BY AIR
Mainland Portugal has three international airports: Lisbon, Porto and Faro, serving respectively the central part, the north and the south of the country. If you're flying in from another continent, you'll arrive at Lisbon, the only airport with direct scheduled flights from the USA. Porto, in the north, is the gateway to Portugal's most heavily populated area, constantly busy with business visitors and a good jumping-off point for the Minho, Douro, Trás-os-Montes and the Beiras. Faro, serving the Algarve, is the busiest in terms of leisure visitors, and also makes a good entry point if you're planning to explore the southern third of the country. Some visitors to Portugal choose to fly to Spain and pick up an air, train or bus connection into Portugal from there.

BY CAR
Driving to Portugal takes time, so, if you are thinking of doing it, weigh up the pros and cons carefully. If you are coming from the UK, you can ferry your car to northern Spain. From elsewhere in Europe, though, you drive through several countries to reach your destination.
If you are driving to Portugal, you will need the following documents:
● Valid driver's licence.
● Original vehicle registration document.
● Motor insurance certificate (at least third-party insurance is compulsory).
● Passport.
From the UK, you can cross the Channel either through the Channel Tunnel (Eurotunnel UK, tel 0870 535 3535; www.eurotunnel.com) or by ferry (▷ opposite). The major routes south to Portugal will take you through France and across Spain. There are two main options: south down the west coast of France on the E5, crossing the Spanish border at Irún; or through the Pyrenees on the E7, crossing into Spain at Candanchú. From Irún, head west across northern Spain on the A8 to Santander, then take

the A67-N634 west to join the E1-A9 motorway (expressway) south to Tui on the Portuguese border, where you'll pick up the A3 to Porto. The Pyrenees route takes you southwest via Zaragoza towards Madrid, then west to Salamanca, crossing the Portuguese border at Fuentes de Oñoro on the E80.

BY BUS
International buses to Portugal from the UK are operated by Eurolines, the international arm of National Express (tel 08705 808080; www.eurolines.com). Destinations include Lisbon, Porto, Coimbra, Bragança, Guarda, Viseu, Beja, Faro and Portimão, with a return (round-trip) adult fare to Lisbon costing around €200; under-12s and senior citizens travel half-price. Passengers from the UK have to change buses in Paris, which sometimes involves a lengthy wait; it may be simpler to travel independently to Paris.
Journey time is 40–45 hours, depending on your destination.

BY FERRY
If you're driving to Portugal from the UK, you can cut down on the driving time slightly by taking a ferry to northern Spain. The main international ferry access points are Santander and Bilbao, from where it is still a long day's drive through most of Spain to reach Portugal. There are no scheduled direct ferry services between Portugal and elsewhere in continental Europe or the UK.

BY TRAIN
From the UK you can travel by train to Portugal via Paris. The other rail option is to enter Portugal by train from Spain—a good choice if you want to see another European country during your visit. Bear in mind that journey times are long (25–28 hours from London to Lisbon) and fares are quite high compared with those of budget and charter flights.
The main route from Paris to Lisbon runs via Bordeaux, Biarritz, Irún, Donostia, Salamanca and Guarda; change at Irún for the Lisbon train and again at Guarda for connections

to Porto and Coimbra. Travelling from Spain (Madrid), the rail route will take you through Cáceres to Marvão-Beirã, Abrantes, Entroncamento and so to Lisbon. From Lisbon you can connect with Porto, Coimbra and the south.
From the UK, it's best to use Eurostar via the Channel Tunnel as far as Paris, from where trains south are fast and frequent. Eurostar trains depart from St. Pancras Station and link London with Paris in under 3 hours. You must check in 30 minutes before departure and you are allowed two suitcases and one item of hand baggage, all of which should be clearly labelled with your name, address and seat number. You will need your passport to clear immigration and customs.
● Eurostar: www.eurostar.com
● Rail Europe: www.raileurope.co.uk

VISITORS WITH A DISABILITY
In Portugal, the major problems for people with a disability often lie not so much in the transportation, accommodation and public buildings as in the actual nature of the old cities and towns. Things are progressing, but disability facilities in Portugal overall still lag behind those in northern European countries and North America. This is partly offset by the helpfulness of the Portuguese themselves, who will make great efforts to render your visit as stress-free and uncomplicated as possible.
Useful Organization
Holiday Care
www.holidaycare.org.uk
Information on accessibility.

GETTING AROUND

BY CAR

Up until the 1990s, Portugal had one of Europe's least developed road networks, with just one incomplete motorway (expressway) open between Lisbon and Porto. Since then, a massive injection of European Union funding into road construction has given the country a network of highways that has provided faster and easier access to main towns and cities as well as to previously remote areas.

Portugal's motorway system is built and run by a private company, Brisa (call free 808 508 508; www.brisa.pt). Motorways run from north to south of the country, from Valença on the Spanish border to Lagos in the Algarve. They link the cities of Braga, Aveiro, Coimbra, Leiria and Lisbon with the Algarve, and there is a further network around Lisbon. In addition, the A23 runs northeast from Entroncamento to Vilar Formoso on the Spanish border; the A6 links Lisbon with Badajoz in Spain; and the A22 runs from the western Algarve to the Spanish frontier at Vila Real de Santo António.

All motorways are clearly signposted and approached via slip roads (ramps) leading to the toll booths. Take the ticket from the automatic booth on the left of the car and the barrier will lift. Keep your ticket safe while you're on the road, as you will need it to pay when you come off. Cash payment is made to the official in the booth at the exit; the amount due is displayed on a screen outside the payment window.

YOU WILL NEED:

- A valid driver's licence; Portuguese law requires everyone to carry photographic proof of identity at all times. If you have an old-style licence without a photo, make sure you have your passport.
- Vehicle registration document.
- Motor insurance certificate; third-party insurance at least is compulsory.
- A first-aid kit, fire extinguisher and spare bulbs.
- It is compulsory to carry a warning triangle sign and to display a nationality sticker (unless you have Euro-plates).

BY TRAIN

Trains in Portugal are operated by CP—Caminhos de Ferro Portugueses (tel 808 208 208; www.cp.pt). Its network, augmented in some areas with connecting buses, covers much of the country, and includes some wonderfully scenic lines. There are different types of trains and services. Local trains can be snail-like, and so you may find some destinations easier and faster to reach by bus, although trains are often cheaper. The best policy is to plan your journey in advance, using the excellent English-language website.

TYPES OF TRAIN

- **Regional and inter-regional** Most Portuguese trains fall into these categories. They run throughout the country, using both first- and second-class carriages (cars) with an acceptable level of comfort. Regional trains stop at most stations; inter-regional ones are faster, stopping only at major stations. On-board facilities are basic, but do include toilets.
- **Intercidades** These are fast, comfortable intercity trains, on which advance reservation is mandatory; this adds around 60 per cent to the price of a normal ticket. On-board facilities include bar/café, telephones and toilets. Both first- and second-class seats are available.
- **Alfa** This fast, luxurious service operates between Lisbon and Porto, with stops at Coimbra and Aveiro. Advance booking is essential, and some Alfa trains are made up of first-class carriages (cars) only, with all the facilities to be expected on a premier service.

TICKETS

- Portuguese trains have first- and second-class *bilhetes* (tickets), which can be purchased online (www.cp.pt) and at railway stations. Different price structures exist for different train categories, with regional trains being the cheapest. Overall, rail travel is relatively inexpensive.

BY BUS

- Buses in Portugal are operated by various different companies, all private, mainly running services within their own region. Privatization has led to hot competition between operators, with a proliferation of more frequent services on the more popular routes, and the inevitable cut-backs or even cessation of many local services.
- There is no national long-distance bus company. Portugal's network of long-distance express buses is run by many different companies, although these do combine their timetables and fare structures. Journeys should be booked, and seats reserved, in advance. For information and reservations, tel 969 502 050 (some operators may speak English). You can also check times, and book and pay for tickets, on line at www.rede-expressos.pt (Portuguese only, but simple to operate). Express buses are comfortable, with air conditioning.

BY TAXI

Taxis are available in cities and towns, including some surprisingly small places. Fares in Portugal are relatively low by European standards. If you don't have a car, taxis are a good option for getting around in rural areas, especially as, away from the major towns and cities, it is acceptable to negotiate for a few hours' hire.

- Portuguese taxis are generally metered, with a minimum fare of around €1.50.
- Any luggage carried in the boot (trunk) is charged as an extra.
- Additional charges are made between 10pm and 6am.
- Tipping is not obligatory, but 10 per cent of what is on the meter is appreciated.
- Check that the meter is working, switched on and set to minimum fare before you set off.
- If there's no meter, agree the price with the driver before you drive off, writing it down if there's any language problem.

GETTING AROUND IN LISBON

Carris runs Lisbon's public transport system, an integrated network that includes buses, trams and funiculars, or street elevators, all of which are frequent, inexpensive and reliable. You will be able to see everything you want by using just a few routes—but make sure they include a tram ride, just for the experience.

You can get information on Carris services at the Carristur office on the Praça do Comércio (tel 213 613 054, daily 8am–8pm, www.carris.pt), at the company's kiosks in Praça da Figueira, Restauradores and Cais de Sodre, or at any tourist office. Travel details, ticket information and free maps of the transport system are available.

Carris introduced a new form of multi-modal ticket in November 2007. Called Zapping, it's a smartcard that electronically stores an amount of money that can be used at fare points to pay for travel on buses, Metro and trams. The cards can be bought and refilled at Carris and Metro concessions, post offices and payshop agents around the city.

BUSES
● *Autocarros* (single-decker buses) cover the whole city, and can be crowded. There are few seats, so be prepared to stand, and, although Lisbon has a low crime rate, watch your pockets and belongings.
● *Paragens* (bus stops) show the route number and list the stops along the line. The stop where you are is indicated inside the bus.
● Board at the front and validate your ticket. Exit towards the rear.

NIGHT BUSES
Carris operates a *madrugada* (night service) along the main routes; buses run between 11pm and 4am, depending on the route.

BY TRAM
Lisbon's wonderful *eléctricos* (trams) are worth taking for the pleasure of the ride. They run along five routes and climb some of the steepest city gradients in the world. Nos 28, 12 and 25 are old-fashioned,

traditional trams that cover the heart of the old city. No. 18 runs west towards Belém, while No. 15 is a new 'supertram' that heads along the river from Cais de Sodre through Belém to Algés.

ELEVADORES
There are three useful funiculars, Bica, Glória and Lavra, which provide quick routes from the Baixa up to the Bairro Alto. Unfortunately, the walkway from the Santa Justa street elevator, which originally linked the Baixa with the Carmo church, has been shut for years as it is unsafe, but the ride is a pleasure in itself.

METRO (METROPOLITANO)
Lisbon's Metro is a slick and efficient way of getting around the city. There are four lines, with interchanges between them at Baixa-Chiado, Marquês de Pombal, Alameda and Campo Grande.
● Trains run 6.30am–1am.
● Entrances are marked with a white 'M' on a red background.
● Tickets (combined bus and Metro) cost €1.15 per journey or €3.50 for a day pass.
● Validate your ticket in the box next to the entrance barrier.
● Clear information boards (green, blue, yellow or red according to the line you're on) indicate direction of travel by the name of the station at the end of the line.
● Metro maps are available at main stations.

LOCAL TRAINS
If you're visiting Cascais, Estoril, Queluz or Sintra, you can get there by local train. Trains run from Cais de Sodre to Estoril and Cascais, and also stop at Belém. For Queluz and Sintra, catch the train at Rossio station.

The Lisbon Card also covers travel on these trains.

FERRIES
Ferries across the Rio Tejo leave from various points throughout the day. Fluvial river station, near the Praça do Comércio, links Lisbon with Cacilhas, Montijo and Barreiro; there's also a service from the Parque das Nações to Cacilhas, and from Belém to Trafaria. Buy your tickets at the ferry point; a return journey costs €1.60.

TAXIS
Lisbon taxis are cream or black and green. A green light indicates the taxi is occupied. All have meters—check to ensure yours is switched on; tips are discretionary. Taxi stands in the city include Rossio, Fluvial, Praça da Figueira, Chiado, Largo da Misericórdia and Avenida da Liberdade.

Taxis themselves are inexpensive, even though fares rise after 10pm and on weekends and public holidays. You can call a cab by telephoning:
Autocoope tel 217 932 756
Rádio Taxis tel 218 119 000
Teletaxis tel 218 111 100.

PORTUGAL

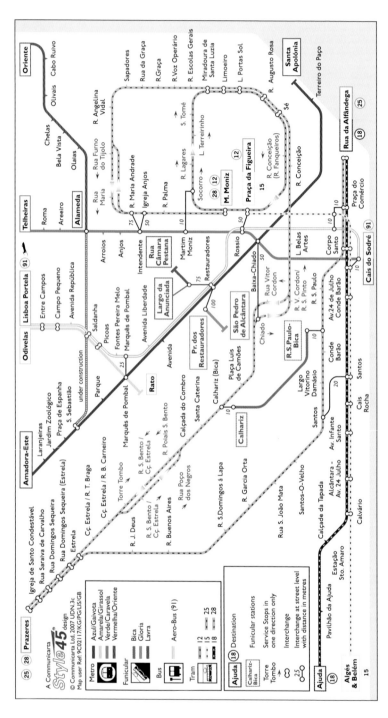

PORTUGAL

SPAIN

A Coruña
La Coruña
Santiago de
Compostela
Gijón
Oviedo
Bilbo
Bilbao
Vigo
Orense
Santander
Donostia-San
Sebastián
León
Pau
Mont-de-
Marsan
F
Toulouse
les Sables-
-d'Olonne
La Rochelle
Limoges
Bordeaux
Brive-la-
Gaillarde
Porto
Coimbra
Valladolid
Burgos
Pamplona
Iruña
Perpignan
Óbidos
P
Salamanca
Ávila
Segovia
Soria
Zaragoza
AND
Lleida
Lérida
Girona
Gerona
Abrantes
MADRID
Barcelona
LISBOA
Toledo
Sines
Badajoz
Mérida
Lagos
Faro
Huelva
Sevilla
Seville
Albacete
Valencia
Eivissa
Palma de
Mallorca
Menorca
Mallorca
Illes
Balear
Cádiz
Málaga
Granada
Murcia
Alicante
Alacant
Cartagena
Formentera
Algeciras
GBZ
Gibraltar
Almería
MA
Ceuta
Melilla
Córdoba

UNDERSTANDING SPAIN

In Spain loyalties are first to home towns and villages, then to regions and only lastly (and not always very strongly) to the country itself. This means there are immense cultural variations and no 'typical' Spain to visit, so your experiences will be truly different depending on which area you visit. The historical cocktail of Roman, Gothic, Moorish, Jewish and Christian civilizations has produced a unique blend of architecture and culture, with some of the most astonishing festivals in the world.

LANDSCAPE

Spain is perhaps Europe's most diverse country geographically, taking in the deserts of Andalucía, the green lushness of Galicia with its Norwegian-like fiords, the plains of Castile and the Pyrenees. This is the highest country after Switzerland, and at its heart is the mighty Meseta, a little-populated agricultural plateau that covers nearly half the country. Water, or the lack of it, plays a continuingly controversial role in Spain so the major rivers—the Ebro, Duero, Tajo (Tagus), Guadiana and Guadalquivir—are vital lifelines. The country also includes the Balearic Islands and the Canary Islands, plus the tiny outposts of Ceuta and Melilla in Africa.

Consuegra's windmills (above) have been immortalized by Miguel de Cervantes

LANGUAGE

Language is an extremely divisive and controversial subject in Spain. The dictator Francisco Franco, who ruled from 1939 to 1975, deliberately tried to eradicate the Catalán, Galician and Basque tongues, and impose Castellano (Castilian, regarded by the rest of the world as 'Spanish') on the entire country. With the transition to democracy, the various regions have used their traditional tongues—which are distinct languages, not dialects—as an emblem of their fight for autonomy: Catalán, Basque and Galician are also official languages of Spain, and mentioned as such in the Constitution. Other Spanish languages include Bable in Asturias and Aragónese in Aragón, plus many regional variants (the people of the Balearics and Valencia speak a close cousin of Catalán).

Larger cities and towns in the autonomous regions mainly have two names: a Castellano version and their original, local language name. Since democracy, local names have once more gained the ascendancy, particularly in the Basque country and Catalonia, but also in other areas such as Valencia and Galicia. Touring throughout the regions, you will see place-names in the local language and also in Castellano, with street signs and general public information also using Catalán, Basque, Galician or Valencian, as well as Castellano.

Spanish today

Spanish (Castilian) has proved to be extremely absorbent: The bedrock vocabulary comes from Latin but the invasion of the Visigoths in the fifth century AD introduced Germanic words (*werra*, for example, became *guerra*, meaning war), the Muslim conquest in the eighth century added many Arabic words (*berenjena*—aubergine/eggplant, *almacén*—shop, *naranja*—orange), French pilgrims on their way to Santiago de Compostela in Galicia brought elements of their language from the 11th century onwards and during the 15th and 16th centuries the Aragónese domination of Italy brought Italian words. Spain also has one of the world's more unusual languages in Silbo, a whistled speech system from La Gomera in the Canary Islands.

CLIMATE

Spain's climate varies greatly and it is certainly not universally Mediterranean. Central Spain has hot summers and bitter winters, but is constantly pretty dry. Rainfall is increasingly scarce the farther south you travel, and given the fiercely hot summers there are very real fears of desertification. The north of the country is wetter, snowier and colder, due mainly to the Pyrenees.

ECONOMY

Disintegration and Francoist mismanagement following the Civil War (1936–39) have largely been overcome and, as the now-famous soundbite by former Prime Minister José María Aznar goes, *España va bien* (Spain's doing well). Spain has particularly benefited from European Union (EU) grants (the impressive AVE train link from Madrid to Seville is one example), although these subsidies are now being cut.

The key industries are tourism and agriculture—especially wine, cereals, oranges and olives—despite the drift of the rural population from the countryside to the cities, which has caused an increase in ghost towns. Hothouse agriculture is growing fast. Manufacturing—especially cars—is also important and Spanish companies, from

THE REGIONS OF SPAIN

Administratively Spain is divided into 17 autonomous regions; in this book we have grouped some of those regions together for convenience. The Canary Islands, lying 1,100km (680 miles) from the mainland, are not included here.

Galicia, Asturias and Cantabria offer a gently green and pleasant land quite different from the usual stereotype of raucous, sun-drenched Spain.

Euskadi (Basque Country) and Navarra are politically controversial, linguistically unique and fiercely independent. Together with **Aragón**, they form Spain's gastronomic heartland.

Barcelona, not a region in its own right but the capital of Catalonia, is the peninsula's chic city and the modern cosmopolitan melting pot of the country.

Catalonia (Catalunya), Valencia and Murcia claim the glorious coastline that inspired Dalí, gave the world paella and set the pace for the tourist industry.

Eating out is a popular and enjoyable pastime (above left). The Puente Nuevo spans the gorge of the Río Guadalevín, which divides Ronda in two (above middle). Victoria Duende dances flamenco (above right)

Castile-León and La Rioja is a largely agricultural area dominated by elegant cities such as Salamanca, but the Sierra de Gredos mountains and the country's most famous wine region are also here.

Madrid has a stately exterior and a spectacular nightlife and its central position makes it a perfect base for exploring the rest of the country.

Around Madrid is not an actual region, but a convenient grouping of a number of historic places that are in easy reach of the capital and make great excursions for a day or two.

Castile-La Mancha and Extremadura enjoy bleakly beautiful landscapes and in the ruins at Mérida provide a step back in time to the days of the ancient Romans.

Andalucía is the archetypal Spanish destination for bullfighting, flamenco, tapas, sun, sea, sand, fiestas, whitewashed villages and extreme heat.

The Balearic Islands—pocket-size Spain—offer a taste of everything from the mainland, including superb food and beaches, fine walks and intriguing archaeological monuments.

clothing giant Zara to the world's biggest lollipop manufacturer, Chupa Chups, are increasingly conspicuous on the international stage. Though connections with South and Latin America are strong, Spain's principal trading partners are other EU countries. At home, unemployment and low pay remain problems. The changeover from the peseta to the euro, however, proceeded relatively smoothly.

DEMOGRAPHY AND RELIGION

While Spain remains an essentially Catholic country, church attendance is dropping; religious freedom is guaranteed by the 1978 Constitution. The birth rate is also dropping, which has huge social implications for the still strongly traditional family-dominated way of life. Spain's population of around 40 million will start to drop within the next couple of decades and in some regions, such as Asturias, the replacement rate is already at crisis point. Into this demographic hole are pouring immigrants from South America and Africa.

POLITICS

Spain is a constitutional monarchy with a central parliament (and a still much-respected and hands-on monarch in Juan Carlos) but with power devolved to 17 autonomous regions, some more autonomous than others and several with extremely strong separatist ambitions.

After a rocky 20th century, Spain has become an important player on the world stage, partly due to former Prime Minister Aznar's foreign policy. His successor, the socialist José Luis Rodriguez Zapatero, won elections in 2004 after terrorist attacks in Madrid, and has introduced modern laws such as those permitting marriage between gays and between lesbians. He has continued with good relations with the UK but is on rockier ground with the US, particularly over the Iraq war. One of his first acts upon election was to pull all Spanish troops out of Iraq. The biggest ongoing conundrum is how to deal with the Basque pro-independence group ETA.

SPAIN

GALICIA, ASTURIAS AND CANTABRIA

Countryside A hike or drive in the dramatic Picos de Europa mountains, home to some of Europe's most endangered wildlife.

Music Enjoy a concert featuring the traditional Galician bagpipes.

EUSKADI, NAVARRA AND ARAGÓN

Museum The Guggenheim in Bilbao lives up to all the hype, both inside and out (▷ 366).

Bulls The San Fermín fiesta in Pamplona in July is a perfect chance to see these enormous beasts in action.

Fiesta Aragón's *Las Tamboradas* festival is a different take on the Easter celebrations, with hours of religious drumming.

Bilbao's Guggenheim Museum (above). Bull advert near Llanes (left)

BARCELONA

Wandering The Barri Gòtic's medieval maze-like streets are full of interesting shops and cafés to explore (▷ 356–357).

Work in progress Gaudí's controversial and unfinished Sagrada Família delights and disgusts visitors to the city in fairly equal measure (▷ 361–363).

Streetlife There's something along Las Ramblas for everyone, from performance artists to caged birds.

Street life on Las Ramblas (above)

CATALONIA, VALENCIA AND MURCIA

History The Jewish quarter in Girona shows a way of life that was once central to Spanish culture.

Religion Montserrat is home to the Black Virgin.

Eating Restaurant El Bulli in Roses is a delicious laboratory of tastes.

CASTILE-LEÓN AND LA RIOJA

Cathedral Spain's loveliest and most spectacular Gothic cathedral is in Burgos.

Architecture Beautiful but restrained, Salamanca's elegant buildings are dotted all around the city.

Drinking The wines in La Rioja are the best known outside Spain.

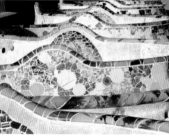

Unusual benches in Gaudí's Parc Güell (above). Street entertainment at its best (left)

MADRID

Park Join the locals for a Sunday pre-lunch wander around the capital's Parque del Retiro.

Shopping Bring back a quintessentially Spanish souvenir.

AROUND MADRID

Memorial Philip II's greatest architectural legacy, El Escorial.

Children Tasty food and dressing up on the summer Strawberry Train outings from the capital to old royal haunt Aranjuez.

Flower stall in Las Ramblas, Barcelona (above)

Barcelona

✚ 4 C4 🛈 Plaça de Catalunya 17, tel 932 853 854; daily 9–9. Closed 1 January and 25 December. www.barcelonaturisme.com. Comprehensive site in English

HOW TO GET THERE

✈ Airport
El Prat International Airport is located 13km (8 miles) from the city centre

🚉 Rail stations
Sants is the main station, located just outside the city centre. Most national and international trains depart and arrive here. The more central Passeig de Gràcia station services regional Catalonia.

The extraordinary architecture of Antoni Gaudí has become an emblem of the city

TIPS

● Do consider the plethora of discount cards available at the visitor information office. You will save a bundle on museum and attraction entry fees.
● The city's hop on–hop off Bus Turístic is highly recommended if you have limited time in the city.
● Try to reserve accommodation well in advance as Barcelona's busy trade fair calendar means many hotels can be booked out at peak times.
● Take extra care with belongings in public areas. Although the situation is gradually improving, tourist-targeted petty crime remains a problem.

SEEING BARCELONA

Barcelona is laid-back, well ordered and blessed with a benign climate. Many choose to spend their time simply meandering the narrow streets and plazas of the Barri Gòtic or the elegant L'Eixample, with its abundance of art nouveau residences. Architecture, in general, is a big draw and best seen on foot. A good pair of shoes is vital, and a stroll around each of the inner-city *barris* (neighbourhoods) will give you a taste of the city's diversity, vibrancy and life. Las Ramblas is where most people start, but the real treasures lie on either side of it.

While the Picasso Museum tends to grab all the glory, there are many more world-class museums. The recently refurbished MNAC holds a millennium of Catalan and Northern European art. Enthusiasts of more contemporary genres should not miss the Tàpies and Miró Foundations—both showcases of Catalonia's most prolific artists—or the MACBA. Art and architecture aside, the city's splendid beaches, highly creative cuisine, vibrant nightlife and cutting-edge shops make a combination that's hard to beat. But it's best not to rush. With so much on offer, you can afford to tailor your visit to your mood.

BACKGROUND

Barcelona sprang to the forefront of international tourism in 1992, when the city played host to the Olympic Games. Savvy city planners took the opportunity to clean up historic buildings, create an outstanding waterfront and open up dank pockets of the old town with a patchwork of plazas and boulevards.

The first of the city's 'golden ages' occurred in the 13th–16th centuries, when Catalonia ruled the Mediterranean, and merchants and traders reaped in the benefits. The splendid Barri Gòtic is living proof of the epoch's mercantile prowess and artisan skill. The next came towards the end of the 19th century. The heady *Renaixença* (or Renaissance) saw the rebirth of Catalan culture, art and above all a unique style of architecture known as *modernisme*. Its champion was Antoni Gaudí and his whimsical work, along with that of other *modernista* luminaries, can be seen in the chamfered blocks of L'Eixample neighbourhood.

Nationalism thrived after the death of Franco and remains today as strong as ever, with Catalonia likely to achieve 'nationhood' status within the Spanish state in the near future. Unless you want to lose friends, never refer to its capital Barcelona as a 'Spanish' city and practise a few words of Catalán during your visit. You will be amazed at the reception you get!

DON'T MISS

THE TEMPLE OF THE SAGRADA FAMILA
Gaudí's awesome (and still unfinished) masterpiece (▷ 361–363)

MUSEU D'ART DE CATALUNYA (MNAC)
From Romanesque chapels to *modernista* furniture under one roof

MUSEU PICASSO
Extensive collection from the genius who was raised in Barcelona (▷ 360)

FUNDACIÓ JOAN MIRÓ
Prolific collection in a stunning, purposely designed setting (▷ 359)

SANTA MARIA DEL MAR
This austere church is the jewel of the city's Gothic period

CASA MILÀ (LA PEDRERA)
Another Gaudí masterpiece; educational, informative and an assault on the senses

SPAIN

BARCELONA

Barri Gòtic

The most complete Gothic quarter on the Continent. A maze of dark, twisting, medieval streets and sunny squares: the city's political hub, formed of grand squares and medieval buildings.

The rose window in Església Santa Maria del Pi (top). Plant-filled, wrought-iron balconies (above)

Traditional Spanish fans make great souvenirs

Els Quatre Gats café, where Picasso and fellow artists met

RATINGS	
Historic interest	●●●●●
Photo stops	●●●●
Shopping	●●●●
Walkability	●●●●

BASICS

☩ 355 D4

🛈 Visitor information office
Ciutat 2, 08002 Barcelona, tel 93 285 38 32 (from abroad 932 85 38 34); Mon–Fri 9–8, Sat 10–8, Sun 10–2
Ⓜ Jaume I, Liceu

www.barcelonaturisme.com
General information but hard to read.

TIP

● Stroll the streets behind the cathedral after sunset, when the faint lighting creates a wonderful atmosphere.

SEEING THE BARRI GÒTIC

Next to modernism, the Gothic period had the greatest influence on Barcelona's architecture. An afternoon's stroll around the ensemble of 13th- to 15th-century buildings, grand plazas and narrow streets of the city's Barri Gòtic is a must.

HIGHLIGHTS

PLAÇA DEL REI

This small, well-preserved, medieval paved square lies in the heart of the Barri Gòtic and once rang with the comings and goings of official visitors and buyers and sellers of flour and hay. It is flanked by the 13th- to 16th-century structures of the Palau Reial (Royal Palace), and the Conjunt Monumental de la Plaça del Rei. The Mirador del Rei, on the square's western side, was used as a watchtower, and the Palau de Loctinent, on the left of the *mirador* (balcony), was the official home of the viceroy after Catalonia lost its independence in the 16th century.

PLAÇA DE SANT JAUME

The Plaça de Sant Jaume, on the Carrer de Ferran, is the city's political hub. The spacious square is flanked on one side by the Casa de la Ciutat, or Ajuntament, and on the other by the Palau de la Generalitat (▷ below), and acts as a backdrop for many spontaneous public events. The Barça soccer team greets ecstatic crowds from the Ajuntament's balcony after major wins, and the two great Catalán folk traditions of *castellers* (human towers) and the *sardana* (a group dance) are played out here on public holidays.

PALAU DE LA GENERALITAT

Plaça de Sant Jaume ☎ 93 402 46 00 🕐 2nd and 4th Sun of each month 10.30–1.30 Ⓜ Jaume I, Liceu 🚌 14, 16, 17, 19, 38, 40, 45, 59 🎫 Free 📷 No tours, visits by prior application
The Generalitat is the name of both Catalonia's autonomous government and the building from which it governs. So far, 115 presidents of Catalonia have ruled from its 15th-century Gothic interior, making it one of the few medieval buildings still in

SPAIN

continuous use for its original purpose. When Generalitat presidents are in town they stay next door at the 14th-century Casa dels Canonges, on Carrer del Bisbe. The hanging enclosed walkway joining the two buildings dates from the 1920s and was styled on Venice's Bridge of Sighs.

CASA DE LA CIUTAT (AJUNTAMENT)

Plaça de Sant Jaume 1 ☎ 93 402 73 64 🕐 Sun 10–1.30 🚇 Jaume I 🚌 14, 16, 17, 19, 38, 40, 45, 59 🎟 Free 🚫 No tours available; advance booking for large groups
The Ajuntament started out as the seat of the Consell de Cent, one of the world's first democratic representative councils, made up of 100 guild leaders and ordinary citizens. Although the Ajuntament is not as spectacular as the Generalitat, its classic early 1900s façade hides a Gothic interior. The highlight is the Saló de Croniques, with murals dating from 1928 by painter Josep Maria Sert, who went on to decorate New York's Rockefeller Center.

PLAÇA DE SANT FELIP NERI

The pretty square of Sant Felip Neri is entered from the Baixada de Santa Eulàlia, the street where Barcelona's patron saint met her grisly death. The square itself is peaceful, with a central fountain and baroque church, but it has a dark past. The bullet holes you see on the church's façade next to the infant school are the evidence of a massacre of 20 children by Fascist forces in 1938.

The Plaça del Pi, with its Gothic masterpiece, the Esglèsia Santa María del Pi, is a good place to take a break. The foundations of nearby Carrer de Petrixol were laid in 1465 and the street now houses some of the most famous of Barcelona's *granjes* (pastry and dairy cafés).

BACKGROUND

The Barri Gòtic dates principally from the 14th and 15th centuries, the zenith of Barcelona's maritime and mercantile power. The area was originally almost entirely enclosed by fourth-century Roman walls, traces of which are still visible along the Via Laietana to the northeast; the southern limits are bounded by Las Ramblas (▷ 358). In this tiny nucleus, the machinery of medieval government and commerce functioned in purpose-built palaces and halls, while a series of squares served as public gathering places—functions they still fulfil today.

Façade of the Palau de la Generalitat

AROUND BARRI GÒTIC
CARRER D'AVINYÓ

Once full of inexpensive hostels and a stamping ground for ladies of the night, Carrer d'Avinyó is now full of hip clothing stores and contemporary galleries.

PLAÇA DE SANT JUST

The tranquil Plaça de Sant Just, with its ornate fountainheads, is home to the fine Gothic church, Eglésia de Sants Just i Pastor, thought to have been founded in 801.

Plaça del Rei, showpiece of the Barri Gòtic

SPAIN

Mosaic salamander in Parc Güell

CATEDRAL

One of the finest examples of Catalán Gothic architecture.

BASICS	RATINGS	
✚ 355 D4 • Plaça de la Seu 3, 08002 Barcelona ☎ 93 315 15 54	Good for kids	● ● ●
🕐 Daily 8–1.45, 4.30–7.30 🎫 Free;	Historic interest	● ● ● ●
special (less crowded) midday visits	Value for money	● ● ●

(1–5) €4, under 8 free 🚇 Liceu 🚌 16, 17, 19, 45 📖 Various available at €2, €3 and €9 🏛 Two shops 🚻 🅿
www.catedralbcn.org

The plans for the interior of the cathedral were first laid down in 1298, and for the next 150 years four different architects worked on the edifice and produced cloisters and chapels that show Catalán Gothic architecture at its best.

THE CLOISTER
The most pleasing part of the cathedral is undoubtedly the cloister, and a few minutes spent among its orange and medlar trees and its shady palms are an effective battery-charger. The pond serves as home to a gaggle of white geese, which are said to represent the purity of Santa Eulàlia, Barcelona's patron saint. Its mossy, central fountain once provided fresh water for the clergy.

THE INTERIOR
The crypt houses Santa Eulàlia's marble tomb, dating from the ninth century. The central choir, with its beautifully carved 14th-century stalls, is worth lingering in. The coats of arms represent members of the chapter of the Order of the Golden Fleece. Peek under the misericords (choir seats) to see the sculptures of hunting scenes, games and other pastimes.

Another highlight is the Capella del Santíssim Sagrament, a small chapel immediately to the right of the main entrance. The chapel's vaulted roof soars to more than 20m (66ft), but its treasure is the 16th-century figurine *Christ of Lepanto*.

On the opposite side of the cathedral's entrance is the baptistery, with a plaque bearing the names of six South American natives said to have been brought back by Christopher Columbus in 1493 and christened in the cathedral. Finally, take the lift (elevator) up to the roof for panoramas over the city and close-ups of the 19th-century spires.

Don't miss The altar has two large sixth-century Visigoth capitals (crowning features on the columns) and an altarpiece with a superb painting of the Crucifixion by Bernat Martorell (1400–52).

PARC GÜELL

✚ 355 off D1 • Carrer d'Olot s/n and Carretera del Carmel s/n, 08014 Barcelona 🕐 Daily 10–sunset. Casa-Museu Gaudí: daily 10–6. Last ticket sold 15 min before closing time 🎫 Free. 🚇 Lesseps 🚌 24, 25, 28, 31, 32, 74; 24 is the only one going directly to the gate. The others stop 10–15 min walk away

This site of 17ha (42 acres) is one of the most magical works by architect Antoni Gaudí (1853–1926), and brims with his singular creativity. The project was commissioned in 1900 by industrialist Eusebi Güell, who intended to use the land to build a large élite residential estate of some 60 houses. Unfortunately only two buyers ever signed up for the scheme.

The park's icon and most popular photo opportunity is a brightly decorated salamander. The main square itself offers sweeping views of the city.

LAS RAMBLAS

✚ 355 D4 ℹ️ Plaça de Catalunya, 17 Soterrani, 08002 Barcelona, tel 93 285 38 32 🚇 Catalunya, Liceu, Drassanes 🚌 14, 18, 38, 57, 59, 64 and all routes to Plaça de Catalunya or the Plaça Portal de la Pau
www.barcelonaturisme.com

Las Ramblas was described by writer Somerset Maugham as 'the most beautiful street in the world' and is without doubt the very heart of the city. It is, however, actually several streets in one, hence the plural, and leads down to the port.

The Canaletes, the fountain in the Plaça de Catalunya, is at the top of Las Ramblas and the namesake of the first section. Legend has it that anyone who drinks from the fountain will return to the city.

SPAIN

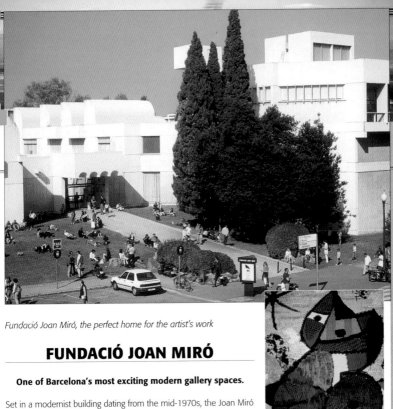

Fundació Joan Miró, the perfect home for the artist's work

FUNDACIÓ JOAN MIRÓ

One of Barcelona's most exciting modern gallery spaces.

Set in a modernist building dating from the mid-1970s, the Joan Miró Foundation enjoys a hilltop position on Montjuïc, with panoramic glimpses of the Barcelona skyline visible from throughout the gallery.

THE MAN AND HIS ART
Joan Miró (1893–1983) was one of the most prolific Catalán artists of the 20th century. He also worked in sculpture and tapestry throughout his life, but rarely deviated from a bright palette of blue, red, yellow and green.

TAPESTRY AND EARLY INFLUENCES
The collections are spread over 10 *salas* (rooms), the first stop being the Tapestry Room. The most spectacular piece here is the *Foundation Tapestry*, which was designed especially for the gallery in 1979. Before you enter the next galleries, don't miss *Mercury*, a fascinating fountain-sculpture created for the Spanish Pavilion at the 1937 Paris World's Fair by American avant-garde artist Alexander Calder (1898–1976).

The Joan Prats Gallery shows Miró's early works and development. Miró was inspired by Van Gogh and Cézanne; Van Gogh's influence, for example, is clearly visible in the charming *Portrait of a Young Girl* (1919). In the 1920s Miró moved to Paris, where he abandoned realism for imagination; the 1925 *A Music Hall Usher* is a key work of this stage. Part of a series known as *The Dream Paintings*, this is one of the 100 works Miró produced between 1924 and 1928.

PILAR JUNCOSA GALLERY
Many of Miró's later works are in the Pilar Juncosa Gallery. A particularly poetic example of this time is *The Gold of the Azure* (1967). In some cases Miró's paintings became mere gestures, as can be seen in the last room, which contains three extraordinary, large-scale triptychs. The most powerful of these is *Cell for a Solitary Man I, II and III* (1968), a trio of irregular black lines on a white background evoking the despair and solitude of a condemned man in his cell. The spectacular sculpture garden on the rooftop terrace is unmissable. *The Caress of a Bird* is one of the quirky works here: a 1967 piece showing how Miró began to introduce bright colours to his bronze sculptures.

Detail of Miro's The Foundation Tapestry, *1979*

RATINGS					
Good for kids	●	●	●	●	○
Specialist shopping	●	●	●	○	○
Value for money	●	●	●	●	○

BASICS
✚ 354 B4 • Parc de Montjuïc, 08038 Barcelona ☎ 93 443 94 70 🕐 Jul–end Sep Tue–Sat 10–8; Oct–end Jun Tue–Sat 10–7; Thu till 9.30, Sun and holidays 10–2.30 💶 Adult €7.50, under 14 free. Temporary exhibitions only: adult €5 🚇 Paral.lel then Funicular de Montjuïc 🚌 50, 55 🎧 Audiotour €3.80. Free tours in Catalán and Spanish only: Sun 11.30 📙 Guidebook €10.20 🍴 Restaurant ☕ Smart café 🛍 Two shops

www.bcn.fjmiro.com
Useful site; tour through the galleries.

TIP
● If you visit after dark, don't attempt the short walk down the mountain afterwards; it is better (and safer) to wait for the No. 50 bus, which leaves from outside the entrance.

Museu Picasso is spread over a number of Gothic mansions

MUSEU PICASSO

A fascinating collection that leads you through some of the most important periods of Picasso's artistic development.

The most popular museum in Barcelona is dedicated to Pablo Picasso (1881–1973), and covers the artist's formative years in the city, his famous Blue Period (1901–04) and his variations on the Velázquez masterpiece *Las Meninas*. The permanent collection is on the top two floors.

EARLY WORKS

The oils that line the walls of the first section are from Picasso's adolescence. They are mainly portraits, such as the famous *Portrait of a Man in a Beret* (1895). Other works include *Carrer de La Riera de Sant Joan* (1900), a view from the artist's studio window, and *Passeig de Colom* (1917), another view-inspired painting. The next rooms deal with the artist's social impressions of his first trip to Paris, and include what must surely be one of the most passionate paintings of all time, *The Embrace* (1900). His ground-breaking Blue and Rose periods are possibly the least represented in the museum, although the space devoted to them does contain *The Madman* (1904), in which Picasso conveys human suffering with unprecedented skill.

THE 'LAS MENINAS' PAINTINGS

The 'Between the Wars' rooms illustrate the artist's first venture into what would become known as cubism in *Figure with Fruit Bowl* (1917). But much of this work acts as a mere interlude to the 'Las Meninas' series of paintings. From the early 1950s Picasso started looking towards the great artists, such as El Greco, Manet and Courbet, but his prime obsession was with Velázquez. The result was a series of canvases on the common theme of the Spanish painter's masterpiece *Las Meninas* (dated 1656, and on show in the Prado, ▷ 388–389).

FINAL YEARS

The final section, 'The Last Years', shows Picasso's need to increase his output. He worked around the clock, producing a spontaneous, almost naïve and infantile style. He also dabbled in ceramic work and collage work; examples of both are in the final room.

RATINGS

Good for kids	◐◐
Specialist shopping	◐◐◐
Value for money	◐◐◐◐

BASICS

✚ 355 E4 • Carrer Montcada 15–23, 08003 Barcelona

☎ 932 256 30 22

🕐 Tue–Sun 10–8

💶 Adult €9, under 16 free. Also free 1st Sun of every month. Entrance to temporary exhibitions only €5.80.

❓ Group bookings must be made before 2pm the day prior to visit; tel 933 19 63 10

🚇 Jaume 1, Arc de Triomf

🚌 14, 17, 19, 39, 40, 45, 51, 59

📖 Guidebook available in all major European languages and Japanese €9.10

☕ Café with outside terrace, although the café at the Textile Museum across the road is better

🏬 Two gift shops

🚻 Although toilets are available on every floor, they can be tricky to find, so use the ones on the ground floor

www.museupicasso.bcn.cat
Plenty of information with clear menus.

La Sagrada Família

The symbol of Barcelona—Gaudí's extraordinary unfinished church, the culmination of his eccentric genius. A controversial building that is still being completed almost a century after Gaudí's death.

The exquisite detail of Gaudí's Nativity Façade

Ornate work enhances La Sagrada Família's exterior

La Sagrada Família has been called a 'catechism in stone'

SEEING LA SAGRADA FAMÍLIA

Love it or loathe it, you cannot ignore La Sagrada Família, or the Temple Expiatori de la Sagrada Família (Expiatory Temple to the Holy Family), to use its full name. Its towers and cranes are visible from all over Barcelona and it is the one must-see item on every visitor's itinerary. Work on La Sagrada Família is progressing continually and what you see will depend on when you go. Entry to the interior is at the Passion Façade on Carrer de Sardenya. After passing the gift shop on your left and the lift (elevator) to the towers on your right, you reach the central nave. The whole area resembles a building site, but the sheer scale of the work will take your breath away.

HIGHLIGHTS

NATIVITY FAÇADE

This is the sculptural high point of the church, begun in 1891 and completed during the lifetime of the architect Antoni Gaudí (1852–1926). The stone carvings on the façade drip with detail, so that at times it resembles a fairy grotto, a hermit's cave or a jumble of molten wax. The theme is the joy of creation at the birth of Jesus, and it deliberately faces east to receive the first rays of the rising sun. At the heart is the nativity scene, featuring Joseph, Mary and Jesus; above them angels play trumpets and sing to celebrate the birth. Three doorways, dedicated to Faith, Hope and Charity, depict other biblical scenes, from the marriage of Mary and Joseph to the presentation of Jesus in the temple. At least 30 species of plants which are native to both Catalonia and the Holy Land have been identified in the façade, echoing the theme that all creation worships Jesus. This theme reaches its climax in the Tree of Life, a ceramic green cypress tree swarming with doves that tops the façade, between the tall towers.

PASSION FAÇADE

In contrast to the richness of the Nativity Façade, the figures on the Passion Façade are harsh and angular, evoking the pain and humiliation of Christ's crucifixion and death. The Catalán sculptor Josep Subirachs (born 1927), who completed these figures in 1990

RATINGS	
Good for kids	● ● ● ○
Photo stops	● ● ● ○
Specialist shopping	● ● ● ○
Value for money	● ● ● ○

TIPS

● Before you go in, take a walk around the exterior of the building and cross Carrer de la Marina to reach Plaça Gaudí, as the best views of the Nativity Façade are from this small park and lake.

● Take a five-minute walk up the Avenida de Gaudí, towards the Hospital de Sant Pau, to get a better view of the overall dimensions of the church.

● If you decide to use the audioguides, you will be asked to leave some identification (passport, driver's licence, etc) as a deposit. If you don't have these on you, you may be asked for a credit card.

SPAIN

A footbridge links two towers of the Nativity Façade

🚻 355 F2 • Carrer de Mallorca 401, 08013 Barcelona ☎ 93 207 30 31

🕐 Mar–end Sep daily 9–8; Oct–end Apr daily 9–6; 25–26 Dec, 1 and 6 Jan 9–2

💶 Adult €8, child under 10 free; elevator €2

🚇 Sagrada Família

🚌 19, 33, 34, 43, 44, 50, 51

📻 Audiotours €3.50 in English, French, German, Italian, Spanish or Catalán. Guided tours €8, child (10–18) €5, child (6–10) €3, held daily but language alternates, phone for details. English: 11am, 1pm, 3pm, 5.30pm

🖼 Large selection available in gift shop

📷 Food and snack machines only

🏬 Shop selling books on the church and Gaudí, plus gift items

🚻 Large toilets at the entrance and smaller ones throughout the site

www.sagradafamilia.org
An easy-to-follow site in English, French and Spanish, but much of it is still under construction.

SPAIN

and still has a workshop on the site, has come in for much criticism, but Gaudí always intended that this should be a bleak and barren counterpart to the joyful scenes of the Nativity. Six huge, leaning columns support a portico containing a series of sculptural groups beginning with the Last Supper and ending with the naked Christ on the cross. The figures of Roman centurions are clearly influenced by Gaudí's chimneys on the roof of Casa Milà. Look for the *Kiss of Death*, a sculpture showing Jesus' betrayal at the hands of Judas, complete with a biblical reference in stone (Mark 14:45) and a 'magic square' whose rows, columns, diagonals and corners all add up to 33, Christ's age at the time of his death.

THE TOWERS
By the time of Gaudí's death in 1926, only one bell tower had been completed, but there are now four towers above each of the Nativity and Passion façades. The final plans show a total of 18 towers, dedicated to the 12 apostles, the 4 evangelists (or Gospel writers), Christ and the Virgin Mary. The dramatic spires, which are up to 112m (367ft) tall, are covered in ceramic mosaics. Gaudí maintained that by looking at the towers, your gaze would be drawn upwards to heaven, transmitting the words of the prayer *Sanctus, Sanctus, Sanctus, Hosanna in Excelsis* (Holy, Holy, Holy, Glory to God in the Highest), which is spelled out in broken ceramic tiles at the top. Spiral staircases give access to the towers, and there is also a lift (elevator) at each end of the building that takes you most of the way. Climbing the towers gives close-up views of the spires and also allows you to look down over the central nave. Another good vantage point is the footbridge linking two towers above the Nativity Façade.

THE CRYPT
The cathedral's original architect, Francesc de Villar, designed the crypt in neo-Gothic style; it is reached by an entrance to the right of the Passion Façade and now contains a museum. Among the items on display are some of Gaudí's scale models and drawings (although most were destroyed during the Civil War), and sketches and casts for the Passion Façade by Josep Subirachs. There is also a confessional box and a tenebrarium (a candle-holder used during Holy Week), both designed by Gaudí. You can look into the workshop where artists are at work preparing plaster casts for the Glory Façade. One of the chapels, dedicated to Our Lady of Carmen, contains Gaudí's simple stone tomb, with the Latin inscription *Antonius Gaudí Cornet, Reusensis*, a reference to his home town of Reus.

BACKGROUND
It is one of the great ironies of Barcelona that a building widely perceived as a triumph of modernism should have been conceived as a way of atoning for the sins of the modern city. The original idea came from Josep Bocabella, a bookseller and conservative Catholic. The first architect, Francesc de Villar, envisaged a conventional Gothic-style church, but when Gaudí took over the project at the age of 31 in 1883 he was given free rein and his fantasies were let loose. It is not always realized that Gaudí, despite the playfulness of his architecture, was a deeply religious man. In his later years he devoted himself totally to La Sagrada Família, living like a recluse in a hut on the site, refusing to draw a salary, wearing simple clothes, eating little food and begging passers-by and rich businessmen for money to allow work on the church to continue.

In 1936, 10 years after Gaudí's death, his plans for La Sagrada Família were destroyed in an anarchist riot, so it is impossible to be certain what the finished building would have looked like. Nevertheless, despite widespread opposition, work on the church resumed in 1952 and it has now taken on an unstoppable momentum, driven by massive worldwide interest and financed by public subscription and the money from entrance fees. The current plan is to complete the temple by 2026, in time for the centenary of Gaudí's death.

La Sagrada Família is impressively illuminated at night

BAD TASTE
Not everyone is impressed by La Sagrada Família. 'I think the Anarchists showed bad taste in not blowing it up when they had the chance,' wrote English novelist George Orwell in *Homage to Catalonia* (1938), his account of the Spanish Civil War.

A CHANGING CHURCH
It is envisaged that the nave will have five aisles, divided by a forest of pillars. Work has already begun on four massive stone columns designed to support the central spire, which will be 170m (558ft) high and topped by a cross, making La Sagrada Família once again the tallest building in Barcelona. Around the spire will be four more towers, dedicated to the evangelists and topped with the symbols of an angel, an ox, an eagle and a lion. As you stand in the nave, look left to see Gaudí's altar canopy and the neo-Gothic wall of the apse; to the right, work has begun on the Glory Façade (which will eventually be the church's main entrance), together with four more towers. Straight ahead, across the transept, a doorway leads outside for a close-up look at the Nativity Façade. The entire church will one day be surrounded by an ambulatory, or external cloister. Despite all the construction work, the completed church seems a long way off, but as Gaudí himself said: 'My client is in no hurry.'

WHAT TO DO

⊕ ADOLFO DOMÍNGUEZ

Passeig de Gràcia 32, 08007
Tel 93 487 41 70
www.adolfodominguez.com
This top Spanish designer's cool linen suits were responsible for a fundamental shift in men's fashion in Spain. Ladies' wear and sportswear too.
⊙ Mon–Sat 10–8.30
⊙ Passeig de Gràcia

⊕ EL CORTE INGLÉS

Plaça de Catalunya 14, 08002
Tel 93 306 38 00
www.elcorteingles.es
This is Spain's most prominent and popular department store, and quite simply a classic. Its superior wares include clothes, food, shoes, electrical appliances, sports gear and more. Perfect if you don't have time for specialist shops.
⊙ Mon–Sat 10–10 ⊙ Catalunya

⊕ LOEWE

Passeig de Gràcia 35, 08007
Tel 93 216 04 00
www.loewe.es
Loewe has always been the ultimate Spanish luxury fashion label, with its classic top-quality leather goods, clothes and accessories.
⊙ Mon–Sat 10–8.30
⊙ Passeig de Gràcia

⊕ MERCAT LA BOQUERÍA

Plaça de la Boqueria, La Rambla 91, 08002
Tel 93 318 20 17
Of Barcelona's markets, La Boquería and Mercat de Sant Josep are the most popular. La Boquería, right in the heart of Las Ramblas, is great for fresh produce. Once you've done your shopping, you can stop at one of the bars and soak up the bustling atmosphere.
⊙ Mon–Sat 8am–8.30pm ⊙ Liceu

⊕ EL TRIANGLE

1 Plaça de Catalunya, 08002
Tel 93 318 01 08
This is one of the busiest shopping malls in Barcelona.

You'll find branches of all the main-street chains here.
⊙ Mon–Sat 10–10 ⊙ Catalunya

⊕ VINA VINITECA

Carrer Agullers 7 and 9, 08003
Tel 93 310 19 56
Vina Viniteca carries about 4,500 different wines and spirits, many of which are exclusive to the shop. All Spain's wine regions are represented, alongside a solid selection sourced from the world's most significant wine-producing countries.
⊙ Mon–Sat 8.30–2.30, 4.30–8.30; Aug 8.30–2.30 ⊙ Jaume I

⊕ BIKINI

Carrer de Deu i Mata 105, 08029
Tel 93 322 00 05
www.bikinibcn.com
Bikini is a classic in Barcelona when it comes to nightlife and the music scene. Its three halls stage many different styles of music such as Latin jazz, pop and rock, as well as DJ sessions. Snacks available.
⊙ From €9 ⊙ Les Corts

⊕ ESPAI JOAN BROSSA

Carrer Allada Vermell 13, 08003
Tel 93 310 13 64
www.espaibrossa.com
Shows here include flamenco, contemporary ballet, magic, poetry and a handful of daring productions not suitable for every audience. The team also performs street entertainment on Sunday.
⊙ From €16 ⊙ ⊙ Arc de Triomf

⊕ PALAU DE LA MÚSICA CATALANA

Carrer Sant Francesc de Paula 2, 08003
Tel 902 44 28 82
www.palaumusica.org
Attending a concert in this flamboyant art nouveau hall is an unforgettable experience. The interior has been designed as if it were a large garden. The building is 100 years old and was conceived and realized by Lluís Domènech i Montaner.
⊙ From €5 ⊙ ⊙ Urquinaona

⊙ CAFÉ ROYALE

Carrer Nou de Zurbarano 3, 08002
Tel 93 412 14 33
Café Royale can best be described as sophisticated and trendy, making good use of modern lighting and a split-level venue. A style-conscious

crowd frequents the bar and dances the night away to soul, funk, bossa and Latin jazz.
⊙ Sun–Thu 8.30pm–2am, Fri–Sat 8.30pm–3am ⊙ Free ⊙ Liceu

⊙ DOT

Carrer Nou de Sant Francesc 7, 08002
Tel 93 302 70 26
www.dotlightclub.com
This dance bar is divided into two main areas. It's busy just about every night, with partygoers dancing to deep house, garage and Latin music. Scenes from cult movies are projected on to the dance floor.
⊙ Sun–Thu 10pm–2.30am, Fri–Sat 10pm–3am ⊙ Free ⊙ Drassanes

⊙ CAMP NOU (FC BARCELONA)

Avinguda de Aristides Maillol s/n, 08028
Tel 93 96 36 00
www.fcbarcelona.com
A great atmosphere is guaranteed here whether you attend a national or Champions League game.
⊙ Guided tours available (phone for details) ⊙ From €25 ⊙ María Cristina

⊙ PARC D'ATTRACIONS TIBIDABO

Plaça del Tibidabo, 08035
Tel 93 211 79 42
www.tibidabo.es
This theme park is one of the world's oldest. The Tibidabo funicular takes visitors to the top of the hill— a great way to start the fun. Attractions here fit in with the *fin de siècle* atmosphere, and there are excellent views over the city.
⊙ Jul–end Aug Mon–Thu noon–10, Fri–Sun noon–11; Jun, Sep Mon–Fri noon–8, Sat–Sun noon–9; Mar–end May, Oct Sat–Sun 12–7; Nov–end Feb Sat–Sun 12–6 ⊙ Adult €24, child (under 1.10m/3.5ft) €11 ⊙ Funicular Tibidabo

EATING

AGUA

Passeig Maritim de la Barceloneta 30, 08005
Tel 93 225 12 72
Agua is so close to the beach that when you are at your table you can even get sand in your shoes! Owing to the location, Sunday lunchtime is busy, with people stopping for a beer and a bite to eat.

SPAIN

Mon–Thu 1.30–4, 8.30–midnight,
Fri 1.30–4, 8.30–1, Sat 1.30–5, 8.30–1,
Sun 1.30–5
🍴 L €25, D €35, Wine €10
Ⓜ Ciutadella-Vila Olímpica

LA BOMBETA

Carrer de La Maquinista 3, 08003
Tel 93 319 94 45
A very popular old fishermen's
bar in La Barceloneta. It's
perfect for those on a budget
who love fresh seafood. You
can either settle at a table or
stand at the bar and dig into
some of the generous tapas.
Choose from steamed
mussels, *esqueixada* (cold cod
with vegetables) or fried squid
and *patatas bravas*, to name
but a few. No credit cards.
🕐 Thu–Tue 10am–midnight. Closed Sep
and last two weeks in Feb
🍴 L €10, D €14, Wine €6
Ⓜ Barceloneta

CA L'ISIDRE

Carrer de les Flors 120, 08002
Tel 93 441 11 12
www.calisidre.com
The menu can change on a
daily basis according to the
seasonal availability of
ingredients, so your duck liver
might be served with plums,
chestnuts, puréed grapes or
Chinese mandarins. The
owner's daughter is the driving
force behind the desserts,
such as chocolate soufflé with
coconut ice cream.
🕐 Mon–Sat 1.30–4, 8.30–11. Closed
holidays and 1–18 Aug
🍴 L €60, D €80, Wine €15
Ⓢ Section
Ⓜ Paral.lel

IL MERCANTE DI VENEZIA

Carrer de Josep Anselm Clavé 11,
08002
Tel 93 317 18 28
The soft classical music,
candlelight and luxurious
curtains conjure up an air of
refinement reminiscent of
Venice. Fillet steak seasoned
with lemon, a range of
seasonal carpaccio and fresh
pasta form the highlights of
the menu.
🕐 Tue–Sun 1.30–4, 8.30–12
🍴 L €12, D €25, Wine €8
Ⓜ Drassanes

MOO

Carrer de Roselló 265, 08008
Tel 93 445 40 00
Located inside the achingly
fashionable Hotel Omm, the
Moo restaurant is the
brainchild of the Roca brothers
of the famed El Cellar de Roca
near Girona. Their second
restaurant is a cutting-edge
affair, serving up *fashionista*
food that embraces style and
substance. Leave room for
their famous perfume-infused
desserts: Chanel No. 5
sorbet, anyone?
🕐 Daily 1.30–4, 8.30–11
🍴 L €40, D €70, Tasting menu (with
wine pairing) €88, Wine €17
Ⓜ Diagonal

QUO VADIS

Carrer del Carme 7, 08001
Tel 93 302 40 72
This restaurant dates back to
the 1950s. Its location near the
Teatre del Liceu has always
made it a popular option for a
post-opera dinner. The choice
of dishes is wide and features
examples of Spanish and
French cuisine with a modern
slant, as well as typical
Catalán fare.
🕐 Mon–Sat 1–4, 8.30–11.30. Closed
Aug
🍴 L €30, D €45, Wine €14
Ⓜ Liceu

<hr>

STAYING

ACTUAL

Carrer de Rosselló 238, 08008
Barcelona
Tel 93 552 05 50
www.hotelactual.com
One of architect Antoni
Gaudí's masterpieces, this
hotel is not only competitively
priced but also has an
excellent location, next to the
Passeig de Gràcia and behind
Casa Milà. Modern and sleek,
and with just 29 rooms, this is
the place to stay if you desire
an intimate atmosphere in a
sophisticated setting. All the
rooms have cable TV, minibar
and internet access.
🏨 €150–€180, excluding breakfast
🛏 29 (12 non-smoking) Ⓢ
Ⓜ Diagonal

CATALUÑA

Carrer Santa Anna 24, 08002 Barcelona
Tel 93 301 91 50
If you are looking for a budget
hotel in the middle of town,
this place is right on target.
It's in the middle of the Barri
Gòtic, next to the Las Ramblas,
Portal de l'Àngel and
Portaferrisa shopping areas.
The rooms are basic but clean,
comfortable and well
equipped, with bathroom,
telephone and TV (local
channels only). Unusually,
breakfast is not served on the
premises: You have to cross
the street to another building.
🏨 €107
🛏 40
Ⓜ Catalunya

CONTINENTAL LA RAMBLA

La Rambla 138, 08002 Barcelona
Tel 93 301 25 70
www.hotelcontinental.com
This 100-year-old, 3-star hotel,
right in the hub of Barcelona,
is where the writer George
Orwell once stayed. It is a
traditional lodging with just
35 rooms, all of which are
equipped with satellite TV,
telephone, fridge, minibar and
fan. There's also room and
laundry service, internet access
and a bar. It's conveniently near
Plaça de Catalunya, L'Illa
shopping mall and Carrer
de Pelai.
🏨 €90
🛏 35 Ⓢ
Ⓜ Catalunya

RITZ HOTEL

Gran Vía de les Corts Catalanes 668,
08010 Barcelona
Tel 93 510 11 30
www.ritzbcn.com
Founded in 1919, this classic
grand hotel in the heart of the
city is the ultimate in luxury
and elegance. The interior is
sumptuous, and some of the
suites have tiled Roman baths.
The service is exceptional and
the staff are multilingual.
Famous patrons have included
surrealist Salvador Dalí. There's
a sauna, beauty salon and
hairdressers on site.
🏨 €380, excluding breakfast (€20)
🛏 85 (60 non-smoking)
Ⓢ 🖥
Ⓜ Passeig de Gràcia

Bilbao

The Basque capital is home to the landmark Museo Guggenheim, with its innovative architecture and extensive collection of modern art.

Paseo del Arenal (top). The Guggenheim Museum (above) and illuminated by night (opposite, top)

RATINGS	
Good for kids	● ● ●
Historic interest	● ● ●
Photo stops	● ● ● ●

MORE TO SEE

ARTXANDRA FUNICULAR
Reached from the Plaza funicular, this gives great cityscape panoramas (daily 7.15am–10.30pm).

PALACIO DE LA MÚSICA Y CONGRESOS EUSKALDUNA
This palace on the riverside by the Puente Euskalduna, at Avenida Abandoibarra 4, is a striking new building, designed to resemble a ship. It is a conference centre and the home of the Bilbao symphony orchestra (tel 94 4035 000 for performance times).

GRAN VÍA DON DIEGO LÓPEZ DE HARO
The new town's bustling main shopping street has some of the city's best department stores.

SEEING BILBAO

The Guggenheim is playing an important part in the makeover of Bilbao (Bilbo in Basque) following the collapse of the traditional steel and shipmaking industries in the 1980s. As a result, this modern city is fast becoming the 'in' place, and with a new tram system and Metro link, it is increasingly accessible. The Guggenheim is flanked at its eastern edge by the massive steel Puente de la Salve bridge and stands on the opposite riverbank to the Universidad de Deusto. Beyond the riverfront there is more than just modernism to this city: The interesting *casco viejo* (old town) preserves the older character of Bilbao and has a good selection of varied sights.

HIGHLIGHTS

MUSEO GUGGENHEIM
Avenida Abandoibarra 2, 48001 ☎ 94 435 90 00 ◉ Jul–end Aug daily 10–8; Sep–end Jun Tue–Sun 10–8 🎟 Adult €10.50, under 12 free

The gigantic mass of the shimmering Museo Guggenheim dominates its setting alongside the Río Nervión. With its towering, curving, titanium folds and huge glass windows it stands symbolically as a modernist introduction to the city. Designed by American architect Frank O. Gehry and opened in October 1997, this vast 24,000sq m (259,000sq ft) museum is a focus for modern and contemporary art. It has become Bilbao's most notable building, and is world renowned for its ground-breaking, iconoclastic design. At its main entrance is the much-loved *Puppy* statue, a huge creation made out of flowers and greenery. Originally intended as a one-off exhibit for the museum opening, it has remained in place, becoming an emblem of the city.

The monumental building revolves around a central axis, an empty space crowned by a metal dome. From this central point, glass lifts (elevators) and curved walkways connect 19 galleries. The permanent collection on show includes works from the last 40 years, including pop art, minimalism, conceptual art and abstract expressionism. Basque and Spanish contemporary art is also represented. The Guggenheim Foundation regularly sponsors impressive special shows. Temporary exhibitions and large-format works are displayed in a gallery 30m (100ft) wide, linked to the main complex via the La Salve bridge.

CASCO VIEJO
Farther along from the Guggenheim Museum, on the eastern bank of the river, is the *casco viejo*, Bilbao's old quarter and the medieval heart of the city. Here, among twisting streets and shady alleyways lined with lively tapas bars, is the Gothic Catedral Basílica de Santiago (Tue–Sat 10–1.30, 4–7, Sun 10.30–1.30) and the arcaded Plaza Nueva. This elegant, entirely enclosed square, reached via arched walkways, is arranged around a neat garden and cornered on each side by stylish shops and balconied apartments. Surrounding it are the lively bars and cafés of Siete Calles, meaning 'seven streets', the city's most renowned nightspot.

Bilbao is not a beautiful city but it has some fine old buildings

Crossing the Río Nervión which runs through the heart of Bilbao

Teatro Arriaga, Bilbao's illustrious opera house

The Museo Arquelógico, Etnográfico e Histórico Vasco (Archaeological, Ethnographic and Basque History Museum; Tue–Sat 11–5, Sun 11–2) is in the nearby Plaza Miguel de Unamuno and includes Basque art, folk objects and photographs. In its cloisters is the *Idol of Mikeldi*, a third-century BC animal carving. Opposite the beautiful 1890s Teatro Arriaga, with its fake rococo semicircular façade, is the Parque de Arenal, a popular *paseo* (promenade) that includes a small open-air stage.

MUSEO DE BELLAS ARTES
Plaza del Museo 2, 48011 ☎ 94 439 60 60 🕐 Tue–Sun 10–8 💶 Adult €5.50, under 12 free; free on Wed

In the newer town is the Museo de Bellas Artes, one of Spain's best regional galleries, with exhibits ranging from 12th-century Catalán masters to modern works. There are also several rooms dedicated to Basque artists, as well as a number of paintings by Goya, El Greco and Murillo. It combines two older museums, the original 1908 museum of the same name and the Museo de Arte Moderno, founded in 1924. Opposite is the city's largest open space, the Parque de Doña Casilda de Iturrizar.

BACKGROUND
Bilbao had humble beginnings in the Middle Ages, but was made a borough in 1300 by Don Diego López of Haro, then Lord of Bizkaia. It grew rapidly on the backs of three industries: iron, fishing and farming. The surrounding iron mines had been worked since Roman times, but their 19th-century development as part of the industrial revolution brought extraordinary power and wealth into the area after the Carlist Wars ended in 1874. The city remains the Basque economic capital today. Its navigable estuary port provided a safer inlet than the ports on the coast itself, and the city established strong trading links with both Britain and America through the export of steel and the import of coal. Although these big industries suffered a decline in the 20th century, the modern city still thrives thanks to its financial and service sectors.

BASICS

➕ 4 B4
ℹ️ Visitor information office
Plaza Ensanche 11, 48009 Bilbao,
tel 94 479 57 60; Mon–Fri 9–2, 4–7.30,
Sat 9–2
🚇 Bilbao

www.bilbao.net
The city council website, in English, Basque and Spanish, with basic visitor information.

TIP

● Make time to see the rest of Bilbao as well as the Museo Guggenheim.

Fresh local fish on sale in Bilbao's fish market

KEY TO SYMBOLS

⊕	**Shopping**
⊕	**Entertainment**
⊕	**Nightlife**
⊕	**Sports**
⊕	**Activities**
⊕	**Health and Beauty**
⊕	**For Children**

WHAT TO DO

⊕ KARTELL-ONN
Alameda Mazarredo 67
Tel. 94 423 24 91
Just in front of the Guggenheim Museum, this sleek shop is the Spanish outlet of the famed Italian interiors and homewares firm. The smaller items from local and international designers are very tempting.
🕐 Mon–Fri 9.30–2, 4–7.30, Sat 10.30–2 🚇 Moyua

⊕ LIBRERÍA ANTICUARIO ASTARLOA
Calle Astarloia 4
Tel 94 423 16 07
Lovers of old books, codices, facsimiles and other gems will appreciate this antiquarian bookshop. Vintage texts, yellowing maps and ancient books line the dusty shelves inside this old *librería*. Weighty tomes describe the history of Bilbao and the region, many in Basque. Several English-language travel books, decades old, make intriguing reading.
🕐 Mon–Fri 10–2, 4–8, Sat 10–2 🚉 Abando Interchange 🚇 Moyua

⊕ LOEWE
Gran Vía 39
Tel 94 479 06 40
Reassuringly expensive unisex fashion in central Bilbao. Loewe is heaven for those who wish to splash their cash on hats, gloves, dresses and scarves.
🕐 Mon–Fri 9.30–8, Sat 9.30–1 🚉 Abando Interchange 🚇 Moyua

⊕ MUSEO GUGGENHEIM
Avenida Abandoibarra s/n
Tel 94 435 90 85
The museum's store should not be missed by lovers of modern art books. Over 2,000 titles are on display in a range of languages. The museum also stocks its own selection of purses, leather diaries, gloves and cutting-edge jewellery.
🕐 Tue–Sun 10–8, also Jul–end Aug Mon 🚉 Abando Interchange

⊕ SALEHI
Calle Ronda 27
Tel 94 416 85 50
One of the few places where *aficionados* can get their hands on Basque music. Rows of cassettes and CDs contain the work of local songsters. The staff can also direct you to artisans still producing traditional Basque instruments.
🕐 Mon–Sat 10–2, 4.30–8. Closed Jun–end Sep Sat pm 🚉 Abando Interchange 🚇 Plaza Unamuno

⊕ SOMBREROS GOROSTIAGA
Calle Víctor 9
Tel 94 416 12 76
Hats for every age and occasion are sold here. Most have a traditional feel, such as the top hats and boaters. You can also buy a traditional Basque beret.
🕐 Mon–Sat 9.30–1.30, 4–8. Closed Jul–end Sep Sat pm 🚉 Abando Interchange 🚇 Plaza Unamuno

⊕ VAJILLA
Gran Vía 24
Tel 94 423 08 32
This brimming store sells everything for the kitchen, from the elegant to the ergonomic. Spanish coffee cups, sets of tumblers and stainless-steel, stovetop coffee-makers make fine gifts.
🕐 Mon–Sat 10–1.30, 4.30–8. Closed Jul–end Aug Sat; Jun, Sep, Oct Sat pm 🚉 Abando Interchange 🚇 Diputación

⊕ ARRIAGA THEATRE
Plaza Arriaga 1
Tel 94 479 20 30
www.teatroarriaga.com
Bilbao's most illustrious theatre has a grandiose façade and a busy calendar. Ballet, classical recitals and opera are performed by both national and international acts.
🎭 Varies 🚉 Abando Interchange

⊕ BARRAINKUA CULTURAL CENTRE
Calle Barrainkua 5
Tel 94 424 49 34
Venue of the International Puppet Festival in November. Puppeteers from around the world use stick, glove, shadow and string marionettes to entertain adults and children.
🎭 €10 🚉 Abando Interchange

⊕ KAFE ANTZOKIA
Calle San Vicente 2
Tel 94 424 46 25
In 1995 this former theatre was overhauled and became a cultural venue with a focus on exciting live music. Basque rock bands play frequently, as do national reggae and pop groups. Each Sunday there is a children's show. The venue turns into a restaurant every lunch time.
🎭 €8 for concerts 🚉 Abando Interchange

⊕ PALACIO EUSKALDUNA JAUREIGA (PALACIO DE CONGRESOS Y DE LA MUSICA)
Avenida Abandoibarra 4
Tel 94 403 50 00/902 54 05 39
www.euskalduna.net
Since 1999 this wackily designed wood, steel and glass playhouse in Bilbao's old shipyard district has hosted music, drama, dance and conference events. Most performances are in Basque.
🎭 €8–€40 🚌 26, 56, 62

⊕ TEATRO BARAKALDO ANTZOKIA
Calle Juan Sebastián Elcano 4, Barakaldo, near Bilbao
Tel 94 478 06 00
www.teatrobarakaldo.com
This is Bilbao's other great theatre, with a distinctive concave and convex modern façade. Drama and dance, rather than concert performances, dominate the playlist here. The frequency of shows shoots up during the summer months. The theatre is also frequently used as a cinema.
🎭 From €12 🚉 🚇 Bilbao

⊕ COTTON CLUB
Calle Gregorio de la Revilla 25 (entrance on Calle Simon Bolivar),
Tel 94 410 49 51
www.cottonclubbilbao.com
Funky DJs and live jazz, blues and rock bands. A mixed crowd is attracted by the unpretentious atmosphere and great cocktails.
🕐 Mon–Thu 4.30pm–3am, Fri–Sat 6.30pm–6am. Closed Sun, Aug 🎭 Free 🚉 Abando Interchange 🚇 Indautxu

SPAIN

ATHLETIC BILBAO FOOTBALL CLUB SAN MAMES

Calle Felipe Serrate
Tel 94 424 08 77
www.athletic-club.net
Athletic Bilbao's illustrious
history speaks for itself, with 23
soccer league championships
to its name. Locals are
intensely proud of their
40,000-seat San Mames
Stadium. Weekend matches
take place every two weeks
from September to May.
€19–€45 📨 26, 56, 62
San Mames

EATING

EL ASADOR DE ARANDO

Calle Egaña 27
Tel 94 443 06 64
Fine Castilian food is dished
up at this friendly, locally
recommended eatery.
Mon–Sat 1–4, 8.45–11.30, Sun 1–4
L €44, D €55, Wine €9
Abando Interchange
Indautxu

BAITA GAMINIZ

Alameda de Mazarredo 20
Tel 94 424 22 67
A fantastic modern restaurant
with an emphasis on cod and
other fresh seafood.
Tue–Sat 1.30–3.30, 8.30–11;
Sun–Mon 1.30–3.30
L €40, D €47, Wine €9
Abando Interchange
Moyua

GUGGENHEIM RESTAURANT

Avenida Abandoibarra 2
Tel 94 423 93 33
This restaurant selling
international food is in the
Museo Guggenheim. You may
be able to get a table if you
chat with the museum staff,
but if you are making the trip
specifically to eat then it's wise
to reserve a table.
Wed–Sat 1.30–3.30, 9–10.30; Sun,
Tue 1.30–3.30. Closed Mon
L €15, D €65, Wine €11
Abando Interchange Moyua

EL MARAKAY CAMPUZANO

Plaza Emilio Campuzano 26
Tel 94 441 30 37
Basque-style tapas are
available at low prices at this
warm, friendly bar-cum-
restaurant.
Daily 7.30am–11.30pm
Tapas from €10, Wine €8
Abando Interchange
Indautxu

EL PERRO CHICO

Calle Arechaga 2
Tel 94 415 05 19
El Perro Chico has become
one of the coolest places to
dine in Bilbao. It serves fine
Basque classics. Reserving a
table is essential.
Tue–Sat 1.30–3.30, 8–11.30. Closed
25 Jul–15 Aug
L €35, D €40, Wine €11
Abando Interchange

YANDIOLA

Campo de Volantín 15
Tel 944 134 013
www.yandiola.com
An unusual restaurant headed
by Chef Ricardo Pèrez. The
atmosphere is intimate yet
modern, perfectly
complementing a menu that
shows off Pèrez's considerable
creative and technical skills.
Tue–Sat 1–4, 8.30–11.30, Mon 1–4.
Closed Easter Week
L €44, D €55, Wine €19

ZORTZIKO

Alameda de Mazarredo 17
Tel 94 423 97 43
www.zortziko.es
Original fare is served at this
cool Bilbao eatery, the best
spot in the city to sample
Basque ingredients cooked
with a twist. Reserve your
table in advance.
Tue–Sun 1–3.30, 9–11.30,
Mon 1–3.30
L €105, D €130, Wine €10
Abando Interchange

STAYING

CARLTON

Plaza Federico Moyúa 2, 48009 Bilbao
Tel 94 416 22 00
www.aranzazu-hoteles.com
This Victorian-era white
mansion positively brims with
21st-century features: The
spacious guest rooms have
comfortable beds, satellite TV,
Wi-Fi and internet access.
€100–€185 excluding breakfast (€15)
148 (6 non-smoking)
Abando Interchange
Moyua

CONDE DUQUE

Campo de Volantin 22, 48007 Bilbao
Tel 94 445 60 00
www.bilbaocondeduque.com
The guest rooms in this
modern, comfortable,
central, 3-star hotel all have
20-channel satellite TV,
broadband internet access,

safe-box and minibar. The
private bathrooms have
modern touches, such as a
waterproof radio, magnifying
mirror and telephone.
€107–€171, weekend offers
available
67 (24 non-smoking)
Abando Interchange

HOTEL LÓPEZ DE HARO

Obispo Orueta 2, 48009 Bilbao
Tel 94 423 55 00
www.hotellopezdeharo.com
This luxury hotel is in a
relatively quiet area of Bilbao
and not far from the Museo
Guggenheim. The tastefully
furnished rooms have marble
bathrooms.There is an on-site
car park.
€103–€270
53
Moyau

PETIT PALACE ARANA

Calle de Bidebarrieta 2, 48005 Bilbao
Tel 94 415 64 11
www.petitpalacearana.com
Each room has a hydro-
massage shower, modem
point, interactive TV and
minibar. Bicycle rental is
available.
€115–€150 excluding breakfast,
check for special offers on their website
67 (14 non-smoking)
€12 (24 hour)
Abando Interchange
Casco Viejo

RIPA

Muelle Ripa 3, 48001 Bilbao
Tel 94 423 96 77
www.hotel-ripa.com
The basic amenities give this
hotel a 1-star rating, but it
does have a telephone, TV and
private bathroom in most of
the rooms. Reserve if possible.
€60
16 Available at €10 per night
Abando Interchange
Casco Viejo

Córdoba

Home to some of Spain's finest examples of Moorish architecture, including La Mezquita, one of the largest and most beautiful mosques in the world.

Decorative plate (top). Córdoba is the heart of flamenco (above)

RATINGS	
Historic interest	● ● ● ● ●
Photo stops	● ● ● ● ●
Shopping	● ● ●
Walkability	● ● ● ●

BASICS

✚ 4 B5

ℹ Visitor information office:
Palacio de Congresos, Calle Torrijos 10, 14003 Córdoba, tel 967 35 51 79, and Plaza Judá Leví, 14003 Córdoba, tel 967 35 51 31

🚉 Córdoba

www.andalucia.org
Includes information in English.

Alcázar de los Reyes Cristianos

SEEING CÓRDOBA

Córdoba is smaller and less frenetic than Seville, and has a number of fine churches, monuments and museums. A less obvious Moorish legacy, and a highlight of the city, are the brightly tiled and flower-filled patios of the houses, which can be glimpsed through wrought-iron grilles. Juxtaposed with the rich history of the old quarters are the stylish shops and restaurants of the modern city, which give this university town a lively air. But without doubt Córdoba's principal attraction is La Mezquita.

HIGHLIGHTS

LA MEZQUITA-CATEDRAL

✚ 371 B2 • Calle Torrijos ☎ 957 47 05 12 ⏰ Mar, Jul–end Oct, Dec Mon–Sat 8.30–7, Sun 8.30–10.15, 4–7; Jan, Feb, Apr–end Jun, Nov Mon–Sat 8.30–6; Sun 8.30–10.15, 2–6 💶 Adult €8, child (9–12) €4, under 9 free

This is one of the most beautiful Arabic monuments in the world. It was started by Emir Abd al-Rahman I in AD785, and further enlarged and embellished over the next two centuries. Only the massive size of the exterior walls gives a clue to the splendour within, as Moorish style does not focus on exterior decoration.

You enter through the Patio de los Naranjos (Courtyard of the Orange Trees), where worshippers washed before praying. As you pass through the Puerta del Perdón, you enter the magnificent interior. There are 19 naves, divided by more than 1,000 columns holding up two levels of arches. The columns are made of marble, jasper and onyx, and the arches are decorated in alternating stripes of red brick and white stone. At the far end is the *mihrab*, a prayer niche indicating the direction of Mecca, although for some reason it faces south rather than east. In 1523 Charles V installed a cathedral in the middle of the mosque, to 'Christianize' the building. He later admitted it had 'destroyed something unique in the world'. Although the cathedral has some exquisitely carved choir stalls and other fine features, the earlier Mudéjar Capilla Real and Capilla de Villaviciosa are far more fitting to this monumental house of worship.

LA JUDERÍA

✚ 371 A2 • Museo Municipal Taurino, Plaza de Maimónides s/n ☎ 957 20 10 56 ⏰ Tue–Sat 10–2, 4.30–6.30 💶 Adult €3, free on Fri. Sinagoga: Calle Judíos ☎ 957 20 29 28 ⏰ Tue–Sat 9.30–2, 3.30–5.30, Sun and festivals 9.30–1.30 💶 Free to EU citizens, otherwise €0.30

Between La Mezquita and the Plaza de las Tendillas is La Judería, the labyrinth of narrow streets and squares that comprised the old Jewish quarter. The Jewish population was ejected from Spain by the Catholic Monarchs, Fernando V and Isabel I, in 1492. A 14th-century Sinagoga (synagogue) in Calle Judíos is the sole surviving Jewish building in the area. At the end of this street is the Puerta de Almodóvar, a 14th-century city gate. Look for the Calleja de las Flores, a flower-bedecked cul-de-sac whose walls frame the belfry of La Mezquita in what has become a classic Córdoba scene. In Plaza Maimónides is the Museo Municipal Taurino (Museum of Bullfighting).

CÓRDOBA

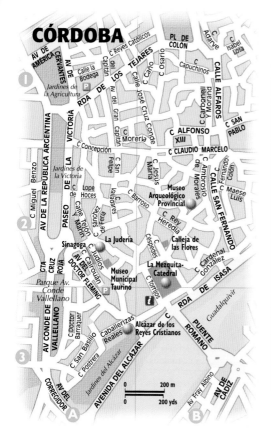

View from the courtyard of the Mezquita (above)

ALCÁZAR DE LOS REYES CRISTIANOS

✚ 371 A3 • Calle Campo Santo de los Mártires s/n ☎ 957 42 01 51 ⏰ 16 Oct–end Apr Tue–Sat 10–2, 4.30–6.30; May–Jun, Sep–15 Oct Tue–Sat 10–2, 5.30–7.30; Jul–end Aug Tue–Sat 8.30–2.30; all year Sun, public holidays 9.30–2.30 💶 Adult €4, free on Fri

The Palace of the Christian Kings was built in the late 13th century by the Christian conquerors to replace the Moor's Alcázar, or fortress, which stood next to La Mezquita. It served as a palace for the Catholic Monarchs, became the headquarters of the Inquisition and was a 19th-century prison. The highlights here today are the magnificent Moorish gardens, a series of terraced ponds in a former orchard.

MUSEO ARQUEOLÓGICO PROVINCIAL

✚ 371 B2 • Plaza de Don Jerónimo Páez 7 ☎ 957 47 40 11 ⏰ Tue 2.30–8.30, Wed–Sat 9–8.30, Sun 9–2.30; closed Mon, public holidays 💶 €1.50

Córdoba's archaeological museum is in the Renaissance Palacio de los Páez, north of La Judería. The arcaded entrance patio is a traditional Córdoban feature, and the building has coffered ceilings and elegant staircases. Córdoba's history is detailed in the fine exhibits of prehistoric, Roman and Moorish art and objects.

BACKGROUND

Córdoba was founded by the Romans around 152BC and was conquered by the Moors in the eighth century. The city became the capital of Moorish Spain for the next three centuries, and was the most cultivated city in Europe in the 10th century, with some 1,000 mosques and 600 public baths, and even street lighting. In 1236 the Christians, led by Fernando III, recaptured Córdoba, marking a long period of decline. It was not until the 20th century that Córdoba flourished once again, this time through agriculture, light industry and tourism.

The famous clustered arches inside the Mezquita (above)

WHAT TO DO

⊕ EL CORTE INGLÉS

Calle Ronda de los Tejares 30
Tel 957 22 28 81
www.elcorteingles.es
You can buy anything from furniture to food, and all the goods are of excellent quality. The fashion department stocks extensive clothing ranges by Spanish and international designers. Not to be missed during the sales!
⊗ Mon–Sat 10–10

⊕ MERYAN

Calleja de Las Flores 2
Tel 957 47 59 02
Meryan has been handcrafting leather for many years, using techniques in accordance with old traditions. The shop sells ready-made items, although most of the work is custom made. Jewellery boxes make excellent presents.
⊗ Mon–Fri 9–8, Sat 9–2

⊕ TURRONARTE

Calle Manrique 1
Tel 957 47 72 79
This delicatessen specializes in all kinds of Andalucían dry goods. Its products are strictly regional and include wines, spirits, oils, confectionery and the exquisite *turrón* (nougat) that gives the shop its name. Some fresh goods are sold during the summer months.
⊗ Mon–Sun 9–9

⊕ ZOCO ARTESANAL

Calle Judíos s/n
Tel 957 20 40 33
www.artesaniadecordoba.com
Zoco Artesanal is a conglomerate of crafts workshops where the biggest association of craftspeople in the province works and markets its products. It offers metal and leatherwork, ceramics in Mozarabic style, and avant-garde designs and crafts in many other media.
⊗ Mar–end Dec daily 10–8; Jan–end Feb daily 10–7

⑪ GRAN TEATRO DE CÓRDOBA

Avenida de Gran Capitán 3
Tel 957 48 06 44, 957 48 02 37
www.teatrocordoba.com
This venue hosts the best artists in town. As well as classical theatre productions, it stages opera and ballet and symphony, chamber and contemporary music. It has a bar.
⑨ Varies according to show ⊗

⑪ SALA QU

Calle Góngora 10
Sala Qu is host to the Córdoba Blues Festival. The modern nightclub is quite small.
⊗ Sat 5.30pm–6am. For other times, email info@salaqu.com ⑨ Varies according to event

⑪ TABLAO FLAMENCO EL CARDENAL

Calle Torrijos 10
Tel 957 48 31 12
www.tablaocardenal.com
A flamenco club, probably the most popular in Córdoba. It features first-class performances by guitarists and dancers, and promises an excellent Andalucían night out.
⊗ Shows Mon–Sat at 10.30pm; closed for a few days in January (phone for details) ⑨ €19 (includes one drink)

⑨ GRIFOS OK

Camino de los Sastres s/n, Ciudad Jardín
Tel 957 45 47 00
During the day this is just another tapas bar, but at night it is the perfect place for a drink while listening to the latest rock and pop on the spacious terrace. The bar has an extensive range of beers.
⊗ Sun–Thu 11am–midnight, Fri–Sat 11am–2.30am ⑨ Free

⑨ LA TERCIA

Calle Llanos del Pretorio 3
Tel 957 47 46 75
www.latercia.net
Charming, modern bar. This is an ideal meeting place for a drink at any time of the day. The spacious terrace is a great setting for a cocktail while listening to the latest music.
⊗ Mon–Thu 7am–3am, Fri–Sat 7am–4am, Sun 7pm–3am ⑨ Free

AL MUDAINA

Jardines de los Santos Mártires 1
Tel 957 47 43 42
www.restaurantealmudaina.com
Housed in a beautiful 16th-century mansion that originally belonged to Bishop Don Leopoldo de Austria, this well-known, reputable restaurant opposite the Alcázar has seven inviting dining rooms serving traditional Córdoban cuisine. House dishes are *salmorejo* (a thick *gazpacho* with ham and egg), *rabo de toro* (oxtail) and sea bass with asparagus sauce. There's a *menú del día* for €21.
⊗ 1 Sep–14 Jun Mon–Sat 12–4, 8.30–12, Sun 12–4. Closed Jun–end Aug Sun
🍴 L €35, D €50, Wine €8

BODEGAS CAMPOS

Calle Lineros 32
Tel 957 49 75 00
www.bodegascampos.com
At this *taberna*, established in 1908, you can sample the house's own montilla sherry and a selection of quality wines accompanied by a selection of tapas. There is also a prestigious restaurant with five dining rooms, serving traditional local cuisine with modern influences.
⊗ Mon–Sat 1.30–4, 8–12, Sun 12.30–4. Closed 24, 31 Dec
🍴 L €40, D €63, Wine €11

EL CABALLO ROJO

Calle Cardenal Herrero 28,
Tel 957 47 53 75
www.elcaballorojo.com
This is one of Córdoba's best-known eateries, with a menu focusing on regional, Sephardic and Mozarabic cuisine. Special dishes include lamb in honey, Mozarabic-style monkfish, and there are delicious desserts. A rooftop patio overlooks the Mezquita. Reserving a table is recommended.
⊗ Daily 1–4, 8–11. Closed 24 Dec
🍴 L €36, D €68, Wine €9

EL CHURRASCO

Calle Romero 16
Tel 957 29 08 19
www.elchurrasco.com
El Churrasco is one of the best restaurants in the city, specializing in traditional Andalucían cuisine. It is most renowned for its *churrasco*

(grilled pork with pepper sauce). The extensive menu (there's even a Braille version) includes fish and meat dishes. Parking is available, and reserving a table is recommended.

🕐 Daily 1–4, 8–12. Closed Aug
🍽 L €40, D €63, Wine €11

PIC-NIC

Calle Ronda de los Tejares 16
Tel 957 482 233

An interesting restaurant that takes an admirably healthy approach to fine dining. Instead of overloading its visitors with rich sauces and heavy food combinations, chef Antonio Canals uses only the freshest, prime ingredients to create an unfussy repertoire that celebrates the simple things in life.

🍽 L €20, D €30, Wine €11.50
🕐 Tue–Sat 1.30–4, 9.30–12, Mon 1.30–4. Closed Easter week and Aug

RESTAURANTE FEDERACIÓN DE PEÑAS (KIKO)

Calle Conde y Luque 8
Tel 957 47 54 27

Generous portions, delicious cooking and reasonable prices are Kiko's main attractions. Most dishes can be shared, unless you opt for *gazpacho* or another soup, or *revuelto* (scrambled eggs).

🕐 Daily 12–4, 7.30–11. Closed 15 Jan–15 Feb
🍽 L €30, D €40, Wine €7

TABERNA RESTAURANTE PUERTA SEVILLA

Calle Postrera 51
Tel 957 29 73 80
www.puertasevilla.com

This *taberna*, decorated with paintings and antiques, is in the old Alcázar area, which takes its name from the western entrance to the district. It is a well-known establishment with a growing reputation for good food. The menu is traditional Córdoban and Mediterranean, with modern Spanish dishes. There is wheelchair access and a parking area.

🕐 Daily 1–4, 8.30–11.30
🍽 L €30, D €45, Wine €8.50

TABERNA LA VIUDA

Calle San Basilio 52
Tel 957 29 69 03
www.puertasevilla.com

In the heart the old city, this tavern offers excellent country-style tapas and raciones including *gazpacho* (soup), *bacalao* (salted cod) and *gambas*. It's a menu that allows beginners to sample a good range of local cuisine. The dining room combines modern lines with traditional motifs, offering a comfortable place for a relaxing rest stop.

🕐 Tue–Sun 1.30–4, 8.30–11.30
🍽 L €12, D €20, W €16

STAYING

ALBUCASIS

Calle Buen Pastor 11, 14003 Córdoba
Tel 957 47 86 25
www.hotelalbucasis.com

Within this hotel's ivy-covered courtyard walls is an eclectic décor comprising old pistols and modern furniture, and there's a comfortable public lounge. The clean, smart rooms all have private bathrooms, telephones, and some have televisions.

🕐 Closed 6 Jan–5 Feb
🛏 €80, excluding breakfast (€5)
🛌 15 ❄ 🅿

HOTEL GONZÁLEZ

Calle Manríquez 3, 14003 Córdoba
Tel 957 47 98 19
www.hotelgonzalez.com

This 16th-century townhouse used to be a Moorish palace. All rooms have private bathrooms; some have balconies overlooking the central courtyard. Breakfast, lunch and dinner are available and can all be taken alfresco. Amenities include a cafeteria (open only for breakfast) and satellite TV.

🛏 €60, including breakfast
🛌 17 ❄

HOTEL MAIMONIDES

Calle Torrijos 4, Córdoba
Tel 957 471 500

Situated right opposite the Mezquita, few places are better located for getting to know the history of this city. Its top feature is a pretty courtyard (where breakfast and dinner are served), and it has pleasant bedrooms and a friendly atmosphere.

🛏 €50–€75, excluding breakfast (€11)

🛌 82 (12 non-smoking) ❄
🅿 €12 day

HOTEL MEZQUITA

Plaza Santa Catalina 1, 14003 Córdoba
Tel 957 47 55 85
www.hotelmezquita.com

This hotel is ideally located opposite the main entrance to the Mezquita. It was formerly a 16th-century palace owned by the painter Julio Romero de Torres. As well as the paintings and antiques, guests can enjoy the lavish bedrooms (all with modern conveniences) and a central patio for dining in the summer.

🛏 €50
🛌 31

LOS OMEYAS

Calle Encarnación 17, 14003 Córdoba
Tel 957 49 22 67
www.hotel-losomeyas.com

Los Omeyas is situated in the old Jewish quarter and the rooms on the top floor have a great view of the Mezquita. All bedrooms are comfortable and have air conditioning.

🛏 €60
🛌 36

PARADOR DE LA ARRUZAFA

Avenida de la Arruzafa s/n, 14012 Córdoba
Tel 957 27 59 00
www.parador.es

There are stunning panoramic views over Córdoba from this opulent 4-star hotel. The guest rooms are large, bright and well decorated, and each comes equipped with a TV, minibar and telephone. Other facilities include a tennis court, bar, lift (elevator), gift shop, garden and playground.

🛏 €140, excluding breakfast (€11)
🛌 94 ❄ 🏊 Outdoor 🅿
🚌 13 every half-hour from Córdoba centre bus terminal
🚌 5km (3 miles) north of Córdoba. From Avenida del Brillante, drive 2km (1 mile) towards Avenida de la Arruzafa. From the junction, continue down the avenue for 500m (550 yards)

Granada

**Home to the Alhambra, one of the world's finest monuments.
Fascinating insight into Islamic Spain.
Plenty of green spaces in which to relax.**

*Mosaic of glazed tiles (above).
Jardines del Partal (left)*

*One of many fountains
scattered throughout the city*

*Decoration on façade (top) of
Palazio de los Nazaríes (above)*

SEEING GRANADA

Granada has both a prosperous new city and a historic older
core, the latter arguably Spain's finest treasure. The city is set at
the foot of Spain's highest mountain range, the Sierra Nevada,
and surrounded by a fertile plain. It rambles over two hills (one
of which is home to the spectacular Alhambra) that lie about
670m (2,200ft) above sea level. The many green areas and
fountains, and the two rivers, the Genil and Darro, make it a
pleasant city to roam around. Although the new city is growing
fast, Granada is easy to explore on foot. However, some sections
can be a bit hilly—such as the lovely walk through the Albaicín
and up to the old gypsy quarter on Sacromonte hill.

HIGHLIGHTS

ALBAICÍN

➕ 376 B2

You could easily spend a day exploring the narrow streets of this old
Moorish quarter. Many of the whitewashed houses here have
delightful secluded interior gardens. Although little remains of the
dozens of mosques that once filled Albaicín's streets, the area has
largely avoided any modern developments. It is increasingly becoming
home once again to immigrants from North Africa, and their influence
is notable in the number of *teterías* (tea shops) and restaurants.

To explore the Albaicín, simply wander up the pleasant Carrera
de Darro, many of whose buildings have notable façades (look in
particular for the Real Cancillería at the bottom and the Museo
Arqueológico at the top). About halfway along is El Bañuelo (Tue–Sat
10–2), Spain's finest Moorish baths, once part of the Mezquita del
Nogal (Mosque of the Walnut Tree), which previously stood here.
The baths were constructed in the 11th century using earlier ruined
Visigothic and Roman building materials—these are most noticeable
in the columns' capitals. Right at the top of Albaicín is the Mirador
de San Nicolás, a lookout point with great views to the Colegiata del
San Salvador, which stands on what was once Albaicín's largest
mosque, and the Iglesia de San Juan de los Reyes, still retaining its
original 13th-century minaret.

RATINGS

Good for kids	●●●○
Historic interest	●●●●
Photo stops	●●●○
Walkability	●●●●

BASICS

➕ 4 B5

ℹ Visitor information office
Plaza de Mariana Pineda 10, 18009
Granada, tel 958 22 688; Mon–Fri 9–7,
Sat 10–2 ❓ There is a smaller office in
the Alhambra

🚉 Granada

www.granadainfo.com/english.htm
Hundreds of links to Granada sites,
including hotels and restaurants,
timetables and statistics.

TIPS

● Although the city is busy
around Easter, the *Semana
Santa* (Holy Week)
celebrations here are
spectacular.
● There are many street
beggars (especially those
carrying sprigs of rosemary
near the cathedral and the
Alhambra). A firm refusal is
usually effective.
● In most bars tapas are free
with each drink you buy.

SPAIN

MORE TO SEE

ALCAICERÍA
✚ 376 A3

The restored former Muslim silk market (next to the cathedral) now has a variety of arts and crafts shops. These tend to be popular among visitors rather than locals, and sell a wide range of good-quality souvenirs.

CASA DE LOS PISAS (MUSEO DE SAN JUAN DE DIOS)
✚ 376 B2 • Calle Convalecencia 1
☎ 958 22 21 44 🕐 Mon–Sat 10–1, Tue–Thu 5–8 💶 €2.50
www.granadamap.com/casapisa.htm
This Renaissance mansion holds a small collection dedicated to San Juan who, legend has it, died on this very spot. The collection itself consists of religious painting and sculpture and treasures in precious metals. The real treat however is the edifice itself, with brilliant forged metal details, wood panelling and a central fountain surrounded by gardens.

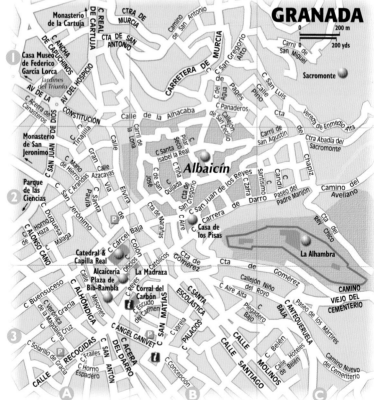

SPAIN

CATEDRAL AND CAPILLA REAL

🔲 376 A2 • Plaza de la Lonja, Gran Vía de Colón 5 ☎ 958 22 29 59 🕐 Oct–end Mar Mon–Sat 10.45–1.30, 4–7, Sun 4–7; Apr–end Sep Mon–Sat 10.45–1.30, 4–8, Sun 4–8 💷 Cathedral: €3. Capilla Real: €3

Taken together, these Christian buildings are almost as impressive as the Alhambra. The very ornate five-nave Renaissance cathedral has a spectacular altar and an enormous central dome, as well as a beautiful façade. Inside are many works by artist Alonso Cano (1601–67), including the west font.

As with many Christian buildings in Granada, the cathedral was built on the site of a former mosque. Construction began in 1518 under Diego de Siloé (1495–1563) but did not finish for another 186 years. Next door, and with a separate entrance, is the late-Gothic Capilla Real (Royal Chapel), which was built as a resting place for the Catholic Monarchs Fernando V and Isabel I (although their bodies briefly spent some time in what is now the *parador* in the Alhambra). Their small, simple, lead coffins are in the crypt with various other members of their close family, including their daughter, Juana la Loca (Joanna the Mad); the tombs themselves are built of much more impressive Carrara marble.

The museum in the chapel's sacristy houses Isabel's art collection, including works by Roger van der Weyden and Botticelli, as well as her sceptre and crown and Fernando's sword.

MONASTERIO DE LA CARTUJA

🔲 376 off A1 • Paseo de la Cartuja s/n ☎ 958 16 19 32 🕐 Apr–end Oct Mon–Sat 10–1.30, 4–8, Sun 10–12; Nov–end Mar Mon–Sat 10–1.30, 3.30–6, Sun 10–12 💷 €3

This early 16th-century Carthusian monastery on the northern edge of the city is one of Spain's gaudiest baroque buildings. Many other styles were also incorporated during the 300 years it took to construct it. In addition to a wonderful frescoed cupola, the monastery's sanctuary and Churrigueresque sacristy are particularly spectacular, decorated with twisting marble columns and a plethora of statues and paintings. Informal guided tours with a resident monk are occasionally available.

CASA MUSEO DE FEDERICO GARCÍA LORCA

🔲 376 off A1 • Calle Poeta García Lorca 4, 18340 Fuente Vaqueros ☎ 958 25 84 66 🕐 Apr–end Sep Tue–Sun 10–7.30; Oct–end Mar Tue–Sun 10–12.30, 4–6.30 💷 €3

www.garcia-lorca.org

This was the airy summer home of the family of poet and playwright Federico García Lorca (1899–1936). He was born here and wrote much of his work in the house. Lorca had something of a love-hate relationship with Granada, but spent much of his free time here and was fascinated by its gypsy population. The house is decorated simply but prettily on the outside—a refreshing contrast to the city's other major sites. Inside, there is plenty of Lorca memorabilia, including manuscripts, furniture, pictures, costumes from Lorca productions, and the great man's bed and ink-stained writing desk. The house is near the airport in the Fuente Vaqueros area, which he described as 'this most pleasant, modern, earthy and liberal of villages'.

SACROMONTE

🔲 376 C1

The network of caves carved out of the clay rock on Sacromonte hill has been home to numerous generations of gypsies, although heavy rain in 1962 forced many to move elsewhere. The caves are close to the Albaicín and offer popular (although not always high-quality) performances of flamenco: Each cave was known by the name of the artists who lived and performed there.

Equally interesting are the caves themselves, many of which have electricity, telephones, plumbing and interiors decorated with copperware and ceramics. There is also a Benedictine monastery on top of the hill, where the ashes of Granada's patron saint, St. Cecilio, are kept.

MONASTERIO DE SAN JERONIMO

🔲 376 off A2 • Calle Rector Lopez Argueta s/n ☎ 958 27 93 37 🕐 Apr–end Sep daily 10–1.30, 4–7.30; Oct–end Mar daily 10–1.30, 3–6.30 💷 €3

Like the cathedral, the Monasterio de San Jeronimo is a prime example of Spanish Renaissance architecture and symbol of Granada's conquest of the Christian forces over the Moors. It served as an army barracks for a century before being handed to an order of nuns in the 1960s and is now dutifully restored. Classical music recitals are often held inside.

The cathedral (above left). Palacio de Carlos V (above). House in the old quarter of Albaicín (below)

PARQUE DE LAS CIENCIAS

➕ 376 off A2 • Avenida del
Mediterráneo ☎ 958 13 19 00
🕐 Tue–Sat 10–7, Sun 10–3. Closed
15–30 Sep 💶 Museum: adult €5,
under 18 €4. Planetarium: adult €2,
under 18 €1.50

This hands-on museum is
especially good for children, with
interactive exhibits such as a
volcano, a tornado and piranhas.

LA ALHAMBRA

➕ 376 C2 • Main access via Cuesta de Gomérez 🕐 Mar–end Oct daily 8.30–8
(also Tue–Sat 10pm–11.30pm); Nov–end Feb daily 8.30–6 💶 Adult €11,
under 8 free

Visitors to the Alhambra can enjoy three main areas—the Palacio
Nazaríes, the Alcazaba and the Generalife—as well as what is
probably Spain's loveliest *parador* (advance reservation absolutely
essential). Throughout, the combination of running water as
decoration, evocative trees such as cypresses and artwork of the
highest standard makes for a unique and relaxing visit.

ALCAZABA

This fortress is the oldest part of the Alhambra, reconstructed over
the ruins of a castle in the ninth century and now little more than a
shell containing ramparts and towers. The most elaborate interiors

*The magnificent Muslim palace
of the Alhambra (above).
Detail on Palacio de los Nazaríes
(below)*

PLAZA DE BIB-RAMBLA

➕ 376 A3

Close to the Alcaicería is one of
the city's most attractive squares
(where people were burned at
the stake during the Inquisition).
Restaurants, shops, street
artists and a generally laid-back
atmosphere.

are those of the Torre de las Armas and the tall Torre de la Vela.
During fiestas, young women in search of husbands traditionally ring
the bell in the latter, from where the views across the surrounding
countryside are fantastic. Towards the southern edge of the Alcazaba
is the delightful Jardín de los Ardaves.

PALACIOS DE LOS NAZARÍES

The star of the Alhambra is the Palacios de los Nazaríes (Nasrid
Palaces), also called the Casa Real (Royal House) and packed with
superb Moorish craftsmanship throughout its various rooms and
courtyards. There are Arabic inscriptions in the stuccowork
everywhere, as well as decorative tiling and intricate wooden carving,
and majestic columns and ceilings, so remember to look up. Simply
wandering around is rewarding, although there are some must-sees
here. In particular, look out for the Salón de los Embajadores (Hall of
the Ambassadors), where all official diplomatic business was
conducted; the Patio de los Arrayanes (Myrtle Court), with its
beautiful pool and myrtle hedges; and the Sala de la Barca (Boat
Room), with an inverted boat-shaped wooden ceiling.

The most famous area is the Patio de los Leones (Court of Lions),
an open arcaded space surrounded by 124 slender columns and
with a central fountain featuring 12 stone lions. Off here are several
important rooms, including the Sala de los Abencerrajes, where the
noble Abencerraje family was murdered as a result of sexual and
political intrigue. The highlight here is the tall, domed ceiling with
geometric vaulting. Opposite is the Sala de las Dos Hermanas (Room
of the Two Sisters, which refers to two marble floor slabs), similarly
richly decorated with a honeycomb dome, where the sultan's
preferred wife lived.

TIP

● A timed-ticket system
operates and it is important to
reserve at least a day in
advance (unless you arrive at
the crack of dawn), either at a
BBVA (Banco Bilbao Vizcaya
Argentaria) bank, online or by
phone. Call 902 888 001
inside Spain or 0034 934 923
750 outside Spain, or go to
www.granadainfo.com

GENERALIFE

Finally, there is the Generalife, a serene collection of walkways, patios
and geometric pools, with beautiful hedges and careful planting. It
was begun in the 13th century but was renovated constantly over the
centuries (the upper gardens were once olive groves). Built as a
retreat from the daily business of the sultan's life, the Generalife is
now the venue for the city's annual music and dance festival in June.
The Patio de la Acequia (Court of the Long Pond) is the complex's
famous focal point, with a long, slender pool over which arch jets of
water; look for the Patio de los Cipreses (Cypress Court).

The Generalife's oriental garden (above). Fountain (right)

BACKGROUND

First settled by native tribes in the fifth century BC, Granada was
later colonized by the Romans, who called it Illibris, a name it
retained until it fell to the invading Moors in AD711. These
Muslim conquerors called it Granada, and it thrived, becoming,
by the 13th century, one of Europe's richest and largest cities,
with a vibrant cultural scene and special expertise in trading.
The Moorish rulers established their power base, the Alhambra,
on a hilltop above the city, the spectacular complex of palaces,
fortress and garden that we see today. It was built mainly under
the Muslim Nasrid dynasty in the 14th century and fell to the
Christian kings, along with the city, in 1492. Ferdinand and
Isabella started a building expansion scheme which continued
until 1526, when Charles V commissioned the vast Renaissance
palace that bears his name.

By the 18th century, the population of the city had declined to
such an extent that Granada became sidelined from national
events, a situation that only changed with the Napoleonic Wars,
when French troops occupied the Alhambra, even blowing up
some of the towers. In 1832 international attention was drawn
to Granada by the publication of Washington Irving's book *Tales
from the Alhambra*, and artists began to live and work in the city.
Foreign visitors followed, and in 1870 the Alhambra was
declared a national monument, a move that marked the start of
the ongoing process of restoration. Granada itself endured a
particularly bloody time during the Spanish Civil War, when
Nationalists ran riot through the city. Among their victims was
the poet and playwright Federico García Lorca.

SPAIN

WHAT TO DO

⊕ EL CORTE INGLÉS
Carrera del Genil 20–22
Tel 958 22 32 40
www.elcorteingles.es
Sells everything except household goods. It is slightly more expensive than elsewhere, but the quality is consistently higher, and there is superior customer service and generous opening hours. There is a good café next to the supermarket in the basement and a restaurant on the second floor.
⊙ Mon–Sat 10–10 ⊟ 7, 10, 11, 13, 33

⊕ GUITARRERÍA BELLIDO Y GIL DE AVALLE
Plaza Realejo 15
Tel 958 22 16 10
www.granadaguitar.com
The best place for handcrafted guitars, although factory-made ones are also sold. Stocks hand-made cellos, violins and double basses, as well as antique string instruments and accessories like books, music scores and CDs. Expect a friendly welcome.
⊙ Jul, Aug Mon–Fri 10–1.30, 6–9; Sep–end Jun Mon–Fri 10–1.30, 5–8, Sat 10–1.30 ⊟ 6

⊕ METRO
Calle Gracia 31
Tel 958 26 15 65
Specialist language bookshop selling a wide range of dictionaries, grammar books and learning materials. Also offers the best selection of English-language fiction, guidebooks and books on Spanish history and culture. The owner speaks English.
⊙ Mon–Fri 10–2, 5–8.30, Sat 11–2 ⊟ 4, 6

⊕ LA OLIVA
Calle Rosario 9
Tel 958 22 57 54
Specializes in extra-virgin olive oils from Andalucía. Also sells fine wines and an excellent range of the best local produce, including organic foodstuffs such as honey, preserves, cheeses, nuts, cakes, herbs and spices. The owner invites you to taste before buying. Search the side streets around Plaza Mariana Pineda to find it.
⊙ Mon–Fri 11–2.30, 5–8.30, Sat 11–3; Jul–end Aug closed Sat ⊟ 23 (Fuente de las Batallas stop)

⊕ ORA ET LABORA
Plaza Pescadería 7
Tel 958 25 81 67
An unusual shop selling expensive delicacies made in convents and monasteries across Spain. These include beautifully presented cakes, pastries, chocolates, wines, liqueurs, honey and preserves. The shop is the only one of its kind in Granada.
⊙ Jul, Aug Mon–Sat 10.30–5.30; Sep–end Jun Mon–Sat 10–2, 5–8.30, Sun 10.30–3 ⊟ 11, 13 (Gran Vía stop)

⊕ SHERPA
Calle Paz 20
Tel 958 52 33 61
www.sherpagranada.com
This shop stocks clothing and equipment for adventure sports enthusiasts, especially walkers, climbers, cavers and skiers. You can try out the gear on the in-house climbing wall before buying. A small noticeboard gives details of trips, courses and second-hand items for sale.
⊙ Mon–Fri 10–1.30, 5–8.30, Sat 10–2

⊕ AUDITORIO MANUEL DE FALLA
Paseo de los Mártires s/n
Tel 958 22 00 22, 958 22 11 44 (tickets)
www.orquestaciudadgranada.es
The modern concert hall, home to Granada's renowned symphony orchestra, stages a variety of symphony music and hosts visiting orchestras.
⬛ €15 ⊗ ⊟ 30, 32

⊕ LA CHUMBERA
Camino del Sacromonte s/n
Tel 958 21 56 47
www.lachumbera.com
This fabulously authentic *peña* (flamenco folk club) in the heart of the *gitano* (gypsy) district is a must for those seeking the spirit of flamenco. Lessons in the art of this brooding dance are available from the nearby Escuela Carmen de las Cuevas.
⊙ Daily 9.30pm–late (check for concert times) ⬛ Entry from €5

⊕ PEÑA FLAMENCA LA PLATERÍA
Placeta Toqueros 7
Tel 958 22 77 12
An authentic flamenco music and dance venue hosting some of Spain's top performers. It attracts real enthusiasts, who help to create a lively atmosphere. It also serves good food and drinks. You'll find it in an alley in the old Moorish quarter of the Albaicín.
⊙ Daily 12–3, 8–1. Performances start at 11pm ⬛ €5 ⊟ 31, 32

⊕ TEATRO ISABEL LA CATÓLICA
Acera del Casino 2
Tel 958 22 15 14
This grand theatre stages events including classical drama, comedy, opera, Spanish light opera, jazz and pop concerts.
⬛ €15 ⊗ ⊟ 11, 13

♥ EL CAMBORIO
Camino del Sacromonte 47
Tel 958 22 12 15
El Camborio is in a real cave in the Sacromonte hillside district. There is a varied selection of music, from techno to flamenco. Since there's nowhere to sit, so dancing is a must! There are views of the Alhambra.
⊙ Daily midnight–7am ⬛ €5 ⊟ 31, 32. Free bus from Plaza Nueva on Thu

♥ ESHAVIRA
Calle Postigo de la Luna 2
Tel 958 29 41 25 or 958 29 08 29
Eshavira is an authentic music club that's been going for 14 years. Live jazz and flamenco are performed at least three nights a week. It's the haunt of local musicians, intellectuals and artists.
⊙ Daily 10pm–5am ⬛ Live performances €5–€8 ⊟ 11, 23, 32

♥ GRANADA 10
Calle de la Carcel Baja 10
Tel 958 22 40 01
Granada 10 fills up with a cosmopolitan mix of people of all ages—singles, couples and groups—for great cocktails and a standard selection of contemporary and classic pop music. It stays open all night.

SPAIN

Thu–Sun midnight–8am 🎫 €6 (one free drink) 🚌 11, 13, 23, 32

⭐ SIERRA NEVADA SKIFIELD

Cetursa-Sierra Nevada S.A., Plaza de Andalucía, Edificio Cetursa C.P
Tel 958 24 91 00, 902 70 80 90 (information line), 958 204 000 (customer services)
www.sierranevadaski.com
Spain's biggest ski resort is just 25 minutes away from Granada. It has 52 lifts and 60km (40 miles) of slopes. The resort is ugly and modern, but the skiing is varied and challenging. Its southern location means there are lots of sunny days, a long season, and bicycling, horseback riding and trekking in summer months. There are several good bars and cafés.
🕐 Mid-Dec–late Apr 💶 Low season: 1-day pass €27.50; 6-day pass €166. High season: 1-day pass €34; 6-day pass €216. Discounts for under 12 and over 65. (Photo required for the 5- and 6-day passes) 🚌 Take the N-420 direct from Granada's ringroad, then follow the signs for the Sierra Nevada

💧 HAMMAM BAÑOS ARABES

Calle Santa Ana 16
Tel 958 22 99 78
www.hammamspain.com
These Arab baths offer a 90-minute session that alternates between the hot and cold pools. Enjoy the Eastern music, Moorish-style decoration and exotic aromas, then complete the experience with a 15-minute massage (reservations essential). Sessions are mixed sex. Reserve in advance and take swim gear (towels and lockers are provided). There's also a tea room upstairs and a restaurant serving local-style food with a Moorish influence.
🕐 Mon–Fri 10am–11pm, Sat–Sun 10am–11.30pm 💶 Baths €17, baths and massage €26 🚌 30, 31, 32

⭐ PARQUE DE LAS CIENCIAS

Avenida del Mediterráneo s/n
Tel 958 13 19 00
www.parqueciencias.com
Parque de las Ciencias is a hands-on, interactive science park. The state-of-the-art building and grounds house a planetarium, an observatory, a Foucault pendulum and a butterfly farm. There's a

cafeteria and a shop.
🕐 Tue–Sat 10–7, Sun and holidays 10–3. Closed Mon, 1 Jan, 1 May, 15–30 Sep, 24–25 Dec 💶 Museum €5, planetarium €2 🚌 4, 5, 10, 11

EATING

CAFÉ FÚTBOL

Plaza Mariana Pineda 6
Tel 958 22 66 62
The Café Fútbol has a pretty terrace set under leafy sycamore trees in a quiet, central square, ideal in summer for home-made ice-creams and *horchata*, a refreshing crushed-almond milk drink. Thick hot chocolate and fresh fried doughnuts *(chocolate y churros)* are served all day during winter. Credit cards are not accepted.
🕐 Daily 6am–3am
💶 Coffee and cake €3
🚌 23

CUNINI

Plaza de la Pescadería 14
Tel 958 25 07 77, 958 26 75 87
The best Mediterranean fish and fresh shellfish from northern Spain are delivered daily to Cunini and cooked to perfection.
🕐 Daily 12–4, 8–12
💶 L €50, D €72, Wine €20
🚌 5, 11

O CAÑA

Plaza del Realejo 1
Tel 958 25 64 70
This is a long-established, cheap and cheerful restaurant that fills with local residents and workers at peak times: mid-morning coffee break, lunchtime and after work. It has four different sections—bustling bar, rustic restaurant, Andalucían patio and private dining room.
🕐 Daily 7am–11pm
💶 L (three-course set menu) €8, D €40, Wine €13
🚌 23

PILAR DEL TORO

Calle Hospital de Santa Ana 12
Tel 958 22 38 47
Pilar del Toro is an impressive 17th-century town house that has been converted into a classy bar and restaurant. Drinks and snacks are served on a delightful Andalucían patio adorned with a fountain and many plants. The restaurant upstairs serves

regional dishes, and there is an extensive list of fine wines. You can sit outdoors in summer.
🕐 Bar: Mon–Sat 9am–2am. Restaurant: Mon–Sat 1.30–4, 8.30–12
💶 L €55, D €68, Wine €10
🚌 31, 32

STAYING

AMÉRICA

Calle Real de la Alahambra 53, 18009 Granada
Tel 958 22 74 71
www.hotelamericagranada.com
Stay in the grounds of the Alhambra palace complex. All bedrooms have private bathrooms, TV and telephone. Parking is at a discounted rate in the nearby public parking area. Reserve in advance.
🕐 Closed 1 Dec–28 Feb
💶 €110 excluding continental breakfast (€7)
🛏 15, plus 1 suite ♿
🚌 30, 32

CASA MORISCA

Cuesta de la Victoria 9, 18010 Granada
Tel 958 22 11 00
www.hotelcasamorisca.com
Some of the rooms in this Moorish mansion have magnificent views of the Alhambra. All have TV and minibar. Buffet breakfast only, served in the cellar.
💶 €114–€196 excluding buffet breakfast (€10)
🛏 12, plus 1 suite and 1 tower room with special views ♿ 🅿
🚌 31, 32

HOSTAL SUECIA

Calle Molinos (Huerta de los Angeles) 8, 18009 Granada
Tel 958 22 50 44
This small hotel with character, is well away from the noise of traffic. The guest rooms vary in size but all are kept spotlessly clean. Four of the eleven bedrooms share a single huge bathroom; the others have private bathrooms. Breakfast is the only meal served.
💶 €55, excluding continental breakfast (€4.50)
🛏 13
🚌 23

SPAIN

Madrid

✚ 4 B4 🏛 Plaza Mayor 3, tel 91 366 54 77; Mon–Sat 10am-8pm, Sun and public holidays 10–3
www.descubremadrid.com. Not a bad site, but hardly complete for a major city

HOW TO GET THERE

✈ Airport
Barajas International Airport lies 15km (9 miles) east of the centre.

🚆 Rail stations
There are three main stations in Madrid: the central Atocha station services southern Spain, most international routes and Barcelona, and Chamartín (also centrally located) serves central Spain. The slightly more out of the way Estación Norte (also the bus station) serves western Spain.

Enjoying the delights of the Museo del Prado

TIPS

• Time permitting, endeavour to make an out-of-town excursion to the palace complex of El Escorial or the medieval town of Toledo.
• You can forget about bottled water here; Madrid's water source is the cleanest in the country.
• Outside of Andalucía, Madrid is the best place to see live flamenco and bullfights (when in season). Check at the tourist office for details of both.
• The sites in Madrid are spread out. Take advantage of the excellent Metro system as the streets are often gridlocked.
• Do remember that Madrid, at 650m (2,132ft) above sea level, is the highest capital in Europe. Temperatures can be extreme and warm clothing is essential in late autumn and winter.

SEEING MADRID

Madrid is Spain's power city. It's the seat of the country's finance and politics, and its classy restaurants, skyscrapers and luxurious hotels reflect its high-rolling lifestyle. That's not to say that the village-like ambience of most other Spanish cities is not to be found here. 'Madrid de las Asturias', the cobbled streets that weave out from the grand centrepiece, the Plaza Mayor, are full of atmosphere, as is the bo-ho inner-city neighbourhood of Chueca, the city's nightlife focal point. The Puerta del Sol, a plaza just south of the city's main artery the Gran Via, is not only the official heart of the city but of the entire country, with all Spanish road distances being measured from here.

Madrid is a monumental city with more than its fair share of spectacular museums and historic buildings. The recently expanded El Prado museum is a challenge to take in during one day, and that's not to mention the contemporary collections of the Centro de Arte Reina Sofía or the sizeable Thyssen-Bornemisza bequest. If it all becomes a little overwhelming, take a break in one of the many parks or time out at a period café. If you do as the locals do and pace yourself, you will soon reap the rewards of this fascinating metropolis.

BACKGROUND

Located in the dead centre of the country, Madrid became the capital of Spain in 1561 when King Philip II decided to move the entire royal household from Toledo to this then-dusty outpost for reasons that remain unclear. During his stay he (and his successors) built dozens of monasteries for the various religious orders, but his greatest legacy lies outside Madrid in the rambling palace of El Escorial. Madrid's beautiful Plaza Mayor was used for hangings, witch burnings and various other atrocities carried out 'in the name of God'. The pious Habsburg kings ruled Spain until 1714 when the French-raised Philip V, the first of the Bourbon dynasty, took over and established such enlightened institutions as the Royal Academy of Language.

A divided city during the Civil War, Madrid emerged badly bruised and with many of its monuments and buildings in tatters. This did not stop Franco from setting up base here (addressing the masses in the Plaza de Oriente from the balcony of the grand Palacio Real) while ruling the rest of Spain during his dictatorship with an iron fist. After Franco's death in 1975, the *movida*, a heady period that revelled in newfound liberalism, took hold. Some of the country's most revered figures in the arts, such as the film-maker Pedro Almodóvar, are a product of this modern-day renaissance.

DON'T MISS

MUSEO DEL PRADO
Fruit of centuries of royal collectors. Highlights include *Las Meninas* by Velázquez (▷ 388–389)

CENTRO DE ARTE REINA SOFÍA
Be moved by Picasso's civil war masterpiece *Guernica*

PLAZA MAYOR
City hub and centrepiece. Best place in the city for an *alfresco* drink

MUSEO THYSSEN-BORNEMISZA
Runs the full gamut of European and American art, from Goya to Warhol (▷ 390–391)

PARQUE DEL RETIRO
The city's much-loved 'central park'

EL RASTRO FLEA MARKET
An authentic slice of *madrileño* street life

SPAIN

Madrid's Royal Palace is best viewed from the Campo del Moro (The Moor's Field)

Façade of Catedral de Nuestra Señora de la Almudena

CAMPO DEL MORO

⊞ 384 B4 • Paseo de la Virgen del Puerto, 28071 Madrid ☎ 91 542 00 59 ◉ Apr–end Sep Mon–Sat 10–8, Sun 9–8; Oct–end Mar Mon–Sat 10–6, Sun 9–6 🚇 Free 🚇 Opera 🚌 3, 31, 50, 65, 148

In 1890 Queen María Cristina of Habsburg landscaped the gardens of the Palacio Real (▷ 392) along the lines of a Romantic English park, renaming them The Moor's Field after the Arab general Ali Ben Yusuf, who supposedly set up camp here while laying siege to the city in 1109. The grotto near the main gate conceals the entrance to a tunnel, which was built for Felipe II as a short cut to the hunting grounds of the Casa de Campo (see below). You can see the royal carriage horses being exercised every day around noon, but the Museo de Carruajes (Carriage Museum) is closed indefinitely for restoration.

CASA DE CAMPO

⊞ 384 A4 • Calle Marqués de Monistrol, Avenida de Portugal, 28011 Madrid ☎ Zoo 91 512 37 70 🚇 Lago, Batán 🚌 33, 39, 41, 65, 75, 84

This vast green lung, on the western side of Madrid, is a relatively natural tract of wooded countryside. During the Civil War Franco's troops were based here, and signs of trenches are still visible. Once a royal hunting ground, it was opened to the public in 1931, and the Casa de Campo now provides the city with a combined zoo and aquarium housing 600-plus species (daily 10.30–sunset), the Parque de Atracciones amusement park (Jul–end Aug Mon–Fri noon–1am, Sat noon–2am, Sun noon–midnight; Sep–end Jun Sat–Sun and festivals noon–9), and the chance to take a boat out on to

the lake. The best way to arrive is by the *teleférico*, or cable-car (tel 91 541 74 50), which runs from the Paseo del Pintor Rosales on the edge of Parque del Oeste and has great views over the city.

CATEDRAL DE NUESTRA SEÑORA DE LA ALMUDENA

⊞ 384 B4 • Calle de Bailén s/n, 28071 Madrid ☎ 91 542 22 00 ◉ Cathedral: daily 10–7.30. Closed during services. Crypt: daily 10–8 🚇 Free 🚇 Opera 🚌 3, 148

Madrid's Roman Catholic cathedral shares its magnificent clifftop setting with the adjoining Palacio Real (▷ 392), and has wide views across the city from the terrace. It was consecrated in 1993 by Pope John Paul II and officially opened a year later.

The most impressive part of the building is its interior, which resembles a medieval church, with (modern) stained-glass windows and painted, vaulted ceilings. The Chapel of the Almudena has a late 15th-century statue of the Virgin. Less pleasing to the eye are the bulky façade and dome, an architectural mixture that reflects the chequered history of the building.
Don't miss The bronze doors were installed in October 2000.

COLEGIATA DE SAN ISIDRO EL REAL

⊞ 384 C5 • Colegiata de San Isidro, Calle de Toledo 37–39, 28005 Madrid ☎ 91 420 17 82 ◉ Mon–Sat 7.30–1.30, 6–9, Sun 9–2. Closed during services 🚇 Free 🚇 Alonso de Mendoza, Getafe Central 🚌 17, 18, 23, 35

The Church of San Isidro, one of the city's most important baroque monuments, dates from 1534, when Jesuits founded a

monastery on the site and, later, a prestigious school, the Colegio Imperial. San Isidro served as the city's cathedral until the completion of the Almudena.

The barrel-vaulted interior, given a neoclassical makeover by the architect Ventura Rodríguez in the 18th century, is impressive, if a little gloomy. The remains of San Isidro, Madrid's patron saint, are preserved in a reliquary above the high altar.

ERMITA DE SAN ANTONIO DE LA FLORIDA

⊞ 384 A4 • Glorieta de San Antonio de la Florida 5, 28008 Madrid ☎ 91 542 07 22 ◉ Tue–Fri 10–2, 4–8, Sat–Sun 10–2 🚇 Free 🚇 Príncipe Pío 🚌 41, 46, 75
www.munimadrid.es/ermita

The walls, vaults and cupola of the Chapel of St. Anthony are decorated with superb frescoes by Francisco de Goya (1746–1828), who is buried here. The church was designed by Italian architect Felipe Fontana in 1792 and completed eight years later. An identical chapel was built next door in 1925 so that the *ermita* (hermitage) could function exclusively as a museum. The frescoes themselves, dating from 1798, cover an area of more than 180sq m (1,937sq ft), and were considered revolutionary in both technique and subject matter. In the apse is *The Adoration of the Trinity*, and the vaults are adorned with sensuous angels and cherubim. The central scene, in the cupola, depicts St. Anthony of Padua bringing a murdered man back to life so that he can clear the name of his own father, who had been wrongly accused of the crime. The models for the frescoes were members of the Spanish Court.

SPAIN

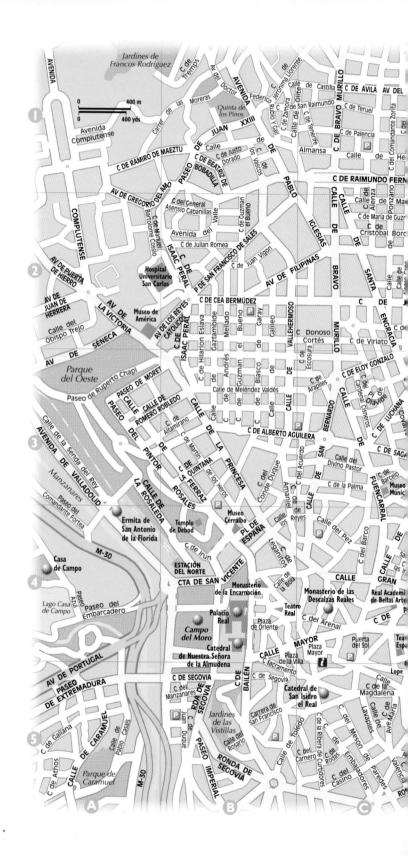

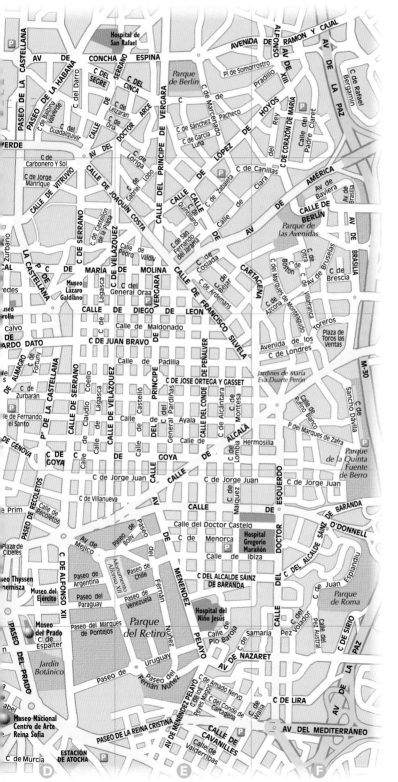

Hospital de San Rafael

AVENIDA DE ALFONSO RAMON Y CAJAL

AV

C de Rafael Bergamin

CONCHA ESPINA

C DEL SEGRE

SERRANO

C DEL CINCA

Pl de Somorrostro

Pradillo

AV XIII

AV

DE

PASEO DE LA CASTELLANA

PASEO DE LA HABANA

C del Darro

DE

C del Leizaran

ARCE

C de

Parque de Berlín

C de Marcenado

Pacheco

DE

del Rey

DE LA PAZ

VERDE

C de Balbina Valverde

C del Guadalquivir

CALLE DEL DOCTOR

C de Oria

CALLE DEL PRINCIPE DE VERGARA

C de Sánchez

C de García Luna

LOPEZ

DE HOYOS

C DE CORAZON DE MARIA

Calle del Padre Claret

P

C de Carbonero Y Sol

AV DEL

C de Loriga

C de Canillas

AMERICA

C de Jorge Manrique

CALLE DE VITRUVIO

CALLE DE JOAQUIN COSTA

C de Gabriel Lobo

CALLE

CALLE

C de Zabaleta

Clara

Av de Baviera

Av de Brasilia

CAL

LA CASTELLANA

C de Castellón de la plana

VELAZQUEZ

Calle de Pedro de Valdivia

DE

C de San Fernando del Jarama

Calle

AV

CALLE DE BERLIN

Parque de las Avenidas

C de Oltra

C de Bruselas

BRASILIA

P C DE SERRANO

DE MARIA DE MOLINA

VERGARA

CALLE DE FRANCISCO SILVELA

C de Coslada

C de Bélar

C de Bosán

Av de Bruselas

C de Brescia

edes

Museo Lázaro Galdiano

Lagasca

C del General Oraá

C de Ardemans

CARTAGENA

C del Marqués de Montesquío

C de Villafranca

C de Azcona

seo olla

CALLE DE DIEGO DE LEON

Calle de Maldonado

Toreros

Plaza de Toros las Ventas

Calvo

DE

ARDO DATO

C de Fortuny

C DE JUAN BRAVO

Calle de Padilla

PRINCIPE

Avenida de los

C de Londres

M-30

es

ALMAGRO

C de Zurbarán

CALLE DE SERRANO

PASEO DE LA CASTELLANA

Coello

Lagasca

C del Castello

C DE JOSE ORTEGA Y GASSET

C del Conde de Peñalver

Jardines de María Eva Duarte Perón

Calle de Rufino Blanco

Sancho Dávila

C de

le de Fernando el Santo

P

CALLE DE VELAZQUEZ

Calle

de

C del General Pardiñas

Ayala

C de Alcántara

C de Montesa

P del Marqués de Zafra

Parque de la Quinta Fuente de Berro

DE GENOVA

C DE GOYA

Calle

Calle

DE

GOYA

CALLE

ALCALA

Hermosilla

C de Lombía

P Prim

PASEO DE RECOLETOS

Calle de Recoletos

C de Villanueva

C de Jorge Juan

CALLE

C de Jorge Juan

DE

ESGUERDO

C de Jorge Juan

Plaza de Cibeles

C DE ALFONSO XII

Av de Melico

Paseo de Bolly

Paseo del

CALLE

Calle del Doctor Castelo

C de Menorca

P

DOCTOR

C DEL ALCALDE SAINZ DE BARANDA

O'DONNELL

Esplandiu

seo Thyssen nemisza

Museo del Ejército

Paseo de Argentina

Paseo de Chile

Hospital Gregorio Marañón

Calle de Ibiza

C de Juan

Esplandiu

Parque de Roma

PASEO

Museo del Prado

C de Espalter

Paseo del Paraguay

Paseo de Venezuela

MENENDEZ

C DEL ALCALDE SAINZ DE BARANDA

CALLE

C del Velador

C DE SIRIO

Jardín Botánico

Paseo del Marqués de Pontejos

Parque del Retiro

Fernán Núñez

Hospital del Niño Jesús

Calle de Pío Baroja

PELAYO

C de Samaria

Pez

Calle del Pez Austral

DE LA PAZ

abel

Museo Nacional Centro de Arte Reina Sofia

Uruguay

Paseo de

Paseo del Fernán Núñez

AV DE NAZARET

C de Amado Nervo

C del Conde de Cartagena

C de Walia

C DE LIRA

n

C de Murcia

ESTACIÓN DE ATOCHA

P

PASEO DE LA REINA CRISTINA

AV DE MENENDEZ PELAYO

C de Reyes Magos

CALLE DE CAVANILLES

Calle de Valderribas

P

AV DEL MEDITERRANEO

D

E

F

Empress Maria of Austria's tomb, above the Madonna in the choir

The austere brick and stone façade of the monastery

BASICS

✚ 384 C4 • Plaza de las Descalzas Reales 3, 28013 Madrid ☎ 91 454 88 00 🕐 Mon–Sat 9.30–5, Sun 9–2. The Chapter Room is currently closed for restoration 💶 Adult €5, child (5–15) €4 🚇 Sol 🚌 3, 5, 15, 20, 50, 51, 52, 53, 150 📷 Compulsory 1-hour guided tour departs every 15 min 🏪 Small shop, selling art books, guides to Madrid, decorative religious objects and mementoes

www.patrimonionacional.es
General site with useful background information.

TIPS

● The guided tour is in Spanish, but questions are answered in English. Be prepared to wait for up to 15 minutes while enough visitors assemble for the tour.
● To get the most out of your visit, focus on the overall impact of the artistic treasures rather than trying to locate particular exhibits.

MONASTERIO DE LAS DESCALZES REALES

This 16th-century convent is a treasure house of artwork.

The monastery has been a working convent since its foundation more than 400 years ago. The building was originally a palace, and in 1554 Felipe II's sister, Juana de Austria, stayed here while acting as regent for her brother. She had the palace adapted for use as a convent, and the Franciscan nuns who live here were originally nicknamed *las descalzas reales* ('the royal barefoot women') on account of their aristocratic backgrounds. The convent has an impressive display of paintings, sculptures, tapestries, *azulejos* (painted tiles) and gold and silver liturgical objects. The only way to see them is on a guided tour.

OUTSTANDING FRESCOES

The Grand Staircase is one of the first stops, and one of the highlights. The stunning frescoes that cover the walls, arches and balustrades were painted at the end of the 17th century by José Ximénez Donoso (1632–90) and Claudio Coello (1642–93). To the right is the Balcón Real (Royal Balcony), with a splendid portrait of Felipe IV and his family. The staircase leads to the Upper Cloister, which is surrounded by chapels. Look for the Chapel of the Virgin of Guadalupe, which has 68 oil panels painted in 1653 by Sebastián de Herrera Barnuevo. The altar facing is made of wood, bronze and glass, and the statue of the Virgin, though not the original, dates from the 16th century.

TAPESTRY ROOM

Next is the antechoir, with its late 15th-century *Virgin and Child*, one of the oldest works of art in the convent. You then go through the choir and to the 16th-century Redeemer's Staircase, which leads to the Tapestry Room. Here is a superb set of 20 Brussels tapestries dating from the 17th century, not all of which are on show. They were commissioned by the Infanta Isabel Clara Eugenia. The cartoons for the tapestries were prepared by Peter Paul Rubens (1577–1640) and include the famous *Triumph of the Eucharist* (c1625).

Don't miss The Spanish and Italian Picture Room has an excellent collection of paintings, among them *St. Francis*, attributed to Zurbarán (1598–1664), and *The Tribute Money* by Titian (1490–1576).

The two external glass elevators are a focal point of the museum

MUSEO NACIONAL CENTRO DE ARTE REINA SOFÍA

The permanent collection here spans the entire 20th century, and includes Picasso's *Guernica*.

Spain's national modern art museum opened in 1992 and is the largest exhibition space in Europe after the Pompidou Centre in Paris. Pride of place goes to Picasso's masterpiece, *Guernica* (1937), but the gallery also has an exceptional collection of work by his contemporaries, including Juan Gris, Joan Miró and Salvador Dalí.

The austerity of the façade is modified by the glass lifts (elevators), which allow visitors a view over the rooftops. The collection, in light and airy galleries, is arranged chronologically and thematically, beginning on the second level with the Basque and Catalán schools of the early 20th century. Art from the post-war period can be found on the fourth level, while the first and third levels are used for temporary shows.

GUERNICA
The focus of the permanent collection is Pablo Picasso (1881–1973). Most visitors make a beeline for *Guernica*. This huge canvas was the artist's response to the aerial bombing of the town of Gernika-Lumo by the Germans, who were allies of General Franco during the Civil War. The impact of the painting was such that it still aroused controversy when it was first exhibited here in 1992. The bulletproof screen, to protect the painting against maverick right-wing attacks, was removed three years later and visitors can now see it as it was meant to be seen. Room 6 shows some of Picasso's earlier work, including the Blue Period painting *Woman in Blue* (1901).

WORKS BY OTHER ARTISTS
The work of Madrid-born painter Juan Gris (1887–1927) is in Room 4. The whole of Room 7 is devoted to the Catalán artist Joan Miró (1893–1983). The artistic evolution of Salvador Dalí (1904–1989) during the 1920s and 1930s is explored in Room 10, where *The Great Masturbator* (1929) is representative of his work during this period.

The post-war generation of Spanish artists is also represented, along with European artists such as Robert and Sonia Delaunay, Max Ernst, Henry Moore and Francis Bacon, and leading American artists Ellsworth Kelly, Barnett Newman, Donald Judd and Bruce Naumann.

One of Madrid's most exciting galleries and exhibition spaces

RATINGS
Good for kids	◕◕
Historic interest	◕◕◕◕
Value for money	◕◕◕◕

BASICS
✚ 385 D5 • Calle de Santa Isabel 52, 28012 Madrid ☎ 91 774 10 00
🕐 Mon, Wed–Sat 10–9, Sun 10–2.30. Closed Tue & public holidays 💶 Adult €6, under 18 free. Free Sat pm and Sun
🚇 Atocha 🚌 All routes to Atocha
🎧 Audiotour €2.40. Free guided tours (Spanish only) Mon and Wed at 5, and Sat at 11; advance reservation required, tel: 91 527 72 05 🏛 Official guide €8. Regularly updated, informative floorplan (English and Spanish) free
🍴 Café-restaurant and bar in basement. Drinks terrace closed for refurbishment 🅿 Calle Sánchez Bustillo, about 2 min walk, open 24 hours

www.museoreinasofia.es
Spanish and English site, with details of collections, a history of the museum and more.

TIP
● In winter, the best time to visit the Reina Sofía is early on Sunday morning, when entry is free and there are relatively few visitors.

Museo del Prado

Madrid's biggest visitor attraction.
Incomparable collection of Spanish art, plus important Dutch and Italian
masterpieces. Holds more than 8,000 paintings.

Lofty gallery space shows off the
Prado's treasures at their best

A statue of Goya (1746–1828)
stands outside the museum

The Marquesa de Santa Cruz
by Goya (1805)

RATINGS

Good for kids	◕◕
Cultural interest	◕◕◕◕◕
Specialist shopping	◕◕◕
Value for money	◕◕◕◕◕

GALLERY GUIDE

GROUND LEVEL
Rooms 50 and 51c: Spanish medieval.
Rooms 56–57b and 63a: Spanish 16th century.
Rooms 60a–62a: El Greco.
Rooms 55–58a: Flemish 15th and 16th centuries: Pieter Breughel the Elder
Room 54: German.
Rooms 56b and 60-63b: Italian 14th–16th centuries. Botticelli and Raphael.
Rooms 64–67 and 71–73: Sculpture. Dauphin's Treasure.

FIRST LEVEL
Rooms 1, 16a–18a, 24–26, 28 and 29: Spanish 17th century. Zurbarán and Murillo.
Rooms 12, 14–16 and 27: Velázquez.
Rooms 7a–11: Flemish 17th century. Van Dyck and Rubens.
Room 7: Dutch 17th century.
Rooms 2–6: French and Italian 17th century.
Rooms 19–22: Spanish 18th century.
Room 23: Spanish 19th century.
Rooms 32 and 34–39: Goya.

SEEING THE PRADO

The museum is in the so-called Golden Triangle of museums, which includes the nearby Reina Sofía and Thyssen-Bornemisza. The main entrance to the central Villanueva building is the Goya door at the north end, but access is also possible by the Murillo door to the south. The layout of this vast space is labyrinthine, so pick up a free floorplan as you enter. A new wing has been added and set aside for temporary exhibitions.

HIGHLIGHTS

GROUND LEVEL
***The Garden of Delights* by Hieronymus van Aeken Bosch (Room 56A)**
The Prado has an unmatched collection of work by Bosch. This is the artist's most famous work. It is divided into creation, earthly pleasures (and sins) and hell—a satirical view of the cyclical nature of humanity.

***The Adoration of the Shepherds* by El Greco (Room 61A)**
This piece is typical of El Greco's later Mannerist work, with the famously awkward hands and posture, elongated bodies and strong use of yellow and crimson. This was painted towards the end of El Greco's career and was earmarked for his own funerary chapel.

FIRST LEVEL
***Las Meninas* by Velázquez (Room 12)**
This is court painter Velázquez' best-known work, painted in 1656 under the original title of *La Familia de Felipe IV*, which refers to the court companions of the monarch's children. Although the royal Infanta Margarita is in the middle (the work was originally intended to hang in the king's private study), *Las Meninas* is full of endless interest, including plays on perception and perspective, an aristocratic self-portrait placed cheekily close to royalty, and copies of Rubens' works within the painting.

***Black Paintings* by Goya (Rooms 38 and 39)**
The *Pinturas Negras* series of 14 works was never really meant for public consumption, having been painted by Goya on to the dining-

SPAIN

Las Meninas *by Velázquez*

and sitting-room walls of his home after he moved there in 1819; it was only long after his death that they were transferred to canvas and bequeathed to the Prado. These violent and disturbing images—including *The Witches' Sabbath* and *Saturn Devouring One of his Sons*—were painted during Goya's later years when he was deaf. They underline his views on the atrocities of war and man's inhumanity to man.

SECOND LEVEL

The Clothed Maja and *The Naked Maja* by Goya (Room 89)

These two matching versions of the same subject—a reclining woman, clothed and then naked—were actually painted at different times and are among Goya's most talked-about works. The sensual nature of the paintings (the pose of the arms behind the head was a recognized sexual come-on) attracted the attention of the Inquisition.

BACKGROUND

The Prado, which means 'meadow' in Spanish, is architecturally impressive in its own right, built in a neoclassical style under architect Juan de Villanueva. Although construction started in 1785, the building has been constantly extended, most recently in 1918 and then again in the 1950s and 1960s. The current renovation schedule has proved controversial, for although the Prado has been notoriously under-resourced for decades, it is seen as a cultural benchmark for Spain in general and Madrid in particular.

SECOND LEVEL

Rooms 76–84: European 18th century.
Rooms 85–94: Goya.

🏛 385 D5 • Paseo del Prado s/n, 28014 Madrid

☎ 91 330 28 00

🕐 Tue–Sun 9–8. Last entry 30 min before closing; visitors are requested to start leaving the galleries 10 min before closing

💶 Adult €6, under 18s free. Free on Sun, 18 May, 12 Oct and 6 Dec

🚇 Banco de España, Atocha

🚌 9, 10, 14, 19, 27, 34, 37, 45

🎧 Audioguide in Rooms 1 and 51 for €3. For licensed private guides, ask at the visitor office. Free floorplan

📖 Catalogues €24, €36, €60

🍴 Self-service café-restaurant and upstairs bar

🏪 Several stands with art books, books on Spain, CD-ROMs and guides to the Prado, plus assorted souvenirs

🅿 Nearest (7 min) is Plaza de las Cortes

www.museoprado.mcu.es

Museo Thyssen-Bornemisza

One of the finest privately amassed art collections in the world, covering 800 years of Western painting and sculpture.

The Thyssen-Bornemisza collection's elegant home

The museum shop is a good place to buy art books

Inside the museum's airy galleries (top and above)

RATINGS

Good for kids	●●
Historic interest	●●●●●
Specialist shopping	●●●
Value for money	●●●●

GALLERY GUIDE

SECOND LEVEL

Rooms 1–2: Italian primitives.
Rooms 3–4: 15th-century Dutch religious paintings.
Rooms 5–9: Italian and Northern Renaissance paintings.
Room 10: 16th-century Dutch painting.
Rooms 11–15: 16th- to 17th-century Italian, Spanish/French late Renaissance and baroque.
Rooms 16–18: 18th-century Italian painting.
Rooms 19–21: 17th-century Dutch and Flemish painting.

FIRST LEVEL

Rooms 22–27: 17th-century Dutch landscapes, interiors and still life.
Room 28: 18th-century French and British schools.
Rooms 29–30: 19th-century North American painting.
Room 31: 19th-century Romanticism and Realism.
Room 32–33: Impressionism and Post-Impressionism.
Rooms 34–40: Fauve movement and Expressionism.

SEEING THE MUSEO THYSSEN-BORNEMISZA

Displayed in a building specially adapted for the purpose, the collection is arranged in chronological order to take you on a fascinating journey through the history of Western art, from the 13th to the 20th centuries. The exhibition has an overall coherence, making it less overwhelming than the Prado, and the layout and clear signing make it easy to find your way around. The tour begins on the second level, as the oldest paintings benefit most from the low ceilings and natural light, while 20th-century art is found on the ground level.

HIGHLIGHTS

THE BUILDING

The handsome 18th-century palace itself formerly belonged to the Duque de Villahermosa, after whom it is named. It was designed by Antonio López Aguado and is considered to be a fine example of the Madrid neoclassical style. The modern architect Rafael Moneo was responsible for restoring and adapting the palace to specific gallery needs in the late 1980s, and for this he won a design award from the Madrid City Council.

SECOND LEVEL

***Portrait of Giovanna Tornabuoni* by Ghirlandaio (Room 5)**
Painted in 1488 by the Florentine master Domenico Ghirlandaio (1449–94), this is the Thyssen's most famous portrait. It had become acceptable to portray secular subjects, and this is an idealized and serene profile of a young girl, elaborately dressed and wearing a magnificent gown. The text behind her back reads: 'If the artist had been able to portray the character and moral qualities there would not be a more beautiful painting in the world.'

Young Knight by Carpaccio (Room 7)

One of the earliest full-length portraits, probably painted around 1510, this languid and beautiful young man is by the Venetian artist Vittore Carpaccio (1460–1523). The plants, animals and figures that surround the central figure are allegorical.

SPAIN

Portrait of George Dyer in a Mirror *by Francis Bacon (left)*

St. Jerome in the Wilderness by Titian (Room 11)

Painted about 1575, this is a late masterpiece by the Venetian painter Titian (*c*1488–1576). It reveals his unsurpassed handling of colour, tone and light and is a superb example of his late work with its almost impressionistic brushwork.

FIRST LEVEL
Expulsion, Moon and Firelight by Thomas Cole (Room 29)

The Thyssen has one of the best collections of American painting outside the US and this huge landscape by Thomas Cole (1801–48), a member of the Hudson River school, perfectly highlights the vision of America as a virgin land shared by 19th-century painters of this movement.

Les Vessenots by Van Gogh (Room 33)

Spanish museums are not, on the whole, strong on Impressionism, but the Thyssen's superb collection goes far towards filling the gap. Vincent van Gogh (1853–90) painted this vivid picture at Auvers in the last year of his life; it displays the explosive colour and brushwork typical of his late work.

GROUND LEVEL
Man with a Clarinet by Picasso (Room 41)

This painting from Picasso's Cubist period is a parallel study with the pictures by Georges Braque and Piet Mondrian which hang on either side of it.

BACKGROUND

German financier and industrialist Baron Heinrich Thyssen-Bornemisza began collecting Old Masters in the 1920s, and by the time of his death in 1947 he had acquired more than 500. His son, Hans Heinrich (who died in 2002), shared his father's love of art and eventually diversified into modern movements, including the 20th-century avant-garde. In 1988 some 775 paintings were loaned to the Spanish government, which bought them outright five years later for the knockdown price of €350 million (their true value was estimated at closer to €1 billion). Hans Heinrich's wife, Carmen Cervera, a former Miss Spain, has offered a substantial part of her own collection of paintings to the museum.

GROUND LEVEL

Rooms 41–44: Experimental European—Cubism, Dadaism, Constructivism.
Room 45: Post-World War I European painting.
Room 46: North American 20th-century abstract Expressionism.
Rooms 47–48: 20th-century Realism, Surrealism and Pop Art.

BASICS

➕ 385 D4 • Paseo del Prado 8, 28014 Madrid ☎ 91 420 39 44
🕐 Tue–Sun 10–7
🎫 Permanent exhibition: adult €6, over 12 €4, under 12 free if accompanied by an adult. Temporary exhibitions: adult €5, over 12 €3.50. Combined permanent and temporary exhibition ticket: adult €9, over 12 €5
Ⓜ Banco de España
🚌 10, 14, 27, 34, 37, 45
🎧 Audiotours €5
📖 Guidebook €12. Floorplan free
🍽 Café serving snacks, plus daily fixed-price menu and à la carte dishes
🛍 Museum publications, art books, guides to Madrid, posters, postcards
🅿 None on site; nearest (5 min) is Plaza de las Cortes

www.museothyssen.org
Spanish and English site, which includes a virtual tour and a special section aimed at children (Spanish only).

Statue of Felipe IV before the long façade of Palacio Real

Statues line the path leading to the palace

PALACIO REAL

The 18th-century Palacio Real is an outstanding historical and architectural monument.

The Royal Palace is the official residence of the royal family. While only a fraction of the 3,000 rooms are in daily use, around 25 of the state apartments are open to the public. These are decorated with frescoes, gilded stucco, Spanish marbles and silk wall-hangings, and are crammed with priceless *objets d'art*.

The current Palacio Real stands on the site of the ninth-century Moorish Alcázar (fort), which, with some modifications, became the preferred royal palace after Felipe II moved his court to Madrid in 1561. In 1734 the palace burned down, and it was rebuilt by Italian architect Battista Sacchetti. It occupies a superb cliff-top site overlooking the Río Manzanares and the Casa de Campo (▷ 383), and the views to the Sierra de Guadarrama are stunning.

THE ROOMS

The most impressive room on the tour is the Throne Room, designed by Giovanni Battista Sacchetti and completed in 1772. The velvet wall-hangings were made in Genoa and decorated with gilded silver thread. Covering the ceiling is the allegorical masterpiece *The Apotheosis of the Spanish Monarchy*, by Giovanni Battista Tiepolo (1696–1770). The Throne Room is still in use, although the present king and queen prefer to stand during audiences.

The Gasparini Room, named after its Neapolitan designer, Matteo Gasparini, was the king's robing room. The restored silk hangings are embroidered with arabesques to match the equally spectacular ceiling, which is encrusted with stuccoed fruit and flowers. The Banqueting Hall dates from 1885. It was created for Alfonso XII by joining together three rooms from the queen's apartments. The ceiling frescoes formed part of the original design, although most of the contents were introduced later. The dining table seats up to 164 guests and can be dismantled for balls and receptions.

PALACE PRECINCTS

The Royal Armoury (reached from the courtyard) has one of the finest collections of arms and armour in Europe. Opposite is the Royal Pharmacy, most of whose exhibits date from the reign of Carlos IV.

RATINGS
Good for kids	● ● ●
Historic interest	● ● ● ●
Value for money	● ● ●

BASICS

✚ 384 B4 • Calle de Bailén, 28071 Madrid ☎ 91 542 00 59 ◉ Apr–end Sep Mon–Sat 9–6, Sun 9–3; Oct–end Mar Mon–Sat 9.30–5, Sun 9–2
💶 Adult €10, child (5–16) €6, under 5 free ◎ Opera 🚌 3, 25, 39, 148
🎧 Guided tour €9, departs every 10 min in groups of about 30. Audioguide in variety of languages €2.30
📘 Official guidebook ☕ Café-bar
🎁 Gift shop on ground floor 🚻

www.patrimonionacional.es
General site with useful background information.

TIPS

● The palace frequently closes for state visits and other formal occasions. Check at the visitor information office.
● The Changing of the Guard ceremony takes place in the Plaza de Armas at noon on the first Wed of the month, Feb–May and Sep–Dec.
● The entrance and ticket office are on Plaza de Armas. Free access to the shop, café and toilets is by ticket, collected from the entrance.

WHAT TO DO

⊕ AGATHA RUIZ DE LA PRADA

Serrano 27, 28010
Tel 91 319 05 01
www.agatharuizdelaprada.com
This Spanish designer has built her name on original and bold clothing. The ladies' collection includes some incredible dresses, and the men's collection is just as impressive. There are also shoes, jewellery, children's clothes and toys, plus towels, feather quilts, chairs, tables and crockery for the home. The prices won't break the bank either.
⊙ Mon–Sat 10–2, 5–8 ⊠ Serrano
⊟ 5, 7, 14, 27, 45, 150

⊕ CASA MIRA

Carrera de San Jerónimo 30, 28013
Tel 91 429 88 95
Luis Mira opened this sweet shop in 1842, and the family still prepares home-made, all-natural *turrón* (nougat). The confectioners certainly know a thing or two about creating delicious marzipan, ice cream and flaky biscuits (cookies).
⊙ Mon–Sat 9.30–2, 5–9, Sun 10.30–2.30, 5.30–9 ⊠ Savilla ⊟ 3, 5, 9

⊕ EL FLAMENCO VIVE

Calle Conde de Lemos 7, 28013
Tel 91 547 39 17
www.elflamencovive.com
One of the best flamenco stores in Madrid. New releases are stocked alongside old songs, books, biographies, collectors' items, sheet music and even some instruments such as the traditional flamenco guitar.
⊙ Mon–Sat 10.30–2, 5–9 ⊠ Ópera
⊟ 3, 50

⊕ PIAMONTE

Piamonte 16, 28004
Tel 913 522 45 80
You will find an enormous selection of handbags here for every occasion: party bags, or something sophisticated, innovative or classically stylish.

You can also choose from hats, shawls and costume jewellery. The designers featured are Isabel Marant, Helena Rhoner, Giorgio Armani, Paco Rabanne and María Calderara.
⊙ Mon–Fri 10.30–2, 5–8.30, Sat 11–2.30, 5.30–8.30 ⊠ Chueca ⊟ 5, 14, 27, 37, 45, 53, 150

⊕ EL RASTRO

Plaza de Cascorro, 28005
Tel 91 540 40 10
One of the capital's most intriguing street markets. Antiques, hand-made clothes and jeans line Calle Ribera de Curtidores, and Plaza del General Vara del Rey is the place to go for second-hand clothes, leather and furniture. Get there early to avoid the crowds and watch your bag carefully. The area is good for bars and tapas.
⊙ Sun and public holidays 9–3
⊠ Tirso de Molina ⊟ 17, 18, 23, 35

⊕ CASA PATAS

Calle de Cañizares 10, 28012
Tel 91 369 04 96
www.casapatas.com
Casa Patas, one of the better places for live flamenco shows, features both established stars and up-and-coming artists. It is both a performance venue and a restaurant.
⊙ Tue–Thu 1–4.30, 8–midnight; Fri–Sat 1–4.30, 7.30–1 ⊞ €20
⊠ Antón Martín ⊟ 6, 26, 32, 50

⊕ SEGUNDO JAZZ

Calle del Comandante Zorita 8, 28020
Tel 91 554 94 37
This bar draws its loyal regulars from Madrid's jazz-lovers. There are live shows and during weekends other genres of music are performed. The atmosphere is very relaxed and the discerning crowd is mostly aged 30 or older. It's a great place for a civilized evening.
⊙ Daily 7pm–4am ⊞ €4–€8
⊠ Nuevos Ministerios, Cuatro Caminos
⊟ 68, 69, 149

⊕ TEATRO REAL

Plaza Isabella II, 28013
Tel 91 516 06 60 or 902 24 48 48 (advance sales)
www.teatro-real.com
Madrid's opera house presents all operatic styles and offers a first-class schedule, including a number of ballet

productions. It also has a nouvelle cuisine restaurant, open for dinner.
⊞ Ballet from €7. Opera from €13
⊠ ⊠ Ópera ⊟ 25, 39

⊕ GOLDFIELD

Calle Ventura Rodríguez 7, 28008
Tel 915 541 59 37
Goldfield is a fashionable nightclub. You'll see plenty of famous faces bopping with Madrid's trendy young things. Themed parties are often held here.
⊙ Fri–Sat 12.30am–7am ⊞ €9–€12
⊠ Plaza de España ⊟ 1, 2, 44, 66, 74

⊕ PACHA

Calle Barceló 11, 28004
Tel. 914 470 128
www.pacha-madrid.com
The world-renowned club Pacha goes from strength to strength. Dress to impress the picky bouncers or pick up a flyer from the city's bars for a smoother entry. The younger generation (ages 14 and up) can party on Friday and Saturdays from 6pm–11pm before the club reopens for the adult ravers.
⊙ Thu–Sat 11.30pm–6am ⊞ €15, including two drinks ⊠ Tribunal, Alonso Martínez ⊟ 3, 10, 21, 35, 149

⊕ PLAZA DE TOROS DE LAS VENTAS

Calle de Alcalá 237, 28028
Tel 913 56 22 00
www.las-ventas.com
One of the most important bullrings in Spain. The major season begins during the San Isidro Festival in May and bullfighting is held daily thereafter. Guided tours are available.
⊙ Bullfights: Sun and holidays around 5pm; May–end Sep during festivals daily at 7pm ⊞ From €3.60 ⊠ Ventas
⊟ 12, 21, 38, 53, 106, 110, 146

⊕ TELEFÉRICO

Paseo del Pintor Rosales s/n, 28008
Tel 91 541 74 50
www.teleferico.com
Take a ride in a cable-car for magnificent views over Madrid. The ride ends in Casa de Campo park.
⊙ Apr–end Sep Mon–Fri 12–9, Sat–Sun 12–9.30; Oct–end Mar Sat–Sun 12–6.30 ⊞ Adult one-way €3.35, round-trip €4.80; child one-way €3.10
⊠ Argüelles ⊟ 21, 74

CAFÉ COMERCIAL
Glorieta de Bilbao 7, 28004
Tel 91 521 56 55
This is one of the city's oldest cafés. It has a long bar and a large, airy (apart from the smoke) space to drink coffee, have a slice of cake and relax.
🕙 Mon–Thu 7.30am–1am, Fri–Sat 7.30am–2am, Sun 10am–1am
🍽 Coffee and cake €3.50
🚇 Bilbao

CAFÉ GIJÓN
Paseo de Recoletos 21, 28004
Tel 91 521 54 25
Established in 1881, this café has been a social hub for artists and intellectuals throughout its existence. The menu represents Spain's many regions with grilled meats and fish such as hake or cod. The wine list is sizeable.
🕙 Mon–Fri, Sun 7.30am–1.30am, Sat 8am–2.30am
🍽 L €33, D €45, Wine €8
🚇 Colón
🚌 5, 14, 27, 37, 45, 53, 150

CASA CAROLA
Calle de Padilla 54, 28007
Tel 91 401 94 08
www.casacarola.com
At this traditional Spanish restaurant *cocido madrileño* (soup with noodles, chick peas, meat and vegetables) is served only at lunchtime, as is the local custom.
🕙 Daily 1–4, 9–11.30. Closed Aug
🍽 L €23, D €28, Wine €7.50
🚇 Núñez de Balboa 🚌 1, 29, 52, 74

LA CASTAFIORE
Calle Marqués de Monasterio 5, 28004
Tel 91 319 42 21
La Castafiore is a special place where the waiters serenade you while you dine. The food is enticing.
🕙 Mon–Sat 2–4.30, 9.30–1
🍽 L €10, D €40, Wine €10 🚇 Colón
🚌 1, 2, 5, 20, 37, 51, 52, 53, 74, 146

CASTELLANA 179
Paseo de la Castellana 179, 28046
Tel 91 425 06 80
www.castellana179.com
This is a sophisticated restaurant in Chamartín serving satisfying Spanish dishes and home-made desserts.
🕙 Mon–Sat 2–4.30, 9–12.30
🍽 L €50, D €60, Wine €15
🚇 Plaza Castilla 🚌 5, 27, 147, 149

CHOCOLATERÍA SAN GINÉS
Pasadizo San Gines 5, 28013
Tel 91 365 65 46
A classic spot for an early breakfast after a night out. As 6am approaches, the café fills up, as this is when many of the city's nightclubs close. *Churros* (fritters) and *porras* (a larger version of the same) come in generous portions. Hot chocolate, coffee and assorted refreshments are also available. Credit cards are not accepted.
🕙 Daily 6pm–7am
🍽 Hot chocolate and *churros* €3.50
🚇 Sol
🚌 3, 50

JOCKEY
Calle Amador de los Ríos 6, 28010
Tel 91 319 24 35
www.restaurantejockey.net
This restaurant is one of Madrid's finest. It has won many awards over the years, and a number of famous people have dined here. The elegant interior is dotted with equestrian objects. The menu features traditional dishes with an exotic touch. Reserving a table is advisable.
🕙 Mon–Sat 1.30–4.30, 9–12. Closed Sun, holidays and Aug
🍽 L €90, D €110, Wine €12
🚇 Colón
🚌 5, 14, 27, 45, 150

O'PAZO
Calle Reina Mercedes 20, 28020
Tel 915 53 23 33
O'Pazo is a top choice if you fancy fresh fish or seafood. Meat doesn't feature on the menu, except for a delicious Iberian ham starter.
🕙 Mon–Sat 1–4, 8.30–12
🍽 L €40, D €70, Wine €9
🚇 Santiago Bernabéu
🚌 5, 43, 149

PRADA A TOPE
Calle Principe 11, 28012
Tel 91 429 59 21
www.pradaatope.es
Rustic and comfortable, the cuisine here originates in León, known for its smoked beef, and this restaurant does it proud.
🕙 Tue–Sun 1–4, 9–12
🍽 L €20, D €28, Wine €12
🚇 Sevilla, Sol
🚌 3, 33, 49, 51

SALVADOR
Calle de Barbieri 12, 28004
Tel 91 521 45 24
This welcoming, comfortable restaurant is far off the tourist trail. It has an excellent selection of typically straightforward Castilian fare, including *rabo de toro* (oxtail) and *solomillo* (sirloin steak) with very salty fries. Try to get a table upstairs, where the dining is more secluded.
🕙 Mon–Sat 1.30–4, 9–11.30. Closed Aug
🍽 L €30, D €50, Wine €9
🚇 Chueca

TRES ENCINAS
Preciados 33, 28013
Tel 91 521 22 07
www.tresencinas.com
This restaurant has other branches in Madrid. Seafood is the order of the day, although there are good meat dishes served here, too. There is valet parking, and you can take your order away with you.
🕙 Daily 1.30–4, 7.30–12
🍽 L €40, D €70, Wine €10
🚇 Callao
🚌 44, 75, 133, 146, 147

LA VACA VERÓNICA
Calle de Moratín 38, 28014
Tel 91 429 78 27
A charming, romantic restaurant, not far from the Prado. Fresh pasta with crayfish and filet Veronica are the house specials. Reserving a table is advisable.
🕙 Sun–Fri 2–4, 9–12, Sat 9–12
🍽 L €30, D €45, Wine €10
🚇 Antón Martín
🚌 6, 10, 14, 26, 27, 32, 34, 37, 45

ASTURIAS
Calle de Sevilla 2, 28014 Madrid
Tel 91 429 66 76
www.chh.es
This hotel is conveniently central, close to Puerta del Sol and not far from Huertas and its many bars and restaurants. The rooms are well turned out: simple, classic and with private bathrooms, safety deposit boxes and satellite TV. There's also a bar, TV lounge and restaurant specializing in traditional Spanish dishes.
🍽 €110–€120
🛏 175 🔲

SPAIN

Ⓜ Sevilla

🚌 5, 15, 20, 51, 52, 53, 150

CROWNE PLAZA MADRID CITY CENTRE

Plaza de España s/n, 28013 Madrid
Tel 91 454 85 00
www.madridcitycentre.crowneplaza.com

A grand building in the heart of Madrid, next to the Gran Vía and providing fine views of the Palacio Real. The interior is elegant. Rooms have safety deposit boxes, interactive TV, internet access and hairdryer. There is 24-hour room service. The hotel's services include money exchange, laundry, sauna and a full-service business centre.

💶 €145–€405, excluding buffet breakfast (€19)

🛏 306 (86 non-smoking) ⬛ 📺 🅿

Ⓜ Plaza de España

🚌 1, 2, 44, 68, 69, 74, 133

INGLÉS

Calle de Echegaray 8, 28014 Madrid
Tel 91 429 65 51

This 2-star hotel dates from as far back as 1853, and is conveniently close to Madrid's Art Triangle (the Prado, Thyssen-Bornemisza and Reina Sofía) and lively Calle de las Huertas. The area can be quite noisy at night, especially if your room looks out onto the main street. Guest rooms are comfortable and fitted with satellite TV and direct telephone lines.

💶 €80–€100, excluding breakfast (€5)

🛏 58 ⬛ 📺 🅿 €12

Ⓜ Antón Martín, Sevilla, Sol

🚌 6, 26, 32, 57

MEDIODÍA

Plaza Emperador Carlos V 8, 28012 Madrid
Tel 91 527 30 60
www.mediodiahotel.com

This is a 2-star hotel opposite the Atocha train station, close to the Reina Sofía and Prado museums and just a stroll away from Parque del Retiro. It's good value for money, is well connected by public transport, and there's a range of tapas bars and restaurants on the square.

💶 €69, excluding breakfast (€2.10)

🛏 173 ⬛

Ⓜ Atocha

🚌 6, 19, 27, 34, 59, 68, 69, 141

OPERA

Cuesta de Santo Domingo 2, 28013 Madrid
Tel 91 541 28 00
www.hotelopera.com

The Opera is about as central as it gets. Rooms include a minibar, safe deposit boxes, internet access and hairdryer, and the hotel also has a bar, a cafeteria (serving fixed-price menus), a laundry service and business facilities. Spanish and international dishes are served at the Café de la Ópera; the restaurant's waiters (professional singers) perform for guests as they serve.

💶 €120–€132, excluding breakfast (€9)

🛏 79 (30 non-smoking) ⬛ 🅿

Ⓜ Ópera

🚌 25, 39

PARÍS

Calle de Alcalá 2, 28014 Madrid
Tel 91 521 64 96

Close to Puerta del Sol, this charming, old-fashioned hotel is set among plenty of restaurants, bars, shops and theatres. It's an old convent, and was first opened as a hotel in 1872 making it one of Madrid's oldest. The interior is decorated in simple, classic style. The rooms are spacious and airy with private bathrooms, TV and safe deposit boxes.

💶 €90 including tax, excluding breakfast

🛏 120 ⬛

Ⓜ Puerta del Sol

🚌 3, 5, 15, 20, 51, 52, 53, 150

RITZ

Plaza de la Lealtad, 28014 Madrid
Tel 91 701 67 67
www.ritzmadrid.com

The Ritz is one of the most beautiful and emblematic of Madrid's hotels. It has played host to royalty and countless aristocrats, writers and musicians. The bold décor features old tapestries, elegant chandeliers, marble bathrooms, exquisitely embroidered linen sheets and a wealth of antiques. The hotel benefits from a garden terrace, and the restaurant serves traditional Spanish cuisine on its daily menu.

💶 €220–€525, excluding breakfast (€25)

🛏 167 (two floors with non-smoking rooms) ⬛ 📺 🅿

🚌 10, 14, 27, 34, 37, 45

TRAFALGAR

Calle Trafalgar 35, 28010 Madrid
Tel 91 445 62 00
www.hotel-trafalgar.com

Trafalgar is a 3-star hotel not far from lively Calle de Fuencarral and its cinemas and shops, and convenient for peaceful Plaza de Olavide. All in all, this a good option for those watching their euros but still keen to stay somewhere pleasant. The building is modern and the rooms comfortable, with TV, direct-dial phone, safety deposit box, private bathroom and hairdryer. Other features include a coffee bar, money exchange, laundry, meeting rooms and a restaurant serving Spanish dishes.

💶 €90–€122

🛏 48 (non-smoking upon request) ⬛

Ⓜ Quevedo, Iglesia, Bilbao, Canal

🚌 3, 16, 37, 61, 149

WELLINGTON

Calle de Velázquez 8, 28001 Madrid
Tel 91 575 44 00
www.hotel-wellington.com

This luxury hotel is in a handsome building with a neoclassical interior and attractive wall hangings. Amenities include a laundry service, 24-hour room service, a hairdresser, internet access and meeting rooms. The elegant guest rooms have a safety deposit box, minibar and satellite TV. The Goizeko Wellington restaurant specializes in Basque cuisine.

💶 €290–€500, excluding breakfast (€18)

🛏 261 (53 non-smoking) ⬛

🏊 Outdoor 🅿

Ⓜ Velázquez, Retiro

🚌 1, 9, 19, 51, 74

Shopping around the lively Plaça Major (above). Decorated glazed tile plate on display in Palma Museum (left)

La Seu, Palma's cathedral (right)

PALMA DE MALLORCA

The stylish and sophisticated capital of the Balearics, with lively streetlife and a thriving cultural scene.

Millions of people pass through Palma each year in their rush for the beaches, yet few bother to stop off in the city. For those who take the time to linger, Palma is something of a surprise. This confident city has great restaurants, buzzing cafés and a thriving modern arts scene. It is the only place in the Balearics with that big city feel, yet it has hidden corners that have changed little in centuries, where Renaissance mansions and patios shelter behind wooden doors.

The city was founded by the Romans in 123BC, who named it Palmaria after the palm trees they found growing here. During the period of Arab rule in Mallorca (AD902–1229), it was known as Medina Mayurqa and was one of the most advanced cities in Europe, with streetlights, covered sewers and heated baths. After the Catalán conquest of 1229 a cathedral was built on the site of the main mosque and the Arab governor's fortress became a royal palace.

THE SIGHTS

Palma sits in the middle of a broad, sheltered bay. A long promenade leads along the waterfront, passing the fishing port, yacht club, restaurants and bars. Viewed from the water, the city is dwarfed by its cathedral, La Seu (Apr–end Oct Mon–Fri 10–6, Sat 10–2; Nov–end Mar Mon–Fri 10–3, Sat 10–2), a triumph of Gothic architecture whose flying buttresses and sandstone walls seem to rise out of the old city walls. Look out for the Portal del Mirador on the south front facing the sea. Some of the best views of La Seu are from the Parc de la Mar, whose artificial lake was designed to catch the cathedral's reflection. To one side of La Seu is the Palau de l'Almudaina (Mon–Fri 10–2, 4–6, Sat 10–2), former residence of the Mallorcan kings; to the other a warren of narrow streets leading into the oldest part of town. Here you will find the Museu de Mallorca (Tue–Sat 10–7, Sun 10–2), with archaeological displays, and the 10th-century Baños Àrabes (Arab Baths; Apr–end Nov daily 9.30–8; Dec–end Mar daily 9.30–7).

Don't miss At Fundació La Caixa (Tue–Sat 10–9, Sun and festivals 10–2), around Plaça Major, shops sell pottery, carved olive wood, Mallorcan sausages, cheese and wine.

SPAIN

PALMA

0 100 m
0 100 yds

AVINGUDA ALEMANYA

Institut Ramón Llull

AVINGUDA DE PORTUGAL

VIA

Carrer Bernat Amer

Plaça Fort

Carrer Coethe

Carrer Elvissa

Carrer Obrador

PASSEIG MALLORCA

Carrer Ruben Dario

Carrer Joaquin Borto

Carrer Santiago

CARRER RAMON I CAJAL

ARGENTINA

Carrer Alos

Carrer Rodriguez de Arias

Carrer Cima

Carrer Menorca

Carrer Mateu Elvissa

Carrer Ruiz de Aida

Passeig Mallorca

Carrer Cerdanya

Carrer Bisbe Campin

AVINGUDA COMTE DE BARCELONA

CARRER INDUSTRIA

Carrer Fray Luis de Leon

MALLORCA

Carrer Menorca

Carrer Conflent

Carrer Omelades

Carrer Carlades

Bonaire

Carrer Esparteres

Carrer Misericordia

Hospital General

Capella de la Sang

Plaça Hospital

Plaça San Magdaler

Carrer Pietat

Carrer Murillo

Carrer Pou

SANTA CATALINA

CARRER CATALUNYA

PASSEIG

Torrent de sa Riera

Passeig Mallorca

Carrer Pere de Fraga

PUIG DE SANT PÉRE

Carrer Aragones

Carrer Joan de Cremona

La Concepció

Concepció

Carrer Catany

Plaça Cavalleria

Carrer Ermita

Sant Ja

CARRER CARO

CARRER TEODOR LLORENT

ARGENTINA

Carrer Fabrica

AVINGUDA JAUME III

Carrer S Marti

Carrer Montcades

AVINGUDA JAUME III

Carrer Pursiana

Carrer Annibal

Plaça la Feixina

Carrer Berenguer de Tornamira

Carrer Protectora

Carrer P

Carrer Can Bordoi

Can Solleric

PASSEIG DES BORN

Carrer Sant Caleta

AVINGUDA

Jardins de la Faixina

Plaça Porta de Santa Catalina

Can Sales

Carrer Polvora

Carrer Santa

Creu

Vi Pau

Carrer Sant

Can Belloto

Carrer Jovelianos

Museu Es Baluard

Santa Creu

Carrer F de l'oliviera

Carrer Sant Llorenc

Chacon

Palau Montenegro

Carrer Caceres

Carrer Montenegro

Carrer Feliu

Paralires

Carrer Const.

Fundació Joan Miró, Castell de Bellver

Carrer Sant Pere

Carrer F de l Gloria

Carrer Estanc

Carrer F. Bauza

Of de Cor

AVINGUDA GABRIEL ROCA (PASSEIG MARITIM)

Plaça Drassanes

Apuntadors

Plaça de la Reina

Palau March

Club Nautic

Carrer Contramoll

Consolat de la Mar

Carrer J Ferrer

Carrer L de Mar

Carrer Vallseca

Carrer S Joan

AVINGUDA D'ANTONI MAURA

Palau de l'Almudaina

Passeig de Sagrera

La Llotja

Plaça Llotja

AVINGUDA GABRIEL ROCA

S'Hort del Rei

Ramón Llull

Port de Pescadors

Barcelona
Ibiza
Menorca
València

Porta Vella del Moll

Escullera

Carrer

AUTOPISTA DE LLEVANT

Parc la M

SPAIN

A   B   C

SPAIN

⊕ Shopping
🅰 Entertainment
🆅 Nightlife
⊛ Sports
✪ Activities
♡ Health and Beauty
⊗ For Children

WHAT TO DO

⊕ LA CASA DEL OLIVO

Carrer Peseataria Vella 4
Tel 971 72 70 25
Olive trees line Mallorca's countryside, and their richly textured, honey-toned wood is prized for decorative use. This shop sells handcarved bowls, dishes and other pieces. The prices aren't low, but the craftsmanship is high.
🅒 Mon–Fri 10–1.30, 5–8, Sat 10–1.30. Closed Jul, Aug 🚍 2

⊕ HERREROS DE VICENTE JUAN RIBAS

Carrer Sant Nicolau 10
Tel 971 72 17 73
Roba de llengues (tongue cloth) is used in everything from tablecloths and curtains to furniture upholstery. This shop is generally considered to be one of the best places to buy the textiles and prices reflect the high level of workmanship.
🅒 Mon–Fri 10–1.30, 4.30–8, Sat 10–1
🚍 Many buses, including lines 3, 7, 5, stop in nearby Plaça Rei Joan Carles I

🅰 AUDITORIUM

Passeig Marítim 18
Tel 971 73 47 35
www.auditorium-pm.com
The Auditorium is a conference centre and performance hall for events such as theatre, opera and orchestral concerts. There's also a cafeteria/bar.
🎫 €18–€50 🚍 EMT; follow directions to Eivissa; the nightclub is halfway along, near San Rafael

🆅 GARITO CAFÉ

Dársena de can Barbarà
Tel 971 73 69 12
www.garitocafe.com
Garito is one of the most fashionable bars in Palma. DJ Nacho Velasco plays jazzy deep house to pre-club drinkers at the end of the week, but you'll hear an eclectic selection of music, from drum 'n' bass to soul and funk, on other nights.
🅒 Daily 7pm–late

EATING

LA BOVEDA

Carrer Boteria 3
Tel 971 71 48 63
This tavern-style tapas bar serves traditional Mallorcan fare such as brown bread with oil, and local olives and sausages. The restaurant has a sister branch nearby called La Taberna de la Boveda.
🅒 Mon–Sat 1.30–4, 8.30–12
🍽 L €35, D €60, Wine €7

PARLAMENT

Carrer Conquistador 11
Tel 971 72 60 26
www.restaurantparlament.com
This old-fashioned, elegant establishment is very busy at lunchtime. Famous for its squid (cooked in its own ink) and *paella ciega* (with no bones), it serves mainly fish and rice dishes, and also has a variety of meats.
🅒 Daily 1–4, 8–11. Closed Aug
🍽 L €30, D €45, Wine €10

RESTAURANTE KOLDO ROYO

Paseo Marítimo 3
Tel 971 73 24 35
www.koldoroyo.com
Koldo Royo has chic surroundings and innovative modern cuisine based on Basque classics.
🅒 Tue–Sat 1.30–3.30, 8–11
🍽 L €60, D €87, Wine €10

RESTAURANTE EL PILÓN

Carrer C'an Cifre 4
Tel 971 71 75 90
This tiny restaurant specializes in local seafood platters.
🅒 Mon–Sat 11–4, 6–12
🍽 L €54, D €70, Wine €7

STAYING

ARMADANS

Marqués de la Cenia, 34,
07014 Palma de Mallorca
Tel 971 22 15 54
www.hotelarmadans.com
One block away from the seafront, the Armadans is marginally cheaper than the other high-rise hotels on the Passeig. It makes up for the lack of sea views by being moderately stylish, for a large hotel. All rooms have private bathroom, television, internet connection, safe and minibar. Breakfast is an expansive buffet in an enormous dining room. The Armadans' clientele tends to be business-orientated, but the hotel is conveniently located for sight-seeing.
🅒 All year
🛏 Double from €80
ℹ 73
🔳 🍽 🛗

GRAN MELIÀ VICTORIA

Avinguda Joan Miró 21,
07014 Palma de Mallorca
Tel 971 73 25 42
www.granmeliavictoria.solmelia.com
The Gran Melià chain is well known for offering quality service. All rooms have a minibar and safe. This branch is just in front of the sea, near the heart of Palma. The guest rooms are plush, though not large, and the bathrooms are new and clean. The restaurant serves food all day. The snack bars are best for drinks and light fare.
🛏 €170–€285
ℹ 171 (24 on one floor for non-smokers) 🛗
🔳 Outdoor and indoor 🍽

PALAU SA FONT

Carrer del Apuntadors, 38,
07012 Palma de Mallorca
Tel 971 71 22 77
www.palausafont.com
A 16th-century palace on the outside, Palau Sa Font is a hip confection of funky colours, modern furniture and distressed ironwork on the inside. Best of all, the youthful guests find it perfectly placed for bar crawls in La Llotja. All the rooms have telephone, televison and central heating. Breakfast, like the decor, is slightly more imaginative than the standard hotel buffet, with tortilla, Serrano ham and smoked salmon. Don't miss the exciting views across Palma from the tower.
🅒 All year
🛏 Double room from €140
ℹ 19
🛗

SPAIN

Seville

**Seville hosts Spain's most exuberant fiestas and has
a fascinating multicultural history.
It is the best place to see flamenco and bullfighting.**

*Tiling on Casa de Piletus (top).
Tour of the bullring (above)*

*Tiled balustrade decorating
footbridge in Plaza de España*

*Seville's cathedral was built on
the site of the Moorish mosque*

SEEING SEVILLE

Because the city's main attractions lie close together and its
network of streets is particularly alluring, walking in Sevilla
(Seville in English) is both sensible and a pleasure. But to see
the city's true character you should visit when its residents are
celebrating, perhaps during the processions of *Semana Santa*
(Holy Week—Palm Sunday to Easter Sunday) or the debauchery
of the *Feria de Abril*, immediately afterwards.

HIGHLIGHTS

ALCÁZAR (REALES ALCÁZARES)

⊕ 402 B2 • Plaza del Triunfo s/n ☎ 95 422 71 63 ◉ Apr–end Sep Tue–Sat
9.30–8, Sun 9.30–7; Oct–end Mar Tue–Sat 9.30–5, Sun 9.30–2.30 💷 €7
Although nominally a fortress dating back to the 10th century, the
highlight here is the Palacio de Don Pedro. Built in the 14th century
by Pedro the Cruel, this spectacular Mudéjar palace is still used by
the Spanish royal family when visiting and for royal wedding feasts.
It is reminiscent of Granada's Alhambra (▷ 378), thanks to its
combination of water, gardens and Islamic detail, including Mudéjar
plasterwork, arches and tiling throughout. Look for the Patio de las
Doncellas (Court of the Maidens), Camara Regia (Royal Chamber),
Patio del Yeso (Gypsum Court) and Salón de Embajadores (Hall of
Ambassadors), the last topped by a dome representing the universe.
There are also lovely gardens that make a good retreat from the busy
city, especially in summer.

BARRIO DE SANTA CRUZ

⊕ 402 B2
This area near the Alcázar was once the city's Jewish quarter. Little
of this period of its history remains, although one of its former
synagogues still stands in the form of the Iglesia de Santa María la
Blanca. Inside the church is *The Last Supper* (1640) by Bartolomé
Murillo (1617–82), who lived in Barrio de Santa Cruz. You could spend
an afternoon just wandering around the *barrio*'s alleyways among the
orange trees, looking at the wrought ironwork and the whitewashed
houses, and stopping for coffee at one of the many cafés or shops.

RATINGS	
Good for kids	●●●○
Historic interest	●●●●●
Photo stops	●●●●○
Shopping	●●●●●

BASICS

⊕ 4 B5
🛈 Visitor information office:
Paseo de la Delicias 9, 41013 Sevilla;
tel 95 423 44 65
🛈 There are also tourist offices at
Oficio Laredo, Plaza de San Francisco
19 and Naves del Barranco, Calle
Arjona 28

www.turismo.sevilla.org

TIPS

● Seville is allegedly the
birthplace of tapas; its bars
have a bewildering choice.
● Avoid the city during July
and August, when it becomes
swelteringly hot.
● Look after your valuables:
Seville has one of the worst
reputations for petty thievery
in Spain.

SPAIN

MORE TO SEE

ARCHIVO DE INDIAS

✚ 402 B2 • Avenida de la Constitución
3 ☎ 95 421 12 34 ◷ Mon–Sat 10–4
🖐 Free

A fabulous collection of maps and documents dating back to 1492, including correspondence between Isabel and Columbus. Changing displays.

CASA DE PILATOS

✚ 402 B1 • Plaza Pilatos 1 ☎ 95 422 52 98 ◷ Mar–end Sep daily 9–7; rest of year daily 9–6 💶 Museum: €8. Patio and gardens: €5 ❓ First level: guided tour only

This 16th-century palace belonging to the Dukes of Medinaceli (the current duke still lives in part of it) is a surprisingly successful mixture of Mudéjar (ceilings and tiles), plateresque (portal), Moorish (arches) and Gothic (balustrade) elements. It was built by the first Marquis of Tarifa, who styled it on the House of Pontius Pilate in Jerusalem. In the main courtyard are three Roman statues dating from the fifth century BC and a fountain imported from Genoa. Around the rooms is a collection of paintings, including works by Italian artist Sebastiano del Piombo (1485–1547) and by Francisco de Goya (1746–1828). As the palace is unusual and slightly off the main tourist trail, it is less hectic than other sights.

Boarding a plane at Seville's airport

The striking monument to Christopher Columbus

Horse and cart in the Parque de María Luisa

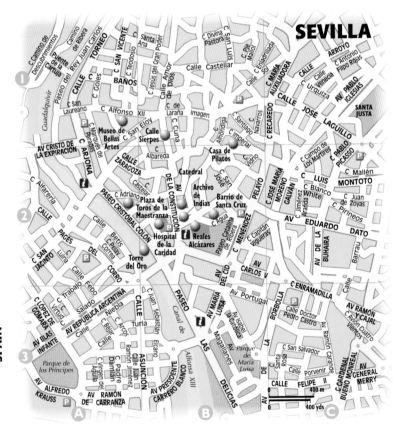

CATEDRAL

✚ 402 B2 • Plaza Virgen de los Reyes, Avenida de la Constitución ☎ 95 421 49 71 🕐 Mon–Sat 11–5, Sun, festivals 2.30–6 💶 €7 (also entry to La Giralda), free on Sun

Depending on the criteria you use, this is the largest church in the world. Built on the site of a 12th-century mosque between 1401 and 1507, the Gothic cathedral claims among many other things to contain the remains of Christopher Columbus (c1451–1506). The overpowering sensation inside the cathedral is of its vastness—it has five naves and equally enormous side chapels, all built simply but impressively. There is plenty to see here, including the 15th-century stained-glass windows, elaborate 15th-century choir stalls, and works by Goya, Murillo and Zurbarán in the treasury. The most imposing part of the cathedral is the Capilla Mayor, which contains an enormous Gothic retablo (altarpiece) with 45 scenes from the life of Christ,

CALLE SIERPES

✚ 402 B1

The best street for one-stop Spanish shopping, whatever you want, with plenty of cafés where you can take a break.

HOSPITAL DE LA CARIDAD

✚ 402 B2 • Calle Temprado 3 ☎ 95 422 32 32 🕐 Mon–Sat 9–1.30, 3.30–7.30, Sun and festivals 9–1 💶 €3

This hospital has been caring for the poor and sick since the 17th century. It contains works by

Dining along the riverside on Calle Betis

Statue on a patio at Casa de Pilatos

Exquisite tiling in Plaza de España

probably the finest altarpiece in the world. Next door, and accessible from the cathedral, is the famous Giralda. This 12th-century minaret is all that remains of the original mosque on which the cathedral stands, and can be climbed via a series of ramps for views over Seville.

PLAZA DE TOROS DE LA MAESTRANZA

✚ 402 A2 • Paseo Cristóbal Colón 22 ☎ 95 421 03 15 🕐 Daily 9.30–7; on bullfight and concert days 9.30–3. Bullfights: mostly Sun, Apr–end Sep

This historic bullring is possibly Spain's most attractive and certainly its most venerable, at almost 250 years old. Bullfighting is central to life in Seville and Andalucía and a visit here, even if not to an actual *corrida* (bullfight), gives some idea of its role. A small bullfighting museum has displays of matador costumes and *corrida*-related art.

BACKGROUND

Seville was an important port city under the Romans (when it was called Hispalis) and a cultural focus when ruled by the Visigoths. During Muslim rule (when it was called Ishbiliya), it was a powerful state that, at its height in the 11th century, stretched from Murcia to Portugal. The city returned to Christian hands after a two-year siege in 1248, when Fernando III of Castile resettled around 25,000 Castilians in the city to create a genuinely tri-cultural mix of Christians, Jews and Muslims.

Seville became Spain's most important city in 1503, when it won a monopoly on Spanish trade with the Americas. Its population tripled and it played an important part in Spain's Golden Age as home to such artists as Zurbarán and Murillo. Plague halved the population in 1649, and as the Río Guadalquivir silted up, the city's fortunes suffered. Mid-19th-century industrialization and the establishment of an exotic stereotype—compiled of images of *Carmen*, bullfighting and gypsies—attracted visitors and helped Seville regain some of its former glory. This was further aided by its first great international fair, the Exposición Iberoamericana, in 1929. The huge Expo World's Fair of 1992 also helped, although the city still faces many problems, not least unemployment.

Bartolomé Murillo (1618–82) and Juan de Valdés-Leal (1622–90), plus courtyards and a baroque chapel.

MUSEO DE BELLAS ARTES

✚ 402 A1 • Plaza del Museo 9 ☎ 95 486 482 🕐 Tue 2.30–8.30, Wed–Sat 9–8.30, Sun 9–2.30 💶 €1.50, EU citizens free

The former Convento de la Merced is now one of the country's most important art museums, with a particular bias towards the Seville school of artists. There are works by El Greco and Zurbarán, but of particular note are the religious paintings of local artist Bartolomé Murillo and the unsettling canvases by Juan de Valdés-Leal. The early 17th-century building itself has three pleasant patios decorated with flowers and *azulejos* (ceramic tiles).

TORRE DEL ORO

✚ 402 B2 • Paseo de Cristóbal Colón s/n ☎ 95 422 24 19 🕐 Tue–Fri 10–2, Sat, Sun 11–2 💶 €1, free on Tue

A defensive lookout since the early 13th century, the 12-sided Tower of Gold was once covered in ornamental tiles. It is now a maritime museum focusing on the port's long history.

WHAT TO DO

⊕ EL CORTE INGLÉS

Plaza del Duque de la Victoria 8
Tel 95 597 000
www.elcorteingles.es
This is the largest of four central city branches of Spain's most prestigious department store chain. There is a cafeteria and good-quality restaurant on the top floor. You'll find a gourmet food shop and an extensive wine cellar located on the ground level.
🅒 Mon–Sat 10–10 🚌 13, 14

🎭 TEATRO DE LA MAESTRANZA

Paseo de Cristóbal Cólon 22
Tel 95 422 65 73
www.teatromaestranza.com
This theatre is a modern and spacious venue with excellent acoustics that complement some of the most prestigious operas in the world. There is also a café and bar.
🎫 From €6 up to €85 🅢 🚌 C4, B2, 43

⚽ PLAZA DE TOROS DE LA MAESTRANZA

Paseo de Colón 12
Tel 95 450 13 82
www.realmaestranza.com
You can take a tour of one of Spain's most notable bullrings or watch a fight.
🅒 Bullfights usually Sun evenings, Apr–end Oct 🎫 €25 🚌 C4, B2, 43
🅷

♡ AIRE DE SEVILLA

Calle Aire 15
Tel 955 010 025
www.airedesevilla.com
This modern-day hammam (Arab bathhouse) offers a salt bath, hydro-massage bath, sauna and other water-based therapies, as well as massage. Try its mud and seaweed wrap treatments. A towel, footwear and locker are supplied, but bring your bathing suit as the facilities are mixed sex.
🅒 Daily noon–2am 🎫 Bath and aromatherapy €20, bath, aromatherapy and massage €31 🚌 C3, C4, 21, 23

✿ ISLA MAGICA

Pabellon de España, Isla de la Cartuja
Tel 902 16 17 16
www.islamagica.es
Isla Magica has a range of activities, although the roller-coasters, gardens and outdoor walking areas are the big attractions. There are several trains and mini-rides for those aged under 10. There are baby-changing facilities.
🅒 Apr–end Jun Sat–Sun 11–8; Jul to mid-Sep Sun–Fri 11–11, Sat 11am–midnight; Oct–end Nov Sat–Sun 11–9 🎫 Adult (over 13) €65, under 13 €34

EATING

CERVECERIA GIRALDA

Calle Mateos Gago 1
Tel 954 227 435
This atmospheric tapas bar is located in an old Arab bathhouse. The selection of tapas is enormous and the jamón ibérico (cured, acorn-fed ham) is in high demand. Excellent views of the Giralda add to the moment.
🍴 L €20, D €25, Wine €7
🅒 Daily 1pm–midnight

CORRAL DEL AGUA

Callejón del Agua 6
Tel 95 422 07 14, 954 22 48 41
www.andalunet.com/corral-agua
Come here for alfresco dining under the citrus trees of the secluded garden (interior seating is also available). Specials include sea bass in dry sherry and leg of lamb with spinach and pine nuts.
🅒 Mon–Sat 12–4, 8–12
🍴 L €40, D €60, Wine €10
🚌 1, 21, 22, 23, C3, C4

DOÑA ELVIRA

Plaza de Doña Elvira 6
Tel 95 421 54 83
www.barriosantacruz.com
A patio terrace extends from a Sevillan house into a small tree-lined square. The tasty combination of Spanish and Mediterranean dishes includes gazpacho, Andalucían paella and oxtail. A fixed price lunch menu is available for €15.
🅒 Daily 12–12. Closed 24 Dec and 1 Jan
🍴 L €28, D €50, Wine €13
🚌 1, 21, 22, 23, C3, C4

EL RINCONCILLO

Calle Gerona 42
Tel 95 422 31 83
Tapas were reputedly born here, in one of the oldest and most atmospheric bars in Seville, dating back to 1670. Hanging hams, stone floors and wooden furnishings decorate the small room. Most people choose to stand, drinking wine tapped from barrels and ordering small platefuls of tapas through a hatch in the wood panelling. However, a small seating area at the back can accommodate four or five tables of diners. Very popular with the locals.
🅒 Daily 1pm–1.30am. Tapas served 1–4.30, 7.30–midnight. Closed 15 Jul–1 Aug
🍴 Tapas around €2
🚌 10, 11, 12, 15, 20, 24, 27, 32

STAYING

AMADEUS

Calle Farnesio 6, 41004 Sevilla
Tel 95 450 14 43
www.hotelamadeussevilla.com
A family-run hotel that caters particularly to a musical clientele tendency—some of the rooms are soundproofed and have pianos. The hotel is close to the Alcázar and La Giralda. Features include internet access and a reading room. All of the rooms have minibar, satellite TV and a personal safe.
🛏 €80–€130 excluding breakfast (€7)
ⓘ 14 🅢
🚌 C3, C4
🚉 Santa Justa

LA CASA DEL REY DE BAEZA

Plaza Jesús de la Rendicion 2, 41003 Sevilla
Tel. 954 561 496
www.hospes.es
This hotel's unique and elegant setting is a well-executed fusion of past and present. The rooms have state-of-the-art features such as CD players and flat screen TVs. There is a rooftop plunge pool, and bicycle rental is available.
🛏 €142–€375, breakfast €14
ⓘ 41 (10 non-smoking) 🅢
🏊 Outdoor

SPAIN

ARRIVING

BY AIR
Spain is well served by international airlines. There are major international airports at Madrid and Barcelona and several smaller international airports in other regions, including Alacant (Alicante), Málaga and Bilbao (Bilbo). Spain's main national and international carrier is Iberia, though most other major carriers, such as British Airways, American Airlines, KLM and Lufthansa, also operate services to at least the two main airports.

BY FERRY
The main international ferry access routes to Spain are from the UK and operate into the north-coast ports of Bilbao and Santander. Other international services run from the southern coast of Spain to North Africa and ferries go to the Balearic Islands from the Spanish mainland. There are no scheduled boat connections between Spain and North America, although many cruise ships visit Spanish ports.

BY TRAIN
There are international train services to Spain from several European countries, including the UK, France, Portugal and Germany. Journey times are generally long and the fares are quite high compared to some of the budget airline flights. However, if you prefer going overland or want to see more than one European country during your visit, then the international train services, with their high levels of comfort and service, are a good choice. Although you can travel to other stations, particularly in some of the bigger cities in the north of Spain, most international services go to Madrid's Chamartín and Barcelona's Sants stations. The Spanish national rail company, RENFE, operates services throughout the country.

BY CAR
Driving into Spain from France and Portugal is very easy—in fact, you may not notice that you have crossed the border at all. There are customs points at all border crossings, varying in size depending on whether it is a main motorway (expressway) access point, such as at Portbou and Hondarribia, or a small mountain crossing point in the Pyrenees, for example. You must stop if requested by a border guard. Crossings are usually not manned, though you must slow down to pass through these areas. The southern crossing from Andorra into Spain is more obviously controlled, and usually takes time to clear. Again you must stop if asked to do so by a border guard and your vehicle may be searched.

Main Driving Routes
On entering Spain you will almost certainly need to head south, as few roads go east to west across the Pyrenees. To make quick progress from east to west there is a motorway (expressway) link running in that direction to the south of the Pyrenees, from Bilbao, via Zaragoza, to Barcelona (following the A-8, AP-68, AP-2 and AP-7). Throughout the rest of Spain, the main roads tend to head to Madrid or along the north, east and south coasts. The A-8/E-70 goes west along the northern coastline from Donostia (San Sebastián), at the main western border crossing, to Oviedo. From the main eastern border crossing at La Jonquera, the AP-7/E-15 heads south through Girona to Barcelona and on to Valencia and beyond.

Car rental
Check your rental car thoroughly before you set off. The smallest marks, scratches or anomalies are worth pointing out, even if they are then dismissed as unimportant by the company's representative. Ensure that any significant damage is marked down on the rental form, or you could face a substantial damage penalty surcharge.

Some rental companies send their cars out with full tanks of fuel; you need to return the vehicle the same way. Other companies send the cars out almost empty (with just enough to get you to a filling station) and these should be returned empty.

Unless you are using the car for minor trips out of the city, it is cheaper to get an unlimited kilometre package. Some companies do not offer this, allowing you only 100km (60 miles) per day and then surcharging for every kilometre over that total. You may need to do some calculations to work out which is cheaper to rent, depending on your requirements.
- To rent a car you need your driver's licence—an international driver's permit is often more useful—and money, or a credit card, for the deposit. If you are leaving cash, the deposit can be quite a significant amount.
- There may be a minimum age (often 21, sometimes higher) and a requirement that you have been driving for at least a year.
- If you rent when you get to Spain, look for local firms in the telephone book under *Aquiler de coches* or *Automóviles alquiler*, or ask at the information office.

VISITORS WITH A DISABILITY
While visitor services in the main cities are active in providing suitable disability access, Spain is on the whole quite poorly equipped compared to other European and North American countries. Things are improving all the time, though, and new public buildings are now legally obliged to include facilities for people with disabilities.
- www.makoa.org has resource links for people with disabilities, including information on travel; look under Travel and Recreation Resources.

GETTING AROUND

BY CAR

Spain is generally easy to drive around. There's a good network of motorways (expressways) and dual carriageways (divided highways); about half of these are toll roads (*autopistas*) and the rest are free (*autovías*). There are also national roads (*nacionales*) and smaller roads (*comarcales*). Many roads, particularly the main motorways, are quiet outside the rush hour. If you are tempted to skip the tolls and head for the main national routes, be warned that many truck drivers think the same way so these roads can be very busy and very slow.

● You need a driver's licence to drive in Spain. Licences from the United States, Canada, the UK and other EU countries are valid.

● It is compulsory to carry your licence with you at all times, as well as the vehicle registration document and at least third-party insurance. If the vehicle is not registered in your name, you should have a letter from the registered owner that gives you permission to drive it.

● Your insurers should also provide you with a Green Card before you travel if your insurance policy requires it.

● It is compulsory for drivers to carry the following equipment in the vehicle at all times: 2 self-standing, warning triangles (to be placed at least 50m/55 yards behind and in front of the vehicle in the case of breakdown); a green safety jacket; 1 set of spare headlight and rear light bulbs; 1 set of spare fuses for lights and electrics; 1 spare wheel; 1 spare fan belt.

BY TRAIN

The major rail network in Spain is run by RENFE (tel 902 24 02 02; www.renfe.es/ingles) and it covers much of the country with its extensive 12,000km (7,440 miles) of track. There are different types of train services, which all serve different purposes, travel at different speeds and often have several different names.

DIFFERENT TYPES OF TRAIN

● **Local (Cercanías)** These services operate around the environs of major cities, calling at most local stations, and are generally slow but pleasant.

The trains are usually red and white and some have double-decker carriages (cars). They offer a simple ticket one-way (*ida*) or round-trip (*ida y vuelta*), and are usually a better and faster, though slightly more expensive, option than taking the bus.

● **Regional** This is a comprehensive network of services covering the entire country. It has reasonable prices, comfort and access to smaller towns, as well as the major cities, without the express speed.

● **Long-distance** (Diurno, Estrella, Talgo, Intercity). These long-distance trains generally run at high speed between major cities on journeys over 400km (250 miles). They are very spacious and comfortable. Passengers board the trains by following a check-in procedure similar to that used at airports.

The standard long-distance services are Diurno and Estrella, which often cost substantially less than the other services, such as Talgo. These trains stop only at the largest cities.

Train-Hotels offer sleeping facilities on overnight services and are the very comfortable. Intercity and Talgo run frequently and have greater levels of comfort between the major cities during the day.

● **AVE** This is the ultimate in speed and luxury, but these services currently run only on the Madrid–Seville, Madrid–Ciudad Real–Puertollano, Lerida–Madrid (which will soon be extended from Barcelona) and Madrid–Zaragoza routes. They have cafés, telephones, music and video entertainment on board and tourist-, first- and club-class seating. These fast trains take just 2 hours 35 minutes to go between the two cities compared with 3 hours 15 minutes on a normal long-distance service,

but may cost more. You get a guarantee that if the train is more than five minutes late, the cost of your ticket is refunded.

● **FEVE** This modern, independent rail network (www.feve.es) operates services along the north coast of Spain from Bilbao to Ferrol and inland from Bilbao to León, plus some smaller, local routes in Murcia, Palencia and A Coruña. It runs on a narrower gauge track than RENFE trains. It has offices in Santander, Bilbao, Gijón and Oviedo, and offers two types of service—the local one, also known as Cercanías, and Regionales for longer trips between the bigger cities. You can buy books of 10 tickets and monthly tickets, as well as the usual one-way and round-trip.

BUSES

Many villages throughout Spain are accessible only by bus. The local train network is comparatively sparse, so going by bus can often be the best, if not the only, way to get directly to a small village or town.

Local bus services tend to emanate from the bigger towns and regional capitals, so you may find yourself having to travel via one of them to get between villages.

There are plenty of bus companies running services, and the best way to find out where a particular bus departs from is to ask at a visitor information office or at the main bus station. Comfort levels vary widely on these services and there are usually no facilities on board.

You can buy a ticket at the station prior to departure or, more often, on the bus itself.

TAXIS

Generally, catching a taxi in Spain is fairly stress-free. In a city, if convenience and speed are important, then a taxi is a pretty straightforward way of quickly getting exactly where you want to go.

GETTING AROUND IN MADRID

Madrid is an easy city to negotiate, with a first-rate public transport network, including a very efficient bus service, an excellent Metro and plenty of taxis. As Madrid's sights are quite spread out, any visit to the city is going to involve using public transport at some stage.

The Madrid city authorities and public transport companies have created a website which brings together all the bus, metro and urban train information in one place: www.ctm-madrid.es has information in Spanish and English.

BY BUS
The bus system is efficient and far-reaching, with regular schedules to all parts of the city and its suburbs. Finding your way is made easy as the various routes and stops are shown at every bus stop on a plan. There are two types of buses—the standard red bus and the yellow microbus. Both operate between 6am and midnight, and charge €1 or €1.75 for a combined bus/metro ticket for each one-way ride in the city, though the *bono* or Metrobus ticket giving 10 rides costs €6.40. You can buy the *bono* (also valid for the Metro system) from the Empresa Municipal de Transportes (EMT) office at Calle Cerro de la Plata 4 (tel 902 50 78 50, open daily 8–2), from any EMT kiosk or Metro station in the city and from some newsstands and tobacconists. Night buses (locally known as *buhos*, meaning owls) operate from Plaza de la Cibeles to many suburbs between midnight and 6am and the tickets cost the same as during the day.

The night bus service is not as punctual as the daytime one. Bus information offices are located in Plaza de la Cibeles and Puerta del Sol, where you can pick up route maps and schedules.

BY METRO
The Metro system is one of the oldest in Europe, but has been modernized. It is easy to follow, and has a central convergence point at Puerta del Sol. There are 13 lines, each with a different colour and number shown on route maps and at stations.

The latest addition is the No. 12 Metrosur line, a major loop extension to the southwest of the city reaching as far as Parque Europa. Metrosur is accessed from Puerta del Sur station on Línea 10.

The system is split into zones, with most of it in Zone A, while the outlying areas and lines are in zones B1, B2 and B3. The one-way fare for any journey is €1 but you can buy a *bonos* or Metrobus ticket (▷ By Bus). There is a separate Metrosur multi-ride ticket giving 10 trips on the Metrosur line and the interconnecting Línea 10 stations, also for €6.40.

The Metro system runs from 6am to 2am; schedule information and a full Metro map are available from www.metromadrid.es (tel 902 444 403). You can also pick up maps at any station. The Metro trains operate around every three to six minutes from Monday to Friday; this extends to every 15 minutes after midnight, and there are slightly fewer trains on weekends. It is very reliable and the best way of getting around the city quickly, but it's best to avoid the rush hours, generally 7–9.30am and 7–9pm, when it gets very busy.

BY TAXI
Getting a taxi from a hotel or hailing one on the street should be quite easy. The official taxis are white with a diagonal red stripe, and a green light on the roof shows when they are free.

There are other private taxi companies, which are legitimate, but beware of pirate taxi cabs, which charge higher

fares and can be less trust-worthy. The prices for official taxis are reasonable, so if you need to get somewhere quickly then it is certainly worth considering.

The standard base taxi fare is €1.85, with a charge of €0.87 for every further kilometre in Zone A. There is a supplement payable for journeys to certain places, such as the rail station (€2.50), airport (€5) and bullring (€0.95), as well as a Sunday and holiday supplement (€1.40) and nighttime supplement (€1). Make sure the meter is turned on and set at the base fare for your journey, otherwise you will pay more. The major private taxi companies in Madrid are TeleTaxi (tel 91 371 21 31; www.tele-taxi.es) and Radio Taxi (tel 91 447 32 32).

BY TRAIN
Chamartín, north of Plaza de Castilla, is the terminus for northern destinations. It is linked by a through line with Atocha, the old southerly station, now rebuilt, at the bottom end of the Jardín Botánico (Botanical Gardens).

There is also a Metro link, No. 8, Chamartín to Plaza de Castilla; then take No. 1 to Atocha RENFE. *Cercanías* refers to local and suburban trains, *largo recorrido* to intercity and long-distance trains.

BY CAR
If you can avoid driving around Madrid then do so. It's always busy, often dangerous and navigating and driving at the same time is challenging.

BY BICYCLE
The Bike Spain bicycle store at Plaza de la Villa 1 (tel 91 559 06 53; www.bikespain.info; Metro Sol, Opera) rents out mountain bicycles at €18 per day, but be careful—the city's motorists are not known for their attention to bicyclists.

SPAIN

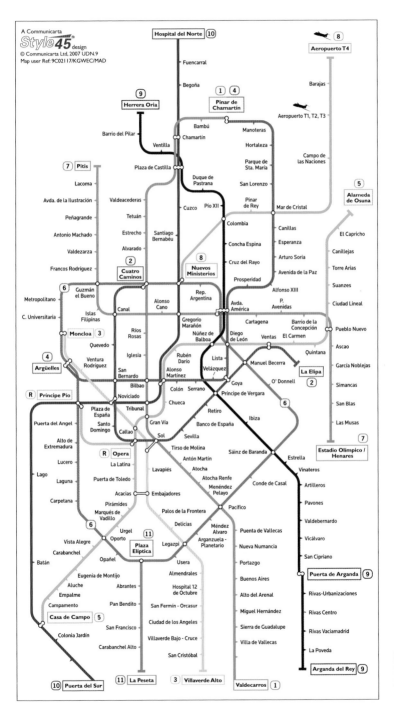

SPAIN

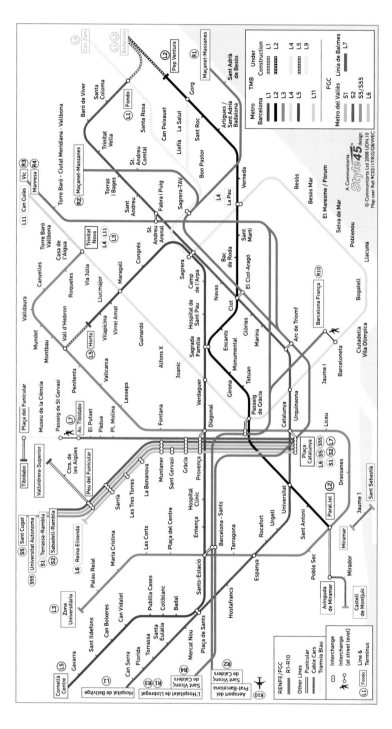

SPAIN

SWITZERLAND

UNDERSTANDING SWITZERLAND

Few nations can match this small country at the heart of Europe for the beauty of its mountains and lakes. But many first-time visitors overlook the country's other attractions: its outstanding art collections, modern buildings by world-class architects, the rich variety of regional vernacular buildings, and the diversity of food and culture that comes from the national influences of its three main languages–French, German and Italian. Its wealth coupled with competent administration and the benefits of a strong environmental awareness have helped to create a country whose main cities constantly rank in the top ten in 'quality of life' surveys.

Snow-capped peaks in the Klausen Pass   Staubbach Falls (above). The Ogre Fountain in Berne (below)

GEOGRAPHY

Switzerland is less than one-third the size of England, and trains cross the country in a few hours. Yet the striking differences between the regions require a stay of disproportionate length to appreciate them. Much of the country is moun-tainous, but the gentle, rounded Jura Mountains straddling the border with France in the northwest are utterly different from the abrupt inclines and dark slopes of the Bernese Oberland or the long idyllic valleys of the Engadine in Graubünden.

To compensate for lack of access to the sea, Switzerland has or shares with neighbours ten substantial lakes and hundreds of smaller areas of freshwater. The larger lakes have fleets of ships, some graceful steam-powered paddle-steamers into their second century of service. The majority of the population lives in the five principal cities and the more gently contoured country of the Bernese Mittelland and the northeast. The largest canton, Graubünden, is also the most sparsely populated. Swiss cities are smart and clean, many with a lake frontage that goes a long way to mitigating the urban feel, but it is the bucolic meadowlands of the countryside that stay in the memory; with vivid green grass-land contrasting dramatic peaks against azure blue skies as beautiful on a sunny day as the images on a thousand chocolate boxes.

The country spans four main climatic regions: continental, Mediterranean, subtropical and marine, so there can be dramatic differences in temperature and weather on either side of moun-tain massifs. At all times of year it is advisable to be prepared for rain and cold as well as taking the vital sunscreen for higher altitudes.

POLITICS AND SOCIETY

The make-up of Swiss society is reflected in the absence of a national language, since opinion on some issues divides along linguistic lines. Enthusiasm for joining the European Union, for example, is stronger in the French-speaking part of the country. Moreover, the country is further divided by the power of the 26 cantons within the confederation, which have considerable authority over day-to-day affairs, taxation and justice, though the local governments are respon-sible to the federal government in Berne. Switzerland has a highly developed and devolved democracy, with referenda on many issues right down to commune level.

Switzerland's neutral status since 1815, coupled with a reputation for probity and decency, has encouraged many international organizations to establish their headquarters in the country, principally in Geneva and Lausanne. Geneva was the chosen headquarters for the Red Cross, founded in 1863, and it has since been joined by the League of Nations, the European headquarters of the United Nations, the International Labour Organization and the World Health Organization. While Lausanne is home to the International Olympic Committee, Zurich has the world headquarters of FIFA and Nyon UEFA.

Ignorance has perpetuated many myths about the Swiss, not least the idea that they invented the cuckoo clock, which Orson Welles articulated

SWITZERLAND

in *The Third Man*; it was actually the Bavarians. In reality the Swiss are so diverse a people that they defy glib generalizations. But they may be described as a remarkably tolerant people who have provided sanctuary for deserving and not so deserving exiles through the centuries, from English regicides and Scots Presbyterians to French Huguenots and Russian revolutionaries. Curiously, some suggest that good governance and the smooth running of public services are indicative of dullness; others see in the Swiss the perfect combination of northern efficiency and southern vitality. The psychiatrist Carl Jung saw the Swiss 'occupying a neutral position between the contradictory aspirations and opinions of the other [European] nations'. A love of nature and the country is deeply embedded in the national psyche, and ostentatious displays of wealth are widely regarded as vulgar.

watch, and so began the major industry of this part of Switzerland.

It was also largely thanks to Britons that the tourism industry developed, leading to close ties between the countries. Writers and artists such as Lord Bryon and J. M. W. Turner created an awareness of the beauty of the Alps and their romantic aspects; the purity of the air at a time when so many diseases were airborne was an added inducement for wealthy families to spend months in the higher parts, leading to a vogue for mountain-top hotels such as those on the Rigi and at Caux on Rochers-de-Naye. Sanatoria were built, particularly for people suffering from tuberculosis, and the peculiar society that congregated in these resorts is described in Thomas Mann's novel *The Magic Mountain*. It was three Englishmen who built the famous Cresta Run near St Moritz for bobsleighs (bobsleds); curling was introduced

Church in the countryside surrounding Appenzell

Glacier Express

ECONOMICS
There is no better illustration of the benefits of peace than the way the Swiss economy has been transformed from a largely poor agrarian base with few natural resources to a prosperous and well-ordered nation within the space of a century and a half. Switzerland is known primarily for banking, watchmaking, chocolate and tourism but it also has major sectors in pharmaceutical products, energy, electrical appliances and machine tools. It also has a thriving food and wine industry despite the large proportion of the country that is unsuitable for agriculture; its famed cheeses and chocolate are the most well-known products.

Theologian John Calvin was indirectly responsible for stimulating watchmaking in Geneva by his puritanical tirades against the craftsmen who made expensive jewellery; those who accepted his accusation of being in league with the devil converted their skills to making clocks and watches. These were very expensive to produce, the skill of making cheaper watches being the preserve of London-based craftsmen, until in 1709 a travelling Englishman with a broken watch called at the blacksmith's shop of Daniel Jean-Richard, who also mended clocks at Le Locle in the Jura; overnight Jean-Richard made a drawing of the

from Scotland; and the Kandahar Ski Club of Mürren, named after its founder Earl Roberts of Kandahar, gave rise to the terrifying Inferno ski race from the Schilthorn and the world's first alpine skiing championships in 1931. Between the two world wars, three out of every five Britons going abroad went to Switzerland.

RELIGION
Though Christianity was introduced by the Romans during their 500-year occupation of western Switzerland from 58BC, it was not until the preaching of the Irish missionaries St. Columban and St. Gall in the late 6th and early 7th centuries that Christianity became well established. In their wake, mostly Benedictine monasteries were founded in St Gallen, Disentis, Einsiedeln and elsewhere, becoming the country's first cultural centres, and the churches and surrounding buildings are today major tourist attractions.

Parts of the country became staunchly Protestant: Zwingli began preaching in Zurich against the Catholic Church, provoking riots between Catholics and Protestants; Geneva was a magnet for Protestants in exile, such as Jean Calvin on his expulsion from Paris, Thomas Bodley, who founded Oxford's Bodleian Library, and John Knox, who preached to the refugee English congregation in the Auditoire Calvin of Notre-Dame-de-la-Neuve. Lucerne in contrast has remained a more Catholic city, and the Jesuit Church of St. Francis Xavier was the country's first large baroque church.

THE BEST OF SWITZERLAND

BERNESE OBERLAND

Ballenberg Devote a day to this open-air museum of more than 90 reconstructed buildings on an 80ha (200-acre) site, with demonstrations of bygone crafts and three restaurants offering regional dishes.

Interlaken Catch the train to Lauterbrunnen and Kleine Scheidegg for the railway to the highest station in Europe at 3,454m (11,329ft) inside the Jungfrau at Jungfraujoch.

CENTRAL SWITZERLAND

Berne Wander the streets of the World Heritage Site old town with 6km (4 miles) of stone arcades sheltering the pavement (sidewalk) beside the many small shops.

Lucerne Board one of the five paddlesteamers on the lake for a lunch or evening cruise around the lake, which has the most striking landscapes of any of Switzerland's navigable lakes.

Meiringen Feel the power of water in the narrow gorge of the Aare river with its exciting footpath, and at the nearby Reichenbach Falls, where Conan Doyle set the death of Sherlock Holmes.

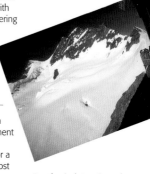

Jungfraujoch terminus, the highest train station in the world (above)

GRAUBÜNDEN

Scuol Travel by the frequent postbuses to the village of Tarasp for one of the country's most dramatically situated castles, built in the 11th century.

St. Moritz Take the train to Tirano, just across the border in Italy, and experience the highest rail crossing of the Alps from an open carriage (in summer), perfect for photographers.

TICINO

Centovalli Walk in the tranquil beechwoods that line the long valley of the River Melezza, joined by numerous side valleys.

Lugano Reserve a seat on the Palm Express, the best-known postbus journey in the country, which weaves along the shore of Lake Lugano and through Italy to reach the Engadine and the resort of St. Moritz.

Collegiate Library in St. Gallen (above)

VALAIS

Gornergrat mountain in Zermatt (below)

Fiesch Board the cable car up to Eggishorn for a walk beside the Aletsch Glacier, the longest in Europe at 23km (15 miles).

Zermatt Get up early and take the rack railway up to Gornergrat to watch the sun rise on the Matterhorn, one of Switzerland's most distinctive and famous mountains.

ZURICH AND THE NORTHEAST

St. Gallen Be overwhelmed by the exuberant decoration of the rococo interior of the Collegiate Library attached to the monastery and cathedral, which are all ranked a World Heritage Site.

Stein am Rhein Admire one of the best-preserved collections of half-timbered and highly ornamented buildings in the country.

Zurich Gain an understanding of Swiss culture and history at the Swiss National Museum (▷ 418), housed in a neo-Gothic building that resembles a castle, then take in the extensive and diverse collection of 15th–20th-century paintings in the Kunsthaus, with changing special exhibitions (▷ 418).

SWITZERLAND

Tourists on a boat trip around Lake Geneva

GENEVA

For centuries Switzerland's most cosmopolitan city, Geneva, with its historic old town, is situated at the western end of Lac Léman with views over the French Alps.

Almost entirely surrounded by France, Geneva looks and feels French, though the district of Carouge has an Italian character thanks to its former ownership by Sardinia and its design by Piedmontese architects. The riverbanks have been partially spoiled by a few monstrous modern buildings, so it is the old town and the area around the lake to which tourists gravitate. The latter curves round Geneva's most famous symbol, the Jet d'Eau, a water spout from the lake, which reaches 140m (460ft) thanks to a velocity of 200kph (124mph) and which can be seen from over 16km (10 miles) away. On the shore is the Jardin Anglais, with its ornate bandstand, fountain and massed bedding plants.

MUSEUMS

Geneva has more than 40 museums and art galleries. Winner of the 2007 Council of Europe Museum Prize, Geneva's new Musée International de la Réforme in Maison Mallet at Rue du Cloitre 4 (Tue–Sun 10–5) uses holograms to describe the development of Protestantism and the role played by exiles from Britain who produced the English Geneva Bible in 1560. Some of the paintings in the Musée d'Art et d'Histoire at Rue Chares-Galland 2 (Tue–Sun 10–5) were bequeathed by British residents; there is a rich archaeological collection and fine art from the 15th century to the present. The story of the red cross on a white background and the Geneva Convention is graphically portrayed in the Musée International de la Croix-Rouge et du Croissant-Rouge at Avenue de la Paix 17 (Wed–Mon 10–5). The skills of Geneva's watchmakers, jewellers and enamellers can be admired at Musée de l'Horlogerie et de l'Émallerie in a 19th-century villa at Route de Malagnou 15 (currently closed for renovation).

Don't Miss Other sights are the city's opera house, the Grand-Théâtre on Place Neuve (tram line 12); the heart of the old town at Place du Bourg-de-Four, where the Romans held their markets; and the Cathedral of St. Pierre, which dates from the 12th century and offers a fine view of the city from the top of the north tower.

RATINGS

Historic interest	●●●●
Cultural interest	●●●●●
Good for food	●●●●●
Walkability	●●●

BASICS

✚ 5 D4

🛈 Rue du Mont-Blanc 18, tel 022 909 70 20; mid-Jun to end Aug Tue–Sun 9–6, Mon 10–6; Sep to mid-Jun Tue–Sat 9–6, Mon 10-6

🚉 Geneva (Cornavin)

www.geneve-tourisme.ch
Comprehensive website in French and English, covering attractions, events, shopping, dining, accommodation, special offers and maps.

TIPS

● Some hotels have seasonal 'three nights for the price of two' offers.

● From Geneva Tourism you can rent a CD player with a tour of 25 places of interest around the city. A passport or ID is necessary.

● All hotel, youth hostel and campsite guests receive a free Geneva Transport Card, conferring free use of the city's public transport by tram, bus, train and boat.

● Enjoy a lake cruise, perhaps aboard one of the elegant paddlesteamers.

SWITZERLAND

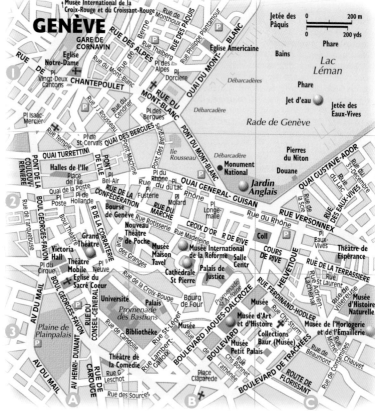

GENÈVE

Musée International de la Croix-Rouge et du Croissant-Rouge

GARE DE CORNAVIN

RUE DES ALPES

RUE DES PÂQUIS

QUAI DU MONT-BLANC

Eglise Notre-Dame

Rue de Monthoux

Berne

Rue Thalberg

Rue de Berne

Rue Philippe Plantamour

Eglise Americaine

Bains

Lac Léman

Phare

Jetée des Pâquis

0   200 m

0   200 yds

CHANTEPOULET

Pl Vingt-Deux Cantons

Pl des Alpes

Pl Dorciere

Rue du Mont-Blanc

Débarcadères

Phare

Jet d'eau

Jetée des Eaux-Vives

RUE DU MONT-BLANC

Pl Isaac-Mercier

Rue J.J. Rousseau

Rue du Cendrier

Pl des Bergues

Débarcadère

Rade de Genève

Rue temple

Pl de St-Gervais

QUAI DES BERGUES

Pont de la Machine

Ile Rousseau

Débarcadère

Pierres du Niton

QUAI TURRETTINI

Pont des Bergues

PONT DU MONT-BLANC

Monument National

Douane

QUAI GUSTAVE-ADOR

Halles de l'Île

PONT DE L'ÎLE

Place de l'île

Pl Bel-Air

Pl du Rhône

Pl du Lac

QUAI GENERAL-GUISAN

Jardin Anglais

Rue de la Scie

Rue des Eaux-Vives

BOUL GEORGES-FAVON

RUE DE LA COULOUVRENIÈRE

Quai de la Poste

Pl de Hollande

RUE DE LA CONFEDERATION

Pl Fusterie

Pl du Molard

RUE DU RHÔNE

Pl Longe-malle

Rue du Rhône

RUE VERSONNEX

Rue de la Plaine

Bourse de Genève

Rue Rôtisserie

Rue Madeleine

CROIX D'OR

R DE RIVE

Coll

COURS DE RIVE

Eaux-Vives

Théâtre de l'Espérance

Nouveau Théâtre de Poche

Grand Théâtre

Victoria Hall

Théâtre Mobile

Eglise du Sacré Coeur

Musée Maison Tavel

Rue des Granges

Musée International de la Réforme

Salle Centr

Cathédrale St Pierre

Palais de Justice

RUE DE LA TERRASSIERE

Rue St Laurent

Rue Adrien-Lachenal

Rue de Villereuse

Musée d'Histoire Naturelle

BOUL GEORGES-FAVON

AV DU MAIL

RUE DU CIRQUE

Pl du cirque

Pl Neuve

Rue de la Croix-Rouge

Université

Palais

Bourg de Four

Promenade St Antoine

HELVETIQUE

RUE FERDINAND-HODLER

Musée

Musée de l'Horlogerie et de l'Émaillerie

Promenade des Bastions

Rue de Candolle

Musée

Rue Chs-Sturm

Musée d'Art et d'Histoire

Rue Michel Chauvet

Plaine de Plainpalais

Bibliothéke

Rue St-Léger

BOULEVARD JAQUES-DALCROZE

Collections Baur (Musée)

Rue de Contamines

Rue de Beaumont

AV HENRI-DUNANT

RUE DU CONSEIL-GÉNÉRAL

Théâtre de la Comédie

Rue G Leschot

Rue Lamberc Caloix

BOULEVARD

Rue Chs-Bonnet

Petit Palais

Rue des Trachères

ROUTE DE FLORISSANT

AV DU MAIL

RUE DE CAROUGE

Rue des Sources

Place Claparede

BOULEVARD DE TRACHES

SWITZERLAND

A   B   C

1   2   3

KEY TO SYMBOLS
- ⊕ **Shopping**
- ♪ **Entertainment**
- ☺ **Nightlife**
- ⚑ **Sports**
- ✪ **Activities**
- ♡ **Health and Beauty**
- ✱ **For Children**

WHAT TO DO

⊕ ANTIQUES SCIENTIFIQUES

Rue du Perron 19
Tel 022 310 07 06
www.perret-antiques.ch
This is a delightfully idiosyncratic shop in the old town selling all manner of scientific instruments, from barometers, microscopes and calculating machines to surveying instruments, cameras and medical equipment.
✪ Mon–Fri 10–12.30, 1.30–6.30, Sat 11–2 ⊟ Tram 12, 16 to Place du Molard

⊕ CAROUGE

This district, reached by tram, is the place to go for small interesting shops–jewellers, milliners, glassblowers, weavers, watchmakers, bookbinders and clothes stylists–who often make on the premises what they have for sale.
⊟ Tram 13 direction Palettes, alight at Marché

⊕ PLAINPALAIS

This large area is the site of a well-established flea market on Wednesday and Saturday mornings, with hundreds of stands.
✪ Wed, Sat from dawn ⊟ Tram 12, 13, 17

☺ LE CHAT NOIR

Rue Vautier 13, Carouge
Tel 022 343 49 98
www.chatnoir.ch
Le Chat Noir is the best jazz and blues club in Geneva, with an eclectic mix of local and international artists. The upstairs bar is a hip hangout, while downstairs is all about the music. After midnight, DJs spin house and techno into the small hours.
✪ Tue–Thu 8–4, Fri 6–5, Sat 8–5. Concerts from 9 or 10 ⊟ Tram 12, 13 to Marché

☺ LEOPARD BAR, HOTEL D'ANGLETERRE

Quai du Mont-Blanc 17
Tel 022 906 55 55
www.hoteldangleterre.ch
This subtly lit bar has the atmosphere of a colonial club library in Nairobi, but with live music. The bar snacks are more like canapés.
✪ Daily 5.30–2, music Tue–Sat 7.30–9, 10.30–12.30

EATING

AU PIED DE COCHON

Place Bourg-de-Four 4
Tel 022 310 47 97
A restaurant for carnivores, the 'Pig's Foot' has the atmosphere of a Lyonnaise bistro, with its white tiles and low ceilings. On the menu are cassoulet, *choucroute*, alpine lamb, tripe and, of course, pigs' feet.
✪ Tue–Fri 6–11, Sat, Sun 9–11
🍽 L CHF41, D CHF55, Wine CHF35

BRASSERIE-RESTAURANT DE L'HOTEL-DE-VILLE

Grand-Rue 39
Tel 022 311 70 30
You need to have a hearty appetite for the good-value *menu degustation*, which offers an *amuse bouche* and four courses, including such dishes as lake perch, Genevese sausage, spiced traditional Genevese pork stew and pear mousse in a cave of spun sugar. This restaurant dates from 1764 and has the charm of a neighbourhood bistro–lace curtains, dark wood, potted plants and all.
✪ 11.30–11.30
🍽 L CHF19, D CHF35, Wine CHF37
⊟ 17

CAFÉ DU CENTRE

Place du Molard 5
Tel 022 311 85 86
www.cafeducentre.ch
A Geneva institution since 1871, this restaurant serves a good range of fish–including various mixed platters–and meat dishes such as veal escalope and lamb cutlet, using produce from the canton of Geneva.
✪ Tue–Fri 6am–1am, Sat 9am–1am, Sun 9am–12am, Mon 6am–12am
🍽 L CHF30, D CHF39, Wine CHF30
⊟ Tram 12, 16 to Molard

STAYING

BEAU RIVAGE

Quai du Mont-Blanc 13,
CH-1201 Genève
Tel 022 716 66 66
www.beau-rivage.ch
The last Swiss family-run five-star hotel in the city and dating from 1865, the Beau Rivage overlooks the lake. Its character has been carefully maintained by descendants of the founders during modernizations to provide contemporary amenities. It has an outstanding restaurant and a cellar of 45,000 bottles.
🛏 CHF620–9,000, excluding breakfast
🛎 93 (some non-smoking)
🚶 10mins' walk from Geneva (Cornavin)

CITY HOSTEL GENEVA

Rue Ferrier 2, CH-1202 Genève
Tel 022 901 15 00
www.cityhostel.ch
Basic but clean double rooms are provided in this backpackers' hostel on a quiet street, eight minutes' walk from the station. There are kitchen and laundry facilities and a movie each night.
🛏 CHF72–86, excluding breakfast
🛎 50 ✱
⊟ Tram 13, 15 to Butini

EDELWEISS

Place de la Navigation 2,
CH-1201 Genève
Tel 022 544 51 51
www.manotel.com
If you don't have time to go to the mountains, this hotel has the feel of a chalet, with lots of natural wood. It offers free WiFi and is on a quiet street close to the lake.
🛏 CHF170–300, including breakfast
🛎 42 (non-smoking floors)
⊟ 1 to Navigation

INTERNATIONAL & TERMINUS

Rue des Alpes 20, CH-1201 Genève
Tel 022 906 97 77
www.international-terminus.ch
Situated on the square outside the main station, the 19th-century building was modernized in 2005. It has a restaurant with an outdoor terrace and is only 0.5km (0.3 miles) from the lake.
🛏 CHF160–280, including breakfast
🛎 60 (some non-smoking)
🚆 Geneva (Cornavin)

View of Zurich showing the twin spires of the Grossmünster and Lake Zurich with the Alps in the background

ZURICH

The country's largest city has the most vibrant cultural life, with a wide range of concerts, museums, galleries and restaurants.

Built in a broad valley around the confluence of the Sihl and Limmat rivers at the northern end of Lake Zurich, Switzerland's foremost financial and business city has an energy and dynamism that make it as attractive to tourists as it is to residents–Zurich consistently tops the Mercer Quality of Life Survey of world cities. Old quarters, such as the former industrial district of Zurich West, are regenerated with an imagination and design flair that attracts residents, entrepreneurs and visitors alike. Besides the museums, opera, concerts, open-air bars, nightclubs and shops, the city is well situated for day excursions to the mountains or nearby walks in the countryside with a backdrop of snow-covered peaks.

AROUND THE OLD TOWN

The Schweiz Landesmusuem (Swiss National Museum, Tue–Sun 11–5) near the station offers a good introduction to the country's history and culture. A walk through the old town on the west bank of the Limmat is a must, stopping off to see the stained-glass windows by Chagall and Giacometti in the Fraumünster on Münsterhof (Apr–end Oct 10–6; Nov–end Mar 10–4), and on the opposite side of the river the twin-towered Grossmünster (mid-Mar to end Oct 9–6; Nov to mid-Mar 10–5). The streets on each side of the river, many pedestrian-only, are lined with small interesting shops and restaurants. Up the hill on the east bank on Heimplatz is the city's principal art gallery; the Kunsthaus (Wed–Fri 10–8, Tue, Sat–Sun 10–6) is reached by trams 3, 5, 8, 9 and has many rooms of Old Masters, Impressionists, Dadaists and Surrealists. You can join a two-hour guided walk through the old town from the tourist office (Nov to mid-Mar Wed–Sat 11am; end Mar–end Oct daily 3pm).

There are footpaths beside the lake, the east side is the more attractive, with plenty of trees and flowerbeds and a Chinese Garden (daily 11–7). At the eastern end of tram line 6 is the large Zoo (daily 9–6) with 2,000 animals and a vast glass-roofed recon-struction of Madagascan rainforest.

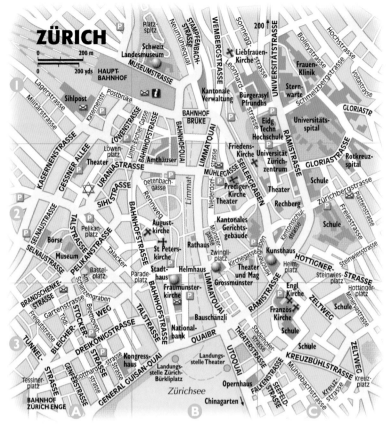

ZÜRICH

Platzspitz

STAMPFENBACH-STRASSE

WEMBERGSTRASSE

Neumühlequai

sonnegg

UNIVERSITÄTSTRASSE

Bolleystrasse

Hochstrasse

200 ↑

Schweiz Landesmuseum

Liebfrauen-Kirche

Frauen-Klinik

0   200 m

0   200 yds

HAUPT-BAHNHOF

MUSEUMSTRASSE

Leonhard-

strasse

Sternwarte

Schmelzbergstrasse

Vorderstrasse

Lagerstrasse

Postbrücke

Kantonale Verwaltung

Burgerasyl Pfrundhs

Militärstrasse

Sihlpost

Kasernenstr

BAHNHOF BRÜCKE

Eidg Techn Hochschule

Universitäts-spital

GLORIASTR

KASERNENSTRASSE

LÖWENSTRASSE

BAHNHOFSTRASSE

BAHNHOFQUAI

LIMMATQUAI

Friedens-Kirche

Universität Zürich-zentrum

RAMISTRASSE

GLORIASTRASSE

Rotkreuz-spital

GESSNER ALLEE

Löwenplatz

Linth-Escher-Gasse

Amthäuser

Schule

Zürichbergstrasse

Freiestrasse

Plattenstrasse

Theater

URANIA STRASSE

MÜHLEGASSE

SEILERGRABEN

Theater

SIHLSTRASSE

Oetenbach-gasse

Niederdorf-

strasse

Rennweg

Prediger Kirche

Theater

Rechberg

Kantonsschul-

strasse

Schule

SELNAUSTRASSE

TALSTRASSE

BAHNHOFSTRASSE

PELIKANSTRASSE

Pelikan-platz

August-kirche

Münster-gasse

Kantonales Gerichts-gebäude

Kunsthaus

HOTTINGER-

Steinwiesstrasse

Börse

Rathaus

Kirchegassegraben

STRASSE

Museum

St Peters-kirche

Zwingli-platz

Theater und Mag

Heim-platz

Steinwies-platz

Hottinger-platz

Bastel-platz

Am Schanzengraben

Parade-platz

Stadt-haus

Helmhaus

Grossmünster

Kantons-graben

RAMISTRASSE

Engl Kirche

ZELTWEG

Schule

Mittenwegstrasse

BRANDSCHENKE-STRASSE

Gartenstrasse

Beethoven-

WEG

LIMMATQUAI

Fraumünster-kirche

Franzos-Kirche

Schule

ZELTWEG

Tödi

STOCKER-

TALSTRASSE

Bauschänzli

THEATERSTRASSE

Stadelhofer-

strasse

Schule

KREUZBÜHLSTRASSE

Freigutstrasse

BLEICHER-

DREIKÖNIGSTRASSE

STRASSE

National-bank

QUAIBR

Schule

kreuz-platz

TUNNEL-

Gotthard-

strasse

Kongress-haus

Landungs-stelle Theater

UTOQUAI

Kreuz-

strasse

Tessiner-platz

GENFERSTRASSE

GENERAL GUISAN-QUAI

Landungs-stelle Zürich-Bürkliplatz

Zürichsee

FALKENSTRASSE

THEATERSTRASSE

Mühlebachstrasse

SEEFELD-

BAHNHOF ZÜRICH ENGE

A

B

Chinagarten ↓

Opernhaus

C

Traditional lakeside boathouse displaying the Swiss flag

SWITZERLAND

WHAT TO DO

⊕ FREITAG
Geroldstrasse 17
Tel 043 366 95 20
www.freitag.ch
An unforgettable shop made out of vertically stacked containers containing displays of the trendy bags created from recycled truck tarpaulins and designed by Daniel and Markus Freitag.
🕙 Mon–Fri 11–7.30, Sat 11–5
🚆 S-Bahn to Hardbrücke

⊕ SCHWEIZER HEIMATWERK
Uraniastrasse 1
Tel 044 222 19 55
www.heimatwerk.ch
This outlet has been selling a wide range of Swiss-made crafts since 1930, from pottery and glass to hand-woven fabrics and jewellery. It also sells quintessentially Swiss products such as army knives and fondue equipment.
🕙 Mon–Fri 9–8, Sat 9–5 🚋 Tram 6, 7, 11, 13 to Rennweg

⊕ SIHLCITY
Kalanderplatz 1
Tel 044 204 99 99
www.sihlcity.ch
This former paper factory has been imaginatively transformed into an urban entertainment complex with hotel, cinema, 80 shops and 13 restaurants with an open courtyard.
🕙 Shops Mon–Sat 9–8 🚋 Tram 5, 13 to Utobrücke

▽ PLATINS
Kalanderplatz 7, Sihlcity
Tel 044 280 03 30
www.platins.ch
On four floors of the new Sihlcity development with a chill-out area and a business lounge, this stylish club offers deep house, dirty house, electro house, funky house and tech house music.
🕙 Wed 6pm–1am, Thu 8pm–2am, Fri–Sat 10pm–5am 🚋 Tram 5, 13 to Utobrücke

▽ YELLOW DOOR BAR
Sihlfeldstrasse 63
Tel 043 811 52 38
www.yellow-door-bar.ch
This music and dance bar is devoted to jazz and blues with themed evenings such as Cuban and Doha.
🕙 Mon–Sat 5–1 🚋 Tram 2, 3 to Lochergut

EATING

HAUS HILTL
Sihlstrasse 28
Tel 044 227 70 00
www.hiltl.ch
Europe's first vegetarian restaurant, Haus Hiltl was founded in 1898 and was reopened in 2007 with restaurant, bar, café, confectionery shop and take-away (takeout). Besides staples such as rösti and farmer's plate, it specializes in incorporating Indian influences, and the Indian buffet has 25 dishes on offer while the salad bar has 50.
🕙 Thu–Sat 6am–4am, Sun, Mon 6am–12am, Tue, Wed 6am–2am
🍴 L CHF31, D CHF40, Wine CHF28
🚋 Tram 6, 7, 11, 13 to Rennweg or 2, 9 to Sihlstrasse

KRONENHALLE
Rämistrasse 4
Tel 044 262 99 00
www.kronenhalle.com
One of the city's most historic restaurants, founded in 1862, the Kronenhalle and its haute cuisine have long attracted celebrities and continue to do so for their few concessions to fashion. Staple dishes include veal steak with morel mushrooms, rösti, and semolina with raspberries. The walls are decorated with original works by Chagall, Bonnard, Braque, Miró, Picasso and Rodin.
🕙 Daily 12–12
🍴 L CHF85, D CHF100, Wine CHF51
🚋 Tram 2, 4, 5, 8, 9, 11, 15 to Bellevue

ZUNFTHAUS ZUR ZIMMERLEUTEN
Limmatquai 40
Tel 044 250 53 63
www.zunfthaus-zimmerleuten.ch
Overlooking the Limmat River, this medieval home of the carpenters' guild now offers alfresco dining beneath arches downstairs or a more expensive wood-panelled first-floor room. Typical Zurich and Swiss dishes feature, such as fish soup of perch and trout.
🕙 Mon–Sun 11.30–2, 6–12
🍴 L CHF40, D CHF70, Wine CHF30
🚋 Tram 4, 15 to Helmhaus

STAYING

GLOCKENHOF
Sihlstrasse 31, CH-8022 Zurich
Tel 044 225 91 91
www.glockenhof.ch
Only seven minutes' walk from the main station, this period building has been tastefully modernized and has an attractive garden restaurant. Many of the bedrooms are generously sized.
🛏 CHF390–520 including breakfast
ⓘ 95
🚋 Tram 6, 7, 11, 13 to Rennweg

LIMMATHOF
Limmatquai 142, CH-8001 Zurich
Tel 044 267 60 40
www.limmathof.com
Overlooking the river and close to the railway station, this hotel has vegetarian and Swiss restaurants.
🛏 CHF158–175 including breakfast
ⓘ 62
🚋 Tram 3, 4, 6, 7, 10 to Central

SORRELL HOTEL ZURICHBERG
Orellistrasse 21, CH-8044 Zurich
Tel 044 268 33 35
www.zuerichberg.ch
In a quiet location overlooking fields and the Alps, the hotel is less than 20 minutes from the city centre at the end of tram line 6. Half the rooms are in the modernized Victorian building, half in the new building next door. There's a good restaurant with alfresco dining.
🛏 CHF230–450 including breakfast
ⓘ 66
🚋 Tram 6 to Zoo

HOTEL ST. GEORGES
Weberstrasse 11, CH-8004 Zurich
Tel 044 241 11 44
www.hotel-st-georges.ch
The rooms in this traditional hotel in the heart of the city have been attractively renovated, though only some have their own bathroom.
🛏 CHF124–159 including breakfast
ⓘ 44
🚋 Tram 2, 3, 8, 9, 14 to Stauffacher

SWITZERLAND

ARRIVING

BY AIR

The number of world and European companies and organizations in Switzerland means that the country is well served by international airlines with flights to the principal hub of Zurich from 135 airports worldwide. Swiss and other airlines offer direct flights to many destinations in North America including JFK airport in New York, Newark New Jersey, Philadelphia, Chicago, Atlanta, Miami, Los Angeles and Montréal. Zurich also offers direct flights to Dubai, Hong Kong and Singapore, all of which act as hubs for the Middle and Far East and for onward connections to Australia and New Zealand. Zurich is followed by Geneva and Basel, with smaller airports and very limited services at Berne, Lugano and Sion. The national airline, Swiss International Air Lines (www.swiss.com), flies to 70 destinations in 42 countries; an advantage of flying Swiss into Zurich and Geneva and proceeding onwards by rail is that the Fly-Rail facility enables your check-in luggage to be consigned through to principal stations in Switzerland, where it is available for collection.

The frequent trains are the quickest and cheapest way to reach the city centres of Zurich (about 17 minutes) and Geneva (6 minutes); both airports have main-line stations beneath them with fast trains to all other principal cities. Basel airport awaits an extension of the tram network; until then bus route 50 runs 2–8 times an hour for a 13-minute journey to the main railway station; outside is the principal interchange on the tram network.

BY BUS

Eurolines (www.eurolines.co.uk/ www.nationalexpress.co.uk) has air-conditioned long-distance buses with reclining seats that travel across Western Europe to Switzerland. It has services to hubs in the east and in west, linking with the efficient domestic rail and bus system. Journey times can be long. From Victoria Station in London,

UK International services to Geneva and the west involve a transfer in Paris with a wait of up to 2 hours (journey time from London around 19 hours). For Zurich and the east, transfers take place at Brussels (journey times are around 17 hours).

BY TRAIN

Lying at the heart of Europe, Switzerland is criss-crossed by international railway routes, but the majority of visitors approach by high-speed TGV trains from France or ICE services from Germany. Trains from Paris Gare de l'Est reach Basel in 3 hours 20 minutes and Zurich in 4 hours 35 minutes, while Lyria TGVs leave Gare de Lyon to reach Geneva in 3 hours 25 minutes and Lausanne in 3 hours 48 minutes. Tickets to and within Switzerland (▷ below) can be purchased through Swiss Travel Service.

BY CAR

Switzerland has excellent motorway (expressway) links with neighbouring France and Germany, making driving easy. In summer, the mountain passes across the Jura from France into Switzerland offer a more picturesque way to cross the border.

There are good links through the Alps with Italy to the south with a picturesque trip along the water's edge of Lake Lugano or Lake Maggiore, which are metaphorically cut in two by the border between the two countries. A motorway is currently being built linking Switzerland with the Italian motorway leading to Milan.

You need a national driver's licence (an international licence will not suffice) and the vehicle registration certificate to take a car into Switzerland. A Green Card is not necessary, but motorists are strongly advised to obtain a comparable level of cover from their insurance company. To use the motorways, you need to obtain a vignette by paying a motorway tax, which can be bought from Switzerland Travel Centres, at border crossings or online from

www.MySwitzerland.com. The minimum age for driving is 18. Unless otherwise posted, speed limits are 50kph (31mph) in built-up areas and on secondary roads, 80kph (50mph) on ordinary roads and for caravans and trailers, and 120kph (74mph) on motorways.

Some major Alpine destinations such as Wengen and Zermatt cannot be reached by car, and the concentration required on mountain roads often leaves little opportunity to enjoy the scenery.

If taking a car in winter, snow chains are compulsory. It's wise to practise putting these on the tyres at home so that you are not struggling with them when you get to the freezing cold mountain roads.

CAR RENTAL

The major car rental companies are found at the three principal airports. Some car rental operators may set a higher minimum age than the national 18. In winter, car rental companies will supply cars with winter tyres or snow chains. This may involve extra cost but they are important to cope with mountain conditions and are a legal requirement.

VISITORS WITH A DISABILTY

Switzerland has good facilities for visitors with disabilities, though difficulties do arise from the low platform levels still common throughout much of Europe (rebuilding is reducing the number). However, 160 stations have hoists and staff to overcome the height difference. A toll-free call within Switzerland (0800 007 102) one hour before the train is due to leave will procure the necessary assistance. Further information is given in the brochure *Travellers with a Handicap*, which is available at all stations or can be viewed as a PDF file on the website mct.sbb.ch/ mct/en/reisemarkt/services/ wissen/handicap.htm. Further information on facilities for the disabled can be obtained from Mobility International Switzerland (www.mis-ch.ch).

GETTING AROUND

BY SWISS TRAVEL SYSTEM

Switzerland has the finest public transport system in the world. It is easy to use, good value, and the best and safest way to enjoy the country's stupendous scenery. The quality of the trains and postbuses (▷ below) is high, cleanliness and punctuality can be taken for granted, and services are frequent and fast. Trains, postbuses, funiculars, cable cars and ships provide a dovetailed system that offers quick connections between each mode. Information, maps and timetables are readily available and well designed.

For visitors there is a range of Swiss Travel System passes that cover a variety of holiday types. Valid for 4, 8, 15, 22 days or 1 month, the Swiss Pass covers unlimited travel on trains, postbuses, boats and the public transport systems of 38 Swiss cities, with 50 per cent discount on mountain summit trains, cable cars and funiculars. For those who will not need a pass every day, the Swiss Flexi Pass covers 3, 4, 5, 6 or 8 days travel within a one-month period. For people up to 26 years old, the Swiss Youth Pass confers the same benefits as the Swiss Pass, but under-16s travelling with one or two parents travel free of charge with a Swiss Travel System Family Card. If you are visiting only one place, the Swiss Transfer Ticket takes you from a border or airport to your destination. The first three passes are also valid as a Swiss Museum Pass, giving free access to more than 420 museums, making them even better value. If two or more people are travelling together, each receives a 15 per cent discount on the purchase price of any passes.

BY TRAIN

The core network is built to standard gauge; most lines have an hourly service and many trains have either double-deck coaches or tilting carriages to allow higher speeds on curved track. This is supplemented by narrow-gauge lines of great character which reach areas where standard-gauge lines would have been too difficult and costly to build. Interchanges are easy, and most stations have ramped access to the platforms for wheeled luggage and wheelchairs.

BY BUS/TRAM

Urban transport services are provided by local companies with modern buses and, in the larger cities, trams. Both are usually of the low-floor type, making access easy.

Outside the major urban areas bus services act as an extension of the efficient rail system, linking more distant towns and villages with the railway station for quick onward transport.

Buses also provide good connections between distant ski slopes and the ski resorts during the winter season with free tickets for those who have bought ski passes.

BY POSTBUS

The iconic Postbus with its distinctive horn reaches outside the urban areas to connect routes and places with the railway network, so at many stations you will see postbuses waiting to meet a train. Though called buses, the vehicles provide the comfort of coaches, and carry luggage and usually bicycles.

Many of the routes thread mountain roads and have become a tourist attraction in their own right, sometimes with double-decker buses. The most scenic routes are served by 'Route Express' buses with limited stops. The best known is the Palm Express between St. Moritz and Lugano; others include the Romantic Route Express between Andermatt and Grindelwald over the Furka and Grimsel passes and the Napoleon Route Express between Saas Fee and Domodossola over the Simplon Pass.

Its possible to buy travel passes by the month or pay per journey, though be aware that passes may only be valid for a limited postbus region, rather than for the whole of Switzerland.

BY BICYCLE

Despite its gradients, Switzerland has excellent facilities for cycling: besides many dedicated, well-signed cycle paths and routes, bicycles can be rented from 100 railway stations. The option of returning them to another station allows you to choose a downhill route to explore a valley, such as the Ticino between Airolo and Biasca. Cities such as Zürich, Berne and Geneva also have free cycle loans; enquire at the tourist office for the locations.

BY CAR

Switzerland's major cities are linked by a modern and well maintained system of motorways (expressways), and all roads are kept in good condition, though country and mountain roads will certainly contain steep and winding sections that can prove challenging. In order to use any roads you'll need to buy a tax vignette (see left). An annual vignette costs CHF40 (www.ezv.admin.ch) and this must be paid whatever the length of your stay–even a one-day trip. The vignette must be placed at specific points on the windscreen of your vehicle in full view for police and traffic regulation enforcers.

If travelling in the mountains with your own vehicle pay extra attention–the magnificent views can be distracting–and only stop/park in specified areas. The Swiss have efficient towing companies if you leave your vehicle in a dangerous or improper place and you'll need to pay a fine or release fee before you get your vehicle back.

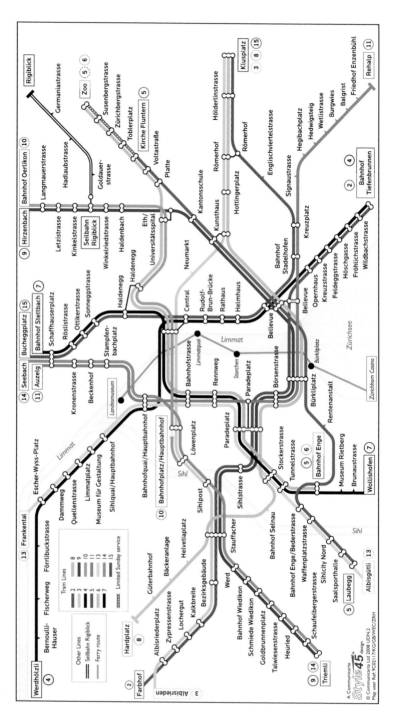

Werdhölzli ④
Bernoulli-Häuser
Fischerweg
Förrlibuckstrasse
Frankental ⑬
Escher-Wyss-Platz
Dammweg
Quellenstrasse
Limmatplatz
Museum für Gestaltung
Sihlquai/Hauptbahnhof
Bahnhofquai/Hauptbahnhof
Bahnhofplatz/Hauptbahnhof ⑩
Löwenplatz
Paradeplatz
Stockerstrasse
Tunnelstrasse
Museum Rietberg
Bahnhof Enge ⑤ ⑥
Rentenanstalt
Bürkliplatz
Wollishofen ⑦

Rigiblick
Germaniastrasse
Zoo ⑤ : ⑥
Susenbergstrasse
Zürichbergstrasse
Toblerplatz
Kirche Fluntern ⑤
Voltastraße
Platte

Klusplatz
③ ⑧ ⑮
Friedhof Enzenbühl
Rehalp ⑪

Hölderlinstrasse
Wetlistrasse
Burgwies
Balgrist
Römerhof
Hegibachplatz
Hedwigsteig
Englischviertelstrasse
Signaustrasse
② ④
Bahnhof Tiefenbrunnen

Bahnhof Oerlikon ⑩
Langmauerstrasse
Hadlaubstrasse
Goldauer-strasse

Hirzenbach ⑨
Letzistrasse
Kinkelstrasse
Winkelriedstrasse
Haldenbach
Eth/Universitätsspital
Seilbahn Rigiblick

Kantonsschule
Römerhof
Kunsthaus
Hottingerplatz
Kreuzplatz

Bucheggplatz ⑮
Bahnhof Stettbach ⑦
Schaffhauserplatz
Röslistrasse
Ottikerstrasse
Sonneggstrasse
Haldenegg
Haldenegg
Neumarkt
Central
Rudolf-Brun-Brücke
Rathaus
Helmhaus

Bahnhof Stadelhofen
Bellevue
Opernhaus
Höschgasse
Feldeggstrasse
Kreuzstrasse
Fröhlichstrasse
Wildbachstrasse

Seebach ⑭
Auzelg ⑪
Kronenstrasse
Beckenhof
Stampfenbachplatz

Landesmuseum
Bahnhofstrasse
Limmatquai
Renngweg
Storchen
Paradeplatz
Börsenstrasse
Bellevue
Bürkliplatz

Limmat
Zürichsee
Zürichhorn Casino

Hardplatz ⑧
Güterbahnhof
Bäckeranlage
Helvetiaplatz
Sihlpost
Stauffacher
Sihlstrasse
Bahnhof Selnau

Farbhof ②
Albisriederplatz
Zypressenstrasse
Lochergut
Kalkbreite
Bezirksgebäude
Werd
Bahnhof Enge/Bederstrasse
Waffenplatzstrasse
Sihlcity Nord

Laubegg ⑤
Albisgütli ⑬

Triemli ⑨ ⑭
Schmiede Wiedikon
Goldbrunnenplatz
Talwiesenstrasse
Heuried
Schaufelbergerstrasse
Saalsporthalle
Bahnhof Wiedikon

Albisrieden ③

Limmat
Sihl
Sihl

Tram Lines
2
3
5
6
7
8
9
10
11
13
14
15
Limited Sunday service

Other Lines
Seilbahn Rigiblick
Ferry route

A Communicarta
Style45 design
© Communicarta Ltd 2008 UDN 2
Map user Ref: 9C02117/KG/GB/WEC/ZRH

PLANNING

WHEN TO GO

AUSTRIA

• You can expect much variation in the weather in Austria. Overall, the country has a moderate central European climate with four distinct seasons. Vienna can be bitingly cold in winter and get stifling hot in summer; Salzburg catches a lot of rain. In Innsbruck and the Tirol valleys, the hot, dry *Föhn* winds of early spring and autumn can cause headaches. There's a Mediterranean influence in eastern Carinthia and Styria. Summers are short in the Alps, with the winter ski season usually spanning December to mid-April, but in winter or summer, the sun is intense at high altitudes.

• May to September are warm and pleasant summer months, with the highest temperatures in July and August. Summer is also the time of the highest rainfall, and July and August are peak tourist season. May and September are usually the ideal months for walking.

BELGIUM

• Belgium enjoys a mild climate with average temperatures in summer around 20ºC (68ºF), and 6ºC (43ºF) in winter. Winters (December through March) see little snow except in the south of Belgium, but a lot of rain and strong winds. It still rains a fair amount in early spring, but by May it gets sunnier and warmer. Summers can be very sunny but there are rainy days. Autumn (September through November) is often very mild.

• The peak tourist season is July and August, and Bruges can get overwhelmed by too many people in its narrow streets. May, June, September and October are the best months to visit without the crowds and in milder weather conditions.

FRANCE

• Paris has cool winters and warm summers. The longest days are in June, when you're likely to find comfortable temperatures and the most sunshine. August is quiet, as many Parisians flee to other parts of France to escape the muggy heat. Some restaurants close for the whole month. Autumn can be pleasant but hotel rooms may be hard to find as the trade fair season is in full swing. If you don't mind cooler winter weather, December can be magical, with the streets sparkling with Christmas lights.

• The northwest is often rainy, with mild winters and cool summers.

• The Vosges are hot in summer, the Massif Central is stormy and the southern Massif is dry. In contrast, the Cévennes get a lot of rain and the northern Massif can become very hot.

• The south of France has hot, dry summers and warm, wet winters. Summer winds are cooling and gentle but the colder and fiercer Mistral can swirl around for days, particularly in March and April.

GERMANY

• Generally speaking, Germany enjoys a mild climate, with average temperatures reaching around 20˚C (68˚F) in July and August and dropping to around 0˚C (32˚F) in December and January. Average rainfall is also fairly seasonal, with most regions receiving up to 120mm (4.75in) a month in the height of summer and less than 20mm (0.75in) in the depths of winter. However, the weather in Germany is changeable, even day to day.

• In cold winters, snow is not uncommon, particularly in the south and southeast. Western Germany tends to experience milder winters, while northern Germany usually feels cooler thanks to bracing winds blowing in off the North Sea.

• The most reliable months for a visit in terms of weather are May to September, although some areas, such as the Rhine and the Mosel, are probably best avoided in July and August, when the tourist tide is at its height. For those who are interested in winter sports, the ski slopes and cross-country trails in the Alps and the Black Mountains are generally open from December to March inclusive.

GREAT BRITAIN

• The wettest areas of Britain are to the west: Cornwall and Wales.

• June to the end of August is the warmest and busiest period, especially during the school holidays (July to early September). Rural and coastal areas—such as the West Country, the national parks and the Scottish Highlands—as well as major tourist cities are very busy at Easter and in July and August. Spring and September are appreciably quieter, although the weather is less reliable.

• Winter (December to late February) is chilly, with snow most widespread in the hills of northern England, Wales and Scotland; Scotland's Highlands have skiable snow most winters. Frosty conditions often do not arrive until November. On average January is the coldest month. The winter months can be a good time for visiting cities; accommodation is often less expensive and sights are less crowded. But note that some attractions close in winter (November to Easter), including most National Trust properties. However, major city museums stay open year-round.

IRELAND

• Ireland does not have extremes of temperature. The average daily temperature is about 50°F (9°C) across the country. The coldest months are January and February with a mean temperature between 39° and 44°F (4° and 7°C), and the warmest months are July and August, although even then average inland temperatures are only between 64° and 66°F (18° and 20°C).

• The main weather factor likely to affect your day is the rain, because despite being mild, Ireland is a very wet country. Irish skies are completely covered by cloud approximately half of the time. You can, and should, expect rain at all times of the year, although the summer is generally not as wet as winter. The parts of the country that receive most rainfall are the west and the hills. The north and west coasts are two of the windiest areas in Europe.

• In winter some visitor attractions close and don't reopen until spring, and it gets dark early, so be prepared for total darkness by 4pm if you travel in December.

● In July and August the roads will be busier as this is the main tourist season. For the best chance of sunny weather, come in May or June.

● Dublin and Belfast are great cities to visit at any time, with attractions open all year round.

ITALY

● Apart from the summer months, when temperatures soar and the sun shines all day, this mountainous country has the full range of conditions. In summer, the area around the Alps experiences numerous thunderstorms, which help clear the air, but inland parts of southern Italy suffer extremely hot nights, often making sleeping difficult.

● The climate is predominantly Mediterranean, with the far north experiencing Alpine trends and the far south arid and hot. Spring is pleasant everywhere, but there's frequent rain right through into May, and temperatures north of Rome only climb in June. Temperatures start to drop everywhere towards the end of September, with increasingly frequent bouts of rain and the first frosts in the Alps.

● Winter in the north is cold, with snow in the mountains, heavy frosts and thick fog on the plains. These conditions are also found to an extent in central Italy, with Tuscany and Umbria both experiencing bitter spells during the winter months. November is dank and wet everywhere. Winter is the wettest season in the south. Mountain regions are colder, with heavy winter snowfalls.

THE NETHERLANDS

● The maritime climate off the coast of northwest Europe brings mild winters and cool summers. It is not a country of extremes. You can experience rain at any time of year, though to improve your chances of fine weather, February and April are the driest months. March and October are the wettest months.

● August is the hottest month, but the average is only 22°C (72°F), and it is also one of the wettest months. Amsterdam and Den Haag are both on the western coast, which makes them cooler in summer, warmer in winter and slightly wetter all year round than the rest of the country.

PORTUGAL

● Despite its Atlantic position, Portugal's climate is predominantly Mediterranean, with warm, dry summers and mild, wet winters. Its geographic position on Europe's western edge ensures that the average rainfall is far higher than that of Spain to the east. Much of the rain falls between November and March, with levels increasing as you move north; showers are possible throughout the year in the far north. In central and southern Portugal, especially on the coast, it's mild throughout the year, though it is often cloudy in winter. Summers are hot and sunny all over the country, the high temperatures pleasantly tempered by cooling breezes along the coast.

● July and August are prime vacation time, with millions of foreign visitors flocking into the country. The Algarve, in particular, is at its busiest: Prices are at their peak, and bars, shops and beaches are packed.

● Most seasoned visitors to Portugal agree that spring and autumn are the best times to go; the weather is warm but not too hot and you'll escape the huge influx of high-summer tourists.

● Lisbon and the southern third of the country have mild winters, so this is an excellent time to explore the capital, the Alentejo and the Algarve. Some tourist facilities may be closed, but there's the huge advantage of dramatically reduced prices and few other visitors.

SPAIN

● During the summer months the temperature in the Mediterranean, northern and central regions can be scorching. Although the bars, shops and beaches are generally packed to bursting point, the guaranteed all-day sunshine and warm, balmy evenings more than compensate. This is also the time to visit the northern coast and the mountainous regions.

● Spring is the season to visit the Balearic Islands and the central regions of Castile, Andalucía and the Mediterranean coast. Early autumn is ideal for almost everywhere in the country, with many sunny days and blue skies.

● Spain is an excellent choice if you are looking for winter sunshine in Europe. Head for the southern and eastern coastal resorts, particularly Almería, which holds the winter sunshine record. The beautiful mountainous regions are ideal for winter sports.

● There is a huge regional variation in rainfall, which is highest in Galicia and the Cantabrian mountains, and in the central areas the winters can be quite cold, with bitter winds coming in off the sierras. Cool, refreshing sea breezes moderate the summer heat in the north, while in the south there is sometimes a hot, dry wind from Africa.

SWITZERLAND

● Switzerland's mountainous terrain makes it changeable at any season. You can enter a long Alpine tunnel in rain and emerge in sunshine. Perhaps the only month to be avoided is November, when many hotels outside cities and large towns are closed and mountain cable cars and chairlifts are being prepared for the skiing season. Skiing at the higher resorts such as Zermatt and Saas Fee can be good into May and even June, though climate change is eroding the dependable season.

● Rainfall tends to be higher in the spring and autumn, but the rain clears the air and produces a clarity that is rare in summer when haze can obstruct views. The Jura region is particularly noted for its high spring rainfall, while the Ticino enjoys the most hours of sunshine.

TIME ZONES		
City	Time difference	Time at 12 noon GMT
Amsterdam	+1	1pm
Berlin	+1	1pm
Brussels	+1	1pm
Chicago	-6	6am
Johannesburg	+2	2pm
Madrid	+1	1pm
Montréal	-6	6am
New York	-5	7am
Paris	+1	1pm
Rome	+1	1pm
San Francisco	-8	4am
Sydney	+10	10pm
Tokyo	+9	9pm

DOCUMENTATION

PASSPORTS

To enter Austria, Belgium, France, Germany, Italy, The Netherlands, Portugal and Spain, foreign visitors must have a passport valid for at least six months or, in the case of EU nationals, a national identification card or passport. Visitors to Swizerland, the Republic of Ireland and the UK (England, Northern Ireland, Wales and Scotland) must have a passport that is valid for at least six months at the date of entry.

Loss of passport

If you lose your passport, contact your embassy in the country you are in. It helps if you have details of your passport number; either carry a photocopy of the relevant pages of your passport, or scan them and email them to yourself at a secure account that you can access anywhere in case of emergency.

VISAS

Citizens of any one of the European Economic Area (EEA) countries—the EU, plus Switzerland, Norway and Iceland—can enter the Republic of Ireland and the UK on leisure or business for any length of stay without a visa. Visitors from the US, Australia, Canada or New Zealand do not require a visa for stays of up to six months. However, you must have enough money to support yourself without working or receiving money from public funds.

Those wishing to stay longer than six months, and nationals of certain other countries, require a visa.

Citizens from the EU, Australia, Canada, New Zealand and the US visiting Austria, France, Germany, Italy, The Netherlands, Portugal and Spain do not require a visa for stays of up to 90 days. EU nationals are not limited by the length of time they can stay in Portugal. However, after 90 days, to remain in the other European countries listed above, a visa, extension, residence or work permit will need to be applied for, depending on the individual country.

Citizens from the EU, US, New Zealand and Australia do not require a visa for stays of less than 90 days in Switzerland.

CUSTOMS ALLOWANCES

Travelling to the EU from outside the EU

The EU countries are: Austria, Belgium, Cyprus*, Czech Republic, Denmark, Estonia, Finland, France, Germany, Greece, Hungary, Italy, Latvia, Lithuania, Luxembourg, Malta, Netherlands, Poland, Portugal, Republic of Ireland, Slovakia, Slovenia, Spain (but not the Canary Islands), Sweden, the UK (but not the Channel Islands).
*Though Cyprus is part of the EU, goods from any area of Cyprus not under control of the Government of the Republic of Cyprus are treated as non-EU imports.

You are entitled to the allowances shown below only if you travel with the goods and do not plan to sell them. If you bring in large quantities of alcohol or tobacco, a Customs Officer is likely to ask about the purposes for which you hold the goods. These allowances do vary slightly from country to country, so check before you travel.

- 200 cigarettes; or
- 100 cigarillos; or
- 50 cigars; or
- 250g (9oz) of tobacco

- 60cc/ml of perfume
- 250cc/ml of toilet water
- 1 litre of spirits or strong liqueurs over 22 per cent volume; or
- 2 litres of fortified wine, sparkling wine or other liqueurs
- 2 litres of still table wine

Travelling from the EU

When exiting the EU, make sure you know the allowances for the country you are travelling to as different coutnries have varying allowances. For example, there are limits on the amount of tobacco products you can bring into the UK from some EU countries, even though the UK is part of the EU.

Visitors from all other countries should contact their local embassy before travelling.

Entry requirements differ depending on your nationality and are also subject to change at short notice. You should always check the requirements prior to a visit and follow news events that may affect your situation.

TAX REFUNDS

For non-EU citizens most countries operate a tax refund system. Visitors spending a minimum amount at a participating store (normally indicated by a Tax Free sign in the window) will receive a form detailing the transaction and amount paid. These forms can be taken to a tax refund office (often at major airports and ports) for an immediate refund or sent by post for an electronic refund into a bank account.

PRACTICALITIES

CLOTHES AND LUGGAGE

Bring a selection of clothing for a wide range of weather conditions. Rainwear and sunscreen are essential, and also recommended are a lightweight waterproof jacket for summer and a small shoulder bag or rucksack for daily use when sightseeing and walking around town. Avoid expensive-looking, cumbersome luggage if you intend to travel around a lot.

ELECTRICITY

Britain and Northern Ireland use 240 volts AC and three-pin plugs, so you'll need an electrical adaptor or converter. The standard electricity supply is 230 volts AC in the Republic of Ireland. Sockets take three-pin plugs, as used in the UK.

Voltage in Austria, Belgium, France, Germany, Portugal, Spain and Switzerland is 220 volts AC. Sockets take plugs with two round pins.

Electricity in Italy and The Netherlands is 240 volts AC, and electrical appliances are fitted with sockets that have two round pins.

British users need an adaptor, and American users need an adaptor and a transformer, to step down the current for US electrical devices.

MEASUREMENTS

Britain officially uses the metric system, with fuel sold in litres, and food in grams and kilograms. However, imperial measurements are used widely in everyday life. Beer in pubs is still sold in pints (just under 0.5 litres), and road distances and speed limits are given in miles and miles per hour (mph) respectively.

The rest of Western Europe uses the metric system. Road distances are measured in kilometres, fuel is sold by the litre and food is weighed in grams and kilograms.

PUBLIC TOILETS

Hygiene standards in public toilets vary within the countries in Western Europe. You'll usually find the most hygienic facilities in museums, restaurants and shopping malls. Toilets in bars, restaurants and department stores are generally free,

CONVERSION CHART

From	To	Multiply by
Inches	Centimetres	2.54
Centimetres	Inches	0.3937
Feet	Metres	0.3048
Metres	Feet	3.2810
Yards	Metres	0.9144
Metres	Yards	1.0940
Miles	Kilometres	1.6090
Kilometres	Miles	0.6214
Acres	Hectares	0.4047
Hectares	Acres	2.4710
Gallons	Litres	4.5460
Litres	Gallons	0.2200
Ounces	Grams	28.35
Grams	Ounces	0.0353
Pounds	Grams	453.6
Grams	Pounds	0.0022
Pounds	Kilograms	0.4536
Kilograms	Pounds	2.205
Tons	Tonnes	1.0160
Tonnes	Tons	0.9842

CLOTHING SIZES

The chart below shows how British, European and US clothes sizes differ.

UK	Europe	US	
36	46	36	SUITS
38	48	38	
40	50	40	
42	52	42	
44	54	44	
46	56	46	
48	58	48	
7	41	8	SHOES
7.5	42	8.5	
8.5	43	9.5	
9.5	44	10.5	
10.5	45	11.5	
11	46	12	
14.5	37	14.5	SHIRTS
15	38	15	
15.5	39/40	15.5	
16	41	16	
16.5	42	16.5	
17	43	17	
8	36	6	DRESSES
10	38	8	
12	40	10	
14	42	12	
16	44	14	
18	46	16	
20	48	18	
4.5	37.5	6	SHOES
5	38	6.5	
5.5	38.5	7	
6	39	7.5	
6.5	40	8	
7	41	8.5	

although it's impolite to use them without buying anything or asking first. There is often a small charge for using public toilets, such as those in some train stations and shopping malls. Public toilets in Italy and Portugal and Spain can be scarce and the facilities are basic, so you might find it worthwhile to carry a supply of toilet paper with you outside the large towns.

SMOKING

In Belgium, France, Italy, Great Britain and Ireland, smoking is banned in pubs, clubs, restaurants, cinemas, offices, all forms of public transport and all other enclosed public spaces.

Smoking is generally tolerated in The Netherlands, with some exceptions, such as public transport. On 1 January 2009 it will become a legal requirement that all restaurants, bars and other service establishments will have to provide a non-smoking area.

Cafés and restaurants with non-smoking sections are the exception rather than the rule in Germany. Although 34 per cent of Swiss adults smoke, one of the highest rates in the developed world, the majority wants to see smoking in public places outlawed. There is little doubt that other cantons will follow the Ticino's lead in March 2008 in doing so. Most hotels have non-smoking rooms, and many restaurants have non-smoking areas. Smoking on public transport is prohibited.

In Austria and Spain some anti-smoking legislation has been passed into law. Smoking is banned in most workplaces and public areas. Small bars and eateries can designate themselves either a smoking or a non-smoking establishment and must display clear signs indicating this choice. Larger bars and restaurants (over a minimum square metreage) must have a clearly designated non-smoking area that is fully enforced.

Smoking is universal in Portugal and is still permitted in most hotels and restaurants. Non-smoking areas are few and far between though smoking is not permitted in museums, inside airports, or on some forms of public transport.

HEALTH

BEFORE YOU GO

- No inoculations are required for visiting Western Europe, although it's a good idea to make sure your tetanus protection is up to date (boosters are required every 10 years).
- If you are on any medication and think you might need a repeat prescription while you're away, ask for it well before you travel, and keep the packaging and/or the prescription in case you run out or lose your medication while you are away.
- EU citizens receive reduced-cost healthcare in other EU countries and Switzerland with the relevant documentation. This is the European Health Insurance Card (EHIC). This gives you access to state-provided medical treatment, and you'll be treated on the same basis as an 'insured' person living in the country you're visiting. You may have to make a contribution to the cost of your care. The EHIC also covers any treatment you need for a chronic disease or pre-existing illness. The EHIC won't cover you if the main purpose of your trip is to get medical treatment. You can apply for an EHIC online. Full health insurance is still strongly advised.
- If you are visiting Western Europe from a non-EU country, private medical insurance is essential; bring the policy document and a photocopy with you.
- If you are planning to stay away from home for a month or more, it may also be a good idea to have a full dental and medical check-up before you go.

WHAT TO BRING

- Take a first-aid kit with you. This should include: assorted adhesive plasters (Band Aids); sterile dressings; a bandage with safety pins; cotton wool; insect repellent; antiseptic cream; painkillers; remedies for constipation and for diarrhoea; antihistamine tablets; sunscreen; personal medicines.
- If you are on regular medication, you should ensure that you have adequate supplies for your trip. Make a note of the chemical name (rather than the brand name) in case you need replacement supplies.
- It is a good idea to take photocopies of all important

- Visitors to Europe from as far as the US, Australia or New Zealand may be concerned about the effect of long-haul flights on their health. The most widely publicized concern is deep vein thrombosis (DVT). Misleadingly labelled 'economy-class syndrome' DVT is the formation of a blood clot in the body's deep veins, particularly in the legs. The clot can be deadly as it moves around the bloodstream.
- People most at risk include the elderly, smokers, the overweight, pregnant women and those using the contraceptive pill. If you are at increased risk of DVT see your doctor before departing. Flying increases the likelihood of DVT because passengers are often seated in a cramped position for long periods of time and may become dehydrated.

To minimize risk:
drink water (not alcohol)
don't stay immobile for hours at a time
stretch and exercise your legs periodically
do wear elastic flight socks, which support veins and reduce the chances of a clot forming

EXERCISES

1 ANKLE ROTATIONS	2 CALF STRETCHES	3 KNEE LIFTS

Lift feet off the floor. Draw a circle with the toes, moving one foot clockwise and the other counterclockwise	Start with heel on the floor and point foot upward as high as you can. Then lift heel high keeping ball of foot on the floor	Lift leg with knee bent while contracting your thigh muscle. Then staighten leg, pressing foot flat to the floor

Other health hazards for flyers are airborne diseases and bugs spread by the plane's air-conditioning system. These are largely unavoidable but if you have a serious medical condition seek advice from a doctor before flying.

documentation, such as travel insurance and, for Europeans, your EHIC, which should be kept separate from the originals. You could scan the photocopies and send them to an email address that can be accessed anywhere in the world.
- Mosquitoes can be a problem in Portugal, so stock up with insect repellent and coils or electric zappers for use in bedrooms at night.
- If you forget any of these items, they are all readily available at pharmacies.

SUMMER HAZARDS

- The sun can be strong in any part of Western Europe between May and September, so pack a high-factor sun block.
- If you are planning on doing any high altitude walks take plenty of water, warm clothing and check weather reports before you go, as sudden changes in weather are not unknown.

MONEY

CURRENCIES
- Austria, Belgium, France, Germany, Italy, the Netherlands, Portugal, the Republic of Ireland and Spain have adopted the euro as their official currency. Euro notes and coins were introduced in January 2002.
- The currency of Britain and Northern Ireland is pounds sterling.
- Switzerland has the Swiss Franc as its currency.

CREDIT CARDS
- Credit cards are widely accepted; Visa, American Express and MasterCard are the most popular, but are still not accepted by smaller establishments or for small purchases. Check with staff.
- Many credit and debit cards in Europe are now allocated a four-digit security number that can be used instead of a signature. If you don't have a security number, you may need to show another form of ID, such as a passport or driver's licence, when paying for goods over the counter.
- Credit cards can also be used

for withdrawing currency at cash-points (ATMs), where you pay a fixed withdrawal fee, making it more economical the larger the amount you withdraw.
- If your credit cards or traveller's cheques are stolen call the issuer immediately, then report the loss to the police; you'll need a reference number for insurance purposes.

AUTOMATIC TELLER MACHINES (ATMs)
- These are widely available across Western Europe and accept most credit and debit cards.
- ATMs often have on-screen instructions in a choice of languages. Among the cards accepted are Visa, MasterCard and Diners Club. You'll need a four-digit PIN number.
- Many are accessible 24 hours a day.

TRAVELLER'S CHEQUES
- Traveller's cheques are a safer way of bringing in money as you can claim a refund if they

are stolen—but commission can be high when you cash them.
- With the growth in the use of plastic cards for payments and cash withdrawals, there has been a decline in the acceptance of travellers' cheques and few places now accept them for payment. The exchange rate for travellers' cheques is most favourable for those issued in euros, but is generally poorer than for banknotes.

BANKS
- There are plenty of banks throughout Western Europe, and most will exchange foreign currency (in France main post offices rather than banks offer this service). International airports also have currency exchanges. You will need your passport to change currency or traveller's cheques.
- Shop around for the best exchange and commission rates.
- Hours vary, but most banks open Monday–Friday, 9–5, but some close for lunch. Some open on Saturday morning.

CASH

There are 100 pence (p) to the pound (£). Coins are in denominations of 1p, 2p, 5p, 10p, 20p, 50p, £1 and £2. Banknotes (bills) are in denominations of £5, £10, £20 and £50. Banknotes issued in Scotland look different, but are generally accepted in England and Wales.

One euro is made up of 100 cents. Euro notes come in denominations of 5, 10, 20, 50, 100, 200 and 500 euros.

Swiss Franc notes are issued in denominations of 10, 20, 50, 100, 200 and 1000 francs.

Coins come in denominations of 1 and 2 euros and 1, 2, 5, 10, 20 and 50 cents.

One Swiss Franc is made up of 100 centimes. Coins come in denominations of 5 francs, 1 franc, 0.5 franc, 20 centimes, 10 centimes and 5 centimes.

COMMUNICATION

Australia	00 61
Austria	00 43
Belgium	00 32
Canada	00 1
France	00 33
Germany	00 49
Ireland	00 353
Italy	00 39
Netherlands	00 31
New Zealand	00 64
Portugal	00 351
Spain	00 34
Switzerland	00 41
UK	00 44
US	00 1

MOBILE PHONES

● Check with your mobile supplier to see if your phone will work in the country you are travelling to.

● Make sure the numbers memorized in your directory are in the international format.

● Check the call charges, which can rise dramatically when you use your phone abroad. You will often be charged to receive calls as well as make them.

● For visitors from North America, only tri-band mobile phones will work in Europe. Again, if you're unsure whether your phone is dual band or tri-band, check with your supplier.

● Don't forget to take a charger and an adaptor.

PUBLIC TELEPHONES

● **Austrian** phone booths are generally dark green and yellow. Most only accept phonecards, which can be bought from post offices and tobacconists.

● For most public telephones in **Belgium** you need a pre-paid phonecard, which you can buy from post offices and some supermarkets.

● Call boxes in **Britain** and **Northern Ireland** accept coins, credit cards, debit cards and BT chargecards. Note that only unused coins are returned.

● Nearly all public payphones in **France** use a phone card (*télécarte*) rather than coins. You can buy these at post offices, *tabacs,* corner shops and France Télécom shops, with 50 or 120 units. Some phones also accept certain credit cards.

● Most pay phones in **Germany** accept only phone cards (*Telefonkarten*), which can

be bought at tourist or post offices, fuel stations and newspaper kiosks. International calls can be made from all pay phones except for those marked '*National*'. Phone calls can also be made from main post offices. If you're using a phone card to call abroad, shop around for the best rates.

● Some phoneboxes in the **Republic of Ireland** accept coins only (minimum €0.50), while others accept coins, Eircom call cards and credit cards. You can buy €5, €10 or €20 Eircom call cards in newsagents, shops and post offices.

● In **Italy** note that some pay phones will only accept coins and others only a *carta telefonica* (phone card). Phones that only take coins tend to be less reliable. Call-centre telephones are often a better bet. You pay for the call when you have finished. Prepaid *carte telefoniche* (phone cards) are used widely. You can buy them from post offices, tobacconists, newsstands and bars.

● Most public telephones in the **Netherlands** accept phonecards from KPN Telecom and some take coins or credit cards. You can buy phonecards at KPN teleboutiques, post offices, newsagents and stations.

● All calls in **Portugal** are most easily made using card-operated *credifones*. Cards are available from post offices, newspaper shops, kiosks and tobacconists. Main post offices also have telephone cabins where you can make your call and pay afterwards.

● Public telephone booths in **Spain** are blue. They operate with both coins and phonecards (*tarjeta telefónica or credifone*), available from newsstands, post offices and tobacconists (*tabacos*). Telefónica also operates public phone stations (*locutorios*); you pay the attendant at the end of your call.

● Public telephones in **Switzerland** take both coins and phonecards. Phonecards can be bought from post offices and many shops.

POST

● Stamps in **Austria** are sold at tobacco kiosks as well as at post offices. Post boxes are yellow.

● Stamps can be bought from

stamp machines and post offices in **Belgium**. Post boxes are red.

● Post boxes in **Britain** and **Northern Ireland** are bright red and are either set into walls or are freestanding circular pillar boxes. Stamps are available from newsagents and supermarkets in addition to post offices.

● In **France** you can buy stamps (*timbres*) at post offices and *tabacs*. Write *par avion* (by air) on the envelope. Mailboxes are yellow. In Paris, some have two sections, one for Paris and the suburbs (*Paris–Banlieue*), and another for national and international mail (*autres départements/étranger*).

● Mail boxes in **Germany** are bright yellow and can be found outside and inside main post offices. Stamps (*Briefmarken*) can be bought from the post office counter or from stamp machines near the entrance.

● AnPost runs mail services in the **Republic of Ireland** and post boxes are bright green.

● Stamps in **Italy** (*francobolli*) are available from post offices and tobacconists. In the latter, the value of the stamps they sell you for a letter will be an approximation of the delivery cost.

● In the **Netherlands** you can buy stamps in many newsagents, some shops that sell postcards and at hotel receptions, as well as in post offices. Dutch post boxes were red but became orange in 2006. Unless you are posting something for the immediate local postal district, use the slot marked 'Overige Postcodes' (Other Postcodes).

● In **Portugal**, *selos* (stamps) can be bought at *correios* (post offices), kiosks, tobacconists, automatic dispensing machines and anywhere that has the 'Correio de Portugal' sign. There are two levels of mail service: *correio azul* for urgent letters, which must be weighed and posted in a blue box; and red boxes for regular mail.

● **Spanish** post boxes are bright yellow. Stamps (*sellos*) can be bought at post offices (*correos*), and tobacconists.

● In **Switzerland**, stamps can be bought in newsagents and hotels as well as post offices. Post boxes are a bright yellow.

FINDING HELP

EMERGENCY NUMBERS

AUSTRIA			IRELAND	
Police		133	**Republic of Ireland**	
Fire		122	Police, fire, ambulance,	**999** or
Ambulance		144	mountain rescue, cave rescue	**112**
			Northern Ireland	**999**
BELGIUM				
Police		101	**ITALY**	
Fire, Ambulance		100	Ambulance	**118**
			Fire Brigade	**115**
FRANCE			Police	**112** or **113**
General emergency number		112		
Ambulance		15	**THE NETHERLANDS**	
Police		17	Police, Fire, Ambulance	**112**
Fire		18		
			PORTUGAL	
GERMANY			Police, Fire, Ambulance	**112**
Ambulance, Fire		112		
Police		110	**SPAIN**	
			All emergency services:	**112**
GREAT BRITAIN			Police (in cities)	**091**
Police, Ambulance,		**999** or	Fire	**080**
Fire Services, Coastguard,		**112**	Ambulance	**061**
Mountain and Cave Rescue				
			SWITZERLAND	
			Police	**117**
			Fire	**118**
			Ambulance	**144**

PERSONAL SECURITY

● Don't keep wallets, purses or mobile phones in the back pockets of trousers, or anywhere else that is easily accessible to thieves. Money belts and bags worn around the waist are targets, as thieves know you are likely to have valuables in them. Always keep an eye on your bags in restaurants, bars and on the metro, and hold shoulder bags close to you, fastener inwards, when you are walking in the streets.

● Carry bags and cameras slung diagonally across your chest rather than over one shoulder, and position them under one arm in busy places. Backpacks might seem like a good idea,

but when they're worn using both straps it's almost impossible to keep an eye on them. If you must use a backpack, make sure that the zips are either lockable (i.e. with a miniature padlock) or hard to access. Again, if you're at all concerned about busy crowds, wear the backpack on your front where you can see it.

● Never carry more cash with you than you need, and keep all valuable and irreplaceable items in your hotel room or, better still, in a hotel safety deposit box. Note down credit card and traveller's cheque numbers and keep them in a safe place.

● At night, stick to brightly lit, main streets whenever possible

and avoid quiet areas.

● Be aware of who is standing behind you when you are withdrawing money from an ATM.

● Always lock your car, even if you intend to leave it for only a short time, and make certain luggage and other valuables are kept securely out of sight in the boot (trunk).

● Take special care if your journey includes a night train, as thieves sometimes target sleeping passengers. Take it in turns with a companion to watch the luggage. Keep an eye on suitcases during daytime journeys as well.

● If you are robbed, whatever you do, don't resist.

LOST PROPERTY

● If you lose money or valuables, inform the police and, depending on the small print of your policy, your travel insurance company as soon as possible (to be covered, lost or stolen belongings often have to be reported within 24 hours). Similarly, if your traveller's cheques are lost or stolen, notify the issuing company and tell them the serial numbers of the missing cheques.

● Airports have dedicated lost-property offices, but contact individual airlines if you lose belongings on board the aircraft.

● If your passport is lost or stolen, report it to the police and your consulate. The whole process of getting a replacement is easier if you have kept a copy of your passport number or a photocopy of the information page.

UK/US EMBASSIES ABROAD

Country	Telephone/Website
AUSTRIA	01 716130, www.britishembassy.at (UK); 01 313390, www.usembassy.at (US)
BELGIUM	02 287 6211, www.britain.be (UK); 02 508 2111, www.usembassy.be (US)
FRANCE	0144 51 31 00, www.amb-grandebretagne.fr (UK); 01 43 12 22 22, www.amb-usa.fr (US)
GERMANY	030 20 45 70, www.britischebotschaft.de (UK); 030 2385 174, www.usembassy.de (US)
GREAT BRITAIN	020 7499 9000, www.usembassy.org.uk (US)
IRELAND	01 205 3700, www.fco.co.uk (UK); 01 668 8777, www.usembassy.ie (US)
ITALY	06 4220 0001, www.britain.it (UK); 06 467 41, www.usembassy.it (US)
NETHERLANDS	070 427 0427, www.britain.nl (UK); 070 310 2209, www.usembassy.nl (US)
PORTUGAL	021 329 40 00, www.uk-embassy.pt (UK); 021 727 3300, www.american-embassy.pt (US)
SPAIN	091 700 83 09, www.ukinspain.com (UK); 091 587 22 00, www.embusa.es (US)
SWITZERLAND	031 359 77 00, www.britishembassy.ch (UK); 031 357 70 11, www.usembassy.ch (US)

FRENCH WORDS AND PHRASES

CONVERSATION

What is the time?
Quelle heure est-il?

When do you open/close?
**À quelle heure ouvrez/
fermez-vous?**

I don't speak French.
Je ne parle pas français.

Do you speak English?
Parlez-vous anglais?

I don't understand.
Je ne comprends pas.

Please repeat that.
**Pouvez-vous répéter
(s'il vous plaît)?**

Please speak more slowly.
**Pouvez-vous parler plus
lentement?**

What does this mean?
Qu'est-ce que ça veut dire?

Write that down for me, please.
**Pouvez-vous me l'écrire,
s'il vous plaît?**

Please spell that.
**Pouvez-vous me l'épeler,
s'il vous plaît?**

I'll look that up
(in the dictionary).
**Je vais le chercher
(dans le dictionnaire).**

My name is…
Je m'appelle…

What's your name?
**Comment vous appelez-
vous?**

This is my wife/husband.
Voici ma femme/mon mari.

This is my daughter/son.
Voici ma fille/mon fils.

This is my friend.
Voici mon ami(e).

Hello, pleased to meet you.
Bonjour, enchanté(e).

I'm from …
Je viens de …

I'm on holiday (vacation).
Je suis en vacances.

I live in…
J'habite à…

Where do you live?
Où habitez-vous?

Good morning.
Bonjour.

Good evening.
Bonsoir.

Goodnight.
Bonne nuit.

Goodbye.
Au revoir.

See you later.
À plus tard.

How much is that?
C'est combien?

May I/Can I…?
Est-ce que je peux…?

I don't know.
Je ne sais pas.

You're welcome.
Je vous en prie.

How are you?
Comment allez-vous?

I'm sorry.
Je suis désolé(e).

Excuse me.
Excusez-moi.

That's all right.
De rien.

USEFUL WORDS

Yes
Oui

No
Non

There
Là-bas

Here
Ici

Where
Où

Who
Qui

When
Quand

Why
Pourquoi

How
Comment

Later
Plus tard

Now
Maintenant

Open
Ouvert

Closed
Fermé

Please
S'il vous plaît

Thank you
Merci

IN TROUBLE

I don't feel well.
Je ne me sens pas bien.

Could you call a doctor?
**(Est-ce que) vous pouvez
appeler un médecin/un
docteur, s'il vous plaît?**

Is there a doctor/pharmacist on
duty?
**(Est-ce qu')il y a un
médecin/docteur/une
pharmacie de garde?**

I feel sick.
J'ai envie de vomir.

I need to see a doctor/dentist.
**Il faut que je voie un
médecin/docteur/
un dentiste.**

Please direct me to the
hospital.
**(Est-ce que) vous pouvez
m'indiquer le chemin
pour aller à l'hôpital, s'il vous
plaît?**

I've been stung by a
wasp/bee/jellyfish.
**J'ai été piqué(e) par une
guêpe/abeille/méduse.**

I have a heart condition.
J'ai un problème cardiaque.

I am diabetic.
Je suis diabétique.

I'm asthmatic.
Je suis asmathique.

I am on medication.
Je prends des médicaments.

I have left my medicine at home.
J'ai laissé mes médicaments chez moi.

I need to make an emergency appointment.
Je dois prendre un rendezvous d'urgence.

I have bad toothache.
J'ai mal aux dents.

I don't want an injection.
Je ne veux pas de piqûre.

Help!
Au secours!

I have lost my passport/wallet/purse/handbag.
J'ai perdu mon passeport/portefeuille/porte-monnaie/sac à main.

I have had an accident.
J'ai eu un accident.

My car has been stolen.
On m'a volé ma voiture.

I have been robbed.
J'ai été volé(e).

RESTAURANTS

A table for…, please.
Une table pour…, s'il vous plaît.

We have/haven't booked.
Nous avons/n'avons pas réservé.

Could we sit there?
(Est-ce que) nous pouvons nous asseoir ici?

Are there tables outside?
(Est-ce qu')il y a des tables dehors/à la terrasse?

Where are the toilets?
Où sont les toilettes?

We'd like something to drink.
Nous voudrions quelque chose à boire.

Could we see the menu/wine list?
(Est-ce que) nous pouvons voir le menu/la carte des vins, s'il vous plaît?

Is there a dish of the day?
(Est-ce qu')il y a un plat du jour?

What do you recommend?
Qu'est-ce que vous nous conseillez?

I can't eat wheat/sugar/salt/pork/beef/dairy.
Je ne peux pas manger de blé/sucre/sel/porc/bœuf/produits laitiers.

I am a vegetarian.
Je suis végétarien(ne).

I'd like…
Je voudrais …

Could I have bottled still/sparkling water?
(Est-ce que) je peux avoir une bouteille d'eau minérale non-gazeuse/gazeuse, s'il vous plaît?

We didn't order this.
Nous n'avons pas commandé ça.

The meat is too rare/overcooked.
La viande est trop saignante/trop cuite.

The food is cold.
Le repas/Le plat est froid.

Can I have the bill, please?
(Est-ce que) je peux avoir l'addition, s'il vous plaît?

The bill is not right.
Il y a une erreur sur l'addition.

HOTELS

Do you have a room?
(Est-ce que) vous avez une chambre?

How much each night?
C'est combien par nuit?

I have a reservation for … nights
J'ai réservé pour … nuits.

Double room.
Une chambre pour deux personnes/double.

Twin room.
Une chambre à deux lits/avec lits jumeaux.

Single room.
Une chambre à un lit/pour une personne.

With bath/shower/toilet.
Avec salle de bain/douche/WC.

Is the room air-conditioned/heated?
(Est-ce que) la chambre est climatisée/chauffée?

Is breakfast/lunch/dinner included in the cost?
(Est-ce que) le petit déjeuner/le déjeuner/le dîner est compris dans le prix?

The room is too hot/cold.
Il fait trop chaud/froid dans la chambre.

Could I have another room?
(Est-ce que) je pourrais avoir une autre chambre?

I am leaving this morning.
Je pars ce matin.

Can I pay my bill?
(Est-ce que) je peux régler ma note, s'il vous plaît?

May I see the room?
(Est-ce que) je peux voir la chambre?

MONEY

Is there a bank/currency exchange office nearby?
(Est-ce qu') il y a une banque/un bureau de change près d'ici?

Can I cash this here?
(Est-ce que) je peux encaisser ça ici?

I'd like to change sterling/dollars into euros.
Je voudrais changer des livres sterling/dollars en euros.

Can I use my credit card to withdraw cash?
(Est-ce que) je peux utiliser ma carte de crédit pour retirer de l'argent?

What is the exchange rate today?
Quel est le taux de change aujourd'hui?

GERMAN WORDS AND PHRASES

There is one official standard German language, *Hochdeutsch* (High German), which is taught in school and which everyone in the country should be able to understand. However, regional dialects, with strong local accents, are widely spoken in many areas. The words and phrases that follow are High German, and the guide below should help you with the pronunciation.

Vowels:

a	short as in hand, or long as in father
e	short as in bet, or long as in day
i	short as in fit
o	short as in lost, or long as in coach
u	long as in boot
ä	short as in wet, or long as in wait
ö	long as in fur
ü	long as in blue

Vowels are always short after a double consonants, and long when followed by 'h'

Dipthongs:

ai	as in mine	ie	as in tree
ei	as in spy	eu	as in boy
au	as in how	äu	as in boy

Consonants:

b is like **p** }
d is like **t** } at the end of a word or syllable
g is like **k** }
ch is either a throaty sound, like the Scottish lo**ch**, after a, o, u and au, or an exaggerated **h** sound after i, e ä, ö, eu, and ie
j is like **y** in yacht
s is either like **z** in zip when the first letter of the word, or like **s** in bus if it goes before a consonant
sch is like **sh** in shut
sp and st are pronounced **shp** and **sht**
v is like **f** in fit when the first letter of the word
w is like **v** in very

CONVERSATION

What is the time?
Wie spät ist es?

I don't speak German.
Ich spreche kein Deutsch.

Do you speak English?
Sprechen Sie Englisch?

I don't understand.
Ich verstehe nicht.

Please repeat that.
Wiederholen Sie das, bitte.

Please speak more slowly.
Sprechen Sie bitte langsamer.

Write that down for me please.
Schreiben Sie das bitte auf.

Please spell that.
Buchstabieren Sie das, bitte.

My name is…
Ich heisse…

What's your name?
Wie heissen Sie?

Hello, pleased to meet you.
Guten Tag, freut mich.

This is my friend.
Das ist mein Freund/meine Freundin.

This is my wife/husband/ daughter/son.
Das ist meine Frau/mein Mann/meine Tochter/mein Sohn.

Where do you live?
Wo wohnen Sie?

I'm from…
Ich komme aus…

Good morning/afternoon.
Guten Morgen/Tag.

Good evening/night.
Guten Abend/gute Nacht.

Goodbye.
Auf Wiedersehen.

How are you?
Wie geht es Ihnen?

Fine, thank you.
Sehr gut.

USEFUL WORDS

yes
ja

no
nein

please
bitte

thank you
danke

you're welcome
bitte schön

excuse me!
entschuldigung

where
wo

here
hier

there
dort

when
wann

now
jetzt

later
später

why
warum

who
wer

may I/can I
darf ich/kann ich

IN TROUBLE

Help.
Hilfe.

Stop, thief.
Haltet den Dieb.

Can you help me, please?
Können sie mir bitte helfen?

Call the fire brigade/police/an ambulance.
Rufen sie die Feuerwehr/ Polizei/einen Krankenwagen.

Where is the police station?
Wo ist das Polizeirevier?

I need to see a doctor/dentist.
Ich muss zum Arzt/Zahnarzt gehen.

Please direct me to the hospital.
Wie komme ich zum Krankenhaus?

I have lost my passport/ wallet/purse.
Ich habe meinen Pass/meine Brieftasche/Handtasche.

I have been robbed.
Ich bin bestohlen worden.

Is there a lost property office?
Gibt es hier ein Fundbüro?

I am allergic to…
Ich bin allergisch gegen...

I have a heart condition.
Ich habe ein Herzleiden.

RESTAURANTS
Waiter/waitress.
Kellner/Kellnerin.

I'd like to reserve a table for… people at…
Ich möchte einen Tisch für... Personen um... reservieren.

A table for…, please.
Einen Tisch für... bitte.

We have/haven't made a reservation.
Wir haben/haben nicht reserviert.

Could we sit there?
Können wir dort sitzen?

Are there tables outside?
Gibt es draußen Tische?

We'd like something to drink.
Wir möchten etwas zu trinken.

Could we see the menu/wine list?
Wir hätten gern die Speisekarte/Weinkarte.

Do you have a menu/wine list in English?
Haben Sie eine Speisekarte/ Weinkarte auf Englisch?

Is there a dish of the day?
Gibt es ein Tagesgericht?

What do you recommend?
Was empfehlen Sie?

I can't eat wheat/sugar/salt/ pork/beef/dairy.
Ich vertrage keinen Weizen/Zucker/kein Salz/ Schweinefleisch/Rindfleisch/ keine Milchprodukte.

I am a vegetarian.
Ich bin Vegetarier.

I'd like…
Ich möchte...

Could we have some salt and pepper?
Könnten wir etwas Pfeffer und Salz haben?

May I have an ashtray?
Kann ich einen Aschenbecher haben?

This is not what I ordered.
Das habe ich nicht bestellt.

The food is cold.
Das Essen ist kalt.

The meat is too rare/ overcooked.
Das Fleisch ist zu roh/ verbraten.

Can I have the bill, please?
Wir möchten zahlen, bitte.

The bill is not right.
Die Rechnung stimmt nicht.

I'd like to speak to the manager, please.
Ich möchte mit dem Geschäftsführer sprechen.

The food was excellent.
Das Essen war ausgezeichnet.

Where are the toilets?
Wo sind die Toiletten?

HOTELS
Do you have a room?
Haben Sie ein Zimmer frei?

I have made a reservation for …nights.
Ich habe ein Zimmer für... Nächte bestellt.

How much per night?
Was kostet es pro Nacht?

Do you have room service?
Haben Sie Zimmerservice?

Is the room air-conditioned/ heated?
Hat das Zimmer eine Klimaanlage/Heizung?

Is there an elevator in the hotel?
Hat das Hotel einen Fahrstuhl?

When is breakfast served?
Wann gibt es Frühstück?

I need an alarm call at…
Ich möchte um... geweckt werden.

May I have my room key?
Kann ich meinen Schlüssel haben?

Will you look after my luggage until I leave?
Kann ich bis zu meiner Abreise mein Gepäck hier lassen?

Where can I park my car?
Wo kann ich meinen Wagen parken?

Could I have another room?
Könnte ich ein anderes Zimmer haben?

Where is the tourist information office, please?
Wo ist dei Touristeninformation, bitte?

I am leaving this morning.
Ich reise heute Morgen ab.

Please can I pay my bill?
Kann ich bitte meine Rechnung bezahlen?

Thank you for your hospitality.
Vielen Dank für Ihre Gastfreundschaft.

MONEY
Is there a bank/currency exchange office nearby?
Ist hier in der Nähe eine Bank/Wechselstube?

I'd like to change sterling/ dollars into euros.
Ich möchte Pfund/Dollars in Euro tauschen.

Can I use my credit card to withdraw cash?
Kann ich mit meiner Kreditkarte Geld abheben?

ITALIAN WORDS AND PHRASES

Once you have mastered a few basic rules, Italian is an easy language to speak: It is phonetic, and unlike English, particular combinations of letters are always pronounced the same way. The stress is usually on the penultimate syllable, but if the word has an accent, this is where the stress falls.

Vowels are pronouned as follows:

a	casa	as in	mat short 'a'
e	vero closed	as in	base
e	sette open	as in	vet short 'e'
i	vino	as in	mean
o	dove closed	as in	bowl
o	otto open	as in	not
u	uva	as in	book

Consonants as in English except:
c before **i** or **e** becomes **ch** as in **ch**urch
ch before **i** or **e** becomes **c** as in **c**at
g before **i** or **e** becomes **j** as in **J**ulia
gh before **i** or **e** becomes **g** as in **g**ood
gn as in on**i**on
gli as in mi**lli**on
h is rare in Italian words, and is always silent
r usually rolled
z is pronounced **tz** when it falls in the middle of a word

All Italian nouns are either masculine (usually ending in o when singular or i when plural) or feminine (usually ending in a when singular or e when plural). Some nouns, which may be masculine or feminine, end in e (which changes to i when plural). An adjective's ending changes to match the ending of the noun.

CONVERSATION

What is the time?
Che ore sono?

I don't speak Italian.
Non parlo italiano.

I only speak a little Italian.
Parlo solo un poco italiano.

Do you speak English?
Parla inglese?

I don't understand.
Non capisco.

Please repeat that.
Può ripetere?

Please speak more slowly.
Può parlare più lentamente?

Write that down for me, please.
Lo scriva, per piacere.

Please spell that.
Come si scrive?

My name is…
Mi chiamo…

What's your name?
Come si chiama?

Hello, pleased to meet you.
Piacere.

This is my friend.
Le presento il mio amico/la mia amica.

This is my wife/husband/daughter/son.
Le presento mia moglie/mio marito/mia figlia/mio figlio.

Where do you live?
Dove abiti?

I live in…
Vivo in…

I'm here on holiday.
Sono qui in vacanza.

Good morning.
Buon giorno.

Good afternoon/evening.
Buona sera.

Goodbye.
Arrivederci.

How are you?
Come sta?

Fine, thank you.
Bene, grazie

I'm sorry
Mi dispiace.

USEFUL WORDS

yes
sì

no
no

please
per favore

thank you
grazie

you're welcome
prego

excuse me!
scusi!

where
dove

here
qui

there
la

when
quando

now
adesso

later
più tardi

why
perchè

who
chi

may I/can I
posso

tomorrow
domani

today
oggi

yesterday
ieri

IN TROUBLE

Help!
Aiuto!

Stop, thief!
Al ladro!

Can you help me, please?
Può aiutarmi, per favore?

Call the fire brigade/police/an ambulance.
Chiami i pompieri/la polizia/un'ambulanza.

Where is the police station?
Dov'è il commissariato?

I have lost my passport/ wallet/purse.
Ho perso il passaporto/il portafogllio/il borsellino.

I have been robbed.
Sono stato/a derubato/a.

I need to see a doctor/ dentist.
Ho bisogno di un medico/ dentista.

Where is the hospital?
Dov'è l'ospedale?

I am allergic to…
Sono allergico/a a…

I have a heart condition
Ho disturbi cardiaci.

RESTAURANTS

Waiter/waitress.
Cameriere/cameriera.

I'd like to reserve a table for… people at…
Vorrei prenotare un tavolo per…persone a…

A table for…, please.
Una tavola pe …, per favore.

Could we sit there?
Possiamo sederci qui?

Is this table taken?
Questa tavola è occupata?

Are there tables outside?
Ci sono tavole all'aperto?

We would like to wait for a table.
Aspettiamo che si liberi una tavola.

Could we see the menu/wine list?
Possiamo vedere il menù/la lista dei vini?

Do you have a menu/wine list in English?
Avete un menù/una lista dei vini in inglese?

What do you recommend?
Cosa consiglia?

What is the house special?
Qual è la specialità della casa?

I can't eat wheat/sugar/salt/ pork/beef/dairy.
Non posso mangiare grano/ zucchero/sale/maiale/ manzo/latticini.

I am a vegetarian.
Sono vegetariano/a.

I'd like…
Vorrei…

May I have an ashtray?
Può portare un portacenere?

I ordered…
Ho ordinato…

Could we have some salt and pepper?
Può portare del sale e del pepe?

The food is cold.
Il cibo è freddo.

The meat is overcooked/ too rare.
La carne è troppo cotta/ non è abbastanza cotta.

This is not what I ordered.
Non ho ordinato questo.

Can I have the bill, please?
Il conto, per favore?

Is service included?
Il servizio è compreso?

The bill is not right.
Il conto è sbagliato.

We didn't have this.
Non abbiamo avuto questo.

HOTELS

I have made a reservation for …nights.
Ho prenotato per…notti.

Do you have a room?
Avete camere libere?

How much per night?
Quanto costa una notte?

Double/single room.
Camera doppia/singola.

Twin room.
Camera a due letti.

With bath/shower.
Con bagno/doccia.

May I see the room?
Posso vedere la camera?

I'll take this room.
Prendo questa camera.

Could I have another room?
Vorrei cambiare camera.

Is there an elevator in the hotel?
C'è un ascensore nell'albergo?

Is the room air-conditioned/ heated?
C'è aria condizionata/riscal- damento nella camera?

Is breakfast included in the price?
La colazione è compreso?

When is breakfast served?
A che ora è servita la colazione?

The room is too hot/too cold/ dirty.
La camera è troppo calda/ troppo fredda/sporca.

I am leaving this morning.
Parto stamattina.

Please can I pay my bill?
Posso pagare il conto?

MONEY

Is there a bank/currency exchange office nearby?
C'è una banca/un ufficio di cambio qui vicino?

Can I cash this here?
Posso incassare questo?

I'd like to change sterling/ dollars into euros.
Vorrei cambiare sterline/ dollari in euro.

Can I use my credit card to withdraw cash?
Posso usare la mia carta di credito per prelevare contanti?

SPANISH WORDS AND PHRASES

Once you have mastered a few basic rules, Spanish is an easy language to speak: It is phonetic and, unlike English, particular combinations of letters are always pronounced the same way. When a word ends in a vowel, an n or an s, the stress is usually on the penultimate syllable; otherwise, it falls on the last syllable. If a word has an accent, this is where the stress falls.

a	as in	pat	ai, ay	as **i** in	side
e	as in	set	au	as **ou** in	out
i	as **e** in	be	ei, ey	as **ey** in	they
o	as in	hot	oi, oy	as **oy** in	boy
u	as in	flute			

Consonants as in English except:

c before **i** and **e** as **th**, *although some Spaniards say it as* **s**
ch as **ch** in church
d at the end of a word becomes **th**
g before **i** or **e** becomes **ch** as in loch
h is silent
j as **ch** in loch
ll as **lli** in million
ñ as **ny** in canyon
qu is hard like a k
r usually rolled
v is a **b**
z is a **th**, *but* **s** *in parts of Andalucía*

CONVERSATION

What is the time?
¿Qué hora es?

I don't speak Spanish.
No hablo español.

Do you speak English?
¿Habla inglés?

I don't understand.
No entiendo.

Please repeat that.
Por favor repita eso.

Please speak more slowly.
Por favor hable más despacio.

What does this mean?
¿Qué significa esto?

Can you write that down for me?
¿Me lo puede escribir?

My name is…
Me llamo…

What's your name?
¿Como de llama?

Hello, pleased to meet you.
Hola, encantado.

I'm from…
Soy de…

I live in…
Vivo en…

Where do you live?
¿Dónde vive usted?

Good morning/afternoon.
Buenos días/buenas tardes.

Good evening/night.
Buenas noches.

Goodbye.
Adiós.

This is my wife/husband/son/daughter/friend.
Esta es mi mujer/marido/hijo/hija/amigo.

See you later.
Hasta luego.

That's all right.
Está bien.

I don't know.
No lo sé.

You're welcome.
De nada.

How are you?
¿Cómo estás?

USEFUL WORDS

yes
sí

no
no

please
por favor

thank you
gracias

fine
bueno

there
allí

where
dónde

here
aquí

when
cuándo

who
quien

how
cómo

free (no charge)
gratis

I'm sorry
Lo siento

excuse me
perdone

large
grande

small
pequeño

good
bueno

bad
malo

IN TROUBLE

Could you call a doctor?
¿Puede llamar a un médico?

I need to see a doctor/dentist.
Necesito un médico/dentista.

Help!
Socorro

Stop thief!
Al ladrón

I have had an accident.
He tenido un accidente.

Call the fire brigade/police/
ambulance.
**Llame a los bomberos/la
policía/una ambulancia.**

I have lost my passport/
wallet/purse/bag.
**He perdido el pasaporte/la
cartera/el monedero/el
bolso.**

Is there a lost property office?
**¿Hay una oficina de objetos
perdidos?**

I have been robbed.
Me han robado.

Where is the police station?
¿Dónde está la comisaría?

I am allergic to…
Soy alérgico a…

RESTAURANTS
I'd like to reserve a table for….
people at…
**Quiero reservar una mesa
para…personas para las…**

A table for…
Una mesa para…por favor.

Could we sit here?
¿Nos podemos sentar aquí?

Waiter/waitress.
El camarero/la camarera.

Where are the toilets?
¿Dónde están los aseos?

I prefer non-smoking.
Prefiero no fumadores.

Could we see the menu/
wine list?
**¿Podemos ver la carta/
carta de vinos?**

We would like something to
drink.
Quisieramos algo de beber.

What do you recommend?
¿Qué nos recomienda?

Is there a dish of the day?
¿Tiene un plato del día?

I can't eat wheat/sugar/salt/
pork/beef/dairy/nuts.
**No puedo tomar
trigo/azúcar/cerdo/ternera/
productos lácteos/nueces.**

Do you have vegeatarian
dishes?
¿Tiene platos vegetarianos?

I'm a diabetic.
Soy diabético(a).

Could I have a bottle of
still/sparkling water?
**¿Podría traerme una botella
de agua mineral sin/con gas?**

Could we have some salt and
pepper?
**¿Podría traernos sal y
pimienta?**

This is not what I ordered.
**Esto no es lo que yo he
pedido.**

I'd like…
Quiero…

May I change my order?
¿Puedo cambiar el pedido?

The food is cold/too rare/over-
cooked.
**La comida está fría/muy
cruda/demasiado hecha.**

May I have the bill, please?
¿La cuenta, por favor?

Is service included?
¿Está incluido el servicio?

The bill is not right.
La cuenta no está bien.

I'd like to speak to the
manager.
**Quiero hablar con el
encargado.**

HOTELS
Do you have a room?
¿Tiene una habitación?

I have a reservation for…
nights.
**Tengo una reserva para…
noches.**

How much per night?
¿Cuánto por noche?

Double room.
**Habitación doble con cama
de matrimonio.**

Single room.
Habitación individual.

Twin room.
**Habitación doble con dos
camas.**

With bath/shower
Con bañera/ducha

Swimming pool.
La piscina.

Air-conditioning.
aire acondicionada.

Non-smoking.
Se prohibe fumar.

Is breakfast included?
¿Está el desayuno incluido?

When is breakfast served?
**¿A qué hora se sirve el
desayuno?**

May I see the room?
¿Puedo ver la habitación?

Is there a parking area
¿Tiene aparcamiento?

Is there a lift (elevator)?
¿Hay ascensor?

I'll take this room.
Me quedo con la habitación.

The room is dirty.
La habitación está sucia.

The room is too hot/cold.
**Hace demasiado calor/frío en
la habitación.**

Can I pay my bill, please?
¿La cuenta, por favor?

Could you order a taxi for me?
¿Me pide un taxi por favor?

MONEY
Is there a bank/bureau de
change nearby?
**¿Hay un banco/una oficina
de cambio cerca?**

Can I cash this here?
¿Puedo cobrar esto aquí?

I'd like to change sterling/
dollars into euros.
**Quiero cambiar libras/dólares
a euros.**

Can I use my credit card to
withdraw cash?
**¿Puedo usar la tarjeta de
crédito para sacar dinero?**

What is the exchange rate?
¿Cómo está el cambio?

PORTUGUESE WORDS AND PHRASES

CONVERSATION
I don't speak Portuguese.
Não falo português.

Do you speak English?
Fala inglês?

I don't understand.
Não compreendo.

Please repeat that.
Por favor repita isso.

Please speak more slowly.
Por favor fale mais lentamente.

My name is…
Chamo-me…

Hello, pleased to meet you.
Olá, prazer em conhecê-lo(a).

I live in…
Vívo em…

Good morning.
Bom dia.

Good afternoon.
Boa tarde.

Good evening/night.
Boa noite.

Goodbye.
Adeus.

See you later.
Até logo.

May I/Can I?
Posso?

How are you?
Como está?

I'm sorry.
Desculpe.

Excuse me.
Com licença.

USEFUL WORDS
yes
sim

no
não

where
onde

when
quando

why
porquê

how
como

open
aberto

closed
fechado

please
por favor

thank you
obrigado(a)

later
mais tarde

now
agora

IN TROUBLE
I need to see a doctor/dentist.
Preciso de um médico/dentista.

Please direct me to the hospital.
Por favor indique-me onde é o hospital.

Help!
Socorro!

I have lost my passport/wallet/purse/handbag.
Perdi o meu passaporte/a minha carteira/bolsa/mala de mão.

I have had an accident.
Tive um acidente.

My car has been stolen.
Roubaram-me o carro.

I have been robbed.
Fui assaltado.

RESTAURANTS
I'd like to reserve a table for… people at…
Gostaria de reservar uma mesa para…pessoas às….

A table for…, please.
Uma mesa para…, por favor.

We have/haven't booked.
Temos reserva/não temos reserva.

Could we sit there?
Podemos sentar-nos ali?

Could we see the menu/wine list?
Pode trazer-nos a ementa/lista dos vinhos?

Are there tables outside?
Há mesas lá fora?

Where are the toilets?
Onde ficam as casas de banho?

We'd like something to drink.
Gostávamos de tomar uma bebida.

Is there a dish of the day?
Tem prato do dia?

I can't eat wheat/sugar/salt/pork/beef/dairy.
Não posso comer trigo/açúcar/sal/carne de porco/carne de vaca/lacticínios.

I am a vegetarian.
Sou vegetariano(a).

The bill, please.
A conta por favor.

HOTELS
Do you have a room?
Tem um quarto?

I have made a reservation for … nights.
Fiz uma reserva para … noites.

How much each night?
Quanto é por noite?

double room
quarto de casal

twin/single room
quarto duplo/individual

with bath/shower/lavatory
com banho/duche/sanita

Is the room air-conditioned/heated?
O quarto tem ar condicionado/aquecimento?

Is breakfast included?
O pequeno-almoço está incluído no preço?

Can I pay my bill?
Posso paga a conta?

ACKNOWLEDGMENTS

Abbreviations for the credits are as follows:

AA = AA World Travel Library, **t** (top), **b** (bottom), **c** (centre), **l** (left), **r** (right), **b/g** (background)

The Automobile Association would like to thank the following photographers, companies and picture libraries for their assistance in the preparation of this book.

6l AA/A Baker; 6c AA/A Kouprianoff; 6/7 AA/S L Day, 7 AA/K Paterson; 8 AA/T Woodcock

AUSTRIA

10l AA/M Siebert; 10c AA/A Baker; 10/11 AA/A Baker; 11 AA/P Baker; 12tr AA/A Baker; 12cr mediacolor's/Alamy; 12br AA/J Smith; 13tb/g AA/A Baker; 13 World Pictures/Photoshot; 16t AA/J Smith; 16l AA/J Smith; 16c AA/C Sawyer; 16r AA/J Smith; 17 AA/J Smith; 21 AA/J Smith; 22t AA/J Smith; 22b AA/J Smith

BELGIUM

24 AA/A Kouprianoff; 26l AA/A Kouprianoff; 26c AA/A Kouprianoff; 26/7 AA/A Kouprianoff; 27r AA/A Kouprianoff; 27b AA/A Kouprianoff; 28l AA/A Kouprianoff; 28tr AA/A Kouprianoff; 28cr AA/A Kouprianoff; 28br AA/A Kouprianoff; 29tb/g AA/A Kouprianoff; 29t AA/A Kouprianoff; 30 AA/A Kouprianoff; 32t AA/A Kouprianoff; 32l AA/A Kouprianoff; 32c AA/A Kouprianoff; 32r AA/A Kouprianoff; 33 AA/A Kouprianoff; 36 AA/A Kouprianoff; 38 AA/A Kouprianoff; 39t AA/A Kouprianoff; 39b AA/A Kouprianoff

FRANCE

42l AA/I Dawson; 42c AA/R Moss; 42r AA/J Edmanson; 43l AA/M Short; 43c AA/C Sawyer; 43r AA/P Kenward; 43br AA/P Enticknap; 44tl AA/C Sawyer; 44tr AA/J A Tims; 44tcr AA/I Dawson; 44bacr AA R Moore; 44br AA/D Robertson; 45t AA/N Setchfield; 45cl AA/N Setchfield; 45c AA/N Setchfield; 45cr AA/N Setchfield; 45b AA/P Kenward; 47 AA/N Setchfield; 49t AA/R Day; 49cl World Pictures/Photoshot; 49c World Pictures/Photoshot; 49cr World Pictures/Photoshot; 50 World Pictures/Photoshot; 51b AA/D Robertson; 52 AA/R Day; 54t AA/J Wyand; 54cl AA/J Wyand; 54c AA/J Wyand; 54cr AA/J Wyand; 56 AA/J Wyand; 58t AA/C Sawyer; 58cl AA/A Baker; 58c AA/A Baker; 58cr AA/C Sawyer; 58b AA/A Baker; 59 AA/A Baker; 61 AA/C Sawyer; 63t AA/R Strange; 63cl AA/A Baker; 63c AA/C Sawyer; 63cr AA/R Strange; 63b AA/R Strange; 64 AA/A Baker; 65 AA/A Baker; 67t AA/R Moss; 67r AA/C Sawyer; 69 AA/P Kenward; 74 AA/M Jourdan; 75 AA/M Jourdan; 76t AA/M Jourdan; 76b AA/M Jourdan; 77t AA/B Rieger; 77cr AA/K Paterson; 78t AA/M Jourdan; 78cl *Mona Lisa*, c.1503–6 (oil on panel), da Vinci, Leonardo (1452–1519)/ Louvre, Paris, France, Giraudon/The Bridgeman Art Library; 79 AA/P Enticknap; 80t AA/M Jourdan; 80l AA/M Jourdan; 81l AA/K Paterson; 81r AA/J A Tims; 82t AA/J A Tims; 82l AA/M Jourdan; 83 AA/T Souter; 87 AA/A Baker; 88 AA/J A Tims

GERMANY

92 AA/J Smith; 93cl AA/M Jourdan; 93c AA/P Bennett; 93cr AA/A Baker; 94l AA/P Bennett; 94tr AA/D Traverso; 94tcr AA/J Smith; 94cr AA/A Kouprianoff; 94bcr AA/P Bennett; 94br AA/C Sawyer; 95 AA/J Smith; 96tl AA/T Souter; 96tc AA/T Souter; 96tr AA/S McBride; 96b AA/A Baker; 97bc AA/S McBride; 97bl AA/S McBride; 100 AA/T Souter; 101t AA/S McBride; 101r AA/C Sawyer; 102 AA/A Baker; 103 *The Dance or Iris* 1719–20 (oil on canvas) Watteau, Jean Antoine (1684–7121) Gemäldegalerie, Berlin, Germany, Giraudon/The Bridgeman Art Library; 104t AA/A Baker; 104l AA/J Smith; 105t AA/J Smith; 105r AA/S McBride; 106t AA/S McBride;

106b AA/J Smith; 107 AA/S McBride; 108t AA/C Sawyer; 108b AA/J Smith; 109t AA/J Smith; 109b AA/T Souter; 111t AA/A Kouprianoff; 111l AA/A Kouprianoff; 111c AA/A Hemmisen; 111r AA/AHemmisen; 112cl AA; 112cr AA/A Kouprianoff; 112b AA/A Kouprianoff; 113bl AA/P Enticknap; 113br AA/A Kouprianoff; 114t AA/A Kouprianoff; 114b AA/A Kouprianoff; 115t AA/A Hemmisen; 115b AA/A Kouprianoff; 116 AA/A Kouprianoff; 118l AA/M Jourdan; 118r AA/M Jourdan; 118/9c AA/A Baker; 119l AA/A Baker; 119b AA/M Jourdan; 122t AA/C Sawyer; 122cl AA/T Souter; 122cr AA/C Sawyer; 122b AA/M Jourdan; 123 AA/M Jourdan; 124l AA/A Baker; 124r AA/T Souter; 125l AA/T Souter; 125r AA/T Souter; 128 AA/T Souter; 130t AA/J Smith; 130b AA/J Smith

GREAT BRITAIN

132 AA; 134l AA/A Baker; 134c Britain On View; 134r AA/S J Whitehorne; 135b AA/M Jourdan; 135r AA/E Meacher; 136l AA/W Voysey; 136tr AA/C Jones; 136tcr AA/N Setchfield; 136cr AA/C Lees; 136bcr AA/S & O Mathews; 136br AA/S J Whitehorne; 137t AA/E Meacher; 137cl AA/E Meacher; 137c AA/E Meacher; 137cr AA/M Birkitt; 137b AA/E Meacher; 138c AA/E Meacher; 138b AA/S L Day; 138/9 AA/E Meacher; 139 Britain On View; 141 AA/M Jourdan; 146t AA/R Strange; 146l AA; 146b AA/G Wrona; 147 Helmet, from the Sutton Hoo Ship Burial, c.625–30 AD (iron & gilt bronze), Anglo-Saxon, (7th century) /British Museum, London, UK/The Bridgeman Art Library; 148 AA/S McBride; 149t AA/J A Tims; 149r AA/P Kenward; 150 AA/S McBride; 151l AA/M Jourdan; 151r AA/R Ireland; 156t AA/A Lawson; 156cl AA/A Lawson; 156c AA/C Jones; 156b AA/A Lawson; 156b AA/C Jones; 157l AA/S L Day; 157r AA/A Lawson; 157b AA/A Lawson; 160 Ian Leonard/Alamy; 161t AA/P Bennett; 161r AA/P Wilson; 161b AA/R Newton; 162t Britain On View; 162b AA/P Bennett; 163 AA/P Bennett; 165t Britain On View; 165r AA; 167t AA/K Paterson; 167r AA; 169t AA/K Paterson; 169c AA/J Smith; 169b AA/K Paterson; 172t AA/S J Whitehorne; 172l www.seeglasgow.com; 173l www.seeglasgow.com; 173r AA/S J Whitehorne; 175 AA/S Gibson Photography; 177 Britain On View; 179 AA/J A Tims

IRELAND

182 Belfast Visitor & Convention Bureau; 184 AA/S McBride; 185cl AA/S Hill; 185c AA/G Munday; 185cr AA/J Blandford; 186bl AA/S McBride; 186tr AA/S L Day; 186tcr AA/L Blake; 186bcr AA/G Munday; 186br AA/J Blandford; 187t AA/S Hill; 187cr AA/S McBride; 187bl AA/C Jones; 188t AA/C Jones; 188l AA/C Jones; 192 AA/SlideFile; 193tl AA/S L Day; 193r AA/SlideFile; 193bl AA/S J Whitehorne; 194bl AA/S J Whitehorne; 194br AA/S L Day; 195bl AA/SlideFile; 195br AA/S L Day; 196t AA/M Short; 196cl AA/S L Day; 197t AA/SlideFile; 197cr AA/M Short; 197br The Caliph Ma'mun (813–833) Bathing, Khusrau and Shirin Khamsah by Nizami, 1529 (936 Hijra) (vellum) / © The Trustees of the Chester Beatty Library, Dublin /The Bridgeman Art Library; 198tl AA/S L Day; 198tr AA/S L Day; 198bl AA/S L Day; 199tl AA/S L Day; 199tr Guinness Storehouse; 199br Guinness Storehouse; 200t AA/S McBride; 200cl AA/S McBride; 200c AA/S J Whitehorne; 200/1 AA/S McBride; 201t AA/S McBride; 201r AA/S J Whitehorne; 202t The Tara Brooch, from Bettystown, County Meath (cast silver with glass, enamel & amber), Celtic (8th century)/National Museum of Ireland, Dublin, Ireland/The Bridgeman Art Library; 202/3 AA/S L Day; 203c AA/S L Day; 203cr AA/S J Whitehorne; 203cb The Ardagh Chalice (detail) early 8th century (silver with silver

gilding, enamel, brass and bronze), Celtic, (8th century)/
National Museum of Ireland, Dublin, Ireland, Photo © Boltin
Picture Library/The Bridgeman Art Library; **204t** MS 58
fol.291v Portrait of St. John, page preceding the Gospel of St.
John, from the Book of Kells, c.800 (vellum), Irish School,
(9th century)/© The Board of Trinity College, Dublin, Ireland/
The Bridgeman Art Library; **204cl** AA/S L Day; **204c** AA/S L
Day; **204/5** AA/L Blake; **205tr** MS 58 fol.291v Portrait of St.
John, page preceding the Gospel of St. John, from the Book
of Kells, c.800 (vellum), Irish School, (9th century)/© The
Board of Trinity College, Dublin, Ireland/The Bridgeman Art
Library; **205br** AA/M Short; **208t** AA/G Munday; **208cl** AA/I
Dawson; **208c** AA/C Coe; **208cr** AA/G Munday; **208b** Belfast
Visitor & Convention Bureau; **209l** Belfast Visitor &
Convention Bureau; **209r** Belfast Visitor & Convention
Bureau; **210cl** AA/C Coe; **210c** AA/C Coe; **210cr** AA/I Dawson;
210b Belfast Visitor & Convention Bureau; **211cl** AA/I Dawson;
211c AA/G Munday; **211cr** AA/I Dawson; **213tr** AA/I Dawson;
213c AA/C Coe; **213b** AA/G Munday; **215** AA/C Jones; **218**
AA/C Hill

ITALY

220l AA/C Sawyer; **220c** AA/M Jourdan; **220/1** AA/T Harris;
221cr AA/K Paterson; **222tl** AA/M Jourdan; **222tr** AA/P
Davies; **222ctr** AA/S McBride; **222c** AA/S McBride; **222cbr**
AA/C Sawyer; **222br** AA/E Meacher; **223** AA/C Sawyer; **225**
AA/K Paterson; **228t** AA/S McBride; **228cl** AA/S McBride;
228c AA/C Sawyer; **228cr** AA/K Paterson; **229** AA/S McBride;
230 AA/S McBride; **231** AA/S McBride; **232t** AA/B Smith;
232cl AA/J Edmanson; **232cr** AA/S McBride; **232br** AA/S
McBride; **233t** AA/S McBride; **233r** AA/S McBride; **234** AA/S
McBride; **235t** AA/C Sawyer; **235r** AA/J Edmanson; **236t**
AA/C Sawyer; **236b** AA/S McBride; **237t** AA/S McBride; **237r**
AA/B Smith; **238t** AA/S McBride; **238cl** AA/S McBride; **238bl**
AA/S McBride; **239** AA/C Sawyer; **242t** AA/P Bennett; **242cl**
AA/C Sawyer; **242cr** AA/M Jourdan; **242b** AA/M Jourdan;
243 AA/C Sawyer; **245l** AA/M Jourdan; **245r** AA/C Sawyer;
248t AA/M Jourdan; **248cl** AA/M Jourdan; **248c** AA/M
Jourdan; **248cr** AA/M Jourdan; **250l** AA/M Jourdan; **250r**
AA/M Jourdan; **253tl** AA/S McBride; **253tr** AA/S McBride;
257t AA/C Sawyer; **257c** AA/S McBride; **257b** AA/C Sawyer;
258t AA/D Miterdiri; **258cl** AA/D Miterdiri; **258cr** AA/P
Wilson; **258bl** AA/A Kouprianoff; **259tl** AA/S McBride; **259tr**
AA/C Sawyer; **259b** AA/P Wilson; **260t** AA/S McBride; **260cl**
AA/J Holmes; **260c** AA/J Holmes; **260cr** AA/S McBride; **260bl**
AA/A Kouprianoff; **261** AA/J Holmes; **262t** AA/S McBride;
262cl AA/S McBride; **262cr** AA/P Wilson; **262bl** AA/S
McBride; **263t** AA/C Sawyer; **263b** AA/P Wilson; **264** AA/P
Wilson; **265t** AA/S McBride; **265cr** AA/S McBride; **265br** AA/S
McBride; **266tr** AA/J Holmes; **266bl** AA/J Holmes; **267c** AA/D
Miterdiri; **267b** AA/S McBride; **268** AA; **271t** 4 Corners
Images; **271cl** Fiat Auto; **271c** Claudio Penna/Marka; **271cr**
John Heseltine; **272** Ermes Lasagni/Marka; **274** AA/S McBride;
275tl AA/C Sawyer; **275tr** AA/S McBride; **278t** AA/C Sawyer;
278cl AA/C Sawyer; **278c** AA/C Sawyer; **278cr** AA/D Miterdiri;
278b AA/C Sawyer; **279l** AA/P Wilson; **279r** AA/C Sawyer;
280t AA/S McBride; **280l** AA/S McBride; **280c** AA/S McBride;
280r AA/S McBride; **281l** AA/S McBride; **281r** AA/S McBride;
281b AA/C Sawyer; **282t** AA/S McBride; **282l** AA/S McBride;
282r *The Meeting of Etherius and Ursula and the Departure
of the Pilgrims*, from the St. Ursula Cycle, originally in the
Scuola di Sant'Orsola, Venice, 1498 (oil on canvas), Carpaccio,
Vittore (c.1460/5–1523/6)/Galleria dell' Accademia, Venice,
Italy/The Bridgeman Art Library; **282b** *The Story of St. Ursula,
the Repatriation of the English Ambassadors*, 1490–96 (oil on
canvas), Carpaccio, Vittore (c.1460/5– 1523/6)/Galleria dell'
Accademia, Venice, Italy, Alinari /The Bridgeman Art Library;
283 *Madonna and Child Enthroned between SS. Francis,
John the Baptist, Job, Dominic, Sebastian and Louis* (the San

Giobbe Altarpiece) c.1487 (oil on panel) (for detail see 61101
and 276359), Bellini, Giovanni (c.1430-1516)/Galleria dell'
Accademia, Venice, Italy/The Bridgeman Art Library; **284t**
AA/R Newton; **284l** AA/S McBride; **284r** AA/C Sawyer; **285c**
AA/C Sawyer; **285b** AA/C Sawyer; **286t** AA/S McBride; **286l**
AA/C Sawyer; **287t** AA/S McBride; **287r** AA/S McBride; **290t**
AA/C Sawyer; **290l** AA/C Sawyer; **290/1** AA/C Sawyer; **291**
AA/P Bennett; **292t** AA/A Mockford & N Bonetti; **292b** AA/A
Mockford & N Bonetti;**293** AA/S McBride; **295** AA/S McBride;
297tr AA/S McBride; **297b** AA/J Holmes

THE NETHERLANDS

300 AA/M Jourdan; **302cl** AA/K Paterson; **302c** AA/K
Paterson; **302/3** AA/M Jourdan; **303r** AA/A Kouprianoff;
303b AA/M Jourdan; **304tr** AA/M Jourdan; **304tcr** AA/K
Paterson; **304bcr** AA/K Paterson; **304b** Brian Hamilton/
Alamy; **305tb/g** AA/K Paterson; **305t** AA/K Paterson; **306**
AA/K Paterson; **311tb/g** AA/K Paterson; **311t** AM
Corporation/Alamy; **313** AA/A Kouprianoff; **314** AA/K Paterson

PORTUGAL

316 AA/C Jones; **318l** AA/A Mockford & N Bonetti; **318c** AA/M
Chaplow; **318r** AA/P Wilson; **319l** AA/J Edmanson; **319c** AA/A
Mockford & N Bonetti; **319r** AA/A Mockford & N Bonetti;
320tr AA/A Kouprianoff; **320l** AA/A Mockford & N Bonetti;
320cr AA/T Harris; **320br** AA/A Kouprianoff; **321** AA/A
Kouprianoff; **322tl** AA/A Mockford & N Bonetti; **322bl** AA/A
Mockford & N Bonetti; **322br** AA/T Harris; **323tr** AA/A
Mockford & N Bonetti; **323ct** AA/A Mockford & N Bonetti;
323cb AA/A Mockford & N Bonetti; **326t** AA/A Mockford & N
Bonetti; **326l** AA/T Harris; **326c** AA/A Mockford & N Bonetti;
326r AA/A Kouprianoff; **327l** AA/A Mockford & N Bonetti;
327r AA/A Kouprianoff; **328t** AA/A Mockford & N Bonetti;
328cl AA/A Kouprianoff; **328bl** AA/A Kouprianoff; **329t** AA/A
Mockford & N Bonetti; **329cr** AA/A Kouprianoff; **329br** AA/A
Kouprianoff; **330t** AA/A Kouprianoff; **330cl** AA/A Kouprianoff;
330c AA/A Kouprianoff; **330cr** AA/T Harris; **330bl** AA/A
Kouprianoff; **331** AA/T Harris; **332t** AA/T Harris; **332l** AA/T
Harris; **333tl** AA/A Kouprianoff; **333tr** AA/A Kouprianoff; **334t**
Museu Gulbenkian; **334/5** AA/A Kouprianoff; **335t** Museu
Gulbenkian; **335b** AA/A Kouprianoff; **336t** AA/T Harris; **336b**
AA/T Harris; **337** AA/A Mockford & N Bonetti; **340/1** AA/A
Kouprianoff; **341r** AA/A Mockford & N Bonetti; **342l** AA/A
Mockford & N Bonetti; **342c** AA/A Mockford & N Bonetti;
342r AA/A Mockford & N Bonetti; **343** AA/A Mockford & N
Bonetti; **345** AA/M Wells; **347c** AA/A Kouprianoff; **347br**
AA/A Mockford & N Bonetti

SPAIN

350 AA/M Chaplow; **351l** AA/M Jourdan; **351c** AA/P Wilson;
351r AA/M Jourdan; **352tl** AA/M Jourdan; **352tr** AA/M
Jourdan; **352tcr** AA/M Chaplow; **352cr** AA/S L Day; **352bl**
AA/M Chaplow; **352br** AA/S L Day; **353** AA/P Wilson; **356t**
AA/S L Day; **356cl** AA/S L Day; **356c** AA/S L Day; **356cr** AA/S
L Day; **357t** AA/S L Day; **357b** AA/S L Day; **358tl** AA/P
Wilson; **358tr** AA/M Jourdan; **359t** AA/S L Day; **359r** P
Wilson/© Succession Miro/ADAGP, Paris and DACS, London
2008; **360t** Ronald Stallard/Museu Picasso, Barcelona 2008;
360l Museu Picasso; **361t** AA/M Jourdan; **361l** AA/S L Day;
361c AA/P Wilson; **361r** AA/M Chaplow; **362** AA/S L Day; **363**
AA/S L Day; **366t** AA/S Watkins; **366l** AA/M Jourdan; **367t**
AA/M Jourdan; **367cl** AA/M Jourdan; **367c** AA/M Jourdan;
367cr AA/S Watkins; **367br** AA/M Jourdan; **370t** AA/M
Chaplow; **370cl** AA/M Chaplow; **370bl** AA/M Chaplow; **371tr**
AA/M Chaplow; **371br** AA/M Chaplow; **374** AA/M Chaplow;
375t AA/M Chaplow; **375cl** AA/J Edmanson; **375c** AA/M
Chaplow; **375cr** AA/M Chaplow; **376** AA/M Chaplow; **377c**
AA/M Chaplow; **377br** AA/M Chaplow; **378c** AA/D
Robertson; **378b** AA/M Chaplow; **379t** AA/J Edmanson; **379b**

AA/M Chaplow; **382** AA/M Jourdan; **383tl** AA/R Strange;
383tr AA/M Jourdan; **386t** AA/R Strange; **386l** AA/R Strange;
387t AA/M Jourdan; **387r** AA/T Oliver; **388t** AA/M Jourdan;
388l AA/M Jourdan; **388c** AA/M Jourdan; **388r** AA/T Oliver;
389 *Las Meninas* or *The Family of Philip IV*, c.1656 (oil on
canvas), Velasquez, Diego Rodriguez de Silva y
(1599–1660)/Prado, Madrid, Spain, Giraudon /The
Bridgeman Art Library; **390t** AA/M Jourdan; **390l** AA/R
Strange; **390c** AA/M Jourdan; **390r** AA/M Jourdan/© The
Estate of Roy Lichtenstein/DACS 2008; **391** AA/M Jourdan/©
The Estate of Francis Bacon/DACS 2008; **392t** AA/J
Edmanson; **392l** AA/M Jourdan; **396t** AA/K Paterson; **393r**
AA/K Paterson; **397** AA/K Paterson; **401t** AA/P Wilson; **401l**
AA/P Wilson; **401c** AA/A Molyneux; **401r** AA/P Wilson; **402l**
AA/A Molyneux; **402c** AA/A Molyneux; **402r** AA/A Molyneux;
403l AA/A Molyneux; **403c** AA/P Wilson; **403r** AA/P Wilson;
404 AA/A Molyneux; **406** AA/J A Tims; **408** AA/R Strange

SWITZERLAND
412l AA/S L Day; **412c** AA/S L Day; **412/3** AA/S L Day; **413r**
AA/A Baker; **413b** AA/S L Day; **414tr** AA/S L Day; **414cr** AA/S
L Day; **414br** AA/A Baker; **415tb/g** AA/S L Day; **415t** Jon
Arnold/Alamy; **416** AA/A Baker; **418tb/g** AA/S L Day; **418t**
Zurich Tourism/Manuel Bauer; **419** AA/S L Day; **421** Zurich
Tourism/Caroline Minjolle; **423** Zurich Tourism/Manuel Bauer

PLANNING
426 AA/A Baker; **428** AA; **431** MRI Bankers' Guide to Foreign
Currency, Houston, USA

Every effort has been made to trace the copyright holders,
and we apologise in advance for any accidental errors. We
would be happy to apply the corrections in the following
edition of this publication.

Project editor
Marie-Claire Jefferies
Design work
Catherine Murray
Picture research
Carol Walker
Internal repro work
Michael Moody
Production
Lyn Kirby
Mapping
Maps produced by the Cartography Department of AA Publishing
Cartographic editor
Anna Thompson
Main contributors for this title
Sue Dobson, Sylvie Franquet, Mike Gerrard, Anthony Lambert (authors), Lindsay Bennett (verifier); Marie Lorimer (indexer); Stephanie Smith, Susi Bailey (copy editors); Marilynne Lanng (proofreader)

Published by AA Publishing, a trading name of Automobile Association Developments Limited, whose registered office is Fanum House, Basing View, Basingstoke, RG21 4EA, UK.
Registered number 1878835.

A CIP catalogue record for this book is available from the British Library.

ISBN: 978-0-7495-5799-7

Colour separation by Keenes, Andover
Printed and bound by Leo Paper Products, China

Find out more about AA Publishing and the wide range of travel publications and services the AA provides by visiting our website at www.theAA.com/travel

A03221
Maps in this title produced from:
Mapping © ISTITUTO GEOGRAFICO DE AGOSTINI S.p.A., NOVARA 2008
Mapping © MAIRDUMONT / Falk Verlag 2008
Mapping © GEOnext (Gruppo De Agostini) Novara

   Mapping data licensed from Ordnance Survey® with the permission of the Controller of Her Majesty's Stationery Office. © Crown copyright 2008. All rights reserved. Licence number 100021153.
Mapping data licensed from Ordnance Survey of Northern Ireland® reproduced with the permission of the Chief Executive, acting on behalf of the Controller of Her Majesty's Stationery Office. © Crown copyright 2008. All rights reserved. Permit number 70135.
Republic of Ireland mapping based on © Ordnance Survey Ireland. Permit number 8430.
© Ordnance Survey Ireland/Government of Ireland.
Mapping © Freytag-Berndt u. Artaria KG, 1231 Vienna-Austria.
Map data © Tele Atlas N.V 2005
Map data © 1998-2003 Navigation Technologies BV. All rights reserved.
Mapping © KOMPASS GmbH, A-6063
Map data from Global Mapping, Brackley, UK. Copyright © Borch GmbH Publishing.
Transport maps © Communicarta Ltd UK.

COVER PICTURE CREDITS

Front Cover: AA/A Kouprianoff
Back Cover, top to bottom: AA/E Meacher; AA/M Siebert; AA/A Kouprianoff; AA/S McBride
Spine: AA/A Kouprianoff

Dear KeyGuide Reader

●

Thank you for buying this KeyGuide. Your comments and opinions are very important to us, so please help us to improve our travel guides by taking a few minutes to complete this questionnaire.

You do not need a stamp (unless posted outside the UK). If you do not want to cut this page from your guide, then photocopy it or write your answers on a plain sheet of paper.

Send to: KeyGuide Editor, AA World Travel Guides
FREEPOST SCE 4598, Basingstoke RG21 4GY

Find out more about AA Publishing and the wide range of
travel publications the AA provides by visiting our website at
www.theAA.com/travel

ABOUT THIS GUIDE

Which KeyGuide did you buy? _____

Where did you buy it?_____

When? _ _ month/ _ _ year

Why did you choose this AA KeyGuide?
❏ Price ❏ AA Publication
❏ Used this series before; title _____
❏ Cover ❏ Other (please state) _____

Please let us know how helpful the following features of the guide were to you by circling the appropriate category: very helpful (**VH**), helpful (**H**) or little help (**LH**)

Size	**VH**	**H**	**LH**
Layout	**VH**	**H**	**LH**
Photos	**VH**	**H**	**LH**
Excursions	**VH**	**H**	**LH**
Entertainment	**VH**	**H**	**LH**
Hotels	**VH**	**H**	**LH**
Maps	**VH**	**H**	**LH**
Practical info	**VH**	**H**	**LH**
Restaurants	**VH**	**H**	**LH**
Shopping	**VH**	**H**	**LH**
Walks	**VH**	**H**	**LH**
Sights	**VH**	**H**	**LH**
Transport info	**VH**	**H**	**LH**

What was your favourite sight, attraction or feature listed in the guide?

Page _____ Please give your reason _____

Which features in the guide could be changed or improved? Or are there any other comments you would like to make?

ABOUT YOU

Name (*Mr/Mrs/Ms*) _____

Address_____

_____

Postcode _____ Daytime tel nos _____

Email _____

Please *only* give us your mobile phone number/email if you wish to hear from us about other products and services from the AA and partners by text or mms.

Which age group are you in?
Under 25 ❑   25–34 ❑   35–44 ❑   45–54 ❑   55+ ❑

How many trips do you make a year?
Less than1 ❑   1 ❑   2 ❑   3 or more ❑

ABOUT YOUR TRIP

Are you an AA member?   Yes ❑ No ❑

When did you book?   _ _ month/_ _ year

When did you travel?   _ _ month/_ _ year

Reason for your trip?   Business ❑ Leisure ❑

How many nights did you stay?_____

How did you travel?   Individual ❑ Couple ❑ Family ❑ Group ❑

Did you buy any other travel guides for your trip?_____

If yes, which ones? _____

_____

Thank you for taking the time to complete this questionnaire. Please send it to us as soon as possible, and remember, you do not need a stamp (*unless posted outside the UK*).

AA Travel Insurance call 0800 072 4168 or visit www.theaa.com

---

Titles in the KeyGuide series:
Australia, Barcelona, Britain, Brittany, Canada, China, Costa Rica, Croatia, Florence and Tuscany, France, Germany, Ireland, Italy, London, Mallorca, Mexico, New York, New Zealand, Normandy, Paris, Portugal, Prague, Provence and the Côte d'Azur, Rome, Scotland, South Africa, Spain, Thailand, Venice, Vietnam, Western European Cities.